W9-BGE-842

Born in exile, **HRH Prince Michael**, 7th Count of Albany (Scotland), is the senior legal descendant of the Stuart Kings of Britain. He is Head of Scotland's legitimate Royal House of Stewart, and in 1992 was elected President of the European Council of Princes. A Scottish resident since 1976, Prince Michael actively promotes a reinstatement of Scotland's Written Constitution to uphold the rights, liberties and welfare of the Nation.

THE FORGOTTEN MONARCHY OF SCOTLAND

The True Story of the Royal House of Stewart and the Hidden Lineage of the Kings and Queens of Scots

HRH
PRINCE MICHAEL
OF ALBANY

This edition published by Barnes & Noble, Inc., by arrangement with Element Books Limited

2000 Barnes & Noble Books

M 10 9 8 7 6 5 4 3 2 1

Cover illustration courtesy of The Edinburgh Room, National Edinburgh Library
Cover design by Mark Slader
Design by Roger Lightfoot
Typeset by Footnote Graphics, Warminster, Wilts
Printed and bound in Great Britain by Biddles Ltd, Guildford and King's Lynn

ISBN 0–7607–2048–7

CONTENTS

Part II THE STEWART MONARCHY

Part III A BLOODY UNION

PLATE ILLUSTRATIONS

Black and white plates

Colour plates

MAPS AND LINE ILLUSTRATIONS

Note. The coat of arms on the book cover was used by James V Stewart, as portrayed on the entrance wall of the Palace of Holyrood House.

GENEALOGICAL CHARTS

APPENDIX XIV: ADDITIONAL CHARTS

NOTE

The following abbreviations have been used in the genealogical charts:

R	reigned	*de jure*	of right
b	born	*de facto*	of fact
d	died	dau	daughter
k	killed	g-dau	granddaughter
exc	executed	bro	brother
dsp	died without issue	god dau	god daughter
	(*decessit sine prole*)	g g-dau	great granddaughter
dep	deposed	g g-son	great grandson
div	divorced	mat	maternal
u/m	unmarried	n	natural
bur	buried	c	about, approximately

PICTURE CREDITS

The author would like to thank the following for their kind permission to use black and white illustrations for which they hold the copyright: National Galleries of Scotland, 1, 2, 3, 5, 6, 7, 8, 9, 10, 11, 12, 13, 14, 15, 16, 17, 18, 19, 20, 22, 23, 24, 25, 26, 27, 28, 29, 30, 31, 33, 34, 35, 36, 40, 41, 44; Stewart Archive 4, 21, 32, 37, 38, 39, 42, 43, 45, 46, 47, 48, 49, 50, 51, 52, 53, 54, 55, 56, 57, 58, 59, 60, 61, 62, 63, 64; and to the following for permission to use colour illustrations: National Galleries of Scotland 1, 2; Historic Scotland 3, 4, 5, 6; © Sir Peter Robson, Kt St Gm 7, Stewart Archive 8, 9, 11; © Anne Grahame Johnstone 10.

ACKNOWLEDGEMENTS

I wish to thank the Knights, Dames and Companions of the Noble Order of the Guard of Saint Germain for their support and encouragement during the making of this book. Special thanks also to Suzannah Kerr and Deborah Hunter of the Scottish National Portrait Gallery for their patience in helping me with the selection of ancestral plates; to Angela Gardner for her assistance with research and the compilation of the typescript; to Jack Robertson FSA (Scot) of Atholldene for his tremendous input and textual additions; and to Joe White of Historic Scotland.

My thanks are due to those librarians, museum curators and archivists the world over, particularly those of the National Libraries of Edinburgh, London, Paris, Madrid, Oporto and Rome for their invaluable help in scouring the National Archives on my behalf. I am similarly indebted to the Genealogical Institute of Italy, the Archival Department of the Vatican, and the several Under Secretaries of the Foreign Ministries of Italy, Belgium, France, Portugal, Poland, Denmark, Spain and the United States of America – all of whom responded so willingly to my numerous enquiries.

My grateful appreciation also to Leo van de Pas for his genealogical assistance; to Antonia Reeves and Michael Deering for their photographic expertise; to the Edinburgh Room of the Scottish Library for supplying the cover emblem transparency; to Gordon Stewart and Victoria Thorpe for their professional assistance; to Jean MacPherson of MacPherson's the Kiltmaker; to Chevalier David Roy Stewart; and to my many European cousins who have lent their support to the Stewart cause during the past six years of my ECP presidency. I am additionally obliged to all those Scots, at home and abroad, who have provided me with so many interesting facts of generally forgotten Scottish history.

DEDICATION

To those, past and present, who have kept the faith in the traditional rights of Scotland to be lawfully represented as a Sovereign Nation

Here Stewarts once in triumph reigned,
And laws for Scotland's weal ordained.
But now unroof'd their palace stands;
Their sceptre fall'n to other hands.

Robert Burns

FOREWORD AND INTRODUCTION

The Forgotten Monarchy of Scotland is among the most forthright and explosive of all historical narratives. It tells not only of the trials and tribulations of a steadfast and loyal Nation, but delves into an amazing web of political intrigue to reveal hitherto untold truths about the bribery, corruption and intimidation which led to the dismantling of Scotland's individual sovereignty. It is a story of parliamentary conspiracy, usurped crowns, assassinations, and the unwarranted concealment of information from the patriotic people of Britain. This is history as it should always have been told: the compelling account of a resolute Scots dynasty, the Royal House of Stewart, whose senior heir, the author of this book, now represents the combined sovereign Council of Europe.

In June 1992, HRH Prince Michael James Alexander Stewart, 7th Count of Albany (Scotland), was elected President of the European Council of Princes, a constitutional advisory body within the European Union. He succeeded the Imperial and Royal House of Habsburg Austria, who had retained the office from 1946. The new appointment held significant political implications for Scotland because, in unanimously electing Michael of Albany, some 32 sovereign houses openly proclaimed the continuing *de jure* (rightful) Scots monarchy to an international audience; a royal dynasty which, according to British academic historians, had long been extinct.

The Council's recognition of a royal Stewart was readily accepted in Europe, but it was a startling revelation to many people in Britain, the Commonwealth, America, and elsewhere, who had heard little about the exiled Stewarts (Stuarts) since the days of Charles Edward Stuart, (*Bonnie Prince Charlie*). However, in a direct line from King Robert II (founder of the Royal House of Stewart in 1371), Prince Michael is the seventh legitimate descendant from Charles Edward Stuart, and is the prior legal claimant in the Scottish succession, as confirmed by document under International Law. Now, in this fascinating book, Prince Michael details the lineal heritage of Scotland's Royal House, weighing the balance of hitherto contrived history in respect of the rightful sovereign descent.

For nearly 200 years it was officially portrayed in Britain that the Scots royal line ended while in exile. But this disinformation was a product of Georgian and Victorian propaganda, a deceit which, until fairly recent times, was sustained by consecutive Westminster Governments. Dutiful historians have long perpetuated the myth that Charles Edward Stuart and his brother, Henry Benedict, were the last of the Stuart succession, claiming that the Scottish heritage was passed to the Royal House of Sardinia in 1807. But the legitimate Stuart line did not become extinct, and the dynastic legacy was legally inherited by no other house. It was transferred only in the minds of fearful Westminster politicians who schemed and plotted to safeguard their alternative Germanic regime: the House of Hanover.

One might ask why there was any need to create a 'diverted succession', for when other royal lines have truly expired they have been allowed to disappear quite naturally. No one politically contrived to preserve their successions in other family descents unless there were relevant female-line marriages. But there was no such marriage in the Stuart succession; the Georgian Parliament quite simply undertook to manufacture a situation by misappropriating wills and testaments to their own strategic advantage. Why would they do that? Because, after nearly a century of Hanoverian rule in Britain, the exiled Stuarts still posed an enormous threat in terms of their continued popularity at a social level, and this was most embarrassing to King George III and his ministers.

As the stirring tale of Scotland's nationhood unfolds within these pages, we gain a captivating new awareness of many notable figures who have been treated very sparingly by academic historians: figures such as Macbeth, Banquo and William Wallace. We learn the facts about the Stone of Destiny, the Knights Templars, and the Celtic Church in Scotland, along with a truly enlightening account of historical Freemasonry. Also revealed are the generally unknown details of the coronation of Bonnie Prince Charlie, and of the Jacobites' active involvement in America's struggle against the Hanoverian Crown.

In order to set an objective historical scene for Prince Michael's narrative, we should perhaps consider how it was that the Royal House of Scots became the overall Royal House of Britain in the 17th century.

When Queen Elizabeth I Tudor of England died in 1603 she had no immediate heir, and so King James VI of Scots was invited to become King James I of England. James's great-grandmother was Margaret Tudor (the sister of Elizabeth's father, Henry VIII), and he was deemed to be Elizabeth's closest living relative. Since 1371, James's forebears of the Royal House of Stewart had been monarchs of the Scots, but from the union of the Scottish and English crowns in 1603, James VI (I) began the newly conjoined royal succession of Britain, which reigned as the House of Stuart.

Eighty-five years later, however, James's grandson King James VII of Scots (James II of England) was deposed by the Whig aristocracy in favour of the Dutch invader William of Orange, who became King William III, ruling jointly with his wife Mary II Stuart. Then, after the subsequent reign of Mary's sister Queen Anne, the German Elector of Hanover was invited to succeed as King George I in 1714. It might be said that the House of Hanover still reigns in Britain today, although it was renamed Saxe-Coburg-Gotha after the Victorian era. Later, in 1917, Britain's House of Saxe-Coburg-Gotha was renamed yet again to Windsor, so as to veil its German heritage during the First World War.

Not surprisingly, the Scots were most displeased at the loss of their rightful Stewart dynasty in 1688, and from that time a series of related revolts, the Jacobite Risings, took place. Perhaps the best-known of these remains the unsuccessful campaign of 1745, led by the deposed King James VII's grandson, Charles Edward Stuart, fondly remembered as *Bonnie Prince Charlie*. The exiled Charles Edward died in 1788, by which time the Stuarts were widely supported not only in Scotland, but in England, Wales and Ireland. Stuart support was also widespread abroad, particularly in America, where Scots Jacobites had been at the very forefront of the War of Independence. It was therefore thought expedient by the Georgian ministers to pretend that the descendant Stuart line had terminated at Charles's death. His royal inheritance was said to have passed to his brother Henry, a childless cardinal of the Roman Church; and when Henry died in 1807 the direct family succession was declared extinct by the Westminster Parliament.

However, not only was Charles Edward legally married before his death, he also had a legitimate son by that marriage, who succeeded him as the 2nd Count of Albany. Both Charles Edward and his brother Henry had specifically nominated this son, Edward James, Count Stuarton, in their wills, but the British Government chose to disregard the nominations. Instead, they submitted that the Stuart heritage had passed to an ex-king of Sardinia, who actually wrote to Westminster denouncing the falsehood because he knew the Stuart heir to be alive and well. Notwithstanding this, the politicians pursued their deceitful course, and now the Stuart legacy is reckoned to have progressed to the Duke of Bavaria.

Had the Stuart line truly become extinct there would have been absolutely no need for any Hanoverian strategy to 'create' a diverted succession; the line would simply have concluded with Charles Edward. As it was, the diversionary tactic was deemed necessary to manoeuvre Prince Edward James out of the picture as far as the British people were concerned.

From that time, there were a number of Jacobite attempts to reintroduce Stuart awareness in Britain, but one way or another those attempts were confounded by Hanoverian agents. In Europe, though, the story has been rather different, and having succeeded as the 7th Count of Albany, Prince Michael Stewart elected to leave Belgium and return to Scotland in 1976. In the footsteps of his illustrious ancestor, Charles Edward Stuart, he returned specifically to champion the Scottish Nation in its continued struggle for justice, and a rightly deserved recognition on the world stage.

On reaching Scotland Prince Michael was heartened to discover that he was largely among friends; but there were those who questioned whether he would stay the course, for he was not likely to be welcomed with any enthusiasm by the governing establishment. But more than two decades later, he is still in Scotland, and has met with no substantial opposition from either the Westminster Government or the reigning Royal House. Prince Michael's titular heritage has been formally confirmed, and the time has come for him to tell the whole Stewart story from the beginning.

To many readers, this book will provide a distinctly new insight into Scottish affairs, and an entirely new historical picture, which is immeasurably different from that portrayed in the conventional history books, will emerge. Herein is a blow-by-blow account of family record and experienced fact, rather than the politically contrived fiction which has become so familiar. This is the true story of the Royal House of Stewart, Europe's longest reigning dynasty. And it is the story of a great Nation, whose proud sovereignty was once the envy of the Western world. It is the most compelling of all accounts relating to the ancient Kingdom of Scots, and it comes directly from the inherited records of Scotland's own lawful dynastic heir, HRH Prince Michael of Albany.

Laurence Gardner
Le Chevalier Labhràn de Saint Germain

Descent to Prince Michael of Albany

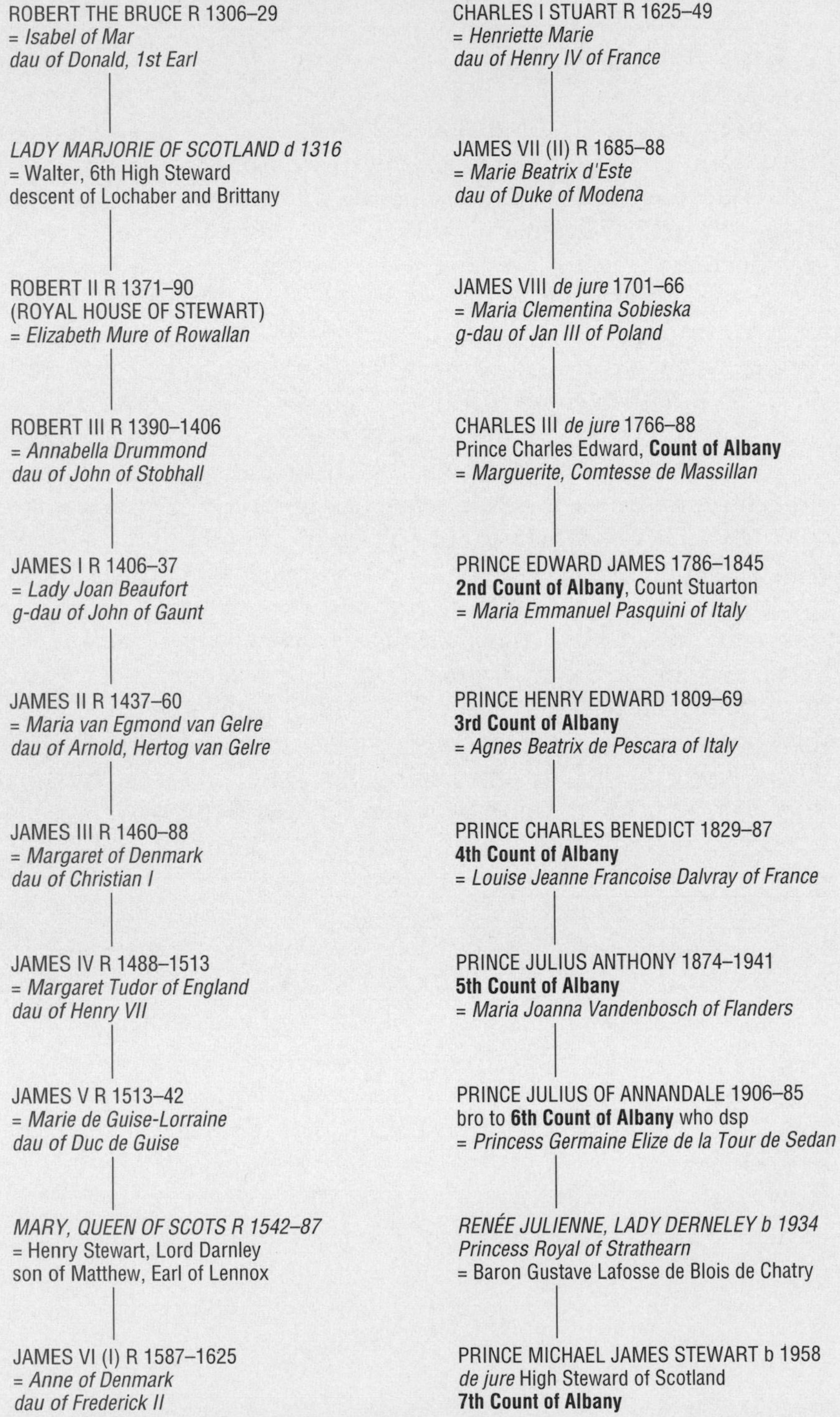

ROBERT THE BRUCE R 1306–29
= *Isabel of Mar*
dau of Donald, 1st Earl

LADY MARJORIE OF SCOTLAND d 1316
= Walter, 6th High Steward
descent of Lochaber and Brittany

ROBERT II R 1371–90
(ROYAL HOUSE OF STEWART)
= *Elizabeth Mure of Rowallan*

ROBERT III R 1390–1406
= *Annabella Drummond*
dau of John of Stobhall

JAMES I R 1406–37
= *Lady Joan Beaufort*
g-dau of John of Gaunt

JAMES II R 1437–60
= *Maria van Egmond van Gelre*
dau of Arnold, Hertog van Gelre

JAMES III R 1460–88
= *Margaret of Denmark*
dau of Christian I

JAMES IV R 1488–1513
= *Margaret Tudor of England*
dau of Henry VII

JAMES V R 1513–42
= *Marie de Guise-Lorraine*
dau of Duc de Guise

MARY, QUEEN OF SCOTS R 1542–87
= Henry Stewart, Lord Darnley
son of Matthew, Earl of Lennox

JAMES VI (I) R 1587–1625
= *Anne of Denmark*
dau of Frederick II

CHARLES I STUART R 1625–49
= *Henriette Marie*
dau of Henry IV of France

JAMES VII (II) R 1685–88
= *Marie Beatrix d'Este*
dau of Duke of Modena

JAMES VIII *de jure* 1701–66
= *Maria Clementina Sobieska*
g-dau of Jan III of Poland

CHARLES III *de jure* 1766–88
Prince Charles Edward, **Count of Albany**
= *Marguerite, Comtesse de Massillan*

PRINCE EDWARD JAMES 1786–1845
2nd Count of Albany, Count Stuarton
= *Maria Emmanuel Pasquini of Italy*

PRINCE HENRY EDWARD 1809–69
3rd Count of Albany
= *Agnes Beatrix de Pescara of Italy*

PRINCE CHARLES BENEDICT 1829–87
4th Count of Albany
= *Louise Jeanne Francoise Dalvray of France*

PRINCE JULIUS ANTHONY 1874–1941
5th Count of Albany
= *Maria Joanna Vandenbosch of Flanders*

PRINCE JULIUS OF ANNANDALE 1906–85
bro to **6th Count of Albany** who dsp
= *Princess Germaine Elize de la Tour de Sedan*

RENÉE JULIENNE, LADY DERNELEY b 1934
Princess Royal of Strathearn
= Baron Gustave Lafosse de Blois de Chatry

PRINCE MICHAEL JAMES STEWART b 1958
de jure High Steward of Scotland
7th Count of Albany

HRH PRINCE MICHAEL JAMES ALEXANDER STEWART

7th Count of Albany

Prince *de jure* of Scotland

Head of the Royal House of Stewart

Count Stuarton

Duke of Kendal and Kintyre

26th Lord High Steward *de jure* of Scotland

Duke of Normandy and Aquitaine

Comte de Blois

Baron Lafosse de Chatry

Titular Prince of France and Poland

Head of the Celtic Church
of The Sacred Kindred of Saint Columba

President of the European Council of Princes

Grand Master
The Noble Order of the Guard of Saint Germain

Patron Grand Officer, The International
Society of Commission Officers for the Commonwealth

Knight Grand Cross and Collar
The Orthodox Imperial Order of Saint George

Knight Grand Commander
The Chivalric Military Order of the Temple of Jerusalem

Knight Grand Commander
The Royal Durrani Order of the Crown of Amanullah

Honorary President
Association of Jewish Students of Glasgow University

Patron of the Albany House Trust

PART ONE

The Birth of a Nation

1

THE SCOTS TRADITION

Farewell to Exile

It is now more than twenty years since I first arrived in Scotland, and it was on Friday 20 August 1976 that *The Scotsman* newspaper published the article entitled 'A Young Pretender from Belgium'. I did not much care for the title, and I was concerned that the article was inaccurate in many respects. But I was pleased enough to have been noticed so quickly, and the inherent journalistic errors were quite understandable since I could speak very little English at the time. The journalist was unfamiliar with French, which had become my family's first language during 288 years of exile, and so the interview was conducted in a rather novel form of *franglais*. Shortly afterwards BBC Radio invited me to debate the political aspects of a possible Stewart restoration in Scotland.

Thereafter, from the age of only 18, I was surrounded by a good deal of sensational press and media reporting. Many wondered about the lad who was descended from the ancient Royal House of Scots, and I became the subject of understandable curiosity, having emerged from Europe after nearly three centuries of imposed Stewart expatriation. My motives were, therefore, questioned by those who found my Scottish affinity somewhat hard to comprehend. Indeed, the Scots were generally unaware that their Royal House still existed; this surprised me greatly, for it had never been any secret abroad. My family had always been well-regarded in Europe, and through each successive generation from the 17th-century Stuart Kings, we had always honoured our Scottish heritage, as had those around us.

Although I knew that England's Hanoverian monarchy had figuratively diverted our Scottish rights to the House of Sardinia in 1807, I also knew that few in Europe took this political manoeuvre seriously. What baffled me, therefore, was that the majority of people in Britain truly believed it had been necessary because Prince Charles Edward Stuart had no legitimate offspring. This, of course, was quite untrue, but the initial propaganda had been so forceful that the British history books and biographies were still quite unanimous in this regard.

My reasons for coming home became more defined once I reached the land of my forebears. Not only did I have to prove my worth, but I also had to convince the people that I was genuine. Although new to Scotland, my heart had long been there, and my ancestors' history was cemented within the very soul of the Scottish nation. Consequently, my motives were very straightforward: to apply myself, by right of my descent, to the welfare and benefit of Scotland. Firstly, though, I had to master the English language, and I am pleased to say that English is now my fourth fluent tongue, in addition to which I have embarked upon the study of Scots Gaelic.

In due course I shall discuss my ancestral forebears and my immediate family at some length. However, it is appropriate to impart some personal details so as to set the scene that exists today. In a direct line from Robert II, who founded the Royal House of Stewart in 1371, my descent from the Stuart Kings of Britain is that of the seventh generation from Charles Edward Stuart (*de jure* Charles III). I was born in Belgium in April 1958, and raised at the Château du Moulin in the Ardennes. My birth certificate identifies me as 'SAR (*Son Altesse Royale*) Prince Michael Jacques Stewart' (that is: HRH Prince Michael James Stewart – the family having reverted to the correct Scottish spelling of 'Stewart' in 1892). My mother is HRH Renée Stewart, Lady Derneley, Princess Royal of Strathearn, and my father is Baron Gustave Lafosse de Chatry.

On the death of my great-uncle, Anthony James Stewart, in 1963, I was confirmed as the 7th Count of Albany, and hold various other hereditary and titular appointments. In the early 1960s my mother and father separated; I was their only child, and from the age of five I was privately educated at our château. But with my parents' divorce imminent, our family finances collapsed, and in 1968 the property and estate were sold. As a result, my mother and I moved to an apartment in Brussels, and I completed my education at a boarding-school in nearby Soignies.

I vividly remember that I fostered one overriding dream throughout those early years: I had always planned for a future in Scotland. Having finished school at 17, followed by a course in catering, I worked for a year in a Brussels insurance firm in order to fund my ambition. It occurred to me, however, that such work could be done just as well in Scotland, and so I made the trip anyway. In no time at all I was confronted by the press and media, but I was ill-prepared for this, being in a somewhat vulnerable position, with no home, no job and hardly any money. I was also faced with a thoroughly different lifestyle, which appeared to incorporate some very strange customs.

A good example of my early bewilderment occurred on my second day in Scotland. I had gone to Elgin at the height of the holiday season, and was fortunate to find a room, having made no reservation. I checked into the hotel late in the afternoon and, following the journey from Edinburgh, my first requirement was a cup of tea. I thought this a pretty ordinary request, having bought tea in Dover, in London, and on the northbound train; but in Scotland things were apparently different. On taking my order, the good lady in reception smiled kindly, saying, 'And would you like an egg with your tea?'

It was a perfectly straightforward question, I suppose – but not to someone fresh from Belgium. What on earth did she mean? An egg! With my tea! My mind conjured up strange images of an egg bobbing around in the mug. Would it be a sort of tea-poached egg, or would the shell still be intact? It must be an old Scottish custom, I thought; but if it was good enough for my kin, then it was good enough for me. And so, undaunted, I said 'Yes'.

To my great delight, when the tea-tray arrived, the pot was accompanied by a wonderful plate of eggs, sausage, bacon, tomatoes and mushrooms. Spread before me was my first Scottish high tea, and I knew then that I would be at home in Scotland, the land where people eat breakfast at any time of day!

Another of my early ports of call was the Edinburgh office of the Lord Lyon, King of Arms, where I lodged necessary copies of my family documents. In contrast I spent that night on a roadside bench in Princes Street, before finding a room and employment at the Carlton Hotel the following day. In seeking to make some personal contacts I soon learned that although I had long planned to settle in Scotland, this was unexpected news for those already living there.

For example, on one occasion I ended up at the Douglas Hotel in Inverness, where I had been taken by car at the behest of Simon Fraser, Lord Lovat. There was nothing especially strange about that, but the events which led to my going there were unusual; in fact, they were wholly indicative of the surprise with which my presence was generally met. Earlier in the day I had taken a train from Elgin to Beauly, and from there a taxi to Beaufort Castle, the Lovat stronghold. The estate was quite the most exquisite I had ever encountered, and the castle, which sits at the head of a long driveway, could easily have been transported from the Loire Valley. I found the place totally deserted, but all the doors had been left open so that anyone could have wandered about with impunity. I called out, but there was no response, and so I waited outside for the return of a Fraser.

At length a gardener appeared, and I asked if I could meet with Lord Lovat. A cheerful 'By all means' was the reply, whereupon I was driven to the Master's residence, a separate villa within the grounds. The Lovat family had been historically Jacobite, and had supported both the *de jure* King James VIII and Charles Edward Stuart during their 18th-century endeavours to regain the crown and kingdom of the Scots. Indeed, it was this that prompted me to get in touch with the present Chief. I had a letter of introduction from my godmother Lady Sarah Stewart, who had been Regent in my name for 13 years until I reached my dynastic majority and became effectual Head of the Royal House of Stewart in 1976. The letter was duly presented to his Lordship, who hurried to greet me. To this day I do not know quite what Lord Lovat thought about my arrival, but in an instant he produced his cheque-book and asked 'What on earth are you doing here?' I could think of no better reply than to quote the well-remembered words of Prince Charles Edward, and answered, 'I am come home'.

I explained that, although appreciative of his generosity, I had not come for his money, but for some moral support in my new environment. 'We, the Stewarts, are the Forgotten Monarchy,' I said in my best *franglais*, and I requested that Lord Lovat might provide me with the names of those who could assist with my rehabilitation in Scotland. But His Lordship was clearly unprepared for such a sudden encounter, explaining that the aristocratic establishment was perhaps now rather too Anglicized to be of any immediate help. That apart, he explained that it was the start of the shooting season, and that the local landowners were awaiting a surge of visitors to their estates, so they would be preoccupied for some time. Having pocketed his redundant cheque-book, Lord Lovat then suggested that I would do better to present myself not to the aristocracy, but to the people at large, at which point I was politely escorted back to the car, and the gardener drove me to the Douglas Hotel. From there, I wrote to the editor of *The Scotsman*, and the long climb from the foot of my ancestral hill had begun.

Kith and Kin

In essence, my coming to Scotland meant the end of a family exile which had commenced in December 1688, when King James VII Stuart (II of England) was compelled to leave the country by the Westminster Parliament. Subsequently the English Whig politicians called upon the Dutch invader William of Orange to replace the rightful King of the Scots. As a result of the surrounding propaganda, most historians have since claimed that it was King James's conversion to Catholicism which lost him the Three Crowns (those of Scotland, England and Ireland), but contemporary evidence proves that there was nothing further from the truth. Long before James succeeded his brother Charles II, his sovereign demise had been organized by his nephew and son-in-law William, the Stadhouder (chief magistrate) of the Netherlands.

King James's wish to emancipate the Jews and free the Catholics and Quakers from their required subservience to the Church of England cannot, under any circumstances, be considered incorrect. In today's environment of more general religious toleration, James's sympathetic views would be regarded as fair-minded and ecumenical, and would be applauded by most of the Christian world. But in contrast, the hard-line attitude of the Anglican clergy and Whig aristocracy of the time supported an immoral persecution of anyone whose beliefs did not conform to the Government standard. This persecution was extended to include anyone who promoted denominational indulgence, and not even the anointed king escaped the puritanical onslaught.

By issuing his *Declaration for Liberty of Conscience* in April 1687, King James made it apparent that he respected the differing beliefs which existed within the realm. He stated, 'We do freely give them leave to meet and serve God after their own way and manner.' Today, such freedom of conscience is taken for granted in Britain, but James was hounded and deposed by fearful Dutch-influenced ministers because of it, at a time when Britain had long been at war with Holland. These days it is plain to most people that James was politically and spiritually ahead of his time, but many narrow-minded Anglicans still talk of the 'Glorious Whig Revolution'! This is not only insulting to their Church's more worthy members, and to those of other denominations, but it is an affront to the Scottish nation, whose system of social toleration was rejected by the English feudalists. It is hardly surprising that so many Scots remained loyal to their successive 'Kings over the water', for under England's dominion they were increasingly suppressed, and many thousands fled to begin new lives in America, Canada and Australia.

The ancient Kingdom of Scots was the oldest socially-operative state in Europe, and the community ideal was a direct inheritance from the family-orientated aspects of the Clan System. This was based on the mutual welfare of groups of people descended from common ancestors, and the fraternal aspect was traditionally maintained by the Kings of Scots in their capacity as 'common fathers' of the Community of the Realm. As such, the kings were obliged to uphold Scotland's Written Constitution of 1320 – the famous *Declaration of Arbroath* established at the time of Robert the Bruce. The Constitution states quite unequivocally that the kings must preserve the rights, liberties and privileges of the Scots and their ancient laws.

The *Declaration of Arbroath* represented a positive statement on behalf of the Scottish nation, with all the people of the land equal in status to their king. Quite unlike the intimidated subjects of England, the Scots were always able to relate personally to their monarchs. With the king being the chief-of-chiefs within the

Clan structure, it was the right of the people to call him their 'kith' (friend and relation); conversely it was the king's privilege to call the people his 'kin' (blood relatives). The Constitution underlined the nation's right to have a king of its own choosing, and it confirmed that sovereignty rested with the people, not with Parliament and the monarchy as is still the case in the English tradition.

Not only did the Whig Government disband the Scots Parliament at the 1707 Treaty of Union, but they also ignored the *Declaration of Arbroath* and enveloped the Scots within the new British constitution. That is to say they were enveloped within no constitution at all, for despite the prerogatives of other Western nations, the English have never had an enforceable written charter to protect individual rights and liberties. At best, all that exists is a loose amalgam of acts, charters and feudal customs which relate to very specific areas of operation.

Britain's present monarchy is certainly not 'constitutional' (as is so often erroneously claimed); it has been expressly contrived by Westminster to be a 'parliamentary' institution. The royal family members operate only with the consent of Parliament, and they are thoroughly constrained by governmental procedure. The present reigning house provides a suitable, though fast-diminishing, ambassadorial service, but has in the course of this become increasingly remote from the nation it is supposed to represent. Whatever their individual merits, the Windsors are quite unable to relate to the day-to-day problems of normal working families. Granted, a number of them do work for a living, but these fortunate royals are not at the mercy of financial institutions who might repossess their homes, or close down their companies – at least not yet. Maybe things will change; there is undoubtedly a prevalent mood to call the hangers-on to account, and to regulate the spending activities of those in the front line.

Irrespective of these prospects, however, there remains a noticeable absence of effective public representation in the face of unwelcome Government dictates. The Windsors may have their offspring wonderfully educated at select private schools, but their education amounts to nothing if they are not allowed to champion the requirements of the people. As things stand England's royals can remain no more than socially ineffectual figureheads in their official capacity. Whether or not the English people are content with this, it certainly was never the Scottish way. In England's feudal and imperial traditions, the people have always been regarded as subordinate subjects of the Crown, but the Scottish custom was founded upon a concept of kith and kin. In such a community-conscious environment, the Kings of Scots were not overlords of society, but were representatives of the nation they were privileged to serve.

2

EARLY SCOTLAND

Scots and Picts

It is perhaps not generally known that Scotland is geologically the most ancient land mass on our planet. When the earth was molten in primordial times, great bubbles would repeatedly build up and explode, and on gradually cooling the earliest solidified rock created the geography that was to become known as Scotland. It is said that the ancient Greeks regarded the bens and glens of Scotland as a sacred domain, while to those of Phoenicia, Anatolia, Macedonia and the Baltic lands our glaciated Highlands were the 'Crown of the Holy Isles beyond the western sea'. Some of the oldest rock in the world (of a type called *Archaean gneiss*) is found at Torridon in Wester Ross, and is reckoned by geologists to be about 20,000 million years old. Clearly, this is a unique heritage that we should treasure and nurture to set a world lead in matters of ecology and environmental conservation.

In the 5th century BC, the Greek historian Herodotus wrote of a sage called Abaros[1], who visited Greece from the 'Winged Temple of the Northern Isles'. This was the Temple of the Sun at Callernish in Scotland's West Lewis, the ancient stone circle called *Teampull na Greine*. Diodorus Siculus, a Sicilian writer of the Heroditus era, said that Abaros also met with Pythagoras. It is apparent, therefore, that some 2,400 years ago Scotland's Druids were of a very advanced culture.

The Druids were generally far ahead of their time, especially in matters of astronomy. According to the 1st-century Greek biographer Plutarch (appointed Procurator of Greece by Emperor Hadrian), 'The Druids celebrate the feast of Saturn once every thirty years because they contend that Saturn takes thirty years to complete its orbit around the sun'. They not only knew that the earth and planets were in orbit around the sun, but they calculated Saturn's orbital time to within six months of correctness some 1,500 years before the Polish astronomer, Nicolaus Copernicus, announced his related heliocentric principle to an astonished academic establishment.

Scotland's royal heritage is the oldest in Europe, and it can be traced back well into the BC era. The legacy of the Scots kings was hewn on the Stone of Destiny, the venerated relic of the Beth-el Covenant (Genesis 28: 18–22). In about 586 BC this stone, known as 'Jacob's Pillow', had been carried to Ireland from Judah during the reign of High King Eochaid of Tara. It became the sacred 'fealty stone' of the Irish kings, and eventually performed the same office in Scotland.

Scottish kingship evolved quite differently from its English counterpart, having been founded in the late-5th century AD by Irish royal immigrants, descendants of King Eochaid, who brought their patriarchal tradition, and the Stone of Destiny, to mainland Britain. The root of Scots kingship was therefore wholly Celtic, and it remained so, whereas the early Celtic kings in England were displaced firstly by Roman overlords, and then by Germanic Anglo-Saxons. In due course, England was invaded and subjugated by the Normans, who established a class-structured feudal regime which is still very apparent today.

To fully understand the problems experienced by the Stewarts after inheriting the English Crown in 1603, it is necessary to consider my ancestors' earlier function as the Kings of Scots, and we need to comprehend the unique nature of Scottish kingship as it developed from its ancient origin. For the most part, Scottish history as taught in our schools would appear to have begun with the 13th-century emergence of Robert the Bruce, but Robert was more than just a hero of the Wars of Independence. He was the upholder of an age-old cultural tradition which has been sidestepped by the English academic establishment – a family-orientated tradition which became the very essence of Scottish nationhood. We shall, therefore, commence our story in early Scotland, following the Kings of Scots through the centuries. We shall meet some fascinating characters whose names have become legendary, but whose wisdom and deeds have been confined to the wings of the historical stage.

During England's period of Roman occupation 45 BC–AD 450 , *the Scots* (Scotii) were actually settlements of the Gaels of Ireland, but in AD 498 three Scots princes of Irish Dal Riàta (north-east Ireland) left their native soil to settle in the Western Highlands of modern Argyll. They were the sons of King Erc, in direct descent from the early Kings of Tara. Once established in their new land they created the kingdom of Scots Dalriada (Dal Riàta), and from Fergus mac Erc (the middle-born son) the Kings of Scots descended. Fergus reigned as the senior king until 501, while his elder brother Loarn governed northern Dalriada (Lorne). Aonghus, the younger brother, controlled the kingdom of Islay and the Western Isles.

Ireland's northern province of Dal Riàta (meaning 'Riàta's share') was situated in Antrim (between modern Portstewart and Ballyclare), and it was but a short passage to Kintyre and the Firth of Clyde, where some Dalriadic settlements already existed before the royal brothers arrived. As the tribal population of Irish Dal Riàta grew, it was very natural to overspill into an underpopulated region across a short stretch of sea. By this means the kingdom of the Scots Gaels was expanded, and in time the overall name of 'Scotland' emerged in place of 'Alba' (Albany) or 'Caledonia', as the country north of the Forth-Clyde isthmus was called.

Beyond the western seaboard of Dalriada, the Highland areas were inhabited by the tribal Picts, who were indeed an ancient race. Originally, they had sailed westwards from Thrace (south-east Europe) through the Mediterranean, to the Atlantic Ocean and Caledonia. The Pictish roots were in Thessaly (Greece) before the coming of the Achaeans, and their forebears included the primitive tribes of the southern Black Sea coast, the Libyan Gulf of Sirte, Majorca (then populated by Libyans), and north-west Galacia.[2] Although the Scots and Picts were culturally quite different, they became one nation in the 9th century, when they were united under a king of the Scots succession.

One major difference between the Scottish and Pictish traditions was that the Scots' heritage of kingship passed from father to son, whereas the Caledonian system of the Picts was

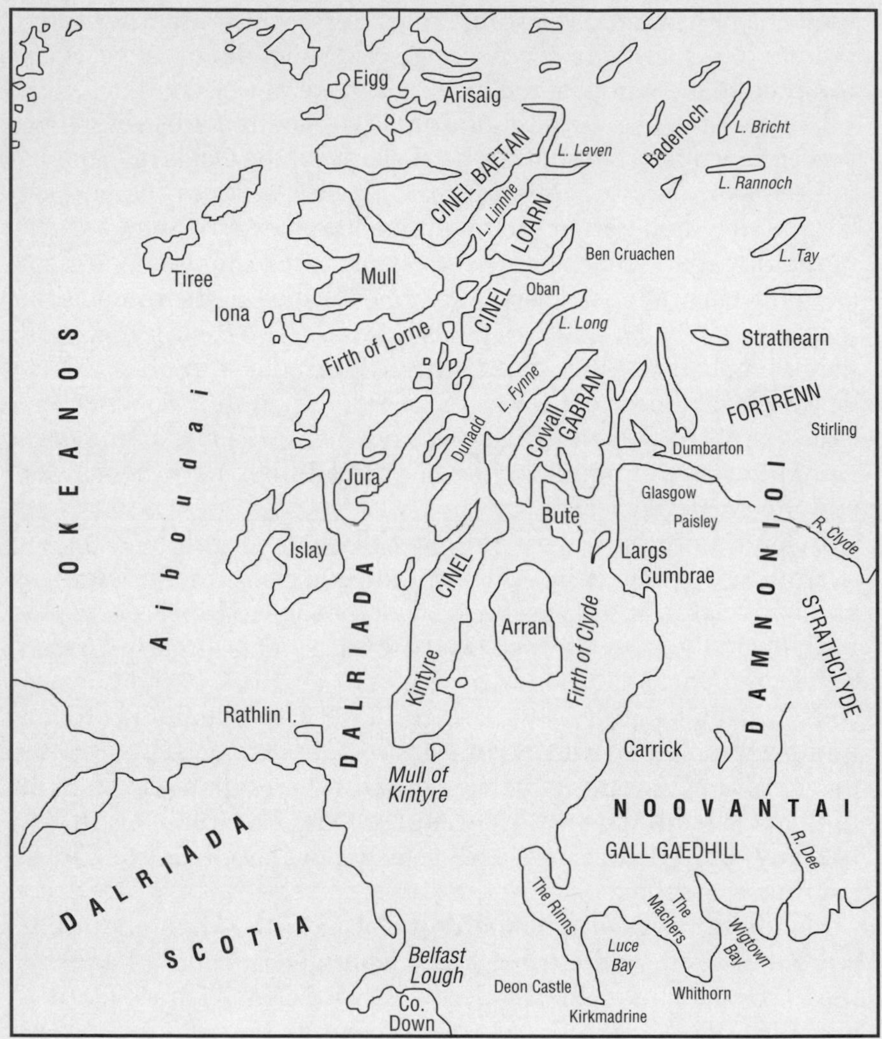

Map 1 Irish and Scots Dalriada

matrilinear (progressing from mother to son). Common to both races, though, was a well-organized and effective community establishment. Neither Ireland nor Alba had been penetrated by the Romans, and there were no lasting vestiges of Roman government as were evident in England and other parts of Europe. In fact, having failed to subdue the fearsome Picts, the Romans had built great walls across the land to keep them from moving south. Hadrian's Wall (finished *c*AD 126) extended from Tynemouth to the Solway Firth, while the Antonine Wall (*c*AD 142) crossed the higher land between the Clyde estuary and the Firth of Forth.

In the Lowland and Border areas below the Scottish and Pictish territories, the regions of Galloway, Lothian, Tweeddale and Ayrshire were governed by Welsh princes of the Gwyr-y-Gogledd (Men of the North) and the tribe of the Votadini. One of these local rulers was the 6th-century King Loth, from whose name Lothian derived. Tradition relates that, in about 518, Loth threw his daughter, Thenaw (Denyw), from a cliff for having an affair with a shepherd, and the spot where she landed became a spring. She was then cast into the Firth of Forth in a coracle, but was rescued by a Culross monk, whom she married. The story of the cliff and the coracle might well be no more than mythology, but the monk whom Thenaw married was, in fact, the Breton nobleman Garthwys de Léon. Their son was the later St Mungo (also known as Kentigern or Cynderyn), who became Bishop of Strathclyde and patron saint of Glasgow. To continue the legend, however, the unhappy shepherd was said to have murdered King Loth, whose grave is now marked by the Loth Stone, which sits at the base of Thenaw's hill (now known as Traprain Law).

Until 844 the separate kingly dynasties of the Scots and Picts prevailed, with the last individual King of Scots being Alpin (839–41). Alpin was also a matrilinear heir to the kingdom of the Picts through his mother, Princess Unuisticc of All Fortrenn (Strathearn, southern Perthshire), and Alpin's son Kenneth duly became King of both the Scots and Picts after defeating Bruide of the Picts at the Battle of Scone.

It was at this stage that the unified nation was truly born, with Kenneth MacAlpin as High King of Alba from 844. However, it was not until the reign of Malcolm II (1005–34) that the term 'Scotia' replaced the old style, so that North Britain as a whole became identified as Scotland. It is interesting to note that although Alba was a united domain under Kenneth I, there was still no king of a unified England at that time. It was not until 927 that Athelstane (the grandson of Alfred the Great) was the first to be recognized as 'Rex Anglorum' by the majority of Saxon kingdoms (Sussex, Wessex, Mercia, Essex, Kent, East Anglia, Deira and Bernicia).

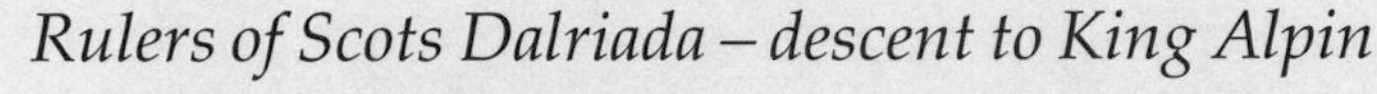

Rulers of Scots Dalriada – descent to King Alpin

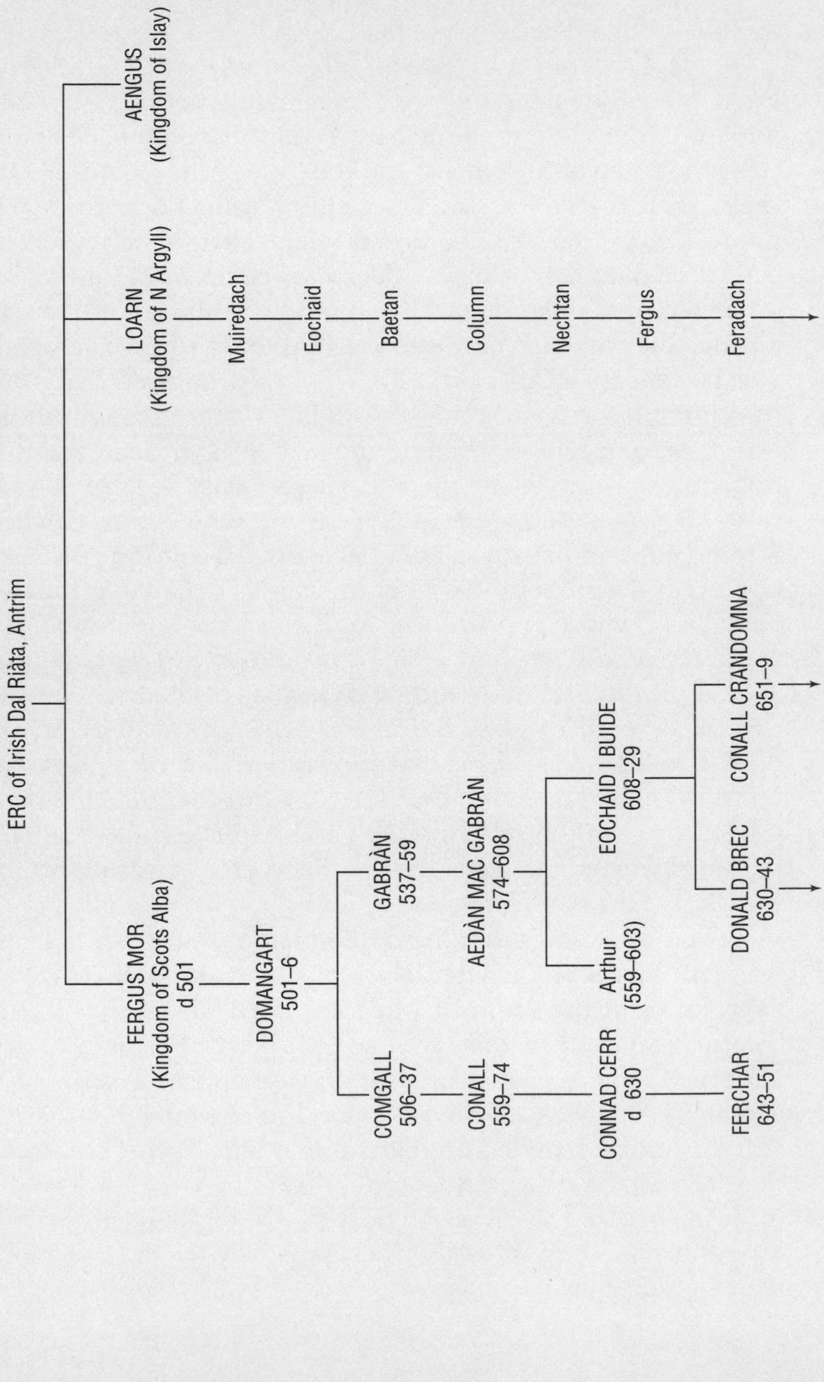

ERC of Irish Dal Riàta, Antrim

FERGUS MOR
(Kingdom of Scots Alba)
d 501

DOMANGART
501–6

COMGALL
506–37

GABRÀN
537–59

CONALL
559–74

AEDÀN MAC GABRÀN
574–608

CONNAD CERR
d 630

Arthur
(559–603)

EOCHAID I BUIDE
608–29

FERCHAR
643–51

DONALD BREC
630–43

CONALL CRANDOMNA
651–9

LOARN
(Kingdom of N Argyll)

Muiredach

Eochaid

Baetan

Column

Nechtan

Fergus

Feradach

AENGUS
(Kingdom of Islay)

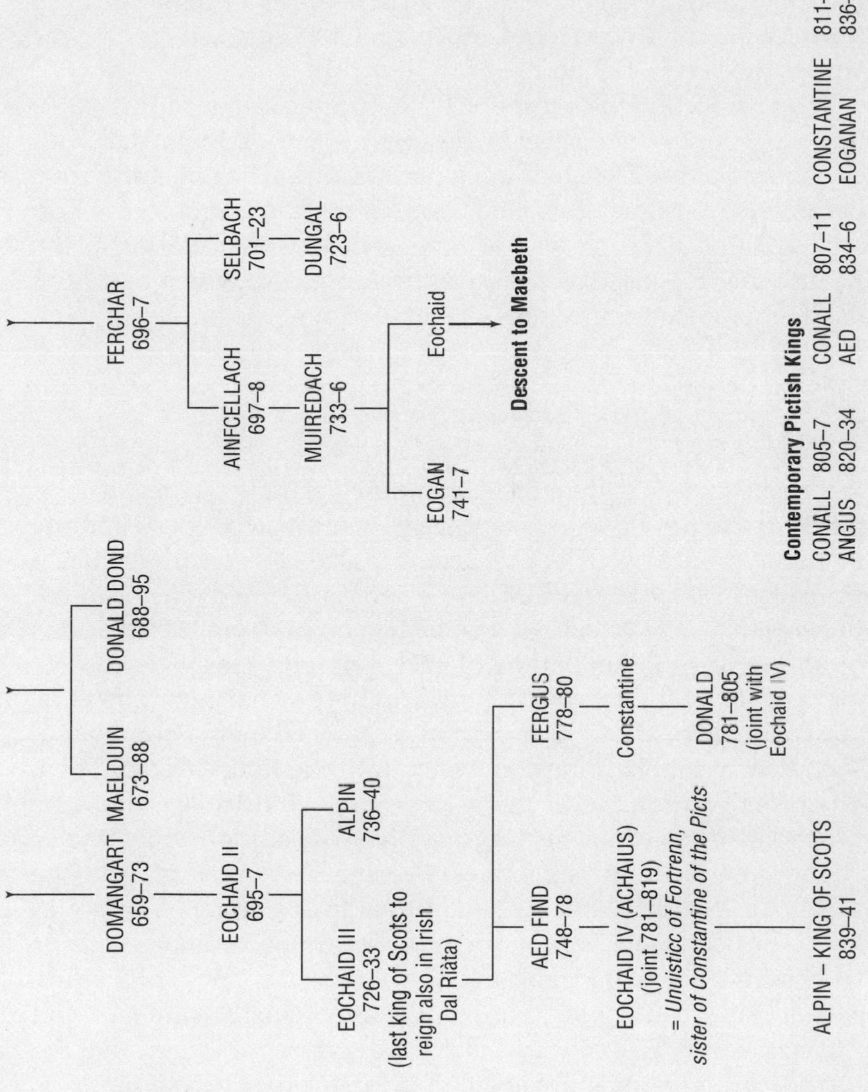
DOMANGART 659–73
MAELDUIN 673–88
DONALD DOND 688–95
FERCHAR 696–7
EOCHAID II 695–7
EOCHAID III 726–33 (last king of Scots to reign also in Irish Dal Riàta)
ALPIN 736–40
AINFCELLACH 697–8
SELBACH 701–23
MUIREDACH 733–6
DUNGAL 723–6
EOGAN 741–7
Eochaid
Descent to Macbeth
AED FIND 748–78
FERGUS 778–80
EOCHAID IV (ACHAIUS) (joint 781–819) = Unuisticc of Fortrenn, sister of Constantine of the Picts
Constantine
DONALD 781–805 (joint with Eochaid IV)
ALPIN – KING OF SCOTS 839–41
Contemporary Pictish Kings
CONALL 805–7 CONALL 807–11 CONSTANTINE 811–19
ANGUS 820–34 AED 834–6 EOGANAN 836–9

The records of Kenneth I's coronation refer to him as being the heir to the royal lineage of Fergus mac Erc, and a descendant of the Queens of Avallon. Also, by virtue of his imperial descent through a female line from Constantine the Great, Kenneth was styled 'Emperor of a Quarter of the World'.

Prior to Kenneth's accession, the traditional burial place of the Scots kings had been at the Celtic See of Iona, but with the advent of the Pictish union a new tradition began, and Scone became the designated location for future coronations. The Hill of Credulity at Scone was of long-standing importance to the Picts, being regarded as a natural power centre which had been used for ancient fertility rites in pagan times.

Tanistry and the Clans

From the time of Kenneth's conjoined kingly status, it was necessary to devise a system of succession which would suit the Pictish nation as well as the Scots. It was decided that Pictish princesses would marry Kenneth's sons and grandsons, with the proviso that new monarchs would be chosen from their various offspring during the lifetime of each reigning king. The choices were made by the prevailing king and his government ministers, which included the Celtic Christian clergy. On being nominated, each heir would become a co-ruler until the king's death. Then, after a period of ruling alone, the new king would follow the same procedure by selecting his successor from a parallel family line.

The inheritors by this process were called 'Tanists', and the system of selection from sons, nephews and younger cousins was known as 'Tanistry'. Compared to the more familiar dynastic succession by primogeniture (father-to-son) this procedure seems rather odd, but it did have a specific advantage, and through nearly two centuries the Tanist system ensured that the Scottish kingdom was never ruled by an inexperienced minor, as was to happen in later times.

When Kenneth died in 859, he was succeeded by his brother Donald. Kenneth's sons, Constantine and Aedh, then ruled in turn, with their respective descendants alternating as the kingship was transferred from cousin to cousin. During the course of this, Cumbria (north-western England) came under Scots control, having declined to recognize the English King Athelstane as overlord. Then, in the reign of Malcolm I (942–54), Edmund of England was obliged to concede the regions of Cumberland, Northumberland and Westmorland to the Scots, as a result of which the overall Scottish domain was about one-third larger than it is today.

Throughout this formative era from the 600s, a very efficient Clan System of related families developed in the Highlands, and by the 11th century numerous clans traced their ancestry from Prince Loarn of Dalriada. A few others were descended from his brother King Fergus, and a couple from the third brother Prince Aonghus. It is apparent, therefore, that the princely sons of Erc were not only important governors but had a significant impact on community development, and many Scottish families emerged with their own royal heritage from the Dalriadic brothers. In this context, the Clan System evolved in a keenly fraternal environment. Everyone belonging to a family clan was cared for spiritually, physically and financially, and there was an inherent community structure consisting of chiefs, chieftains, priests and kin. The clansmen were never classified as the chiefs' subjects, however, because they were all descended from a common ancestor. The chiefs were simply the senior representatives by way of hereditary descent from leaders who had been chosen in the early days.

In the 10th century, King Malcolm I's son Kenneth II married a daughter of the Duke of Normandy, and at that time the Saxon king, Edgar of England, conceded the Northumbrian Lothians to Kenneth II, so that yet another slice of England's former realm was granted to the Scots House of Alpin.

By then, the Celtic Church was firmly established as a governmental institution, and from 906 (when King Constantine III and Bishop Cellach stood together on the Hill of Credulity near Scone) the law and disciplines of the Celtic faith were maintained. The Holy Supper was celebrated once a year only, at Easter (by the old calendar), and there was no communion at any other time of year. In direct contrast to England's Roman Church practice, there were no infant baptisms and no images of the crucifix in Scotland. By virtue of their apostolic heritage, the Celtic Christians rightly claimed a closer affinity than Rome to the original followers of Jesus, and while seeking to convert

Scotland's pagan believers to Christianity, they diplomatically pledged not to destroy the time-honoured customs of the land.

Tanistry came to an end in the early-11th century when Malcolm II seized the Sceptre of Justice and elected to retain the succession within his own line, rather than pass his crown to a younger cousin. As a result, he instigated Scotland's first full-blooded civil war, and the various contenders battled for position. Indeed, Malcolm II had previously hacked his own route to the throne in 1005 by murdering not only his cousin Kenneth III, but also Kenneth's son Boede of Duff. The problem was, however, that Malcolm had no son, only three married daughters, each of whom had a son of exceptional ability and ambition.

Malcolm's eldest daughter, Bethoc, was married to Crinan, Thane of the Isles, Head of the House of Atholl and dynastic Abbot of Dunkeld. Crinan was also successor to the hereditary Bishops of All Fortrenn, and Archpriest of the Celtic Church of the Sacred Kindred of Saint Columba. The son of Bethoc and Crinan was Duncan, Prince of Cumbria.

Bethoc's younger sister was Donada, whose husband was Finlaech, Mormaer of Moray, Thane of Ross and Cromarty, a descendant of Prince Loarn of Dalriada. Finlaech and Donada's son was Macbeth.

The third and youngest sister was Olith, the wife of Sigurd II, Prince and Jarl of the Norse kingdom of the Orkneys. Their son was Thorfinn II, Earl of Caithness.

Macbeth

The names of Macbeth, Lady Macbeth and Banquo are rarely heard outside William Shakespeare's famous tragic play, but they were three of the most important characters in Scotland's history. Indeed, were it not for King Macbeth and his stalwart queen, Scotland could so easily have fallen into anarchy as a result of Malcolm II's demolition of the Tanist system.

In addition to Malcolm II's three daughters there were two other powerful women with regal aspirations; one was Kenneth III's granddaughter Gruoch, the heiress of Duff (Dubh), who was married to Finleach's cousin Gillacomgen of Moray. Not only did Lady Gruoch front her own claim by the law of Tanistry, but she was pregnant at the time, and her husband was related to more than a dozen Clan chiefs, each with a descent from Prince Loarn of Dalriada. The other woman was King Malcolm's own sister Dunclina; she was married to Kenneth, Mormaer of Lochaber – a descendant of King Aedh, with a secondary claim to the crown, being a cousin of the murdered Boede. Their son was Banquo, who became Thane of Lochaber.

In the event, Malcolm II selected Bethoc's son Duncan to be his successor, as a result of which a most important new Scottish custom was born, a custom which was later inherited by the Stewart Kings, and which led to their eventual troubles in England. This was the establishment of 'Priest-Kings' in the Scottish line for, as we have seen, Duncan was the son and heir of Crinan, Archpriest of the Sacred Kindred of Saint Columba. Not only was Duncan destined to become King of Scots, but he would also become hereditary Archpriest of the Sacred Kindred – a joint-status quite unparalleled in Europe.

Notwithstanding this prospect, many were critical when Malcolm announced his successor; they did not object to Duncan's nomination as such, but to the fact that King Malcolm had made the decision alone. This was against the law, which insisted that the succession should be settled in collaboration with the Celtic Church and the Government. Not surprisingly, a furious dispute arose, and Boede's daughter Gruoch lost no time in organizing fierce opposition to Malcolm. He responded by killing her husband Gillacomgen, and Gruoch fled to the Ross-shire protection of her late husband's cousin, the son of Donada and Finlaech. There, she gave birth to Gillacomgen's son, Lulach, and shortly afterwards, in 1032, she married her faithful cousin and protector to become Lady Macbeth.

When Malcolm II died in 1034, his grandson duly succeeded as King Duncan I (the Gracious), whereupon Lady Macbeth persuaded her husband to challenge Duncan's succession. She was not alone in her resentment, for individual clan rebellions were already underway, and not even Banquo (a commander in Duncan's army) could contain the riots. Consequently, a military council was convened, at which Macbeth was given overall control of the King's troops.

Macbeth managed to subdue the commotions, gaining respect and popularity not only from those who had suffered in the riots,

Kings of Scots from Alpin to Malcolm III

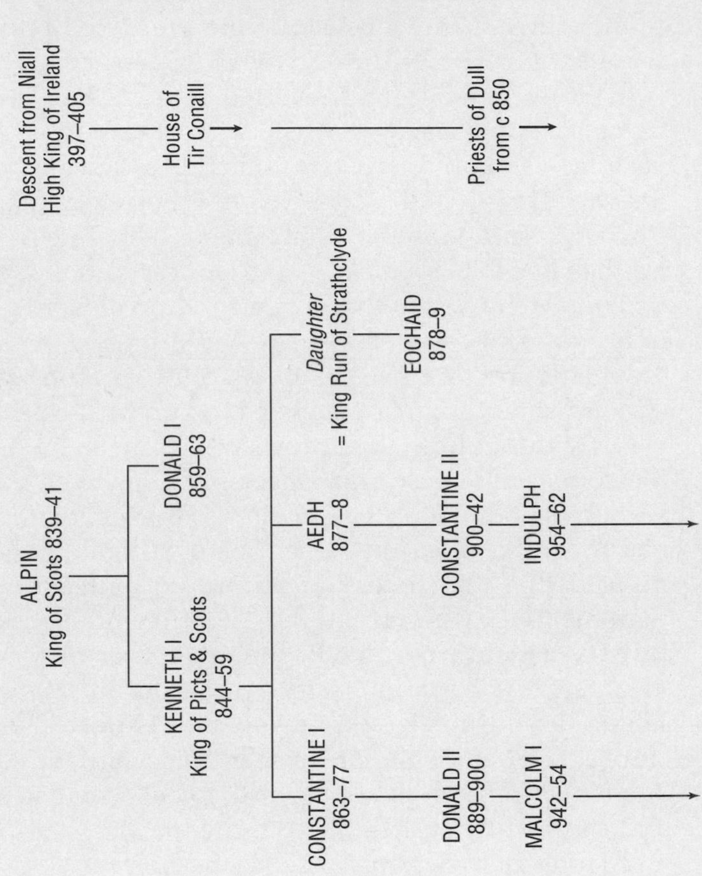

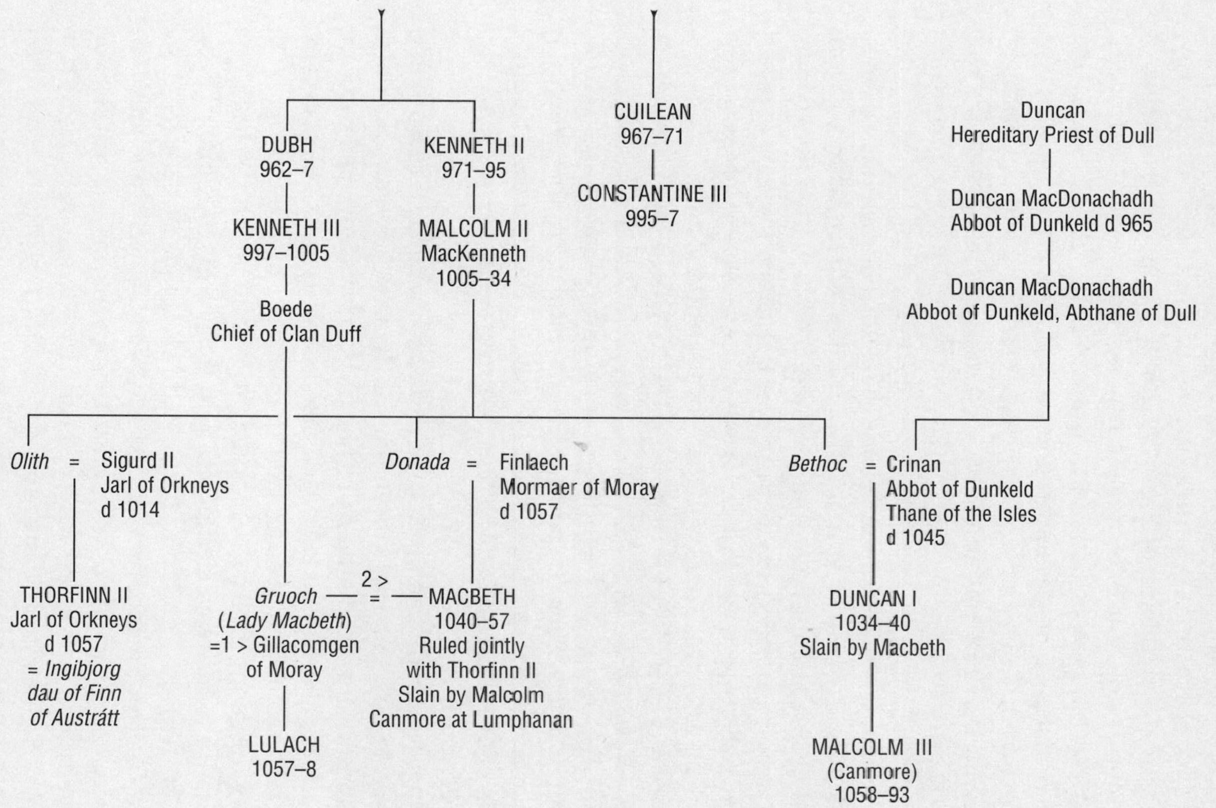
DUBH
962–7
KENNETH II
971–95
CUILEAN
967–71
CONSTANTINE III
995–7
Duncan
Hereditary Priest of Dull
KENNETH III
997–1005
MALCOLM II
MacKenneth
1005–34
Duncan MacDonachadh
Abbot of Dunkeld d 965
Boede
Chief of Clan Duff
Duncan MacDonachadh
Abbot of Dunkeld, Abthane of Dull
Olith = Sigurd II
Jarl of Orkneys
d 1014
Donada = Finlaech
Mormaer of Moray
d 1057
Bethoc = Crinan
Abbot of Dunkeld
Thane of the Isles
d 1045
THORFINN II
Jarl of Orkneys
d 1057
= *Ingibjorg*
dau of Finn
of Austrått
Gruoch
(*Lady Macbeth*)
=1 > Gillacomgen
of Moray
2 > =
MACBETH
1040–57
Ruled jointly
with Thorfinn II
Slain by Malcolm
Canmore at Lumphanan
DUNCAN I
1034–40
Slain by Macbeth
LULACH
1057–8
MALCOLM III
(Canmore)
1058–93

but from those who had instigated them. Much to Lady Macbeth's pleasure, the crown was within her husband's grasp, and in 1040 King Duncan was murdered by an unknown hand at Bothnagowan (the house of the smith), now Pitgavenny, near Elgin. Macbeth then became King south and west of the Tay, being proclaimed King of Scots at Scone, under the protection of the clans of Ross and Moray. His cousin, Thorfinn II of Caithness, ruled the balance of Scotland, guarding the Orkneys and the Western Isles against Scandinavian interference.

Banquo of Lochaber was not impressed by this inheritance, and although not pursuing his own route to kingship, he was determined to regain the crown for Duncan's son Malcolm Canmore. Macbeth and Banquo became bitter enemies, and Macbeth had two of Banquo's sons (Malcolm and Kenneth) slain. Then, while Banquo and another of his sons, Fleance, were hunting in 1043, they were ambushed by Macbeth's henchmen. Banquo was stabbed to death in the fight, but Fleance escaped to the Welsh Court of Prince Gruffyd ap Llewelyn of Gwynedd and Deheubarth. There, in the comparative safety of Wales, he became the first husband of Gruffyd's eldest daughter, Princess Nesta.

We shall return to Banquo, Fleance and Nesta in due course, for they were each important to the story of the emergent Stewarts. Indeed, as Shakespeare's three Weird Sisters foretold in his 17th-century play *Macbeth*, Banquo would himself beget a line of kings.

King Macbeth ran a disciplined and peaceful realm, and proved to be a very able monarch for the next 17 years. Scotland can thank him for the basis of her judicial system, and through his efforts the nation emerged as a strong European power. Macbeth remodelled the Celtic Church, and kept it from becoming engulfed by Catholicism, while at the same time maintaining his respected position in the streets of Rome.[3] There, in 1050, he was reported to have made generous donations to the poor, 'scattering money like seed'. Lady Gruoch Macbeth was equally popular at Court, and the problems of succession seemed to be under control – but old rivals were still at hand. In 1055 Earl Siward of Northumbria invaded Scotland on behalf of Malcolm Canmore; then in 1057 Malcolm led his own army of 10,000 men against Macbeth, forcing the King's entrenchment

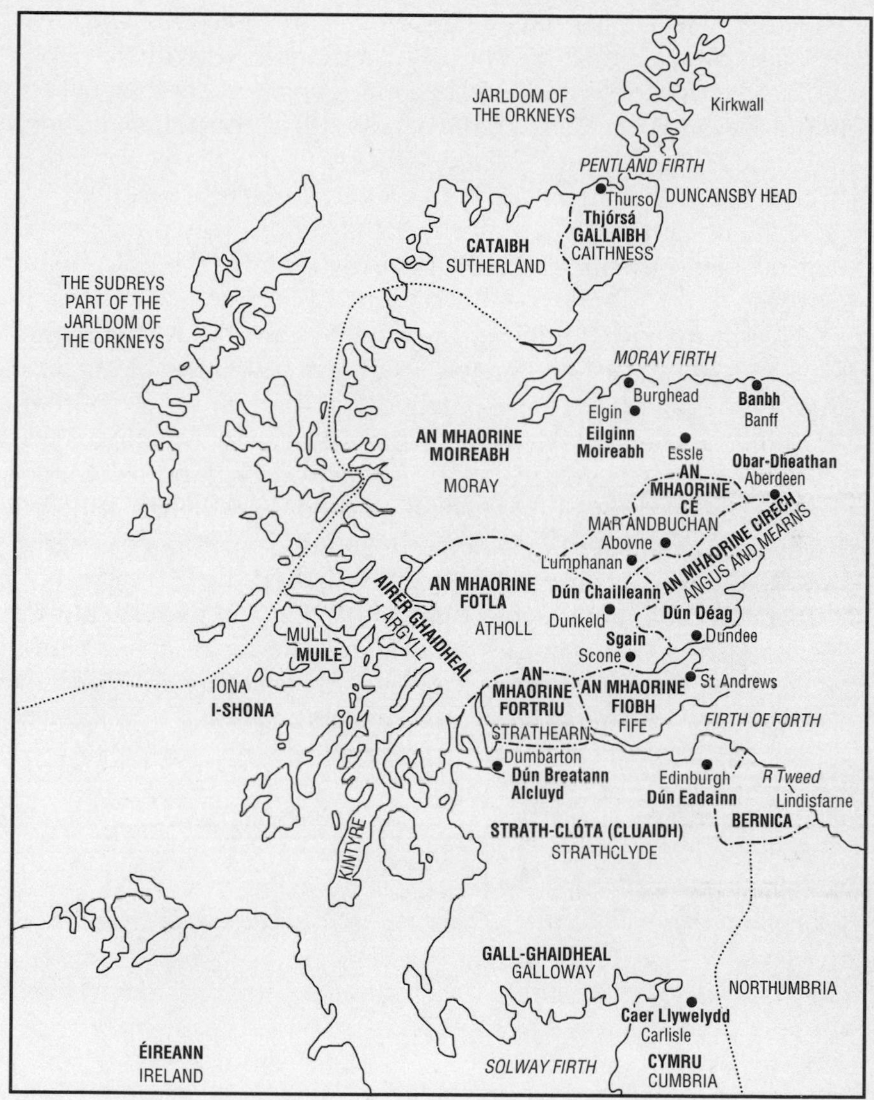

Map 2 Macbeth's Alba

behind a stockade on Dunsinane Hill. As the formidable opposition advanced under camouflage from Great Birnham Wood, Lady Macbeth realized that her husband's days were numbered, and she committed suicide. Macbeth fought a rear-guard action, retreating to Lumphanan, Aberdeenshire, where he was caught and slain.

Thorfinn was also killed in the battle, and his widow, Ingibjorg, was claimed by Malcolm Canmore. Notwithstanding his victory, Malcolm did not become King for another seven months because the Macbeth party was still in control, and upon their leader's death they placed Gruoch's son Lulach upon the throne. Not long afterwards, however, Lulach was killed at Strathbogie, and in 1058 Malcolm III Canmore was proclaimed King of Scots, inheriting also the priestly legacy of the Columban Kindred.

Malcolm married Ingibjorg in order to gain the fealty of the Isles, and she gave him three sons. But in 1066 Ingibjorg was unfairly displaced and dispatched to the Orkneys so that Malcolm could marry the Saxon heiress Margaret Atheling. This was the year of the Norman Conquest of England when, in October, the Witan Council proclaimed Edgar Atheling King of the English in spite of William of Normandy's victory over King Harold. Edgar was descended from Aethelred the Unready, but William the Conqueror sent Edgar into exile, and then set out to decimate the Saxon families of England. Some escapees came to Scotland, but many were not so lucky, falling to Norman swords as the invaders subjugated the land.

3

Priest-Kings and the Church

Saint Margaret

Among those who escaped to Scotland was Edgar's sister, Princess Margaret Atheling. She had been born and raised at the Court of her grandfather King Stephen of Hungary, and had spent some time with her great-uncle Edward the Confessor (King of England 1042–66) during his reign. During this latter period she had been introduced to Malcolm Canmore, who was himself in English exile for 17 years prior to 1057. News of Margaret's arrival in Scotland reached Malcolm in December 1066, and early the following year they were married.

Much has been written in favour of the lady who became Saint Margaret of Scotland, and it has been said that she was considerably more sophisticated than her husband: but this is nonsense. Having been educated in a constrained Catholic environment, Margaret could only converse in Latin and Hungarian, and she cared little for her Saxon heritage, whereas Malcolm was raised to be King. He could read, write, and negotiate very effectively with foreign ambassadors and diplomats. On becoming Queen of Scotland, Margaret set out to undermine everything that was foreign to her – the Gaelic language, the Clan System, and the Celtic Church – bankrupting the State in the process. It was essentially during Margaret's term as Queen that Scotland's traditional Church became Romanized, and she installed her eldest son, Ethelred, as lay Abbot of Dunkeld to facilitate the process.

Margaret is traditionally reputed for her benevolence but, in truth, her ostensibly charitable behaviour was centred around financial bribery in an effort to buy allegiance in an alien environment. Malcolm may have been besotted with Margaret, but when she died in 1093 the people of the Highlands breathed a sigh of relief; if ever there was a personal divide created within the Scottish nation, it was created by Margaret Atheling. Prior to her arrival there was little conflict between the people north and south of the Tay, but by the time of her death the Highlanders and Lowlanders were barely able to understand one another. Despite her Papal sainthood (granted 150 years after her death for services rendered in Romanizing the Celtic Church), Margaret was a Scottish disaster, and her beguiled husband was quite ineffectual in her company.

Before Margaret's death, a major territorial dispute had arisen between the Scots and the Norman conquerors of England. According to the Norman King, William II Rufus, the territories of Cumberland and Northumberland were held by Malcolm III as a vassal of the English Crown, and Malcolm was expected to give an Oath of Allegiance to the King of England. Actually, Malcolm had been King of Cumbria since 1057 when Edward the Confessor sat on the English throne, and Cumberland, Northumberland and Westmorland were designated Scottish territories from the days of Malcolm I. If anyone should have rendered 'homage' it should have been the Norman usurper William Rufus, who ruled England by might of the sword, not by any right of descent or affinity. Indeed, as confirmed at the Council of Gloucester, the true heirs of England were Margaret Atheling's sons by Malcolm III. William Rufus knew this, but he paid no heed to the truth, and the result was an Anglo-Scottish war.

In November 1093 Malcolm III, with two of his sons by Margaret (Edward and Edmund), left Edinburgh for the battlefield of Alnwick in the north of England, but their army was defeated by the Norman troops of William II. Both Malcolm and Edward were slain in the conflict, and for a time Edmund was also presumed dead, though he had actually fled the field. When news of the disaster reached Margaret, she had a nervous breakdown and died very soon afterwards. Once again, there were a number of contenders for the Scottish Crown.

Although Margaret's sons were the rightful heirs of England, they were effectively junior to Malcolm's sons by his first wife,

Ingibjorg, in the Scots succession. The claimants were: Duncan – the first son of Malcolm III and Ingibjorg, whose claim was supported by the King of Norway; Edgar – the fourth son of Malcolm and Margaret, supported by the Anglo-Saxons; Donald Ban – Malcolm III's brother, whose support came from some northern clans, and from his nephew, Edmund, who had disappeared from Alnwick.

As it transpired, in five short years from 1093, they all ruled in turn. Firstly, Donald Ban was proclaimed King by the Highland law of Tanistry, but Duncan II deposed him a few months later. After a very brief rule, Donald and Edmund had Duncan assassinated, whereupon Donald stepped in again, only to be defeated and exiled by Edgar, who threw his brother Edmund into gaol at the same time. By then it was 1097, and Edgar reigned for ten years, but he was slain by his brother and successor Alexander I (the Fierce), who died peacefully at Stirling in 1124. In time the dust of this chaotic era settled, and with Alexander's brother, King David I, came a much needed period of reform and consolidation – a period that was to see the emergence of the Stewarts in Scotland.

The Sacred Kindred of Saint Columba

The most ancient royal and ecclesiastical seat of the early Celtic Kings of Scots was the Church of Dull, near Aberfeldy in Perthshire. After Iona and Dunkeld, Dull was the primary seat of the Celtic Church in Scotland, and it was held by the Kings of Scots in their capacity as Lay Abbots of Dunkeld and Abthanes of Dull.

As we have seen, Crinan, Abthane of Dull, Abbot of Dunkeld and Seneschal of the Isles, was married in the year 1000 to Lady Bethoc of Alban, the eldest daughter of Malcolm II. Crinan's ancestors had maintained the hereditary priesthood of Dull for well over five generations since 850. He was of Irish descent from the 5th-century King Conall Gulban of Tir Connail, and Saint Columba (521–97) was of this same family. Hence, in the early 11th century, Crinan became Head of the Sacred Kindred of Saint Columba. He was later slain by Vikings at the sacking of Dunkeld in 1045.

Saint Columba had brought the original Christian message

(preserved by the Syrian bishop Nestorius) into Ireland and Scotland from the Middle East, so that both the Old and New Testaments received equal status within the Celtic Church. Indeed it was Columba who, in 574, had crowned and anointed King Aedàn mac Gabràn of Dalriada (Celtic Pendragon[1] and father of King Arthur) – the first British monarch to be installed by priestly ordination – and this greatly upset the Church of Rome. Following Columba's death in 597, the Pope sent St Augustine to dismantle the Celtic Church in Britain, but although he became England's new Catholic Archbishop of Canterbury, his mission failed in Scotland, Ireland and Wales, where the Celtic Church prevailed.

Unlike their Catholic counterparts, the priests of the Celtic Church were allowed to be married, and their hereditary offices were passed from father to son. Within this structure, however, there were enclaves of celibate monks who perpetuated the Eastern tradition of anchorites, and Saint Columba was an example of this sect.

Although considered austere by the ostentatious Roman Church, the Celtic Kindred was popular throughout Europe, and the Russian Old Faith believers have traditionally referred to the Celtic faith as their 'Sister Church'. Some Celtic priests and culdees (monks) took up vacant Aryan bishoprics in Europe, while others were substituted for Italian bishops at the people's request. The last Celtic Abbot of Iona, where Columba built his original monastery, was John MacKinnon, who died sword-in-hand in 1500.

Early Celtic Christianity was the closest of all religious teachings to the original doctrines of Jesus, and it had emerged within a few years of the Crucifixion as the foremost Church of the Christian world. Christians of the Celtic Church were recorded in Ireland in the latter reign of Emperor Tiberius (AD 14–37), long before St Peter went to Rome. Given that Jesus' own teachings formed the basis of the faith, the Mosaic structure of the Old Testament was duly incorporated. Judaic marriage laws were observed, together with the celebrations of the Sabbath and Passover, while Easter was correctly held as the traditional feast-day of the Spring goddess, Eostre, long before the Roman Church foisted a new significance on the old Celtic festival at the Synod of Whitby in 664.

Contrary to traditional belief, Emperor Constantine the Great (AD 274–337) did not embrace Christianity as the religion of Rome; he adapted Christianity into a new form which was implemented as the religion of Rome. Constantine's reign as Emperor was actually related to the Syrian Sol Invictus cult of sun worship, but he determined to create a purpose-built religion to divert Christianity from its Judaic origins. He redefined Jesus' birthday to comply with the Sun Festival on 25 December, and substituted the sacred Sabbath (Saturday) with the Sun-day. Indeed, by a series of such manoeuvres, the high-points of Judaic Christianity were conveniently merged with the pagan tradition, and the Persian cult of Mithras, which stressed the concept of final judgement, was also partially enveloped.

The outcome, from a purely political base, was the uniquely contrived and controllable State 'hybrid' of the Roman Church. On being formalized at the Councils of Nicaea and Constantinople, the new Roman doctrine proclaimed all alternative faiths heretical, all except for the Celtic Church, which was too well-established to provoke. Any such attempt would have been tantamount to a declaration of war, particularly against Ireland; and at that time Rome did not have the military capability to confront the fierce troops of the Irish kings.

Knights Templars and the Celtic Order

When David I acceded in the early 12th century, the Cistercian Order of St Bernard de Clairvaux became the natural inheritor of the Celtic Church, whose elders felt it could best survive within the wrap of this financially influential Order. In general terms, Western Christianity had become highly Catholicized, but the Cistercian Order was not attached to the High Church of Rome, and was therefore compatible with the Celtic Church. The Cistercians were strictly monastic, and were concerned with education, agriculture and the sacred arts. Not the least of mutual concerns was that St Bernard supported the ideals of the Scottish Priest-Kings, and was the foremost patron of the Knights Templars of Jerusalem. Today, the Church of Dull stands on Cistercian land inherited from the old Celtic Order. In

1203 a new Cistercian monastery was founded on Iona (where Columba's monastery had been demolished by Norsemen in 807), and at length all the Celtic abbacies became Cistercian.

St Bernard had been appointed Patron and Protector of the Knights Templars at the French 'Council of Troyes' in 1128. At that time, he had drawn up the Order's Constitution, and had since translated the *Sacred Geometry* of the masons who built King Solomon's Jerusalem Temple. Consequently, the secrets of their own Grand Master, Hiram Abiff, were lodged with the Order of the Temple.

Also in 1128, Saint Bernard's cousin Hugues de Payens, founder and Grand Master of the Templars, met with King David I in Scotland, and the Order established a seat on the South Esk. A firm bond was thus cemented between the Cistercians and the Celtic Church of Saint Columba. Indeed, as we shall soon see, both David and his sister were maritally attached to the Flemish House of Boulogne, so there were direct family ties between David, Hugues de Payens, and the Crusader Kings of Jerusalem. It is interesting to note that soon afterwards, in 1147, a Charter of Templar Constitution was granted in Dublin, the capital of Columba's native Ireland.

The Flemish Connection

Although some Normans ventured into Scotland at the time of Malcolm III and the Battle of Alnwick, there was no effective penetration until the reign of King David I (1124–53). But even then this controlled immigration was engineered for specific reasons when David invited the sons of Norman and Flemish aristocracy to his realm. The resultant settlement was far more Flemish than Norman, even though some of the noble families of Flanders (like those of de Brus and Balieul) had been granted lands in Normandy before the conquest of England.

King David (the Saint) recognized that, during the recent years of turmoil, Scotland had fallen behind the European countries in many ways; her systems of government, trade, manufacture and urban development were all outmoded, and the economy was suffering. Flanders, on the other hand, was at the forefront of a significant commercial urbanization which provided substantial rental and mercantile income. The Flemings were also advanced in agricultural expertise, and had a greatly superior weaving industry. All in all, David deemed their knowledge and updated techniques necessary to aid Scotland's survival on the international stage.

The Normans too were very experienced in matters of government and land management. King David, therefore, sought their aid in all manner of administrative affairs: sheriffdoms were created, new communication networks were developed, and the powers of the judiciary were considerably strengthened. Also, the prerogatives of the Crown were redefined so as to be more socially effective and financially viable.

Generally, the incoming nobles of Flanders and Normandy married into Celtic stock, and conversely King David had himself married Maud de Lens of the Flemish House of Boulogne. Maud was the daughter and heiress of Waltheof, Earl of Huntingdon, and the widow of Simon de Senlis (St Liz). In fact, Maud was the richest woman in Britain, and the marital alliance facilitated a valuable trade arrangement between Scotland and Flanders.

David's sister Matilda was married to Maud's Norman cousin, King Henry I of England. David's other sister, Mary, married Eustace III, Count of Boulogne (brother of the Crusade commander, Godefroi de Bouillon, King of Jerusalem), and their son-in-law was Stephen, Comte de Blois (later King of England). Stephen was a female-line grandson of William the Conqueror.

In administrative, trading and economic terms, David's practical strategies worked well, but there were associated problems on the political front. These rose to the fore when the King of Scots became Earl of Huntingdon, succeeding his father-in-law Waltheof. Huntingdon was of course an English earldom, and so when King Henry I died, David was required to give an Oath of Fealty to Henry's daughter, Matilda (known as the Empress). She had been married to Emperor Henrich V of Germany (died 1125), and her second husband (from 1128) was Geoffrey Plantagenet, Count of Anjou.

Empress Matilda was the sole inheritor of the English crown, but at her father's death, Stephen de Blois raced to England from Boulogne and seized the throne. This was a great embarrassment to King David of Scots because Stephen was his nephew-in-law, and so David pledged his allegiance to Matilda in an attempt to aid the situation on her behalf. Eventually, a compromise was reached through David's mediation, and it was settled that Stephen would keep the English crown during his lifetime, following which it would revert back to Matilda or her heirs.

At the time of this debate, Walter Fitz Alan (a forebear of the Stewarts) was a senior adviser to King David. He was of Scottish-Breton lineage, and having successfully repelled a Norse incursion from Cowal and Bute, had been granted extensive lands in Renfrewshire and East Lothian. Walter was a witness to the Charter when King David granted Annandale to Robert de Brus (forebear of Robert the Bruce).

Walter Fitz Alan and Robert de Brus wisely advised David against taking too strong a stand in favour of Empress Matilda. They pointed out that Matilda's heritage was expressly Norman, whereas Stephen's support (irrespective of his descent from the Conqueror) came mainly from the Flemish nobles. Indeed, it was the Flemish House of Boulogne to which Stephen's wife (David's niece) was the heiress. In essence, the men said, this war was actually a battle between Normans and Flemings, and it was not in the Scottish interest for the Normans to succeed. The advisers were particularly concerned that if David made a stand against Stephen's forces he would be setting his loyal Flemish nobles against their own kinsmen and colleagues. The result, said Robert de Brus, would be disaster, and he was adamant that David should sidestep the dispute.

The Lion of Louvain

It is often presumed that Robert de Brus was a Norman from Brix in the hinterland of Cherbourg, but this is quite wrong, as proved by his original Flemish arms. When Matilda of Flanders entered Normandy to marry Duke William in 1053, many nobles of the Flemish houses accompanied her, and numerous others followed. The family of Robert de Brus had been granted lands in Normandy, but when Robert came to Britain he carried the azure Flemish lion of Louvain. This device was originally that of Count Lambert I of Louvain, who had died in 1015. Lambert's granddaughter and heiress was Maud de Louvain (the wife of Eustace I of Boulogne), and her son was Lambert of Lens, whose granddaughter Maud married King David I of Scotland.

When Jocelyn de Louvain (son of Count Godefroi of Lower Lorraine) came to England in the mid-12th century, Robert de Brus yielded the Louvain arms to him as the senior family representative in Britain. Instead, Robert adopted the well-known saltire arms in the red and gold colours of Boulogne. These were the arms of the Castellans of Bruges, and Robert de Bruges (Brus) had been Castellan from 1046 until 1053 when many of the nobles moved to Normandy with Matilda of Flanders. (The earliest Roll of Scottish Arms is the *Armorial de Gelre*, held at the Bibliothèque Royale in Brussels.)

When Maud de Lens married King David, she was accompanied by many kinsmen of her Boulogne house; these included representatives of Walter the Fleming (now Seton), Gilbert de Ghent d'Alost (now Lindsay), Robert de Commines de St Pol (now Comyn and Buchan), Arnulf de Hesdin (now Graham), the Advocate of Bethune (now Beaton), and numerous others. It was largely through these family connections that David managed to implement his concept of active Flemish nobility in Scotland[2]. Apart from de Brus and those named above, other Scottish families with Flemish ancestry are Abernethy, Anstruther, Baird, Balliol, Boswell, Brodie, Cameron, Campbell, Crawford, Douglas, Erskine, Fleming, Fraser, Hamilton, Hay, Innes, Leith, Leslie, Murray and Oliphant.

Battle of the Standard

In 1138, King Stephen of England came to blows with Empress Matilda's half-brother Robert of Gloucester, and King David of Scots (despite having been warned against involvement) felt obliged to confront Stephen's troops at Cuthen Moor, near Northallerton. There, the Scots were sadly defeated at the Battle of the Standard, having been fooled by the English that their King was dead. At a point when victory was strategically in the balance, a severed head, claimed to be that of King David, was held aloft on an English pike. Consternation quickly swept through the Scottish ranks, and the battle was lost. David was taken captive and ransomed to his son Henry, who later married

Princess Matilda's cousin Ada de Warenne, a daughter of the Earl of Surrey.

In the following year, Matilda and Stephen were militarily opposed, and a period of civil war erupted in England. Then in 1153 the campaign was joined by Geoffrey and Matilda's son, Henry of Anjou, who gained the throne after Stephen's death a year later. Using his father's surname, Henry II began the new Angevin dynasty of 'Plantagenet' kings, and the rule of the Norman invaders was seemingly over. In practice, though, it was Matilda's heritage which prevailed, and the Norman barons continued their feudal regime just as before.

For some while Scotland was left in relative peace as the people of England battled among themselves. But eventually the Plantagenets became more of a threat to the Scots than had any previous rulers south of the Border. King David died in 1153 before the English dynastic change took place, but not before he had installed his trusted adviser, Walter Fitz Alan, as Lord High Steward of Scotland (*Dapifer Regis Scotiae*).

PART TWO

The Stewart Monarchy

4

Rise of the High Stewards

Stewart Origins and Descent

For some generations there has been much debate as to the true origin of the Stewarts. Various modern writers claim that we are of Scottish descent, while others maintain that we come from Brittany. The fact is that both versions are correct; Walter the Steward had two parents and two sets of immediate ancestry, just like everyone else. On the Scottish side, Walter's paternal descent was from Kenneth mac Alpin, through King Aedh and the Thanes of Lochaber, while on the Breton side his maternal lineage was from the Seneschals (Stewards) of Dol and Dinan in northern Brittany.

The error which is often apparent in published charts occurs because, within the ranks of King David's European nobles, Walter was styled 'Fitz Alan' (Son of Alan). It has been supposed, therefore, that his father must have been Alan the Breton Seneschal, but this is wrong. In making such a presumption the whole chronology is upset, and a generation is completely missed; Walter's father was Alan of Lochaber, who married into the Breton succession.

Through many decades, and especially since Victorian times, chartists and registrars have been so preoccupied with drafting male lines that the importance of wives and daughters has largely been dismissed. Because of this, many family genealogies have been incorrectly published, and as far as the Stewarts are concerned, the female so often ignored was Walter's own mother,

Adelina of Oswestry, the daughter of Alan Fitz Flaald de Hesdin, Sheriff of Shropshire.

Alan de Hesdin's father, Flaald, was the hereditary Steward of Dol in Brittany. In the early 1100s he was Baron of St Florent, Saumur (in the diocese of Angers)[1], and his early forebears were the Counts of Brittany, who were kin to the Merovingian Kings of the Franks. It is with Flaald and his wife that the genealogical problems normally begin. Flaald was married to Aveline, the daughter of Arnulf, Seigneur de Hesdin of Flanders; but some peerage registers (including *Burke's*, along with the 1858 *History of Shropshire*) show Aveline, quite erroneously, as the wife of Flaald's son Alan. The fact is, however, that Alan Fitz Flaald was born with the 'de Hesdin' distinction readily inherited from his mother, Aveline (Ava) of Picardy. Her status is confirmed in the Cartulary of St George, Hesdin. (*See* Chart: Stewart Origins and the Early High Stewards, pages 44–7).

When Aveline's father, Arnulf (brother to Count Enguerrand de Hesdin), joined the Crusade in 1090, Aveline became his nominated deputy in England. She was known as the 'Domina de Norton' (Lady of Norton), and her son Alan Fitz Flaald was Baron of Oswestry during the reign of King Henry I. As correctly detailed in Chalmers' *Caledonia* (1807), Alan was married to Adeliza, the daughter and heiress of Sheriff Warine of Shropshire, thereby inheriting that same office.

Alan de Hesdin's uncle (the brother of Flaald) was Alan, hereditary Seneschal of Dol, who died a Crusade commander in 1097. From his son, William Fitz Alan, the Fitzalan Earls of Arundel descended, while his daughter Emma married Walter, Mormaer of Lochaber – the son of Fleance, and grandson of Banquo. Walter of Lochaber died fighting alongside Malcolm Canmore at Alnwick in 1093. Some registers make the error of showing Walter of Lochaber as being King David's 1st High Steward, which is quite illogical since Walter, the 1st Steward, did not die until 1177.

From this initial marriage between the Scots and Breton families (*c*1085) emerged Alan, Thane of Lochaber. He was born in about 1088, and later cemented a further alliance with the Breton house by marrying Adelina, the daughter of Alan Fitz Flaald. It was their son Walter who succeeded to the Shropshire inheritance. By virtue of his Lochaber heritage and responsibilities,

Walter was summoned to Scotland by David I prior to 1138, and his task was to guard the western coast (from Loch Linnhe to the Firth of Clyde) against Norse invasion.

As we have seen, Banquo's son Fleance was the first husband of Princess Nesta of Gwynedd, but after Fleance's death Nesta married Osbern Fitz Richard, the grandson of Guiomarc, Comte de Léon, who held substantial estates in Dol. In his later life, Guiomarc became a Benedictine monk of St Florent, Saumur, where Flaald of Dol was to become the Baron. Indeed, the family ties were very close, which is how Osbern came to marry Nesta.

In 1080 Flaald and his brother Alan, Seneschal of Dol, consecrated St Florent Abbey. Then in 1082 their younger brother, Rhiwallon of Dol (hitherto a monk), became Abbot. In 1102 Flaald was present at the dedication of Monmouth Priory, and Flaald's son Alan de Hesdin founded Sporle Priory in Norfolk as a Cell of St Florent Abbey. Osbern and Nesta's son Hugh married Eustachia de Say of Clun, while William Fitz Alan married her sister Isabel de Say. As previously mentioned, William's own sister, Emma, married Walter of Lochaber, the son of Fleance and Nesta.

From Steward to Stewart

WALTER, 1ST LORD HIGH STEWARD

When King David died in 1153 he left no surviving heir, his only son Henry of Huntingdon having predeceased him by a year. Nevertheless, Henry left three sons and three daughters, whereby Scotland's succession was assured. His eldest son became Malcolm IV (1153–65), whose reign was the most uninspired in Scottish history. Known scornfully as 'the Maiden', Malcolm vowed his life to Jesus and, although he did have an illegitimate son, he refused to marry. Seizing his opportunity with the ineffectual young king, Henry II Plantagenet demanded that Malcolm should pass over his Cumbrian and Northumbrian rights to the Crown of England. Malcolm IV, who was then only 13, duly complied without argument, and then went to Toulouse, to spend most of his remaining years in France.

It was just as well for Scotland that Walter the Steward remained at the forefront of political, military and financial

The Lion of Scotland

affairs in the King's absence. His management became particularly vital in 1164 when the western coast was invaded by 160 warships of Somerled, Thane of the Isles. Somerled arrived at Renfrew with more than 6,000 warriors; they were bent on conquest, but once ashore were thoroughly defeated by a much smaller force under Walter's Household Knights. Details of the impassioned Battle of Renfrew (in the *Chronicles of Man, Holyrood* and *Melrose*) are confirmed in William of Glasgow's manuscript at Corpus Christi College, Cambridge. This eyewitness account states that Somerled was wounded early in the combat, following which the Norsemen were routed with heavy slaughter.

In that same year Walter Fitz Alan founded Paisley Priory for Cluniac monks, and as the Lord High Steward of Scotland he was also Chancellor of Treasury Revenues. This appointment gave rise to the familiar armorial bearing of the Stewarts, the 'Fesse Chequey' – a representation of the chequered board which was used for computing financial accounts; hence the State Treasury Department became known as the 'Exchequer'.

At the age of 24 Malcolm IV died, to be succeeded by his brother William, who was a couple of years younger. Chivalrous, and much stronger in character, William was nicknamed 'the Lion', and before long he sought to regain Northumberland and Cumberland from Henry Plantagenet. The armies came together at Alnwick in 1174.

At that time Henry II of England was married to Eleanor of Aquitaine (the divorced wife of Louis VII of France), but their sons (with Eleanor's approval) sided with King William of Scots in the northern dispute, standing against their father on the battlefield. Unfortunately, while making a reconnaissance in the fog, William's horse was killed beneath him, and he was taken captive, whereupon the Scots lost the day. Subsequently, in 1174, William was obliged to sign the *Treaty of Falaise*, which recognized the English King as Lord Paramount of Scotland. The castles of Roxburgh, Berwick, Edinburgh and Stirling were passed to King Henry, and the Scots barons and clergy (along with William's brother David of Huntingdon) were required to give Oaths of Allegiance to the House of Plantagenet. Once more, Scotland lacked her king while William was detained as a hostage-vassal of England; and Walter the Steward was again left to pick up the pieces.

William was the first king to carry Scotland's Red Lion on a field of Gold, and so he acquired his nickname, 'the Lion'. The Arms were used to identify Scotland's traditional trading links with Flanders, in the same way that the subsequently added double-tressure and fleury-counter-fleury commemorated the Franco-Scottish alliance.

As previously stated, the Flemish union had been cemented through David I and his wife Maud de Lens, but few historians comment on the importance of the resultant trading advantage. Scotland was actually attached to a monopoly situation, for Maud was not only a cousin of the Count of Flanders, she was also a cousin of Godefroi de Bouillon, Guardian of the newly created kingdom of Jerusalem. David's policy had been to implement a mercantile strategy that would link Scotland to a trading empire centred upon Bruges and managed by Flemish families throughout Eastern and Western Christendom. Indeed, when Scotland began negotiations with the Hanseatic League (a North German trading confederation), she was empowered to negotiate for Burgundian Flanders as well. As recently as 1997 the people of Geel in Flanders organized a festival, with pipers and Highland dancing, to celebrate their nation's traditional links with Scotland. The town mayor welcomed Scots representatives in an official 'ceremony of friendship', and a possible town-twinning[2] is now being discussed to perpetuate the age-old alliance.

Although William the Conqueror had married Matilda of Flanders, the Norman dukes were a constant threat to the Flemish nobles, as was identified by Robert de Brus before

Stewart Origins and the early High Stewards

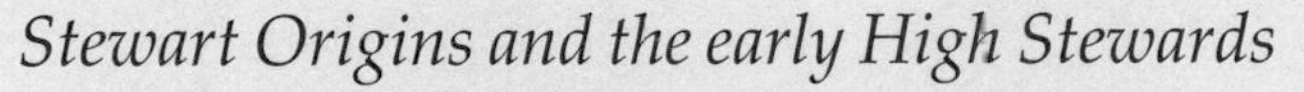

Descent from Faramund of the Sicambrian Franks 419–30
Cousin line to Merovingian Kings
Froamidus
Count of Brittany 762
Frodaldus
Count of Brittany 795
Frotmund d 850
Flotharius
Adelrad
Frotbald c 923
Alirad
Frotmund c 985
Fretaldus c 1008
Nominoé
Duke of Brittany
826–51
= *D'Argentael de Léon*
Espoé
Duke of Brittany
851–7
KING ALPIN OF SCOTS d 841
King Kenneth mac Alpin d 859
King Aedh d 878
Thanes of Lochaber
Doir b 870 d 936
= *dau of King Osbert*
of Northumberland
Murdoch b 900 d 959
Constantine I d 877
Donald II d 863
Malcolm I d 954
Kenneth II d 995
Malcolm II d 1034

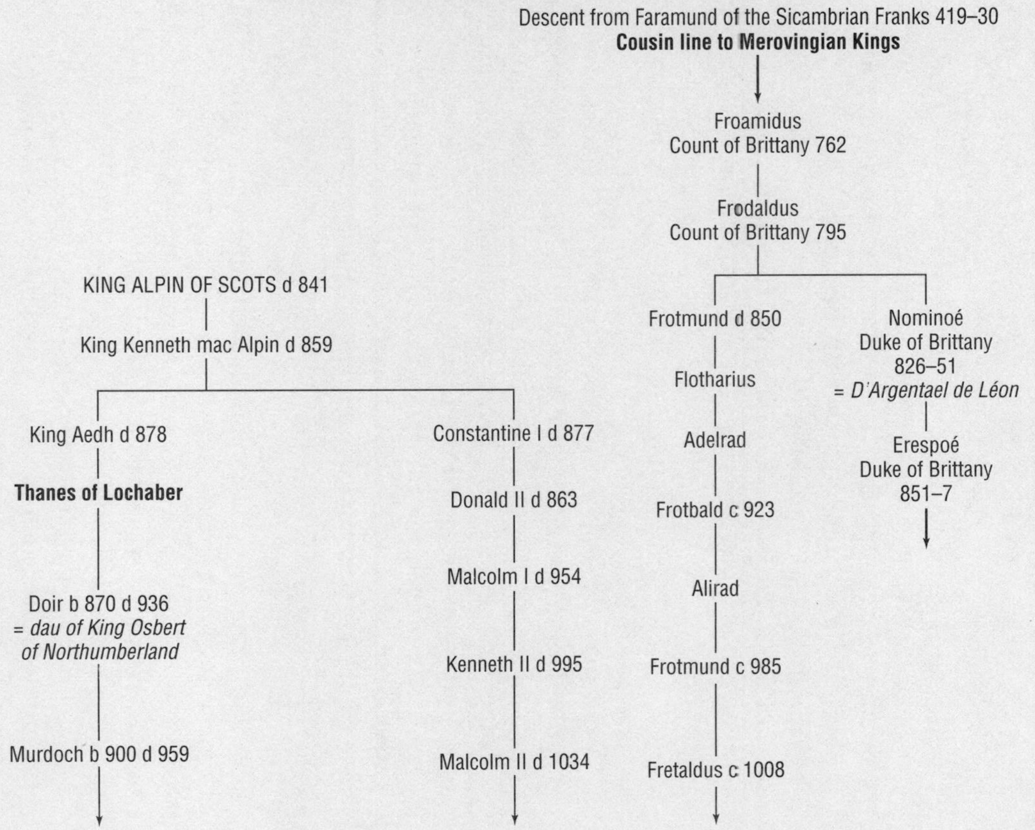

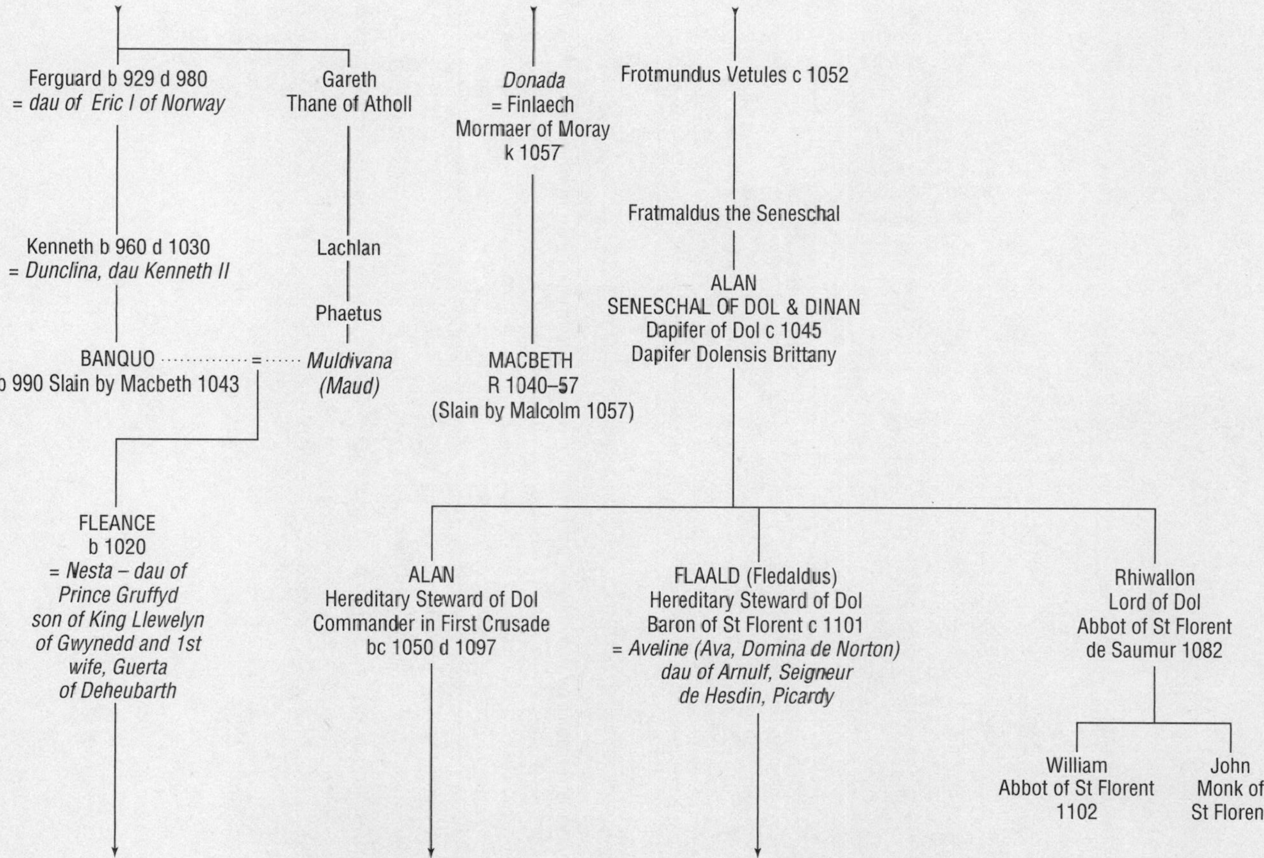
Ferguard b 929 d 980
= *dau of Eric I of Norway*
Gareth
Thane of Atholl
Donada
= Finlaech
Mormaer of Moray
k 1057
Frotmundus Vetules c 1052
Fratmaldus the Seneschal
Kenneth b 960 d 1030
= *Dunclina, dau Kenneth II*
Lachlan
Phaetus
ALAN
SENESCHAL OF DOL & DINAN
Dapifer of Dol c 1045
Dapifer Dolensis Brittany
BANQUO
b 990 Slain by Macbeth 1043
Muldivana
(Maud)
MACBETH
R 1040–57
(Slain by Malcolm 1057)
FLEANCE
b 1020
= *Nesta – dau of*
Prince Gruffyd
son of King Llewelyn
of Gwynedd and 1st
wife, Guerta
of Deheubarth
ALAN
Hereditary Steward of Dol
Commander in First Crusade
bc 1050 d 1097
FLAALD (Fledaldus)
Hereditary Steward of Dol
Baron of St Florent c 1101
= *Aveline (Ava, Domina de Norton)*
dau of Arnulf, Seigneur
de Hesdin, Picardy
Rhiwallon
Lord of Dol
Abbot of St Florent
de Saumur 1082
William
Abbot of St Florent
1102
John
Monk of
St Florent

Stewart Origins and the early High Stewards – continued

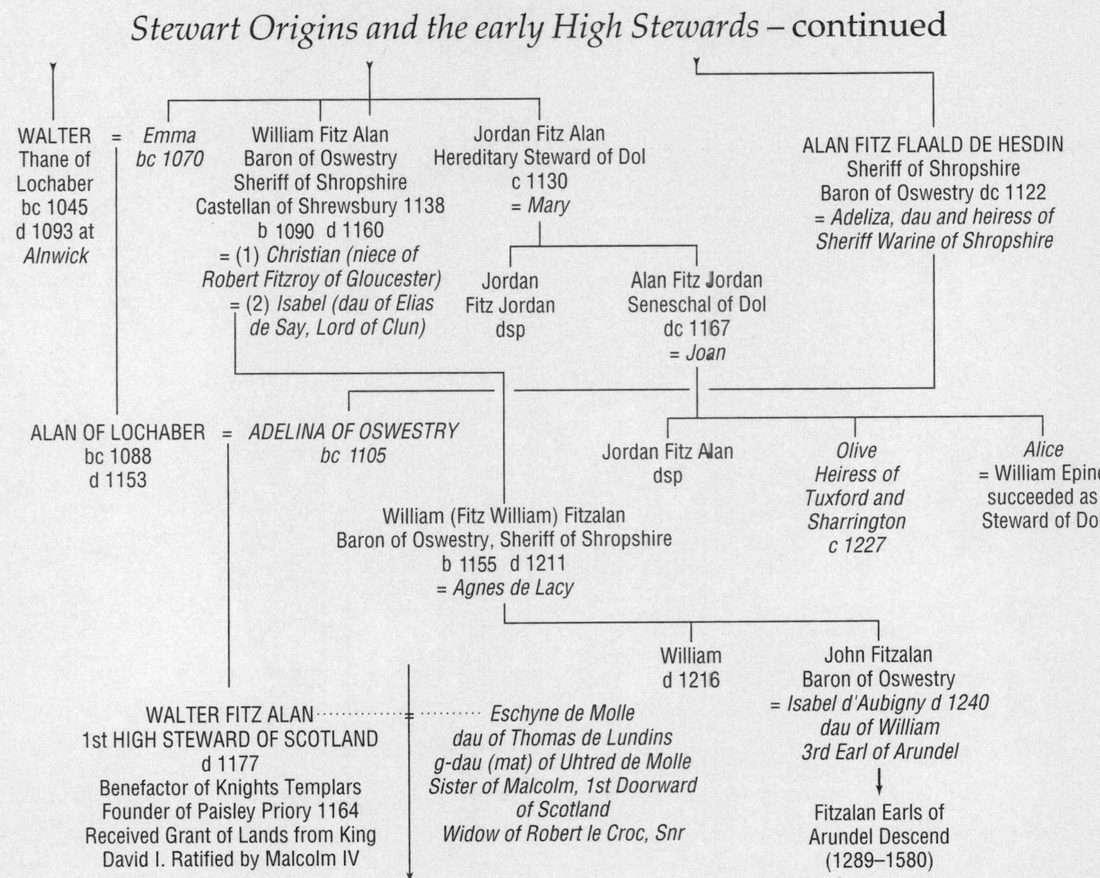

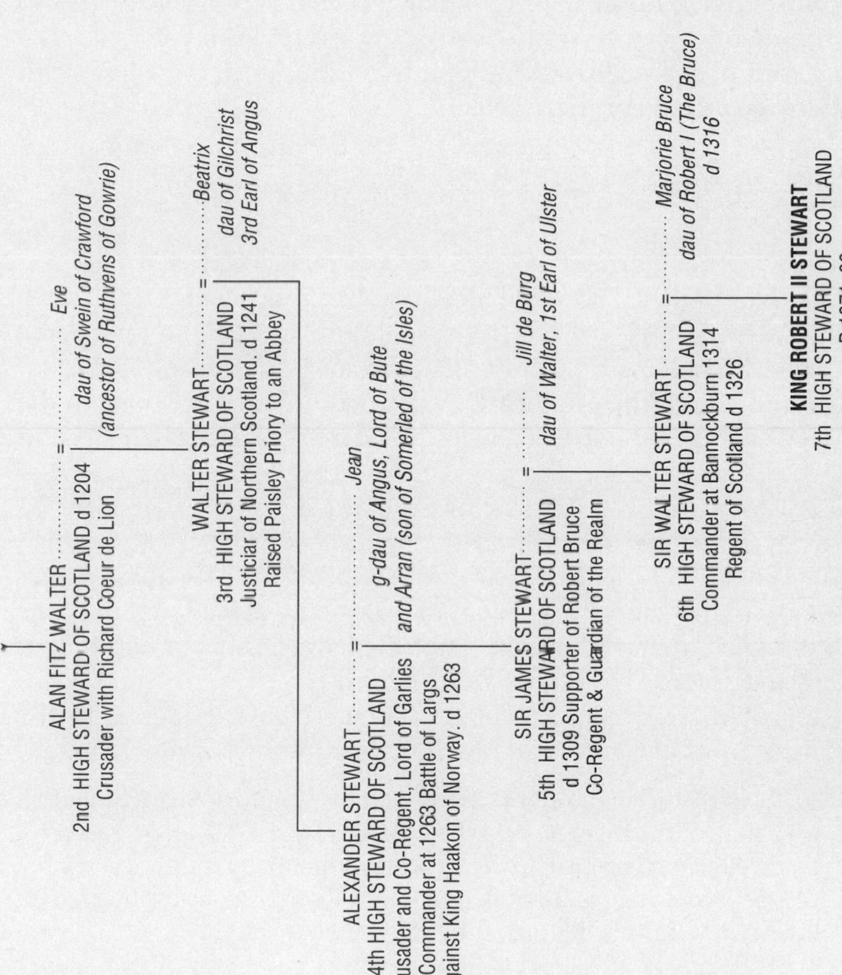
ALAN FITZ WALTER = Eve
2nd HIGH STEWARD OF SCOTLAND d 1204
Crusader with Richard Coeur de Lion
dau of Swein of Crawford
(ancestor of Ruthvens of Gowrie)
WALTER STEWART = Beatrix
3rd HIGH STEWARD OF SCOTLAND
Justiciar of Northern Scotland. d 1241
Raised Paisley Priory to an Abbey
dau of Gilchrist
3rd Earl of Angus
ALEXANDER STEWART = Jean
4th HIGH STEWARD OF SCOTLAND
Crusader and Co-Regent, Lord of Garlies
Commander at 1263 Battle of Largs
against King Haakon of Norway. d 1263
g-dau of Angus, Lord of Bute
and Arran (son of Somerled of the Isles)
SIR JAMES STEWART = Jill de Burg
5th HIGH STEWARD OF SCOTLAND
d 1309 Supporter of Robert Bruce
Co-Regent & Guardian of the Realm
dau of Walter, 1st Earl of Ulster
SIR WALTER STEWART = Marjorie Bruce
6th HIGH STEWARD OF SCOTLAND
Commander at Bannockburn 1314
Regent of Scotland d 1326
dau of Robert I (The Bruce)
d 1316
KING ROBERT II STEWART
7th HIGH STEWARD OF SCOTLAND
R 1371–90

the Battle of the Standard. From the time of the Norman Conquest until Tudor times England had few reliable trading partners, and the Scots' commercial coup was a key reason for the Plantagenet endeavours to exercise control north of the Border. Scotland's international trade was conducted largely from Berwick-upon-Tweed, which is why Berwick featured so prominently in the Anglo-Scottish wars. Eventually, when the fortified port was lost to the English, Edinburgh's Port of Leith succeeded in the primary role.

Alan, 2nd Lord High Steward

Walter Fitz Alan died in 1177, and was succeeded by his son Alan Fitz Walter, 2nd High Steward. Like his father, Alan was a benefactor of the Knights Templars, and in 1189 he joined the Third Crusade with Henry II's son and successor, Richard I Coeur de Lion (the Lionheart). Alan was on good terms with the new Plantagenet king, and before leaving for the Holy Land Richard declared the *Treaty of Falaise* cancelled, giving back the Scottish castles and estates to William in return for a 10,000 merks contribution towards the Jerusalem cause. [A Scottish silver merk had a sterling currency value of 13s 4d – about 66½p. Hence, 10,000 merks was equal to around £6,650, which in terms of today's inflation-adjusted equivalent value, based on Bank of England records, would be about £2.5m.]

On delivering his Charter of renewed independence to the King of Scots at Canterbury, Richard the Lionheart proclaimed:

> To the Archbishops, Abbots, Earls, Barons, Justices, Sheriffs, and all Ministers and Lieges of the whole of England, Greetings. Know ye that we have given back to our brother William, by the Grace of God, King of Scots, his castles of Berwick and Roxburgh, as his by right of inheritance, to be held forever by him and his heirs.

Having made his gesture, Richard I then departed for the Third Crusade along with the 2nd High Steward, Alan Fitz Walter, and the Scots heir-presumptive, David of Huntingdon.

A few years before his reinstatement, William the Lion had married Ermengarde, the daughter of Richard de Beaumont. It was 12 years before they managed to produce a son, but fortunately William's long reign lasted until he was 71. His son duly succeeded as Alexander II in 1214, prior to which Richard the

Lionheart had been killed in 1199. Having battled with Saladin the Saracen for long enough, Richard had not succeeded in wresting Jerusalem from the Muslims, and so he had returned to Europe, only to be held for ransom in Austria. Thereafter, he spent most of his life defending his French estates, and was slain by an archer in the process.

When Alexander II gained the throne of Scots, Richard's brother John had been King of England for 15 years. He had become unpopular with the nobles, the merchants and the Church through his strategic revisions of the tax system, and because of his disputes with the Pope. And so in 1215 (the year after Alexander's accession) King John's avenging nobles presented him with the Magna Charta (Great Charter) at Runnymede. From that moment, England's feudal structure was redefined because the barons became attached to the Church and the wealthy merchant-class, rather than being allied to their king.

In the midst of all this, Alexander of Scots decided to make a show of strength, and he travelled south with his army to meet with his ally, the Dauphin of France, in England. (King John's violent behaviour and the murder of his nephew and claimant, Arthur, had alienated the Barons of Anjou and Poitou, as a result of which John had lost most of his French lands.)

Having concluded their strategic meeting, the Scots and French troops went their separate ways, but King John died of poisoning (apparently administered by a monk) while Alexander was travelling northwards. Subsequently two Papal legates, with bell, book and candle, arrived in Scotland to excommunicate King Alexander and the whole Scottish nation for taking arms into Catholic England. In practice, though, nobody cared very much what the Pope thought, and hardly noticed when the interdict was lifted a year later.

Walter, 3rd Lord High Steward

Alan the High Steward had died in 1204, to be succeeded by his son Walter, who became Scotland's 3rd Lord High Steward, and who was the first of the family to use the surname Stewart. He raised Paisley Priory to the status of an Abbey in 1219, and became Justiciar north of the Forth as well as being Scotland's High Steward and Chancellor.

The Arms of Walter, 3rd High Steward of Scotland

King Alexander II married Joan of England (the daughter of King John) in 1221, but 17 years later, on a visit to the Saint Thomas shrine at Canterbury, Joan died, without having given Scotland an heir. The following year (1239) Alexander married Marie de Couci of Picardy, who was brought over from France by the Archbishop of Glasgow and Walter Stewart. Within two years Marie bore a son, but not long afterwards Alexander died and Marie returned to France, where she married Jean de Brienne, son of the titular King of Jerusalem.

Alexander III was only eight-years-old when he succeeded as King of Scots in 1249, and two years later he was married to his cousin Margaret, the daughter of King John's son Henry III Plantagenet. At the wedding ceremony, Henry intimated that Alexander should pay homage to him, but the young King of Scots was very aware of the agreement made between William the Lion and Richard the Lionheart more than 60 years before. Confronting the English king, Alexander explained that he had come to celebrate a marriage, not to deal with matters of State.

Alexander, 4th Lord High Steward

In time, Alexander III was to become one of Scotland's most impressive kings, but during his minority his co-Regent was the new 4th High Steward, Walter's son Alexander Stewart. By 1263 the Norsemen were becoming troublesome again, and warships from King Haakon's Norwegian fleet arrived at Clydeside. They were successfully defeated by Scots forces under the overall command of Alexander Stewart at the Battle of Largs, and the High Steward was duly rewarded with the lordship of Galloway.

Succession and the Maid of Norway

In 1266 a treaty was signed, whereby the Western Isles and the Isle of Man were ceded to King Alexander by Magnus VI of Norway in return for a nominal quit-rent of 100 merks [today's equivalent value: about £25,000]. Then, in a continued effort to maintain peaceful relations with Norway, Alexander III's daughter Margaret was married to the future Eric II in 1281. Unfortunately she died in childbirth soon afterwards, two years before the death of her father, who broke his neck in a riding accident. At this event, some Catholic believers proclaimed that he should have known better than to make his journey during Lent!

James, 5th Lord High Steward

Although Alexander fathered two sons, they had also predeceased him, and the sole heiress to the Kingdom of Scots was his motherless granddaughter Margaret, the Maid of Norway. She was only three-years-old, and the prevailing 5th High Steward, Sir James (Alexander Stewart's son), became the co-Regent of Scotland, as his father had been before him.

In England, Henry III had been a pretty incompetent king, and his heavy spending caused a Barons' Council (headed by the Frenchman, Simon de Montfort, Earl of Leicester) to rule the country for a year. It was during this period that de Montfort implemented the concept of a Parliament in England. Henry's son Edward I (1272–1307) was rather more capable, and during his reign the English Parliament was formally defined to manage the king's taxation and expenditure. Two categories of government were then introduced to handle the distinct classes of society; designated the 'House of Lords' and the 'House of Commons', both are still operative today despite their feudal origins.

In an attempt to prevent Edward I's lordship of Wales, Prince Llewelyn of Gwynedd led an unsuccessful rebellion against the English king, whereupon Edward (the Lawgiver) passed the *Statute of Wales* which brought the Welsh nation firmly under Plantagenet rule. In order to emphasize the fact he built imposing castles at Harlech and Caernarvon, and gave the title 'Prince of Wales' to his own new-born son. Henceforth the distinction has remained with the eldest son of England's reigning monarch.

Ireland was rather less of a problem for Edward I, having already been subjugated by Henry III. With the express approval of the Pope (who was pushing to overthrow the Celtic Church), Henry had launched a great military invasion to bring Ireland's ruling classes under his dominion; he then drained the land of its wealth to support his effort to gain control in Scotland. This endeavour was continued by Edward I, who saw his own great opportunity when the little Maid of Norway acceded to the Scottish throne.

It was evident to all that the Scots faced a very delicate situation, but they were not too concerned with the Plantagenet threat at first. The greater problem was that, given Margaret's Nordic-Scots status, the nation could so easily come under rule from Norway. The Bishop of Glasgow decided to approach Margaret's uncle, Edward I of England, for advice on the matter, but in view of Edward's Scottish ambition his response was not difficult to predict. He suggested that the young Queen should be betrothed to his own son, Edward Caernarvon, and that she should be raised at the Plantagenet Court in England. King Edward even prepared a treaty alluding to a marital alliance, but the Scots were not altogether convinced. Four years later, however, the Scots resolved to bring the Maid to Scotland in any event, free from matrimonial entanglement, and the Norwegian King agreed.

Margaret, Queen of Scots, was then seven years old, and in September 1290 her ship sailed from Norway. But upon reaching Orkney Margaret died, having been 'seized by a mortal disease'.

It was a most unexpected and mysterious death, the true cause of which has never been discovered, and in Scotland there was a widespread suspicion of foul play. Many believed that the young Queen had been poisoned, while others asserted that she had been abducted, and sold into the hands of her enemies. But when the small coffin was taken to Norway, King Eric accepted the body as that of his daughter, and had her buried beside her mother in Christ's Kirk at Bergen.

In the aftermath of this unfortunate incident the co-Regent, Sir James Stewart, endeavoured to keep the peace within a very troubled society, but the resultant Wars of Succession and Independence were destined to plague Scotland for many years. Initially there were numerous claimants to Margaret's inheritance but, ultimately, there were three main contenders: John (the Black) Comyn – in descent from King Donald Ban; John Balliol – in descent from Prince David, Earl of Huntingdon; and Robert Bruce, Lord of Annandale – in another descent from Prince David.

It seemed that Bruce, who had been selected as Tanistair by Alexander III, had the best claim to the Scottish crown, but Edward of England decided otherwise. As far as he was concerned, his own son had been betrothed to Queen Margaret, and that gave him privileged personal rights over Scots' opinion. Apart from that, the Bishop of Durham had said to Edward, 'This Robert is of the noblest stock of all England, and with him the Kingdom of Scotland will stand very strong'. Hence, Bruce was far from the favourite in Edward's mind. Edward's own favourite was John Balliol, whose wife Isabel de Warenne's grandmother was King Edward's own grandmother, Isabella of Angoulême. Bruce, on the other hand, was of Flemish-Celtic stock, and he was clearly not open to a policy of anglicizing Scotland.

Edward then travelled north and declared himself Lord Paramount of Scotland; he informed the Scottish nobles that he had given weighty consideration to Scotland's predicament, and requested that his lordship be acknowledged so that justice could be done. On being challenged by one of the assembly, Edward's mood changed, and he proclaimed, 'By Saint Edward, whose crown I wear, I will maintain my just right or die in the cause'. Clearly his request was more of a demand, and when the Scots asked for an opportunity to confer among themselves,

Edward replied, 'You are all sufficiently informed by the tenor of my summons, but you shall have until tomorrow'. The nobles responded that this was insufficient time, and finally wrested three weeks from the obdurate monarch. In return, he instructed that Scotland's chief fortresses be surrendered into his hands; he then appointed his own committee of English councillors, and prepared to select a king for the Scottish nation.

The proceedings began in June 1291, but it was not until the November that Edward, having consulted with his advisers, was ready to deliver his verdict. There was only one important consideration for the Plantagenet king and his council: the appointed King of Scots must be prepared to rule under the seniority of the King of England. Robert Bruce refused, saying:

> If I can get the aforesaid kingdom by means of my right and a faithful assize, well and good. But if not, I shall never, in gaining that kingdom for myself, reduce it to thraldom.

In the light of this, Bruce was duly dismissed, but John Balliol agreed to the fealty, and swore the required oath:

> I, John, King of Scotland, shall be true and faithful to you, Lord Edward, by the grace of God, King of England, the noble and superior Lord of the Kingdom of Scotland, the which I hold and claim to hold of thee . . . And I shall bear to you my fidelity of life and limb and worldly honour against all men.

This was precisely what Edward wanted to hear, and John Balliol gained the throne of Scots in 1292.

Sir William Wallace

Before long, King Edward was compelling Balliol to provide Scottish money and men for the English army, and Edward's general treatment of the Scots caused even Balliol to question the undue pressures of Plantagenet dominion. And so Edward elected to rule Scotland himself; he deposed Balliol in 1296, whereupon the hitherto vassal-king repudiated his earlier Oath of Fealty, and was stripped of his royal robes in Strathcarro churchyard on 10 July, signing his deed of abdication at Brechin three days later. King Edward then had Balliol imprisoned in the Tower of London and, in company with a guard of his royal army, he called a Parliament at Berwick. There, the subservient nobles, knights and squires of Scotland signed the infamous *Ragman Roll*, proclaiming their acceptance of Edward's kingship. Edward then placed English governors and garrisons into the Scottish castles, banishing all Scots in the process. As for John Balliol, he was released, destitute, from the Tower after a couple of years, and eventually died in Normandy. (*The Ragman Roll* was so called because of its ragged appearance due to the numerous appendant seals. Hence, the word 'rigmarole'.)

One man who was to foresee an unsatisfactory outcome almost immediately was the Abbot of Scone who, in a moment of inspiration, hid the sacred Stone of Destiny (the traditional fealty stone of the Kings of Scots). The Abbot recognized that the true legacy of the kingdom lay with the ancient Stone which, at all costs, must be preserved north of the Border. But Edward took the Stone! – some might say. The fact is, however, that he did not. What he took was a substitute; the true Stone of Destiny is still in Scotland where it has always been, precisely where the Abbot concealed it. On secreting the relic in 1296 he prophesied, 'Four scores and six hundred years will it take before the Michael comes back to his inheritance'.

A signature which was noticeably absent from the *Ragman Roll* was that of the Paisley-born knight Sir William Wallace. He was a colleague and attaché of the prevailing 5th Lord High Steward, Sir James Stewart, and a strong opposer of King Edward's government. William was the son of Malcolm Wallace of Edersley, Ayrshire, and the great-grandson of the Welshman Richard Walays who had arranged the marriage between James Stewart's ancestor, Alan of Lochaber, and Adelina of Oswestry. Richard had left Wales after the marriage, and travelled to Scotland with Alan who granted him lands in Ayrshire. The Walays (Wallace) descendants subsequently became hereditary knights of the élite Household Guard of the High Stewards.

William Wallace was raised at the French Court, and came to Scotland to uphold a military alliance made between John Balliol and Philippe IV of France in 1295. By this time, William had lost both his father and brother against the English, while his mother was obliged to travel the country in disguise for fear of seizure.

Duly inheriting his father's Ayrshire estates, William took up his aristocratic position as a Household Knight of James Stewart, 5th High Steward, and before long he had gained a fine reputation, being described as bold and strong, while also noted for his fine dress in the French manner. As can be seen from this, the noble and influential Sir William Wallace was very different from the somewhat uncouth character portrayed by Mel Gibson in the recent film *Braveheart*. However, whilst full of historical inaccuracies, this very moving film has certainly done much on the world stage to underline the plight of the Scottish nation in those days.

With many of Scotland's immigrant nobles allied to the Plantagenet oppressor in typically feudal style, Wallace formed a strong resistance movement in favour of a Free Scotland. He was soon outlawed by the English king, but his following was considerable. John de Warrenne of Surrey (the English governor of Scotland) was so concerned about Wallace's military strength that he offered him a pardon if he would lay down his arms. 'We are not here to treat for peace', answered Wallace, 'but to abide battle and restore freedom for our country. Let the English come . . . We defy them to their very beards'.

And so the English came, to meet with Wallace's troops on Cambuskenneth Bridge, Stirling, in 1297. The wooden bridge broke and collapsed as the Scots drove Surrey's men into retreat, pursuing their victory into England, and taking castles as far south as Newcastle and Carlisle. Thereafter, Wallace was justly proclaimed 'Warden of Scotland' and 'Guardian of the Realm'.

But the triumph was short-lived, and in the following year Wallace was defeated by Edward's longbowmen at Falkirk, whereupon he went to France to enlist help for his country. In the absence of Wallace, the Pope took his opportunity to announce that Scotland was a fief of the Holy See; but Edward of England responded, 'At no time has the Kingdom of Scotland belonged to the Church . . . the King of England is independent of Papal authority'. Indeed, Wallace went to Rome in 1300 to plead Scotland's case with Pope Boniface VIII, but his mission was in vain, for Boniface claimed his own personal sovereignty over all kings, including those of France, England and Scotland. This enraged Philippe IV of France, who promptly seized and publicly humiliated the 68-year-old Pope, who died of shock soon afterwards. His successor, Benedict XI, died a few months later in July 1304, and the Church was without a Pope for many months until Philippe's ally, Bertrand de Got, followed as Pope Clement V in June 1305.

On his original voyage from Kirkcudbright to France, Wallace encountered a flotilla of pirate ships, and the captain of the lead vessel leapt aboard the Scottish ship. At this, Wallace seized him by the throat and threw him to the deck, declaring, 'I have never taken as a prisoner any man who was my foe; for God's sake I grant thee thy life'. Duly humbled, the pirate captain swore no injury to Wallace, who discovered that he had captured a notorious rogue called Thomas de Longueville. He had previously been exiled by King Philippe IV for slaying a prominent French nobleman, and had become a pirate of the high seas, known as the 'Red Rover' because of the colour of his sails.

De Longueville ordered his ships to sail to La Rochelle where, by arrangement with Wallace, he would surrender to the French authorities. But when Wallace arrived to a hero's welcome, with de Longueville in his company, he decided to intercede on the Red Rover's behalf, and using his considerable influence at Court he obtained a royal pardon from the French King. The former pirate subsequently came back to Scotland with Wallace in 1305, and married the heiress of Charteris of Kinfauns, many of whose family became Provosts of Perth. De Longueville then assumed the family name of Charteris, and was eventually granted lands in Perthshire as reward for his assistance in regaining the fair city from the English.

Sir William Wallace was not so fortunate, and soon after his return he was captured in Scotland and removed to London. There, at the Great Hall of Westminster, he was charged with treason, sacrilege, homicide, robbery and arson. On being found guilty, separate punishments were implemented for each apparent crime, whereupon Wallace was dragged to Smithfield, branded, and hanged till unconscious. He was then revived, drawn, castrated and disembowelled, and his parts burned before his eyes, before he was finally beheaded and quartered. His head was then impaled upon London Bridge as an example to all who would challenge King Edward's supremacy. What remained of Wallace was dispatched to Scotland and the north:

his right arm to Newcastle, and his left to Berwick; his right leg and torso to Perth, and his left quarter to Aberdeen. All of this was supposed to compel the Scots into compliance but, instead, a more fervent hatred was born, and the Scots were more determined than ever to promote their own chosen king.

5

The Written Constitution

Robert the Bruce

In March 1306 Robert the Bruce was crowned Robert I of Scots. Crowning was the traditional right of the Macduff Earl of Fife, representing the Sacred Kindred of St Columba. However, young Duncan of Fife was opposed to Bruce, and so his sister, Isabel, Countess of Buchan, performed the honour.

King Robert was the grandson of Robert Bruce the contender and, during Wallace's earlier absence, had become joint Guardian of the Realm with Sir John (the Red) Comyn, the son of John Comyn the contender. Like their forebears, however, Bruce and Comyn were arch-rivals, and their feud had led to a violent quarrel in which Bruce slew Comyn on the high altar at Dumfries. Edward of England proclaimed Bruce an outlaw, and duly informed the Pope, whereupon Bruce was excommunicated, with an interdict levelled against the Scottish nation. But the people of Scotland cared nothing for the Papal decree, and immediately countered Edward's proclamation by having Robert the Bruce crowned at Scone.

At this, the excommunication of Bruce's adherents was formally confirmed, with the sentence passed at St Paul's Cathedral, London. Bruce's second wife, Elizabeth of Ulster, was seized and taken under guard to be detained in England with her 12-year-old stepdaughter Marjorie. They were held in various convent locations, to be finally housed (1313–14) at Shaftesbury Abbey in Dorset. Isabel of Buchan was also taken, along with Bruce's sisters, Mary and Christian, but they were very harshly treated. Isabel was confined in a turret at Berwick Castle for having crowned the King. There, she was hung in a cage, communicating with no one for four years; even the guard who brought her food was forbidden to speak. Mary Bruce was similarly caged at Roxburgh Castle while her sister Christian was confined in a convent in Lincolnshire.

A proscribed fugitive in Plantagenet eyes, Bruce avoided the fate of Wallace, even though some Comyn supporters, such as the Macdougalls of Lorne, were set against him at that time. Edward I Plantagenet (known as the 'Hammer of the Scots') died in 1307, prior to which he ordered that his bones should be carried before the English army until Scotland was subdued. He was succeeded by his son, Edward II, but nothing changed, and the Plantagenet effort against Scotland continued year-upon-year. Under Bruce, however, the Scots managed to regain most of the key fortresses, until only three of Scotland's strongholds remained in English hands. One of these was at Stirling, where Edward II took his mighty force to confront the troops of King Robert I, the Bruce, on the nearby field of Bannockburn.

Here, on 24 June 1314, some 1,354 gallant warriors gave their lives for the freedom of the Scottish realm, destroying and humiliating an army far stronger than their own. 'Let Edward of England bring every man he has, and we will fight them were they more', had been the Scots' cry. And Edward did just that, but he lost thousands of men that day, and was forced to flee the field. Once more, the Pope asserted his decree of excommunication against Bruce and his supporting nation, but notwithstanding this Bruce's wife Elizabeth, and daughter Marjorie (born to Robert's first wife Isabel of Mar), were released from England after eight years of confinement.

Bruce and the Knights Templars

When Hugues de Payens and the Knights Templars had first returned from Jerusalem in 1128, they brought with them the secrets of Master Mason, Hiram Abiff, the builder of King Solomon's Temple. However, their Jerusalem excavations had also led to other important discoveries, including some ancient documentation which enabled them to challenge certain Roman

Church doctrines and New Testament interpretation, particularly in relation to the Crucifixion and Resurrection. For this reason, the Knights refused to bear the upright Latin Cross, and wore an eight-pointed, centred red cross as their emblem.

Their documentary discoveries were substantial, including numerous books from the East, many of which had been salvaged from the burned library of Alexandria. There were ancient Essene works predating Jesus Christ, and volumes from Arabian and Greek philosophers, all of which were destined to be condemned by the Church. There were also countless works concerning numerology, geometry, architecture and music, along with manuscripts pertaining to metals and alloys. In all, the Templars returned to Europe with the combined knowledge of thousands of years of study.

When transporting their auspicious find through Europe prior to the 1128 Council of Troyes, St Bernard de Clairvaux wrote:

> The work has been accomplished with our help, and the Knights have been sent on a journey through France and Burgundy, under the protection of the Count of Champagne, where all precautions can be taken against all interference by public or ecclesiastical authority.

But in addition to the revelationary documents, the Knights returned with a significant wealth of treasure, found in the deep vaults beneath the Jerusalem Temple site. This had been buried during the 1st-century Jewish revolt against the dominion of Imperial Rome.[1] With this resurrected hoard to form a collateral base, the Order became the most successful financial organization the world has ever known. Within a short space of time, the Knights Templars became advisers and bankers to monarchies and parliaments throughout Europe.

By the time that Robert the Bruce was crowned in 1306, the international influence of the Knights Templars was truly feared by Pope Clement V, and he endeavoured to eliminate the Order. In this he was aiding King Philippe IV of France, who owed a fortune to the Templars; and Philippe's son-in-law was none other than King Edward II of England.

A fact not generally realized is that the Knights Templars were established as an Order of Warrior Monks, monks of St Bernard's Cistercian Order, an independent offspring of the Benedictines. In 14th-century France and Flanders most aristocratic families had sons within the Church, if not as bishops, then as abbots of various allied Orders. The Chaplain of the Manor of La Buzadière (District of Mans)[2] was one of these noblemen. Shortly before the Papal edict against the Templars there were seven Templar guests at the Lord of the Manor's castle. At this gathering, the Knights were alerted to the impending Inquisition, and they raced to Paris, where they informed their hierarchy of the Pope and King Philippe's plan. Then, with an auxiliary contingent, they travelled to St Malo, spreading the word abroad. (The seven Knights were Gaston de la Pierre Phoebus, Guidon de Montanor, Gentilis de Foligno, Henri de Montfort, Louis de Grimoard, Pierre Yorick de Rivault and Cesare Minvielle.)

The edict came into force on Friday 13 October 1307, from which date the Knights Templars were hounded and persecuted in Europe and England. [As a result we are still averse to the unlucky date of Friday 13th.] The prevailing Grand Master, Jacques de Molay, was arrested at the outset in France, but in Scotland the Papal Bull was quite ineffective because of the prevailing excommunication of Bruce and the Scottish nation. However, the Papal Inquisition was not simply a matter of persecution, it was also designed to root out the Templar treasure from its hiding-place, which was known to be in France. Armies and agents searched far and wide, but to no avail. Prior to 13 October the treasure had actually been safely locked in the Chapter House treasury vaults of Paris, but by that date the hoard had been loaded aboard eighteen galleys of the Templar Fleet, which set sail immediately from La Rochelle. Their main destination was Scotland, although some of the ships went to Portugal.

When the Dead Sea Scrolls were translated in 1956, the 'Copper Scroll' (which gives details of the fortune hidden beneath the Temple at Jerusalem) revealed that, along with a vast stockpile of bullion and valuables, an 'indeterminable treasure' was buried. French Masonic ritual stemming from the Middle Ages states that the treasure was the specific responsibility of the Templar Grand Knights of St Andrew, instituted by King Baldwin II of Jerusalem, who succeeded in 1118. They were called the 'Guardian Princes of the Royal Secret', and it was they who selected Scotland to be the place of refuge for the Templar treasure. Furthermore, their chosen hiding-place was said, in itself, to determine the very nature of the Royal Secret.

According to Masonic tradition, the Knights of St Andrew were the inheritors of an Order established in 586 BC. They were the Temple Guard of Jerusalem, who were gathered by the High Priest Hilkiah before the Temple of Solomon was destroyed by King Nebuchadnezzar of Babylon. Their task at that time was to secrete the treasure from the invader, and to carry away certain items of express significance. This was, of course, the very year when the sacred Stone of Destiny found its way to Ireland with the prophet Jeremiah.

In 1307 fifty or so Knights Templars from France settled on Scotland's Mull of Kintyre. Later, on 24 June 1313 (realizing that their Grand Master, Jacques de Molay, could soon be executed in Europe), they applied the provisions of the Order's revised Constitution of 24 June 1307, and appointed a Knight called Pièrre d'Aumont as their Scottish Grand Master. On the nearby island of Islay, and at Kilmartin on the mainland, there are numerous Templar graves still to be found, and some of their

Knight Templar tombstone slab on the Isle of Islay

distinctive tombstone slabs depict the occupants as Knight Officers of the original Templar Fleet.

Under the auspices of Robert the Bruce and the excommunicated clergy, the Order was restructured into a Church, with a hierarchy quite independent of Rome. The Templar Church had abbots, priests, and even bishops – but no cardinals, and certainly no Pope. Indeed, Papal authority was rejected totally, emphatically, and forever. The Knights began to train the army of Robert the Bruce in the hit-and-run tactics of warfare established in the Crusades. And, in preparation for battle against the English, a new arms supply was manufactured in Ireland, to be paid for with Templar gold. (Robert's brother, Edward Bruce, was King of Ireland from 1314 until his death in 1318.)

If ever England's House of Plantagenet had designs on the Scottish realm, these were dramatically heightened from the arrival of the Templars in 1307, and the eventual result was the 1314 Battle of Bannockburn. This battle was fought only three months after Grand Master Jacques de Molay was burned at the stake in France for refusing to reveal Templar secrets to the henchmen of King Philippe IV, the father-in-law of England's King Edward II.

At an earlier Inquisition hearing in 1309, Bishop William Lamberton of St Andrews had been ordered, under edict of Pope Clement V and Edward II, to expose all the Templars in Scotland, but the good Bishop struck a contrary deal at Holyrood House in the December of that year. The Templars would receive sanctuary in Scotland, in return for arms and monetary expertise. The input of arms was apparently substantial, for King Edward complained about the extent of weaponry imported from Ireland at this time, and the Templars were outlawed by the Pope in 1312.

It is on record that the Papal Legate, John de Soleure, judicially examined two English knights at Holyrood in 1309. They were Walter de Clifton, Preceptor of Ballantradoch, and William de Middleton, both of whom were sentenced to house arrest for the duration of the Legate's visit.

In Scotland the Templars were free men, able to swear personally before God, rather than be subjected to Papal whims and commands. This was a traditional concept of the Scots, and the Coronation Oath of Robert the Bruce was firstly to God, and then to the Community of the Realm of Scotland. This Oath had been sworn by all Kings of Scots from the 9th-century King Constantine I. The established Roman Church may have betrayed the Templars, but in Scotland they found something far more trustworthy and tangible: a sacred royal house, and a Priest-King of the Celtic Church succession.

Subsequent to Bannockburn, where the Templars comprised the participatory section that very largely carried the day for Scotland, the Knights became part of the Scottish Government as the appointed Royal Bodyguard, with the Order established as 'Guardian of the King of Scots by day and by night'.

The year 1317, however, saw a change in the administration of the Templars. Many had died at Bannockburn and, with their ranks depleted, it was thought advisable to invite Scottish Companions into the Order. The King of Scots was installed as the hereditary Sovereign Grand Master, and from that time, whichever descending King held the office, he was to be known simply as 'Saint Germain'. A new Order was then formed, called the Elder Brothers of the Order of the Rosy Cross, and several of the Rosy Cross Knights then sailed to France for a meeting with Pope John XXII at Avignon.[3] Despite the Templars' relinquishment of Papal control, this new Order was not apparently Templar to outsiders, and since the Pope held the international reins of Chivalric Orders, a meeting was necessary for registration. Gaston de la Pierre Phoebus was the senior representative for the mission, and the Pope agreed to issue a Charter so long as his own nephew, Jacques de Via, became the operative Grand Master. However, Jacques de Via died on 6 May 1317, and the position immediately became vacant, whereupon the Knights elected Guidon de Montanor (who was still in Scotland), and they duly returned with the necessary Charter of Incorporation.

In the event, the Papal edict of Scots excommunication did not last indefinitely, and it was lifted in 1323 when Pope John XXII recognized Robert the Bruce as the true King of Scots. Many historians have presumed therefore that the Knights Templars must have been disbanded in Scotland, but this was not the case; it was simply that Bruce had contrived the secret Order to become even more secretive. Indeed, the Order of the Knights of the Rosy Cross had been established by Bruce for Templars who had been valiant at Bannockburn, and this was a very successful cover. The prevailing 'Royal Order' associated with the Rosy

Cross in Scotland was that of Kilwinning, Ayrshire (possibly founded by King David I), for which James Stewart, 5th High Steward, had been a Grand Master.

The Declaration of Arbroath

A long-sought period of consolidation ensued after the Battle of Bannockburn, and in May 1328 England finally acknowledged Scotland's independence at the *Treaty of Northampton*. Meanwhile, the Scottish nation was provided with a unique privilege in the form of the first ever 'Written Constitution'. This prized Constitution, the 1320 *Declaration of Arbroath*[4], was upheld by Robert the Bruce, and is now at Edinburgh's Register House. It is a closely-knitted and passionate document, written almost in the form of a prayer. Constructed in Latin, it embodies a good deal of early history, detailing Scottish origins from the people of the Black Sea region of Greater Scythia in the time of Jesus, people who moved westwards across the Tyrrhenian Sea. It continues:

> And, as the historians of old time bear witness, they have held it free of all bondage ever since. In their kingdom they have reigned one hundred and thirteen kings of their own royal stock, the line unbroken by a single foreigner. The high qualities and deserts of these people (were they not otherwise manifest) gain glory from this: that the King of kings and Lord of lords, our Lord Jesus Christ, after his Passion and Resurrection, called them, even though settled in the uttermost parts of the earth, 'almost the first' to his most Holy Faith. Nor would he have them confirmed in that Faith by merely anyone but by the first of his Apostles – by calling, though second or third in rank, the most gentle Saint Andrew (who preached in Scythia), the Blessed Peter's brother, and desired him to keep them under his protection as their patron for ever.
>
> The most Holy Fathers, your predecessors, gave careful heed to these things, and bestowed many favours and numerous privileges on this same kingdom and people, as being the special charge of the Blessed Peter's brother. Thus, our nation under their protection did indeed live in freedom and peace up to the time when that mighty Prince and King of the English, Edward, the father of the one who reigns today (when our kingdom had no head and our people harboured no malice or treachery, and were then unused to wars or invasions) came in the guise of a friend and ally to harass them as an enemy.

> The deeds of cruelty, massacre, violence, pillage, arson, imprisoning prelates (*ecclesiastical dignitaries*), burning down monasteries, robbing and killing monks and nuns, and yet other outrages without number which he had committed against our people, sparing neither age nor sex, religion nor rank, no one could describe nor fully imagine unless he had seen them with his own eyes.

Ever since 934, when the Wessex Saxons (Sassenachs) invaded Scotland, the Scots had been under threat from England, suffering various degrees of harassment. But it was not until the time of Edward I that the threat became insurmountable.

On the day that Sir William Wallace died, true Scottish Nationalism was born, and Robert the Bruce regained his nation's independence in 1314. A few years later, in April 1320, the Scots clergy met at Arbroath, declaring that the people would never again be subjected to English dominion. It was pronounced that, henceforth, the people's right to 'choose' a king to uphold their individual liberties would be reserved:

> But from these countless evils we have been set free, by the help of Him, who though he afflicts and restores by our most tireless Prince, King and Lord, the Lord Robert (the Bruce). He, that his people and his heritage might be delivered out of the hands of our enemies, met toil and fatigue, hunger and peril, like another Maccabaeus or Joshua, and bore them cheerfully. Him, too, divine providence, his right of succession according to our laws and customs which we shall maintain to the death, and the due consent and assent of us all have made our Prince and King. To him, as to the man by whom salvation has been wrought unto our people, we are bound both by law and by his merits, that our freedom may be still maintained, and by him, come what may, we mean to stand.
>
> Yet, if he should give up what he has begun, and agree to make us or our kingdom subject to the King of England or the English, we should exert ourselves at once to drive him out as our enemy and a subverter of his own rights and ours, and make some other man, who was well able to defend us, our King. For as long as but a hundred of us remain alive, never will we on any conditions be brought under English rule. It is in Truth, not in glory, nor riches, nor honours, that we are fighting, but for Freedom – for that alone, which no honest man gives up but with life itself.

This document made it perfectly apparent that the 'choosing' of a King of Scots was the prerogative of the Scottish nation and people. It was certainly not the business of the Pope, nor the King of England, nor of France. It was, in essence, a declaration of fraternal nationhood as against the otherwise feudal concept of monarchical ownership of a country and its people. The message of the *Declaration of Arbroath* rang out loud and clear: 'Do not interfere, or else'!

The Mystery of Scota

It is worth considering at this point the historical content of the *Declaration of Arbroath,* with particular reference to its statement that the Scots originally came from Greater Scythia, by the Black Sea.

Few children in today's Scottish primary schools are taught Scottish history in any depth. They receive selected titbits about Mary, Queen of Scots, and perhaps some veiled references to the Battle of Bannockburn and other events. Maybe even *Bonnie Prince Charlie* gets a mention, but that's about it. For the most part, our children are taught an overall British history, as if Scotland had existed forever as a department of England. Consequently, when statements such as the Scots emerging from Scythia come to the fore, they are by-passed very quickly by the indoctrinated academic establishment. The same applies to the traditional belief that the tribal name of the early Irish 'Scots' came from Princess Scota of Egypt, as given in the ancient histories of Ireland.

When compiling the material for this book, I decided to investigate the Scythia and Scota traditions, only to discover that these two names have a similar root. Some modern dictionaries describe that 'Scythia' is pronounced 'Sith-ia', but older documents indicate that it was originally pronounced 'Skudda' or 'Skota'. (It's rather like the word 'Celtic', which has a hard 'C' [Keltic], although it is sometimes corrupted as if it were 'Seltic'.)

My first point of contact was my family's royal historiographer, Laurence Gardner, le Chevalier Labhràn de Saint Germain. We discussed the old traditions at length, and it was revealed that there were two separate Princess Scotas in the history of the Scots, with hundreds of years between them, and so we embarked upon a quest to find them both.

The Irish-Scottish annals record that the earliest Scota was a daughter of the Egyptian Pharaoh Cinciris (again, hard Cs – therefore, 'Kinkiris'), but we could find no reference to such a Pharaoh. Nevertheless, we discovered that each of the ancient Pharaohs had more than one name: a birth name, a throne name, a Horus name, etc. Suddenly our investigation had become enormously complex, but the Irish histories gave us a clue to the relevant Egyptian dynasty. It was the 18th dynasty, that of Akhenaten and Tutankhamun. The problem was that, in the name Kinkiris, we were dealing with an English phonetic translation of something written in old Irish Gaelic, which meant that the original name was probably only something similar.

As luck would have it, the discovery was mine: I awoke suddenly one night, knowing precisely who Kinkiris was. I immediately rushed to the *Guinness Book of Kings, Rulers and Statesmen*, and there indeed was our man: Pharaoh Akenkheres (A-Kenkeres). No one made the connection before because this Egyptian king (1364–62 BC) was better known as Smenkhkare.

I telephoned Laurence next morning with the good news, only to be asked, 'But did he have a daughter called Scota?' Once more we set to work and, although we found no daughter by this name, we managed to discover Scota's identity. Originally, she was Akenkheres' daughter Merytaten, who had married Prince Niul of Greater Scythia. Hence, she became Princess of Scythia (pronounced 'Scota').

But what of the second Princess Scota, who ended up in Ireland, and whose probable grave is to be found there? Having discovered her ancestral forebears, she was actually easy enough to find simply by following the family line forward from the 1300s BC. It transpired that twenty-one generations later, a descendant Prince of Scythia married the sister of Pharaoh Psamtic II (595–89 BC), who sent a fleet of Phoenician ships to circumnavigate the African continent. This sister duly became Princess of Scythia (Princess Scota). Her husband was Prince Galamh (known also as Milidh), and their son was Djer Amon (Beloved of Amon), cited in the Irish annals as Eirhe Ahmon.

It was Eirhe Ahmon's son Eochaid, High King of Ireland, who married Tamar Tephi, the daughter of King Zedekiah of Judah, in about 586 BC. With her father a captive in Babylon, and her brothers murdered by Nebuchadnezzar, Tamar had escaped to

Ireland with the prophet Jeremiah, and with them came the Stone of Destiny. As we have seen, this event coincided with the Jerusalem Temple Guard's instruction to remove sacred treasures from the grasp of the invading King of Babylon, and it is therefore apparent that Jeremiah was rather more than just a prophet. Indeed, as given in the Old Testament (Jeremiah 1.1), he was the son of Hilkiah, the very Zadok High Priest who created the Order of the Temple Guard, the Order which eventually became the Knights of St Andrew. Hilkiah was also the High Priest who first discovered the Mosaic *Book of the Law* hidden within the Temple (2 Kings 22.8).

From Tamar and Eochaid were descended most of the royal lines of Ireland, not the least that of Dal Riàta – the Royal House of Dalriada, through which all Kings of Scots traced their succession from the biblical Kings of Judah, from the Princes of Greater Scythia, and from the Pharaohs of ancient Egypt.

1 *Macbeth*
One of Scotland's greatest Kings. He preserved the independence of the Celtic Church from Catholic interference and brought Scotland firmly into the European political scene.

2 *Sir William Wallace*
Guardian of Scotland. His appointment ensured that the newly-made alliance between France and Scotland would survive the conquering ambitions of Edward I of England.

3 *Robert I, Bruce*
The Patriot and Warrior-King used Templar knights to train Scotland's army against the might of England. His victory at Bannockburn in 1314 regained Scotland's independence.

4 *Walter, 6th High Steward, greeting Marjorie Bruce, Lady of Scotland*
They were married in 1315 to become the parents of Robert II Stewart.

5 *Robert II Stewart*
The people's choice, and founder of the Royal House of Stewart. He is remembered as 'A king of such constancy, he seldom spoke a word which he performed not'.

6 *Robert III Stewart*
Born John, Earl of Carrick, his reign was constantly harassed by his younger brother, the Duke of Albany.

7 *Annabella Drummond of Stobhall*
On predeceasing her husband, Robert III, she was sadly mourned by the Scots, who said she was 'among the best of our queens'.

8 *James I Stewart*
A reformer of Scottish politics, he modernized the State, introducing sheriffdoms and updating laws to suit the needs of the many rather than the few.

9 *Lady Joan Beaufort*
Wife of James I, and a formidable woman. James wrote the *Kingis Quhair* on falling in love with Joan while he was a prisoner in England.

10 *James II Stewart*
Fascinated by artillery, he was killed when a bombard exploded next to him while besieging Roxburgh Castle.

11 *James III Stewart*
More concerned with arts, architecture and music than with politics, but James strove for success in unfortunate economic circumstances.

12 *Margaret of Denmark*
Wife of James III. She brought the Orkneys and Shetlands within Scotland's realm as her marriage dowry.

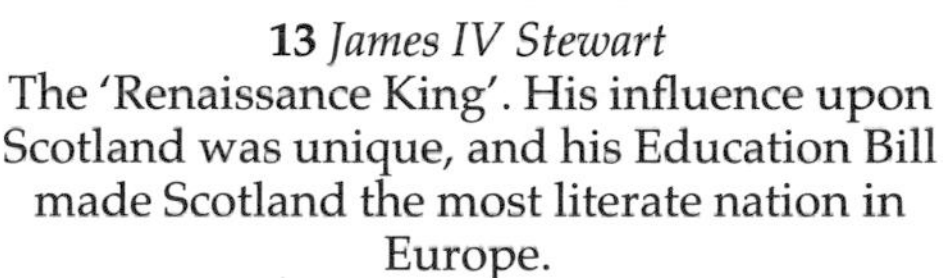

13 *James IV Stewart*
The 'Renaissance King'. His influence upon Scotland was unique, and his Education Bill made Scotland the most literate nation in Europe.

14 *Margaret Tudor*
Her marriage to James IV was called the 'Wedding of the Thistle and the Rose', and was intended to create an *entente cordiale* between Scotland and England.

15 *James V Stewart*
Known as 'The guid man of Ballengeich', he moved among the people in disguise so as to gain insight into their needs.

16 *Marie de Guise-Lorraine*
The second wife of James V. It was during her regency that French people gained dual nationality with the Scots.

17 *Mary Stuart – aged 16*
Queen of Scots and Dauphiness of France, Mary's upbringing was French, but she was kept informed of affairs in Scotland by the Earl of Bothwell.

18 *Francis II of France*
The first husband of Mary Stuart, but he was rather more a brother by virtue of Mary's upbringing at the French Court.

19 *Mary Stuart, Queen of Scots*
Held captive in England for 19 years by Elizabeth I Tudor and beheaded at Fotheringhay Castle in 1587.

20 *Henry Stewart, Lord Darnley*
Cousin and second husband of Mary Stuart. He would have become King of England after Elizabeth I, but his violent demise was the beginning of the end for Mary.

21 *Mary, Queen of Scots, and John Knox*
Mary agreed to recognize the Presbyterian Kirk as Scotland's National Church on condition that Catholics were granted their own right of worship. Knox, in the pay of Elizabeth I of England, refused the condition.

22 *James VI Stuart of Scots*
Mary and Darnley's son, he introduced Episcopacy into Scotland to weigh the balance against the growing power of the Kirk.

23 *James VI as James I of England*
Succeeding Elizabeth I Tudor in 1603, James was faced with unfamiliar English monarchical concepts. Consequently, he was at loggerheads with Parliament throughout his reign in England

24 *Anne of Denmark*
By way of her marriage to James VI, the Orkneys and Shetlands were confirmed as Scottish territories by the King of Denmark.

25 *Charles I Stuart*
James VI's younger son, Charles, rose to prominence following the death of his brother Henry, Prince of Wales. Intended for a Church career, he successfully administered the realm for many years – but Cromwell and the Puritans contrived the judicial murder of the Stuart king.

26 *Henriette Marie of France*
Daughter of a Protestant king who had converted to Catholicism to gain the French Crown. Her marriage to Charles I was accepted by Scots as being good for trade, but the Anglicans viewed it with suspicion.

27 *Charles II Stuart*
First crowned King of Scots at Scone in 1651, and then King of England in London, 1660. His reign was one of treaties with France, war with Holland, and trade with Portuguese and South American outposts.

28 *James Stuart, Duke of York and Albany*
Brother of Charles II. A General in France during the days of his exile, James became England's Lord Admiral and Scotland's Lord High Chancellor.

29 *Anne Hyde of Clarendon*
The first wife of James, Duke of Albany (later James VII/II). Like her husband, she converted to Catholicism after reading a history of the Church of England.

30 *James VII Stuart of Scots (II of England)*
Successor to his brother Charles II. Although capable, and popular with the people, the Anglican Church saw his conversion to Catholicism as a threat to its own position.

31 *Mary d'Este of Modena*
The second wife and Queen of James VII/II, Mary's Italian background brought a new artistic impetus to Scottish court life. She also introduced tea-drinking in Edinburgh.

32 *King James and the Great Seal*
By throwing the Great Seal into the River Thames, James VII/II ensured that William of Orange and his wife Mary (James's daughter) never truly attained kingship.

33 *James Francis Edward Stuart*
James, Prince of Wales and Duke of Rothesay (later James VIII of Scots), was born in London, 1688, but spent much of his life in exile in France and Italy.

34 *Louise, sister of James Francis Edward*
The Noble Order of the Guard of St Germain was created by James VII/II upon the birth of his daughter, Louise, at the Château de St Germain en Laye in 1692.

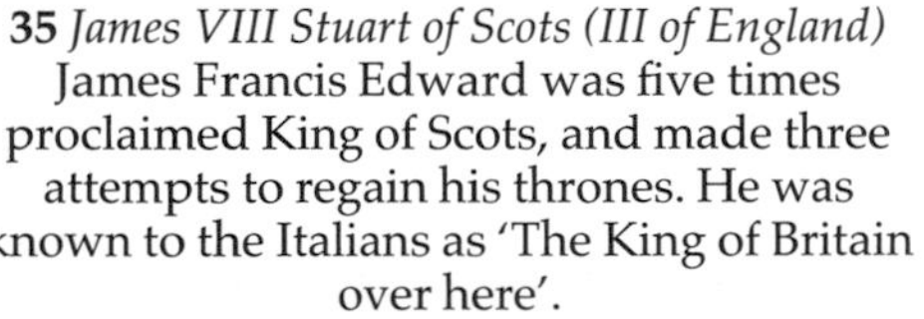

35 *James VIII Stuart of Scots (III of England)*
James Francis Edward was five times proclaimed King of Scots, and made three attempts to regain his thrones. He was known to the Italians as 'The King of Britain over here'.

36 *Maria Clementina Sobieska*
Wife of James VIII. The granddaughter of King Jan III of Poland, she was Europe's richest heiress, bringing her husband both money and a claim to the Polish Crown.

37 *Château de St Germain en Laye*
The palace at St Germain, near Paris, where Mary Stuart lived as Queen of France. It was the home in exile of James VII/II until he died in 1701, and of his son James VIII/III until 1717.

38 (*below left*) *The Palace of Urbino*
Following the Treaty of Utrecht, which required James VIII's expulsion from France, the papal estate at Urbino became his official residence from July 1717 to 6 October 1718.

39 (*below right*) *The Palazzo Muti*
Pope Clement XI's wedding gift to James VIII and Maria Clementina. It was the Roman residence of the Stuarts through the lifetimes of James and his son, Charles Edward.

40 *Charles Edward Stuart*
Prince of Wales and Duke of Rothesay, Charles Edward became the Jacobite focus from 1735, and was symbolically crowned in September 1745. His army penetrated England, but on retreating to Scotland from Derby, was defeated at Culloden on 16 April 1746.

41 *Henry Benedict Stuart, Duke of York*
The younger brother of Charles Edward in 1746.

42 *Henry Benedict in 1748*
Henry, Duke of York, became a Roman Church cardinal in 1747. Subsequently, he and his brother Charles were not on speaking terms until their father's death in 1766.

43 *Clementina Walkinshaw of Barrowfield*
The mother of three of Charles Edward's children. The Catholic records of Liège in Belgium state that Charles and Clementina were man and wife.

44 *Charlotte, Duchess of Albany*
Born in Liège, 1753, Charlotte was the legitimated daughter of Charles Edward Stuart and Clementina Walkinshaw. Though unmarried, she had three children by Ferdinand de Rohan, Archbishop of Bordeaux.

45 *Charles Edward in his latter years*
Charles suffered from asthma and from epilepsy after a physical breakdown in the wake of Culloden. These illnesses and their medicaments facilitated Hanoverian reports of his drunkenness.

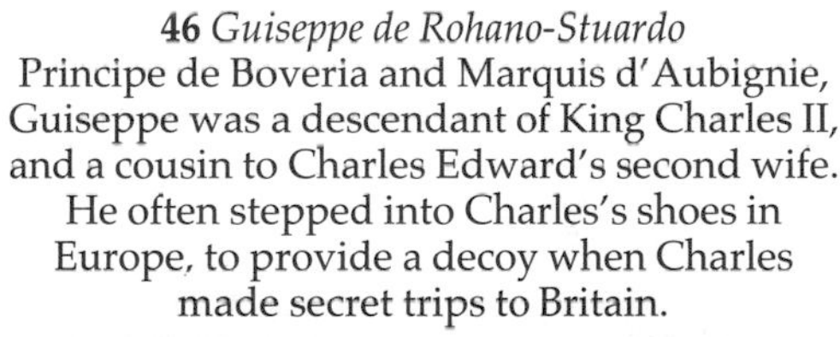

46 *Guiseppe de Rohano-Stuardo*
Principe de Boveria and Marquis d'Aubignie, Guiseppe was a descendant of King Charles II, and a cousin to Charles Edward's second wife. He often stepped into Charles's shoes in Europe, to provide a decoy when Charles made secret trips to Britain.

47 *Marguerite Marie Therese O'Dea d'Audibert de Lussan, Comtesse de Massillan*
From a portrait, 1785, by Court Painter, Laurent Pecheux (1729–1821). When Charles Edward's wife, Louise of Stolberg, left him in 1780 for Vittorio, Count Alfieri, Charles's cousin Marguerite stepped into the royal household. She and Charles were married in December 1785 and she bore him a son in October 1786. Charles Edward died in Rome, January 1788.

6

The Royal House of Stewart

The Dynasty Begins

Walter, 6th Lord High Steward

Sir James Stewart, 5th High Steward, died within three years of Bruce's coronation, to be succeeded by his son Walter. Like his father, Walter was also a Bruce supporter, and at the young age of 21 had commanded the left wing of the Scots army at Bannockburn.

Walter Stewart of Scotland lyne
That then was but a beardless hyne,
Came with a rout of noble men,
That might by countenance be ken.

He was knighted by King Robert on the field of battle, and when Edward II made another attempt at Scotland he was driven back by Sir Walter's army at Berwick.

In 1315 Walter married King Robert's daughter Marjorie, and some months later, when Bruce went to Ireland, he left Walter as his Commissioner in Scotland. Unfortunately, though, within a year of her marriage Marjorie Bruce died in a riding accident; she was pregnant at the time, but her unborn child was quickly saved by Caesarean operation. Her husband Sir Walter Stewart, 6th High Steward, died in 1326, and King Robert I died in 1329, to be succeeded by his son David, Earl of Carrick, who was only five-years-old. Although Walter and Marjorie's son Robert was also quite young, he was already the 7th hereditary High Steward.

Before he died, Robert the Bruce had requested that his heart should be carried to the Holy Land, and Sir James Douglas and Sir William St Clair of Roslin sought to perform the office. They sailed from Montrose (with Sir Robert Logan, Sir Walter Logan, Sir William Keith and Simon Lockhart of Lee), carrying the royal heart in a gold casket, and were joined by some English knights at Sluys. A week later they set sail for Spain, where King Alfonso solicited their aid in his war against the Saracens. At the Battle of Tebas de Ardales, on 25 March 1330, Douglas and his knights were in the vanguard of the Spanish army which forced the Saracen Moors to flee the field. However, in pursuing the foe, they were unaware that the majority of Spaniards had stopped to loot the abandoned camp. When the fleeing Moorish cavalry realized they had an advantage, they turned about and then slew the charging Douglas contingent. Bruce's heart, nevertheless, was subsequently returned to Scotland in an enamelled case, and was laid to rest at Melrose Abbey. The skull and leg-bones of Sir William St Clair were eventually laid at Rosslyn Chapel, and Sir James Douglas' heart at Lee Castle.

At about that time England was launched into a protracted war with France. The struggle began as a dispute between Edward II and the French king, to whom Edward (being the Duke of Aquitaine) was effectively a vassal. Edward refused to acknowledge the French Crown, and in 1324 King Charles IV of France annexed a part of Gascony, ruining England's trading effort. Edward threatened to cease his trade with Flanders, and formed an alliance with another reluctant vassal, the Duke of Burgundy. The irony was that Edward II (through his wife Isabella) was Charles IV's brother-in-law, but Isabella became so isolated in England that she returned to France in 1325. There, she and her English lover Roger Mortimer, Earl of March, plotted the overthrow and murder of Edward II in 1327.

In the following year Charles IV died, and a new French dynasty began under his cousin Philip VI, Duke of Valois. England's new monarch, Edward III, challenged this accession and claimed that he was himself the true King of France, being the grandson of Isabella's father, Philipe IV. Edward had Mortimer executed, confined his mother to a convent, and in 1346 took his bowmen to Crecy, to decimate the French knights with a hail of arrows. Thus began the Hundred Years' War, which was hardly

The trumpets blew, the cross bolts flew
The arrows flashed like flame
As spur in side and spear at rest
Against the foe we came

And many a bearded Saracen
Went down both horse and man
For thro' their ranks we rode like corn
So furiously we ran

But in behind our path they closed
Though fain to let us through
For they were forty thousand men
And we were wonderous few

We might not see a lances length
So dense was their array
But the long fell sweep of Scottish blade
Still held them hard at bay

Make in, Make in! Lord Douglas cried
Make in my brethren dear
Sir William of Saint Clair is down
We may not leave him here

But thicker, thicker grew the swarm
And sharper shot the rain
And the horses reared amid the press
But they would not charge again

Now Jesu help thee said Lord James
Thou kind and true Saint Clair
And if I may not bring thee off
I'll die beside thee there

Then in his stirrups up he stood
So lion like and bold
And held the presious heart aloft
All in its case of gold

He slung it from him far ahead
And never spake he more
But pass thee first thou dauntless heart
As thou went of yore

We'll bear them back into our ship
We'll bear them oer the sea
And lay them in the hallowed earth
Within our own countrie.

Guardians of the Dauntless Heart

underway when the Great Plague of the Black Death struck England in 1348.

One might imagine that, in the midst of such turmoil, the Plantagenets would have left Scotland to her own devices, but such was not the case. Back in 1320, Edward II had announced that he was only prepared to give the Scots a 13-year truce, and by 1333 the time was up. With this in mind, Edward Balliol (son of ex-King John Balliol) had launched his own claim to sovereignty in 1332, but when his attempt failed he fled to England and reminded Edward III about his father's deadline, destined for the following year.

Some time earlier, in an effort to prolong the peace, David II Bruce (then aged four) had been contractually married to King Edward's sister Joanna, but to no avail. Having begun open hostilities against the French in 1329, Edward III decided also to launch an assault against Scotland; he won the day at Halidon Hill, and duly proclaimed Edward Balliol King of Scots, whereupon young David II was hurriedly removed to France, in 1333.

During David's minority, Robert Stewart had (from the age of 19) been Regent of Scotland, and remained so until David was 17 in 1341. Edward III's Scottish campaign and the war against France were very hard upon the English people, whose taxes were substantially increased to pay for it. England's ongoing French conflict was, however, of great advantage to Robert Stewart, who seized his opportunity to deal with Balliol in Edward's absence. In one fell swoop, he sailed from Bute, attacked Dunoon, and overthrew the usurper, forcing Edward Balliol out of Scotland. Then in 1341 King David II Bruce returned from France. The balance of the English occupation was dealt with in the following year, when the Scots re-captured their strategic fortress at Roxburgh – but that was not the end of it. With the English expelled from Scotland, David then took up the French cause against King Edward III, only to be defeated and captured at Neville's Cross in 1346. Once again, Robert the High Steward, elected Guardian of the Kingdom, was left in charge north of the Border.

The next step was to retrieve King David II, and so the Scots seized Berwick-on-Tweed, which they lost almost immediately again to the English. Nevertheless, Edward Balliol formally surrendered his interests; a truce was negotiated, and David's freedom was gained for 90,000 merks [today's adjusted equivalent value: about £22.5m]. Having been King in name from 1329, it was only from 1357 that David reigned in his own right; but what the Scots did not know was that he had previously come to an arrangement with Edward III. Meeting the Scottish Parliament for the first time, David Bruce announced that should he die without issue the Crown of Scotland would pass to the King of England or his son, the Duke of Clarence. In reply, he was informed, 'So long as one of us can bear arms, we will never permit an Englishman to reign over us'.

David's wife, Joanna Plantagenet, died childless during the succession debate, and soon afterwards David married Margaret of Logie. But she was a badly chosen woman, who persuaded David to levy an unjust Scots property tax, and then absconded abroad with the money. Margaret and the King were later divorced, and in 1371 David died in Edinburgh. Irrespective of his arrangement with Edward III, the Scots knew there was only one man who could possibly succeed him – the man who had kept Scotland afloat for 36 years, and whose forebears had been Regents and Kings' deputies for six generations. Their choice was of course Robert the Bruce's grandson Robert Stewart, 7th Lord High Steward, Earl of Atholl and Strathearn.

Choice of the Nation

Robert (being the progeny of Marjorie Bruce) had previously been nominated in 1318, but this had been shelved upon the birth of Marjorie's brother, David Bruce. Although Robert was the natural successor to David, he was, nevertheless, 'chosen' by an assembly of the Three Estates (Nobles, Clergy and People's Representatives) which sat at Linlithgow on the very morning of his coronation. And so it was that on 26 March 1371 the Royal House of Stewart was founded by King Robert II, in worthy descent from the Kings of Scots Dalriada, the Thanes of Lochaber, the Breton Seneschals of Dol, and the House of Bruce.

The installation procedure for a King of Scots from the time of Robert the Bruce was rather different from the ceremonies of England and France. Firstly, the King-to-be was passed through a ritual of purification, to become an ordained people's priest. He

Kings of Scots – descent to Robert II Stewart

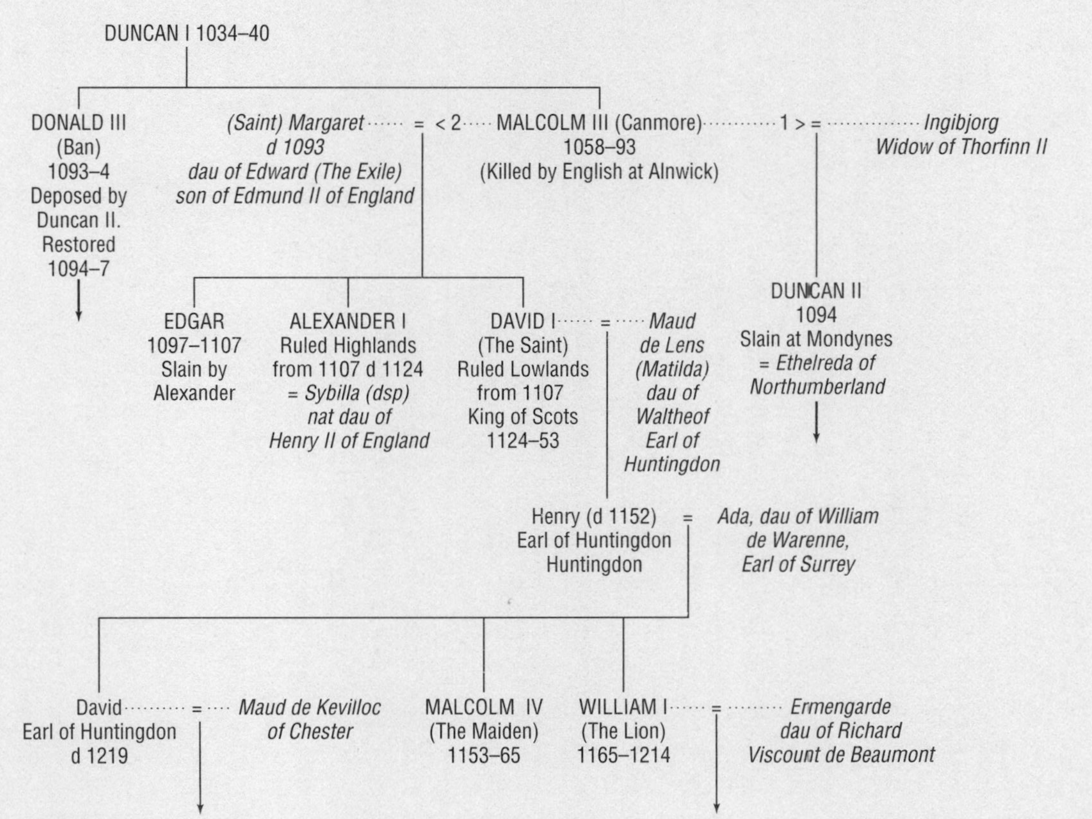

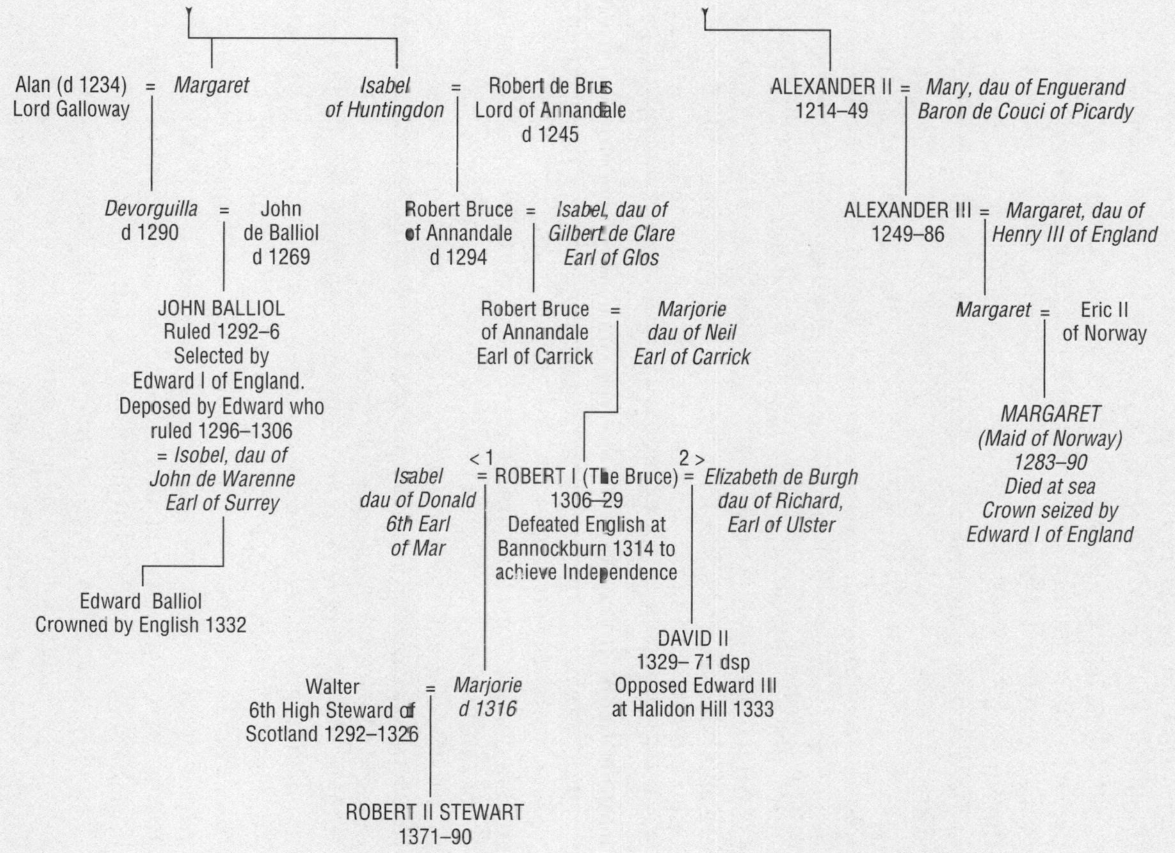
Alan (d 1234) Lord Galloway
= Margaret
Isabel of Huntingdon
= Robert de Brus Lord of Annandale d 1245
ALEXANDER II 1214–49
= Mary, dau of Enguerand Baron de Couci of Picardy
Devorguilla d 1290
= John de Balliol d 1269
Robert Bruce of Annandale d 1294
= Isabel, dau of Gilbert de Clare Earl of Glos
ALEXANDER III 1249–86
= Margaret, dau of Henry III of England
JOHN BALLIOL Ruled 1292–6 Selected by Edward I of England. Deposed by Edward who ruled 1296–1306
= Isobel, dau of John de Warenne Earl of Surrey
Robert Bruce of Annandale Earl of Carrick
= Marjorie dau of Neil Earl of Carrick
Margaret
= Eric II of Norway
MARGARET (Maid of Norway) 1283–90 Died at sea Crown seized by Edward I of England
Isabel dau of Donald 6th Earl of Mar
< 1 =
ROBERT I (The Bruce) 1306–29 Defeated English at Bannockburn 1314 to achieve Independence
2 > =
Elizabeth de Burgh dau of Richard, Earl of Ulster
Edward Balliol Crowned by English 1332
Walter 6th High Steward of Scotland 1292–1326
= Marjorie d 1316
DAVID II 1329– 71 dsp Opposed Edward III at Halidon Hill 1333
ROBERT II STEWART 1371–90

would then appear at the Church Abbey of Scone, dressed in white as a symbol of integrity, to be conducted to the Fealty Stone (traditionally, the Stone of Destiny) by a Bishop, followed by seven priests. With his hand upon the Stone, the King would swear his Oath of Fealty as the people's champion. He was duly anointed, and then sat upon the separate and much larger Coronation Stone, following which an 'Assembly of Friends' (seven nobles – symbolic of the Seven Earls of Scotland) would gather round as the Macduff Earl of Fife placed the crown upon the King's head. (In Robert II's case, this office was performed by Isabella, Countess of Fife, the daughter of Earl Duncan whose sister had crowned King Robert I Bruce.)

In the early days of the Kings of Scots the crown was no more than a circlet of gold, and its symbolic concept was to catch the eye of God, whose wisdom would be embraced within the circle. Subsequently, the circlet was heightened to a more conventional crown shape, but it was still open-topped. The crown of Alexander III was stolen by Edward I of England, and a new open crown, with fleury and fleur-de-lys, was made for Robert the Bruce, to be used by his successors thereafter, until it was remodelled by James V.

Once crowned, the King would receive the White Rod of Strength (the Sceptre) and the Sword of Justice. Having been invested with the Honours of the Realm (Crown, Sceptre and Sword), the King's Senachie (then known as Leo Rex Armorum, and today as the Lord Lyon, King of Arms) recited the pedigree of the new King, in reverse sequence. Certain interesting aspects of family history were also recounted.

Only at that stage would any religious ceremony begin, led by the Bishop and the seven priests. There were readings from Old Testament scriptures, along with prayers for the King's wise rule; also for the people, the nobles and the Church (some of which prayers were still used by the time of King Charles I in 1625). Then, after a formal dismissal, there was a grand banquet, and the general revelries lasted for up to a week or more.

Having undergone such an installation, Robert II succeeded not only as King, but also as a hereditary priest of the royal line. From the time of King Duncan I, son of Archpriest Crinan MacDonachadh, the concept of the monarch's dual priest-kingly role (both as sovereign and religious patriarch) had remained at the very root of Scottish culture. In this regard, Robert the Bruce had instructed that the relics of Saint Columba should be brought to the field of Bannockburn prior to the battle in 1314.[1] The relics were formally presented to the men of the Scottish Army, who knelt before them in prayer. Conventional history ignores the fact that Bruce was not only the Patriot King of his people, but was also Head of the Columban Kindred of their ancient Church. This inheritance was passed to his Stewart grandson Robert II when he succeeded in 1371. At that time, others belonging to the sacred family included the MacNabs, Rosses, Sinclairs, Robertsons, Dunbars, Dundasses, Wemysses, Abernethys, MacDuffs, Leslies, and Mackenzies, along with the Chiefs of Clan Chattan, the Cummings of Altyre, the Celtic Earls of Atholl, the Mackays of Strathnaver, and the Lindsays of Crawford.

As a dynastic family, my forebears of the Stewart royal house were a pretty interesting lot; but it is also important to remember that we were the specific 'choice' of the Scottish nation. Through successive generations this choice was never amended, and it was still widely supported after the English Whigs manoeuvred us out of position more than three centuries later. Quite unlike the violent changes in England's kingly successions, the Stewart kings did not emerge suddenly by force-of-arms or political intrigue; we had stood beside former Scottish monarchs for more than 200 years, and our mettle was well-known. We had been Commissioners, Guardians of the Kingdom, Ambassadors, Chancellors, Justiciars and Generals[2]; we had respected the Community of the Realm on all occasions, and were supporters of the very Constitution which confirmed the Nation's right to 'choose' future Kings of Scots, and to change them if necessary.

The Stewart Kings

Robert II

Plainly, David Bruce did not understand the Scottish Constitution as applied to kingship, and in consideration of his insulting arrangement with Edward of England, he was lucky to keep his crown. He seems also to have forgotten that his mother was Robert the Bruce's second wife (Elizabeth), whereas his father had a daughter by his first wife (Isabel). Moreover, that daughter's Caesarean son had been David's own Regent through the best part of his ineffectual reign. Undoubtedly, fortune had smiled early on Robert II, for neither he nor any of us would have existed were it not for the skilful surgeon who released him from his dead mother's womb on 2 March 1316.

Robert Stewart was 55-years-old when he was crowned and anointed, at the Abbey of Scone, on 26 March, Our Lady Day in Lenten. He had been twice married and had a number of sons – the eldest of whom, John of Carrick, was proclaimed Prince and Lord High Steward of Scotland. These titles were held by all heirs-apparent to the Scottish Crown thereafter. John's mother was Elizabeth Mure of Rowallan, who had died around 1354.

For 29 years Robert II struggled to curb the troublesome powers of the aristocracy, many of whose lines were strongly connected with the Norman and Plantagenet families of England. This had been apparent when the earlier *Ragman Roll* was presented, and throughout Europe the noble class had risen through more than three centuries of baronage and land tenure, as promoted by the Norman-led feudal machine. The Normans (although generally associated with France) were not of French or Flemish stock; they were descended from Norse invaders who had seized a part of northern France in the 10th century. Indeed, William the Conqueror was himself only a few generations removed from marauding Viking pirates, and the name 'Normans' was simply a corruption of 'Norsemen'.

Scotland, unlike England, had never been conquered by the Normans; she had simply acquired Norman immigrants because King David I had brought some of the families into the realm during the 12th century. Consequently, Scotland did not escape a share of the feudal experience, but Scotland's Norman nobles and their descendants were rather more controllable than their free-handed cousins elsewhere.

The Scots had also firmly rejected serfdom[3], but the immigrant aristocrats were particularly meddlesome in their attempts to tamper with the socially-created Clan System. It was, however, this very system, combined with a suitable Written Constitution, which enabled the Stewart kings to keep the Norman nobles in better check than was possible in other lands. By virtue of this, the Stewarts were popular among the Scots at home, and were individually respected by the people of other nations. In later times, however, it was our family tradition of standing alongside the community (rather than with the avaricious nobles and high-minded clergy) that caused the Stewart (Stuart) Kings of Britain to be manoeuvred from the 17th-century stage. This left the British populace forever after at the destructive mercy of unsympathetic monarchs and competitive party politics.

Robert III

In 1388, at the age of 72, Robert II withdrew from active government, and died 18 months later. Buried before the High Altar at Scone, his obituary notice read, 'Robert II was a Prince of such constancy in promise that he seldom spoke a word which he performed not'. His son John, Earl of Carrick, succeeded as King Robert III, but he did not have his father's strength, and the effective governor was actually his interfering younger brother Robert, Duke of Albany.

King Robert III's wife was Annabella Drummond of Stobhall, and when their eldest son David (Duke of Rothesay and heir-apparent) was 21, a move was made to reduce Albany's influence by appointing David as the King's Lieutenant. The King's jealous brother then took revenge by imprisoning his nephew at Falkland, and David was found dead in his cell a few weeks later.

The kingdom was then invaded once more by the English, who defeated the Scots at Nesbit Muir in June 1402, and again three months later at Homildon Hill. In the course of this, Albany's son, Murdoch, was taken prisoner and held to ransom.

A most extraordinary incident in 1396 was the 'Battle of the Clans', fought near Perth before King Robert, Queen Annabella and their Court. With 30 clansmen to each side, the feuding Chattans and Kays fought to the death with bows-and-arrows and battleaxes – and the affray was commenced with ceremony and bagpipes. One fellow, brought in at the last to make up the Chattan number, was not actually of the Clan, but took part for a small payment. Then, when he had killed one of the Kays, he drew aside stating that the numbers were now even, and that he had done quite enough for half-a-crown!

Falkland Palace

Following the death of King Robert's son David, his only surviving son was James, and out of concern for his safety Robert arranged for the nobleman Henry St Clair to take the Crown Prince to the French Court of Charles VI. During the passage, however, St Clair's ship was captured off the English coast, and young James was taken prisoner to England. On learning the sad news, Robert III (already in poor health) died at the age of 69. He had not been a great king by traditional standards, but there was nothing wanting in him as a compassionate man, and he was fully aware of his own shortcomings; he even wrote his own sad epitaph: 'Here lies the worst of kings and the unhappiest of men'. Robert III was buried in April 1406 at Paisley Abbey.

James I

Subsequent to his seizure, James I Stewart was confined by the English for 18 years, and during this period the reins of government in Scotland were usurped by Robert of Albany and his son Murdoch. But in 1424 James married the English princess, Lady Joan Beaufort, and was released to be crowned at Scone in May of that year. He had first seen Lady Joan from his cell window, and although she was the daughter of the Earl of Somerset, James set his heart on her from that moment, writing:

And there I spied, beneath my prison tower,
The fairest and the freshest young flower
That ever I beheld before that hour.
Entranced I gazed, and with sudden start,
Rushed instant, all my blood into my heart.

Although somewhat late in the day, King James I emerged in a blaze of retribution as James 'the Lion' of Scots. He immediately set out to deal with the self-serving nobles who had feathered their own nests at the people's expense, and put the nation's finances into chaos. James vowed to dismantle the realm of the nobles, and return Scotland to the people, 'though I myself must lead the life of a dog to do it'.

James sat sternly in his Parliament, with his sword ever-ready before him, and ran private surgeries at which the people could address him personally with their complaints. One Highland woman, with sorely wounded feet, had been brutally shod like a horse by a Macdonald assailant. Consequently, James had the man brought before him, to be similarly shod by a blacksmith. As far as James I was concerned the punishment should equal the crime, and he became renowned for his Solomon-like judgement. By 1425, he had received diplomatic emissaries from the Courts of France and Flanders, and word of his determination to uphold common rights and liberties was spread far and wide.

The Church of Rome was not at all happy that James managed things so well, and his reputation was such that the Pope feared other kings might follow his example by applying laws of justice rather than governing by implementing the laws of the Church. As a result, the papal ambassador Aeneas Sylvius was sent to Scotland, but his ship was caught in a North Sea storm, and he vowed that, should he be saved, he would walk to offer prayer at the first holy place. He came ashore at Aberlady in East Lothian, but had to walk a full ten miles, barefoot through the snows of winter, to a shrine at Whitekirk. By that time he had acquired a particular dislike for Scotland, and could not believe that the towns were unfortified, and that churches were offering arms to the poor.

King James I received Sylvius very graciously; he paid all his expenses, and gave him two horses, but still the ambassador was unhappy, and upon his return to Rome he reported how Scotland was so destitute that the people had to burn black sulphurous rocks on their fires![4] The black rock which had baffled Sylvius was 'coal', a domestic fuel quite unknown in Europe. Conclusive archaeological evidence from the locale of Prestonpans now affirms that coal had been used in Scotland from the time of the Bronze Age. Eventually, in 1458, Aeneas Sylvius became Pope Pius II.

One of the despotic aristocrats who fell to James's justice was his own cousin, the treacherous usurper Murdoch of Albany, who was duly beheaded at Falkland. Subsequently, James routed the troublesome Lord of the Isles at the Battle of Badenoch, only to be defeated by Donald Balloch of Isla at Inverlochy in 1431. Against the persistent English, however, James won the day at Piperden, near Berwick, in 1436 – but his own sudden end came soon afterwards.

While James I was in conference with his uncle, Walter of Atholl, at the Dominican Convent in Perth, the midnight proceedings were interrupted by a body of armed men led by Sir Robert Graham. The surprised King was slain there and then on 21 February 1437. The noblemen's plot was seemingly devised by Atholl himself, with intent to secure the crown for his own grandson Robert of Atholl. However, despite the assassination, the overall scheme was unsuccessful, and both Walter and Robert of Atholl were executed. The King was buried in the Carthusian monastery at Perth, and his widow, Queen Joan, later married Sir James Stewart, the Black Knight of Lorne, son of Lord Innermeath. From them descended the new Stewart House of Atholl. Initially, King James's heart was taken on a pilgrimage to the East, but it was subsequently returned from Crete by a Knight of St John, and granted to the Charterhouse of Perth, which James I had founded.

By 1444, some years after James I's murder, the English under Henry VI Plantagenet endeavoured to upset the trading alliance between Scotland and Flanders. The problem was solved, however, by way of a marriage between James's daughter, Mary, and Wolfaert van Borselen, Count of Grand Prés and Lord of Veere in Zeeland[5], one of Bruges' greatest trading magnates.

James II

Notwithstanding the Atholl plot, James was succeeded by his rightful son and heir James II (nicknamed the 'Fiery-face' because of a birthmark). He was only seven-years-old when crowned, and he was carried amid throngs of cheering people through the streets of Edinburgh, from the Castle to Holyrood Abbey. His mother, Joan Beaufort (who was Regent until her remarriage in 1439) had elected not to risk her son's life to any aristocrat's ambush on the road to Scone. Indeed, on one later occasion, Queen Joan had to secrete the young king from the capital to Stirling, hidden in a box of her clothes. (Edinburgh became the capital of Scotland following James I's murder at Perth in 1437. Prior to that date, Perth was the capital.)

In the manner of his forebears, James II grew to be far more popular with the clans and the people than with the aristocracy. Meanwhile, the Anglo-Scots dispute continued, and in 1448 the English burned Dunbar. The Scots retaliated at Alnwick, following which Dumfries was assaulted by the Earl of Salisbury, but James II's troops eventually won the Battle of Clochmaben Stone. In 1449 James married Maria van Gelre (Marie de Gueldres – a cousin of the King of France) at Holyrood House. Then two years later James obtained sanction for the foundation of Glasgow University, while that of St Andrews had been founded during the reign of his father.

In the continuing struggle against English oppression, King James launched a successful southern invasion in 1455 – but he was not so fortunate in his later attempt to besiege Roxburgh Castle. There, on 3 August 1460, James II (always fascinated by artillery) was killed by chance when one of his own cannons blew up beside him. Buried in the Chapel of Holyrood at the age of 29, James was succeeded by his eldest son.

James III

James III was yet another Stewart to gain his kingship as a minor, and he was only nine-years-old when crowned at Kelso. In total disregard for the Scots' Clan tradition of social community, the self-serving nobles saw another chance for supremacy, and the Earl of Ross made a pact with Edward IV for Scotland's subjugation to England. He conspired that the lands north of the Forth would be divided in his favour, but fortunately the plot failed. Two years later James's mother, Queen Maria, founded Trinity College Church in Edinburgh. In 1465 the appointed Governor of the Kingdom (Bishop James Kennedy of St Andrews) died, and James III became an operative king on his 16th birthday. He subsequently married Princess Margaret of Denmark, bringing Orkney and Shetland into the Scots domain.

Amid all this, the internecine struggles continued as various nobles battled to gain prime positions from one another. Edward IV of England pursued his imperious course, and ruled that James's younger brother, Alexander of Albany, was the true King of Scots. He issued a Charter to that effect in 1482, following which a number of James's colleagues were seized and hanged before his eyes on Lauder Bridge.

A month later, Berwick was taken by the English, and at that time the aristocrats were positively split into pro- and anti-James factions. On 11 June 1488 these met in battle at Sauchieburn, and it was the intention of James's enemies to replace the King prematurely with his own son who, at the age of 15, was taken to face his father on the battlefield. He requested that no one should lay hands on his father, but the King's troops were forcefully scattered, and James III rode, defeated and possibly slightly wounded, from the scene. However, that was not the end of it. The propagandist story which followed claimed that James found shelter in a cottage at Miltown, Stirlingshire, whereupon a priest was summoned to his aid. A supposed priest duly arrived, but he was actually one of James's pursuers from the battle, who promptly drew his dagger and struck down the King. The truth was, however, that James and a small riding party were hunted down, and James was killed fighting for his life, sword in hand.

James IV

James III was aged 36 when slain, and he was buried at the Abbey of Cambuskenneth alongside his wife, Queen Margaret, who had died two years earlier. As a result, young James IV inherited the crown as the saddest of all kings, and inflicted a penance upon himself by placing an iron-chain belt around his waist. He wore this for the rest of his life, adding a new link to the chain each year.

Notwithstanding his unfortunate circumstance, James IV became greatly admired, and was described as 'a very humane king, who could speak Scots, Latin, Gaelic, French, German, Flemish, Spanish and Italian'. Indeed, he was hailed as 'Defender of the Faith' in 1506 by Pope Julius II, long before Henry VIII Tudor of England received that same distinction. James's papal honour was gained because of his fervent ambition to lead a great Crusade to the Holy Land. In Scotland, crop taxes were set aside to fund the campaign, and James endeavoured to gain support from the Christian princes of Europe. One influential prince who responded with enthusiasm was Vlad IV (the Monk) of Transylvania, brother of Vlad III 'the Impaler' (so-called because he had impaled a number of aristocrats on wooden stakes for rebelling against his family). Vlad III was also called Dracula (his father, Vlad II, being Dracul) because of his traditional descent from the Priests of Dracul the Dragon. They were the attendants of the Egyptian Queen Sobeknoferu (*c*1785 BC), a scientific leader of her age. Indeed, it was Vlad III of Transylvania who was the prototype for the fictional Count Dracula in Bram Stoker's famous 19th-century Gothic novel.

In 1507, Pope Julius also sent James IV the famous Sword of State, with its metre-long blade and golden scabbard. Previously, Pope Alexander VI had given him the Sceptre (later refashioned for James V, whose initials were engraved on the rod). These are now displayed in Edinburgh Castle, together with the Stewart Crown – the original golden crown of Robert the Bruce, remodelled with stones and top-arches to house a crimson bonnet for James V in 1540. (Charles V, King of Spain and Holy Roman Emperor, was the first to attach top-arches to his crown, and then Henry VIII Tudor, who was married to Charles V's aunt, Catherine of Aragon, did likewise. The new style was considered to be 'Imperial', and it was soon adopted by the French, and then by James V of Scots.) Earlier, in 1489, James IV had been presented with a sword and dagger by Spanish ambassadors[6], but these were later stolen by the English, and are now held at the Herald's College of Arms in London.

Quite apart from his obvious social awareness, James was also held in great regard by military men for his prowess in arms. He was a noted exponent at jousting, and knights came from home and abroad to compete in his famous Edinburgh tournaments, proclaiming that James was 'even more courageous than a king should be'.

So of his court through Europe spread the fame,
Of lusty lords and lovesome ladies ying,
Triumphant tourneys, justings and knightly game,
With all pastime according for ane King
Who was the gloir of princely governing.

In terms not only of Scotland, but of Europe in general, James IV was a socially amazing monarch who totally reformed educational and workers' rights to unparalleled levels of operation. He also ratified the Constitution of the College of Surgeons, and instituted the University at Aberdeen, with King's College founded in 1495. But, through all of this, his punitive iron belt was a constant reminder of his duty to his father's people. James IV was particularly revered in religious circles, being admitted as a lay canon of Glasgow Cathedral, and a lay brother of the Friars Observant at Stirling.

James IV was additionally responsible for improving the Scottish Navy, and won two significant sea-battles against the formidable English fleet in 1489 and 1504. He built many ships including his own favourite, the *Margaret*, named after his wife Margaret Tudor. In anticipation of his great Crusade, James also built the *Great Michael* – the largest warship of the era, with capacity for 300 crew, 120 gunners, 300 ordnance pieces, and 1,000 men-at-arms (*see* Appendix I). This impressive vessel was used to subdue the warlike Lord of the Isles, and also took part in the sacking of Carrickfergus, an English garrison in Ireland.

Flowers of the Forest

In August 1503 James IV had married Margaret Tudor, the eldest daughter of England's Henry VII. By way of this alliance, James inherited an ultimate claim to the English crown of Saint Edward, a claim which was destined to fall so harshly upon his

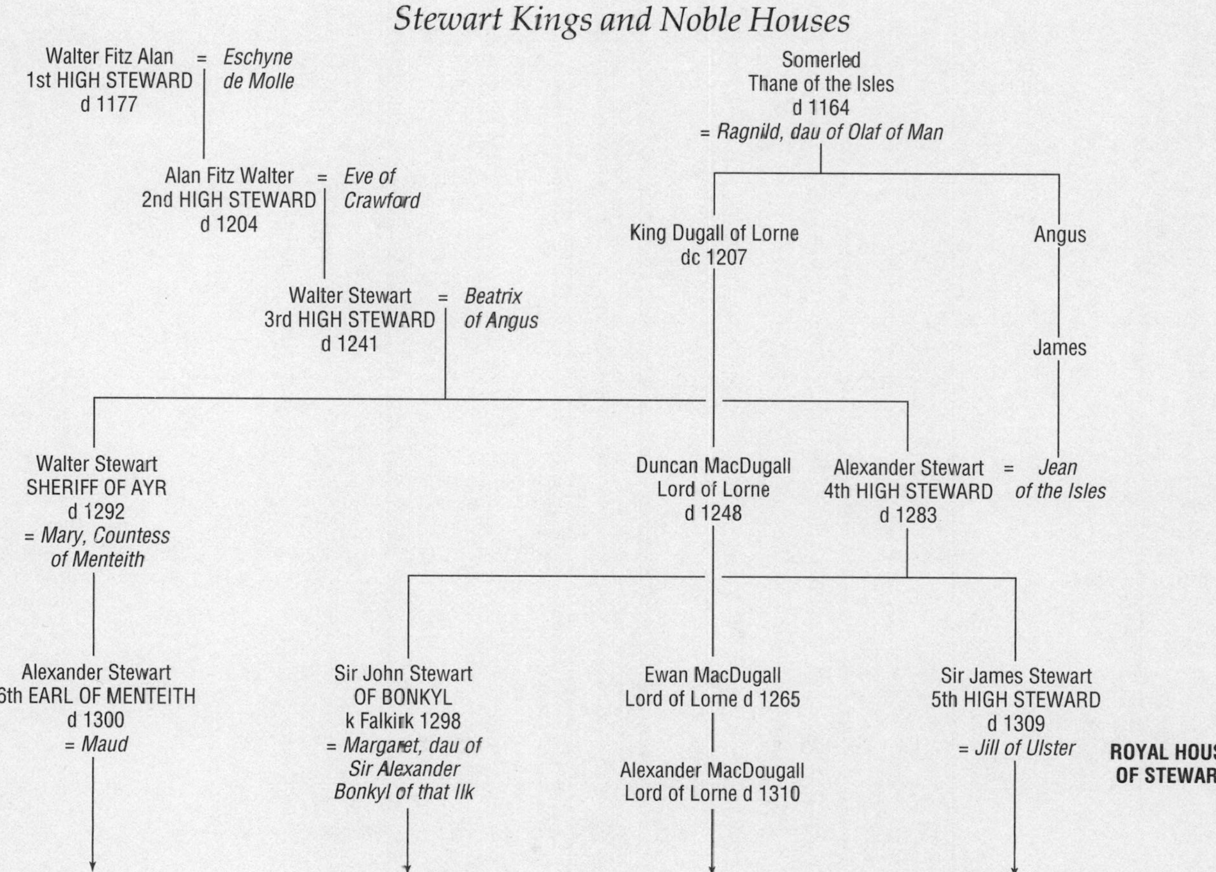
Stewart Kings and Noble Houses
Walter Fitz Alan
1st HIGH STEWARD
d 1177
= Eschyne de Molle
Somerled
Thane of the Isles
d 1164
= Ragnild, dau of Olaf of Man
Alan Fitz Walter
2nd HIGH STEWARD
d 1204
= Eve of Crawford
King Dugall of Lorne
dc 1207
Angus
Walter Stewart
3rd HIGH STEWARD
d 1241
= Beatrix of Angus
James
Walter Stewart
SHERIFF OF AYR
d 1292
= Mary, Countess of Menteith
Duncan MacDugall
Lord of Lorne
d 1248
Alexander Stewart
4th HIGH STEWARD
d 1283
= Jean of the Isles
Alexander Stewart
6th EARL OF MENTEITH
d 1300
= Maud
Sir John Stewart
OF BONKYL
k Falkirk 1298
= Margaret, dau of Sir Alexander Bonkyl of that Ilk
Ewan MacDugall
Lord of Lorne d 1265
Alexander MacDougall
Lord of Lorne d 1310
Sir James Stewart
5th HIGH STEWARD
d 1309
= Jill of Ulster
ROYAL HOUSE OF STEWART

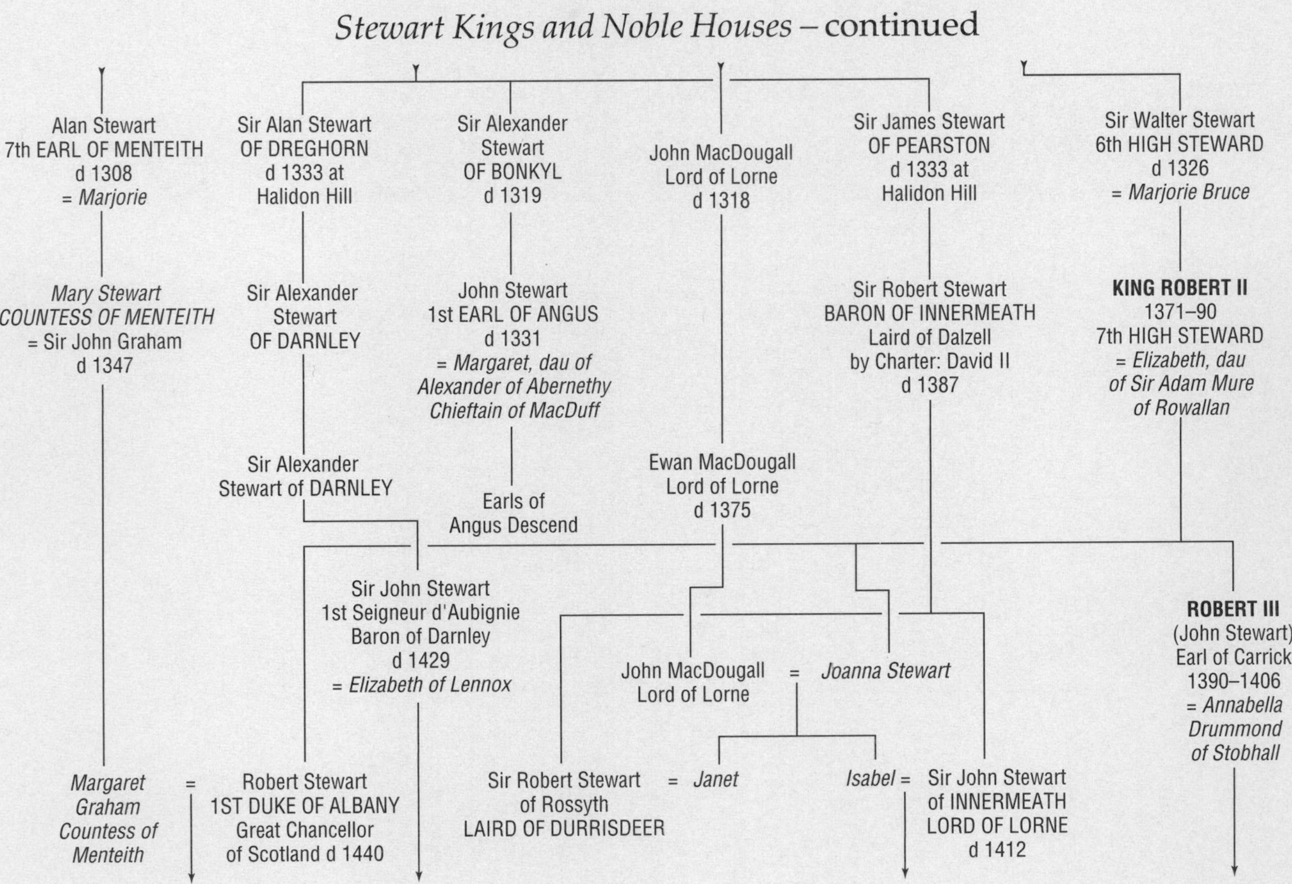
Stewart Kings and Noble Houses – continued
Alan Stewart
7th EARL OF MENTEITH
d 1308
= Marjorie
Sir Alan Stewart
OF DREGHORN
d 1333 at
Halidon Hill
Sir Alexander
Stewart
OF BONKYL
d 1319
John MacDougall
Lord of Lorne
d 1318
Sir James Stewart
OF PEARSTON
d 1333 at
Halidon Hill
Sir Walter Stewart
6th HIGH STEWARD
d 1326
= Marjorie Bruce
Mary Stewart
COUNTESS OF MENTEITH
= Sir John Graham
d 1347
Sir Alexander
Stewart
OF DARNLEY
John Stewart
1st EARL OF ANGUS
d 1331
= Margaret, dau of
Alexander of Abernethy
Chieftain of MacDuff
Sir Robert Stewart
BARON OF INNERMEATH
Laird of Dalzell
by Charter: David II
d 1387
KING ROBERT II
1371–90
7th HIGH STEWARD
= Elizabeth, dau
of Sir Adam Mure
of Rowallan
Sir Alexander
Stewart of DARNLEY
Earls of
Angus Descend
Ewan MacDougall
Lord of Lorne
d 1375
Sir John Stewart
1st Seigneur d'Aubignie
Baron of Darnley
d 1429
= Elizabeth of Lennox
John MacDougall
Lord of Lorne
=
Joanna Stewart
ROBERT III
(John Stewart)
Earl of Carrick
1390–1406
= Annabella
Drummond
of Stobhall
Margaret
Graham
Countess of
Menteith
=
Robert Stewart
1ST DUKE OF ALBANY
Great Chancellor
of Scotland d 1440
Sir Robert Stewart
of Rossyth
LAIRD OF DURRISDEER
=
Janet
Isabel =
Sir John Stewart
of INNERMEATH
LORD OF LORNE
d 1412

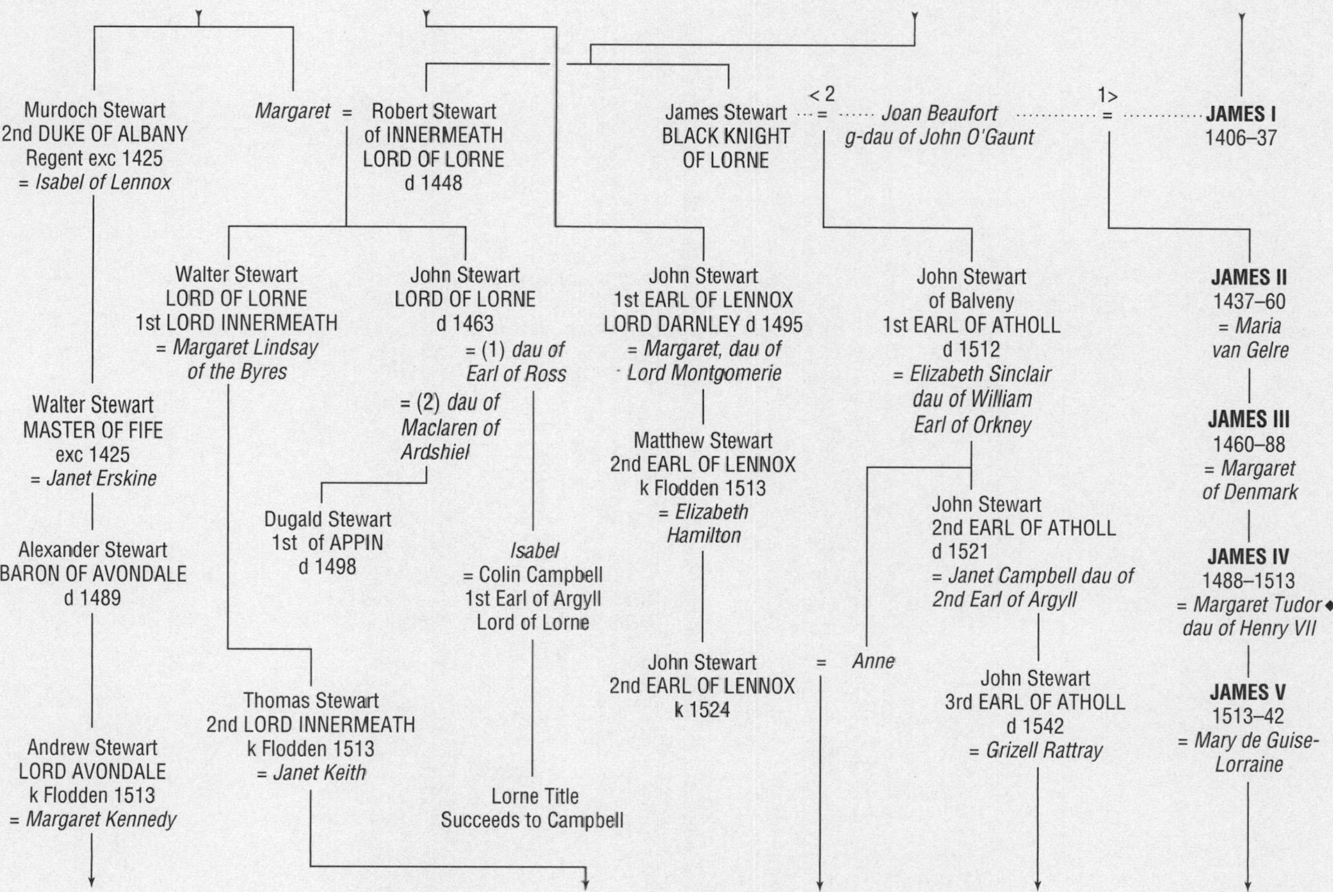

Murdoch Stewart
2nd DUKE OF ALBANY
Regent exc 1425
= Isabel of Lennox
Margaret =
Robert Stewart
of INNERMEATH
LORD OF LORNE
d 1448
James Stewart
BLACK KNIGHT
OF LORNE
< 2 = Joan Beaufort
g-dau of John O'Gaunt
1> = JAMES I
1406–37
Walter Stewart
LORD OF LORNE
1st LORD INNERMEATH
= Margaret Lindsay
of the Byres
John Stewart
LORD OF LORNE
d 1463
= (1) dau of
Earl of Ross
= (2) dau of
Maclaren of
Ardshiel
John Stewart
1st EARL OF LENNOX
LORD DARNLEY d 1495
= Margaret, dau of
Lord Montgomerie
John Stewart
of Balveny
1st EARL OF ATHOLL
d 1512
= Elizabeth Sinclair
dau of William
Earl of Orkney
JAMES II
1437–60
= Maria
van Gelre
Walter Stewart
MASTER OF FIFE
exc 1425
= Janet Erskine
JAMES III
1460–88
= Margaret
of Denmark
Matthew Stewart
2nd EARL OF LENNOX
k Flodden 1513
= Elizabeth
Hamilton
Dugald Stewart
1st of APPIN
d 1498
John Stewart
2nd EARL OF ATHOLL
d 1521
= Janet Campbell dau of
2nd Earl of Argyll
Alexander Stewart
BARON OF AVONDALE
d 1489
Isabel
= Colin Campbell
1st Earl of Argyll
Lord of Lorne
JAMES IV
1488–1513
= Margaret Tudor ◆
dau of Henry VII
John Stewart
2nd EARL OF LENNOX
k 1524
= Anne
John Stewart
3rd EARL OF ATHOLL
d 1542
= Grizell Rattray
Thomas Stewart
2nd LORD INNERMEATH
k Flodden 1513
= Janet Keith
JAMES V
1513–42
= Mary de Guise-
Lorraine
Andrew Stewart
LORD AVONDALE
k Flodden 1513
= Margaret Kennedy
Lorne Title
Succeeds to Campbell

Stewart Kings and Noble Houses – continued

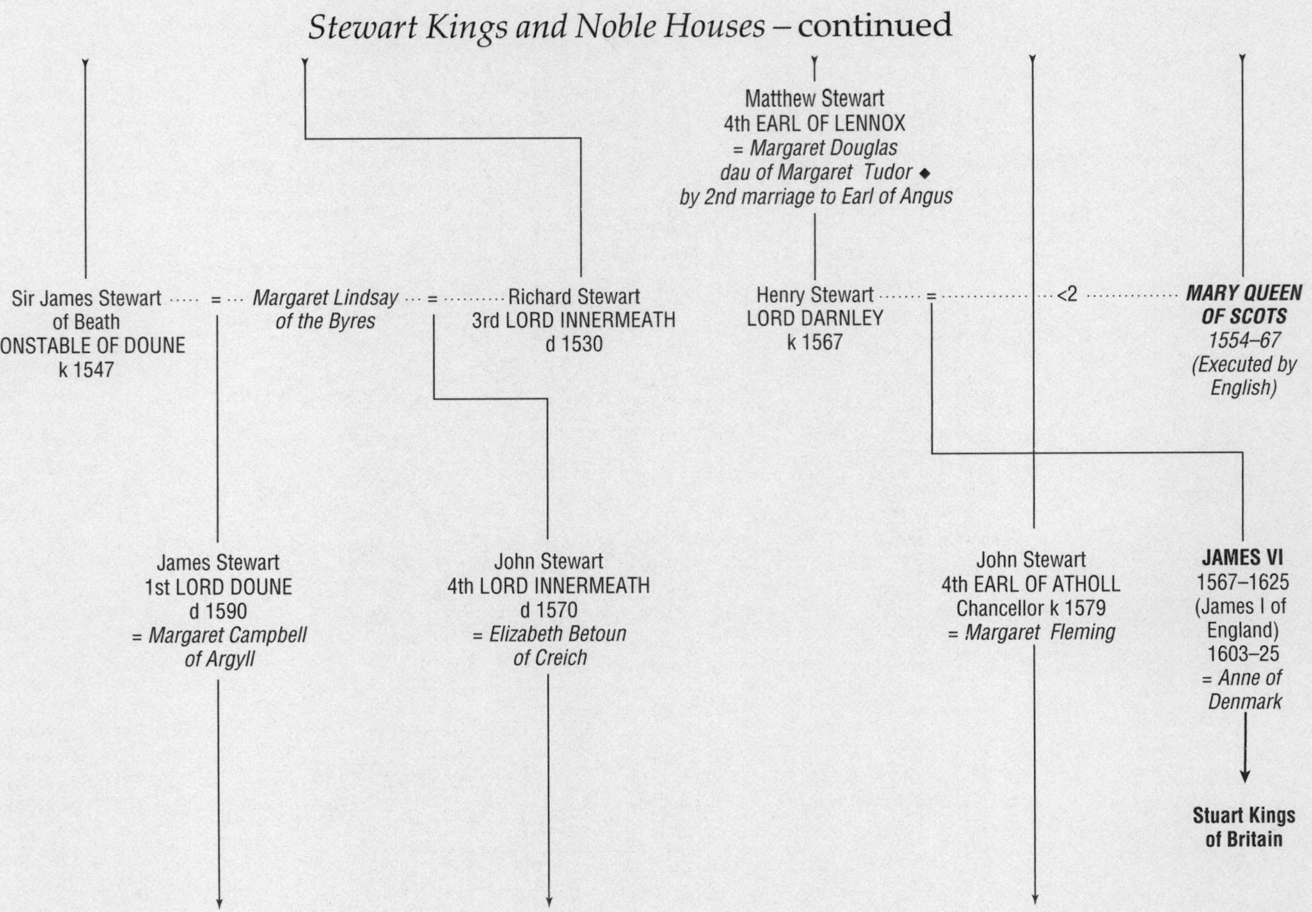

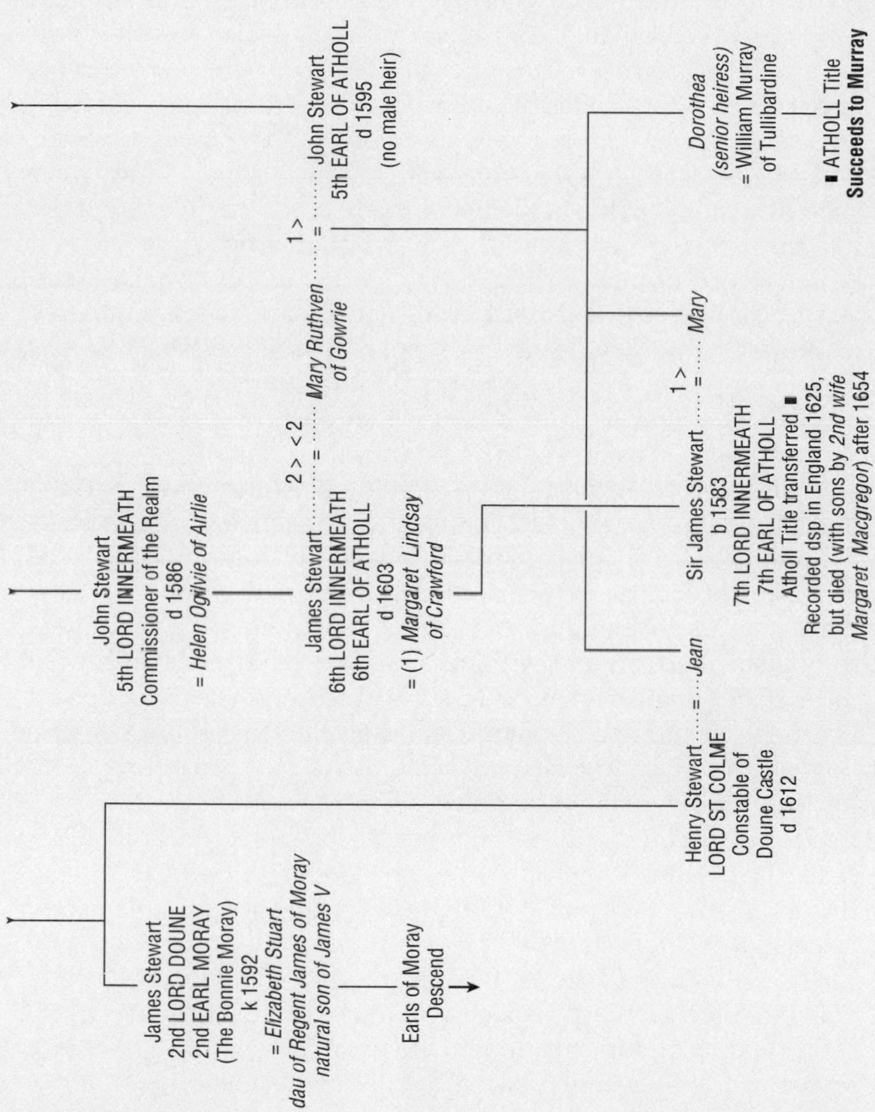
James Stewart
2nd LORD DOUNE
2nd EARL MORAY
(The Bonnie Moray)
k 1592
= Elizabeth Stuart
dau of Regent James of Moray
natural son of James V
Earls of Moray
Descend
John Stewart
5th LORD INNERMEATH
Commissioner of the Realm
d 1586
= Helen Ogilvie of Airlie
James Stewart
6th LORD INNERMEATH
6th EARL OF ATHOLL
d 1603
= (1) Margaret Lindsay
of Crawford
2 > < 2
= Mary Ruthven
of Gowrie
1 > =
John Stewart
5th EARL OF ATHOLL
d 1595
(no male heir)
Henry Stewart
LORD ST COLME
Constable of
Doune Castle
d 1612
= Jean
Sir James Stewart
b 1583
7th LORD INNERMEATH
7th EARL OF ATHOLL
Atholl Title transferred ■
Recorded dsp in England 1625,
but died (with sons by 2nd wife
Margaret Macgregor) after 1654
1 > = Mary
Dorothea
(senior heiress)
= William Murray
of Tullibardine
■ ATHOLL Title
Succeeds to Murray

Stuart descendants. Indeed, Henry Tudor had actually promoted the alliance on the basis that, if a union of kingdoms followed, then the lesser realm (Scotland) would be subordinate to the greater (England).

Some years later, Margaret's brother, Henry VIII (prior to his dispute with the Pope) was in league with the Holy Roman Emperor, Maximilian I Habsburg, in a territorial dispute with France. In the course of this, the *Auld Alliance* between the Scots and French was strengthened in both military and financial terms. Henry saw his chance to gain some lands across the water, and so he and his troops landed in France, where they were successful at the Battle of the Spurs in 1513. Meanwhile, James IV had placed the Scots Fleet at the disposal of King Louis XII, and he sent word of this to King Henry, who was completely taken aback by the *Great Michael*'s dimensions. He immediately commissioned the building of a similar vessel, the *Henry Grace à Dieu* – or as more commonly known, the *Great Harry*. But, in the event, this ship was so top-heavy that she could only sail on short voyages in calm weather and in sight of land.

In his effort to expand the English Navy, Henry later built the flagship *Mary Rose*, but she fell to the vengeance of the Knights Templars in 1545. In conjunction with his dissolution of the monasteries, Henry had also issued an edict of dissolution against the Templars in England, particularly in London. The Knights duly disbanded, but not without a parting gesture: they scuttled the *Mary Rose*, and she sank off Spithead on her maiden voyage. (It was because of Henry's Templar dissolution that there were no English Knights at the siege of Malta, when for three long years the Knights of other nations held the Turks at bay.)

Having granted his Naval services to the French in 1513, James IV was then approached by the Queen of France, Anne of Brittany, who sent him a blue-stone ring as a token. She requested that, on her behalf, he should advance 'one step' onto English soil, in defiance of the Tudor monarch. Queen Margaret was horrified at the prospect, but James sent his Lion Herald (Lord Lyon) to inform King Henry of his intention. Henry responded with indignation, stating that James had no authority to side with the French because Scotland was only a department of England, held by Scots under grant of dispensation from the House of Tudor with himself as the 'verie owner'! 'Furthermore,' yelled Henry, 'I shall, at my return, expulse him from his realm.'

Unlike his father, Henry VIII Tudor did not believe that war and glory were bad for business. He had long endeavoured, in true Plantagenet style, to bring Scotland under his authority – and here was another chance. Without delay, England's Earl of Surrey led his army to the Scottish Border, and 13 English ships sailed into Leith – setting the scene for the most ill-fated day in Scots history.

When Surrey arrived, James IV had no intention of going to war against the English, but Surrey's brother, Sir Edward Howard, threw repeated insults at the King of Scots, taunting him over the earlier death of a certain Captain Andrew Barton, who had been a close friend of James. Two years earlier, Barton had been Master of the Scottish ship *Lion,* which was sailing off the English coast in company with the smaller, faster ship *Jennet Pirwyn.* They were attacked by English ships under the command of Edward Howard, and at the height of battle Andrew Barton climbed the rigging to direct the Scottish guns. He was soon struck by a cannon-ball which tore off his legs, and he plunged to the deck; but the bold Captain Barton was not finished, and he ordered his sailors to place him in a barrel of sea-water. 'Fight on brave lads', he cried from the barrel. 'So long as you hear my whistle, you'll know I'm with you'. However, Barton died in the brine, and the English won the day, seizing the Scottish ships for their Navy.

As it transpired, Howard's mocking of the gallant captain was too much for James, whose army stood behind him – and the result was immediate war. It was 9 September 1513 when James IV's soldiers, and Henry VIII's troops under the Earl of Surrey, met at Branxton Moor, Northumberland.

The Scots were ready and in position, but while Surrey's men were still on the move and seemingly not mustered, James forbade any advance or shot, for he had agreed to meet on equal terms. However, unbeknown to James, the mobile English had already begun the battle, and were actually exerting a flanking manoeuvre which resulted in a sudden, devastating attack. A Scottish eyewitness report stated,

> The fight began about four o'clock in the afternoon. The armies joined very awfully, and fought very cruelly for a long time with uncertain victory. The King was fighting in the multitude, and no one knew what was happening.

Better known as the Battle of Flodden Field, the fierce conflict, which began in torrential rain, claimed the life of King James, 12 of his earls, 13 barons and more than 10,000 of his soldiers, forever remembered as the 'Flowers of the Forest'. Also killed was the Archbishop of St Andrews, along with the Bishops of Caithness and the Isles, and at least 50 clan chiefs and gentry. When the sun set beyond the Moor, the armies withdrew, and the numbed survivors from the Scottish ranks took their leave of the blood-soaked field. By morning, the Scots had departed, and the English were alone amid the deserted Scottish guns (including the famous 'Seven Sisters of Borthwick'), with the dead piled around. So many had been slain that hardly a family in Scotland did not mourn its youth that day.

Never was read in tragedy or story,
At one journey so many nobles slain
For the defence and love of their sovereign.

Enigma of the Tomb

History books tell that King James had been struck down when an arrow entered his throat, and as he lay mortally wounded the English rushed to finish him. In an effort to defend himself James raised his right arm, whereupon the hand on which he wore Anne of Brittany's ring was severed by a ferocious blow from a battleaxe. But did James IV actually die at Flodden? This is a question which has long puzzled researchers, for there is an amount of evidence which suggests that he did not.

James's body was seemingly found within a heap of corpses, and was taken to Berwick for identification. Subsequently disembowelled and embalmed, the body was dispatched to Richmond, Surrey, on a cart, for presentation to the English Queen, Catherine of Aragon. Henry VIII then asked Pope Leo X for permission to bury James in the consecrated ground of St Paul's Cathedral, but this was not done, even though the request was approved.[7] The body was, in fact, left unburied and wrapped in lead at Sheen Monastery in Surrey. Some years later, in 1598, a Londoner named John Stowe wrote in his *Survey of London* that he was shown the body of the King amid the rubble of a waste-room, prior to which some workmen had lopped off the head. Apparently a glazier had taken the head to London, where it was later interred with other bones at the Church of St Michael in Wood Street. When Sheen Monastery was demolished in 1750, the body and its lead casing had gone; and when St Michael's Church was demolished last century, the head had also disappeared.

What no one has ever understood is why the King of Scots was not buried in consecrated ground as Henry VIII had requested with the Pope's approval. This strange anomaly is understandable, however, if it was discovered that the corpse brought to Surrey was not that of James after all.

The body removed from Flodden had an arrow through the cheek, a severed hand, and had been sliced from ear to ear with a bill; but no Englishman could be sure that it was the King's body because ten Scotsmen had been clad in copies of the King's armour that day. Indeed, the historian Lindsay of Pitscottie wrote in 1560 that four Scottish knights, with straw tied to their spears for identification, had cut through the chaos of Flodden to remove their live King from the carnage of the field. Furthermore, when James's Queen, Margaret Tudor, was attempting to divorce her second husband, the Earl of Angus, in 1525, she confirmed in State Papers that James had lived for three years after his supposed death in battle.

The most puzzling feature of all was the fact that the body removed from Flodden bore neither a chain nor any chain-marks, yet it was known that James always wore his iron belt of penance next to his skin, a chain fastened and welded by a blacksmith.

After the battle, there were rumours in Scotland that King James had actually been murdered off the field by the Earl of Home, who had failed to take an active part at Flodden. In fact, one of Home's servants alleged that Home had 'taught the King that he was mortal', and when Home was later executed for rebellion, the people accused him again of assassinating the King. Some years after this, another condemned prisoner told the Regent Albany that he could show him where James was buried along with his iron belt, but it was recorded that 'Albany desired not that such things should be known'.

In a recent *Scots Magazine* article Archie McKerracher

concluded that Home may well have been discovered looting the battlefield by James, and probably did assault the King, as reported, for fear of being charged with treason. Having struck James a mentally incapacitating blow to the head, Home then confined him for three years until he died. Of particular significance in this regard is a document written by the Earl of Nithsdale, and preserved at the Scots College in Douai, France. This manuscript history of Scotland relates:

> During the usurpation of Cromwell, a skeleton, girded with an iron chain, and enclosed within a bull-skin, was found amongst the ruins of the old castle of Roxburgh; and that the iron chain, which James IV did at no time lay by, made people believe that it was the body of the prince that had been discovered. But, the nation being then in subjection, there was no way to make a further trial of the matter, so that the skeleton was interred without any ceremony in the common burial place.

James V

Having achieved so much in his reign, James IV was still only 40 at the Battle of Flodden, and when Parliament was convened after the toll of the slaughter, more than half the seats were empty in silent testimony. Nevertheless, James's Queen, Margaret Tudor, wasted no time in having her 17-month-old son crowned James V at Stirling Castle, and she immediately became Regent of Scotland. Then, in compliance with James's will, she married Archibald Douglas, Earl of Angus. If the King had survived, Margaret obviously did not know it at the time, even though she later confirmed the fact.

Given Henry VIII Tudor's failure with his ship the *Great Harry*, he had long been endeavouring to gain ownership of James IV's *Great Michael*, and had even sent an ambassador to Scotland requesting the world's foremost warship to enhance the English Navy. Consequently, after their loss at Flodden, the Scottish Three Estates Parliament promptly relieved Henry of his ambition by selling the *Great Michael* to the French in 1514.[8]

Young James V had been born at Linlithgow on Easter Day 1512, and cemented his sovereign position at the age of 14 in 1526. In continuation of his father's interest in people's wages

Linlithgow Palace

and conditions of employment, James kept an avid, incognito eye on the situation, and he was said to have been 'delighted to move about disguised as a farmer'. Unfortunately, much of his father's success in breeding a better temper among the nobles had been lost on the field of Flodden, following which the Regency prevailed for too long, with the Duke of Albany having succeeded Queen Margaret as Guardian of the Realm. By the time that James V was of age to take the reins, the aristocrats were battling with each other as before. As for James, he concentrated his social efforts among the people, acquiring his affectionately deserved appellation, 'The Poor Man's King'.

In an effort to maintain a diplomatic relationship with England, James V made a number of ambassadorial visits to London, where a large house was set aside for him at the Palace of Whitehall. Its main entrance was approached across a large courtyard which was designated Scottish territory, by an Act of Parliament in 1534, and subsequently named Scotland Yard. It was here that in 1829

Sir Robert Peel established his original police department, retaining the old name from the Stewart era. Subsequently there have been two changes of location, but the definition 'Scotland Yard' (now New Scotland Yard) has remained synonymous with the Metropolitan Police headquarters.

In 1535 King James V received the Order of the Garter from his uncle Henry VIII, the Order of the Golden Fleece from Emperor Charles V, and the Order of Saint Michel from King Francis I of France, whose daughter Madeleine he married in the following year. Unfortunately, the new Queen of Scots died within six months at Holyrood House; then in 1538 James married Marie, Duchesse de Guise, Princesse de Lorraine, the widow of Louis II d'Orléans.

Despite James's endeavour to maintain peace with the English, trouble brewed again when Henry VIII demanded that James should pay homage in England. He deemed this only right and proper because his own sister, Margaret Tudor, was the King of Scots' mother. James, of course, refused, and in August 1542 Henry's army advanced northward. Initially, they were defeated by the Scots under the Earl of Huntly at the Battle of Hadden Rig, but the situation reversed at Solway Moss in the November. Slightly wounded, the popular King James V was taken to Falkland Palace where, following a nervous breakdown, he died at the age of 30 on 14 December. He was buried at Holyrood Abbey little more than a week after his daughter and heiress, Mary, was born at Linlithgow Palace.

Knights Templars and Knights Hospitallers

One of Scotland's most prominent families of the early Stewart era was the old Norman family of St Clair, who had arrived in the 11th century, sometime before the Norman Conquest of England. In 1057, they had received the Barony of Roslin, south of Edinburgh, from Malcolm III Canmore; and Sir William de St Clair, Sheriff of Edinburgh, was a close colleague of Alexander III. Also, as we have already seen, it was a later Sir William de St Clair who was entrusted with the heart of Robert the Bruce.

The St Clairs (from the Latin, *Sanctus Clarus,* meaning Holy

Light) were appointed Scots Ambassadors to both England and France, and some of the Templar treasure of Jerusalem was taken to the vaults of their castle at Roslin in 1307. However, not all of the Knights Templars went to Scotland with the fleet at that time; a good number went to Portugal where, in 1317, they were reincorporated as the Knights of Christ by King Dinis (ratified by John XXII in the following year). By 1394 Prince Henry the Navigator was that Order's Grand Master, and other notable seagoing explorers, such as Vasco da Gama, were knights of the Order. Indeed, oceanic navigation was a great attribute of the Templars, and in 1398 twelve ships of Henri St Clair, Prince of Orkney, sailed across the Atlantic to Nova Scotia, Massachusetts and Rhode Island a century before Christopher Columbus was said to have discovered America. On his return from America, however, St Clair was killed by English raiders at Kirkwall in 1400. (This Henry St Clair was the father of Henry St Clair who attempted to remove Crown Prince James [James I] to safety in France in 1406.)

Evidence of the St Clair voyage can be seen at each of these places. At Louisburg, Cape Breton, is a cannon of the Venetian type used by the St Clair fleet, a type long obsolete by the time of Columbus. At Westford, Massachusetts, the grave of one of Henry St Clair's knights is still discernable. Punched into a rock ledge is the seven-foot effigy of a 14th-century knight wearing a basinet, chain-mail and a surcoat. The figure bears a sword of the 1300s, and a shield with heraldry of the Chief of Clan Gunn.

At Newport, Rhode Island, is a well preserved two-storey medieval tower, constructed as an octagon within a circle, and eight arches around. This is based on the circular model of the Templar churches, and a similar example is to be found at the 12th-century Orphir Chapel on Orkney. The Newport architecture is Scottish, and its design is reproduced at the St Clair Church, Corstorphine, where Henry St Clair's daughter has her memorial. Rhode Island was not officially founded until 1636, but its founding was no chance event. At the Public Records Office in London, a text dated four years earlier describes the 'rounde stone towre' at Newport, proposing that it could be used as a garrison for the soldiers of Sir Edmund Plouden who colonized the area.

By the time of James II Stewart, the St Clairs had changed their name to Sinclair, and William Sinclair, Earl of Caithness, Grand Admiral of Scotland, was appointed Hereditary Patron and Protector of the Scottish Masons by King James in 1441. The document of appointment, signed by James, is held by the Grand Masonic Order of Scotland, and is lodged at Freemasons Hall in Edinburgh. Also in Edinburgh is Lawrie's *History of Freemasonry* (1804) which gives details of the hereditary appointment. William was a Knight of the Golden Fleece, a most prestigious European Order, founded on 10 January 1429 by Philip the Good, Duke of Burgundy, with St Andrew as its apostolic patron. William Sinclair was also a Knight of the Coquille St Jacques, the Knights of Santiago di Compostella, a 12th-century Order with strong Templar connections. (Templars entering the Order today are dressed as pilgrims returning from Compostella, Spain, with the clamshell badges of Santiago [Sant Iago = St James] on their hats.)

The masons of William Sinclair were not the speculative Freemasons that we know today, but operative stonemasons, privy to the Sacred Geometry held by the Knights Templars. Because of this, William was enabled to build the now famous Rosslyn Chapel; the overall work, with its abundance of intricate carvings, was begun in about 1446. In 1475 a Charter (The Incorporation of St Mary's Chapel) was ratified, and Rosslyn became known as 'Lodge Number One' in Edinburgh. The magnificent Chapel – still used by Knights Templars of the Scottish Grand Priory, and by the Scottish Episcopal Church – stands above the Esk Valley, near the original Templar centre at Ballantradoch (House of the warrior).

By way of a Charter dated 19 October 1488, James IV confirmed the administrative consolidation of the Scottish Knights Templars with the Knights Hospitallers of St John of Jerusalem. They continued to function as independent Orders, but their property administration was conjoined under William Knollis, Preceptor of the Scottish Hospitallers at Torpichen (the senior residence of the Knights Hospitallers in Scotland). The sequence of events was as follows: Knollis was appointed Treasurer by James IV on 18 June 1488 (one week after the Battle of Sauchieburn), and was installed as Governor of Blackness Castle, near Bo'ness on the Firth of Forth. On 19 October all Templar properties were settled under Hospitaller administration, and three years later, on 10 January 1491, Knollis was granted a permanent parliamentary seat as Lord St John.[9] Subsequently, he received a royal appointment as tutor to James Stewart, Earl of Mar, and he eventually died on 11 March 1503. (The 'Lord St John' title was held by each successive Hospitaller Preceptor of Torpichen until 1560.)

Although not ratified until 1488, the amalgamation of Templar and Hospitaller property interests had actually taken place sometime after 1314, when Templar lands and preceptories in England were confiscated and granted to the Hospitallers. Indeed, Pope Clement V had issued a Bull demanding that this should be done. Although the directive was not implemented in Scotland, the Templars certainly became more secretive from that date, shielding themselves behind the Hospitallers and other Orders under the patronage of Robert the Bruce. Nevertheless (because of the increasing difficulties of administration), it was subsequently deemed necessary to have jointly managed Scottish property accounts for the Orders from 1488, even though the Knights Templars still functioned quite separately from the Hospitallers.

The early transfers of English holdings had taken place as far south-west as Bagworthy, on Exmoor, where the old Templar-owned settlement was granted to the Hospitallers of St John by edict of Edward II Plantagenet. It was to this place that Sir James Stewart of Lorne, 7th Lord of Innermeath, later brought his family in 1623. He had been banished from Scotland by the Privy Council for sheltering fugitive Macgregors within the confines of Atholl. Known as 'Sir Eoin Ciar' (Sir John the dusky), the exiled Lord Innermeath became immortalized as 'Sir Ensor' in R D Blackmore's classic novel, *Lorna Doone.*

The Knights Hospitallers had been founded in the Holy Land shortly before the Templars, and under their Grand Master, Raimond Dupuy, they provided welfare and medical aid for pilgrims and victims of the Crusades. In fact, their Jerusalem hospital existed before the First Crusade of 1096, having been established in about 1050 by a Frenchman known as Gerhard the Holy. From 1530, the Knights Hospitallers of St John were re-established as the Knights of Malta, having left the Holy Land after the Crusades terminated in 1291. As distinct from the Knights Templars' familiar eight-pointed cross (red on white), the Knights of Malta bore their similar device, white on black. (A later offshoot of the Order, chartered in 1888, created Britain's St John Ambulance Association.)

As well as having insignia of different colours, the Knights Templars and Knights Hospitallers also each wore the robe colours of their respective Orders: The Templar mantle emulating the white cassock of the Cistercians, and the Hospitaller mantle emulating the black cassock of the Benedictines.

The Thistle and the Unicorn

In parallel with the Templar and Hospitaller Orders, two other notable chivalric bodies were founded in Stewart Scotland. The first appeared in 1452 when King James II created 12 knights in a General Assembly at Edinburgh, instituting the Order of St Andrew or the Thistle. The *Theatre of Honour* details that this Order was established upon an original foundation by Eochaid IV of Scots (King Achaius) in 807. In 1470, James III introduced a badge for the Order, and James V later introduced a collar for the restyled Most Ancient and Noble Order of the Thistle.

In the course of this, King James III also instituted the knightly Order of the Unicorn[10] under the private seal of his royal signet which bore a Unicorn with the legend *Tout a Une*. A prominent knight of the Order was Anselm Adornes, a Flemish member of the Greek Adorno trading family, and related to the Genoese Doge, Prospero Adorno. He became Baron of Cortachy, and was James's agent in Bruges, the key centre of Scotland's trading alliance in Flanders. Sir Anselm's gravestone at Bruges still bears the Arms of Adornes surrounded by the collar of the Order of the Unicorn. (The *Aberdeen Guild Court Book*, 1441–68, shows the Unicorn signet being used for legal work as early as 1460 by King James II.)

7

The Union of Crowns

Mary, Queen of Scots

Prior to his death, James V is reputed to have said, 'It cam wie a lass; it'll gang wie a lass'. And what a lass! Succeeding her father at only one-week-old, Mary Stuart was crowned in September 1542, aged only nine months. With her French mother as Regent, and James, Lord Hamilton, as the State Governor, Mary was kept safe enough from the clutches of her grand-uncle Henry VIII, but this did not deter his jealous effort against her realm. In 1543 Henry's troops (under the Earl of Hertford) invaded Scotland and fired Edinburgh, destroying vast tracts of the city along with the Abbey and Palace of Holyrood House. Two years later the Scots (led by the Earl of Angus) resisted the English at Ancrum Moor, Roxburghshire, and Henry VIII responded with great vengeance, burning Kelso and Melrose.

By that time the Presbyterian Kirk was becoming established in Scotland, and the Catholics (against advice from the Regency) executed the reformer George Wishart at Saint Andrews. His supporters then murdered Cardinal-Archbishop David Beaton, and the scene was set for an ongoing conflict between the opposing denominations. Then in January 1547 Henry VIII Tudor died, to be succeeded by his son Edward VI, whereupon the Earl of Somerset arrived in Scotland with a great army, demanding that young Queen Mary should marry the new King of England. Marie de Guise knew that she could only respond with a show of strength, but in the continuing sad aftermath of Flodden there were very few men with experience in warfare.

Nevertheless, Marie promptly sent the Fiery Cross to towns and villages throughout the land, calling every able-bodied man to take up arms. (A burning hazel-wood cross, fastened to a spear, was the traditional call to arms.)

Thirty-five thousand Scots were mustered, and they met Somerset's army at Pinkie on 10 September 1547. But the Scots, being largely untrained, and without a competent military leader, lost the day, whereupon Mary Stuart was hurriedly dispatched to the French Court of Henri II. She set sail from Dumbarton with four playmates, Mary Beaton, Mary Seton, Mary Livingstone, and Mary Fleming – henceforth known in history as the 'Four Maries'.

From the age of six, Mary was educated in France by the sophisticated Diane de Poitiers, the influential mistress of King Henri II. It was Diane who ministered to Mary during her periods of childhood sickness, and she who taught her skills in art, music, poetry, play-writing and politics. In fact, women truly ruled Europe in those days: Catherine de Medici in France, Marie de Guise Lorraine in Scotland, Elizabeth I in England, and Joanna (the Mad) of Castile in Spain – with her son Carlos I holding the reins of kingship.

From Stewart to Stuart

In her 16th year Mary was married to Francis the Dauphin, and by way of this alliance she was not only Queen of Scots, but also the Queen-consort-apparent of France. Indeed, she became Queen of France soon after her marriage, but in the following year (1560) young Francis II died and Mary returned to Scotland. By that time, the name Stewart had become Stuart in the royal line. This alternative spelling was a French corruption, first used by the 15th-century Stewart Seigneurs d'Aubignie[1], who were Darnley descendants of Alexander, 4th Lord High Steward.

Edward VI's Protestant half-sister, Elizabeth Tudor, was then on the English throne. In the meantime (since young Edward VI's death) Lady Jane Grey had come and gone, and *Bloody Mary* (Mary I Tudor of England) had promoted her fanatical Catholicism, burning all who dissented. In Scotland, Governor Hamilton had resigned his authority in full to the Regent Marie de Guise who (when the Kirk held its first Edinburgh congregation) promptly confirmed that the House of Stuart would gladly tolerate both the Protestant Kirk and the Catholic Church within the realm.

When Mary Stuart returned to Scotland in 1561 her mother had lately died, but the new Queen of Scots soon discovered that Marie's declaration of tolerance was very much a one-sided affair. John Knox, the narrow-minded protagonist of the Kirk, showed no such indulgence, and he also declared that, according to God's law, no woman was capable of ruling the kingdom! Mary soon found another unwelcome enemy in the person of her half-brother James, Earl of Moray. Being 11 years Mary's senior, he was her chief adviser for a while, but then (in the light of Mary's weak position against the Kirk) Moray decided to claim the crown for himself. In 1565 he raised an army to oppose the Queen of Scots, but was unsuccessful and was exiled to England.

Darnley and Bothwell

Earl Moray's position was dampened by the fact that, in that same year, Mary had married her younger kinsman Henry Stewart, Lord Darnley. He was an English-born descendant of James II through the Earls of Lennox, and had a strong claim to the Tudor crown of England through his grandmother Margaret Tudor (widow of James IV) and her second husband, the Earl of Angus. Against Mary's better judgement, she had styled Darnley 'King of Scots', but she sensibly refuted his sovereign rights later on. From a safe distance, Moray fed information through his agents to the gullible Darnley, insinuating that Mary was rather too closely involved with her personal secretary David Riccio. Consequently Darnley had the Queen's confidant dragged from her presence and stabbed to death. At the same time, though, he aided Mary's escape from his own accomplices, and took her to Dunbar, where she gathered her troops for a triumphant return to Edinburgh. Soon afterwards, on 19 June 1566, their son (later King James VI) was born at the Castle.

A new character then appeared on the scene: James Hepburn, Earl of Bothwell, Great Admiral of Scotland, whose sister Jean was married to another of Mary's half-brothers. With Earl Moray out of the picture Bothwell made his own bid for recognition, and with the support of the Privy Council he suggested that Mary should divorce Darnley because of his involvement in the Riccio murder. But Mary refused, and so an alternative plan was put into action: at around 2 o'clock in the morning of 10 February 1567, Bothwell and his henchmen blew up the Kirk o'Field House where Darnley was sleeping.

By some chance warning Darnley and his manservant Tayler managed to escape from a gallery window before the explosion. They were then confronted by Archibald Douglas and his men who (quite coincidentally) were the instruments of a separate plot to murder Darnley. This had been instigated by the Earl of Morton, who was angered that Darnley had betrayed the Douglases for their part in the Riccio affair. Having let themselves down to the alleyway with a rope and chair, Darnley (still in his nightgown) and Tayler entered the neighbouring garden, where Archibald Douglas gave the order, and both men were strangled.

Bothwell was probably initially unaware that his gunpowder plot had failed, but Darnley was dead, and Bothwell was brought to trial. Under the circumstances, however, the influential Earl was acquitted, and shortly afterwards he and Mary were at his castle in Dunbar, where the Queen remained for ten days. Quite what occurred at Dunbar is still a matter of debate, but within a few weeks Mary and Bothwell were married. For all that had transpired in respect of the faithless Darnley, Bothwell's loyalty to Mary had never faltered, and he was the only one she could really trust. Mary had known Bothwell (a Protestant) ever since she was the Dauphiness of France, and he had always been dependable in her times of need. Even Marie de Guise had said that Bothwell was 'unbribable and totally loyal'.[2] It was Bothwell (along with Riccio) who had always given Mary the best advice, and it was Bothwell who had kept the peace in the Scottish Border lands. Quite apart from that, he was Mary's cousin, being descended from Sir James Stewart, the Black Knight of Lorne, whose wife, Lady Joan Beaufort, was the widow of King James I.

Not long after the marriage of Mary and Bothwell a rebellion of jealous nobles erupted, and Bothwell's army was defeated at Carberry Hill in 1567. Mary was pressured into leaving her husband, and taken hostage to the island castle of Lochleven, whose custodian was married to the mother of the illegitimate Earl of Moray. There, Mary was illegally compelled to abdicate in favour of her one-year-old son on 24 July. At this, the scheming Moray emerged once more to be proclaimed Regent of Scotland, but Mary was rescued from Lochleven by William Douglas the Younger[3], and within a few days she had raised her army. Regrettably, they were vanquished by Moray's troops at Langside on 13 May 1568, but Mary managed to escape in a fishing boat. However, instead of going to France where she had money and property, she went to England, seeking protection from her kinswoman Queen Elizabeth I. In the event, however, she was confined as a house-prisoner at various locations for 19 years.

The problem was that not only was Mary Stuart the lawful Queen of Scots and the Queen Dowager of France, she was also deemed to be Elizabeth's closest living relative, and heiress-presumptive to the English crown. Thus, although manoeuvred from Scotland, she could still emerge as the next Queen of England – a prospect that was quite unacceptable to the newly styled Anglican clergy since Mary's French upbringing had been Catholic. However, when the French authorities questioned the reason for Mary's confinement, they were simply told that she had broken the law by entering Britain without a passport![4]

Trial and Execution

Given Mary's defenceless position, various attempts were made to implicate her in treasonable actions, and these became ever more desperate as the unmarried, childless Elizabeth grew older. To begin, Darnley's murder was laid at Mary's feet, and letters were produced at court (the so-called 'Casket Letters'), insinuating that she had been Bothwell's mistress before the event. The documents included some love sonnets and a communication described as 'ane horrible long letter containing foul matter'. It transpired, however, that the letters proved absolutely nothing except their own dubious origin. Mary was then blamed for Catherine de Medici's 'Saint Bartholomew's Day Massacre' of Huguenots in France, even though she was locked away in Sheffield Castle at the time!

Ultimately, a *Bill of Attainder* was passed against Mary in 1572, denying any rights of accession to the English throne; but she had never made any claims in that direction, and she was hardly capable of doing so in her contained situation. The only positive move made in that context was a marriage proposal sent to Mary by the Duke of Norfolk, whose advisers were attempting to have the English succession settled upon him. Needless to say, Queen Elizabeth had Norfolk locked away in the Tower of London, and subsequently executed.

It is worth dwelling for a moment on the matter of the English succession because, although Mary had not herself made any claim in this regard, claims had previously been made on her behalf. From the very moment that Elizabeth's predecessor and Catholic half-sister, Mary Tudor, had died, the Catholic world proclaimed Mary Stuart as her natural successor. But Mary Stuart was certainly not the natural successor to Mary Tudor. Both Henry VII and Henry VIII (Mary Tudor's father) had obliged the Westminster Parliament to pass a Bill whereby only a member of the English Royal Family, born on English soil, could succeed to England's crown of St Edward. Mary Stuart was born in Scotland, and raised in France. However, the de Guise family (the family of Mary's mother) decided to approach the Pope, and he agreed to recognize Mary Stuart as the lawful Queen of England – as if it was anything to do with him!

In protesting her innocence time and time again, all Mary ever stated was, 'I came to England on my cousin's promise of assistance against my enemies and my rebel subjects, and was at once imprisoned'. She begged Elizabeth to believe that the Casket Letters had been forged, and asked even to be banished to France rather than 'consume away in tears and regrets at receiving this evil when I came in request of aid'. But her pleas were ignored.

The unfortunate Queen of Scots had landed in an enemy nest from which there was no escape, while typically Tudor-style plots and counter-plots evolved around her. The most famous of these were the 'Throgmorton Plot' and the 'Babington Plot' which led to Mary's execution. The Englishman, Anthony Babington, had organized a scheme with members of Elizabeth's household to assassinate the English Queen, but the plan was foiled by the Secretary of State, Sir Francis Walsingham, in 1586.

Three years earlier, Walsingham had uncovered a similar intrigue led by Francis Throgmorton, who was duly executed.

After 19 years of virtual imprisonment Mary, Queen of Scots, was brought to trial following Babington's arrest; she was convicted of treason, and sentenced to be beheaded at Fotheringhay Castle, near Peterborough, on 8 February 1587. However, she did not have to suffer having her warrant of execution read to her as was the custom; she was simply required to sign it in acknowledgement of the fact. Hence the document which authorized Mary's judicial murder bore only two signatures: that of Queen Mary herself, and that of her treacherous assailant, Queen Elizabeth of England.

On the day before her execution Mary gathered her possessions for gifting to her closest friends, and she wrote her will, along with a few letters: 'They are now at work in the hall, erecting, I think, the scaffold on which the last act of my tragedy is to be performed'. Mary wrote to her cousin, Queen Elizabeth, asking that her body should be buried in holy ground, and that her end should not be conducted in secret: 'For the sake of King Henry VII, your grandfather and mine, and by the honour of the dignity we both hold, and of our sex in common, do I implore you to grant these requests'. Her final letter was to the Pope, with whom she entrusted the well-being of her son James.

While concerning herself with these administrative affairs, Mary had set her ladies to making her a blood-red dress, along with similarly dyed petticoats and hose. They also shaved Mary's head to make her a wig from her own hair. Then, early next morning, Mary's attendants dressed her in the red attire, and she made her solitary communion, having refused the Last Rites offered by an Anglican chaplain. She then veiled her gown with a long black cloak and a white ruffle, and sat by her fireside to await the Sheriff, who eventually conducted her to the Castle hall. Before leaving, however, she tucked her little dog inside her bodice to gain courage from the animal's warmth, and she duly entered the arena with her retinue at hand.

Upon Mary's entry, the Earl of Salisbury presented the signed warrant, and having prepared herself for death, Mary sent a last message to her son James, willing that he should serve God and the Church, and keep his country in peace – adding, 'Let him speak no evil of the Queen of England'.

Mary's ladies-in-waiting conveyed her to the dais, where she let fall her cloak and ruffle to reveal the blood-red gown as a final gesture of contempt for those who had labelled her a whore and a scarlet woman. As a general rule, women of royalty, if and when executed, would meet their end wearing white, but Mary's dress signified her ultimate scorn for the lies told against her: 'You may take my blood against my will, but I shall not show it to you'. She then asked for a priest of her own Catholic faith, but was told, 'It has been ordained otherwise', whereupon the Anglican Dean of Peterborough was dismissed by the Queen of Scots, who prayed aloud in Latin. She then asked that a keen-edged French sword might be used for her beheading instead of a clumsy axe, but this request was also denied.

At this, Mary's executioner and his assistant knelt to beg her forgiveness. 'I forgive thee with all my heart', said the Queen, and she arranged that the blow would not be struck until she gave the signal by extending her arms. And so Mary's head went to the block, and as she outstretched her arms, the axe-man's assistant held tight the hands in which she clasped her crucifix. But the blow was not accurate, and Mary was left alive and choking. A second blow was dealt with little more effect, and then a third before the Queen's head was severed from her body.

At length, the deed was done to cries of 'God save Queen Elizabeth'. 'And so perish all her enemies!' exclaimed the Dean of Peterborough. 'Amen', added the Duke of Kent. But when Mary's head was to be held aloft before the audience, only her wig was pulled from the basket, at which point the headless body began to move, with a muffled sound – and the onlookers were terror-struck, for there was no blood visible on the scarlet gown. Then out came Mary's dog from her bodice, and despite the apparent enthusiasm of the guests for her end, the executioners were at that moment moved to desolation by the forlorn little pet who sat whimpering against the Queen's body.[5] As the axe had fallen upon Mary's neck, she cried, 'In my end is my beginning' – and in this she could not have been more correct, for she has since become one of history's most enigmatic heroines.

Throughout the court proceedings, Mary had attested her ignorance of any plot against Elizabeth, but her pleas were in vain. The flimsy case against her rested on certain incriminating letters – supposedly written to and from Babington – and on the strength of these Mary was strategically implicated. It was to be another 250 years before a related collection of Government documents was discovered, which threw considerable new light on the fateful conspiracy.

At the time of the Throgmorton and Babington plots, the Leighs of Somerset were lawyers to Francis Throgmorton, and they were also concerned with the Babington case. In 1836 a succeeding lawyer, Robert Leigh, found a small chest when clearing the archives of his family's Bardon House at Old Cleeve, Somerset – a chest which has since become known as the 'Throgmorton Box'. The box and its contents – State papers relating to the incrimination and trial of Queen Mary of Scots – were submitted to the British Museum, where they were authenticated and are still held.

The *Bardon Papers* detailed the list of contrived complaints against Mary, but more importantly they set out her repeated denials and the unpublished truth of her innocence. The various manuscripts disclosed the treacherous actions of Mary's persecutor, Francis Walsingham, and his confederate High Treasurer, Lord William Cecil of Burghley. During the course of her trial, Mary had stated, 'I am alone, without council or anyone to speak on my behalf. My papers and notes have been taken from me, so that I am destitute of all aid, taken at a disadvantage'. With the discovery of the Throgmorton Box, however, the true nature of Mary's disadvantage was revealed; the supposed correspondence between her and Babington was found to be counterfeit and concocted at Walsingham's own office. It became blatantly apparent that the incriminating letters were fabrications, and Mary's signatures thereon had been forged – but it was 250 years too late!

Quite recently, the 1587 Elizabethan death warrant that sealed the fate of Mary, Queen of Scots, came up for auction at Sotheby's in London. It sold for £45,500, and was purchased by none other than the Lambeth Palace headquarters of the Church of England. This is the very Anglican Church which claims that it is short of funds, and is forever endeavouring to extract increased contributions from its hard-pressed, dwindling congregations. The rather more responsible Keeper of the Records for Scotland stated that he did not even bid for the Warrant because such money was better spent on worthwhile purchases.

Mary, Queen of Scots (my great$^{\times 10}$-grandmother) is undoubtedly my favourite ancestor, and she is certainly to be numbered among the most romantic characters of world history. So much has been written about Mary and the mistakes she made, but she undoubtedly coped as best she could with the odds stacked so heavily against her. Being raised in France was Mary's biggest downfall, and it is perfectly understandable that she would have been swept into the trappings of French tradition as if they were her natural birthright. The French royal family was very forceful then, and few people realize how horrendous the French Court really was at the time. Wilful poisoning was a common occurrence, and Mary's mother-in-law, Catherine de Medici, was an expert in this regard. Indeed, French historians firmly believe that Mary was twice poisoned as a child. A French film which accurately portrays the Court life of the era is *La Reine Margot* (Queen Margot) – a true reflection of the appalling environment into which little Mary was placed.

James, King of Britain

The great irony was that, following Elizabeth I's death in 1603, Mary's son James VI of Scots was invited to become King of England. The English succession appeared to be a matter of debate, but Elizabeth's chief minister, Robert Cecil (son of Lord Burleigh), and other senior officials had actually made their decision some time prior to their Queen's death. Strictly speaking, although Mary had been considered Elizabeth's closest relative, her son James VI was not the rightful heir of England. The true successor should have been Edward Seymour, Lord Beauchamp, in descent from Henry VII's sister, Mary Tudor. This points, of course, to a strategic plot to gain dominion over the Scottish succession.

Bringing James to London was in fact a political manoeuvre to sever the alliance between Scotland and France; it was designed to bring Scotland and England together under one monarch, just as the English had been attempting to do for centuries. Albeit the sovereign position was reversed with a Scots king overall, such a technicality could be amended once the precedent had been established, and this is precisely what happened some time later. Meanwhile, the arrangement enabled the Privy Council to announce a dynastic change that would put an end to cross-Border conflicts, and the people were happy enough with that concept.

Although James VI barely knew his mother, he had lived with a haunting dilemma while she was alive, for he knew that his Scots kingship was illegal because of Mary's forced abdication. When asked to ratify this supposed abdication in England, Mary had refused, stating, 'the last word I shall speak in this life will be that of a Queen of Scotland'. She had demanded to see the original abdication document, but was shown nothing.

Mary's death was a sad loss, but in the event it was probably a deliverance for both mother and son. Not only had Mary's years of torment and frustration come to an end, but James's own mind was set at ease, and in 1587 he became in practice what he had previously been in theory alone: King of Scots.

James was just over one-year-old when he had acceded to the Scottish throne, and he was crowned within the week at the Parish Kirk, Stirling, on 24 July 1567. The Regency was firstly held by the Earl of Moray, who abolished Papal authority in Scotland and ratified the Kirk's supreme position. This earned him Queen Elizabeth's support, for she had been personally excommunicated by Rome. Moreover, she had dispensed with Henry VIII's English branch of the Catholic Church and instituted her own Protestant Communion. In January 1570 Moray was murdered by Hamilton of Bothwellhaugh, and the Scottish Regency passed to Lord Darnley's father, the Earl of Lennox. In the meantime, Mary's husband and confederate, the Earl of Bothwell, had left the country, and he died some years later in the Danish castle of Dragsholm.

In September 1571 Lennox was killed in a skirmish at Stirling, whereupon the Regency fell to the Earl of Mar, who died a year later, to be succeeded by the Earl of Morton. He lasted for six years, but was finally tried, convicted and beheaded in 1581 for being an accessory to the Darnley murder.[6] From that moment, young James VI (still only 15-years-old) was on his own. In less than a year he founded Edinburgh University, but within a few months he was abducted at Ruthven by the Earl of Gowrie, whose father had been party to the stabbing of Riccio. Eventually, James escaped to St Andrews, and Gowrie was executed after plotting to seize Stirling Castle. However, in August 1600, James was led into a trap by Gowrie's sons, and was lucky to escape with his life.

Following his mother's execution, James sailed for Denmark, and in November 1589 he married Frederick II's daughter Anne at Oslo, Norway. Subsequently, he ratified the foundings of Fraserburgh University and Marischal College, but all the while his personal situation was that of an impoverished monarch, and he was severely constrained by the Presbyterian Kirk elders. They kept a very tight rein on his ability to govern, and so when he was offered England's Crown of Saint Edward in 1603 he was more than ready to accept. After being crowned and anointed in Westminster Abbey on 25 July, James VI of Scots reigned thereafter as King James I Stuart of Britain and Ireland until 28 March 1625 when he died at Theobalds, Hertfordshire, aged 58. Buried in Henry VIII's Chapel at Westminster, James was succeeded by his son King Charles I, and by his grandsons Charles II and James VII (II).

Knights Templars and Freemasons

As we have seen, from 1488 the Knights Templars and the Knights Hospitallers were administratively conjoined in Scotland under the jurisdiction of the Grand Preceptor of the Hospital and Temple. However, in 1560, the Scottish Three Estates Parliament decreed that any Chivalric Order which paid lip service to the Pope had to be disbanded, with their lands taken over by the State (but not by the Crown). In this regard, the Templars found a route of avoidance, but the Hospitallers fell to the edict, and in recompense their Preceptor, James Sandilands (the prevailing Lord St John), was granted the estates and hereditary barony of Torpichen by Mary, Queen of Scots. In the event, however, the Knights were not at all happy that Sandilands had given up their cause so easily. (Torpichen was the traditional chief residence of the Knights Hospitallers in Scotland.)

As for the Knights Templars, they came under the new leadership of David Seton (a kinsman of Lord George Seton and his sister Mary Seton, one of the Four Maries who accompanied Mary Stuart to France in 1548, and returned with her to Scotland in 1561). In order to safeguard Templar interests, David Seton reconstituted the Scottish Order under a new identity: the Order of the Knights Templars of St Anthony. At the same time, he dispensed with the traditional red 'Cross Pate', substituting the 'Tau' symbol (T), the Cross of St Anthony, as the new badge of knighthood. (St Anthony [*c*AD 300] was the founder of Christian monasticism in Egypt.)

From 1590 there were two grants made by King James VI to the Templars of St Anthony[7], and each required that the Knights should found an operative hospital. The second of these land grants, awarded in about 1593, was for a chapel, monastery and hospital at Leith. The hospital, founded in 1614, was called 'King James's Hospital', and bore the royal arms. At that stage, the Edinburgh lands of the Order of St Anthony were transferred by James to the Kirk Session of South Leith in order to support the hospital which bore his name.

By that time there were speculative Freemasons (as against operative stonemasons) in Scotland. It is generally reported that Freemasonry did not emerge in Britain until the mid-17th century, but the Lodge of Aberdeen was part-speculative from 1541. Indeed, according to the Rite of Strict Observance, speculative Masons from operative French guilds were in Aberdeen as early as 1361. Also, the lodge at Stirling was reputed to have had a Masonic chapter as early as 1590, at which time various higher degrees were being worked, including Rose Croix, Royal Arch, and Knight Templar.

As previously indicated in respect of the Masonic patronage granted to Sir William Sinclair in 1475, it is evident that there were trade and craft Guilds in Scotland at that time. Indeed, notwithstanding any earlier Guild Charters in Perth (capital of Scotland until 1437), King James III had granted numerous Charters in Edinburgh that year, as did his successors thereafter:

Date	**Guild**	**Chartered by**
1475	Weavers	James III
	Cordwainers (leather-workers and shoemakers)	
	Wrights (artificers and metalworkers)	
	Masons (stone-workers and builders)	
	Bowyers (bow-makers)	
	Glaziers	

Date	Guild	Chartered by
	Upholsterers	
	Painters	
	Slaters	
	Sievewrights (sieve- and basket-makers)	
	Coopers (barrel-makers)	
1483	Hammermen (blacksmiths, goldsmiths, saddlers, cutlers and armourers)	
	Fleshers (butchers)	
1500	Wakers (clothiers and millers)	James IV
1505	Surgeons	
	Barbers	
1530	Bakers	James V
	Bonnet-makers	
1581	Goldsmiths (separated from Hammermen)	James VI
1586	Skinners	
1635	Post Office	Charles I
1640	Dyers (incorporated with Bonnet-makers)	
1672	Hatters (incorporated with Wakers)	Charles II
1681	Merchant Company	

Following the execution of Charles I, revenue from the Post Office was awarded to Oliver Cromwell and his heirs, but this was repealed and settled by Parliament upon King James VII (II) and his male heirs, forever – a settlement which was later ignored when James was deposed.

These early guilds formed the very basis of early Freemasonry, wherein the members were 'speculative' (that is to say, notional or theoretical), as against being active (or 'operative') workers in the various trades and crafts. A few Guilds such as these had previously existed in France, but in the Middle East their traditions dated back for hundreds of years. Even the Western banking system introduced by the Knights Templars was originally an Islamic concept based on the idea of using letters of authorization (cheques), enabling the bearer to withdraw from banks other than that of the drawer.

During the Crusades the Templars had learned that Christian Europe lagged far behind the Muslim world in terms of business practice, and this was mainly due to the strict controls and narrow-minded outlook of the Roman Church. The Templars endeavoured to emancipate the various nations by implementing fraternal Guilds with access to a monetary agency that charged a fixed rate of interest on loans. Hence, in financially aiding businesses, the Order of the Temple became a business itself, and it was the success and international prestige of this business which upset King Philippe IV of France and Pope Clement V. Philippe had borrowed enormous funds from the Order, but did not want to repay, and so he looked for a means to avoid his debt. Consequently, from 1307, Philippe and the Pope launched their Templar Inquisition with the only charge that the Catholic Church could hope to sustain – and the charge levelled against the Knights was heresy![8]

From the Church's point of view this charge was ideal because it was not a general matter of law, and only the Church could define it. Similarly, the Church dictated the surrounding procedures, in that a defendant had no right to a defence, neither any right to know his accusers or their specific accusations. It was also possible for prosecution witnesses to be paid, and so there was rarely a shortage of willing perjurers. The tortures inflicted upon seized Knights were absolutely horrendous. One report details a Knight whose feet were spread with fat, and then cooked over an open fire.[9] If a Knight confessed to heresy as a result of torture, he was burned alive. But if he refused to confess, as did the majority, then the torture continued until he died anyway. Others never even got as far as a trial by torture, and were simply left to rot, chained in their cells.

In conjunction with their banking network, the Templars had sought to modernize Europe more generally by creating a structure of regulated Guilds for tradesmen, craftsmen and certain professionals. They also conceived the practice of apprenticeship, so that large and small businesses alike could be perpetuated beyond their original foundations. But it was not until the Knights were in Scotland that their ideal really took shape, and this occurred because Scotland was outside Papal control.

Quite apart from the Guilds, the Knights also received lay-people into their allied confraternities and, for a small annual subscription of a few pence, men and women alike were afforded numerous privileges by way of personal and family support in times of need. This was, in fact, the beginning of the insurance and life assurance industry, and it is the reason why so many of today's leading British underwriting institutions emanated from Scotland.

From the ranks of the newly created, operative Guilds, the Knights Templars selected certain members who were keen to extend their minds to matters of science, geometry, history and philosophy, as detailed in the ancient manuscripts which the original Order had brought out of Jerusalem and the Holy Land. Those who taught were the Elder Brothers of the Order of the Rosy Cross[10], and as a result of their effort Scotland became a beacon of enlightenment. The new brotherhood of 'Free' Masons supported their less fortunate neighbours, and their respective Guilds set money aside for the poorer members of society, thereby beginning the establishment of charitable organizations in Britain.

King James VI became a speculative Freemason at the Lodge of Perth and Scone in 1601[11], and on becoming James I of England two years later he introduced the concept south of the Border. This was, in large measure, a political tactic because the English Treasury coffers were empty following the high spending of Queen Elizabeth, and James needed a route to cash. Also James's fellow Scots were not allowed to sit in the Westminster Parliament, and he needed allies outside the self-serving English aristocracy. These he found within the trade and craft Guilds which had emerged in England. The first official inductions into English Freemasonry are recorded from about 1640, when rituals were formalized during the reign of Charles I. Nevertheless, it was Charles's father, King James, who had previously established the fraternal ideal on an informal basis.

8

Community of the Realm

The Kingdom of Scots

Up to the time of James VI, Scottish kingship had traditionally been approved and granted by the 'Three Estates' Parliament to the monarch's eldest son, or to the eldest living heir or heiress. There was, however, an inherent right for the people to 'choose' another monarch if needs be, according to the terms of the Written Constitution. (The 'Three Estates' comprised nobles, clergy and people's representatives called 'burgesses'.) The English monarchy, on the other hand, was not a people's institution; it was the express property and prerogative of the royal family themselves, and this had enabled usurpers and opposing family branches to grab the sceptre while annihilating their kingly cousins. Such regular transfers by force-of-arms were an integral part of English history, and the people had no say in the ongoing battles for sovereignty.

These changes were manifest in the Norman Conquest of Duke William, who ousted the Anglo-Saxon regime to become King William I. Later there followed the internecine quarrels between Empress Matilda and Stephen de Blois, which culminated in the substitute Plantagenet succession. Richard II (of the Clarence branch) was usurped by his cousin Bolingbrook (a Lancastrian), who became Henry IV. Then the York faction took issue with the House of Lancaster and civil war erupted (the Wars of the Roses), as a result of which the crown was transferred to the Yorkist, Edward IV. After his death, his two young sons were murdered in the Tower of London, and the crown was seized by their uncle, Richard III (of Gloucester). At this, another challenger with a distant claim appeared; he was the partly Welsh Duke of Richmond, who defeated Richard to become Henry VII of the new House of Tudor. In the midst of the Tudor era was the *coup d'ètat* which installed the Protestant noblewoman Jane Grey on the throne of England, but she was displaced by the Catholic majority in favour of Henry VIII's daughter Mary Tudor, who burned Protestants and plotted to murder her half-sister Elizabeth. Before too long, though, *Bloody Mary* died, to be succeeded by Queen Elizabeth I.

While all this was going on south of the Border, things in Scotland were entirely different, and the Stewart kings had progressed through a straightforward dynastic succession. The medieval Scots were the first nationals to adopt a Written Constitution – the 1320 charter which became known as the *Declaration of Arbroath*. Its message was forthright in that the King of Scots (at that time, Robert the Bruce) and his successors would uphold the civil rights and liberties of the Community of the Realm of Scotland. The Community embodied the sovereignty of the people, the king, the government, the judiciary and the nation. Should a Scots monarch betray the interests of the Scottish people in favour of those of England, the nation (through law enacted by the 'Three Estates', answerable to the judiciary) had the right to displace that monarch and substitute another family member who was willing to uphold the Constitution.

When Scotland's independence was ratified at the 1328 *Treaty of Northampton* her adopted form of Constitutional Monarchy was not only the first in Europe, but the first in the world. The overriding principle was manifest in the description 'Kings of Scots' – not Kings of Scotland. In other words, they were chosen monarchs of the Scottish people, rather than being overlords of the land, as was the position in England's feudal regime. It was not until James VI Stuart of Scots also became James I of the English that the southerners referred to him (quite erroneously) as the King of England and Scotland.

Scotland's socialist concept had its roots in the original Clan System, whereby individual clansmen and women accepted representation by family chiefs. Like the office of the kings, the appointment of chiefs was hereditary, and since the Kings of Scots were the chiefs-of-chiefs[1], they were truly the 'common fathers' of the Scottish Nation. In general terms the system rarely failed the people, although (due to unfortunate periods of regency and minority inheritance) some problems were experienced at the hands of the competitive nobility. But as for actual strife within the royal family, the Scots can boast a limit of only two *coups d'etat* within their Middle Ages history. The first was in 1488, when James III was unseated by jealous nobles in favour of his son James IV, and the second occurred when the Presbyterian faction deposed Mary, Queen of Scots, supposedly to install her infant son James VI. In reality, this latter incident was contrived to seize the Regency for Mary's half-brother, the Earl of Moray; it was an unprecedented act of political treason, and Mary always refuted her alleged abdication. She had fully recognized the Kirk as a lawful entity within the Scottish Parliament, but the puritanical clerics and aristocrats determined to seize power by constraining religious choice to their own advantage.

Despite the episodes of individual Stewart misfortune, we were certainly not cursed in Scotland as some books suggest. The records show that we fared rather well considering the persistent intrigues of uncooperative nobles. This subversive element was a constant plague to the Clan System which, being a socially conceived ideal, offered community rewards according to merit, as against the English system which was based on privilege by wealth and ownership. Since a proportion of Scots nobility were of the same Norman blood as their mischievous cousins south of the Border, they were easily influenced, and consequently they adhered not to the rule of merit, but to the precept of might. They deduced that whoever managed the kings' affairs during periods of minority was likely to hold the reins of power thereafter.

Not only was Scotland continually troubled by English invasions, but the Plantagenets and Tudors took an unhealthy delight in disrupting our commercial trade with France, Spain, Scandinavia and the Low Countries. Even the Auld Alliance with France was often more of a hindrance than a help, and it was a very one-sided affair for a good while. It was designed to operate on a continuing give-and-take principle, but we seemed to do all the giving, while the French were glad to do the taking.

The Auld Alliance was said to date back to the time of Charlemagne, who had concluded a mutual Treaty (The League

Offensive and Defensive) with Eochaid IV of Scots in 807. At that time Scots Dalriada and Pictish Caledonia were not united, and the overall kingdom of Scotland did not exist as such. After the Treaty, however, joint trade and military enterprises became common between the Scots and French, and Princess Margaret Stewart (a daughter of James I) was married to Louis, the Valois Dauphin (son of King Charles VII of France), in 1436.

By the reign of Louis XII (1498–1515) France housed several Scots Colleges and, in view of the close relationship, King Louis granted French nationality to his Scottish allies in 1513.[2] In return, the French gained their Scottish nationality from Marie de Guise-Lorraine, Regent of Scotland and mother of Mary, Queen of Scots, in 1552.

From the time that Robert the Bruce regained Scotland's independence, the Stewarts were aware that Scottish unity was paramount in resisting England's plans for territorial expansion. Scotland was also the back door which enabled France and Spain to keep England from ruling the Western world; thus, in fighting our own battles to protect Scotland from successful invasion, we were also protecting the rest of Europe.

Scotland was the first country to introduce minimum wage rights after James IV had laboured personally in the fields. James established that some workforces were insufficiently paid by the nobles, and so he arranged that employers should remunerate their workers in accordance with a minimum wage scale approved by Parliament. Subsequently his son James V adopted the same method of scrutiny and commitment, thereby upholding the true nature of a publicly-geared Constitutional Monarchy, wherein the king's overriding concern is the welfare of the community.

James IV also introduced funded schooling for the eldest heir of every free household, and this was backed by the founding of early printing and publishing centres. Scottish families, rich and poor alike, were provided by the kingdom with educational insight into Scots, Latin and French languages, and Scottish law. The immediate recipients were required to pass some of this knowledge on to their families, and by the late 1400s Scotland was the most literate nation in Europe. One cannot begin to compare these socially advantageous features of Stewart Scotland with the primitive working conditions and meagre educational prospects that persisted even 400 years later in Victorian England.

Throughout the Hundred Years' War between France and England, the former always recognized Scotland as a separate military power, as indeed she was. The famous Scots Guard was formed in that era for the French House of Valois. It was a time of great upheaval, with the Plantagenet kings claiming that France was an English domain, while the Scots actively supported the French position. Joan of Arc originally resisted the idea of Scottish assistance, but soon realized that it was essential to facilitate the Siege of Orléans in 1429. When France was liberated, the Valois king, Charles VII, elected to keep the Scots Guard in his service, and they (100 men-at-arms and 200 archers) became the élite royal security force as the Garde Ecossais.[3]

Knights Templars and Scottish Gold

Scotland was the perfect haven for the Knights Templars of Jerusalem. The Stewart kings, the Setons and the Sinclairs were all hereditary Knights Templars, and Scottish Rite Freemasonry was later created as a sub-structure of the organization. The hereditary right of the Stewarts came by virtue of Robert the Bruce having granted the Knights asylum in Scotland. The Sinclairs gained their privilege because they had afforded half the Templar Fleet safe anchorage at Orkney, and the Setons had given valuable financial assistance during the Order's hour of need. In Scotland, the Templars were the moral guardians of the kings, and the Scottish national banking system (the oldest in Europe) evolved from Templar principles of monetary supply and demand.

It was known that Scotland's soil held significant gold reserves, and the Order was quick to put these resources to use. This underground wealth was one of the primary reasons why the English were so keen to become the masters of this land. To subdue a poor country for the sheer sake of it is hardly the route to an asset, but Scotland had an amazing monopoly on pure gold. Scottish trade routes to Nova Scotia were operated long before Columbus discovered America, and (although neither we nor the English were aware of it at the time) offshore Scotland was also a wealthy oil and gas repository.

From the time of Robert the Bruce, the Order of the Temple in Scotland had, in effect, been a recognized State within a State, and the Order supervised the mining of Scottish gold, which was of paramount importance to Scotland's international trade. All too often, historic Scotland is portrayed as a poor country with an economy based on sheep and cattle rearing – but it was not this that underpinned our commerce with France, Russia and the Baltic nations, but gold, along with silver from the Bathgate and Leadhills area.

In the Middle Ages we were importing large quantities of highly expensive spices from the East, and the Scots people were buying these for their own consumption. This is hardly the image of a poor country dependent on sheep farmers and cattle-traders. Consider our ancient Celtic artifacts, many of them made with pure Scottish gold, as is the Crown of Scotland, with its magnificent Scottish gems, and pearls from the River Tay. Consider the famous Paris banquet of King James V and his first wife, Madeleine de France, where over 300 French guests were each presented with a medieval goblet filled to the brim with Scottish gold dust.[4]

It was not until the reign of King James VI of Scots (I of England) that the Knights Templars lost their right to statehood, and at the same time they lost their mining rights, although the English never discovered where the key mines were located. The current story is rather different though, for a recent geological survey of Scottish reserves detailed that Scotland could well be regarded as the potential South Africa of the north, and there are two gold mines currently being worked in Perthshire, as reported in the *Mail on Sunday*, 20 June 1997.

Catholics and Protestants

From the mid-16th century, Presbyterianism (which was sponsored by Queen Elizabeth's English cash) did much to undermine Scottish influence in Europe. Its promoter, John Knox (previously a Catholic, and a Deacon of St Andrews), had been Edward VI Tudor's private chaplain[5] before being sent back to Scotland by Elizabeth I. Knox had his orders, and he duly liaised with the English Queen to further his own enterprise, which was to set Scotland into denominational turmoil for very many years.

Plainly, it suited Elizabeth to have an allied religious hierarchy across the Border, and it suited Knox to be associated with a monarch who was not logistically placed to interfere with his activities. It was as a result of an inflammatory speech by Knox that Scone Abbey (the traditional coronation Abbey of the Kings of Scots) was wilfully destroyed on 27 June 1559.

Despite her own French Catholic upbringing, Queen Mary of Scots had recognized the customary Stewart principle of religious indulgence. She was happy, therefore, to accommodate the Protestant Kirk, and to acknowledge Presbyterians in Parliament. Her admirers called her a 'champion of denominational toleration', but John Knox had other views, and sought to impose his discriminatory beliefs on everyone. These were uncomfortable times, not only in Scotland but throughout Christian Europe, as the Protestant Church emerged alongside its traditional Catholic neighbour.

In England the Catholic Church had long prevailed, but Henry VIII separated the English Church from Rome to aid his divorce from Catherine of Aragon, and to acquire Church property for himself. He did not become a Protestant; he simply made himself Head of England's branch of the Catholic Church. His daughters split the religious family in two, however, for they were severely at odds; Mary Tudor was a convinced Catholic, and Elizabeth was a committed Protestant. This manner of division was prevalent throughout the realm, and Elizabeth endeavoured to amalgamate the dissenters by creating the separate Anglican Church, a Protestant version of the Roman episcopal concept. She implemented her *Thirty-nine Articles* of the English doctrine in 1563, and was duly excommunicated by the Vatican in 1570.

In Scotland the Presbyterian Kirk emerged in a somewhat different guise, as an austere institution in its early days, controlled by elders rather than bishops. By virtue of this, Scotland's Protestant alternative was significantly different to England's, for when compared with the Anglican Church, the Kirk was considerably more removed from traditional Catholicism.

From the time of Henry VIII, English monarchs were established as Heads of the English Church, as is still the case. But in Scotland the position was more flexible since the monarchy and religion were not formally affiliated, except for the Scots kings' nominal attachment to the ancient Celtic Kindred. Everyone in

Scotland had been free to choose his or her religion according to conscience, until John Knox sought to change the rules in 1560. Queen Mary of Scots was a Catholic, while her cousin Elizabeth of England was a Protestant, and during their era the two denominations perpetuated a violent antagonism – a ludicrous conflict of dogmas which persists today.

There was a significant difference between the customary religious allegiance of Scotland and those of other 16th-century nations, for Scotland had cut the umbilical cord with Rome long before the Anglican or Presbyterian Churches were conceived. In Scotland, Papal decrees were acknowledged only if they were within the precepts of the Scottish Constitution and in the interests of the community. Indeed, it had been an excommunicated clergy that crowned and anointed Robert the Bruce in 1306. Not only the clergy, but the Patriot-King and the entire Scottish Nation had received Papal damnation for rebelling against Edward I of England.[6] (This is why the anti-Templar Bulls were ineffective in Scotland.) Although this excommunication of all Scots was lifted 17 years later in 1323, the *Declaration of Arbroath* had already been compiled by the disinherited clerics, and their unanimous message was that the Pope should mind his own business!

The Stuarts and Religion

James VI (I)

When James VI of Scots arrived in London as James I of England, three distinct problems confronted him, not the least of which was the matter of religion. Although both Scotland and England were essentially Protestant, James had a Presbyterian background, while England was officially Anglican. Notwithstanding this, James (who held no seniority within the Scottish Kirk) was automatically designated Head of the Church of England.

The second difficulty was the fact that the Westminster Parliament was wholly English, and although hundreds of supporters had followed James to the south, all Scots born before his English accession were debarred from holding parliamentary office. This meant that, with the operative age being sixteen, no Scot could become an MP in England before 1619.

The third predicament was caused by England's long-standing desire to control affairs in Scotland; and with the King of Scots conveniently subjected to Westminster's rules, the Anglican Parliament perceived a new route to this end.

Elizabeth I had been an authoritative queen, and had ruled without too much parliamentary reliance, putting the Crown into considerable debt. James was, therefore, obliged to implement higher taxation, a measure to which Parliament agreed, with the proviso that new laws should only come into force by Act of Parliament. Having already been a successful king for many years, James disagreed with this restriction, claiming that he was not answerable to his own ministers but to God and the Nation. Furthermore, he expressed his dislike for the fact that power in England was vested in the wealthy upper-classes rather than in the community as a whole.

For 22 years James battled against pressures from Westminster and the Anglican Church. After his death in 1625, his son and heir Charles I found himself in an equally unenviable position. Apart from being styled Kings of England and Scotland, the Stuarts were also designated Kings of Ireland, which was an intrinsically Catholic domain. Hence, with three major denominations to consider, an amount of religious toleration was vital on the kings' part, but this toleration was not welcomed by the sectarian Anglicans. It similarly annoyed the unbending Presbyterians of the Scottish Kirk.

Throughout the whole Stuart era, religious conflicts persisted between rival factions of the Christian Church, with each successive king criticized for his liberal forbearance. In enforcing the *Acts of Uniformity* in respect of the Common Prayer Book, James VI (I) upset the Catholics and prompted the unsuccessful 'Gunpowder Plot' to blow him up in Parliament. Conversely, in introducing his Authorized Version of the Bible, he caused the Protestants to assert that he was siding with Rome! As for the National Kirk elders, they were more than displeased by James's concept of a new Scottish Episcopal Church, which was neither Anglican, Presbyterian, nor Catholic.

Charles I

When Charles I succeeded, his immediate concern was to rid the administration of the parliamentary subversion and dishonesty that had plagued his father. The self-serving politicians were far more of a hindrance than a help to the Crown, and Charles gained an amount of early popularity by suppressing their troublesome influence. Additionally, by looking to his own devices, he balanced the national budget for the first time in centuries. But on the religious front a fast-growing Puritan movement had risen to the fore in competition with the Anglican Church. Even by Presbyterian standards, the Puritans were intolerant extremists; they were wholly non-conformist, and stood against all forms of episcopy.

At that stage, the high-handed Anglican ministry was justifiably disliked by large sectors of the community, and the locally preaching Puritans gained a good amount of public support. Charles I, nonetheless, perceived them as potentially dangerous insurgents, and so he lent his personal support wholeheartedly to the Church of England. As it transpired, his perception of the Puritans was correct, but at the time his very noticeable Anglican leaning alienated him in many quarters. Concurrent with this (as a strategic manoeuvre in the struggle against Spain) Charles allied himself with France by marrying Henri IV's daughter, Princess Henriette Marie. But Henriette was a Catholic, and so, regardless of Charles's open affiliation with the Anglicans, this marriage disturbed the intolerant English clergy.

As time progressed, Westminster became increasingly dominated by the Puritans, who had split from the Anglican Church in order to become more religiously 'pure'. As a result, they restricted Parliament's financial grants, and subjected the King to their express demands. Accordingly, Charles dissolved his Parliament in 1629, and then surprised everyone by raising his own finances and successfully managing affairs by himself for 11 years. During this period he became more generally accepted by the people than had any monarch since Henry VII.

In the course of this, Charles's Anglican alliance with Archbishop Laud annoyed the Scottish Kirk, and led to the Bishops' Wars of 1639–40. These were sparked by Laud's endeavour to introduce the English Prayer Book into Presbyterian Scotland, and the financial requirements of the conflict caused Charles to reconvene Parliament. The 'Short Parliament' of April and May 1640 was a worthless exercise, as was the ultimately fatal 'Long Parliament' convened in the following November.

However, irrespective of the Scottish conflict, the Puritans were not about to assist the Anglican community whom they opposed. Instead, they seized their parliamentary opportunity, impeached the Archbishop, and had him beheaded along with the King's deputy Viscount Strafford. In the wake of this, the Puritans then abolished the traditional King's Council of the Star Chamber, and produced *The Grand Remonstrance* – a list of complaints against the King himself.

Civil War

There had been significant unrest in Ireland from Tudor times, and at the peak of Charles Stuart's political misfortune in 1641 rebellion erupted in Ulster. The Irish Catholics had decided to make a stand against the increasing number of Protestant settlers who were taking over their towns and cities. This infiltration had begun at the auspices of Queen Elizabeth who, in forcing her Protestant control on the Catholics of Ireland, had sold Ulster to the London Guilds. The incoming merchants then compelled the Irish to become their servants or leave their homeland.

On learning of the bloody insurgency, Charles I endeavoured to raise an army to quell the riots, but Westminster refused him the resources, fearing that he would turn his military force against Parliament. Charles sought to arrest five MPs for their obstructive behaviour, but the gates of London were locked against him, whereupon he moved to Nottingham and mustered an army of volunteer Royalists to support him against the troublesome Puritans. The result was the ill-fated Civil War.

At the forefront of the Parliamentary Army was Oliver Cromwell, a politically ambitious farmer's son who had represented Huntingdon and Cambridge in the House of Commons. He raised a cavalry troop which met the King's Cavaliers at Edgehill; the battle ended indecisively, but in 1643 the Royalists were successful in the north and west of England. As against the King's colourful Cavaliers, the puritanical Westminster politicians, with their short haircuts, were dubbed 'Roundheads', while Cromwell's armoured troopers were nicknamed 'Ironsides'.

Following Edgehill, the Westminster Roundheads negotiated the 'Solemn League and Covenant' with the Scottish Kirk, and promised to introduce Presbyterianism into England and Ireland. In return for a bribe of £30,000 a month (about £2m a month in today's terms), the gullible Kirk elders fell for the stratagem and supplied Parliament with additional soldiers, facilitating a Puritan victory at Marston Moor in 1644. The Episcopal Scots, however, found their own place within the Royalist faction, and Scotland became sorely divided by way of religious persuasion – but not for long. In 1645 Parliament's 'New Model Army' defeated King Charles at Naseby, and it was at this stage that the true despotic nature of Cromwell and his pseudo-religious followers became fully apparent. It was reported:

> The parliamentary Roundheads slaughtered without hesitation all the Irish women found in the Royalist camp after Naseby, and disfigured their English sisters by cutting open their faces. They took the Scotsmen prisoners, dug out their eyes, cut off their ears at the roots with razors, and nailed down their drawn-out tongues.

Because of the indifferent and patronizing attitude of the Anglican ministers, a large number of English people had initially supported the Puritan cause. At first this seemingly temperate religious sect appeared more akin to the humble nature of the community – but the Puritan concept had been shamefully distorted to create a brutal Parliamentary Army, whose sole purpose was conquest and religious persecution. Following the Civil War, Cromwellians swept through Ireland, killing more than 6,000 Catholics in Drogheda and Wexford alone. Unfortunately, though (as with Queen Elizabeth's earlier subjugation of Ireland), the innocent people of England were blamed as a whole for this hideous outrage, and retribution is sought to this day.

However, Charles I had always maintained that politics and religion should be identified as separate issues. Members of Parliament, he claimed, should represent 'all' the people of their constituencies, not simply the Protestants – for surely the Jews, Catholics and others were also citizens with a right to ministerial representation. Charles also contended that, although the devotional affiliations of nation were the natural concerns of a king, such matters should be of no legislative consequence; Parliament, he asserted, should apply itself to politics.

It was a long-standing Scottish custom that the Kings of Scots were also hereditary priests of the Columban Kindred. The whole psyche of the Scottish Nation was embodied in this priest-kingly tradition, but it was that very ideal which caused such problems for the Stuarts in England. Such a socially-geared concept was quite unknown to the English ministers, to whom religion was no more than a political weapon to wield against the people. Hence the Stuarts were constantly plagued with the misunderstanding of their primary responsibilities to God and the nation before Parliament, and as a result their dynastic positions as spiritual ambassadors became thoroughly misinterpreted as the much-maligned *Divine Right of Kings*.

In 1646 King Charles was defeated at Newark and taken into parliamentary custody. In June 1647 he escaped to the Isle of Wight, and six months later he began desperate negotiations with the National Kirk elders who had betrayed him. The Presbyterian Scots recognized that their misguided affiliation had greatly assisted the demolition of their own ancient kingly heritage. But despite their efforts to make amends, it was too late, and the Scots Royalist army was crushed at Preston in August 1648.

King Charles I was tried by the Puritans at Westminster, and beheaded in Whitehall on 30 January 1649. However, unlike his grandmother Mary, Queen of Scots, who wore red for her execution, Charles elected to wear white. But, in view of the cold weather, he donned two white shirts to avoid shivering, 'lest they think I am frightened on facing my maker'.[7]

Firstly, the English had executed Queen Mary, and now her grandson Charles! Without further ado the Scots installed the late King's son, Charles II Stuart, who was crowned at Scone on 1 January 1651. Needless to say, the Puritans violently objected, and in that same year Cromwell defeated the new King at Worcester, whereupon Charles II escaped to France. Scotland was then brought firmly under the rule of Cromwell's kingless Commonwealth, and 280 years of legitimate Stewart/Stuart succession were ruthlessly terminated.

With no one to oppose him, Oliver Cromwell became so powerful that, in 1653, he elected to rule by martial force alone. He dissolved Parliament, and appointed himself 'Lord Protector' so that Britain was in the grip of a ruthless military dictator with greater powers than any king had ever known.

Having disposed of Parliament and the monarchy, to substitute them with his own all-powerful army, Cromwell then sought to demolish the Anglican Church as well. At his order, the Common Prayer Book was forbidden, as were the celebrations of Christmas and Easter. His self-styled military Protectorate was more severe than any previous regime, and his puritanical directives lasted throughout the 1650s. Games, sports and entertainment were restricted, dissenters were tortured and banished, houses were sequestrated, punitive taxes were levied, universities were constrained, theatres and inns were closed, freedom of speech was denied, adultery was made a capital offence, and mothers of illegitimate children were imprisoned. No one was safe, even at home, and any unwitting group of family or friends could be charged with plotting against an establishment that empowered crushing fines to be imposed at will by the soldiers. It was not surprising that people prayed for 'a speedy deliverance from the power of the major-generals, and a return to the protection of the Common Law'.

PART THREE

A Bloody Union

9

The End of an Era

The Stuart Restoration

Charles II

After Oliver Cromwell's death in 1658, the Protectorate was continued for a time by his less ambitious son Richard. But it was not long before representatives were sent to Charles II's Court of exile at The Hague, and the young King was invited to return. In 1660 Charles Stuart was restored to his kingdoms, by which time even the regular Puritans sought protection from the cruel dominion of the Cromwellian regime. Charles did not disappoint them; he was a most skilful monarch, who created a Parliament with royal limitations on its powers, and re-established the Church of England. Moreover, he endeavoured to promote a religiously tolerant environment wherein all denominations were accepted with equal status.

King Charles II managed the nation's affairs popularly and well, leading the country into a comfortable era of internal peace – but the high-minded Anglican clergy soon fell upon him when he married the Portuguese princess, Catherine of Braganza. Despite Charles's wholehearted support in the reinstatement of the English Church, the bishops presumed that, because of his chosen wife, he must have a Catholic leaning. In view of this, and in total disregard of Charles's tolerant viewpoint, Parliament passed the 1673 and 1678 *Test Acts*, preventing anyone but Anglicans from holding public office. In Scotland the 1681 *Test Act* compelled all those in public office to commit themselves to the Protestant faith. This time, however, the public were unconvinced, and they united in welcoming their King's just ministry, so that Charles II was probably the most popular and diplomatic monarch ever to sit upon the British throne. (It was during the colourful reign of Charles II that Frances 'la belle' Stuart, granddaughter of Lord Blantyre, modelled for the famous Britannia portrait which was used on British pennies until decimal currency was introduced in 1971.)

Prior to the restoration of Charles II, his brother James (the future King James VII/II) had also spent his years of Commonwealth exile in continental Europe. He had entered into military service with various European monarchs, and earned himself a significant reputation, becoming a General and then an Admiral. After the 1660 Stuart Restoration, James (Duke of York and Albany) returned to Britain, where he was appointed Lord High Admiral of England. However, the Navy had fallen into ruin during the Protectorate; the ships were rotting and their crews were ill-trained. Nevertheless, Parliament still expected James to keep England's trade routes free from the constant attacks of the Dutch.[1] The task was enormous since Holland was one of the foremost naval powers, and James was obliged to go cap-in-hand to the Westminster politicians. Unfortunately, memories of the Cromwellian era persisted, and the ministers were financially opposed to supporting a well-equipped force that could perhaps be turned against them at some time.

As a result James was provided with meagre funds to keep his ships afloat and pay his seamen. The British Navy was sparse and poorly armed, and the Dutch took due advantage to establish settlements on the Hudson River among the English colonies of North America. This posed an unacceptable threat to England's fish-traders, and the merchants duly appealed to Parliament for assistance. Accordingly, New Amsterdam (later New York – so named after James, Duke of York) was seized by the British, and in 1665 war was formally declared against Holland. Initially, James's Navy won a good victory in a battle of 300 ships off Lowestoft, but after that expensive endeavour James was unable to put his fleet to sea because there were no supplies. This enabled the Dutch to sail into the River Medway, raid Chatham, and capture the flagship *Royal Charles* in 1667.

At that time, James's close colleague and Secretary to the Navy was the noted diarist Samuel Pepys. Between them, and against seemingly insurmountable odds, they managed to keep the worst of the Dutch advances at bay, and for this valiant effort James became enormously popular with the people. They had not the vaguest notion that only 23 years later James Stuart and his family would be disinherited by Parliament, and their country handed on a plate to the hated Dutch enemy, William of Orange.

Amid all of this, the poverty of the harsh Protectorate was still evident, but Parliament was loath to apply funds to much needed areas of public service. Consequently in the early 1660s the towns and cities were in a terrible state of filth and decay, while the aristocracy were building themselves fine mansions with public money. Not the least controversial estate of the period was the massive Clarendon House, built in London by the Lord Chancellor himself. The people openly accused Chancellor Clarendon of using Government money which should have been better spent, and this was singularly embarrassing to James of Albany, for he was married to Clarendon's daughter, Anne Hyde, until she died in 1671. Lord Clarendon was also blamed for purposely obstructing James's financial management of the Navy, and to save his brother James further embarrassment, Charles II removed the irresponsible Chancellor from office.[2]

Fire and Plague

An unforgivable outcome of Parliament's reluctance to acknowledge the pressing social requirement was that, in 1665, London was ravaged by another great plague of the Black Death. This terrible disease, carried by rats and fleas, killed nearly 70,000 people in the capital (about 15 per cent of the city's population). Within a year came the Great Fire of London, which caused 100,000 residents to become homeless. But who was there to direct the fire-fighters when the politicians fled and Samuel Pepys found the Lord Mayor skulking in Canning Street? In the smoke-laden streets the chief director of operations was King Charles II himself. Hose-in-hand, he laboured earnestly among the firemen, while his brother James organized the clearing of strategic areas to prevent an outward spread of the blaze.

Through a period of many years James's considerable efforts on behalf of the nation earned him a well-deserved respect and legitimate popularity as a man of the people. But as a result he acquired numerous enemies in high places, and the aristocrats and Anglican clergy viewed him as a personal threat to their ongoing wealthy status. James held very radical views that were based upon his European experience and influenced by the sad catalogue of events that had sent his father to the scaffold. He was convinced that men of talent, ability and true intellect were perfectly able to work together for the common good of a nation. He maintained that religious differences were no crucial barrier to cooperation, and that the finest achievements were possible when those of influence put their community duties before their sectarian interests.

Albeit that James had despised the ruthless Cromwellian regime, he was not blinkered against certain aspects which displayed their individual merits. As a practised soldier, he was certainly impressed by the strategic qualities of the 'New Model Army'. He also spoke well of the honest Puritan administrators of the original Commonwealth; they had been efficient and had withstood the corruption which followed during the Protectorate. He constantly pressed his brother, Charles II, to introduce reforms to free public appointment from the constraints of religious denomination; but Parliament stood firmly against such measures, even though Charles issued an unapproved *Declaration of Indulgence* in 1672. Some years later, in 1681, Charles was specifically asked to disinherit his brother, so as to ensure that he did not accede to the throne. The Edinburgh Parliament, on the other hand, voted that 'only' James and his heirs had any rights to the Scottish Crown.

James VII (II)

By that time it had become increasingly clear that Charles would have no legitimate heir by his wife Catherine of Braganza, but he did have a number of children by his various mistresses. One of these, James, Marquis d'Aubignie (the son of Marguerite, Duchesse de Rohan), had been specifically legitimated for the British succession in 1667. However, Charles II maintained a personal allegiance to his brother, and when Charles died in 1685, James Stuart of York and Albany duly succeeded as King James VII of Scots (II of England).

James was undeniably popular in the north, and for the most part he was welcomed in the south. That is to say, he was wholeheartedly welcomed by the people at large, but not by the self-serving clergy and the parliamentary aristocrats. James was challenged almost immediately by the Anglican party who put forward their own contender, the Duke of Monmouth.

The Pitchfork Rebellion

The Duke of Monmouth was an illegitimate son of King Charles II and Lucy Walters, who had been Charles's mistress in exile some 13 years before his marriage to Catherine of Braganza. The Chancellor, Lord Shaftesbury, had long declared that Monmouth was the legitimate heir, but Charles and his retainers vigorously denied the fact. The Chancellor's main problem was that, whereas both Charles and James were popular, Monmouth had a most unworthy reputation, having been banished in 1683 after masterminding a plot to murder his father and uncle in Hertfordshire. His plan was to have Charles and James slain at Rye House, Hoddesdon, where they were to stop on their journey from Newmarket to London. When the attempt failed, Monmouth was censured and expelled, while his fellow conspirators (the politicians, Lord William Russell and Algernon Sidney) were executed.

In opposition to Shaftesbury's intrigue, King Charles II had formed his own 'Court Party' under Lord Danby in 1673. The Chancellor's opposing 'Country Party' referred to the King's ministers as Tories (bandits), whereupon the royalists labelled the others Whigs (rustlers). Thereafter, there were two effective 'parties' in Parliament, and their individual nicknames prevailed.

In spite of Monmouth's notoriety, the Whigs were content in the knowledge that he was a Protestant, and they funded his return from exile. He landed at Lyme Regis in the summer of 1685 expecting a great army to meet him, but there was none. He then had himself proclaimed King at Taunton, Somerset, and tried to raise his own militia, but the country gentry were not interested. At best, he mustered about 6,000 local inhabitants, the majority of whom were armed only with crude weapons and farming tools, and had never been trained for fighting. London and Taunton were a few days apart on horseback, and the people of Somerset were not well versed in current affairs. They were, in fact, largely dependent on the clergy for information, and Monmouth was fully aware of this. He also knew that the rural people took their lead and direction from the Anglican clerics, and so much of his recruiting was done in the local churches, with the so-called servants of God preaching the downfall of their anointed King. What they succeeded in doing, however, was to send many hitherto innocent parishioners to their deaths.

The Duke of Monmouth's ambitious cause was lost on 6 July 1685, when his 'Pitchfork Army' was defeated at the Battle of Sedgemoor. They had hoped to surprise the King's men, but were sadly disappointed when they met the royal troops on an expanse of marshland that was drained by huge ditches. King James's soldiers were no strangers to trench warfare (many of them had desert experience from training in Tobruk), and they won the day with ease. Soon after the battle, Monmouth was captured and taken to London where he was lodged in the Tower.

From his prison, Monmouth wrote to his uncle James begging that his life be spared; he promised to honour the King's future position, and to live in perpetual exile wherever James might choose. King James was presented with quite a dilemma, for this potential usurper had been the lad with whom he was associated during his early years of exile, the same youth he had taken on sea-patrol when commanding the pitiful English Navy. But he was also the same man who had attempted to assassinate him at Rye House. All things considered, and being a merciful man, James was quite willing to spare the young Duke, but in spite of his submissions to this effect, Monmouth was charged with treason and executed by the very men who had brought him to England in the first place. They had not acquired a puppet-king as envisaged, and so they turned their attentions to the alternative concept of creating a martyr, and duly sent Monmouth to the block.

Judge George Jeffreys was sent to the West Country to try the Sedgemoor prisoners and other captured rebels. The public records state quite plainly that King James required Jeffreys to show mercy to all but the most criminal offenders; he was to take care in separating the true sinners from those local recruits who were sinned against. It appears that, for the most part, Jeffreys carried out his duties as required, but histories of the affair compiled some time after the event make much of the ensuing trials, grossly exaggerating them as the *Bloody Assizes*. In fact, only 100 or so rebels were executed from an original force of about 6,000, while others were not hanged but expatriated to the colonies. (Compare this with the brutal mass slaughter of Highland families as the Duke of Cumberland's marauding troopers swept across Scotland in the wake of the Hanoverian victory at Culloden in 1746.)

Many latter-day writers have wondered how it was that King James's public reputation emerged unscathed from the so-called *Bloody Assizes*, whereas history records Judge Jeffreys as a heartless rogue. The question is not difficult to answer: firstly, the Assizes were not so bloody as portrayed; secondly, it was James who had kept Jeffreys' ministry within bounds as far as he was able – and the people at large were fully aware of this.

Religious Toleration

Apart from general attempts to uphold specific values within a multi-denominational structure, it is quite impossible to label James VI (I), Charles I or Charles II as anything but simply 'Christian'. Yet one-by-one they were the victims of individual jealousies, with each religious faction pursuing its own sectarian ambition. It was not until Charles II was succeeded by his brother James VII (II) in 1685 that any Stuart king actually declared his personal conviction. Plainly, James was not destined to be a Puritan, and since the Anglican Church was disliked by the people (having done so much to obstruct James's brother, father and grandfather), it was not really surprising that he announced his preference for the Catholic doctrine. The Anglican Parliament had tried to persuade Charles II to disinherit his brother and heir on numerous occasions, but King Charles remonstrated each time, maintaining that kingship was a sanctified office of the people, and that Parliament had no right whatever to interfere.

Even though James VII (II) announced his personal Catholicism, he was actually more religiously flexible than his predecessors; he was probably the most tolerant king in the history of Britain. In 1687 he decided to introduce an *Act of Indulgence*, which was designed to give everyone freedom in matters of conscience, but Parliament declined to accept the bill, and so the King presented it again the following year. Meanwhile, he even went so far as to issue a written *Declaration for Liberty of Conscience*, which conveyed the ideal of 'religious freedom for all' (*see* Appendix II for a full transcript). The people were delighted, but they were not in control, and Parliament's ambition for Anglican religious supremacy remained unchanged. Also unchanged was the English power-lords' desire to fully subjugate the Scottish Nation. Despite the strategic 'Union of Crowns', this enterprise was forever thwarted while a hereditary King of Scots reigned overall, and what the scheming politicians needed was a controllable monarch – preferably someone from abroad who would not care too much about his British kingdoms.

As a result, James VII (II) became yet another victim of fervent extremists – not Puritans this time, nor even straightforward Anglicans of the old school, but Dutch-influenced Whig Protestants who had become very powerful at Westminster. They not only persecuted the King, but had him deposed for daring to acknowledge the alternative faiths of the Catholics, Jews, Presbyterians, Quakers or whatever. The Whig ministers centred their accusations on the fact that James gave his consent to Catholicism,[3] but such a charge was quite illogical on its own. In practical terms, his tolerance of the Jewish faith would have been a far more appropriate target for fervent Christians. It is clear, therefore, that the attack had little to do with religion; it was more precisely concerned with the fact that, in granting a denominational choice, James was challenging the dogmatic supremacy of the English Parliament over the people.

The Test Acts

In attempting to grant an equality of conscience, King James VII (II) sought to repeal the restrictive *Test Acts*, which bound those in public office to communion with the Church of England. His action was, therefore, seen to oppose the distinct privileges of the

Anglican clergy, as well as affording people the choice to adopt a religion over which Parliament had no control. In this, the King's public popularity counted for nothing, neither did his earlier courage on the battlefields of France and Flanders, nor his years of relentless work for the British Navy. However, James's personal leaning was of no importance to the people; they had already stood by him when his illegitimate nephew, the Duke of Monmouth, endeavoured to seize the Throne in 1685. Monmouth was a 'Protestant' but, as proven by his futile Pitchfork Rebellion, very few were sympathetic to his cause.

In December 1688 the fearful Whigs deposed King James and drove him from England, so illegally terminating Scotland's access to her own traditional Royal House. Resultant history has been constructed to suggest that James was dismissed because he was a Catholic, but in truth he was displaced to guarantee future power to a Parliament that was not elected by the majority vote of the people, and to ensure the continuing supremacy of the Anglican bishops. The fact that James was a Catholic was of no individual relevance since the 1678 Act (which tied public officials to the Anglican Communion) had specified James by name as an 'exception' to the rule. Everyone except James had been happy enough with this; he not only disliked the law in general terms, but disapproved of the fact that he was personally exempt from its limitations, while others were bound by them.

Much later, in 1828–9, the English *Test Acts* were repealed in favour of Catholics (with the exception of the office of Lord High Chancellor). Then in 1858 the provisions were relaxed in respect of Jews, and the Scottish Act was overturned in 1889. In Britain today all religious denominations (Christian or otherwise) are afforded the right to worship according to their beliefs and conscience, precisely as King James VII (II) envisaged 300 years ago. Few would now claim that James was wrong in promoting an outlook of liberal toleration, and it is apparent that he was considerably ahead of his time in this regard. However, this fair-minded man was lost to the people of Britain, to be replaced by an uncompromising Dutchman, and in time by an autocratic German dynasty.

10

By Force of Arms

The Dutch Invader

Anne Hyde of Clarendon, the first wife of James VII (II), had borne two daughters, Mary and Anne. However, after Anne Hyde's early death James had married Mary Beatrix d'Este de Modena in 1673. Within a few years their first son was born, only to die a month later. But shortly before James's deposition, Queen Mary d'Este gave birth to the new royal heir, James Francis Edward Stuart, giving the ambitious politicians another reason to panic. They had hoped that, with no direct successor, it would be possible to select their own King of England, rather than continue with a dynastic King of Scots on the Throne. It was therefore determined that, one way or another, James must go.

In the period surrounding James's departure, King Louis XIV and the French were threatened by the ever-growing menace of the Holy Roman Empire, headed by the Emperor and the Pope. James had sided with Louis in resisting the Papal and Imperial pressures, but his alliance with the French monarch in this regard was not welcomed by the Anglican Whigs at Westminster. Consequently they began to show favour towards James's Protestant daughter Mary and her ambitious Dutch husband, Prince William II of Orange.

The Holy Roman Empire was, of course, a Catholic institution. Its opposers, James VII (II) and Louis XIV, were also both Catholics at heart, but neither desired their countries to be swallowed by Rome, for that was hardly a route towards sympathetic religious toleration in their lands. What today's establishment historians conveniently ignore is that Holland (although part of the newly independent Netherlands) had long been affiliated to the Holy Roman Empire[1], despite the apparent strength of the nation's Protestant faction. In recognizing this, Prince William II the Stadhouder (chief magistrate of the Netherlands) emerges in a wholly different light from that generally portrayed. Notwithstanding his wife's personal religious allegiance, he was no Protestant champion, but a protagonist of the Papal empire to which his House of Orange was related.

King James VII (II) Stuart was the last reigning British monarch to actively defend and uphold the rights, liberties and welfare of the people throughout Scotland, England, Ireland and Wales – and he lost his crown because of it. From the moment of James's departure, the nation was sold into centuries of subservience, to be ruled by various powerful factions who, generally speaking, have had their own interests at heart, rather than the interests of the people they were supposed to represent.

Having been denied the privilege of an effective peacetime army, King James was in no position to resist Parliament's approved Dutch invader, and Prince William duly arrived from Holland with his soldiers. Almost immediately he issued violent threats against the Stuart Royal Family, and on 21 December 1688 Queen Mary d'Este and the infant Prince of Wales were secreted by night from the capital. Amid howling gales and driving sleet, they were taken to the coast, where they embarked in a small boat to Calais. Fortunately, the weather was such that the Dutch militia bands were unaware of their escape. Mary then wrote to her cousin Louis XIV of France, who sent courtiers to fetch the Queen of Britain to his Royal Court.[2] Having spent a night near Beauvais, the group reached Paris, whereupon Mary was met by King Louis and presented with the keys to the Château de Saint Germain-en-Laye. Some 140 years before this had been the residence of Mary, Queen of Scots, but from that moment in late 1688 this historically important palace became the recognized Court of the Stuart 'Kings over the water'.

Meanwhile, in London, James received a letter of ultimatum from his son-in-law, William of Orange. The letter stated that if James did not give up his crown at once, then his family would be at risk. Little did William know that the Royal Family were already gone. In due accord, and perfectly resigned to the situation, King James left Whitehall, depriving his usurpers by throwing the Great Seal of England into the Thames. (This was a very pointed gesture, for William could not achieve effective kingship without this constitutional device.)

James also made the voyage to Calais, and thence to Paris, where the people flocked to meet him; and once at Saint Germain he was greeted by his good friend King Louis XIV of France.

With the support of the Whigs, Prince William convened an illegal Parliament at Westminster on 26 December 1688. The Tory party endeavoured to prevent the Dutch intrusion, but to no avail, for the ministers who were gathered to vote in respect of a dynastic change were constrained at gunpoint by William's armed Orangemen. The *Nineteenth Century Review* of September 1897 reported that the Convention Parliament was in no way at liberty to vote according to conscience because Prince William's soldiers were stationed within the House and all around the Palace of Westminster. With regard to the effect that this militarily-obligated Parliament had on the monarchical structure thereafter (from Orange to Hanoverian times), the report continued:

> Nothing else can equal the fact, commonly overlooked, that the parliamentary vote, by which alone the title of the Hanoverian dynasty was obtained, was in no sense a vote representative of the will of the people . . . King James was gone, and William was present with the Dutch Guard at Westminster to overawe, and with power to imperil the fortunes and lives of those who stood in the way of his advancement . . . William employed actual intimidation which resulted in majorities of '*one*' vote, in two of the most important divisions in the history of Parliament . . . In our time, governments have resigned when their majority over a censuring opposition has not been so small. Yet a majority of '*one*' is held to be adequate justification for a revolution involving the fundamental principle of primogeniture upon which our social fabric is based!

William did not immediately get his own way, however. Following a preliminary Commons debate, the House of Lords was separately concerned as to whether the Throne could be deemed legitimately vacant, and it was suggested that a Regency was the best way to preserve the Crown during James Stuart's lifetime.

Interestingly, not all of the Anglican Church hierarchy were opposed to King James, and the Lords' Regency suggestion was supported by the most senior churchman of all, Archbishop Sancroft of Canterbury. In agreement with him were the Bishops of Bath and Wells, Ely, Gloucester, Norwich, Peterborough, Worcester, Chichester and Chester. Also in favour were Lords Nottingham and Clarendon, and numerous others who sought King James's return. They were similarly backed by many who were actually opposed to the King's *Declaration for Liberty*, but who did not uphold Parliament's assumed power to depose him. Lords Halifax and Danby led the faction against the Regency motion, but they lost the debate. Consequently it was ruled that since there was an original compact between the King and the people, the throne was 'Not Vacant'. The vote in favour of this decision was carried by 55 to 41 – a majority of 14.

This result was of no use whatever to William of Orange; he specifically required to have authority in England so as to preserve Holland's international trade monopoly, particularly against a significant challenge from Louis XIV and the merchants of France. In order to ensure his success against any Stuart-related opposition, the ambitious Dutchman had brought sufficient troops to London to deter James's supporters, and the unforgettable hypocrisy of the situation was that two-thirds of William's supposedly Protestant army were paid Catholic mercenaries![3]

With his soldiers about him, Prince William summoned Lords Halifax and Danby. He explained that he had absolutely no intention of becoming a Regent, neither would he consent to sharing in government. So explicit was the nature of his declaration that there was an immediate fear of war, and many thought that William would seize the crown regardless. Accordingly, a panic conference ensued between the Lords and the Commons, giving rise to an alternative decision: maybe the Throne was vacant after all!

Hence, it was uneasily resolved that the Prince and Princess of Orange should become King and Queen of England and her dominions. They were installed on 11 April 1689, and William reigned for 13 years until his death in 1702.

And so it was that the rightful Stuart monarch and a traditional royal dynasty were set aside for the sake of fear and convenience at the behest of a foreign intruder, and by way of an illegal convention. Archbishop Sancroft and his confederate bishops refused to swear an Oath of Allegiance to the incoming monarchs, claiming that it would be in defiance of their solemn commitment to King James, and against the lawful constitution of the realm. But constitutional laws, commitments and moral issues had no place in the new Orange regime, and the dissenting Anglican churchmen were all deprived of their sees and incumbencies. This was, however, a short-sighted move, for later on it backfired, precipitating a schism within the Anglican Church.[4]

The Bill of Rights

With James Stuart out of the picture, the 1689 *Bill of Rights* laid down the conditions on which the British Throne was granted to William and Mary. There was an ambiguous Stuart heritage retained by this manoeuvre since Mary was the daughter of King James VII (II) and his first wife, Anne of Clarendon. Also, William (whose father was William of Nassau) was a son of King Charles I's daughter Mary, and so the pair were granted equal rights to reign as King William III and Queen Mary II.

The *Bill of Rights* stipulated that future monarchs could only rule with 'Parliamentary Consent', and that Government ministers should be freely elected. But ministers of the era (and for a good while to come) were certainly not freely elected; only a limited number of male property-owners on high incomes were allowed to vote, and the House of Commons was far from characteristic of the people it was supposed to represent.

Knights Templars and the Irish Campaign

During the days of his adversity in England, King James had made many new friends, but he also lost some old ones; even his first wife's daughters, Mary and Anne, deserted him for the Orange cause. But one body of men who stood firmly behind their King was the Order of Knights Templars of the Grand Priories of Scotland and Ireland. The Templars had been given asylum in Scotland by King Robert the Bruce, and 432 Knights had fought at Bannockburn under the command of Chevalier Hugues de Crecy. Thereafter the Order was justifiably honoured in the kingdom of the Scots, and successive heirs to the crown were Knights of the Temple from birth.

Templars were prominent in the ranks of Cavaliers who fought alongside King Charles I, and they also supported James VII (II) in his hour of need. When James was deposed in 1688, the Knights and the Scots in general were most displeased at the loss of their dynastic king – and in the very next year came the first Jacobite Rising. On 27 July 1689 the Grand Prior of the Scottish Knights Templars, Viscount Graham of Claverhouse (known as *Bonnie Dundee*), led a force of Highlanders against King William's troops at Killiecrankie. The Scots' charge was successful, but Dundee was mortally wounded and died without knowing he had been appointed King's General. A few weeks later the Highlanders were less fortunate when defeated at Dunkeld. When Viscount Dundee fell at Killiecrankie he was wearing the Grand Cross and Sash of the Templars[5], and despite what the indoctrinated history books say about the Order having been extinct since 1307, the Order of the Temple of Jerusalem is still flourishing in Scotland and Europe today.

In Ireland too, the Templars were quick to raise forces in opposition to 'Wee Billy Windmills', as William of Orange was called. The fighting persisted until 1 July 1690, when James's supporters were overrun by William's Orangemen at the Battle of the Boyne near Drogheda. This was followed by another Jacobite defeat at Aughrim, Galway, in 1691, whereupon some 10,000 Scots and Irish accompanied James back into exile. The Scots who followed James to France went there not only because of their king, but also by right of their traditional dual-nationality under the terms of the Auld Alliance.

In all, more than 50,000 Jacobites left Britain between 1688 and 1692 – but King James was quite impoverished, and so his supporters formed their own Scots and Irish regiments, offering their services to the rulers of Europe. By virtue of this, the European monarchs were provided with well-trained armed forces, and the military alliance persisted to the time of the 19th-century Napoleonic empire. (Even Napoleon I retained his own Scots Guard[6], and employed many Irish and Scots Jacobites as agents, diplomats and advisers in his ministry.)

Not all the Knights Templars went to France, however, and those who remained to continue the Order in Britain were enabled, by virtue of their secret network, to establish a very efficient intelligence service. They liaised closely with their confederates at the Court of Saint Germain, and managed to thwart many of Westminster's attempts to assassinate prominent Jacobites and members of the Royal Family.

With King James in France, the French had, in effect, two lawful monarchs in residence (Louis and James), for the Stuarts were traditionally designated 'Kings of Britain, France and Ireland'. Strange as it may seem, Louis XIV permitted James to continue with the ambiguous 'King of France' style even though he was an exile in his cousin's domain.[7] Louis saw this as a device to facilitate his avoidance of King William's demand that James should be expelled from France; for a king cannot be expelled from his own kingdom at the whim of a hostile foreign power. Hence, James was afforded the right to retain his theoretical position, although he was actually a pensioner of Louis XIV.

In his early exile, James had fully intended to return to Britain, and it was this which led to his Irish campaign of 1690. With the exception of some Ulster regions, Ireland was no supporter of William III, and the island provided a satisfactory stepping-stone between France and the British mainland. Both the Scots and Irish acknowledged the strategy, and agreed to await their King's instruction. In late February 1690, James set sail for Ireland with a French fleet, and on arrival he established his Court in Dublin. In accordance with his well-known principle, James was explicit that Catholics and Protestants had equal rights of worship and members of each denomination supported his campaign.

All commenced well enough, but the effort failed at the Battle of the Boyne. Once again, King William's opposing force largely consisted of Catholic mercenaries, who had been granted special dispensation by the late Pope Alexander VIII and the incoming Pope Innocent XII.[8] It is quite ludicrous for supposedly intelligent historians to persist with the disinformation that James's 'Catholic' troops were at war with William's 'Protestant' army; there were members of both religious denominations on each side.

It cannot be overemphasized that William of Orange and the Pope were the closest of allies.[9] In confronting the might of the Dutch trading-machine, Louis of France was really challenging the avaricious pursuits of the Holy Roman Empire.

In this regard, he was personally resisting the supremacy of the Catholic Church in France. Had King James been afforded the finance and facilities to fully support Louis XIV in his enterprise, then the international significance of the Papacy would have been severely diminished at that time. The Spanish would likely have followed the lead of France and Britain, and the Roman Church would have been manoeuvred out of the imperial front-line, to find its rightful place as a spiritual institution, rather than an international political organization.

Although there was absolutely no chance for the Empire to dethrone King Louis, both Holland and the Papal State knew it would be easy enough to topple James and replace him with an anti-French monarch. All they had to do was to wave Mary's Protestant flag before the gullible Whigs and they were in business. As it transpired, James's last hopes were dashed in Ireland, and the Battle of the Boyne is still remembered each year by the Orange Order as if some great Protestant victory had been won. In truth, it was quite the reverse, and because of it the Roman Church has retained a power in international politics that is quite unacceptable to those of other denominations.

Granted, we now have the 'Anglo-Irish Agreement', which will perhaps lead to an eventual unification of Ireland. It is also true that the Irish Free State (established in 1921) recognizes the Northerners' right to vote in the Republican Elections. But, inasmuch as genuine attempts are being made to subdue the Catholic protagonists from within, so too must the Protestant extremists understand their historical position and do likewise. The fact is that Westminster is never likely to tell them the truth, and it is sadly inevitable that the Ulster Protestants will end up feeling hurt and confused at being discarded by the very establishment to which they thought they were being loyal. Indeed, by supporting the Orange cause their battling ancestors inadvertently assisted the Papal endeavour. As a result, denominational intolerance is more prevalent in Ireland than in either France, Scotland, England, Wales, or anywhere else today.

It has to be remembered that the English Parliament cared nothing for Protestants in general. Neither did it much care for England's episcopal Protestant ally, the Church of Ireland. Plainly, it cared little for Catholics or Jews. Westminster's primary concern was, and still is, the ultimate supremacy of the Anglican

Church; this is proven time-after-time by the sectarian coronation ritual of its monarchs.

Queen Mary II was undoubtedly a convinced Protestant, but William's banner of appeasement did not confirm that he shared her heartfelt conviction. It simply stated in great embroidered letters, 'I will maintain the liberties of England and the Protestant religion'. Indeed, King James had said as much – and far more. Yet the Churches of England and Ireland were satisfied that Mary's personal influence was sufficient, which is precisely why she was granted joint royal status.

William's famous banner did not mention Ireland at all, and it was not long before the Protestant Church of Ireland was placed in a most unenviable position by William. It was compelled to enact his Government's *Penal Laws* against the Catholic majority, laws whereby Catholics were deprived by statute of their civil rights, liberties, and property rights. This engendered a lasting hatred of the Protestant Irish Church by the Catholic community, and although the Church was reluctant to apply the restrictions, they had no choice.

In 1699 the Protestant Irish Church was further hindered by the crushing English law prohibiting all export of Irish-manufactured wool. This embargo was designed specifically to safeguard the interests of English manufacturers, and it was ruinous to the people of Ireland. Many have wondered why the Protestants of Ireland were so shamefully treated by the monarch they had served so well. The answer is simple: the trade sanction was imposed in 1699, but Queen Mary had died in 1694, leaving William as the sole ruler. His interests were not with Britain or Ireland, and certainly not with the Protestants. His mission throughout was to maximize Holland's trading position against that of France, and to increase his personal dominion by subjecting Britain and her colonies to the will of the Holy Roman Empire.[10] Yet still the unscrupulous William of Orange is revered by many as if he were a heaven-sent champion of the Protestant cause!

Massacre at Glencoe

King James's forced departure was very hard on the Scots, particularly since it was insultingly called an 'abdication'. In denying Scotland's crown to the Stuart dynasty, the very fabric of the Constitution was rent, and the Clan chiefs were then expected to swear an *Oath of Allegiance* to an egotistic Dutch invader. Such a declaration was unfamiliar to the Scots, for their kings had always sworn fealty to the nation, rather than the reverse. Not knowing how best to deal with the situation, many of them travelled to France to ask the advice of their King. James realized that, should he refuse to grant his consent, William would retaliate by letting loose his vengeance on entire families, and so he gave the chiefs permission to swear the oath.

One aged chief who returned from France was MacIain, whose clan of MacDonalds were settled at Glencoe. For technical reasons, MacIain failed to meet the *Allegiance* deadline of 1 January 1692. He had endeavoured to register his oath at Fort William, and went there for that very purpose on 30 December, but no Crown officer arrived from Inverary, and so MacIain was sent home. As a result, he did not manage to fulfil his obligation until 6 January – a week later. Meanwhile, Sir John Dalrymple (King William's Secretary of State for Scotland) was criticized at Westminster for being slow to implement the Highland policy. William required a show of strength, and it was ruled that Dalrymple should persecute an individual clan as an example to the others. He chose the MacDonalds of Glencoe.[11]

Among the few notable clans who betrayed Scottish interests to find favour with the Orange regime were the Campbells of Argyll, and on 1 February Dalrymple sent two companies of Argyll's Regiment, under Robert Campbell of Glenlyon, to slaughter the unsuspecting MacDonalds. The soldiers marched from Fort William to the mountainous valley of Glencoe, and arrived as if on a peaceful mission. They were greeted well, and were fed by the hospitable families with whom they lodged for many days. Then on the bitter morning of 13 February the soldiers rose to a man and cut down every MacDonald they could find, including Chief MacIain. They spared not the women, the elderly, or the young, and the families were hacked to death, whether in their beds or huddled by their firesides. Those who managed to escape were confronted by the most ferocious winter in memory.

In consequence of this brutal event, the Campbells have acquired a notorious reputation. However, in the fairness of hindsight, this reputation must be justly refuted. Apart from being a Campbell-led regiment, the military listing clearly shows that the soldiers concerned were generally not of Clan Campbell extraction.

The savage 'Massacre of Glencoe' has never been forgotten in the Highlands, nor should it be, for it lingers as a permanent reminder of the despotic William of Orange. Not surprisingly, this hideous outrage had the opposite effect to that expected, and instead of intimidating the reluctant Scots, it caused them to form a strong Jacobite confederacy against Westminster and the usurping monarchy.

The Knights of Saint Germain

On 18 June 1692, the very day that Queen Mary d'Este gave birth to her last child in Europe (a daughter, christened Louise Marie Thérèse), King James VII created 'The Most Noble and Ancient Jacobite Order of Saint Germain'.[12] Modelled on the Stewart Order of the Thistle (revived by James VII in 1687 at Windsor), the new Order was divided into two categories – Knights and Companions. Some exiled Thistle knights and loyal Templars were enrolled, together with their brothers of the Order of Lorraine, the Order of Sion, and several knights of the French Orders of Saint Louis and Saint Michel. It was the primary responsibility of the Knights and Companions of Saint Germain to keep safe the Royal Family and the members of their immediate Household in exile. In December 1692 the élite Household Guard was elevated to become a Sovereign and Hereditary Order of the Royal House of Stewart/Stuart, receiving recognition and consent from King Louis XIV in 1693.

On 31 December 1703, England's succeeding Queen Anne presumed to reconstitute the Order of the Thistle in Scotland, whereupon the Order of Saint Germain became the primary Stuart Order in Europe, bearing St Andrew as its insignia. Then in 1715 the incoming King George I of Britain confirmed the statutes of Queen Anne, and purloined the St Andrew insignia for the Hanoverian Thistle collar. Henceforth, both Orders have carried the same insignia, with the Hanoverian riband and sash being green, whereas the Stuart Order retained the colour blue.

As detailed in the *Declaration of Arbroath*, St Andrew had preached in Scythia in the 1st century, and his cult became widespread in Scotland. His relics were originally found in Northumbria, from where they were brought to Fife by Bishop Acca in the 8th century. He presented them to King Angus mac Fergus of the Picts (729–50) who dedicated a church at Kilrymund, later renamed as St Andrews. Tradition has it that King Angus (Hungus) had seen a huge saltire cross formed by clouds in a blue sky when he met Athelstane of England in battle in East Lothian. He took this cross of St Andrew to be a significant omen and duly won the battle, whereupon the Scottish national flag was born. The battlefield was the later named village of Athelstaneford, where the blue-and-white saltire is still permanently flown at the local church to mark the occasion.

Subsequently, St Andrew became the patron saint of Scotland, and his famous saltire cross appeared on Scotland's Seal of the Guardians in 1286, at which time Bishop Fraser of St Andrews was the Chief of the six appointed Guardians of the Realm. St Andrews Cathedral was almost finished after 150 years of building, and although ready for consecration by 1304 its roofing lead was stripped to provide munitions for the war against Edward of England. As a result the consecration was delayed until Friday 5 July 1318, after the victorious Battle of Bannockburn. The office was performed by Bishop William Lamberton, with King Robert the Bruce in attendance to present an endowment to the Cathedral.[13] Never was a patron saint so important to a nation as was St Andrew to Scotland – but still King George I appropriated the St Andrew insignia for the House of Hanover in 1715, and the insult persists to this day.

An express duty of the Knights of Saint Germain was to preserve the honour of Stuart heritage against the detrimental propaganda which subsequently emerged from Westminster and the Palace of Saint James in Hanoverian times. The Knights became renowned as international champions of liberty, and were actively involved in the War of Spanish Succession (1701–14), the War of Austrian Succession (1740–8), and the American War of Independence (1775–83). In the later days of Charles Edward Stuart, the prestigious Knights were front-line diplomats and ambassadors, providing a valuable counter-intelligence service for the Stuart Court. The Household Knights were respected and granted protection by the Kings of France, Spain, Sardinia, Portugal, Saxony and Poland, along with the Austrian Emperors, the Tsars of Russia, and the Sovereign Dukes of Italy. From the time of James VII, the Stuart Kings *de jure* and Counts of Albany have remained Hereditary Grand Masters of the Order, which is extant today as the Noble Order of the Guard of Saint Germain.

* * *

King James VII's life ended on 16 September 1701. Before his moment of death, his trusted friend and kindred spirit, Louis XIV of France, assured him that young James, Prince of Wales, would be honoured as his heir and successor. Furthermore, Louis undertook to protect the new King's interests as far as was possible.

On the following day, James's widow, Mary of Modena, departed for the Convent of Chaillot, where the Abbess and the Sisters received her at the gate. The convent church was draped in black, and a solitary bell rang as Mary, stunned by her sorrow, entered in silence. At length the Abbess addressed the Queen, and declared how fortunate she was to have had such a holy prince for a husband – but that husband had not willed her into a convent. Indeed, his last testament had nominated Mary as Regent during their son's minority. This was a most important Regency, explained the Abbess, for it was the tie that would bind the family for generations to come. At this, Mary smiled her thanks, and duly made her way back to Saint Germain-en-Laye.[14]

11

The Treaty of Union

Queen Anne and the Scots

The most significant constraint encountered by King William was the 1689 *Bill of Rights* and its inherent *Declaration of Rights*. Despite his famous banner and outwardly routine aspirations, Parliament had determined that, having facilitated his invasion, they were in a position to impose certain restrictions for the future. The ministers laid immediate ground rules, and the *Bill of Rights* stipulated that Parliament retained absolute rights of consent over the monarchy, the judiciary and the people. Furthermore, it was henceforth illegal for a monarch to retain a standing army, or to make or amend any laws of the land. The provisions of the bill are still applied today.

Although William made a great show of strength at his initial Convention Parliament, the politicians maintained the upper hand by granting his kingship on a conditional basis. These measures, coupled with Queen Mary's Protestantism, curtailed William's imperial ambitions, but following Mary's childless death in 1694 the inevitable dilemma of succession arose. The fact that Mary had no offspring by William was no surprise to anyone, for their 1677 marriage had been one of political convenience, and William's sexual deviancy was a constant embarrassment to both his Court and Parliament. The *Encyclopedia of Scotland* gives a relevant contemporary quote: 'William III is odious but not silly, and with a penchant for choir-boys which protects his person from syphilis and his country from a Dutch heir'.

At that time, there were 50 legitimate claimants to the crowns of the British Isles, and at the top of the list was the exiled King James VII (II), followed by his son, James Francis Edward Stuart. When King James died in 1701 his son moved into primary position, whereupon the Government deemed it necessary to prevent his right of accession, and the result was the 1701 *Act of Settlement*, which was passed to secure the Throne of Britain for Protestants alone. It is still in force today, even though it was passed in the Commons by a majority of only one vote (118 for, and 117 against). Not only that, but the earlier *Act of Abjuration* (requiring all Government officials to renounce King James) was similarly passed by one vote only (193 to 192). There was no true parliamentary majority for either of these Acts which set a permanent scene for everything that has followed concerning the British monarchy, and once again many of those who voted in favour of the two Acts were forcibly cajoled by physical duress under force-of-arms.

Notwithstanding King William's own doubtful religious affiliation, young James Stuart was being nurtured in a Catholic environment, and so the Act stipulated that the future British succession was to be confined to Protestants. King William's sister-in-law, Anne Stuart, therefore emerged as his successor, and she became Queen in 1702. Prior to her accession, however, the Scottish Parliament had opted for a monarch of its own choosing in accordance with the nation's Written Constitution. The members' choice was, quite naturally, the Stuart heir James Francis Edward, Duke of Rothesay.

In no time at all Queen Anne discovered that the national Anglican and Presbyterian Churches were divided on the matter of her succession. Not only that, but the Church of England was itself facing a schism, and the eminent churchmen who had been ousted after William and Mary's coronation were now heading an influential non-juring party. In their former roles the key figures were William Sancroft, Archbishop of Canterbury; Francis Turner, Bishop of Ely; John Lake, Bishop of Chichester; Thomas Ken, Bishop of Bath and Wells; William Lloyd, Bishop of Norwich; William Thomas, Bishop of Peterborough; and Robert Frampton, Bishop of Gloucester.

When, on 1 February 1690, these men were deprived of their sees and incumbencies for refusing to swear an *Oath of Allegiance* to William of Orange, Parliament had not anticipated that well over 400 dissatisfied clergymen would follow their leaders out of the Anglican establishment[1], together with an attached laity of many thousands. Prior to this, a *Toleration Act* had been passed in 1689, giving rights of worship to nonconformists, but this had largely backfired on the Anglicans and actually facilitated the dissenters' actions. In essence, the Church of England was split, but Archbishop Sancroft declared his breakaway faction to be the true Church since he had held the most senior position as the Primate of Canterbury. As a result, when Queen Anne was crowned by the new clerical regime, she was not fully convinced that she had truly achieved the Throne since the Old Guard of the English Church and the elders of the Scottish National Kirk were both in opposition.

The Protestants of the Church of Ireland thought they would fare rather better under Queen Anne, but she hindered them further by tightening the *Penal Laws* against Catholics and renewing the antagonism. Catholics were excluded from the electorate, and from every corporate or public office. They were forbidden to own horses worth more than £5 each, and were debarred from universities and higher education. They were not allowed to be school teachers, and their terms of employment were generally constrained. Not surprisingly, these impositions affected Catholics and Protestants alike, particularly since the Catholics were in the majority as employers, tradesmen, shopkeepers, farmers and businessmen. They were, therefore, obliged to look to their own, and the unfortunate Protestants of the Irish Church laity found themselves wanting for jobs, services and provisions.

The limited extent of Anne's so-called Protestantism became especially marked when her Government introduced the 1704 *Irish Test Act* against the Ulster dissenters. These Presbyterians and Reformists – the very same who oppose the Catholics today – were ostracized from all forms of civil and military employment under the Crown. In short, Queen Anne's Government was no more interested in Protestants than in Catholics. Then, as now, the only sacrament that was officially tolerated was that of the Anglican Communion.

In the wake of the Battle of the Boyne and King James's attachment to Louis XIV, William had pursued a course of aggression against the French. Queen Anne inherited this active enmity, but the continuing dispute was disrupting Scotland's trade with France, and the Scots were far from happy. Although Anne had significant Whig support, she faced continuing resistance from the Tory benches, and from Scotland. But instead of confronting the Scottish problem by way of a personal visit and parliamentary negotiations, she decided to rid herself of the difficulty by bringing the Scots firmly to heel from the safety of London.

Subsequent to the *Irish Test Act,* Queen Anne wrote to the Scottish Parliament declaring her intention to dissolve the ancient institution.[2] On receipt of her letter, the ministers sought to discover a precedent which could invalidate the Queen's intention, and found the solution in the 1320 *Declaration of Arbroath,* which stated that if a monarch should

> make us or our kingdom subject to the King of England or the English, we should exert ourselves at once to drive him out as our enemy and a subverter of his own rights and ours, and make some other man, who was well able to defend us, our king.

It was obvious that Anne's plan to disband the independent 'Three Estates' Parliament would fully subject the kingdom to domination from Westminster. Therefore, under the terms of their Written Constitution, the Scots were afforded the legal right to elect a sovereign from a royal line other than that chosen by England. In keeping with this, the 'Three Estates' introduced a *Bill of Security,* whereby the Scottish Nation was not bound to accept Anne's chosen heir. The bill was passed with a majority of 59 votes, but to the indignation of the community, Anne refused to give it her royal assent. This aroused such a resolute backlash that the measure was forced through in another session, and Queen Anne was advised not to abstain from granting her formal acquiescence.

Since Anne had no surviving children by her husband Prince George of Denmark, her own nominated choice of successor was the German Electress, Sophia of Hanover. She was the daughter of Frederick V, Elector Palatine of the Rhine, whose wife was Elizabeth Stuart, a daughter of King James VI. However, irrespective of the Stuart maternal connection, the Scots vigorously opposed the concept of a German ruler to the extent that England readied herself for a Border war. Parliament then implemented express trade limitations against the Scots, and in March 1705 Westminster passed the *Alien Act*[4], which demanded that the Scots must accept Sophia of Hanover as Anne's nominated successor, or all trade between the North and South would cease. The importation of Scottish coal, linen and cattle into England would be forbidden, and there would be no continued export of English goods into Scotland. It was a straightforward case of political blackmail.

Bribery and Corruption

Regardless of all this pressure, Queen Anne realized that she would never get the support of the Scottish people; but she could at least 'buy' some allegiance from the aristocracy. Subsequent to the arrival in 1603 of James VI in London, many lines of Scotland's nobility had become quite Anglicized, having been bribed with land and special privileges in the South. Also, King William had restructured Scotland's Three Estates – Parliament ousting the clergy in favour of a baron's estate. Queen Anne therefore plied even more wealth in their direction. The Church of Scotland realized what was afoot, and claimed that the disaffected nobles were about to betray Scottish interests and the Constitution; but there was little the Church or the people could do about it. Ultimately, when the Scottish Parliament met to vote on unification with England, the treacherous aristocrats were there in force. Parliament House was completely surrounded by the armed soldiers of Queen Anne's regiments, and the motion for subjugation to Westminster was carried by conspiracy, bribery, duress and browbeaten votes.

In order to secure the Three Estates' vote in favour of the 1707 *Treaty of Union*, various monetary awards were granted by Queen Anne. The most significant payment went to Her Majesty's Commissioner James Douglas, 2nd Duke of Queensbury KG, who was directly responsible for managing the whole affair. Queensbury's award and allowance was £12,325, in addition to which he was granted the English titles Baron of Rippon, Marquess of Beverley and Duke of Dover. According to the Bank of England's current *Table of Equivalent Values*, Queensbury's cash receipts were equal to about £750,000 in today's terms.

John Murray, 2nd Marquess of Atholl, was a constant

opponent of the Union, even though Queen Anne had created him Duke of Atholl, Lord Privy Seal and KT in 1703. To soften the strength of his persistent opposition, Atholl was offered £1,000 [£60,830 at present values] to vote in favour of the Union – but the bribe had no effect, and he did not change his views. Most of the financial inducements were successful though, and those recorded were as follows [approximate present equivalent values are shown in brackets]:

Earl of Marchmont (former Chancellor) – £1,104. 17s 7d [£67,200]
Marquess of Tweedale – £1,000 [£60,830]
Earl of Balcarres – £500 [£30,415]
Duke of Roxburgh – £500
Earl of Seafield (Lord Chancellor) – £490 [£29,807]
Earl of Cromarty – £300 [£18,249]
Earl of Dunmore – £300
Lord Anstruther – £300
William Stewart of Castle Stewart – £300
Sir William Sharp – £300
Earl of Eglinton – £200 [£12,166]
Lord Preston Hall – £200
Lord Ormiston – £200
Duke of Montrose – £200
John Campbell of Mammore – £200
Earl of Kintore – £200
Lord Fraser – £100 [£6,083]
Earl of Findlator – £100
Earl of Forfar – £100
Sir Kenneth MacKenzie – £100
Earl of Glencairn – £100
John Muir (Provost of Ayr) – £100
Major Cunningham of Eckatt – £100
Alexander Wedderburn – £75 [£4,562]
Treaty of Union messenger – £60 [£3,650]
Lord Cresnock – £50 [£3,042]
Lord Forbes – £50
Lord Elibank – £50
Patrick Coultrain (Provost of Wigton) – £25 [£1,520]
Lord Banff – £11.2s [£675]

Subsequent to the granting of these monetary payments and supplementary awards, there were various stages to the voting procedure. The first vote, which took place on 4 November 1706, concerned *Article Number 1* – the Union of the Scots and English Kingdoms. Debates ensued over matters of trade, political representation, and the Hanoverian succession, in respect of which other key votes followed. Among these was the all-important issue in respect of *Article Number 3* – the Union of the Scottish and English Parliaments. The voting results for *Articles 1* and *3* were:

	Vote on Union of Kingdoms		**Vote on Union of Parliaments**	
	Yes	*No*	*Yes*	*No*
Nobles	46	21	44	21
Barons	37	33	37	33
Burgesses	33	29	33	27
	116	83	114	81
Majority	33		33	

Discounting the money offered to the reluctant Earl of Atholl, and the sums paid to the Duke of Queensbury and the non-voting messenger, there were 29 members whose 'Yes' votes were openly bought with cash. These did not include those additional voters whose names are not individually recorded on the financially corrupted list, nor those who received distinctions and various benefits in kind for their support of the Union. What we do know is that a substantial sum was secretly transferred for immediate use through the Scottish Treasury from England; this was the money received by Queensbury and the nominal list. Numerous personal debts were extinguished for others, and a separate fund was put aside for compliant members' pensions. It is very apparent that the number of members bribed to vote in favour of the Union was considerably greater than the contrived majority which caused the *Treaty of Union* to be passed on 16 January 1707.

Given in Appendix III is the list of 'for' and 'against' contenders in the vote concerning the Union of Parliaments. It is interesting to note that around 68 per cent of the Nobles voted in favour of the Union, while the Barons and Burgesses were far more evenly divided. Precisely how many of the originally anti-Union members switched their allegiance for personal reward is unknown, but those who resisted the temptation also resisted the Queen's armed soldiers, who were present to intimidate the House.

Farewell to all our Scottish fame,
Farewell our ancient glory.
Farewell even to the Scottish name,
So famed in martial story.

But faith and power! To my last hour,
I make this declaration:
We're bought and sold for English gold.
Such a parcel of rogues in a nation!

Robert Burns

So it was that Queen Anne got her way despite the *Bill of Security*, and from 1 May 1707 the Scottish Parliament was no longer active. The crowns of Scotland and England were not simply united, they became 'one' as Westminster took control of the conjoined kingdom of 'Great Britain' under the terms of the *Treaty of Union*.

JAMES VIII

When the Union was formalized, and the 'Three Estates' dissolved, 16 Scottish peers were selected for the House of Lords in London, and only 45 Scottish seats were granted in the House of Commons. (Prior to the Union, Scotland had 305 elected members.) In May 1707 this blatant anti-Scots discrimination prompted the angered Scottish Covenanters to officially depose Queen Anne, and at the Mercat Cross in Edinburgh they proclaimed her exiled half-brother (James Francis Edward Stuart) King James VIII of Scots. The Presbyterian Covenanters cared nothing for the individual religious persuasion of their King, and (together with the similarly Protestant Episcopalians) they sought only to preserve their traditional Royal House without the confining yoke of English supremacy. Historically, true Jacobitism became apparent from that moment. This was not because the Stuarts were in exile, but because the 1707 *Treaty of Union* and the abolition of the 'Three Estates' Parliament were illegal under Scottish Law. The familiar Jacobite tartan emerged

1 (*left*) Malcolm Canmore welcoming Margaret Atheling at Queensferry in 1066. (Painted by William Hole, 1846–1917.)

2 (*right*) The Battle of Stirling Bridge, 1297. Following a Scots victory, Sir William Wallace was appointed Guardian of the Realm. (William Hole.)

3 Edinburgh Castle – the birthplace of King James VI of Scots.

4 Lochleven Castle, where Mary, Queen of Scots, signed her abdication under duress.

5 Stirling Castle – the dowry of the consorts of the Stewart Kings.

6 Arbroath Abbey, where the 1320 *Declaration of Arbroath* was signed.

7 *The Forgotten Monarchy of Scotland* – by Chevalier Peter Robson, Court Painter to the Royal House of Stewart.

(*see* Appendix XV on page 482 for details of characters portrayed)

8 Prince and Princess Julius of Annandale (with their daughter Renée, Lady Derneley), entertained by the Mayor of Brussels on their 50th wedding anniversary in 1982.

9 Prince Michael and the Honours of Scotland, 1990.

10 *Bonnie Prince Charlie* – Equestrian portrait by Anne Grahame Johnstone.

11 HRH Prince Michael of Albany – official portrait, 1997.

at that time, to be worn as shawls and dresses by women, and as kilts or trews by men. The wearing of this tartan was expressly designed to demonstrate a national protest against the Scots' subjugation to the unlawful Union of the Parliaments.

The document bearing the Scottish parliamentary assent to unite with England was not signed in Parliament House as is commonly believed, but in an Edinburgh cellar at the corner of North Bridge and the Royal Mile. Before adding their signatures, the ministers retired to lunch, taking the document with them. But on making their way to the Castle, with the document carried before them on a cushion, they were confronted by a large number of enraged citizens. At first the people shouted their disapproval, but almost immediately they turned to physical action against their betrayers. With the mob close on their heels, the ministers found refuge and barricaded themselves in the cellar, where the instrument of betrayal was duly signed. The ministers were then firmly trapped, and it took some hours for a troop of soldiers to secure their release.

With the imposition of the Treaty, the cross-Border trade restrictions were relaxed, and the Scots were allowed to keep their own Kirk, along with their separate legal system. But then came a series of wholly new impositions to purposely disadvantage the Scots against the English. The disproportionate tax implemented on income from manufactured linen provides a good example; this was of little concern in the south, but linen was a major industry in Scotland.

Parliament Adjourned

Copies of the unacceptable Articles of the Treaty were openly burned in Scottish cities, towns and villages. An ambassador was then sent to Paris, inviting the *de jure* James VIII to re-establish his inheritance in Scotland, but the scheme came to nothing. Accompanied by 6,000 troopers, James made the passage from Dunkirk, and reached the Firth of Forth in March 1708. However, the winds were contrary, and the English Navy lay in wait, so the campaign was abandoned. Once returned to France, James entered into military service and won his spurs at Oudenaarde and Malplaquet in the War of Spanish Succession.

It is interesting to note that the Minutes of the last Parliament of Scotland do not record the institution as terminated. They simply state, 'Parliament adjourned'. The first act of the newly-styled British Parliament was the supposed ratification of the *Treaty of Union* by 1 May 1707. On that date, the Union became effective, and Scotland's Parliament was postponed – yet the records indicate that the new Parliament did not actually ratify the Treaty.[5] Hence, the Union is no more than a theoretical entity, and by the standards of Scottish and International Law Scotland's Parliament is merely dormant, as against being extinct. In practice, it could always have been legally recalled by the people at any time.

PART FOUR

The Jacobite Struggle

12

THE HOUSE OF HANOVER

The German Nomination

Perhaps surprising to many is the fact that, during the 18th-century Jacobite campaigns, Presbyterians worked hand-in-hand with the Jesuit Order in an attempt to restore the Stuarts to their ancestral throne. Similarly, the Scottish Episcopal Church and the Presbyterian Cameronians joined forces to promote a Stuart return to Scotland.

Religion was plainly no divider of the Scottish nation; on the contrary, the active denominational unification added a particular strength and impetus to the Jacobite cause. Queen Anne realized this, and when making her will she decided to bow to the general feeling by forsaking her earlier German nomination, and declaring her half-brother James Stuart as her chosen heir. From that moment, Anne declined to sign any document with her own name alone; she always added James's proxy signature as well.[1] This action was assisted by the fact that the anti-Union Tories held the upper hand for a while, and when Queen Anne died on 1 August 1714 the Tory ministers ruled that her wishes should be honoured. However, the proceedings were delayed while the Whigs regained their supremacy, and disregarding Anne's last will they enacted her earlier 1705 nomination. As a result, Sophia's son, Georg Von Brunswick, Elector of Hanover, duly arrived in London to take the crown as King George I.

North of the Border passions were understandably roused, and the Scots quickly nicknamed George I the 'Wee wee German lairdie'. Clan-by-clan, the Jacobites united, wearing their emblem of Stuart support, the 'White Cockade' (*see* Jacobite Clans in Appendix IV). King George's contemporaries in both Germany and England depicted him as a cold, selfish libertine, and one lady of the English Court referred to him as 'an honest blockhead, who spoke no English, nor ever learnt any, and who showed no inclination whatsoever to meet his new subjects'.

Although designated King of England, George openly mistrusted the English since they had already rid themselves of two kings in the previous 65 years. He preferred, therefore, to rely on his German ministers, and spent most of his time in Hanover. But what manner of man is it that divorces his wife, and then imprisons her in the Castle of Ahlden for 32 years, to die without ever seeing her children again! He accused her of adultery, but was quite content to retain his own buxom mistresses. During the reign of George I, the Government was managed by wholesale bribery and the unabashed manipulation of parliamentary seats. This was the main reason for the creation of an embryonic parliamentary 'Opposition' in the 1730s.

The 'Fifteen'

George I of Hanover may well have suited England's Whig aristocracy and the die-hard Anglican clergy, but he was not welcomed by the Tories or in the Jacobite north. Soon after King George's coronation, James Francis Edward Stuart was proclaimed the rightful King of Scots for the third time in Aberdeen, Brechin, Dundee, Montrose, Perth, St Andrews and Edinburgh. He then sailed again from Dunkirk on his second voyage to Scotland.

In September 1715, James VIII's standard was raised at Braemar, and the Jacobites captured Inverness and Perth. But they failed to take Edinburgh Castle which, along with Stirling, kept the Earl of Mar busy against the Duke of Argyll's Government troops. South of the Border, the Earl of Derwentwater and others mustered the English Jacobites, but within a few weeks the Rising was pretty well over. The southern Jacobite army surrendered at Preston, Lancashire, on 14 November, while in the north, Mar was prevented from moving below Sherriffmuir. There is little point in dwelling on the 'Fifteen' except to say that, despite its outward enthusiasm, it was one of the worst campaigns ever organized. By the time that King James landed in Scotland, the battles of Sherriffmuir and Preston had already been fought, and although both sides had claimed victory at the former, the Jacobites were well and truly contained by the Hanoverian troops.

Having landed at Peterhead on 22 December, James Francis was taken ill, and did not reach Perth until 9 January 1716. He then journeyed with the deflated Earl of Mar to Scone, where he was destined to be crowned in spite of the Scots' failure to topple England's new King. But of all things, the elders of the National Kirk required James's individual Oath of Allegiance, and James refused to swear his indulgence away solely to the Presbyterians. Such a discriminatory requirement was no better than the Anglican practice in England, and James maintained that it was contrary to the Scots Constitution. While the argument prevailed, the Duke of Argyll was nearing Scone with his army, and rather than lose their King to a Campbell axe, the Jacobites hurriedly returned him, uncrowned, to France.

Prior to the inglorious Rising, James's younger sister Louise had died of smallpox in 1712, and this left James and his mother, Mary of Modena, as the only survivors of the Royal Family in exile. King Louis XIV, therefore, pressed the Jacobite party to find a suitable bride for their King *de jure*, since an heir was vital to the succession. The names of various well-connected women were put forward, but James was uninspired, being more concerned with looks and personality. He was particularly fond of his cousin Benedicta d'Este, Duchess of Modena, the daughter of his great-uncle Rinaldo III. Sadly for James, Rinaldo would have none of it because James's position as an uncrowned monarch was not that impressive. Louis XIV of France then suggested that Princess Maria Clementina Sobieska of Poland would make a suitable Queen.[2]

Maria Clementina and her grandmother, the legendary Maryenska Sobieska (Marie Casimire Louise de la Grange, Princess d'Arquien), were then residing at the Château de Blois, near Paris. Through her grandmother, Maria Clementina was French, and King Louis was very satisfied with his choice, especially since she had the looks and personality to please James. Maria's mother, Hedwige Elizabeth of Pfalz-Neuburg, was a younger sister of the dowager Empress of Austria, and Maria's maternal aunts were similarly influential. One aunt was Maria Anna, dowager Queen of Spain – the widow of King Carlos II Habsburg, and mother of the illegitimate Comte de Saint Germain. Another was Dorothea Sophie, Duchess of Parma – the mother of Queen Elizabeth of Spain, and wife of Philip V, grandson of Louis XIV.

Maria Clementina's uncle, Karl III Philip, became the Elector Palatine, while his younger brothers, Alexander Sigismund and Franz Ludwig, were respectively Bishop of Augsburg and Archbishop of Trier. Through her paternal aunt Therese Kunigunde, Electress of Bavaria, Maria had important connections with the Court of Munich, and she was also a first cousin to both the Emperor and the Queen of Portugal. On the financial front, Maria Clementina's prospects were significant, and the entire fortune of the Sobieski family of Poland was settled equally between her and her sister Marie Charlotte. It comprised a vast fortune of cash, jewellery and estates, plus a claim to the Polish Crown. All things considered Maria Clementina seemed the perfect choice for James, but the Jacobite party advisers declined the idea of marriage. They determined that the proposed Sobieski wedlock would not be of any great advantage to the Stuarts at that particular time – and so the plan was shelved.

The year of James's 1715 campaign had also seen the tragedy of Louis XIV's death, and the beginning of decline for the House of Bourbon. His 72-year reign was the longest in French history, and he is still fondly remembered as the 'Sun King'. On behalf of his people, Louis XIV was the constant challenger of the Holy Roman Empire and Papal supremacy. Indeed, through no other era has France shone with such a brilliance of intellect, art and architecture. Unfortunately Louis' longest-surviving son by Queen Maria Theresa had predeceased him in 1711, and other family deaths from smallpox left only a five-year-old great-grandson to succeed. Louis XIV's France was undoubtedly the world's foremost nation – but this legacy was destined to crumble into ashes during the balance of the 18th century.

Contrary to Louis' will, Philip, Duke of Orléans, became Regent during the minority of young Louis XV, and this era sowed the original seeds of decadent rule by the aristocrats of the latter Bourbon era. Louis XIV had long been at war with Holland in an attempt to reduce their maritime monopoly[3], and this had been very hard on the French Treasury. However, Philip sacked all the experienced Government ministers, and replaced them with his own incompetent friends, so that by 1720 the State was actually bankrupt. Given that France was unable to continue her trading effort against England and Holland, a 'Triple Alliance' had been struck in 1717, and in order to placate King George I of Britain, the unscrupulous Regent unlawfully expelled James VIII Stuart from France.

On this occasion it was Pope Clement XI who held out his hand to James Francis Edward. Despite the historical ups and downs between the Scots and the Papacy, Clement had long admired the tenacity of the Stuart Kings, and he was deeply in awe of the loyal Jacobite network. It was indeed fortuitous that a kindly Pope was installed at the time, and he duly welcomed James into Italy, greeting him with all honours as the rightful King of Great Britain, France and Ireland. Moreover, since the Stuart misfortunes were largely due to matters of the Faith, Clement offered James the Palace of Urbino and a pension of 12,000 scudi (about £192,000 in today's value).[4] In truth, James's personal Catholicism did not equate at all with the Roman variety; it was more of the style adopted by Henry VIII Tudor when he separated the English Church from Rome. Even so, this proved to be no barrier to Pope Clement, and James Stuart gladly accepted the residential offer.

Urbino was very impressive, standing high and almost inaccessible on a great outcrop of rock. However, the Duchy of Urbino was itself quite small, and the inhabitants were accustomed to a gentle daily routine which seldom included a lord of the manor. Curious, they awoke from their usual inactivity and made their way to welcome the new arrival, who had lived very informally at Saint Germain and always enjoyed entertaining company. James found his new neighbours much to his liking, and he was well received in turn, so that life was generally comfortable enough for a while – until 18 May 1718. On that unfortunate day a courier galloped his breathless horse up the hill, bringing sad tidings to the palace gate: at the age of 61 James's mother, Mary of Modena, had died at the Château de Saint Germain-én-Laye.

Stuart and Sobieski

Mary Beatrix's final months had been very cruel to her; she had suffered from terminal cancer, and apart from the physical pain she had been without her son and closest friend in her last days. Mary had hoped to see James succeed where his father had failed, but she had witnessed only another chapter of misfortune. At his mother's express wish, James had not been informed of her fast decline, and the news of her death took him very much by surprise – unlike her last written message. In a hurried note she reminded him once again of the importance of marriage and succession. The Royal House of Stewart had prevailed for nearly 350 years, and had held the reins of Scots kingship for more than 500 years. However, James was the last surviving heir, and it was essential that he considered the future – so the search for a royal bride was renewed.

Since James was still not quite 30, there was no immediate panic; yet even Pope Clement recognized that the Queen's death was best compensated by a new birth. In applying himself to the matter, Clement's own considered choice was none other than Maria Clementina of Poland, the very same Princess Sobieska who had been selected three years earlier by Louis XIV. As the granddaughter of the popular King Jan III Sobieski, Maria Clementina's heritage was impeccable and, along with her sister, she was the richest princess in Christendom. Her temperament appeared well-suited to James's easy-going nature, and her father, Prince Louis James Sobieski, Castellan of Crakow, was most agreeable to the union.

So early in 1719 the betrothal of James VIII and Maria Clementina was arranged, and James set out to meet his future bride at Ferrara. His impending marriage was unwelcome news in England, and King George I urged the Holy Roman Emperor, Charles VI, to prevent any wedlock between the Houses of Stuart and Sobieski. George of Hanover perceived that such an alliance (supported by the Pope, the Elector of Bavaria, and the Elector Palatine) would considerably enhance Stuart prestige in Europe. The Papal States were therefore threatened with full-scale invasion by the English Navy. In the face of this threat, Emperor Charles had Maria Clementina and her mother seized at Innsbruck, where they were confined in a German convent.

Emperor Charles VI was not personally against the Stuart-Sobieski marriage, but he was politically constrained by the recent 'Quadruple Alliance' between England, France, Holland and Austria. By virtue of this political arrangement he could not be seen to stand against the Hanoverian Court of Saint James.

Although Maria Clementina and her mother were kept under house arrest, they had been forewarned of the Innsbruck seizure by Maria Clementina's uncles, Karl III Philip (Elector Palatine) and Alexander Sigismund (Bishop of Augsburg). They, in turn, had been advised by their sister, the dowager Empress Eleanore, who was the mother of Emperor Charles VI. Despite her son's action, she acted very openly in favour of the Polish princesses, laying plans for their escape.[5] Hence Emperor Charles was perceived to comply with the British Government's wishes, even though a rescue plan was being organized by his mother.

At the same time, following ongoing hostilities in the Mediterranean, the Spanish decided to invade Britain, and they duly sent word to the Pope that King James VIII's presence was required. In late February 1719 James landed at the Porto di Rosso, near Barcelona, and was greeted by King Philip V of Spain. Early in March the Spanish fleet sailed from Cadiz; the winds were favourable to begin, and the armada was suitably prepared for success. On the next day, the Jacobite Duke of Ormonde sailed from San Sebastian with arms, money, supplies and additional troops, while the Earl Marischal, George Keith, created diversions in Scotland. Leading Jacobites also sailed from France to meet with Marischal on the Isle of Lewis, but fierce storms beset and scattered the Spanish fleet near Cape Finisterre. In the event the weather was so bad that the ships were forced to return home, taking James with them.

Yet again Jacobite hopes were dashed in Scotland, but on the Isle of Lewis the unsuspecting Marischal joined forces with the Marquis of Tullibardine, and they sailed their troops to the mainland with plans to assault Inverness. The Hanoverians had been forewarned, however, and the city garrison was reinforced, while the Navy blocked any retreat by sea. For a short while the Jacobites held out at Glenshiel, but surrendered for want of the anticipated Spanish support. Marischal and Tullibardine then returned to the Continent and, once more, an ill-planned Rising against the German overlord had failed.

Rome and the Palazzo Muti

Thanks to the Irish knight Sir Charles Wogan, Chevalier de Saint Germain (and his romantically styled 'Three Musketeers', Misset, Gaydon and O'Toole), Maria Clementina and her mother were freed from their confinement, and the former was safely conducted to Rome. Once there, she was attended by the Scotsman John Walkinshaw, Laird of Barrowfield, and she met also with the Pope. While awaiting James's return from Spain, Maria Clementina took residence at the Convent of the White Ursuline where, using the style Madama di San Gorgio[6], she was visited by cardinals, princes, ambassadors and the Roman aristocracy.

The royal couple were eventually married on 3 September 1719 at the Italian Cathedral of Monte Fiascone. Pope Clement's wedding gift was the Palazzo Muti in Rome, which became the new Stuart residence, and on 31 December 1720 Maria Clementina gave birth to their first child, Prince Charles Edward Louis John Casimir Silvester Severino Maria Stuart, Prince of Wales, Duke of Rothesay. Five years later, on 6 March 1725, their second son was born; he was Prince Henry Benedict Maria Clement Thomas Francis Xavier Stuart, Duke of York. Subsequent to this Maria Clementina was twice pregnant, but miscarried each time.

Although seemingly well suited, there was one area of constant dispute between James and Maria Clementina. James, like his father, was religiously tolerant, but Maria Clementina was not: she was an ardent daughter of the Roman Church, to the extent that she even objected to having Protestants in her service. James found solace in the more liberal company of the Duchess of Inverness and, soon after Henry's birth, word spread in Rome of the King's affair. Queen Maria Clementina promptly packed her bags, and in November 1725 she entered the Convent of Santa Cecilia. There is little doubt that there was a liaison between the King and the Duchess, although the extent of the relationship is unknown. James, nevertheless, endeavoured to suppress the rumours in order to regain his wife, and Maria Clementina returned to the Palazzo Muti. Her return was strictly conditional, though, and she insisted that the Duke and Duchess of Inverness be dismissed, along with all the other Protestants of her Court.

Descent to Charles Edward Stuart

JAMES V (STEWART) OF SCOTS
b 1512 R 1513–42 d 1542 Falkland
= 2nd 1538 Marie de Guise-Lorraine
d 1560 dau of Claude, Duc de Guise

|

MARY (STUART) QUEEN OF SCOTS
b 1542 R 1542–67 (abdicated)
Beheaded 1587 Fotheringhay Castle
= 2nd 1565 Henry Stewart, Lord Darnley
Duke of Albany, Master of Lennox, murdered 1567

|

JAMES VI (STUART) OF SCOTS
b 1566 R 1567–1625 d 1625 Herts
JAMES I OF ENGLAND 1603–25
= 1589 Anne d 1619 dau of
King Frederick II of Denmark & Norway

|

CHARLES I (STUART) OF BRITAIN
b 1600 R 1625–49 Beheaded 1649 London
= 1625 Henriette Marie d 1669
dau of King Henri IV of France

|

JAMES VII (STUART) OF SCOTS (II OF ENGLAND)
b 1633 R 1685–8 (deposed, Whig Revolution)
(Succeeded brother, Charles II Stuart)
d Saint Germain 1701
= 2nd 1673 Mary Beatrix D'Este d 1718
Dau of Duke Alphonso IV of Modena (Italy)

|

JAMES FRANCIS EDWARD STUART (JAMES VIII OF SCOTS)
(Chevalier Saint George) b 1688 Proclaimed 1701 d 1766
= *1719 Maria Clementina Sobieska d 1735 dau of Prince*
James Lewis Sobieski (son of King Jan III of Poland)

|

CHARLES EDWARD LOUIS PHILIP CASIMIR STUART (CHARLES III OF SCOTS)
b 31 Dec 1720. Symbolically crowned 22 Sept 1745. Succeeded 1766. d 31 Jan 1788
= (1) *Clementina Walkinshaw of Barrowfield, Comtesse d'Alberstroff (refuted 1766)*
= (2) *1772 Princess Louise de Stolberg-Guedern (divorced 1784)*
= (3) *1785 Marguerite de Lussan, Comtesse de Massillan d 1820*

The royal marriage displayed little harmony from that time, and Maria Clementina's unduly pious devotion led her into a life of extreme abstinence. By 1734 she had become very frail, and she died on 18 January 1735. Her funeral was august in the traditional Roman fashion, and she lay in state at the Church of the Holy Apostles, to be buried in the garb of a nun. Her Papal devotion was to have a lasting effect on her younger son Henry, but not so on Prince Charles Edward, who eventually renounced the troublesome Roman religion in favour of the Anglican faith.

13

Culloden Moor

The 'Forty-five'

James's health and spirits began to decline after the Queen's death, and in view of his ill-fated campaigns he became rather less confident about his own role in the Scottish endeavour. In consequence, the Jacobite adherents began to fix their hopes upon his sons, Charles Edward and Henry Benedict. The princes were both mentally and physically active, showing considerable promise in their early years. It had been observed that, unlike his father, young Charles Edward resembled the earlier members of his family, and his gentle but high-spirited disposition made him a great favourite at Court. Even in his youth Charles despised the lazy, effeminate habits of his Roman peers, and whenever granted leisure from his studies he preferred the outdoor life. Seemingly impervious to the Italian sun and heavy rains, he would be out from dawn till dusk, returning home blistered with heat, or wet through from a day's shooting in the Campagna. At a very young age he was adept on horseback, and by the age of six had learnt to shoot accurately with a crossbow. In 1734, aged only 13, Prince Charles had his first battle experience at Gaeta, fighting for the King of Naples. Though complimented for his courage, it is worth noting that those few days of conflict were the full extent of his military experience before landing at Loch nan Uamh, near Moidart, on 25 July 1745, to begin his Scottish Rising.

Charles entered the wider social arena in his 17th year, embarking on a tour of northern Italy with a few colleagues and attendants. The trip was a great success, and he was granted full royal honours throughout, with security guards placed at his disposal. In Bologna the Prince was received by a deputation from the Senate; in Venice he was greeted by the Doge in person, and invited to the Assembly of the Grand Council, as well as being afforded the French Ambassador's personal gondola. In Genoa and Milan he was lavishly entertained with grand receptions, and he was the centre of interest from Piacenza to Florence, where he stayed at the Palazzo Corsini. Returning to Rome by way of Lucca, Pisa and Leghorn, his journey was one of continual popularity and triumph – but the British Government agents watched his every move with interest and trepidation.

In 1727 George II of Hanover had succeeded his father in Britain, only to display the same lack of learning and wit. But, despite moves from the Tory benches to bring James III Stuart back to Britain, the Whig aristocrats were content that George was equally as manageable as his father, and was therefore more suited to their self-serving interests. By that time the Whigs considered that they controlled not only the King and the people, but the rest of the world, and in 1742 a new national song emerged: *Rule Britannia; Britannia rule the waves*.

This was all very well for those living off the ill-gotten fat of their fast-growing Empire across the waves – but what about the people at home? There were no drains in the unlit, garbage-strewn streets, and in London only one child in four lived to become an adult. There were no welfare or employment rights, no representation for people at large in Parliament, and no general education system apart from the charity schools run by Jacobites and Tory benefactors. So much for '*Britons never never never shall be slaves*'! The British people were already slaves, treated no better than the misused workers in King George's colonial plantations abroad.

George II meddled in politics, and flaunted his burly German mistresses, but his greatest claims to notoriety were his irrational outbursts of wrath. When others disagreed with him they were violently kicked, and then had to thank him for the privilege! If people were not available to assault, this tempestuous king would boot whatever else was in range. Not surprisingly, in 1740, Charles Edward Stuart declared that he would try once more to regain the British kingdoms for his father. His brother

Henry had no such ambition, though, for his heart was set more firmly towards Rome than Scotland.

Four years later, Charles left Italy for France, where he stayed for a year, planning the most impressive of all attempts at a Stuart Restoration – an incredible campaign which has become one of the most debated events of British history. From quite small beginnings, the venture grew to an almost complete reconquering of the island; but it then transformed into a strategic retreat, culminating in the unforgettable Jacobite defeat at Culloden.

CHARLES III

Having learned their lesson at the attempted coronation of James VIII, the Scottish Kirk elders had accepted the principle of Stuart toleration by the time Charles Edward first arrived in 1745. On Sunday 22 September, following his victory at the Battle of Prestonpans, the clergy were wholly supportive when representatives of the Presbyterian, Catholic and Episcopal Churches were united to witness and approve the figurative crowning of King Charles III. The proceedings were conducted within the precincts of the Abbey of Holyrood House by the Episcopalian Rev William Harper of Old Saint Paul's, Edinburgh. (He was described in a Commissioners of Excise report dated 7 May 1745

Holyrood House

as, 'William Harper, Episcopal Minister at Bothkiner ... very active in aiding and assisting the rebels, and waited for the Pretender's son at Falkirk'.)

Since the Crown and Honours of Scotland were held by the Hanoverian Court, a substitute laurel wreath was placed on Charles's head by Laurence Oliphant of Gask. Oliphant's *Memoir* confirms that, earlier that day, a preparation for this event had been made at Charles Edward's State apartment, where the laurel crown lay in readiness. Indeed, all Edinburgh was in a fever of excitement, and Charles had already been proclaimed King by members of the Lyon Court who, needless to say, lost their jobs because of it.

It was evident to those assembled that Charles was the necessary catalyst to weigh the balance of Scotland's crippled nationhood. As a King, he could restore Parliament and the Constitution, and he was similarly determined that the English people should be afforded identical rights of political and religious freedom. In his first proclamation, issued in Edinburgh, 9 October 1745, Charles Edward stated, 'With respect to the pretended Union of the two nations, the King cannot possibly ratify it, since he has had repeated remonstrances against it from each kingdom'.

In the Audience Room of Holyrood Palace, on Tuesday 24 September 1745, King Charles III was invested as Grand Master of the Order of the Temple of Jerusalem. In this regard, he succeeded the Order's Regent, James Murray, Duke of Atholl, who had held the reins since the death of Grand Master John Erskine, Earl of Mar. It is recorded in the *Statutes of the Order of the Temple* that, on taking his vow in the presence of ten Knights, Charles declared, 'You may be sure that, when I truly come into my own, I will raise the Order to what it was in the days of William the Lion' (King of Scots 1165–1214).

It is often suggested that the Battle of Culloden was the inevitable conclusion of a defeat which began at Derby, but this perception is manifestly wrong, for there was no defeat at Derby: the Jacobite army simply retraced their steps northward. In point of fact, the Jacobites were never closer to completing their victory than when they engaged the Duke of Cumberland on 16 April 1746. At that stage Charles III faced his enemy with two significant victories behind him, and a force of loyal men who had not previously lost a single battle. First General Cope at Prestonpans, and then General Hawley at Falkirk, had capitulated against the Jacobite onset, and the Scots had constantly eluded General Wade. The important feature of the Falkirk battle was that it was fought *after* the Scots had returned to the north from Derby. The Duke of Cumberland was, therefore, the Government's last hope, since the Hanoverians had no recourse if he also failed them. Had Charles won at Culloden, he could have marched to London virtually unopposed.

With Perth, Edinburgh, Carlisle and Manchester already behind them by 1 December 1745, the Jacobites made their much debated retreat from Derby. But they could well have crossed the country and seized the capital with some ease – or so it is reckoned. Although Sir John Ligonier's Hanoverian cavalry and infantry had been recalled from Flanders to protect the Midlands and the route to London, there were actually few Government troops to hinder the Scots advance, but the Jacobite commanders could not be sure of this. Hanoverian propaganda suggested a very different state of affairs, even though the Duke of Cumberland had been temporarily diverted towards Stafford.

Whatever the case, Charles always knew he would have to confront Cumberland's men if his mission was to succeed. Having marched from Scotland to Derby without such a confrontation, the Jacobites were fully aware that the Duke was still at large and, numerically, his military weight was superior. Let us suppose that Charles had moved successfully to London from Derby – what then? If the main Hanoverian force was not encountered *en route*, it would soon appear. Charles would then have to await the combined might of General Wade and the Duke. For any number of reasons, London was no place for a final battle, certainly not a battle which the Prince might lose.

The Jacobites had long been anxious to engage General Wade's northern force, which had not yet managed to intercept them, although known to be moving south-west from Newcastle. The Scots also knew that Cumberland was heading westwards. What they did not want was to meet them both at once on alien fighting ground, whether at Derby, on the road, or in London. Lord George Murray, therefore, proposed an organized retreat, and the Clan chiefs agreed to his practical strategy. In military terms there can be no doubt that this logistical manoeuvre offered a better chance of ultimate success, even though Charles Edward was personally shocked at the idea. With the Welsh and English Jacobite reinforcements slow to arrive, it was plain that Murray was correct in his judgement; by moving back to the north, the Scots stood some chance of swelling their ranks while dictating some of their own battle terms. For the most part, the strategy worked; additional French troops had landed in Scotland, and new Jacobite recruits were indeed forthcoming.

The northward pursuit began on 7 December 1745; Cumberland overtook Wade in the chase, but Murray's Scots rearguard defeated his advance party at Clifton. The Scots then left their Manchester Regiment to defend Carlisle, and moved north again in fierce weather conditions. This bought them some good time, and once Cumberland had taken Carlisle, he returned south to meet an anticipated French invasion. General Hawley remained on the Jacobites' heels, and his dragoons joined with Wade's men and others in Edinburgh. Meanwhile, the Jacobites besieged Stirling Castle. With the Government's northern troops split from Cumberland's army, the Jacobite strategy was effective enough, and on 17 January 1746 Charles Edward defeated Hawley at Falkirk. Hawley retreated to Edinburgh, while George Murray took his men back to Stirling. So far, so good – but the return to Stirling was a positive blunder, though perhaps not necessarily disastrous at that stage.

Defeat at Drummossie

After the Falkirk success, some of the Jacobites were in favour of pursuing the remnants of Hawley's army, while others favoured an immediate march to London. A third faction maintained they should first cement their position at Stirling, so as to secure communications in the north. An engineer, Mirabelle de Gordon, was said to be responsible for persuading the Prince to take the last course, as a result of which three valuable weeks were lost, during which time Cumberland arrived in Edinburgh. At this, Charles Edward saw his chance to confront the Duke, but Murray advocated a regrouping further north to seize the Highland forts in the winter. Having had little success at Stirling, the Prince reluctantly agreed, particularly since he was informed that his army had suffered a large number of desertions. However, by way of a subsequent muster at Crieff, Charles discovered that those who had left to rejoin their families were fewer than had been intimated, and his relationship with Lord Murray became increasingly strained thereafter. That apart, they marched onwards to Inverness, and were successful in defeating the troops of Lord Loudon on 18 February. Within a few days, Cumberland's army was at Aberdeen, and his additional Hessian soldiers had arrived from Germany to defend Perth.

In March, independent clan regiments captured Fort Augustus, and pursued Loudon into Sutherland, taking Dornoch. Loudon fled to Skye, and Murray raided Blair Castle, but meanwhile a north-western landing of French arms and Jacobite supplies was intercepted. Early in April the outlying Scots detachments were recalled to Inverness in readiness to confront Cumberland, who was at Nairn by 14 April. The Jacobites then marched by night to surprise the Duke's men, but could not reach Nairn before day-break, and so they took up their position on Drummossie Moor (*see* Appendix IV). This was certainly not an army in retreat, for despite a few disappointments they had experienced victories in battles and skirmishes alike on the way south and after their return to Scotland. Their appetites were suitably whetted, and they were eager enough to meet the supreme Hanoverian commander on their own home-ground. In practice, however, their immediate enemy was not the Duke of Cumberland, but hunger and tiredness – and from that moment of arrival at Drummossie Moor, Culloden, judgements began to fail.

Initially, three suggestions were made: the first was to decline from engagement until they had rested and eaten. Some men, therefore, vacated the camp in search of food, leaving others to await reinforcements which were known to be on the way. The second suggestion was to fall back to better ground south of Nairn Water. Thirdly, it was proposed that Cumberland should be attacked before he had time to bring his men to order – but this decision was delayed for too long. And so the 5,000-strong Jacobite army confronted their ready enemy without the necessary reinforcements, and on the most unsuitable terrain. The Scots were already exhausted, and many were half asleep, while others were still absent foraging for food. For some unaccountable reason, Charles relied on a blind faith in the abilities of his clansmen, but they faced a refreshed and well-fed force of some 9,000 men. The enemy ranks contained regiments of dragoons, foot, and militia with heavy guns. Clearly, the Scots' task was impossible, and the rest of the story is legend.

The true significance of Culloden is not that it was the culminating point of defeat, but that it could well have been the final threshold of victory. Disaster did not begin at Derby as is so often suggested – it began and ended at Culloden. Had the Stuart Cause triumphed at that time, King James VIII fully intended to abdicate in favour of his popular son Charles Edward, who had been symbolically crowned in readiness during the previous year. Long before this James had already issued a *Royal Declaration and Regency Commission* in December 1743 (*see* transcript in Appendix V). If Charles had become King, British history would have taken a different course, and such was the panic which had beset the House of Hanover when the Jacobites were in Derby that George II had even loaded the Crown Jewels onto a Thames barge, in readiness for a quick and ignominious getaway to Germany. 'Your ancestor was quite wrong', said the later King George V to Lord Murray of Atholl, 'the Jacobite army should have continued straight on to London, and a Stuart would be today's King of Scotland and England, with each country having its own Parliament'.

With the Stuarts restored, the American War of Independence would never have been necessary. It was additionally well within the bounds of possibility that (with the Bourbons in decline) Charles would also have become King of France – not just in theory but in practice. The long and painful martyrdom of Ireland would certainly have been averted; the decline of Scotland into a provincial appendage of England would have been avoided, and national religious toleration would have been an early achievement. The harsh community exploitation of the industrial age would never have occurred, and the hideous Victorian 'poor houses' would have been unknown. People would have been educated and encouraged instead of suppressed, and a Written Constitution would have been implemented to protect the civil rights and liberties of all. But as fate would have it, these prospects were all dashed by the supporters of German autocrats, whose establishment is still defended by a dictatorial parliamentary institution that has failed everyone.

Once removed from the battlefield of Culloden, Charles was destined to be helped and hidden by all concerned. Despite the impressive price of £30,000 on his head [over £2m in today's terms], he was never betrayed, and while in the Hebrides (during which period Flora MacDonald aided his escape to Skye) the Scots insisted that he had returned to France. When Charles was back in the Highlands, his pursuers were diverted to the east coast, while on 20 September he sailed from the west coast aboard the French corvette, *l'Heureux*. The ship left for the Isle of Rathlin, and then continued to North Donegal. At that stage, although Charles realized he had lost a significant battle, he still thought he had another chance, and with this in view he had organized a future rendezvous with the Scottish chiefs at Fort William.[1] The plan was for French ships to launch a mainland assault from the Irish coast, but Louis XV preferred that the bold Chevalier be repatriated to France. And so the 'Forty-five' was well and truly at an end – or was it?

Subjugation of the Highlands

On 15 May 1746 it was decreed that all Jacobite prisoners should be taken to England for their trials, specifically to London, York and Carlisle. Away from the jurisdiction of the Scottish courts, the trials were superficial, and the sentences brutal. In London, the prisoners were hanged and publicly disembowelled, after which their severed heads were placed on the railings at Temple Bar. At St Margaret's Court, the Justice proclaimed that his victims must be

> severally hanged by the neck, but not till they be dead, for they must be cut down alive; their bowels must be taken out and burned before their faces; then their heads must be severed from their bodies, and their bodies severally divided into four quarters; and these must be at the King's disposal.

While Charles Edward was busy avoiding his pursuers between April and September 1746, the Duke of Cumberland had continued the battle, way beyond the confines of Culloden Moor. A *Disarming Act* was passed, along with other statutes which banned the wearing of Highland dress, the playing of pipes, and the use of Scots Gaelic. Indeed, bagpipes were specifically denoted as 'instruments of war'. Even the traditional Clan System was overturned by the abolition of heritable jurisdictions[2], and General Hawley was instructed to pursue and exterminate the wounded Jacobites.

Meanwhile, from a base at Inverness, the Duke organized a course of brutal subjugation across the land, and no one was safe from the vicious reprisals of the Highland Clearances. From glen to glen men, women, children, livestock and property were all ruthlessly assaulted by Cumberland's marauding soldiers. Back in London there were executions galore – beheadings and hangings, while numerous victims were drawn and quartered. Close to 1,000 Scotsmen were sold into slavery abroad, and others simply disappeared without trace. Such was the unwarranted savagery of it all that there was no regimental pride in claiming the Battle Honour, and no regiment in the British Army presently carries Culloden on its Battle Colours. The Westminster Government did originally strike a medal for issue to the troops after Culloden, but in the aftermath of Cumberland's brutal Clearances, the medal was withdrawn. Consequently, the romantic *Bonnie Prince Charlie* is remembered with fond emotion, but King George's son William Augustus, Duke of Cumberland, is forever recalled (north and south of the Border alike) as 'The Butcher'. His career ended in well-deserved disgrace after his capitulation to the French in the Seven Years War (1756–63).

In addition to the Highland Clearances, prohibitive laws were passed by the Whig Government which forbade the bearing of arms in Scotland, along with the wearing of tartan and the playing of bagpipes. For 46 years after Culloden, anyone found breaking these *Acts of Abolition and Proscription* was liable to imprisonment or transportation to the colonies – that is, if he avoided being shot on sight. Those Scots who were deemed likely to attempt evasion of the laws were hauled before the authorities and forced to take the following terrible oath[3]:

> I swear, as I shall answer to God at the great day of judgement, I have not, and shall not have, in my possession any gun, sword or arms whatsoever, and shall never use tartan plaid, or any part of the Highland garb. And if I do so, may I be accursed in my undertakings,

family and property; may I never see my wife, nor children, nor father, nor mother, or relations; may I be killed in battle as a fugitive coward, and lie without a Christian burial in a foreign land, far from the graves of my forefathers and kindred. May this all come upon me if I break this oath.

Lochiel and the Armistice

With the knowledge of Charles Edward's stop-over in Donegal prior to his return to France, we can take Donald Cameron of Lochiel off the proverbial hook, for it is sometimes presumed that the Duke's violent post-Culloden rampage was partly Lochiel's fault. The unwarranted accusation is fuelled by a submission dated April 1747 (held in the Archives Nationales, Paris) from the Duke of Perth to King Louis XV. The communiqué states that after Culloden the Duke of Cumberland sent a message to Donald Cameron at Lochaber, offering a full amnesty if the Highlanders would lay down their arms. Lochiel refused, and another letter (now with the *Stuart Papers* at Windsor), from Drummond of Balhaldy to James VIII, confirms the same offer and response. However, the fact was that Lochiel had no reason to lay down his arms because he had no reason to suppose that the war was over. As far as he and the other chiefs knew, Charles Edward was planning an imminent return to the Highlands with French and Irish support. In 1869 a confirmatory letter in this regard was deposited in the Louvre Museum, Paris – a letter written in Donegal by Charles Edward, and dispatched to Louis XV of France aboard the ship *l'Heureux*. The letter was to no avail; King Louis was unwilling to assist further at that stage, and the Prince was duly collected and carried to France. In later times, a poem was written in memory of the event:

From Hebrides to Rathlin Isle,
And thence to Inishowen.
But keeping far from Derry walls
Where uncle James was known.

Then straight across the county
To Glencolmkille's wild shore.
Where still is seen Prince Charlie's bed,
In a cave near Malinmore.

A man of the MacGinley clan,
His name was Charlie too,
Here sheltered him while waiting for
The French corvette, l'Heureux.

Dominic O'Kelly (extract)

Last Martyrs of the 'Forty-five'

Traditional history tells that the last Englishman to be executed for his Jacobite activities was Charles Radcliffe of Derwentwater, who fell to the headsman's axe on Tower Hill on 8 December 1746. But more than six years after this a Yorkshireman was charged with treason and shot at Shrewsbury because he had been an agent for the Stuart cause.[4] He was Lieutenant Thomas Anderson from Gales, an officer in the 2nd Dragoon Guards (previously the Queen's Horse, and later the Queen's Bays). The regiment's commander from 1749 was Sir John Ligonier, whose earlier troops had been at Falkirk and Culloden. During the 1745 Rising, Anderson had been attached to King George's Black Watch Regiment, but had been granted a special pass in Perth so that he could move freely in Jacobite circles.

When Ligonier took up his new post in 1749, Anderson promptly deserted the Dragoon Guards, and went to Prague and Vienna with commissioned powers to enlist men for the continuing Jacobite endeavour. On returning to Scotland, however, he was arrested at Perth in June 1752. This was very shortly after the Appin murder of Colin Campbell of Glenure, the Government factor for the sequestrated Stewart estate of Ardsheil. At that time, the Hanoverian redcoats were searching houses throughout Perthshire in pursuit of the fugitive Allan Breck Stewart (as portrayed in Robert Louis Stevenson's classic novel, *Kidnapped*). On being seized under suspicion Anderson was taken to Edinburgh Castle and examined by the Lord Justice-Clerk, Charles Erskine – an internal security officer for the Duke of Newcastle, brother of the Whig Prime Minister Henry Pelham. Erskine duly sent Anderson, under guard and on foot, to Worcester for court martial, and he was subsequently executed at the age of 32 by firing squad on 11 December 1752 at Kingsland, a military depot near Shrewsbury.

Anderson was shot with three musket balls to his breast and one to his head. He was laid to rest in St Mary's churchyard, Shrewsbury, and his executioners described his ultimate behaviour as that of 'a Christian, a gentleman, and a true soldier to the end'. His gravestone epitaph reads:

Stop Traveller!
I have passed, repass'd the seas and distant lands;
Can find no rest but in my Saviour's hands.

The last Scottish martyr of the 'Forty-five' was Dr Archibald Cameron, who was executed six months after Anderson, having been arrested on 20 March 1753. Dr Cameron of Glenkenzie was the brother of Donald Cameron of Lochiel, and was taken at Brenachyle, near Loch Katrine, by redcoats from a garrison at Inversnaid. It was said that he had been commissioned to prepare the clans for another rising – but the original information which led to Dr Cameron's seizure came not from any English spy, but from a fellow Scotsman working with Hanoverian Intelligence. He was Archibald Campbell, 2nd Duke of Argyll, Lord Justice General. His manuscript report to London, dated 1 November 1752 at Inverary, reads as follows:

> Doctor Cameron, brother to the late Lochiel, has had several meetings with those of his Clan, and was twice at Glenahurrick in Sunart, 15 miles of where there was a considerable meeting. He remained some days in the Glen above Fassifern's (this man [ie John Cameron of Fassifern] was brother to the late Lochiel, and remained at home during the Rebellion in order to serve the Clan in the shape of an innocent man, and is now the chief director of them), and was supplied with provisions from the family. Fassifern was with them on Wednesday and Thursday last (viz 25th and 26th of October) from morning till nine at night; their conversation was about the probability of an invasion, and the news of the Young Pretender turning Protestant which is spread among the common people and firmly believed.
>
> There has of late been great prices given for broadswords. Whether they have any hopes given them from abroad, or whether these practices are only artifices to keep up the spirits of the Jacobites, it is certain that they are at present flushed with hopes and

> expectations, and are so insolent as to say that the present rigorous measures (as they call every rational act of Government) will soon be at an end.

Following his arrest, Dr Cameron was carried to London, where his wife pleaded for mercy from King George II, only to be thrown into prison herself. Then, in the face of a great public outcry against Prime Minister Pelham and the King, Archibald Cameron was sentenced under Act of Attainder for high treason, and sent to the scaffold on 7 June 1753. He was dragged on a sled from the Tower of London and hanged at Tyburn, whereupon his head was struck off, and his heart torn out and burned before the crowd. Let it be said, however, that in deference to public sentiment, the Government at least allowed him to hang until dead. The English novelist, Tobias Smollet, who witnessed the execution, wrote: 'The populace, though not very subject to tender emotions, were moved to compassion and even to tears'. Those who remembered the good doctor's part in the 1745 Rising said, 'He never refused his assistance to anyone that asked it, whether friend or foe'.

In view of the English people's anger against the Government, it was decided to conduct Archibald Cameron's funeral in private, and at midnight on 9 June his body was laid to rest in the vault of the King's Free Hospital Chapel of the Savoy. Indeed, the Rev John Wilkinson refused to accept any Hanoverian payment, and was happy to pay the fee himself. In 1846, Dr Cameron's grandson, Charles Hay Cameron, installed a memorial to his popular ancestor, but this was destroyed in the Chapel fire of 1864. It was replaced in 1870 by a commemorative stained-glass window, designed by the Pre-Raphaelite artist Sir Edward Burne-Jones, and this was in turn destroyed during the bombing of World War II. The good Doctor's final resting place seemed doomed to oblivion, but recently, in 1993, a new brass plaque was installed at the instigation of the present Lochiel and The 1745 Association, and set into the altar plinth by the generosity of the Duchy of Lancaster who administer the Chapel. A very moving Service of Dedication was held in the presence of some seventy of the Doctor's descendants and admirers, and an address was given by David Lumsden of Cushnie, a direct descendant of Charles Edward's faithful secretary Andrew Lumisden.

The Invisible Spirit

At home and abroad, the Jacobite dimension has often been described as an 'Invisible Spirit', and as such it existed long before the 1688 Whig Revolution that deposed James VII (II). Subsequent to the Rising of 1745, the House of Hanover considered the spirit extinguished, but this has been far from the case.

The word 'Jacobite' derives from the Latin *Jacobi, Jacobus* or *Jacomus* (James) – stemming from the original Hebrew name *Jacob* – hence 'Jacob-ites'. With the Stewarts/Stuarts as the dynastic focus, the Jacobite movement looked forward to a restoration of the Royal House of Scotland, but the original concept can be traced back to Robert the Bruce, who honoured the 1320 *Declaration of Arbroath* as Scotland's Written Constitution – as did his Stewart successors who remained the nation's chosen dynasty.

The Scots concept of 'choosing' a king to represent and uphold the civil rights and liberties of the people was not totally unique, but despite the logic of the principle, Scotland was the only country in medieval Europe to operate the system both in theory and practice. The Scottish notion of 'people's rights' was intrinsically Celtic, and it rejected all forms of feudalism. Instead a patrimonial social regime was preferred – to be upheld by the Kings of Scots and the inherent Clan System. The recognition of individuals by earned entitlement or merit award was paramount, for status was not determined by wealth and property as was the case south of the Border. Consequently, when the English system of power by land ownership was introduced by the Dukes of Argyll on behalf of the Orange and Hanoverian regimes, it was quite foreign to the Scottish people.

However, the Scottish patrimonial spirit has survived all attempts to be conquered and subdued. In many ways the English mentality is so historically different that it simply cannot come to terms with the heritage and personal bonds of the Scottish ideal. Hence, as is often the case with things that do not conform or are misunderstood, the fearful alternative is to discredit and usurp them.

Jacobitism is not just a desperate struggle to save a way of life pertaining to the Highlands alone; it emerged as a purposeful effort to save Scotland's Written Constitution. This was a straightforward and fair concept which suited the Scottish temperament, but which terrified the autocratic ruling classes of England.

Another aspect of Jacobitism which is seldom mentioned is its reverence towards a right to education, and for centuries the Scots were the only truly literate nation, with a right to formal schooling. But to the Hanoverians a national education structure was perceived as a check on their self-presumed rights to govern in the dictatorial German manner. Indeed, the Georgian and Victorian politicians knew full well that informed, literate citizens would pose a significant threat to their underlying methods of thraldom.

Charles Edward, like his father before him, was brought up and educated by Scots exiles such as Andrew Michael Ramsay, who made it quite clear that the Prince's right to be educated was a product of his Scottish heritage, not a privilege of the monarchical system. In 1745 Charles was not surprised, therefore, to discover a scholastic nation in Scotland, with many people able to read, write and speak both English and French. They were also well-versed in Scots prose, and able to keep the old Gaelic language alive in the Highlands. The fact that Charles also made an effort to master Gaelic says much for him as a champion of the Scottish people.

The Jacobite dimension afforded Scots the right to be represented by a king of their choice – yet neither William III, Queen Anne, George I, nor any monarch since has been the Scottish choice as a natural inheritor. Furthermore, these monarchs have certainly not been upholders of the Constitution of the Community of the Realm of Scotland. On numerous occasions the Scottish Parliament pronounced the people's right to choose a king – different from England's if needs be[5] – and James VII was immediately reconfirmed as the King of Scots when deposed as James II of England. Following the 1707 *Treaty of Union*, even the Presbyterian Covenanters rejected Queen Anne[6], and declared her half-brother James Francis Edward to be the rightful King James VIII of Scots.

Kingship and the Church

This action by the Covenanters displayed an individual aspect of Jacobitism which, according to critical history, should have been impossible. It proved that Presbyterianism was no bar to being a Jacobite. Indeed, the spirit of Jacobitism was never about religious denominations – it was about Scottish nationhood.

Prior to the Westminster Confession of Faith in 1647, the Anglican party (who opposed the Confession) stayed away during the deliberations which began in 1643. However, although Scotland's National Kirk had no rights to vote in the matter, the Presbyterians not only attended, but greatly influenced and generally led the proceedings. The fact was that these Kirk representatives had originally been trained, even ordained, by the Scottish Episcopal Church, and the episcopalian influence was very apparent within the Kirk, even though not forming a part of it. The Episcopal Church was wholly Jacobite, and the common inference that the Kirk of Scotland was anti-Stuart during the 1745 Rising has no foundation whatever.

The Kings and Queens of Scots were required by the Constitution to uphold the rights and liberties of the sovereign nation, and they were inherently obliged to support the right of individuals to worship according to conscience. As designated 'common fathers' of the people, the Stewart kings were unifiers of denominations, and the descendant Stuarts in England were severely misunderstood because of it. James (VII) II's intention to liberate the Catholics, Jews and nonconformists caused him to be condemned by the narrow-minded protagonists of the Church of England. But whatever one's religious denomination, it is not difficult to recognize the social importance of forbearance and toleration. In comparison with the autocratic mentality of William of Orange, along with the blinkered attitude of the Whigs and the unbending disposition of Hanover's Anglican bishops, King James emerges as a wholly just and liberated humanitarian.

As we have seen, though, not all the Church of England clergy were in agreement with the new regime after James's departure, and many (including Dr Sancroft, Archbishop of Canterbury) refused to swear the Oath of Allegiance to King William. Consequently, they were illegally deprived of their Anglican offices on 1 February 1689.[7] Dr Hickes, the displaced Dean of Worcester, met with King James at the Court of Saint Germain, in an attempt to have the deprivations annulled, but the exiled Stuart was quite powerless to assist. From 31 May 1691 replacement appointees were introduced (outside of ecclesiastical law) to the vacant sees – but in time the unseated non-juring bishops were themselves instrumental in providing canonical succession for the Episcopalian Churches of Scotland and America.

True Jacobitism took the Stuart concept of religious toleration fully into account, and the Scottish clergy were wholly supportive. In September 1745, when the Episcopal Church symbolically crowned Charles III, representatives of both Catholic and Presbyterian Churches were also there to witness and approve the event. The short-term divisionary wheel had come full circle, and in this regard the separately denominated Churches were united.

In Europe, Scottish Jacobitism became the bedrock of the people's right to reject absolute monarchies. It facilitated the liberty to replace them with Constitutional Monarchies or even Republics. While the Stuarts reigned in England, they were also defined as Kings of Scotland and Ireland, and theoretical Kings of France. Each of these countries had supported a Parliament which was structurally different from the others, but only Scotland's 'Three Estates' actually upheld individual rights until it was adjourned in 1707.

Knights Templars and the Jacobite Lodges

In France, the exiled Charles Edward and his supporters fostered a political persuasion which the people of that country knew was theirs by right, and whenever required Charles negotiated with Courts throughout Europe. Along with his cousin, the Comte de Saint Germain, and others, Charles left indelible traces of his doctrines and Masonic activity throughout the European continent, and he provided social incentives for ministerial cabinets as far afield as Russia.

Fenelon François de Salignac de la Mothe, Archbishop of Cambrai (the political mentor of James VIII), laid the foundations of French Jacobitism – but before and after the 'Forty-five' Charles Edward was its living catalyst. Andrew Michael Ramsay, a Scottish Freemason, pursued the same course in Italy, adding his Jacobite influence to a nation wherein many regarded the Stewarts as their Biblical kings. Prior to becoming High Stewards of Scotland, the Stewarts' maternal forebears were

Seneschals in Brittany, and they were of the same ancestral stock as the earlier Merovingian Kings of the Franks, in descent from the ancient Royal House of Judah.[8]

The French writer Voltaire (a tremendous admirer of Charles Edward) was overwhelmed by the open-minded toleration of the Stuarts, who called to all nations for an alliance of Christian religions. Throughout Europe and America, the scattered Jacobite exiles identified greatly with the Jews – each longing for a national home to call their own. From the 18th century, Russian, Swedish, French, Spanish and Italian Freemasons (all of whom followed the Jacobite tradition) came to regard Charles Edward and his heirs as their natural spiritual leaders, and they decided, through long-term policies, to follow the Jacobite model of the people's 'right to choose'.

Scottish Rite Freemasonry rests upon a written constitution which, throughout the world (like the State Constitutions of France and America), hinges upon the fundamental principles of the 1320 *Declaration of Arbroath*. Today, as the recognized Count of Albany and *de jure* Lord High Steward of Scotland, I remain the Sovereign Grand Master of all Jacobite lodges extant in Europe.

Scottish Freemasonry had been introduced into England at about the time that James VI of Scots succeeded as James I of England – and when Charles II was in exile in Holland the lodges acted as his intelligence service in Britain, keeping him abreast of Cromwellian policies. Soon after being restored to the Throne in 1660, King Charles became Patron of the Royal Society, whose influential members (under cover of their so-called *Invisible College*) had been the most active in securing the Stuart Restoration. (The Stuart Royal Society had been established by Charles I in 1645, and was incorporated under Royal Charter by Charles II in 1662.) The early members of the Royal Society were all Freemasons, while many of them were also Brothers of the Rosy Cross. During the 17th century they included such notable figures as Robert Boyle, Robert Hooke, Isaac Newton, Christopher Wren, Samuel Pepys and Edmund Halley.

When Charles II's brother, James VII (II), lost the Throne in 1688, the prevailing Society members took up the Stuart flag to become a wholly Jacobite organization, creating Masonic lodges throughout the country that would support the 'King over the water'. During the late 1600s, tens-of-thousands of Jacobites emigrated to France, from which time Stuart Freemasonry was promoted all over Europe. In Italy they created the Carbonari, in Germany they perpetuated the Order of the Rose Cross, and in Spain there were the Alumbrados Illuminati. In England, however, the lodges were infiltrated by Hanoverian agents, and by 1738 the Pope was persuaded to prevent Catholics from joining Masonic lodges, worldwide. Jesuits, on the other hand, ignored the edict, and continued to join European lodges so as to keep the original Stuart ideals alive.

PART FIVE

The Hanoverian Conspiracy

14

THE COUNT OF ALBANY

Arrest at The Opéra

Prior to the Seven Years' War (1756–63) there were eight years of strained armistice between Britain and France. The earlier War of Austrian Succession had raged from 1740 to 1748, and Charles Edward's Jacobite Rising was set firmly in the midst of this. The Austrian hostilities centred around the succession of Archduchess Maria Theresa, whose inheritance was facilitated by the *Pragmatic Sanction* of her father, Emperor Charles VI. Maria Theresa's female right to succeed was challenged by various nations, and Frederick the Great of Prussia annexed the Austrian province of Silesia. Europe then became locked in war, with Austria supported by England and Holland, against Prussia in alliance with France and Spain. The net result was that when the war ended in 1748 Maria Theresa had managed to retain her heritage; her husband Francis of Lorraine became Holy Roman Emperor, and Frederick the Great held on to Silesia.

In October 1748 the French and British met to sign the *Treaty of Aix-la-Chapelle,* which obliged Louis XV to honour the Hanoverian succession. In so doing he was required to forsake his allegiance to Charles Edward Stuart (who was then living in Paris) and Charles was asked to leave the country, even though he was a Prince of France in his own right.

Not wishing to be compromised by King Louis' submission to the will of Westminster, Charles ignored the instruction, and rented a new Paris house on the Quai des Théatins, opposite the Louvre. King George II complained that the treaty was not being observed, but Charles was openly supported by the French people at large; he was actually more popular in Paris than King Louis himself. Apart from that, he preferred to remain in France because of a prevailing love affair with his cousin Marie Louise de la Tour de Rohan-Guéméné, Duchesse de Montbazon.

On the evening of 11 December 1748, 1,200 men of the Garde Royale, with auxiliary constables and grenadiers, were deployed to ambush Charles Edward as he rode to the theatre. The Dauphin protested that his father's strategy was politically and socially unwise, but King Louis' plan went ahead and Charles was seized on the steps of The Opéra. He was bound hand-and-foot, to be carried to the Château de Vincennes, while his companions were taken to the Bastille. It transpired, however, that the Dauphin's fears were well-founded, and the arrest of the popular Stuart enraged Parisians to such an extent that, by this very action, Louis XV rang the death-knell of his own dynasty. Forty years later, the House of Bourbon collapsed in the French Revolution.

From Vincennes, Charles was escorted to the borders of Savoy, from where he travelled to the Papal State of Avignon. But England's George II was still not content, and he threatened the Pope with a naval assault of Civitavecchia. Charles then left Avignon, and within days of his original departure he was back in France. For a number of years thereafter he was the constant bane of Hanoverian Intelligence, travelling, in various disguises, to promote his cause in Britain and throughout western Europe.

By April 1749 Charles was in Paris again; moving incognito, he braved the police and took a room in the apartments of the Convent of Saint Joseph. There he resurrected an earlier liaison with Princess Marie Anne Louise de Talmont, while other admirers acted as envoys and general go-betweens. In September 1750 he was in London, and by March of the following year (some 15 months from his Paris removal) he made it at last to The Opéra.[1]

So much has been written about this thoroughly romantic period of Charles Edward's life that there is little point in duplicating a mass of information here. However, it is worth drawing attention to the fact that between 1748 and 1755 Charles made numerous visits to England and Wales, making good use of doubles and completely outwitting the Westminster agents who endeavoured to keep track of him. (One of these doubles was his cousin Guiseppe de Rohano-Stuardo – *see* 46 in plate sections.) Additionally, in 1753 he was in Ireland again.

Outside Scotland, Jacobitism was smouldering from Northumbria, through the Midlands, and down to the very south of the country. Across the land there was an active network of Jacobite societies and lodges, flourishing even in such major centres as London, Liverpool, Preston, Norwich, Bristol and Manchester (*see* Appendix VI: Jacobite Societies). In Wales there were the renowned 'Sea Serjeants' of Pembroke and Carmarthen, while the legendary 'Cycle of the White Rose' operated from Wrexham. Even the Newcastle colliers proclaimed their mass allegiance to King Charles III in 1750.

Wherever Charles Stuart travelled in England and Wales there were prestigious safe-houses at his disposal, including Arlingham Court, Cornbury Hall, Stoneleigh Abbey, Marbury Hall, Westbrook House, Llangedwyn, and Berse Drelincourt where the children of some notable Jacobite exiles were raised (*see* Appendix IX). It was at the Essex Street home of Ann Drelincourt, Lady Primrose, that Charles stayed while in London concerning the unfulfilled 1751–2 'Elibank Plot' to assault St James's Palace. Apart from Lady Primrose, his English supporters included Baroness Leigh, Earl Cornbury, Earl Barrymore, the Lords of Chesterfield, Bath, Sandwich, and Pultney, along with the Dukes of Beaufort and Westmorland, and perhaps most surprisingly King George II's own son Frederick, Prince of Wales.

By 1756 the *Treaty of Aix-la-Chapelle* had collapsed[2], and intent on regaining Silesia, Maria Theresa of Austria formed an alliance with France and Russia against Prussia. This time King George II sided with his Prussian and Hanoverian colleagues, so that England and France were opposed once again in the ensuing Seven Years War.

Charles and Clementina

Through all of this, King James VIII and the Jacobite party in Rome were becoming increasingly concerned about the continuity of the royal line. In September 1750 Charles Edward was reacquainted in London with his mother's god-daughter, Lady Clementina Walkinshaw of Barrowfield. They had originally been introduced at the Edinburgh Ball, Holyrood House, on 23 September 1745. Subsequently, Clementina had nursed Charles's cold after the Battle of Falkirk[3], and the couple were lovers for a while (*see* Appendix IX).

Under pressure from his peers to find a wife, and having split from his mistress, the Princess de Talmont, Charles duly sent for Clementina in June 1752. She joined him in Ghent, but her arrival was not welcomed by his colleagues because her sister, Catherine, was employed by the Hanoverian Court in London. They considered that Clementina might be a spy, irrespective of the fact that she was of good Jacobite stock with an illustrious noble ancestry. She was descended from Esmé Stuart d'Aubigny, Duke of Lennox (died 1583); she was a cousin to both the Douglas and Hamilton families, and her distant ancestors included none other than Sir William Wallace, Guardian of the Realm. Although the liaison between Charles and Clementina was considered unsuitable by James VIII and others, they elected to live as man and wife. By that time Charles was suffering from fits of epilepsy which had begun after his return to France, and it suited him to have a companion with whom he was already familiar.

In the summer of 1753 the couple moved to Belgium and settled near the Pont Magen in Liège. Then, early in October, Clementina gave birth to their daughter Charlotte. Although Charles had converted to the Anglican faith in 1750, Clementina was a Catholic, and the Pope urged Charles to marry her. Charlotte was baptized in the church of Sainte Marie des Fonts, and the records confirm that, by the rule of Canon Law, the Church considered her parents to be man and wife. Yet to the world at large Charlotte was illegitimate, and the Pope maintained that only through legitimating Charlotte by way of a proper marriage could she become the legal Stuart heiress in the anti-Hanover contest. As an added complication, Charles's brother, Henry of York, had become a cardinal of the Roman Church, and was clearly not in a position to marry. Hence the Stuart hopes for future generations rested firmly with Charles Edward – but he and Clementina did not formalize a church marriage.

By 1760 malicious pressures from numerous Jacobite partisans had made life quite unbearable for Clementina. They criticized Charles for giving her priority over the Stuart cause, and the relationship became increasingly strained, as a result of which Clementina and young Charlotte left Charles for the Paris Convent de la Visitation de Sainte Marie in the Rue de Bac.

Once again Charles immersed himself in travelling to promote the Jacobite Cause. In the course of this, he arrived twice in Edinburgh, where he stayed in the Royal Mile, from where he paid a visit to Glasgow. During that same period he also went to Russia, where he met the Tsarina, Elisaveta Petrovna. Then on 2 January 1766 his father, James VIII of Scots (James III of Great Britain, France and Ireland), died in Rome – and Charles duly made his way to the Palazzo Muti.

Although symbolically crowned some 11 years before in Scotland, Charles Edward now finally succeeded as the *de jure* Charles III on the world stage. However, since he was known to have forsaken Catholicism for the Protestant Church, Pope Clement XIII refused to acknowledge his sovereign distinction. The Vatican later recognized him as the Count of Albany (Scotland), but Charles did not need any Papal blessing to succeed his father; he had been ritually proclaimed King in the presence of an ordained bishop of the Episcopal Church, and had been formally accepted into the Church of England.

In the continued endeavour to find Charles a suitable wife, his French advisers proposed a seemingly favourable union with the 19-year-old Princess Louise Emmanuelle Maximilienne de Stolberg-Guedern. It was 1771, and Charles was nearly 51, whereas his suggested wife was much the same age as his daughter Charlotte. Nevertheless, the match appeared satisfactory, and arrangements were made for the marriage. Louise was of German extraction, but was maternally descended from the Bruces of Elgin.[4] Her family were Catholics, but were quite content for their heiress to marry a King of swayed persuasion. Cardinal Henry, on the other hand, was none too pleased by his brother's prospect since, by that stage, he fostered his own ambition to succeed in the kingly line; it has been suggested that Henry even had delusions of becoming Pope. In Britain, the late George II had been replaced in 1760 by his grandson George III, who preferred to trust that the Stuart line would terminate with Charles and Henry. As a cardinal of the Roman Church,

Henry could not officially propagate; he could perhaps achieve special dispensation for this purpose, but an heir from him was most unlikely.

Like his Hanoverian predecessors, George III is remembered for his stubborn autocracy, and he was equally dull. True, he lacked his forebears' lust for lechery, but his puritanical outlook was such that he despised anything remotely colourful or romantic. He was unhealthily moralistic on the surface, although hypocritical enough when it suited him. This was made clear when he appointed his mother's lover, Lord Bute, as his first Prime Minister. Bute (a Jacobite with a small 'j') recognized that he had not the stomach for political intrigue, and resigned his primary position to accommodate the King's own lackeys, of whom there were no less than five within ten years. It was reported in the press that 'ministers were no longer the public servants of the State, but the private domestics of the sovereign, and the King should remember that, while he plumes himself on the security of his title to the crown, it was, after all, acquired by one revolution and may be lost by another'.

The general ill-will felt against King George III was summed up very well by Robert Burns, who composed the following verse in relation to Stirling Castle:

Here Stewarts once in triumph reign'd,
And laws for Scotland's weal ordained.
But now unroof'd their Palace stands;
Their sceptre fall'n to other hands.

The injured Stewart race is gone,
A race outlandish fills their throne;
An idiot race, to honour lost,
Who know them best despise them most.

Throughout the Hanoverian era, and especially since George II's Highland Clearances, life had been particularly hard for working people in Scotland. Notwithstanding the fact that the Duke of Cumberland wanted Westminster to pass a law whereby all Highland women should be sterilized[5] (a law which Parliament refused to implement), thousands of Scots had been driven from their own farms, and forced to work as labourers for other landowners. Many had to seek employment in the emergent factories, gaining barely enough wages for their families to survive. Others, especially the older men, were destined never to work again, and were left to beg favours from house-to-house. It was no use appealing to the authorities, for the Whig politicians were themselves the farm and factory owners, and there was not even the opportunity to remove them from Parliament by electoral vote: there were only 2,624 registered voters in the whole of Scotland. Indeed, only politicians and council members were allowed to vote in the cities, and in Bute the only authorized voter was the MP who elected himself into office.

The Georgian era also saw the height of the international slave trade, with England taking the market lead. By 1772 there were not only tens-of-thousands of slaves in the British colonies, but there were also about 10,000 in England. A typical advertisement from the *Liverpool Chronicle* of 15 December 1768 reads:

> To be sold
> A fine negro boy of about 4ft. 5ins. high.
> Of a sober, tractable humane disposition.
> Eleven or twelve years of age, talks English,
> and can dress hair in a tolerable way.

Britain's loss of the American colonies in the War of Independence was entirely blamed on King George III and his avaricious ministers – and rightly so, given their attempts to levy unfair taxes and import duties on the Americans, who were not themselves represented at the Westminster Parliament. In fact, Charles Edward Stuart and the Jacobites played a leading part in ensuring that the United States would be lost by the House of Hanover. Thousands of Scots families had fled their homeland after the Battle of Culloden, and a great many found their way to America. They had not managed to defeat the Hanoverians at home, but in assisting their American cousins they certainly found another chance – and this time the campaign was successful. Throughout the War of Independence, the Americans sent regular reports of battles and troop movements to Charles Edward Stuart, who was also kept well informed by the American press. One of Charles Edward's primary contacts was Augustus Edward Maximilien, the eldest son of his cousin and double Guiseppe de Rohano-Stuardo. Augustus was an American agent within the Royalist faction, under the alias Lord Wentworth Smyth.

Marriage to Louise

During the course of the Stuart marriage arrangements, threats of assassination from Westminster forced Charles Edward to leave France before the due date. He and Louise were married, by proxy, in Paris on 28 March 1772, subsequent to which the couple met in Italy, where an official wedding ceremony was held at Macerata. Afterwards they travelled to Rome, where the scheming Cardinal Henry had organized a grand reception. A few weeks later, the non-juring Bishop Gordon received a letter in England. It described the proceedings in Rome, and read, in part, as follows:

> The Cardinal York paid a visit to the princess next morning, had a conference with her for an hour, and made her a present of a gold snuff-box, set with diamonds of great value. But what shall I tell you? The outside, beautiful as it was, was nothing in comparison of the beauty within. Oh! my dear Lord! It contained an order upon his banker to pay her down 40,000 Roman crowns, near equal to 10,000 pounds sterling, with a settlement of 4,000 pounds sterling a year on her. What think you of this affair? [£10,000 in 1772 was the equivalent of over £500,000 in today's terms. Similarly, £4,000 a year in 1772 exceeds £200,000 a year today.]

Many in France and Italy praised Henry's great generosity, but the Jacobites wondered what motive was hidden behind the enormous settlement. Moreover, they were concerned about the purpose and content of the private meeting. It was known that King Louis XV (with whom Charles was then on better terms) had offered Louise a pension to provide the House of Stuart with an heir, and Charles Edward's attendants were, therefore, troubled that Cardinal York's gift would eclipse the French award. What did Henry want Louise to do for such a considerable income? More importantly, what did he want her *not* to do? What she did not do, of course, was to produce a Stuart heir, and it is evident that in the light of Henry's arrangement the French payments to Louise were never made.

A few years earlier, in 1766, Henry had also come to an agreement with Clementina Walkinshaw, and he was supporting her by way of a regular income in return for her sworn testimony that she and Charles had never been married. Thus, by 1772, Charles Edward's two most prominent ladies were both in the Cardinal's pay.

In 1773 Charles and Louise moved from Rome to Siena, where British Intelligence operatives under Sir Horace Mann kept a close watch on the Royal Household, awaiting any sign of a pregnancy. In 1774 the couple moved again to the San Clemente Palace in Florence, but by the late 1770s their marriage was in ruins. Louise had embarked on an affair with the noble poet Vittorio, Count Alfieri, and Cardinal Henry was intriguing with Louise against the interests of her husband. Having been declared barren by the Cardinal's doctors, Louise went to live at Henry's palace, while her host organized a 50 per cent cut in Charles's Papal income. Then in 1780 Louise left to reside openly with her lover, Alfieri.

Robert Burns

Robert Burns was very open about his loyalty to the House of Stewart. English historians often state that this was no more than a romantic attachment, but Burns was of ancient Scottish royal stock, with a wholly Jacobite and Masonic family background.

In a letter which Burns wrote to Lady Winifred Maxwell Constable, he saluted the good lady as 'a common sufferer in a cause where even to be unfortunate is glorious'. He continued, saying,

> Though my fathers had no illustrious honours and vast properties to pass down; though they left their humble cottages only to add so many units more to the unnoted crowd that followed their leaders; yet what they could they did, and what they had they lost. With unshakable firmness and unconcealed political adventure, they shook hands with ruin for what they esteemed the cause of their King and their Country.

Most biographies of Robert Burns (1759–96) conveniently skip the details of his parents and paternal grandparents, to portray him simply as a somewhat undefined son of an Ayrshire farmer. However, Burns' paternal grandmother was Isabella Keith, whose father was James Keith of Criggie, a cousin of George

Keith, Earl Marischal of Scotland. Both were 'out' in the 1715 Jacobite Rising, and entertained King James VIII at the Keith estates of Feteresso and Inchbreck. The Keith ancestry itself can be traced through a line from Lady Mary Bruce, sister of King Robert I, whose gravestone Burns knelt to kiss at Dunfermline Abbey. It can also be traced through Margaret Douglas, the Fair Maid of Galloway, a descendant of Robert III Stewart. Burns had Comyn ancestry too, tracing back to Donald Ban, the brother of King Malcolm III Canmore – and he was related, within five generations, to many of the greatest names in Scotland. Such matters are not particularly significant these days, but they were important in 18th-century Scotland where a 'family' was deemed to comprise a more complete heritage than the legacy of its immediate members.

In view of the very socially minded opinions of Robert Burns, the Russian people regard him as the first true socialist. They celebrate Burns Night every year, just as we do – and his poetry (translated into Russian) is passionately recited on the commemorative anniversary of his death. It is of particular interest to note that James Keith (younger brother of Scotland's Earl Marischal George Keith) became a provincial Grand Master of Freemasonry in Russia.[6]

The Jacobite poems and songs of Robert Burns have been an inspiration for Scots at home and abroad for more than two centuries – songs which uphold the aims and ideals of the Kings of Scots, and which support a return of the Royal House of Stewart. *A man's a man for all that* conveys his belief that everyone, kings and all, has failings.

On 31 December 1787, Robert Burns took part in a celebration of Charles Edward Stuart's birthday – and this was in itself a treasonable act under Hanoverian law. But he was in good company, sharing the dinner table with Lady Nairne (daughter of Charles Edward's aide-de-camp), the Earl and Countess of Seaforth, the Duke of Perth, James Murray of Abercairney, Oliphant of Gask, Thriepland of Fingask, Lord Provost James Stewart, and others. Burns also risked imprisonment, transportation, or even execution, by writing an ode for General George Washington's birthday during the American War of Independence. In this, he even referred to Britain's King George III as a tyrant:

See gathering thousands, while I sing,
A broken chain exulting bring,
And dash it in a tyrant's face.

Robert Burns is well remembered, and highly revered for his great literary achievement – and he is also remembered for the Jacobite sentiments which he so firmly promoted. His *Address to Edinburgh,* along with his *Lament to Mary, Queen of Scots; There will never be peace till Jamie comes home; Charlie, he's My Darling; The Bonnie Lass of Albany* and *Bonnie Dundee,* are all indicative of the heartfelt, Stewart-centred initiative of the great Bard.

The winter of 1788–9 marked the centenary of the Whig Revolution that had deposed King James VII (II) Stuart, and Burns wrote to the *Edinburgh Evening Courant* in support of the Royal House: 'Let every man who has a tear for the many miseries incident to humanity, feel for a family illustrious as any in Europe, and unfortunate beyond historic precedent'.

Charles III and the Crown of America

Following the unhappy Battle of Culloden, the international influence of the Stuarts could easily have lessened – but this was far from the case, even though some indoctrinated historians would have it otherwise. In practice, the political impact which Charles Edward made on his contemporaries was such that 36 years after the Rising he was considered worthy of no less than the Crown of America.

In October 1781 General Charles, 1st Marquess, Cornwallis surrendered his British force at Yorktown, Virginia, and this led to the conclusion of the American War of Independence, thereby ending British rule in the old colonies. But in the winter of 1782 four American gentlemen arrived at Charles III's Florentine residence, the Palazzo San Clemente. They were Mr Galloway of Maryland, two brothers named Sylvester from Pennsylvania, and Mr Fish, a lawyer from New York. On requesting a royal audience, they were accommodated and taken to Charles by his secretary, John Stewart.

Coincidentally, King Charles had been in discussion that day with the Hon Charles Hervey-Townshend (Britain's later

Ambassador to The Hague), and had been debating the pros and cons of monarchy. Being a particularly interested party, Hervey-Townshend remained present for the American interview, witnessing the presentation of *letters of credence,* and listening to the details of a dilemma which existed across the Atlantic.

The content of this interview is well documented in the USA Senate Archives, and in the Manorwater Papers. Sir Compton Mackenzie, Sir Charles Petrie and others have also written of the time when Charles Edward, *de jure* King Charles III of England, Scotland, France and Ireland, was asked by George Washington's envoys to become King of the Americans. In truth, the offer came as no great surprise to Charles, for some years earlier he had been approached in Holland by the men of Boston at the outbreak of the American Revolution.

Having defeated the Jacobites at Culloden in 1746, it would have been a great irony for the House of Hanover to lose America to the Stuarts, and doubtless this thought occurred to Charles on being offered the American crown. For a number of reasons, though, he was obliged to decline the invitation. At that time in 1782, Charles was separated from Louise of Stolberg – but whether or not he could obtain a formal divorce was uncertain. His prospects of remarrying and fathering a legitimate male heir as his successor were, therefore, equally uncertain. He could, of course, have accepted the regal position simply to score a point over King George III, but in so doing he would perhaps have opened the American door to Hanover again at his death. In this regard, Charles was not about to spoil the Americans' future chances to suit his own ends – and so the United States Republic was born.

The Hon Charles Hervey-Townshend later wrote to his aunt, Lady Molly Carteron, Countess of Manorwater, detailing the conversation which took place on that historic day. The meeting was conducted, he explained, in the King's salon at the Palazzo San Clemente, Via San Sebastiano, in November 1782. He stated that, apart from King Charles and the four American representatives, there were two of Charles Edward's cousins present. One was Guiseppe de Rohano Stuardo (a descendant of James, Principe de Boveria, Marquis d'Aubignie – a natural son of Charles II). The other was Marguerite, Comtesse de Massillan, who took part in the interview (*see* Appendix VII for a transcript).

15

A Duplicity of Wills

Divorce from Louise

To that point, Louise de Stolberg had managed to convince Cardinal Henry that her husband, Charles Edward, had been mistreating her, and even the Pope had been seduced by her stories. She maintained her deception for some while, until they learned the truth about her outrageous affair with Vittorio Alfieri. In March 1783, Sir Horace Mann of British Intelligence wrote, 'The tables are now turned. The cat is, at last, out of the bag. The Cardinal York's visit to his brother [who was recovering from a fit of apoplexy] gave the latter an opportunity to undeceive him, proving to him that the complaints laid to his charge of ill-using her were invented to cover a plot formed by Count Alfieri'.

The Pope wasted no time in banishing Alfieri from Rome, and Louise was left to suffer the consequence of her mischief until she was reunited with her lover more than a year later. Earlier, in 1782, Charles Edward had applied for a divorce, but was refused by Rome. Nonetheless, in order to thwart Henry's intrigue with regard to the succession, Charles formally legitimated his daughter Charlotte, who was henceforth the Duchess of Albany.

King Gustavus III of Sweden, travelling under the title of Count Haga, then decided to assist King Charles in his quest for a marriage annulment, and put forward two bases for the proposed divorce. Firstly, he claimed that Louise's inability to produce an heir made her unsuitable for the purpose intended; secondly, her open involvement with Alfieri rendered her quite unworthy of her marital office. With the help of these submissions, the Papal objections were overcome, and on 3 April 1784 Pope Pius VI formally annulled the marriage of Charles and Louise.[1] Simultaneously, Charles made a will nominating Charlotte as his sole heiress, and he published a letter (worded by an Italian notary) in full repudiation of his former wife. Following the legal divorce, a Roman lawyer prepared the formal document of restrictions: Louise would no longer bear the King's name, but would be granted a royal pension. Other than that, she may live wherever she pleased. In August 1784, she married Vittorio, Count Alfieri, at the Castle of Martinsbourg Colmar, which belonged to Louise's friend Madame de Meltzam.

Marriage to Marguerite

During the divorce proceedings, Charlotte had joined Charles Edward in Florence, and they subsequently moved to the milder climate of Rome, where they arrived in December 1784. According to Hanoverian-contrived history, the divorce from Louise de Stolberg was the end of married life for Charles Edward – but it was not. It is recorded in the church annals of Rome, and in our family archives, that on 26 December 1785, at the age of nearly 65, he was married again to the Comtesse de Massillan, a cousin by descent from King Charles II. She was Marguerite Marie Thérèse O'Dea d'Audibert de Lussan, and had stepped into the Royal Household after Louise's departure in 1780. In fact, it was the Countess who had persuaded Charles to formally legitimate his daughter Charlotte.[2] Charles and Marguerite were both musicians of some renown, and they performed with Domenico – Charles on cello and Marguerite on violin. Charles was also a very competent composer in his own right, and at the request of King Louis XV and the Marquise de Pompadour, Charles and his brother Henry had given a concert performance at the French Court in 1747.

When Charles and Charlotte moved to the Palazzo Muti in Rome, Marguerite moved with them, and her marriage to Charles was conducted at the Church of the Holy Apostles, opposite the Palazzo. Until 1769 Marguerite had been a ward at the Ecclesiastical Court of her great-uncle Louis Jacques d'Audibert de Lussan, Archbishop of Bordeaux (died 1769). Her family background was totally Jacobite, with a number of specific mentions in the records of St Germain, and her cousin Guiseppe de Rohano Stuardo was 'out' with Charles Edward in the 'Forty-five', acting occasionally as Charles's double thereafter.

Comtesse Marguerite's paternal grandmother, Theresa, Marchesa d'Aubignie, was the daughter of James de Rohano Stuardo, Marquis d'Aubignie, Prince of Boveria, Italy. He was the natural son (legitimated in 1667) of King Charles II Stuart and Marguerite, Duchesse de Rohan. James d'Aubignie[3] was married to Thérèsa Corona of Naples, who was descended through the princely families of Orsini and Corsini. The Marchesa's husband (Marguerite's grandfather) was Thomas O'Dea (born in Naples), Baron of Ida, Ireland. His ancestry was from Maurice, the 11th-century Green Knight of Kerry (son of a Welsh Princess and a Norman Baron). Cornelius O'Dea (died 1434) was Archdeacon of Killaloe and Bishop of Limerick, and the family were still churchmen in the 18th century when Marguerite's relative Father Peter Joseph O'Dea was a priest in the Breton diocese of Nantes. On her mother's side, Marguerite was of descent in the family line of d'Audibert; they held the titles Comte de Lussan and Baron de Valros. Additionally, the d'Audiberts were Comtes of St Andres d'Olerargues and St Martin de Careiret.

A Latin extract from the marriage entry of Charles and Marguerite at the Church of the Santi Apostoli in Rome reads:

> Quod Heic XXVI Kal Dec. ANRS MDCCLXXXV Hospes Hospiti Carolus III Rex Mag. Brit. Fran. et Hib. Fid. Def. Porrexerit Dexteram Margaretae Mariae Teresae Fil. Ferdinandi Dea d'Audibert de Lussan et Francescae d'Audibert de Lussan, Comitessa de Massillan, etc., Eamque, Servatis SRE Ritibus Duxerit in Matrimonium.
>
> *Translation*: On this day of the 26th December in the year of our Redemption and Salvation 1785, Charles III, King of England, France and Ireland, Defender of the Faith, extended the hand of friendship to Marguerite Mary Theresa, daughter of Ferdinand Dea d'Audibert de Lussan and Frances d'Audibert de Lussan, Countess of Massillan, etc, and with the rites of the Holy Roman Church married her.

The Stuart Heir

A year later, on 15 November 1786, the 37-year-old Countess gave birth to a son, Edouard Jacques Stuardo (Edward James

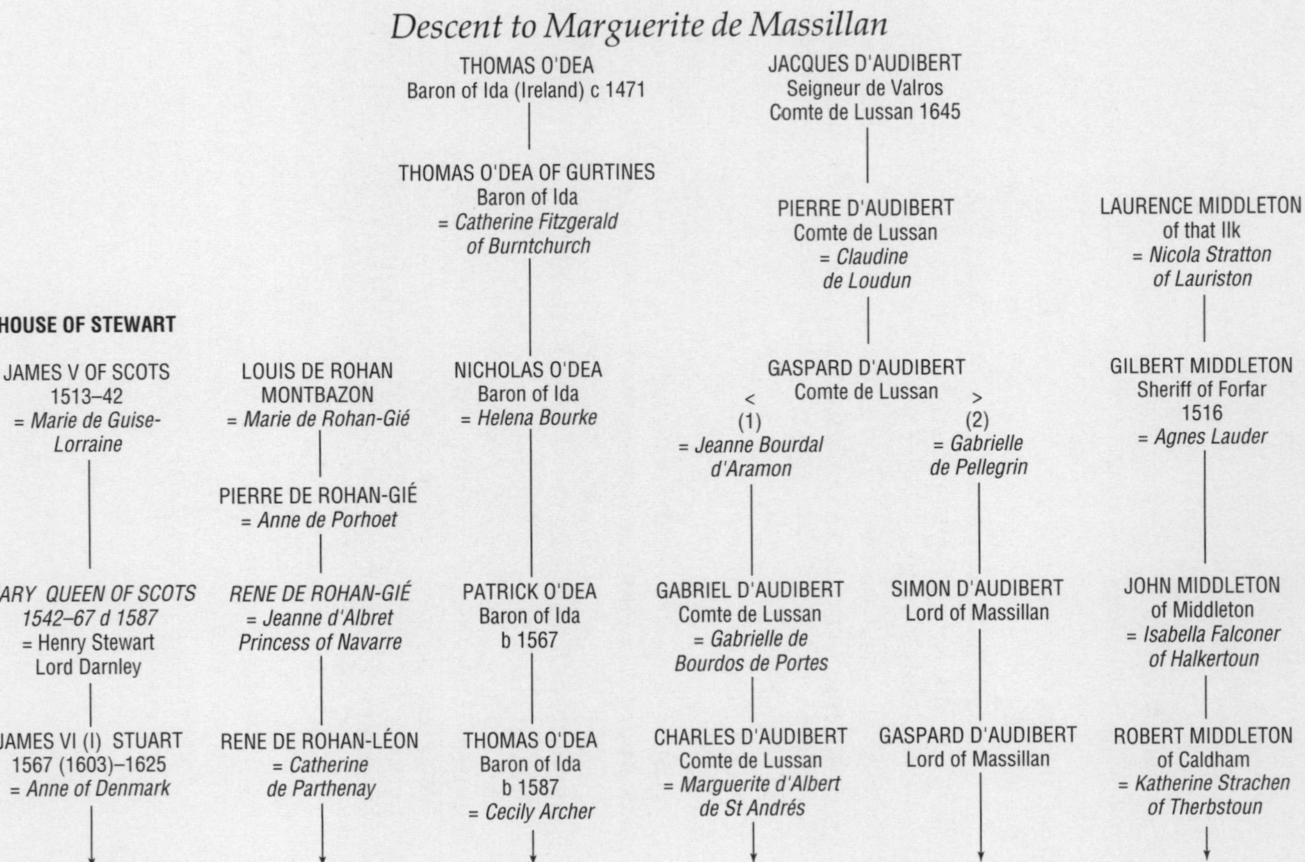
Descent to Marguerite de Massillan
HOUSE OF STEWART
JAMES V OF SCOTS
1513–42
= Marie de Guise-Lorraine
MARY QUEEN OF SCOTS
1542–67 d 1587
= Henry Stewart
Lord Darnley
JAMES VI (I) STUART
1567 (1603)–1625
= Anne of Denmark
LOUIS DE ROHAN
MONTBAZON
= Marie de Rohan-Gié
PIERRE DE ROHAN-GIÉ
= Anne de Porhoet
RENE DE ROHAN-GIÉ
= Jeanne d'Albret
Princess of Navarre
RENE DE ROHAN-LÉON
= Catherine
de Parthenay
THOMAS O'DEA
Baron of Ida (Ireland) c 1471
THOMAS O'DEA OF GURTINES
Baron of Ida
= Catherine Fitzgerald
of Burntchurch
NICHOLAS O'DEA
Baron of Ida
= Helena Bourke
PATRICK O'DEA
Baron of Ida
b 1567
THOMAS O'DEA
Baron of Ida
b 1587
= Cecily Archer
JACQUES D'AUDIBERT
Seigneur de Valros
Comte de Lussan 1645
PIERRE D'AUDIBERT
Comte de Lussan
= Claudine
de Loudun
GASPARD D'AUDIBERT
Comte de Lussan
(1)
= Jeanne Bourdal
d'Aramon
(2)
= Gabrielle
de Pellegrin
GABRIEL D'AUDIBERT
Comte de Lussan
= Gabrielle de
Bourdos de Portes
SIMON D'AUDIBERT
Lord of Massillan
CHARLES D'AUDIBERT
Comte de Lussan
= Marguerite d'Albert
de St Andrés
GASPARD D'AUDIBERT
Lord of Massillan
LAURENCE MIDDLETON
of that Ilk
= Nicola Stratton
of Lauriston
GILBERT MIDDLETON
Sheriff of Forfar
1516
= Agnes Lauder
JOHN MIDDLETON
of Middleton
= Isabella Falconer
of Halkertoun
ROBERT MIDDLETON
of Caldham
= Katherine Strachen
of Therbstoun

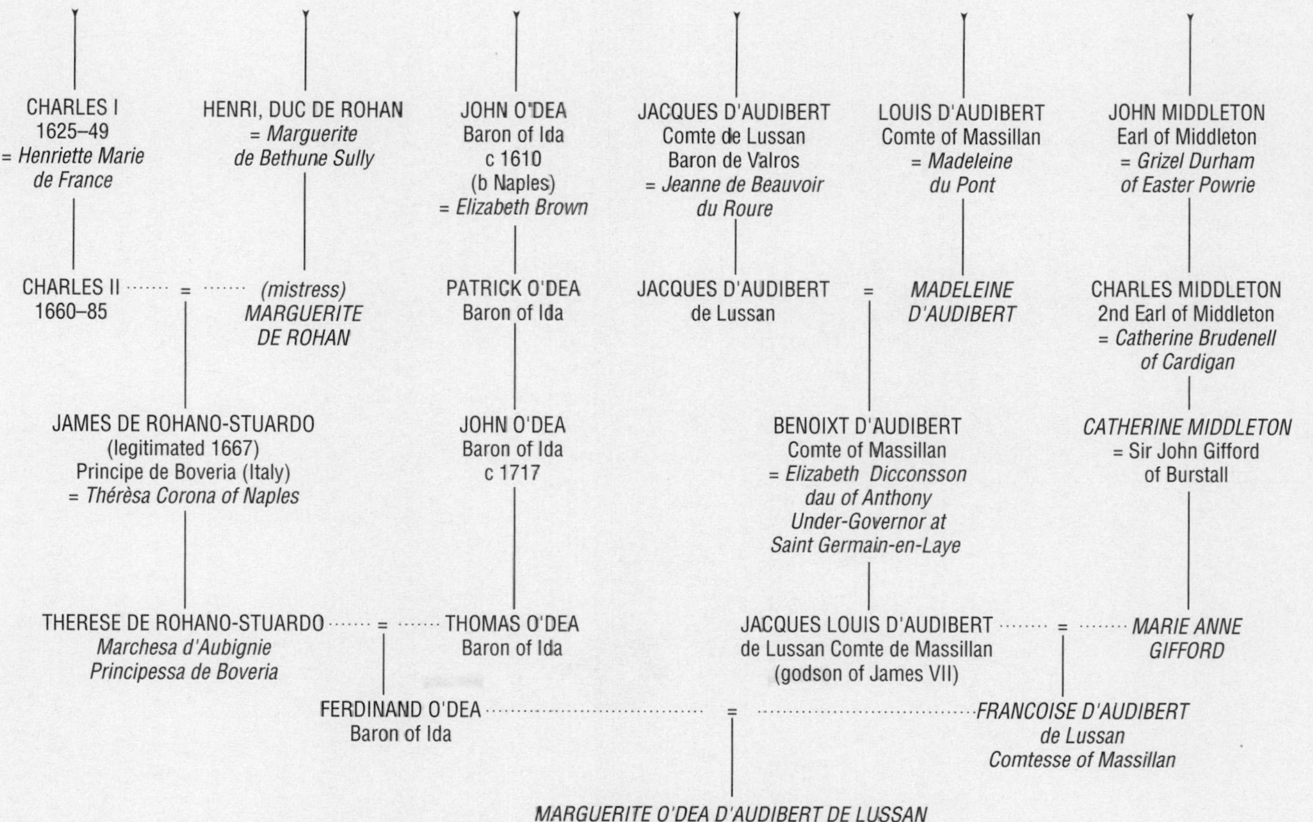

See also APPENDIX CHARTS

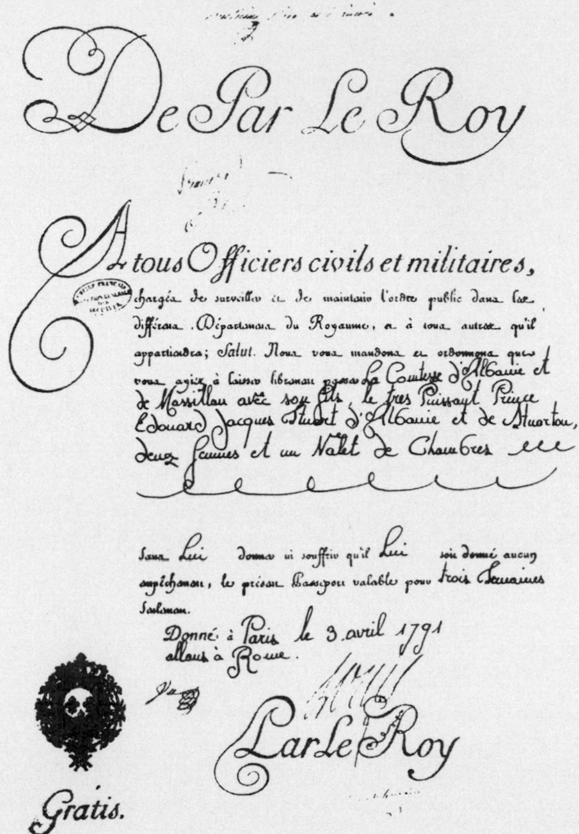

De Par Le Roy

A tous Officiers civils et militaires, chargés de surveiller et de maintenir l'ordre public dans les différens Départemens du Royaume, et à tous autres qu'il appartiendra; Salut. Nous vous mandons et ordonnons que vous ayez à laisser librement passer La Comtesse d'Albanie et de Massillan avec son fils, le tres Puissant Prince Edouard Jacques Stuart d'Albanie et de Stuarton, deux femmes et un Valet de Chambres

sans lui donner ni souffrir qu'il lui soit donné aucun empêchement, le présent Passeport valable pour trois Semaines seulement.

Donné à Paris le 3 avril 1791
allant à Rome.

Par Le Roy

Gratis.

Passport in the names of Marguerite, Comtesse de Massillan, and her son Prince Edward James Stuart of Albany (the wife and son of Charles Edward Stuart), signed by King Louis XVI, and authenticated by the Archives of the French Empire: the Archives Napoleon.

Translation:

By Order of the King

To all officers, civil and military, policing and maintaining public order in the different Departments of the Kingdom, and all others to which this appertains, Greetings. We are asking and commanding you that you let pass freely *the Countess of Albany and Massillan, with her son the high and mighty Prince Edward James Stuart of Albany and Stuarton, two maids and a valet.*

To her must not be given any problem; to her must not be given any impeachment; the present passport valid for *three weeks* only.

Given at Paris 3 April 1791. Going to Rome.

(Signature) *Louis*

Stuart), Duke of Kendal and Kintyre. The 'Kendal' title had first been given to Prince Charles Stuart (born 1666), the son of James VII (II) and his first wife, Anne Hyde (when they were Duke and Duchess of York and Albany). The 'Kintyre' title was originally granted to Prince Robert Stuart (born 1602), the son of King James VI (I)[4]. Prince Edward James was christened by the Sovereign Pontiff in the Church of Saint Peter, and Louis XVI sent his own representative to the baptism – a representative whose daughter was later to become Sir Walter Scott's wife in Britain.

Throughout the period of Charles's earlier marriage to Louise, Hanoverian murder-squads had been equipped and ready to terminate the Stuart line in Italy at any time. In addition to our own family annals, even the *Stuart Papers* at Windsor attest to this fact, and it is well enough reported that Louise's dirty linen was regularly checked by spies to see if her menstrual cycle was broken. Prior even to living with Clementina Walkinshaw, Charles had fathered a son in 1748 by his mistress, Marie Louise de Montbazon – a son who was removed to safety and reported to have died so as to safeguard him from King George's assassins. Initially, Charles's marriage to Marguerite de Massillan, and the birth of Edward James, were well-guarded secrets. For reasons of security, Marguerite gave birth to her son at the Roman residence of her cousin Prince Corsini, where they both remained for a while after Marguerite had recovered. Some weeks later they returned to the Palazzo Muti, where Edward James became an incognito addition to the sons and daughters of Charles Edward's retainers at the Jacobite Court.

News of the birth did not escape the Hanoverians for very long, though, and (as is well documented) it was in that same month of November 1786 that Charlotte of Albany met with King George III's brother William, Duke of Gloucester, at the house of the Prince Santa Croce in Rome. Since Charlotte's mother, Clementina, had been obliged to deny any marriage alliance with Charles Edward, the Duchess was concerned about the strength of her own position as a 'legitimated' daughter of King Charles. She, therefore, informed Gloucester of the recent legitimate birth, and sought his advice in the matter. The Duke confided that Charlotte's personal status was probably safe enough, since it would take the agreement of both the French Parliament and the Pope (with whom her own legitimation had been lodged)[5] to reverse the decision, and such a prospect was too unlikely to consider.

Gloucester's own main concern, however, was a letter which had been sent to Charles Edward by King George III in 1784, following the Stolberg divorce. It suggested that Charles could return to England as the Count of Albany. Charles had not taken up the invitation, but the issue was now complicated by the new-born son who, in time, would be entitled not only to claim his inheritance, but also to sit in the House of Lords. George III had thought the invitation safe enough at a time when Charles had no legitimate male heir, and (on advice from Gustavus III of Sweden) he had lodged the contents of the *letters patent* with the Courts of Spain and France, and with the Pope. Thus, Gloucester knew there was no way in which the correspondence could be denied or rescinded.

The Duke of Gloucester wrote to his brother George III about the Santa Croce meeting, and Charlotte informed her mother, Clementina, about the birth of Edward James. By that time Clementina had become the Comtesse d'Alberstroff, a title conferred in 1768 by the Bishop of Metz at the behest of the Holy Roman Emperor Joseph II. Other documents of the period (once with the *Stuart Papers* at Windsor) attest to the fact of Clementina's knowledge, in that she sent a letter to Charles congratulating him on his good fortune, followed by another dated January 1787 which also referred to the birth of his son.

Suppression of the Evidence

Although word of the marriage and the legitimate royal birth reached Westminster and the Hanoverian Court in a very short time, the facts were quickly suppressed by the Georgian Government. As a result, Prince Edward James has since been totally ignored by academic historians in Britain. There is no doubt of the purposeful concealment of fact, and ignorance cannot be claimed on account of recorded information in England and on the Continent. The concealment was perhaps easy enough in the early days, but there was the prospect of Charles III's eventual death to consider, and somehow the House of Hanover had to find the means to eliminate Edward James's succession from the

PAUL MANNES
NOTAIRE

BRUXELLES 3 Juin 1965
Avenue de Tervueren, 138b
TEL.: 33.16.80
C.C.P. 759.59

Je soussigné, Paul Mannes, Notaire retraité du Roi et de l' Etat Belge, déclare et confirme par la présente l' existence parmi les archives de l' Eglise des Saints Apotres, Place des Apotres, Rome, Italie, du certificat de mariage de Sa Majesté, le Roi Charles III Edouard Louis Philippe Silvestre Casimir Severino Marie Stewart (Stuart), Roi Titulaire des couronne de Grande Bretagne, de France et d' Irlande, fils ainé et héritier du Roi Jacques VIII d' Ecosse, III d' Angleterre, de France et d' Irlande et de sa femme, la Princesse Marie Clémentine Sobieska de Pologne, et de Marguerite Marie Térèse Dee d' Audibert de Lussan, fille unique et héritiere de Ferdinand Dee d' Audibert de Lussan, Comte de Massillan, et de Son Altesse Sérénissime, la Princesse Terese Lucie de Boveria de Rohano Stuardo, Marquise d' Aubignie. Le certificat de mariage contient le texte suivant:

'Qvod Heic XXVI Kal Dec. A H R S MDCCLXXXV Hospes Hospiti Carolus III Rex Mag. Brit. Franc. et Hiberniae, Fid. Def. Porrexerit Dexteram Margareta Maria Teresa Fil. Ferdinando Dee d' Audibert de Lussan, Comes Massillanae, et Teresa Lucia Princ. de Boveria de Rohano Stuardo &c, Eamque, Servatis S R E Ritibus Duxerit in Matrimonium.'

De par la présente, je confirme l' existence du certificat de naissance et de baptème de la posteritée de ce mariage, le Prince Edouard Jacques Stewart, né le quinze Octobre 1786. Le certificat de naissance contient le texte suivant:

'Eduardo Jacobi, Dux Kintyriis et Kendalae, Scot, Angl. Franc. Hib. et Pol. Princeps. Fil. Carolus III Stuartus Fid. Def. et Margarita de Massillanae, Mag. Brit. Franc. et Hibernia Rex et Regina, Natus XV Kal Oct. Anno M DCCL XXXVI.'

Ecrit et approuvé personellement.

Paul Mannes

VILLE DE BRUXELLES – STAD BRUSSEL

Pour extrait conforme : – Voor gelijkluidend uittreksel :
Bruxelles II, le 04/06/1965
Brussel, II,
Pour l'Officier de l'Etat civil,
Voor de Ambtenaar van de Burgerlijke Stand,
Le fonctionnaire délégué,
De gemachtigde Ambtenaar,

F. Devrient

One of a set of notary's letters prepared on 3 June 1965 for Prince Michael's grandfather, Prince Julius Joseph James Stewart of Annandale, by the family lawyer, stamped and authenticated by the City of Brussels authority. This document confirms an extract from the Church archive concerning the marriage of Charles Edward Stuart and Marguerite de Massillan in December 1785. It also confirms the certificated record of the baptism of their son Edward James in October 1786.

This letter, along with various other documents of Stuart/Stewart record and certification not included in this book may be found on the Royal House of Stewart Internet web-site, http://www.mediaquest.co.uk/rhsfmb.html

official records. Indeed, they had to suppress knowledge of his very existence, but the young prince was well guarded. Only by having the Scottish line formally declared extinct could the long-standing German *coup* be accepted by the British people as an unavoidable change of dynasty, rather than an act of possession without entitlement.

George III was not in a strong position at that time; he was unpopular with the people, and his empire was crumbling around him. Not only had Britain been obliged to surrender at Yorktown, Virginia, in 1781, but while the American war was waging colonial India had fallen into anarchy, with the French allying themselves with Hyder Ali of Mysore in 1780. Additionally, Spain had captured Minorca from Britain in 1782, while Gibraltar had been under constant siege from Spanish and French troops. The last thing George and his ministers were prepared to suffer was a resurgence of Stuart popularity in Britain – a popularity that would certainly be heightened by knowledge of the new Jacobite heir.

As things transpired, a suitable scheme fell neatly into place for King George, and after more than four centuries of Stewart sovereign descent, a purposeful duplicity of Wills held the solution. This enabled knowledge of the royal marriage and birth to be shamefully concealed from the British public throughout the balance of the Hanoverian era. For whatever reason, the concealment was then perpetuated in respect of descending heirs through the continuing succession of Saxe-Coburg-Gotha–Windsor.

Should one make enquiries of today's establishment as to who is the present heir to the Royal House of Stuart, the likely answer will be Franz of Bavaria, who succeeded his father, the late Prince/Duke Albrecht. Should one further ask how a Bavarian prince has the right to succeed to the Scottish Honours, the reply will refer to the Will of Charles Edward Stuart's younger brother Cardinal Henry, Duke of York, Bishop of Frascati. It is purported that this Will, made by a childless cardinal of the Roman Church, nominated Charles Emmanuel IV, ex-King of Sardinia, as the Stuart successor.[6] By way of marriages in the female lines from Charles Emmanuel's brother Victor Emmanuel I, Prince Albrecht of Bavaria has long been the commonly recognized heir to the Stuarts, with a somewhat tenuous ancestry back to Henrietta, a daughter of Charles I. Prince Albrecht died quite recently, to be succeeded by his eldest son Duke Franz, who is now said to hold the Stuart distinction. However, the fact is that, despite the propaganda concerning this pseudo-Stuart succession, Henry's Will did not name Charles Emmanuel as his successor. This fantasy, which has made its way into the history books, was a purposely contrived deception by Britain's Hanoverian Government.

This deceit was made possible by creating the belief that Charles Edward Stuart had no son and heir (legitimate or otherwise). In truth, he had fathered more than one son before Edward James; he also had daughters, one of whom, Charlotte of Albany, had been legitimated. Both the Abbé Felicé of Frascati and the Stuart Secretary of State, James Edgar, confirmed in writing that Clementina Walkinshaw had borne more than one child to Charles III, and it was a generally held opinion that Charles and Clementina had been married by Scottish Declaration back in 1746. (*See* Appendix VIII for a list of the Stuart Secretaries.) This belief was supported by the letters between them. Also, the French Register concerning the years 1752–60, when Clementina lived with Charles Edward in Europe, states: 'She was always treated and regarded in public as his wife, bore the same name as the Prince and made honourable his house'.

A marriage declaration by Scottish custom would not automatically have held good with the Roman Church but, nevertheless, Charlotte's baptismal record indicates that her parents, Charles and Clementina, were formally united. It was for this very reason that, under duress instigated by Cardinal Henry, Clementina was pressured into abrogating any such marital commitment by sworn statement in 1766.

In 1784, at the time of the Stolberg divorce, Charles made a Will, nominating his brother Henry as his royal heir, along with Charlotte as his sole estate beneficiary. This event is well enough documented in the historical accounts of his life, but what those accounts fail to mention (because the truth was concealed by the Hanoverian regime) is that this Will was not Charles's final testament: it was superseded by another before his death.

On 30 January 1788, the 67-year-old King Charles III died of an apoplectic fit at the Palazzo Muti in Rome. Queen Marguerite (together with her brother-in-law, Cardinal Henry) was informed of the death by her cousin, Princess Palestrina, and she was then visited by the two Franciscan brothers who had attended Charles at the last. At Marguerite's instruction, and with Cardinal Henry's agreement, Fathers James and Michael MacCormick returned to the Palazzo Muti to make a death mask of the King. His body was duly embalmed and regally vested, with a crown on his head, a ring on his finger, and a sceptre in his hand. He was then placed in a coffin of cypress wood, and the Royal Family (brother, wife, daughter and son) assembled to pay their last respects before Charles was removed to his resting-place at Frascati. At that time, because of Charles's earlier conversion to the Anglican faith, the Pope would not accept his body within the Vatican, but some time later the restriction was relaxed, and Charles was moved to the vault of St Peter's in Rome.

The *Statutes of the Order of the Temple of Jerusalem* confirm that, on the death of Charles III, he was succeeded as Grand Master by John Oliphant of Bachilton.

Last Will and Testament

Shortly before his death, Charles had written in his diary his last Will and Testament; this was witnessed on 13 January 1788 by Father O'Kelly (his Dominican confessor) and the Abbé Consalvi, both of whom were appointed executors. This final Will and the details of Charles's last weeks were removed from the diary (which eventually became the property of the House of Windsor) as soon as it came into the hands of George III. It stated, however, that the royal children, Edward James (Edouard Jacques) and Charlotte, were to be co-heirs to the remainder of the Sobieski inheritance. Furthermore, that his son Edward was to succeed as King *de jure* on his 16th birthday, while Henry of York was to be Regent for his nephew in the meantime:

> My brother Henry is to act as Regent in the interests of my lawful son; and both my children, Edouard Jacques and Charlotte are co-heirs of what is left of the Sobieski inheritance; Edouard to succeed in name on his 16th birthday [ie 1802]. My wife will be the guardian of my son during his minority.

Notwithstanding this, when Charles Edward died in 1788 the ambitious Cardinal Henry wasted no time in declaring himself King Henry of Scots (Henry IX of England). He issued a manifesto[7] proclaiming his rights to the Four Crowns (Scotland, England, Ireland and France), and sent a copy to every European Court. He then modified his Coat of Arms, deleting the silver crescent (the heraldic mark of the second son), and blazoned the Royal Crown in place of his ducal distinction. In signing letters and documents he used the royal signature, 'Henry R', along with his title Duke of York, and had medals struck to commemorate his regal status. Meanwhile, Henry's nephew Prince Edward James (though awaiting his sovereign majority) succeeded as 2nd Count of Albany, Count Stuarton, and Head of the Royal House of Stuart.

To support his audacious claim to the honour of 'Majesty', Henry produced not Charles's last Will and Testament of 1788, but the earlier Will of 1784. This suited Britain's Hanoverian Government because, as a cardinal of the Roman Church, Henry was not likely to have any children. By virtue of this, the cessation of the recognized Stuart line was in sight, with Henry of York at the end of it. Both O'Kelly and Consalvi were party to Henry's intrigue in return for rapid promotion within the Church hierarchy. In no time at all the former became Dominican Procurator, while the latter Abbé was raised to the Cardinalate. Charlotte was provided with an income and a home in Frascati, while the Palazzo Muti was kept available for Marguerite de Massillan and her son Prince Edward.

Another cleric who was involved in the complicity was the Abbé James Placid Waters, Procurator of the Benedictine monks in Rome (1777–1808). He later became adviser to Charlotte of Albany, who died at the age of 36. Upon her death from cancer in November 1789, Waters was plagued with obstruction from Cardinal Henry in respect of Charlotte's own Will. He therefore wrote to Clementina d'Alberstroff, requesting that she tell Lady Stuart (Marguerite de Massillan) to bear with him owing to Cardinal York's interference in the matter.[8]

At the time, both Cardinal Henry and Abbé Waters were quite unaware that Charlotte, though unmarried, had borne three children by her cousin Prince Ferdinand de Rohan, Archbishop and Duke of Cambrai. Two were daughters, Aglae and Marie (who were legitimated by the Duc de Montbazon), and the third was a son, Charles Edward Maximilien, Count Roehenstart. He spent his early life with Baron Korff in Germany, and some later time in America, but died in care following a coach accident in Scotland in 1854, and was buried at Dunkeld Cathedral (*see* Appendix IX).

The claiming of the Stuart Crown instead of the Regency was not the first time that Henry had put his own interests before his family's cause. He had greatly upset his brother and the Jacobites some years earlier when he accepted his cardinal's hat. Plainly, the Roman religion was at the core of the Stuarts' problems, and the 1701 *Act of Settlement,* which had paved the way for the Hanoverian succession in Britain, stipulated that future monarchs must be Protestant. Even so, after the Jacobite defeat at Culloden, Henry chose to make a blatant representation of his own Catholicism on being raised to the Cardinalate in 1748. The Jacobites were distraught, and Charles was so disappointed that, in September 1750, he formally converted to the Anglican faith in London, renouncing the Roman Church altogether.

Count Stuarton

Edward, 2nd Count of Albany

It is evident that with regard to Charles's Will Henry sought only to dismiss the immediate Regency clause, and in so doing he declared himself King *de jure.* However, he had every intention of rectifying his selfish manoeuvre by reverting the inheritance to his brother's son Edward James, Count Stuarton. Accordingly, a year later in January 1789, Henry made his own Will, whereby all that he possessed – the claims of Scotland, England, Ireland and France, the Stuart library at Frascati, his private properties in Italy, France and Mexico, and the Sobieski jewels – were bequeathed to his sole heir, Edward James: that is 'to my nephew Count Stuarton',[9] a title which Henry had bestowed upon Edward that same month. Both Cardinal Ercole Consalvi and Cardinal Angelo Cesarini were privy to the contents of the Will and were nominated executors, as attested in their memoirs.

In early 1798 Rome was invaded by the French, at which time (until 1802) Prince Edward James and his mother were living at the Court of King Charles Emmanuel IV of Sardinia. When the French arrived, both Henry and Pope Pius VI were compelled to flee into exile, but the Pope died *en route* to Naples. Ironically, in 1791 Henry had welcomed the Princesses Adelaide and Victoire of France to Rome. Then, at the executions of Louis XVI and Marie Antoinette in 1793, a requiem had been sung in his Church at Frascati. But now Rome had been proclaimed a Republic, and the power of the Papacy had temporarily collapsed.

In 1799 Henry returned to Rome, and Pius VII was elected Pope. Napoleon, who was a distant cousin to both Henry and his nephew, obliged the Pope to sign the *Treaty of Talentino,* which exhorted financial indemnity from the Holy See. To assist, Henry sold the 'Gold Coin of Poland' which had come to him on the death of his brother, and which should have become the property of Edward James. It was inherited originally from the Sobieski family, and it was probably the Great Seal of King Jan III. Henry also sold the embossed gold shield which had been given to Jan III by the Holy Roman Emperor for having prevented the Turks from invading Vienna. Additionally, he sold a magnificent jewel (the size of a pigeon's egg) called the 'Balas Ruby' for £60,000 [about £1.5m in today's terms]. Then, when the Pope was unable to meet the financial demands of the French Directory, Henry sold most of the Stuart fortune on the Pope's behalf, and emerged totally ruined.

After Charles Emmanuel IV's Sardinian abdication to become a Jesuit monk, Edward James and his Stuart cousins travelled to Rome, to be entertained by Pope Pius VII. As for Henry, having lost his personal wealth and property during the French Revolution and Napoleon's advance into the Papal States, he was induced to become a pensioner of the Hanoverian Crown, and it was then that the Westminster machinations against the Stuart succession heightened.

Henry's agreed British pension was £5,000 per annum[10] [equivalent to about £250,000 per annum in today's terms], but in return for this he had provisionally agreed to two conditions imposed by King George III. Firstly, he was to send the Coronation Ring back to London, which he conceded to have done at his death; secondly, but more importantly, he was required to restructure his Will of 1789 – the Will that named his 'nephew, Count Stuarton', as the Stuart royal successor. Henry confirmed that he would do this once he had spoken with the party concerned, whereupon Lord Minto (acting on behalf of King George) agreed to this proviso.

In 1802 Cardinal Henry met with Charles Emmanuel, the Pope, Marguerite de Massillan, and her son Edward James, in Frascati. They pondered over George III's demand, and agreed that the Will could indeed be rewritten so as to facilitate Henry's pension, but only in accordance with their specified terms. That year of 1802 was the very year of Edward James's 16th birthday – the year of his legal inheritance as determined by his father's Will – and this meant that he would inherit his sovereign rights in the December, regardless of Henry's secondary nomination.

In accordance with the meeting, and in order to retain his British income, Henry was enabled to change the text of his Will in a manner that satisfied King George. This was done by way of a cleverly structured rewording so that it remained in Prince Edward's favour, even though it would become obsolete from the December as far as the pre-destined sovereign rights were concerned. The new document simply substituted the nomination 'to my nephew Count Stuarton' with the words, 'in favour of that prince to whom it descends by virtue of *de jure* blood relationship'.[11]

Those immediately concerned were content at this, for there was only one blood-related prince. Cardinals Consalvi, Cesarini and Fesch all knew perfectly well that the wording could only relate to Henry's one legitimate nephew and closest blood relative, Prince Edward James of Albany, Count Stuarton.

16

The Diverted Succession

Napoleon and the Stuarts

Irrespective of the fact that the Stuarts have been ignored by the British authorities since the death of Cardinal Henry, the descendant royals of Charles Edward's line have been continually active in social, political, military and sovereign affairs abroad. Through the past two centuries, we have been held in high esteem in many countries. Napoleon Buonaparte was a great supporter of the Stuarts, and Cardinal Fesch (half-uncle to Napoleon I) wrote that Prince Edward James represented the Stuart family in Paris during the Sacre (coronation) of the Emperor in 1804.[1] Indeed, on the eve of Napoleon's coronation he received the prized Sobieski sabre of Jan III of Poland from the hands of Prince Edward James Stuart. Edward had originally received the sabre at the time of Charlotte's death from one of her closest friends, Mrs O'Donnel. In turn, Napoleon I bequeathed the sword to his son Napoleon François, Duke of Reichstadt (known as l'Aiglon – the Eaglet). But l'Aiglon did not receive the bequest, and the whereabouts of the famous sabre are still unknown.

Prince Edward James, Count Stuarton, was an appointed observer of battle tactics for the Emperor at his numerous victories: Austerlitz (1805), Saalfeld and Jena (1806), Friedland (1807), Eckmul and Wagram (1809). He was present at Bayonne when Carlos IV of Spain abdicated in 1808, and was with Napoleon at Waterloo in 1815.[2] While at Saalfeld in 1806, Prince Edward stayed at the house of Duke Francis of Saxe-Coburg

(Queen Victoria's grandfather). In 1809 (with the blessing and support of Napoleon I), Edward of Albany married Maria Pasquini, the granddaughter of an Italian aristocrat, and great-granddaughter of the noted composer Bernardo Pasquini.

In 1815 Prince Edward James, 2nd Count of Albany, was involved in a curious affair which completely by-passed the academic historians. Today it provides a good example of how history has so often been manipulated to suit the purposes of the moment. The story relates to the courageous Michel Ney, Prince of Moscow, Marshal of France, whom Napoleon described as 'the bravest of the brave'. Marshal Ney won the great victory for Napoleon at Elchingen (1805); he also fought at Jena and Friedland, and showed extraordinary courage, commanding the rearguard, in the Emperor's retreat from Moscow (1812–13).

Subsequent to the retreat, Napoleon was defeated at Leipzig, and exiled to the Isle of Elba, but he returned to France in 1815. Marshal Ney was duly sent to arrest him, but instead he deserted to join Napoleon again, and fought alongside him at Waterloo. The history books all tell that, subsequent to this, Ney was seized and shot for treason in 1815 – but this was not the case. In fact, Prince Edward James Stuart, together with Napoleon's cousin Pascal Luciani, and Ney's fellow Freemason the Duke of Wellington, aided the Marshal's escape to North America.

The Polish Colonel Lehmanowski of the Great Army told of how the three men bribed Ney's guards and intended executioners with gold. Ney's shooting was faked, and he was removed to the Hospital de Luxembourg, where another body was substituted for burial. Taking the forenames Peter Stuart, Marshal Ney was then conveyed on a British ship to America, where he settled in Brownsville, South Carolina, to become a French teacher.[3] Colonel Lehmanowski became a Protestant minister in Knightown, Indiana. Ney's son also emigrated to America, and several members of the United States Senate visited the family regularly with news from France. Even today there are Ney descendants in America, and within private circles they are still referred to as Princes of the Moskova.

Following Napoleon's eventual defeat at Waterloo and his resultant abdication, the Stuarts came under the protection of Prince Charles de Bourbon, Duc de Berri, subsequent to which the Belgian Baron Surlet de Choquier used the services of Prince

Edward in promoting the idea of having a French prince as King of the Belgians.[4]

Napoleon I was a lineal descendant in a male line from King Charles II Stuart. Prior to marrying Catherine of Braganza, Charles had a liaison in exile with Marguerite, Duchesse de Rohan, and their son, James de Rohano Stuardo, was legitimated in 1667. He married Thérèsa Corona of Naples, a descendant of the princely families of Orsini and Corsini, and Napoleon was descended from this relationship.

Napoleon's real name was not Buonaparte, but 'de Boveria de Rohano Stuardo'. His grandmother was Marie de Neuhoff, titular Queen of Corsica, and his father, Charles Marie, was born at Kinvalla, Brittany, in 1746. In his early teens Charles Marie returned to Corsica in order to manage the family estate and, due to the political circumstance of his Corsican residence, he assumed the name of his family lawyer Giuseppe di Buonaparte. However, neither Charles Marie nor Napoleon were related to the Corsican lawyer who, as confirmed by his brother Luciano, Canon of Ajjacio, died childless.[5]

It is generally suggested in England that most of the French aristocracy were resentful of Napoleon I, but this was far from the case. Many of the younger French nobility, and the more rational sons of the ousted Bourbon regime, entered the service of the Emperor after his *coup d'état* brought an end to the French Revolution in 1799. Among those who were close to Napoleon were Louis de Rohan-Guéméné and his brother Ferdinand (Charlotte of Albany's former lover).

The brothers were both clerics of the Church and barons of the Empire. In 1809 Napoleon consulted them about one particular natural son of Charles Edward Stuart – a son who had been born in 1748 to Charles's cousin and mistress, Princess Marie Louise de Rohan-Guéméné, Duchesse de Montbazon. Seemingly, the boy, Charles Godefroid de Rohan, had lived a mere six months and was buried at the Church of St Louis in Paris – but there had been no period of family mourning at the time, and no mention of his death in the society press as would normally have been the case. The de Rohan brothers confided to Napoleon that the boy did not die, but had been secreted into safe custody (in fact he was brought to Berse Drelincourt in England, the family home of Lady Anne Primrose). Upon learning this, the Emperor had the

60-year-old coffin examined, and found it completely devoid of any bones or dust.[6]

This is just one such instance concerning a well-documented natural child of Charles Edward, but there are other similarly recorded accounts (*see* Appendix IX) – and apart from his wives, Charles had quite a few mistresses at various stages of his life. It is, therefore, strange to consider that, without any foundation except for Hanoverian propaganda, the history books in Britain continue to claim that Charles had little association or success with women.

Having established that Louise de Stolberg had not given Charles III a child, Napoleon gathered the prevailing Stuart family together in 1804. In May he was crowned at the Cathedral of Notre Dame in Paris, for which occasion Edward James and his cousins (Charlotte's daughters) Aglae and Marie were present. At that time, Prince Ferdinand de Rohan-Guéméné (the father of Charlotte's offspring) asked for the Emperor's blessing so that his daughter Aglae Clementine, Comtesse de Rohan, could marry her cousin Jehan de la Tour d'Auvergne, Comte de Bouillon. Jehan was a natural son of the last Sovereign Prince of Bouillon, and had been legitimated in 1800. Napoleon was happy to comply with the request[7], and the couple were married in 1810. Two years later their daughter, Marie Louise, became Duchesse of Bouillon and Albany in her own right. For both personal and political reasons, Napoleon was a great patron of the Stuarts, and it was his own brother, General Joseph Buonaparte, who had forewarned the family about the impending French advance into Rome in December 1797.[8]

Stuart Papers

When Cardinal Henry Benedict Stuart died on 13 July 1807, King George and the British Parliament applied exactly the same strategy that Henry had used in respect of his own brother's Will. They completely ignored his revised 1802 Will, which was by then deemed insufficiently changed to suit their immediate purpose, and reverted to Henry's original Will of 1789. However, certain subtle adjustments were made to its published content. The direct reference to Henry's 'nephew' was excluded, as was the fact of the intended royal succession. Instead of 'nephew', the word 'relation' was introduced in translation, but no one in England thought to enquire who this 'relation, Count Stuarton' might be! An example of a typical press report is that of the *Gentleman's Magazine,* September 1807:

> He [Henry] possessed before 1798 a very valuable collection of curiosities at his villa, where many scarce tracts and interesting manuscripts concerning the unfortunate House of Stuart were among the ornaments of his library. In his Will, made in January 1789, he had left the latter to his relation Count Stuarton; but they were all, in 1798, either plundered by the French and Italian Jacobins at Rome, or confiscated by the French Commissaries for the libraries or museums in Paris.

In fact the said manuscripts had not been purloined by those accused; some are at the Vatican, some are in Roman libraries, and others – said to have been stolen – were actually withheld by the British Government. As to why the documents were removed from Henry's library some while prior to his death, the reason is very straightforward. It was known to the Stuarts in December 1797 (by way of information from General Joseph Buonaparte) that Rome was to be invaded by the French. Steps were therefore taken by the family to secrete some items of value and historical reference from the city, and these included Henry's books and papers. Then, in February 1798, Rome fell as predicted.

According to the memoirs of Henry's executors, Cardinals Consalvi and Cesarini, Henry's library collection was of small relevance as an individual bequest, since he bequeathed All he owned to his 'nephew, Count Stuarton', including the sovereign rights to England, Scotland, France and Ireland.

Interestingly though, the *Gentleman's Magazine* report did confirm the true position with regard to those rights being supposedly diverted to Charles Emmanuel of Sardinia, who was not immediately related to Henry, nor had he ever held the title Count Stuarton. Word had been spread by Hanoverian ambassadors and agents in Europe that the ex-King of Sardinia was Henry's chosen heir (a deceit which is still maintained in some British establishment circles), and this news was reported in the French press. However, the English *Gentleman's Magazine,* being rather less gullible, announced quite correctly that

> the statements in the French papers concerning Cardinal York's bequests to the King of Sardinia are void of all truth.

Houses of Rohan and Sobieski

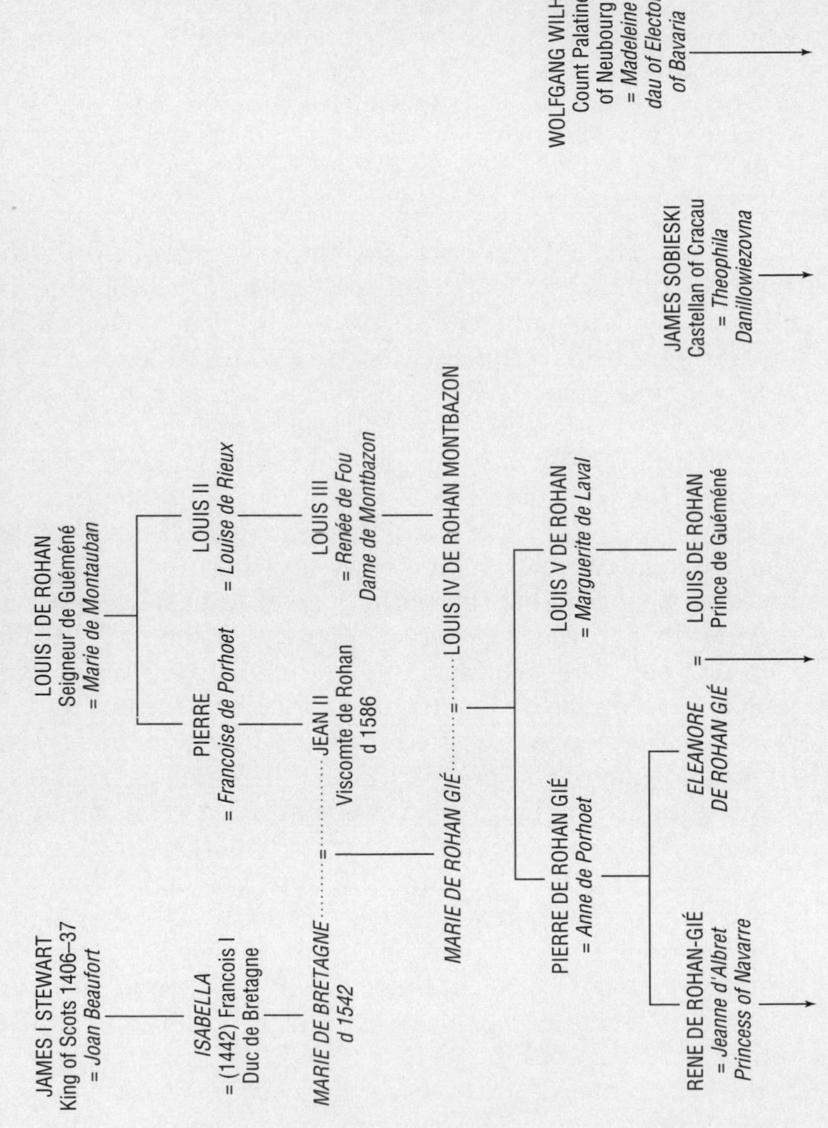

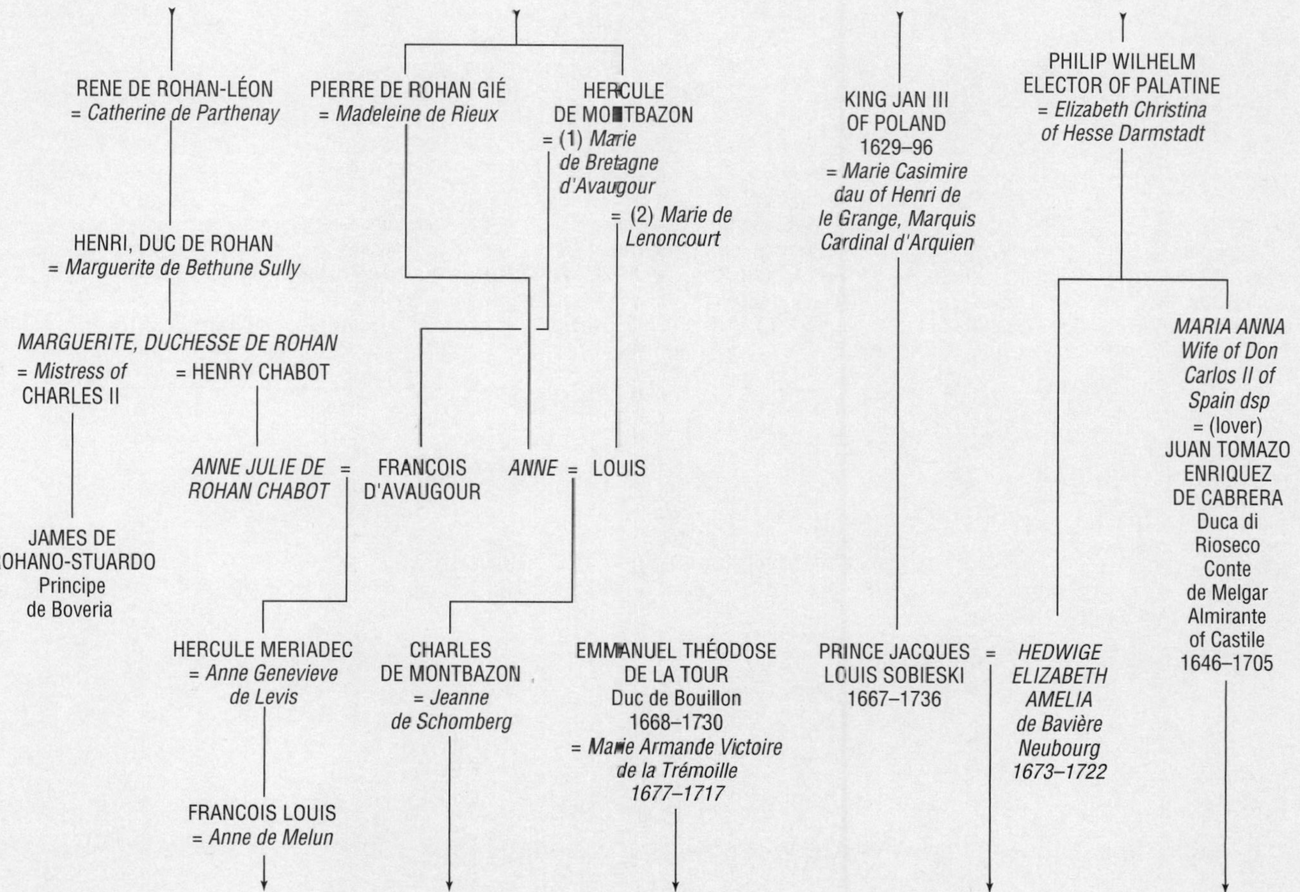

RENE DE ROHAN-LÉON
= Catherine de Parthenay
PIERRE DE ROHAN GIÉ
= Madeleine de Rieux
HERCULE
DE MONTBAZON
= (1) Marie
de Bretagne
d'Avaugour
= (2) Marie de
Lenoncourt
KING JAN III
OF POLAND
1629–96
= Marie Casimire
dau of Henri de
le Grange, Marquis
Cardinal d'Arquien
PHILIP WILHELM
ELECTOR OF PALATINE
= Elizabeth Christina
of Hesse Darmstadt
HENRI, DUC DE ROHAN
= Marguerite de Bethune Sully
MARGUERITE, DUCHESSE DE ROHAN
= Mistress of
CHARLES II
= HENRY CHABOT
MARIA ANNA
Wife of Don
Carlos II of
Spain dsp
= (lover)
JUAN TOMAZO
ENRIQUEZ
DE CABRERA
Duca di
Rioseco
Conte
de Melgar
Almirante
of Castile
1646–1705
ANNE JULIE DE
ROHAN CHABOT
=
FRANCOIS
D'AVAUGOUR
ANNE
=
LOUIS
JAMES DE
ROHANO-STUARDO
Principe
de Boveria
HERCULE MERIADEC
= Anne Genevieve
de Levis
CHARLES
DE MONTBAZON
= Jeanne
de Schomberg
EMMANUEL THÉODOSE
DE LA TOUR
Duc de Bouillon
1668–1730
= Marie Armande Victoire
de la Trémoille
1677–1717
PRINCE JACQUES
LOUIS SOBIESKI
1667–1736
=
HEDWIGE
ELIZABETH
AMELIA
de Bavière
Neubourg
1673–1722
FRANCOIS LOUIS
= Anne de Melun

Houses of Rohan and Sobieski – continued

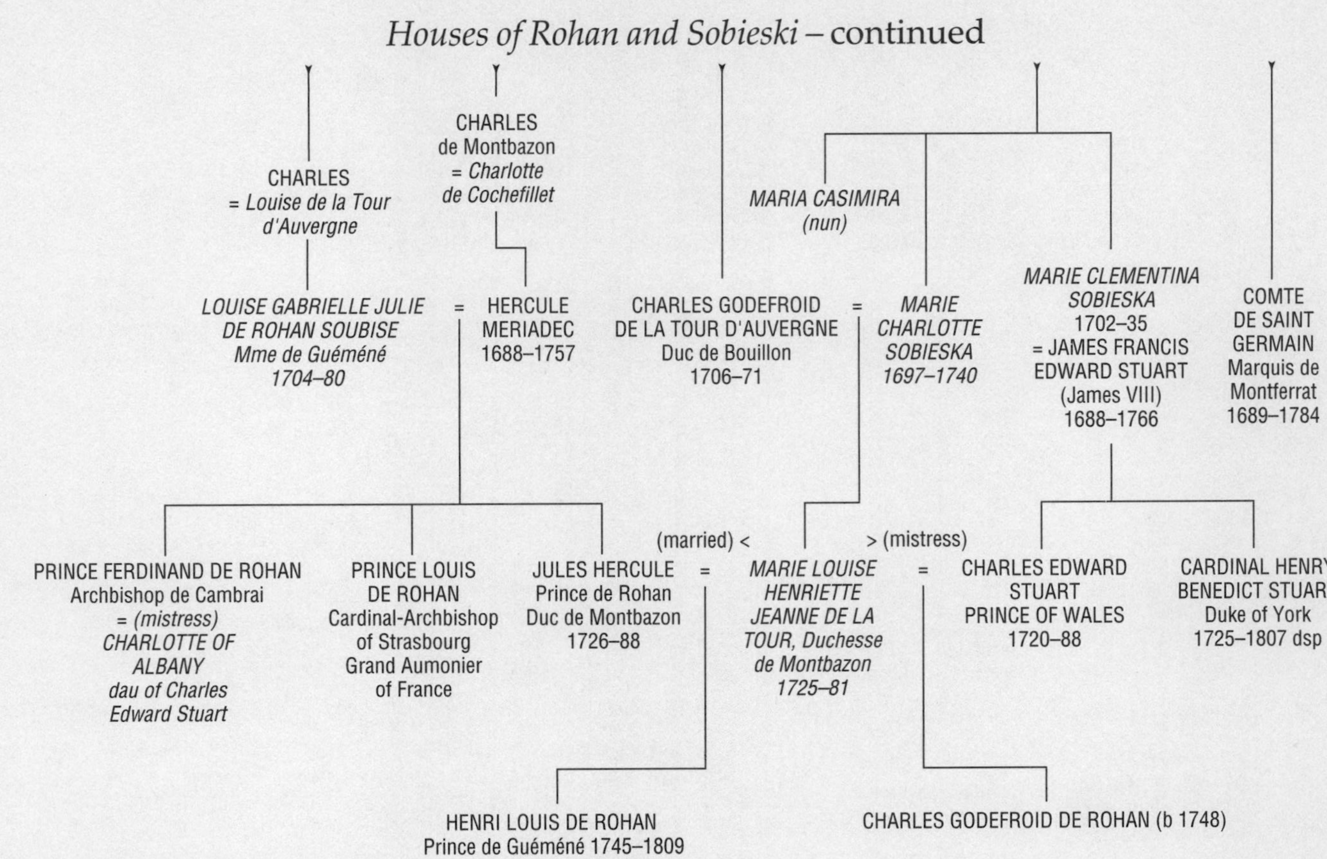

Ignoring the facts of the matter, the Hanoverian ministers proclaimed Charles Emmanuel to be Henry's royal heir. Henry's amended 1802 Will was then produced, and the revised wording was strategically implemented (by virtue of its looseness) in favour of the abdicated King of Sardinia. And so the Stuart inheritance seemingly passed to a childless monk of the Jesuit Order.

Charles Emmanuel, of course, recognized the absurdity of the nomination, and wrote to King George's Parliament denouncing the strategy as fallacious because he knew the Stuarts to be alive and well. He had given Countess Marguerite and Prince Edward James his hospitality in Sardinia from 1798 to 1802, and then built a house for them by the Corso in Rome, near to the Albergo di Roma. Charles Emmanuel sent a copy of his letter to every European monarch[9], yet still the London ministers managed to disguise the issue in Britain. Strategically contrived history books now record the 'diverted succession' as having progressed from Sardinia, through Modena, into Bavaria.

When Charles Emmanuel died in 1819, the diverted Stuart title passed to his brother Victor Emmanuel I. It was all perfectly convenient because Britain's *Act of Settlement* prevented Victor, or others of his Catholic line, from staking any official claim to the spurious inheritance. Victor's Stuart succession was generally accepted by the unsuspecting British public (including the emergent Royal Stuart Society in London), as were the related inheritances of the successive Francis V of Modena and Ruprecht of Bavaria who died in 1955. Nevertheless, when Ruprecht came to Scotland for a holiday prior to the 1953 coronation of Elizabeth II, he was obliged by Parliament to sign a formal declaration stating that he had no intention of claiming the Four Crowns while on British soil.

The story of Cardinal Henry's elusive manuscripts is particularly interesting since it is entirely relevant to the intrigue of this whole chain of events. A large consignment of Stuart documents was discovered near Rome in 1817 by Dr Robert Watson of the Scots College, Paris. He purchased them for £23 [about £610 in today's value], and prepared to write the story of the subverted dynasty. However, before he had the chance to collate the files, they were seized by the Papal Police and sent to Hanoverian Intelligence in London. The *Jacobite Peerage Register* of 1904 records that this was done specifically to avoid their content becoming known to Charles Emmanuel of Sardinia.

Many years later, Watson received an *ex gratia* payment from the British Government for having been deprived of his property. But, still intent on publishing the contents, he pursued his right to study the papers. Needless to say he was refused access, and in 1838 he was found dead in a manner that was reported to be suicide. The ultimate fate of the incriminating papers discovered by Watson remains a matter of conjecture, as does the precise nature of his death – but neither is difficult to presume.

Prior to Cardinal Henry's death, the Abbé Waters (who had lost his possessions in the Napoleonic advance) had also been manoeuvred into receipt of a pension from King George. Not surprisingly, as with Henry, his income also had a price. Following the proclamation of the Roman Republic in 1798, Henry had left Rome, but Waters remained to become the custodian of another significant collection of Stuart papers which Henry had retained since the death of Charles Edward. These documents were the price of the Abbé's Hanoverian pension, and in 1805 he was obliged to pass them to the British Government. In time, they were deposited (in whole or in part) at Windsor Castle. Some of these letters and documents have since been made available for study and publication; but as for the rest, their whereabouts or existence are again open to speculation.

As a result of these important documentary acquisitions, the way was deemed clear for Prince Edward James (the legitimate heir of Charles Edward Stuart) to be totally excluded from historical writings in Britain, as if he never existed! However, despite these losses, and quite apart from additional records which are still held in the Stewart archives, the life of Prince Edward James is well documented. He was the subject of writings by Vicomte René de Chateaubriand, Abbé James Waters, Princess Caroline Murat (Napoleon's sister), the French Government minister O'Farrill, and many others including Mr Denis, the British Consul in Rome (1817), in his personal correspondence with the Prince Regent (later George IV). The whole of my legitimate family line through Charles Edward and Edward James is fully detailed in a signed, stamped and authenticated document issued by the City of Brussels Registrars as recently as December 1990. By that time the Stuarts/Stewarts had been permanent Belgian residents for about 100 years.

Knights Templars and the Strategy of Hanover

Prior to the late 18th century, the inherent secrecy of the Jacobite lodges in Britain had provided the perfect facility for undercover intrigue against the Government and the German succession. Throughout the land, the Stuart societies and Tory lodges had been closely entwined, as a result of which they became prime targets for Hanoverian Intelligence, whose high-ranking Secret Service operatives duly infiltrated the fraternities.

One of these agents was an illegitimate son of George II, who became known as Thomas Dunkerley. Born in 1724, he served (from the age of ten) in the Royal Navy, and his royal birthright was not announced until he was over 40. Having been initiated into Freemasonry in 1754, he formed lodges in many of the ships in which he served, and when his parentage was recognized he was granted a personal income and rooms at Hampton Court Palace. Subsequently he became Provincial Grand Master in numerous provinces, and formed the Supreme Grand and Royal Conclave in 1791. In this regard, he invited George III's young son, Prince Edward (the later Duke of Kent), to be the overall Patron of the Order which assumed control of the high degrees in England. Dunkerley died in 1795, by which time Edward of Kent was committed to English Freemasonry, which was brought firmly under Hanoverian control.

One of the Duke of Kent's brothers was Augustus Frederick, Duke of Sussex, who (despite his Hanoverian status) married twice into Jacobite families. He was first married in Rome to Lady Augusta Murray, daughter of the 4th Earl Dunmore, on 4 April 1793. But this marriage was formally annulled in the following year because (having not been sanctioned by Augustus' father, King George III) it contravened the *Royal Marriages Act* of 1772. Secondly, he married Lady Celia Saunders, daughter of the 2nd Earl of Arran, on 2 May 1831. She was granted the style Duchess of Inverness, but the marriage was similarly deemed to be in breach of the Act. However, in 1793 (the year of his first marriage), Duke Augustus had resigned his right of succession to the British Crown[10] in favour of Henry Benedict Stuart, whom he doubtless met in Rome, and he therefore pursued his own course irrespective of the restrictive Hanoverian statute.

Charles Edward Stuart had died in 1788 but, as we have seen, the French Templar intelligence service operated well for the Stuarts in conjunction with the ambassadorial Knights of Saint Germain. Henry Benedict Stuart was alive and well, but the general public in Britain had no confirmed knowledge of Henry's young nephew Prince Edward James, Count Stuarton. The self-serving Henry had been given a substantial Hanoverian pension for his silence in 1802, and numerous key lodges had been infiltrated by Georgian agents, so it remained only for the House of Hanover to await Henry's own demise, at which time Kent and his allies could take over the Templar organizations in Britain. However, as Henry grew older, so did his nephew – and by the time Henry died in 1807, Edward James was 20-years-old and politically active.

In 1809, within two years of Henry Stuart's death, a heated dispute over sovereign loyalties arose between George III's sons, Edward and Augustus; it became known as the 'War of the Brothers'. As explained, Prince Edward, Duke of Kent (the father of Queen Victoria), was a Freemason, but his brother Prince Augustus Frederick, Duke of Sussex, was a Knight Templar. In fact, having resigned his sovereign rights in 1793, Augustus had become Grand Master of the English branch of the French Templars. Edward's problem was that the Templars were Stuart supporters, and he therefore endeavoured to sway their allegiance to the reigning House of Hanover. In the event he failed, but compromised by creating a Templar-styled branch within the existing Masonic structure. This fell under his own Kent protectorate, and followed the English York Rite of Freemasonry. The Knights Templars, however, pursued the Scottish Rite under the protectorate of Henry Stuart's nephew, Prince Edward James Stuart, 2nd Count of Albany.

It was no secret that the Knights Templars had supported the Kings of Scots from the 12th century when they were first allied to David I. They had fought with Bruce at Bannockburn, and were Stewart (Stuart) adherents thereafter. But in 1809 their continued Stuart support was a real embarrassment to the House of Hanover because there were not supposed to be any Stuarts to support! The Stuart heritage may have been strategically diverted, but the traditional Templar heritage was a different matter, and the best Edward of Kent could do was to establish his own branch of Templarism within English Freemasonry.

In the course of this, a seal-engraver called Alexander Deuchar conspired with Major Müller of the 1st Royal Foot to approach Edward of Kent for a Charter of Dispensation[11] to establish an anti-Jacobite Templar authority in Scotland. Deuchar's brother, David, was an officer in the Peninsula War (Britain against France in Portugal 1808–14), and during the campaign at Leira, Portugal, he stole the altar cross from a Templar chapel within the Castle of Tomar in order to aid his brother's endeavour.

In the old days, the Deuchars had served Scotland well and, from the time of Bannockburn and beyond, the great sword of Deuchar, with its family coat-of-arms, was a welcome sight on any battlefield. By 1745, however, the tables had turned, and the Deuchar allegiance swayed, so that Lyon of East Ogil (a Jacobite supporter of Charles Edward) made it his business to carry off the prized heirloom. The sword was, nevertheless, retrieved again after Culloden, to be held by the Hanoverian supporter Alexander Deuchar when he opened negotiations with the Duke of Kent in 1809.

The Duke agreed to Deuchar's request, and the new establishment became known as the Scottish Conclave, with Deuchar as its Grand Master. However, the Duke of Kent asserted that the English Masonic rules should be followed, and agreed that he would himself be the Royal Grand Patron of the Conclave established 'in that part of Great Britain called Scotland'. Not surprisingly, within a few decades (in typically non-chivalric Hanoverian style), influential non-Templars were allowed to buy their way into the Conclave. The Duke of Leeds, for example, (who had no Templar training) was admitted in 1848, to become Steward of the Great Priory within a few months; and the Episcopal Bishop of Edinburgh was similarly admitted.

Falling under the banner of Deuchar's Scottish Grand Conclave (established in 1811) were several Templar lodges of the Irish Grand Encampment – but it was recognized that, hitherto, many Scottish lodges had been granted warrants from Ireland since 1798. Also, as we shall see, the Irish had proclaimed their open support for the Stuarts in 1799. From 1826, their autonomous Grand Master in Scotland was the Jacobite Robert Martin, who wanted nothing to do with the upstart Deuchar interlopers who were denounced by the Dublin Encampment on 28 December 1827. All Encampment Templars who had succumbed to the unethically created Hanoverian protectorate in Scotland were instructed to surrender their original Irish warrants to Robert Martin. In condemning the establishment of the Scottish Conclave, the Irish document stated, 'Every ancient Sir Knight knows that the Duke of Kent had no more authority to do so than Deuchar himself'.

Following Alexander Deuchar's death in 1844, some officers of Scotland's Grand Lodge called for a reinstatement of the hereditary Sinclair Grand Mastership, as established in 1441 by James II Stewart. A William Sinclair (who died in 1778) had been the first Grand Master of the Grand Lodge of Scotland prior to Deuchar's intervention. He was buried at Rosslyn Chapel, which was built by his great ancestor Sir William Sinclair, Patron of the Scottish Masons in the 15th century. The early Sinclair Grand Masters had sat at the head of an annual Guild Court in the role of Solomon the Judge, and the 15th-century leather-bound *Rosslyn-Hay Manuscript,* which includes the *Book of the Order of Knighthood,* is the earliest existing work of Scottish prose. The 19th-century Grand Lodge officials duly produced the antique *St Clair Charters* which substantiated the hereditary appointment under the Stewart kings. They called for its reinstatement, but to no avail, for the House of Hanover's Kent protectorate was too firmly established.

Quite apart from all the Hanoverian intrigue, the exiled Stuarts were quite separately involved with the general growth and dissemination of legitimate Templarism and Freemasonry in France and Italy. They were the instigators of the exported Scottish Rite, which had higher degrees and held more profound mysteries than other Masonic systems. Prominent in this movement had been Charles Edward Stuart who, in 1747, under his signature as 'King of Scotland, England, France and Ireland', had established the Chapitre Primordian de Rose Croix in France. Also notable in the movement was Charles Edward's cousin and mentor, the Comte de St Germain, who died in 1784. The Stuarts' involvement was firmly based on established rights and privileges, with a desire to initiate brethren into the true antiquity and pedigree of the Rite.

Needless to say, the Duke of Sussex was quite put out that Scottish Rite Masons in France were operating without his involvement, and he had no way of infiltrating the Stuart-related activity. To this end, he made an arrangement in 1819 with the Supreme Council of France to form a Supreme Council for high degrees in Britain. The fact was, however, that at that time there was no Supreme Council in France!

Outside legitimate Jacobite Masonry, there were actually four opposing groups each claiming supremacy in France, and the Duke's arrangement was made with one of these. By way of a thoroughly dubious charter, he duly established his fanciful Supreme Council, making sure that its Constitution was worded so that he appeared to have a Scottish Rite establishment in Britain. But it was not Scottish Rite at all; it was no more than a pretence – a self-contrived Hanoverian Rite of very doubtful legality. Moreover, in setting up his Council for Britain, the name of 'Scotland' was very pointedly omitted from the title: 'The Supreme Council for England, Ireland, and its possessions in America and the Indies'. From that moment in 1819, however, the Council (which had no Masonic authority whatsoever) was permanently inactive, and the Duke was suitably embarrassed.

In more recent times, English Freemasonry has apparently dispensed with political intrigue to become more concerned with allegorical representation and the codes of brotherly love, faith and charity. But in Europe many scientifically-based intellectual lodges of the traditional style are still operative. The problem with mainline Freemasonry today is that, although it provides a fraternal worldwide club, it no longer challenges the minds of its members as did the Masonry of old. Hence, although there is a good deal of ceremony and ritualistic learning, there is very little real scientific advancement. This is hardly surprising because, in England at least, too many self-serving politicians and State administrators hold the reins of power – and they, by way of their biased political oath, have ensured that instead of pursuing the original ideal of enlightenment, an effective status quo has been achieved. Consequently, an organization which once championed certain privileges in the face of the establishment has now become a very controlled part of that establishment.

It is interesting to note that, until 1799, Scotland's Kilwinning Lodge (as mentioned earlier in connection with Robert the Bruce) worked Templar ritual. In that year the Minutes record that a charter to work Templary and Royal Arch was granted to the Kilwinning Lodge in Ireland. However, Kilwinning ceased to practise these higher degrees soon after 1800 because they were under threat of prosecution under the Hanoverian *Secret Society Act* of 1799.

As confirmed in the Masonic Articles of Grand Lodge in London (founded in 1717), the honourable Royal Order of Scotland was active from 1741, and it was elevated to the rank of Grand Lodge of the Royal Order of Scotland in 1767. The King of Scots was deemed to be the Order's Hereditary Grand Master, and his seat (draped in a purple robe, and bearing a replica of the open-topped crown of James IV) has since been held vacant at all meetings. A branch of the Order was close to the heart of the Jacobite Cause during the 18th-century Risings, but the remnants of this branch dispersed into France and America during the Stuart exile. The Royal Order of Scotland membership certificate of Robert, 4th Earl of Roslin (1833–80), is held at Rosslyn Castle.

The ceremony of the Royal Order of Scotland incorporates two degrees, these being The Heredom (Holy Mount) of Kilwinning, which originated within Templarism during the reign of King David I of Scots, and the Knighthood of the Rosy Cross, introduced by Robert the Bruce in 1317. This degree contains the ceremonial of admission formerly practised in the Most Ancient Order of the Thistle: Scotland's equivalent to England's Most Noble Order of the Garter.

Today there are numerous branches of Templarism outside Freemasonry, with many of the organizations claiming supremacy over the others. In France, for example, there are over 100 registered Templar institutions but, at a State level, the only chivalric body recognized by the French Republic is the Legion d'Honneur. The position is similar in Britain, which houses a number of Templar priories – but under Hanoverian ordinance none is recognized by the Scottish Lyon Court or the English College of Arms. This is the reason why so many British reference books claim the Order of the Temple to have been long extinct, and the Order's post-1307 history has been removed from academic sources ever since the House of Hanover's 1799 *Secret Society Act*. It is no coincidence that this Act was passed in the very year that Cardinal Henry Stuart returned, destitute, to Rome, and was subsequently offered a Hanoverian income in return for amending his Will – the Will that specifically nominated his 'nephew Count Stuarton'.

48 *Marshal Michel Stuart Ney, Prince of Moscova*
Having rejoined Napoleon I upon his return to Paris in 1815, Ney avoided execution after the Battle of Waterloo through the assistance of his fellow Freemasons, the Duke of Wellington and Prince Edward James Stuart of Albany.

49 *Stephen James Alexander MacDonald, Duke of Tarentum*
The son of Charles Edward's doctor, and one of many Jacobites within the Napoleonic government.

50 *King Charles X of France*
A keen supporter of the Stuarts, he asked Prince Henry Edward of Albany to bring the last Dey of Algiers to safety in Europe.

51 *Jules de Polignac*
First minister for Charles X of France. His policies afforded a participant role for the Stuarts in European politics.

52 *Pope Pius IX arrives at the Albergo di Roma*
The residence of Empress Charlotte of Mexico during her stay in Rome. Through the intervention of Prince Henry Edward of Albany, the Pope visited Charlotte to discuss her husband's plight in Mexico.

53 *Château de Miramar*
Here, Empress Charlotte ended her days in insanity, having been repatriated to Belgium by the Counts of Albany and Flanders.

54 *John Sobieski-Stuart*

55 *Charles Sobieski-Stuart*
The brothers, John and Charles, were the grandsons of Charles Godefroid de Rohan-Stuart. They were entertained by Lord Lovat, who built a house for them in Scotland.

56 *The Wedding of Edward James Stuart, 2nd Count of Albany*
In 1809, the son of Charles Edward Stuart and Marguerite de Massillan married Maria Pasquini in Rome. From a painting by Baron Gerard, commissioned by Julie Buonaparte, Queen of Naples. The original passed to Queen Julie's son, Lucien (1803–78), and then to Cardinal Antonelli in 1865. On his death, in 1876, the painting was transferred to the Vatican Collection.

57 *Casa Stuardo (Stuarton House), Rome*
Built for Prince Edward James Stuart of Albany in 1802 by Charles Emmanuel IV, ex-King of Sardinia. The house was sold in 1892.

58 *Henry Stuart, 3rd Count of Albany, repatriates the Dey of Algiers*
Following the French invasion of 1830, the unseated Dey took up residence on a papal estate in Piedmont, where he and his family were placed under Stuart protection.

59 *Anthony James Stewart, 6th Count of Albany*
Prince and High Steward of Scotland, he was a courier for the Belgian Government during World War II – originally based in North Africa and then in London. He died in 1963.

60 *Julius Joseph Stewart and Germaine Eliza de la Tour d'Auvergne*
Styled Lord of Annandale, Prince Julius was married on 21 May 1932. Like his elder brother Anthony, Julius was active in the Belgian Resistance during World War II.

61 *Renée Stewart, Lady Derneley, and Baron Gustave Lafosse de Chatry*
Styled Princess Royal of Strathearn, from 1956, Renée's marriage to Gustave conjoined the lines from two of Charles Edward Stuart's offspring. It was mutually agreed that she would be by-passed, with the Stewart succession settled upon her son Michael.

62 *Château du Moulin*
The Stewart residence in Belgium from 1892 and the childhood home of Prince Michael. It was originally gifted by Louis XIV of France to his god-daughter, Louise Marie Therese Stuart, and was vacated by the family in 1968.

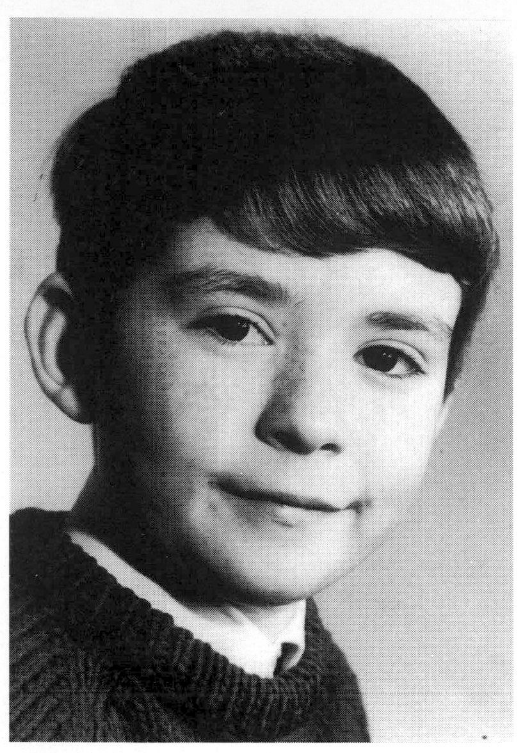

63 *HRH Prince Michael of Albany – aged 10 in 1968*
Already Head of the Royal House of Stewart for five years.

64 *Michael Stewart of Albany in Edinburgh, 1989*

The most apparently recognized Templar Orders currently in existence are those of the Order of Christ, whose Grand Master (by virtue of recognition from the Portuguese State) is the President of Portugal, and the Orthodox Order of the Temple of Jerusalem, whose Grand Master (under grant of a Bull by the Patriarch of the Orthodox Church) is the Head of the Portuguese House of Braganza.

Character Assassination

For the majority of people in 17th-century Britain, King James VII's objective of 'religious freedom for all' had been a very welcome innovation. It appealed greatly to the nation's sense of individual liberty, yet this fair-minded toleration was too much for the Whigs and many of the Church of England hierarchy to accept. Similarly, James's intentions to free the Crown from the magnates who controlled the militia, and to increase the size of the peacetime army, were well received by the community because there were prevailing threats from abroad, particularly from Holland. But James's request was seen by the aristocrats and bishops as a move towards something over which they would have no control. However, despite James's powerful opposers, the Stuart Cause received so much support that, more than half-a-century after losing the crown, his grandson Charles Edward came within an ace of recovering it again. It was, therefore, seen as imperative that to preserve their own status and dominion, the Whig oligarchs should denigrate the memory of King James, and so a maliciously conceived political campaign ensued to depict him as a veritable ogre.

In historical terms, the anti-James machinations of Hanover were not that unusual; the last monarchs of previous fallen dynasties had often been treated in like manner by their successors. History is generally geared to the attitudes and values of the time when written, rather than to those of the time to which it relates – and because of this history is selective. To this extent, recorded history is strategically biased. The Tudor writers so blackened the character of King Richard III that to this day we have no real concept of the man; we only know that the stories told of him were written by his enemies.

The main difficulty encountered in assailing King James VII (II) was that he was not actually the last in his succession. Prior to the Whig Revolution, his son James Francis Edward had been born, and a legitimate continuation of the Stuart line was assured. As a result, it was considered necessary to defame not only King James himself, but the Stuarts as a whole – past, present and future. Ostensibly, this course of personal attack began with James's wife, Mary d'Este; she was the daughter of Alfonso IV, Duke of Modena, but the official Hanoverian line was that she was to be portrayed as an illegitimate child of the Pope!

Even before this denigration of Queen Mary d'Este, the ministers of William of Orange had directed a very specific campaign against Robert II, who founded the Royal House of Stewart in 1371. They endeavoured in 1692 to assert that King Robert's marriage to Elizabeth Mure of Rowallan was not formalized, and that the whole Stewart dynasty was, therefore, illegitimate. However, without delay, Thomas Innes of Drumgask, Principal of the Scots College in Paris, produced the ancient *Glasgow Charters* from the archives. Herein was a Charter of King Robert II's founding of a chaplainry in Glasgow to fulfil express conditions imposed by the Pope. The document provided positive proof that Robert's marriage to Elizabeth had received the requisite Papal sanction, and the accusations against his memory were routed at a single stroke.

There was not much that could be said to impugn King James's brother and predecessor Charles II, for he was still highly regarded in people's memory. But King James VI (I) and Charles I were deemed to be good subjects for assault, and so the Cromwellian annals were carefully scoured for suitably destructive content. The reputedly wise James VI (I) had been known to all as the 'British Solomon', but the 18th-century Whigs soon changed this image, calling him the 'Wisest fool in Christendom'. His unfortunate intestinal illness was used to create the impression that he was a vulgar glutton, and the most common of all Puritan charges was resurrected against him – that of presumed sexual deviancy. This arose because he had been seen to embrace and kiss members of the French Court – a common enough European custom, even today. These maligning allegations stemmed from vindictive nobles and churchmen, but they were especially prevalent in the *Puritan Manifestos*, which made equally vigorous attempts to discredit James's son Charles I.

Clearly the bold Chevalier, Charles Edward Stuart, was an enormous threat to George II, and even after his defeat at Culloden the *Bonnie Prince* retained his popularity among Jacobites in Britain and Europe. In this regard, the greatest of all character assassinations was commenced by the Hanoverians at home, and by their dutiful ambassadors abroad. While George II's son, the Duke of Cumberland, pursued his violent subjugation of the Highlands, Charles Edward was portrayed in England as a rash and treacherous adventurer. In fact, he was labelled as a potentially dangerous usurper, even though it was his own family who had been usurped!

Before long the whole scene was set against the Scots King *de jure.* Charles III was described as a burdensome drunk, a brawler and a woman-hater, who lived a life of pathetic depredation. His various offspring, apart from Charlotte, Duchess of Albany, were excluded from the British history books, so too were his numerous lady companions, except for his childless marriage to Princess Louise de Stolberg, and his ongoing relationship with Charlotte's mother, Clementina Walkinshaw. In fact, even Louise and Clementina were not mentioned for quite a while, since the romantic side of Charles's character, coupled with his very apparent popularity with women, did not suit the destructive task at hand. His later sufferance of both asthma and epilepsy did, however, make it easy enough for the image of drunkenness to be sustained.

English establishment history was devised to portray Charles III as a troublesome pawn of Rome, but he was certainly not that. His rapport with various Popes was often far from amicable, as was proven when he formally converted to the Protestant faith at the age of 29. His relinquishment of Catholicism took place at 'the new church in the Strand' (probably St Mary's-le-Strand, London), and some years afterwards, in 1759, he wrote:

> The Roman Catholic religion has been the ruin of the Royal Family . . . In that religion was I brought up and educated as other princes . . . Had motives of interest been able to make me disguise my sentiments upon the material point of religion, I should certainly, in my first undertaking in the year of 1745, have declared myself a Protestant. As to the motive which dissuaded me from it, it was no other than a persuasion of the truth of my religion. The adversity I have suffered since that time has made me reflect, and has furnished me with the opportunity of being informed.

> In order to make my renunciation of the Church of Rome the most authentic, and the less liable afterwards to malicious interpretations, I went to London in the year 1750, and in that capital did then make a solemn abjuration of the Romish religion, and did embrace that of the Church of England as by law established in the Thirty-nine Articles in which I hope to live and die.

After Charles Edward's death in January 1788, the accounts of his life slowly began to appear. In the first instance they were compiled from the original Georgian sources, and then later Victorian books amalgamated information from the earlier works, and added snippets of further vilifying content. All this provided a base library for future reference, and now there are any number of such biographies, with new ones regularly appearing. They are, in large measure, adapted from one another, and are generally based (intentionally or otherwise) on the contrived portrayal of Charles III by the Hanoverian propaganda machine. The disinformation has thus been perpetuated into and through the 20th century. But despite all this, Scotland has retained her own legacy of pride in the noble Prince, and the registers of Europe tell a very different story about Charles Edward Stuart and his legitimate descendants.[12] These various archives hold the complete and fundamental details of my own heritage – the dynastic bloodline of the Scots Royal House of Stewart that was kept secret in Britain by way of Government conspiracy for nearly 200 years.

In 1763 (17 years after Culloden, and 12 years before the American War of Independence) the political journalist John Wilkes accused the Georgian Government of misrepresenting facts in the King's speech following the Seven Years War. Today, such open challenges are a common enough newspaper occurrence, but Wilkes was arrested, charged with libel, and flung into the Tower of London. Upon his release, a French correspondent asked to what extent the liberty of the press extended in England, and John Wilkes replied, 'I cannot tell, but I am trying to find out'. He found out soon enough: there was no liberty or freedom of speech for the press or the public! Nevertheless, during that time of controlled and politically manufactured information, a vast amount of general history was being written – and it was this contrived history which set the scene for the majority of later publications concerning the exiled Stuarts.

17

CONSTITUTIONAL MONARCHY

People or Parliament?

In contrast to Scotland's 1320 *Declaration of Arbroath,* which supports the ideal of a 'people's monarchy', the present British constitution is that of a 'parliamentary monarchy'. Sovereignty is vested not in the people, but in the Monarch, the House of Lords and the House of Commons. It is not a 'Written Constitution' in terms of being a single document detailing basic civil rights and liberties as in other countries, but comprises an accumulation of customs and precedents concerning parliamentary sanctions, together with a number of laws defining specific aspects. Among the most relevant constituents of the said British constitution are:

Magna Carta (1215) – The Great Charter was granted by King John at Runnymede, and imposed by the Norman barons. It affirmed the privileges of the Church, prevented infringement of the feudal system, defined the barons' legal obligations, and checked the arbitrary implementation of justice. By Tudor times, discernible feudalism had declined, but during the Protectorate it was revived by Oliver Cromwell's parliamentarians, who reinterpreted the Charter to suit their own ends.

Petition of Rights (1628) – This Petition declared martial law illegal, along with imprisonment without trial and taxation without parliamentary consent. The statute was ignored by Cromwell, who pursued the first two illegal courses with impunity, and he was specifically enabled to take advantage of the third proviso since he controlled Parliament.

Habeas Corpus Act (1679) (Latin: 'Have the body') – The Act limits unauthorized imprisonment by way of a Writ. It directs custodians to present prisoners before the court and to explain the reason for custody.

Bill of Rights (1689) – The Bill (which embodies the *Declaration of Rights*) was drawn up by the House of Commons. It was presented to William of Orange and his wife Mary before their installation as King William III and Queen Mary II in place of James VII (II). Because of King James's endeavour to supersede the *Test Acts* by way of his *Declaration for Liberty of Conscience,* the Bill made it illegal for laws to be made or amended by the reigning monarch. It also prevented the maintenance of a royal army in times of peace, and gave Parliament ultimate rights of consent over the monarch and the people.

Act of Settlement (1701) – The Act confines the British succession of monarchs to Protestants alone.

Parliament Act (1911) – This Act limits the powers of the House of Lords, in that the House may delay a Commons Bill for debate, but it retains no right to reject it.

Ireland and the Constitution

The Parliamentary misuse of the *Habeas Corpus Act* provides a very good example of how 'unconstitutional' is the so-called British Constitution in Hanoverian practice. Following the French Revolution (1789–99), it was suggested by the British author Thomas Paine, in his *The Rights of Man,* that people should have the right to appoint and change their own Governments. But to think that people at large should be able to vote was too much for the despotic Westminster politicians. Paine was indicted for treason, and fled to Calais in 1792. By that time almost every town in Britain had a Constitutional Information Club, or a Society of Friends of the People. In 1793 the British Convention of People's Delegates was held in Edinburgh, and in response to the Convention's plea for better representation the Government transported the leaders to the colonies. Hostilities were then commenced against the people of France who, along with the Americans, were said to have fuelled the anti-Hanover mood in Britain.

Subsequently the 1679 *Habeas Corpus Act* was suspended by Prime Minister William Pitt in 1794, so that without any need for a trial, citizens could be kept in prison indefinitely. Government spies roamed the country, bringing in anyone whose views posed a problem for Westminster, and they were duly sentenced without any hearing. Even the Royal Navy's sailors did not escape the harsh parliamentary judgements. Most were press-ganged into service, and they were treated abominably with miserable pay, and despicable food provided by villainous contractors. But when seamen of the Fleet at Nore (near Sheerness) demonstrated for a revised ship-board policy, and a grant of two meals a day instead of one, their leaders were hanged.

At that time, Britain was in a somewhat desperate position: France had conquered the Netherlands, and controlled the Dutch fleet. She had made an alliance with Spain, and practically controlled the Spanish fleet too. Britain had been deserted by her allies, Prussia, Austria and Russia, and was left alone to confront the enemy. And in the midst of all this, the Westminster Government was hanging sailors! During the surrounding fiasco, the British kept up their blockade of the Dutch fleet with only two ships; all the others mutinied. But in full view of the Dutch, Admiral Duncan kept making signals to the mutinous ships as if they were still his under operative command, and as a fortunate result the Dutch fleet did not stir.

Then Pitt made it unlawful to speak, write, or to have any opinion against the Government. He sent German troops into Ireland in 1797, prompting an Irish rebellion in the following year, which led to the arrest and death of the prominent leader Lord Edward Fitzgerald. In the course of this, the Irish proclaimed Henry Benedict Stuart as their rightful King, and this was supported by the French.[1] Pitt duly took immediate action with his *Secret Society Act* in 1799, whereupon Trade Unions and unlicensed public meetings of any kind were forbidden anywhere in Britain. The 'combination' of working-men into any form of club or society for negotiation of improved working conditions or wages was henceforth defined as punishable conspiracy.

In order to establish control over the Irish people, Britain and Ireland were united in 1801, and the Dublin Parliament was closed. To facilitate this union, the Irish Catholics were promised voting rights, but after the documents had been signed and sealed

George III and his lackeys changed their minds! In consequence of this William Pitt resigned, and Ireland's parliamentary representation at Westminster was confined to Protestant landlord gentry.

Later, from 1845 to 1847, the Irish potato crop failed completely, and potatoes were the main food of the working people. About 20 per cent of the population died from hunger, but at the same time Ireland had enough wheat to feed the entire population. However, this wheat went to England while the Irish were starving, and Westminster decreed that the crop had been grown for export, being the property of the English landowners in Ireland!

More than a million people left Ireland during that period, and many more left during the balance of the century. The majority went to the United States, which received nearly 5 million Irish immigrants between 1841 and 1920. Even today, the population of Ireland is less than it was before this scandalous episode – and the Irish-Americans have still not forgotten how badly their ancestors were treated by the House of Hanover.

Irish voting rights did not reach satisfactory proportions until 1885, and by the beginning of the First World War Westminster had agreed to introduce Home Rule for Ireland. But the introduction was strategically delayed so that Irishmen could be called into the Army, prompting a republican movement whose members protested in Dublin for full independence at Easter 1916. The so-called 'Easter Rising' was swiftly put down, and its leaders executed, an act which was criticized from London to the United States. As a result the Republicans won the 1918 elections in almost every area except Ulster – and they reconstituted their own Parliament, the Dail, in Dublin.

Recognizing the extent of its 1916 blunder, the British Government conceded to the independence of southern Ireland from 1921, but insisted that Ulster would remain within the Union. Under the terms of the *Anglo-Irish Treaty* that year, the new Irish Free State accepted Britain's continued use of the key ports, and retained the sovereignty of the British Crown. But in 1932 the new, staunchly republican Fianna Fail party won the election, and the incoming Prime Minister, Eamon de Valera, declared southern Ireland an independent Republic in 1937. Henceforth, the British monarch was no longer sovereign outside Ulster – but mutual relations were maintained so that today, although Ireland and Britain are entirely separate States, their citizens are not considered foreigners in each other's country.

Within the Republic the majority have long believed that one day the whole of Ireland should be united by a process of peaceful cooperation. However, ever since the dark events of 1916, a minority faction has unfortunately pursued a violent course to this end.

Presidents and Princes

The oldest Written Constitution in operation is that of the United States of America; it was adopted in 1787, ratified in 1788, and effected in 1789.[2] In that same year of 1789 began the French Revolution which abolished despotic feudalism in that country, although a system of democracy did not immediately prevail. Even so, France and practically all European States have adopted Written Constitutions since then. These protect the rights of individuals in many important areas. In the context of the various struggles for universal suffrage, the general alternative to absolute monarchy or dictatorships has been found in republicanism. However, in most cases, this arose purely as a democratic substitute for autocracy, not in place of an underlying affinity with monarchy.

In the wake of the French Revolution, King George III and his Westminster Parliament were justifiably fearful of a similar uprising in Britain. Their fears had been greatly heightened by the guillotining of Louis XVI, Marie Antoinette, and their children. There was, indeed, an uprising in Ireland, and the Georgian Whigs knew the Scots would be next – so Britain declared war on the French, and arrested (to sentence without trial) anyone suspected of sympathy with France. In Scotland, hanging was a common result of arrest, while many were imprisoned for life, or sent off to slavery in Australia's Botany Bay.

The American Republic was born from the base requirement of freedom from the tyranny of Britain's House of Hanover. However, despite all that had happened to justify their martial action, the Americans remembered how well they had previously fared with the Stuarts on the British Throne. Even today, there is no doubt of the American people's uncertain fascination with the concept of monarchy, for no matter how republican the spirit, there is always the need for a central symbol – a living focus for the unification of patriotic sentiment. No 'flag' alone can ever fulfil this requirement, nor indeed can any president, for by virtue of the party system presidents are always politically motivated and cannot, therefore, be impartial.

Republicanism is perceived as a democratic ideal of equality for all, yet the visionary 'classless society' cannot become a reality while there remains an inherent desire to display social eminence. In such an environment this takes the form of symbolic displays of standing by degrees of wealth and possession. Hence, the true republican spirit is overtaken by a heightened competitive instinct, and in the final event there is still no equality.

The majority of those conscientious and morally-inspired men responsible for the United States Constitution were Freemasons, and in establishing the Constitution they used the Scottish model that was denied to their fellow countrymen in Britain. The overall American establishment was perceived as a personification of the lodge, with its structure of government reasoned from rites of Freemasonry. Yet even those who conceived and designed it could not escape the ideal of a monarchy to which all citizens would feel an attachment, whatever their individual political party sympathies.

Having led 13 individual colonies to independence, George Washington was unanimously offered the status of King. But, in turn, he recognized the singular importance of a hereditary bloodline, and so at his behest the American crown was offered to Charles III Stuart. Washington knew that the true nature of a people's monarchy rests in the heritage of a dynastic principle; this affords a necessary continuity of security and belonging through whatever governmental changes may occur. Such an affinity provides a life-force of civilized cultural identity within a nation, and its concept is inbred in kingdoms and republics alike. No gallant young president on fiery steed has ever championed the honour and dignity of politically oppressed subjects – for this, in life and legend, is the social realm of princes and their appointed knights.

This then is the crux of Scotland's dilemma – whether portrayed by outrage, sadness or nostalgia. Scotland's dynastic succession of priest-kings was truly hereditary through centuries of operation; it functioned in alliance with a proven Clan System, and with a Written Constitution that was the envy of the Western world. Sovereignty was vested in the people of the land, and the kings stood before God to serve the rights, liberties and welfare of the sovereign nation. This was indeed an environment of continuity, security and belonging – but it was wantonly usurped, demolished and discredited by those who had not the slightest understanding of its merits or meaning.

The Gag Acts

By 1812 George III 's sanity was so impaired that his son George, Prince of Wales, was granted the Regency by Westminster. But these were very turbulent times, and despite the previous actions of William Pitt and the aristocrats to curb the aspirations of working people, demonstrations and riots against unscrupulous employers had become commonplace. The Government stood firmly with the employers, to the extent that any worker who damaged factory machinery was sentenced to death. In one instance, a boy of 15 was sent to the scaffold for acting as a sentry for his disruptive workmates.

The politicians were absolutely paranoid about the possibility of an anti-aristocratic revolution, and every effort was made to force the populace into a greater subjugation than ever before. As a result, the desperation of poverty and hunger led to a significant increase in petty crime, so that before long over 200 offences carried the death penalty – including sheep stealing and picking pockets. Indeed, so harsh was the regime that Prime Minister Spencer Perceval was assassinated in the lobby of the House of Commons in 1812.

Britain's years of expensive involvement in the Napoleonic wars came to an abrupt end on 18 June 1815, when Emperor Napoleon I was defeated at Waterloo. But the ensuing peace brought with it a great depression. The nation was £860m in debt [about £25,000m in today's terms], and the annual interest alone on this was more than half the national budget. Corn prices and rents had doubled, while gold values fell by 50 per cent, and Britain's currency was completely undermined. The Navy was cut in one year from 100,000 men to 33,000, and the hitherto sailors flocked home with the similarly demobilized soldiers to swell an already starving populace. Parliament's first instinct was to protect its own interest, and in 1815 a *Corn Law*[3] was introduced, prohibiting the entry of foreign corn until the home price was high. This, of course, made bread very expensive, and there was a great surge of national feeling against Lord Liverpool's Westminster Government, and against the Foreign Secretary, Viscount Castlereagh, in particular.

Robert Owen, a Manchester cotton-spinner, fought ardently for the rights of citizens, and laid many attacks on his fellow industrialists for their intolerable treatment of employees. Children of nine were working well in excess of 12 hours a day in the factories, where conditions were insanitary and the wages minimal. In London during November 1816, a great crowd gathered in Spa Fields, Bermondsey, demanding a citizens' right to vote. They marched in procession, intent to seize the Tower of London, and although easily dispersed they terrified the Government ministers who remembered the French citizens' assault on the Bastille. Riots were reported from the Midlands to Glasgow, and Parliament imposed the most rigorous methods of control, once again suspending the *Habeas Corpus Act* – one of the supposed great safeguards of British liberty. This meant that Government henchmen could pounce on citizens at will, and imprison them indefinitely without trial or redress.

On 16 August 1819 the radical orator Henry Hunt gathered an audience of 80,000 people in St Peter's Field, Manchester, to hear his ideas for political reform. No one in the crowd was armed, and according to reports they were 'ordinary people listening in an orderly manner' – but the authorities sent in the cavalry with sabres drawn. Hundreds were severely injured, and 11 killed, including two women and a child. The incident (in an allusion to the Battle of Waterloo) became known as the 'Peterloo Massacre'. Clearly, the national scene was set for constitutional change – but the Government was quick to recognize this, and implemented a series of 1819 statutes, which became known as the *Gag Acts*. Not unlike the enforced restrictions of Oliver Cromwell's Protectorate, these Acts forbade freedom of speech and public meetings, while suppressing the press by way of a newspaper duty. Magistrates were given express powers to limit people's rights and liberties, and judicial short-cuts were introduced to speed up sentencing.

In 1820 a band of men led by Arthur Thistlewood met in London's Edgware Road to discuss plans to demolish the Cabinet, capture the Tower of London, and establish a Republic. Needless to say, they were discovered and executed.

The 1820 Rising

The last Jacobite Rising was not the 1745 campaign of *Bonnie Prince Charlie,* as generally told, but took place in Scotland 75 years later in 1820. The period from the French Revolution (1789–99) saw a revitalizing of patriotic sentiment in Scotland, and learned men of the day pronounced that the French revolutionary ideal of 'liberty, equality and fraternity' was no more nor less than a time-honoured Scottish concept. In 1820 there were riots at King George's birthday celebrations in Edinburgh, and the people called for the return of their rightful King. Enlivened by the works of the late Robert Burns (1759–96) a new sense of nationalism had emerged, with the Stuarts as a living focus, and the Jacobite movement gained new inspiration in Scotland. Once more, the Scots decided to pursue a course towards the ideal of a Constitutional Monarchy leading a Republican spirit.

The 1820 revolt, which was thoroughly veiled by the Hanoverian chroniclers, was organized by Stephen James MacDonald, Duke of Tarentum, Marshal of the Empire[4], and it was arranged on behalf of Charles Edward's son, Prince Edward James Stuart. In Scotland, MacDonald's colleagues were James Wilson, John Baird and Andrew Hardie (ancestor of Keir Hardie, founder of the Labour Party). From a Glasgow base, these men were to gather the people into open rebellion, for which Marshal MacDonald would provide the necessary arms. The Rising was enthusiastically commenced on 1 April with a written 'Proclamation and Call to the People' (*see* Appendix X for complete transcript), to which the entire central belt of Scotland rallied:

> Equality of rights – not of property – is the object we contend . . . Liberty or death is our motto . . . Come forward then at once to free your Country and your King from the power of those who have held them too long in thraldom.

Almost at once, the factories and mills were closed, and public services were curtailed. Bands of armed militia were formed, but the scheme was betrayed to the Government in its early stages by the author Walter Scott. He had a most dispassionate attitude towards Jacobites, despite the paradox of his romantic writings.

The 'Committee of the Rising' in Glasgow made plans to seize the city and capture the Falkirk artillery works, but in the light of Walter Scott's information Parliament clamped down with a vengeance. A *Militia Act* was passed to suppress the privately armed bands; Government troops marched into Glasgow from all directions, and dragoons were alerted across southern Scotland. The Government ranks were strengthened at Edinburgh Castle, and the City Guard marched westward. There were rallies, parades, skirmishes and a good deal of spilt blood, at the end of which Wilson, Hardie and Baird were arrested and hanged. Marshal MacDonald then returned to Denmark, where Prince Edward James Stuart was waiting with his ships at the port of Esberg.[5] But the battle was lost before it had begun, and the 1820 Rising collapsed.

For some time the city of Glasgow was under military occupation, and the Government suppressed all Jacobite-related press. Once again history was distorted, and irrespective of the positive mention of their 'King' (Edward James Stuart) in the Committee's *Proclamation,* the whole affair has since been portrayed as a short-lived and unimportant workers' revolt. In the aftermath, however, a new wave of Jacobite feeling swelled in Europe. Pictures of Charles Edward Stuart and Flora Macdonald were even resurrected and displayed in shop windows. Despite his coercive methods, Britain's Prime Minister Jenkinson, 2nd Earl of Liverpool, was left in no doubt that the Stuarts were still able to rally public, political and military support when needed.

The Prince of Whales!

In the wake of this, Secretary Viscount Castlereagh was so hated by the people that he cut his own throat in 1822. The mob jeered with delight as his coffin was carried through the streets of London, and his burial at Westminster Abbey was a scene of great rejoicing.

Walter Scott was created a Baronet for his pains, and was further allowed to organize George IV's 1822 entry into Edinburgh, presenting him with the Constitutional Honours of Scotland. To placate some of the Scottish nobility, two brothers, John and Charles Allen, known as the Sobieski-Stuarts (second-generation descendants from Charles Edward's illegitimate son, Charles Godefroid de Rohan), were formally presented to King George. They were later afforded the Scottish island of Eilean Aigas, and now lie buried beneath a Celtic cross at Eskdale (*see* Appendix IX). Yet, when all the ceremony was over, Sir Walter Scott was totally discarded by King George and the Hanoverians he had served. This came as no surprise to those who knew the faithless George IV; he was criticized so often for his despicable treatment of colleagues and mistresses once they had served their purpose. By 1826 Scott was quite insolvent, and his publishers, Constable, fell into bankruptcy, along with his own printing partnership Ballantyne & Co. Thereafter, he spent his remaining years, until 1832, writing frantically to pay off £120,000 to his creditors [more than £3.5m in today's purchasing terms].

George IV, the so-called 'First Gentleman in Europe', was the epitome of the principle, 'Me, Me, Me again, and encore Me!' He was scented, powdered, slept on feathers, and never took up a cause in his life. At best, he was well-practised in designing elaborate military uniforms that were the laughing-stock of Europe. He ate and drank to the extreme, was unpleasantly obese, and was styled by his own subjects the 'Prince of Whales'. When George IV came to Edinburgh in 1822, he even wore pink silk-stockings beneath his kilt; he was garbed with padding, stays, a coat with ornate frogs and a fur collar, all surmounted by one of Truefitt's best oil-drenched, nutty-brown wigs.

Throughout his reign this arrogant monarch despised everyone, and accrued huge debts to the detriment of his cooks, tailors, barbers, furnishers and the like. Although a member of the strategically Protestant succession, George had secretly married the Roman Catholic Maria Fitzherbert prior to his coronation, but was obliged to discard her in favour of Caroline of Brunswick, whom he could not stand. In no time, he tried to introduce a *Bill of Pains and Penalties* by way of which he could divorce Caroline, but his own immorality was so open and

King George IV, House of Hanover – the 'Prince of Whales'

notorious that popular sympathy was with the Queen, and the Bill was dropped.

In effect, George's second marriage lasted less than a year, and produced but one child, Charlotte. She was born in January 1796, but after her birth the royal couple lived separately, and by 1820 George's solace was jointly found in the company of Lady

Conyngham and heavy doses of laudanum. His death in 1830 was certainly not mourned by the people of the industrial cities or by the rural community; their economic plight had deteriorated year by year, while the King was content to live in the lap of vulgar luxury. The noted diarist Charles Greville had this to say about George IV of the House of Hanover: 'There have been good and wise kings, but not many of them . . . and this I believe to be one of the worst'.

It is ironic that, just before he died of dropsy, one of George IV's last acts was to give his Royal Assent to the *Catholic Emancipation Bill*[6] – the very concept which had cost the last Stuart monarch his throne!

For want of a son, George was succeeded by his brother William, Duke of Clarence – a Naval man by training – and of all the Hanoverians he was the only one deserving of community respect. William IV enjoyed the simple things of life, and achieved a harmonious marriage to Adelaide of Saxe-Meiningen from 1818. He was the first popular sovereign of his House because he truly behaved like a father to his nations – strolling down St James's Street in the early days to rub shoulders with his new subjects. He calmed the fears of his attendants by claiming that the people would soon become accustomed to his new style, and this socially-aware King would actually have gone without an expensive coronation were it not for Parliament's insistence in the matter.

William IV's reign was an era of reforms, which slowly led to an age of ostensibly representative democracy. But for all that, England's leaders have still not since drafted any form of Written Constitution. What meagre version of a Constitution exists is still monarchical, and the monarchy remains 'parliamentary'. Thus, the nation's allegiance is required to be given to the Monarch, the Lords and the Commons. Even the Government ministers are sworn to a hierarchical allegiance, rather than an allegiance to the people they are elected to represent, and Britain's *National Anthem* was originally composed to support this feudalistic concept.

The music for the British *National Anthem* is attributed to Dr John Bull (died 1628), an organist at Antwerp Cathedral. However, the lyrics are of Hanoverian origin (from the time of George II in 1745) and, quite unlike the anthems of other cultures, Britain's song of allegiance is specifically directed towards honouring the monarch, rather than honouring the country and the nation. In fact, Britain is the only country in Europe wherein the constitutional head does not swear an 'Oath of Fealty' to the people. Moreover, the so-called 'British' *National Anthem* was very pointedly composed as an 'English' anthem, with its lyrics directly worded against the Scottish nation, as in the fourth verse:

God grant that Marshal Wade
May by Thy mighty aid
Victory bring.
May he sedition hush
And like a torrent rush
Rebellious Scots to crush.
God save the King.

18

Forsaken Heirs

The Albany Succession

Some years prior to the 1820 Rising, Prince Edward James Stuart's wife, Maria Pasquini, had given birth to a son. He was Henry Edward Benedict, born on 18 November 1809, and Princess Caroline Murat of Naples was chosen to be his godmother. In 1811 their second child was born – a daughter christened Louise Henriette Marie. Her godparents were Charles Emmanuel IV (ex-King of Sardinia) and Princess Marie Terese, Duchess of Angoulême (the surviving daughter of King Louis XVI and Queen Marie Antoinette). Unfortunately, Louise died from smallpox at the age of 5. Later, in the luckless year of the Glasgow Rising, Charles III's widow, Marguerite de Massillan, died of fever.

In 1827 Edward James Stuart's son, Prince Henry Edward Benedict, Duke of Kintyre, married the Italian noblewoman Agnes Beatrix de Pescara – and the Duchesse de Berri gave the 'Mary, Queen of Scots' Ball' in Paris to commemorate the occasion. Within two years Agnes presented Henry with two sons: Prince Charles Benedict James, born 19 October 1829, and Henry Frederick Alexander, Count of Derneley, born 12 July 1831.[1]

In April 1830, shortly before his abdication, King Charles X of France sent word to the Stuarts in Rome, requesting that he might meet with Prince Edward James and his son in Paris. The letter was signed by the King's statesman Jules de Polignac. At the meeting, the Stuarts were informed that the French Government wished to employ Henry Edward Benedict as an observer in the French offensive against Algers (Algiers).

The Prince (aged 21) accepted, and emerged as a superb diplomat in the campaign. However, on learning that Charles Edward's grandson was to be involved with the Polignac ministry, Britain's George IV asked Lord Bute (his ambassador in Paris) to let the French know of his extreme displeasure.

Bute duly said his piece, but having listened to the Georgian recriminations, the Princes Schwarzenberg and Poniatowski, Colonel Filos, Baron de Haussez and Baron Leclerck merely shrugged their shoulders. Bute (thinking they had not understood him) began to shout his message again, only to be strongly answered by Baron Haussez, as detailed in the Polignac report to Charles X:

> My lord, I have never suffered that, against myself – a gentle man by nature – one should use such a tone of voice. Nor would I permit anyone to take that same tone against the Government of which I am a member. I have already told you that we did not wish to treat this event diplomatically, and you will find proof of our action within the verbal terms I am going to use – France, Sir, does not give a damn what England thinks!

Despite the diplomatic hostilities between England and France, the good relations between the Stuarts and the French were reciprocal. Within a few months of this meeting Charles X of France, Count of Artois (brother of Louis XVI and Louis XVIII), abdicated in August 1830. He then travelled through the Highlands of Scotland with the Stuarts, and the French poet and novelist, Victor Hugo, commemorated the event with a poem dedicated to the Stuarts, who had loaned their Edinburgh residence to Charles X de Bourbon. Perhaps something is poetically lost in the English translation of Hugo's poem, but the sentiment remains:

> *Be blessed, o palace; be blessed, o ruin.*
> *May a majestic halo of glory illuminate you forever.*
> *Facing your bleak battlements, pious, we bow ourselves,*
> *For the old King of France has found under your shadow*
> *This melancholic and sombre hospitality,*
> *Which one receives and returns from Stuarts to Bourbons.*

Prior to this, and under the joint-commands of Admiral Duperre and General de Bourmont, Prince Henry Stuart had duly boarded *The Provence* and sailed from the south of France on 25 May 1830. Algers was reached on 13 June, and the Battle of Staeouli was fought and won by the French on the next day. The French placed Hussein Ibn El Hussein (the last Dey of Algers) and his family under Stuart protection, and they were conveyed to Italy by Prince Henry.[2] Thereafter they lived in dignified exile at an estate in the Piedmont, where Hussein died in 1838 – a friend of the Stuarts to the last.

In May 1843 Prince Henry fought alongside the Duc d'Aumale (son of Louis Philippe I) at the Battle of Abd-el-Kader, following which d'Aumale's officer St Amand wrote, 'Prince Henry was not even perturbed by the heat and, though not compulsive in battle, he kept an attitude of constancy while fighting the Arabs'.

By that time the Belgians had revolted against the Dutch and declared their independence. Baron Surlet de Choquier (temporary Regent in Belgium) sent an ambassador to Rome and offered the Crown of the Belgians to Prince Edward James of Albany. Edward declined on the grounds that a Stuart kingdom in Europe would be seen as a potential danger to England, and the Hanoverians would then do their utmost to keep Belgium under the yoke of Holland. However, the Prince was willing to discuss the appointment with ex-King Charles X and the new King Louis Philippe of the French. His idea was to place the Duc de Bordeaux or the Duc de Nemours on the Belgian throne. But on learning of this, the Westminster Foreign Secretary, Lord Palmerston, arranged for a German of British nationality to take the Crown. Hence, King George IV's son-in-law, Leopold of Saxe-Coburg, was accepted by the Regency on behalf of the Belgian people, but he then had to swear to a Constitution, based on the 1320 model of Scotland's *Declaration of Arbroath*. He also had to confirm the Stuarts' title to their traditional estate in the Belgian Ardennes[3] – a 17th-century gift from King Louis XIV.

Henry, 3rd Count of Albany

On 21 September 1845, Edward James Stuart (titular King James IX of Scots) died in Rome, and his son Henry Edward Benedict succeeded as *de jure* Henry X (II of Scots), 3rd Count of Albany, 2nd Count Stuarton.

HRH Prince Henry Edward Benedict Stuart, 3rd Count of Albany, from a painting by Guiseppe Isola c1835

In 1866, the Stuarts repatriated Charlotte of Belgium (Empress of Mexico and wife of Emperor Maximilien I) to Brussels. Having returned from Mexico, however, Charlotte visited her cousin Napoleon III Buonaparte in Paris – an event which was to lead to an unfortunate Stuart embarrassment. Her objective was to convince him not to abandon Maximilien in his struggle against the Mexican revolutionaries, but she was unsuccessful, and Buonaparte withdrew the French legions from Mexico. She then went to Rome to seek an audience with the Pope, but the cardinals and aristocrats ignored her earnest mission, treating her as if she were a mere tourist.

Charlotte took temporary residence in the Albergo di Roma, and awaited a representative of the Pope. In due time Cardinal Giacomo Antonielli arrived, but the meeting was disastrous, and she sent him packing. At that, Charlotte's companion, Madame del Barrio, appeared with Prince Henry Stuart, who had used his influence to organize a Papal audience for the Empress, but not before Henry discovered why everyone had been avoiding her: the poor woman was quite insane, and she was convinced that Napoleon III and the others were out to poison her! With Henry to assist, she conducted her interview after a fashion, but would only eat from the Pope's own plate, even though he refused to help with the Mexican situation. Somewhat embarrassed by the whole affair, Prince Henry asked the Count of Flanders to collect his distraught sister, and on 9 October Empress Charlotte was removed to Miramar.[4]

By then, Henry's two sons, Charles Benedict and Frederick Alexander, had both found wives. Frederick, Count of Derneley, had married Emmanuela Vercatti on 10 August 1855, and their son Alexander James Edward was born two years later on 6 April. Charles, Duke of Kintyre, had married Louise Jeanne Françoise Dalvray on 3 June 1864; she was the daughter of a noted French banker, and a descendant of Louis XV. Prior to this, Charles Benedict had been involved in establishing the Kingdom of Italy, where Victor Emmanuel of Sardinia was installed as overall King at Turin in 1861.

Charles, 4th Count of Albany

Henry Edward Benedict died in Rome on 12 December 1869, and his eldest son Charles Benedict duly succeeded as 4th Count of Albany. On 12 August 1874 his wife Louise gave birth to their first son, Prince Julius Anthony Henry. The name 'Julius' was chosen to honour one of the late Princes de Conde; the name 'Anthony' related to the late Prince of Angoulême, and 'Henry' to the Prince's

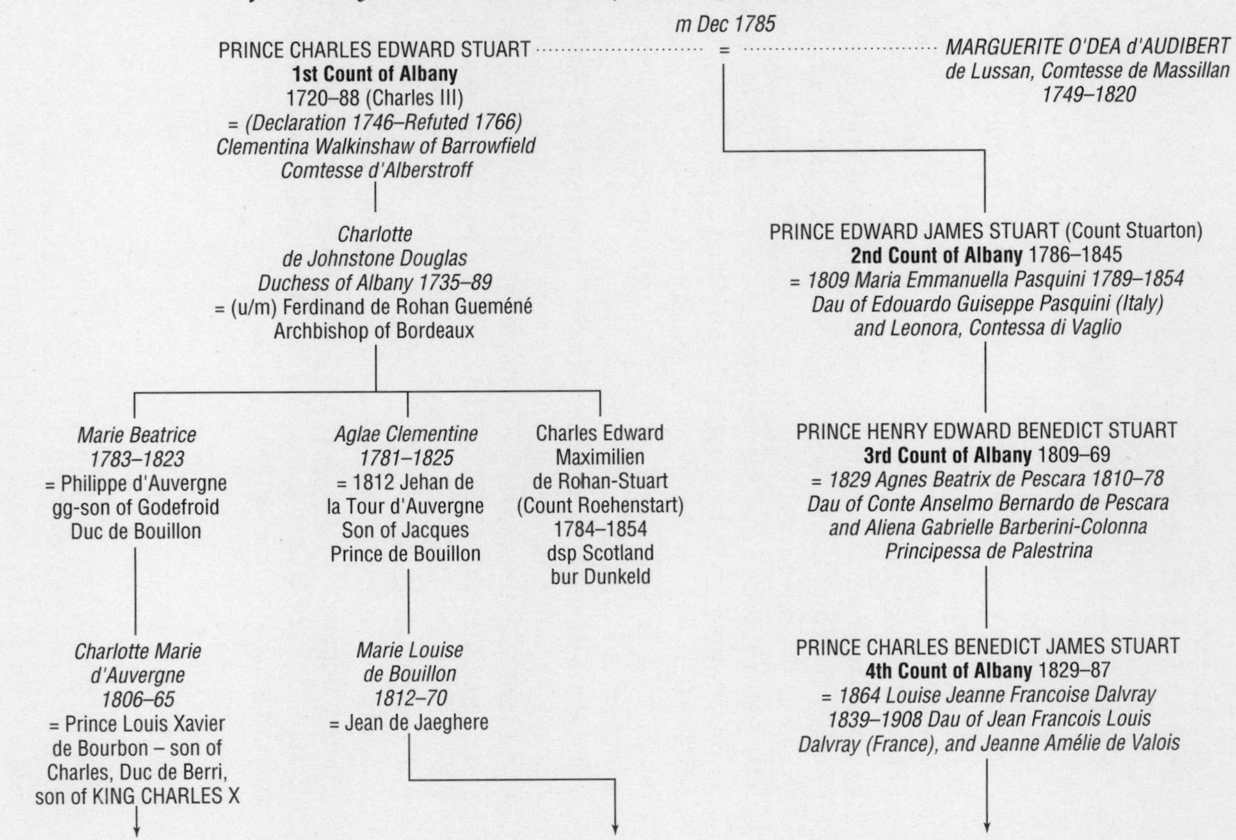
Counts of Albany – Princes and de jure High Stewards of Scotland
m Dec 1785
PRINCE CHARLES EDWARD STUART
1st Count of Albany
1720–88 (Charles III)
= (Declaration 1746–Refuted 1766)
Clementina Walkinshaw of Barrowfield
Comtesse d'Alberstroff
=
MARGUERITE O'DEA d'AUDIBERT
de Lussan, Comtesse de Massillan
1749–1820
Charlotte
de Johnstone Douglas
Duchess of Albany 1735–89
= (u/m) Ferdinand de Rohan Gueméné
Archbishop of Bordeaux
PRINCE EDWARD JAMES STUART (Count Stuarton)
2nd Count of Albany 1786–1845
= 1809 Maria Emmanuella Pasquini 1789–1854
Dau of Edouardo Guiseppe Pasquini (Italy)
and Leonora, Contessa di Vaglio
Marie Beatrice
1783–1823
= Philippe d'Auvergne
gg-son of Godefroid
Duc de Bouillon
Aglae Clementine
1781–1825
= 1812 Jehan de
la Tour d'Auvergne
Son of Jacques
Prince de Bouillon
Charles Edward
Maximilien
de Rohan-Stuart
(Count Roehenstart)
1784–1854
dsp Scotland
bur Dunkeld
PRINCE HENRY EDWARD BENEDICT STUART
3rd Count of Albany 1809–69
= 1829 Agnes Beatrix de Pescara 1810–78
Dau of Conte Anselmo Bernardo de Pescara
and Aliena Gabrielle Barberini-Colonna
Principessa de Palestrina
Charlotte Marie
d'Auvergne
1806–65
= Prince Louis Xavier
de Bourbon – son of
Charles, Duc de Berri,
son of KING CHARLES X
Marie Louise
de Bouillon
1812–70
= Jean de Jaeghere
PRINCE CHARLES BENEDICT JAMES STUART
4th Count of Albany 1829–87
= 1864 Louise Jeanne Francoise Dalvray
1839–1908 Dau of Jean Francois Louis
Dalvray (France), and Jeanne Amélie de Valois

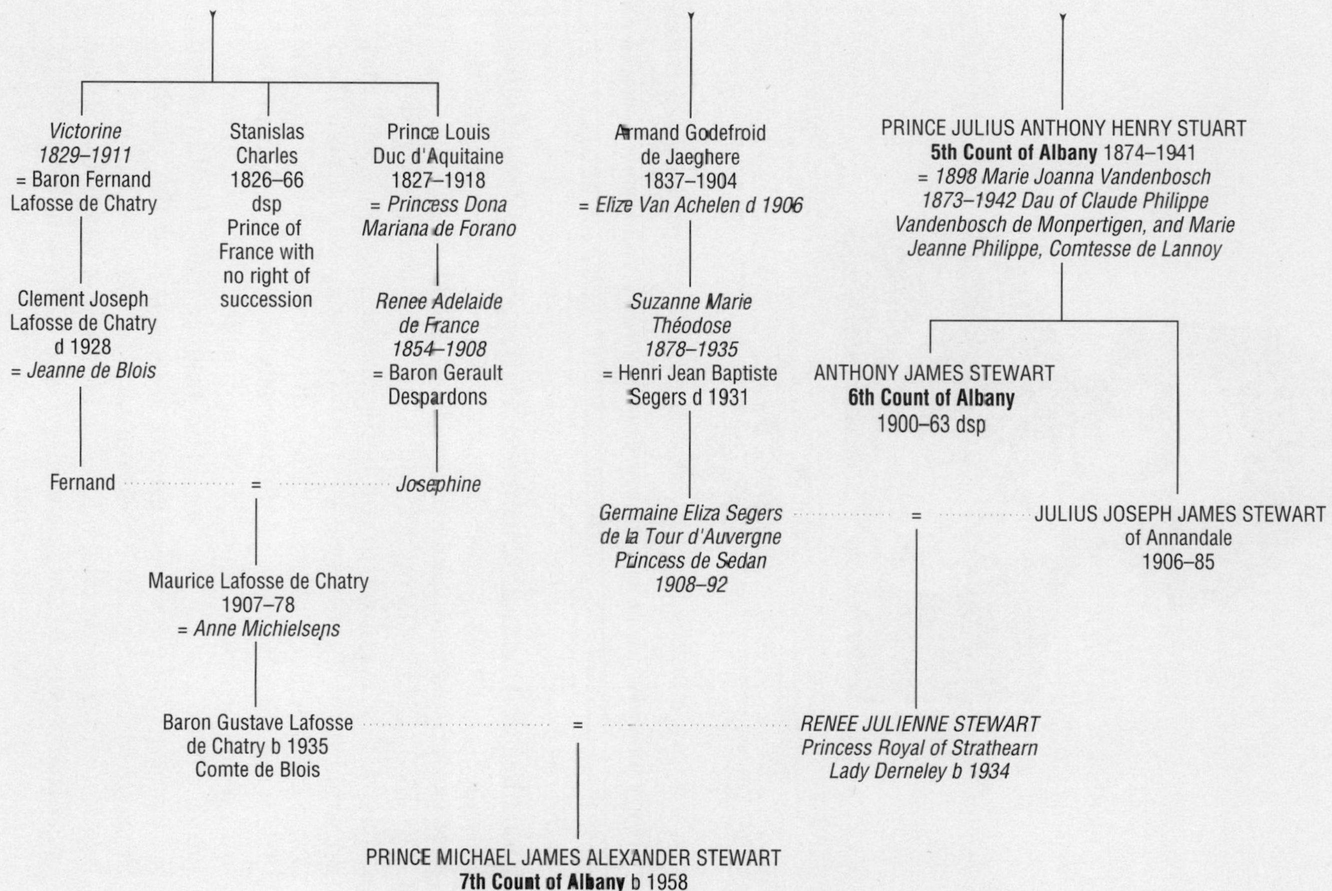
Victorine
1829–1911
= Baron Fernand
Lafosse de Chatry
Stanislas
Charles
1826–66
dsp
Prince of
France with
no right of
succession
Prince Louis
Duc d'Aquitaine
1827–1918
= Princess Dona
Mariana de Forano
Armand Godefroid
de Jaeghere
1837–1904
= Elize Van Achelen d 1906
PRINCE JULIUS ANTHONY HENRY STUART
5th Count of Albany 1874–1941
= 1898 Marie Joanna Vandenbosch
1873–1942 Dau of Claude Philippe
Vandenbosch de Monpertigen, and Marie
Jeanne Philippe, Comtesse de Lannoy
Clement Joseph
Lafosse de Chatry
d 1928
= Jeanne de Blois
Renee Adelaide
de France
1854–1908
= Baron Gerault
Despardons
Suzanne Marie
Théodose
1878–1935
= Henri Jean Baptiste
Segers d 1931
ANTHONY JAMES STEWART
6th Count of Albany
1900–63 dsp
Fernand
=
Josephine
Germaine Eliza Segers
de la Tour d'Auvergne
Princess de Sedan
1908–92
=
JULIUS JOSEPH JAMES STEWART
of Annandale
1906–85
Maurice Lafosse de Chatry
1907–78
= Anne Michielsens
Baron Gustave Lafosse
de Chatry b 1935
Comte de Blois
=
RENEE JULIENNE STEWART
Princess Royal of Strathearn
Lady Derneley b 1934
PRINCE MICHAEL JAMES ALEXANDER STEWART
7th Count of Albany b 1958

HRH Prince Charles Benedict James Stuart, 4th Count of Albany, from a painting by Michele Cammarano c1868

godfather, the Comte de Chambord. On 3 September 1880 Charles Benedict's nephew, Prince Alexander James Edward, married Marie Coucy – a relative of Princess Louise (Dalvray).

In 1883, Charles Benedict and Louise left Rome in order to catch the first ever train to run between Paris and Istanbul; they departed from the Gare de l'Est on Thursday 4 October. Their company included Missah Effendi (First Secretary to the Ottoman Embassy), along with a variety of ministers, journalists and diplomats, and George Nagelmackers, the designer of the esteemed 'Palace on Rail'. The train reached Bucharest on 7 October, whereupon the guests were taken to the Castle of Sinaia to meet King Carol of Romania. A further eventful journey by train and ship took them to Constantinople, where the Sultan organized visits to the palaces of the Ottoman Empire. By 16 October, Charles Benedict and Louise were back in Paris, having travelled 1,975 miles (about 3,186km).

The Stuart Exhibition

Charles Benedict and the Duchess of Buccleuch then contrived an interesting scheme to canonize Mary, Queen of Scots, through the intercession of the Scottish Jesuits in Rome.[5] The idea was to have the Papal Bull read within the walls of Holyrood House, Edinburgh, while at the same time Prince Charles Benedict of Albany would be introduced to the Scottish nation. Queen Victoria gave permission for the use of the Holyrood residence, but on hearing about the second part of the scheme put a firm end to it.

Undaunted by the Edinburgh affair, the endeavour to bring Charles Benedict to Britain was pursued, and in the autumn of 1886 a select number of prominent people received by post a pamphlet marked 'Private and Confidential'. It was from the Order of the White Rose – a revival of an earlier Jacobite society which had existed a century before in Wrexham. An extract from the communication reads as follows:

> For a long time past, it has seemed desirable that some efforts should be made to bring together those who, by hereditary descent or community of sentiment, are in sympathetic accord on the subject of history and the misfortunes of the Royal House of Stuart. It is now close to two-hundred years since the Revolution of 1688 dispossessed that House from the Throne of Great Britain. The chivalrous devotion of so many Englishmen and Scotsmen to that House which they regarded as their lawful Sovereign, has never received a fitting tribute of respect and honour from those who, with an affectionate intensity, admire and reverence the disinterested loyalty of the noble men and women who freely gave up life and fortune for a Sacred Cause.

This approach gave rise to a number of supportive replies, and plans were made for a grand 'Stuart Exhibition' in London.[6] Relics and relevant documents arrived from all over Britain and Europe, and arrangements were formalized to hold the display at the New Gallery in 1888. At the forefront of the White Rose organization was Bertram, 5th Earl of Ashburnham, along with Henry Jenner FSA, the Hon Stuart Erskine, Herbert Vivian (the Order's President), and Melville Massue, 9th Marquis de Ruvigny.

By 1887 the well-publicized proceedings were underway, and the Duchess of Roxburgh (along with Archbishop William Smith of Edinburgh and others) had organized a coinciding event for the Prince in Scotland. But then Charles Benedict of Albany was found dead in Italy; the circumstances were very suspicious, and there was a common belief that he had been murdered. Charles had supposedly fallen from his horse, but as pointed out by Father Torquato Armellini (Postulator of the Jesuits in Rome), his mortal injury was in no way consistent with the presumed fall. The post-mortem revealed that Charles Benedict had been smothered, and had died from suffocation.[7]

The 'Stuart Exhibition' was still held as planned, although in 1889, a year after the due date. However, significant changes had been made to its format, and the Order of the White Rose was politically manoeuvred from the line of sponsorship. Instead, the New Gallery display opened under the patronage of Queen Victoria herself, and its whole purpose was turned to Hanoverian advantage, being ultimately publicized to celebrate the bicentenary of the anti-Stuart Whig Revolution of 1688! Many of the donated Stuart documents and records were never seen by the public as originally intended; they conveniently disappeared altogether.

The Order of the White Rose had been infiltrated by Government agents, and Ruvigny, Vivian and Erskine therefore resigned to found the Legitimist Jacobite League of Great Britain and Ireland. The League's ceremonial attempt to lay a wreath at the Charing Cross statue of King Charles I in 1892 was, once again, confounded by Queen Victoria, and so both Lord Ashburnham and the Marquis de Ruvigny departed from the political stage to direct their future interests towards the chivalric Jacobite Order of the Realm of Sion. This international organization later merged with its allies, the Knights Protectors of the Sacred Sepulchre, and the Order of the Sangréal (Blood Royal/Holy Grail) – a long-standing dynastic Order of the Scots Royal House of Stewart.

Victoria and the Age of Discretion

Queen Victoria, Regina et Imperatrix, had succeeded her uncle William IV in 1837, and she was a discernible ornament in the Hanoverian Crown. Victoria was an independent girl, with a somewhat brutal streak that was manifest in stubborn opposition to anything she could not comprehend. Small and pleasant to behold, Victoria was not particularly well educated, and her understanding of State affairs was somewhat lacking. She therefore relied heavily on her Whig Prime Minister, Lord Melbourne – but the disconcerted Tory politicians began to feel that, due to the obvious closeness of the pair, Victoria would become known as 'Queen of the Whigs', rather than Queen of England.

From 1840 Melbourne was ousted, and the Queen was asked by the emergent Tories in Parliament (led by Sir Robert Peel) to dismiss most of her Whig ladies-in-waiting, but Victoria refused. Her Court was colourful enough, though never overburdened with intellect, and early on she was quite happy in this environment; but this was all to change from 1840 when she married her first cousin, the austere Prince Albert of Saxe-Coburg-Gotha. To that point, the Hanoverian kings had all married German princesses to whom they were related in the first or second degree. Victoria's mother, the Duchess of York, was herself a Princess of Saxe-Coburg, and she ensured that her daughter maintained the tradition. Prince Albert retained his own group of German advisers, and his influence over Victoria (though hard won) was total – if Albert disapproved of something or someone, so did Victoria. Consequently, the once debonair Victorian Court became cold and strait-laced, to be drilled and controlled like a military institution.

It must have been a great disappointment to Albert that he was not elevated to become King Consort, but such a status was probably too much to expect. Nevertheless, he retained dual-nationality so as to preserve his right of succession to Saxe-Coburg and Gotha. With Albert on the scene, Victoria became increasingly uncertain of her national standing in Britain. She sought, therefore, to adopt a borrowed identity with which they could both be comfortable, and so the couple came to Scotland, where they quickly overwhelmed themselves with everything Scottish. Balmoral Castle (the Royal Family's extravagant mansion) was wallpapered from top-to-bottom in tartan, carpeted in tartan, and furnished in tartan. Evidently, they perceived this as the customary way to behave in Scotland! To this day little has changed at Balmoral and with all the trappings of a Disneyland castle, it remains a typically Hanoverian version of a Scottish retreat.

When Albert died in 1861, Victoria's own light was extinguished, and she became a theoretical recluse for the next 40 years, buoyed only by her international status as an Empress. With the heightened surge of British imperialism, Victoria was truly convinced that by marrying her daughters into foreign royalty she did those noble families a favour! But in England, the only marriage which inspired the press and public with its romantic quality was that of Princess Louise to the Scots Marquess of Lorne. Not surprisingly, despite the contrived European marriages, at no time were descendants of the Stuart royal line ever married into the House of Hanover–Saxe-Coburg-Gotha.

Notwithstanding her early qualities, Victoria emerged as Empress of an Empire that she never saw, nor ever tried to see. The last opening of Parliament that she attended in person was in 1886, and five days later the Parliament collapsed due to the intrigue of Liberals and Irish Nationalists.

To believe that Victoria's reign was one of national glory is a concept based entirely on Hanoverian propaganda: one should consider the not-so-impressive Victorian values which the 'all-knowing' Queen condoned. The poverty-stricken lifestyles of the majority of British people were the worst in Europe; they were poorly rewarded for working incredibly long hours in unsafe conditions, and their lodgings were generally squalid and insanitary. The *Poor Houses* flourished, and child slave-labour was a thriving route to the financial success of the burgeoning entrepreneurs. The death-rate from disease, hypothermia, despair and suicide was disgustingly high, and unless one was of the aristocracy, or in some form of public, financial or industrial office, there was little chance to survive far beyond middle age.

As so often dubbed, this was indeed the 'Age of Discretion' – discretion, on the part of both Queen and Parliament, to ignore the plight of the people! And for all Victoria's supposed personal love of Scotland, our folk were as mistreated as their southern neighbours.

When comparing the historical legacies of the Stewarts and the Hanoverians, the differences are quite striking. The early Georgian line was sombre, with little sense of romance and no humour. For the most part, they were egotistic spendthrifts, with poor manners and no great liking for the British people. Such accusations cannot be laid against the Stewart Kings of Scots, nor against the successive Stuart Kings of Britain; their reigns were colourful, economical, tasteful, and always socially motivated. Yet the Stuarts were plagued with assaults from religious and parliamentary extremists. Ultimately, we were deposed to make way for a disinterested German house, whose ambition was despotic empire building at the expense of the British populace.

It is apparent that, despite the destructive machinations in England, the Stewart legacy is what made Scotland the Jewel of the European Crown. Long before the creation of the British Empire, the Scots were fighting against incoming oppressors. They sought to preserve the rights and liberties of many nations in Europe, including France, Poland and Bohemia. Scotland is internationally renowned for her social integrity, whereas England's reputation is one of self-styled imperialism. Trade and political alliances between Scotland and other realms were durable treaties – one of which, the Franco-Scottish *Auld Alliance,* lasted through the centuries from 1513; it was one of the longest-standing arrangements in the history of Europe, whereby (until 1906) Scots entered France as French citizens, and vice versa.

There are few worthwhile traces of the Hanoverian dynasty in the chronicles of Europe, whereas the Stewarts are consistently remembered in a multitude of State archives. Similarly, the Hanoverians are noticeable absentees in the recorded life of Scotland, except for their trips to Balmoral Castle, a week's annual stay at Holyrood Palace and their occasional weekends on Deeside.

PART SIX

The Forgotten Kingdom?

19

THE LATTER HANOVERIANS

From Saxe-Coburg-Gotha to Windsor

Queen Victoria died in 1901 after a lengthy reign, to be succeeded by her son, Edward VII of Saxe-Coburg-Gotha. He was a financial and sexual profligate, who cost the State and his mother an embarrassing amount in monetary debts to clubs and gambling houses. In 1864 Edward had married the Danish princess, Alexandra of Schleswig-Holstein-Sonderburg-Glucksbürg, who was considered by Edward's father to be the most eligible princess in the *Almanac de Gotha.* Initially, Victoria had not considered the match to be suitable, but she was very impressed when she met the girl. What bothered the Queen was that Denmark was no friend of her beloved Prussia which, for some reason, Victoria believed she owned – and because of this Alexandra's family were considered a rather bad lot. So poor Alexandra was scrutinized at Windsor by the Matriarch of England, who finally gave consent to her son's wedding.

Subsequently, the unfortunate Princess Alexandra was regularly faced by her husband's mistresses at Court; she also had to put up with the fact that he was twice called to the witness-box in cases of divorce and libel. Edward gained some limited popularity during his tours to India and the USA, but at home he was frequently admonished by the public for his indiscretions. To Edward's personal credit, however, was the signing of the *Entente Cordiale* following his French visit in 1903. This 'friendly understanding' did not give the English the same rights as the Franco-Scots *Auld Alliance,* but in terms of overall

European relations it was probably the most worthwhile achievement of the Hanoverian era.

Edward VII was succeeded by his second son George V, whose elder brother Albert, Duke of Clarence and Avondale, had died in 1892. George married his brother's fiancée Princess Victoria Maria Wurtemberg Von Hohenstein. Perhaps better known as Mary of Teck, she was a formidable woman with strong German values. It is not a generally known fact that this

The 1917 Windsor Proclamation: Henceforth the House of Saxe-Coburg-Gotha will be known as Windsor

family (from George I to George V) often corresponded and conversed in German, and they were far less Anglicized than the history books tell. By the time of George V's accession, the First World War was looming, and people believed there was a German 'Fifth Column' in Britain, so that shopkeepers and businessmen of German extraction – even the Lord of the Admiralty, Louis Battenberg – found themselves at the wrong end of public opinion. By 1917, with the war well underway, the situation was so bad that King George and the Germanic royal family of Britain changed their name from Saxe-Coburg-Gotha to 'Windsor', and those who refused to comply lost their rights to title and British nationality.

Germany and Abdication

With George V's son and successor, Edward VIII, we come to an especially sensitive moment in British history, and we are told that this socially extrovert king gave up his crown for love. However, according to contemporary documentation, had Edward VIII not been compelled to abdicate in 1936, we might all be speaking German in Britain today. To what final extent this assertion is correct cannot be ascertained, but its basis cannot be denied for it is on film that Edward consorted on amicable terms with Nazi leaders. Historical records pertaining to the Second World War indicate that certain Windsors were associates of Nazi officials such as Joachim von Ribbentrop and Hermann Goering, and it was for this reason that Edward was obliged to vacate his throne – to be cut adrift from the desired public image of the Royal Family.

Philip of Hesse, Honorary General of the Storm Troopers, was specifically earmarked by Adolf Hitler as the Third Reich's contact with Edward Windsor. After the war, embarrassing records of meetings between Edward and Hitler were found at a Hesse castle, and these documents were brought secretly to England by two officers of Edward's brother and successor, King George VI, to be placed under lock-and-key. One of those officers was the notorious Anthony Blunt; he was suitably rewarded with a knighthood, but was stripped of it in 1979 when he was discovered to have been a Russian agent during the Cold War.

Among the 1,000 pages of documentation brought from Hesse were papers concerning Hitler's suggestion that Edward should hold himself 'in readiness to return to the throne'. Allied to this was the added promise of 50m Swiss francs. The Führer maintained this ambition until 1943, but the plan was never realized, and fortunately George VI remained king.

Edward and his American wife (the former Mrs Wallis Simpson) were discarded, to be diplomatically forgotten in an oblivion of house parties, travel and the Arcadian social whirl of the Duke and Duchess of Windsor. Nonetheless, their legacy remains to haunt the Royal House even today – not only because of the German affair, but because of their irresponsible spending of public resources. These hard-earned funds were provided by British taxpayers to support a disgracefully opulent lifestyle which persisted until the 1980s – a far cry from the kith-and-kin principle of the Scots. This contemptible practice of making citizens foot the bill for aristocratic excesses is a perfect example of a Parliamentary Monarchy in operation. Such a practice would be anathema to a true Constitutional Monarchy. Royal Houses are supposed to serve the people – not the other way about!

As an interesting aside, the *Daily Mail* of 15 November 1995 brought to light the fact that Edward's marriage to Mrs Wallis Simpson could actually have been bigamous, for it is contended that he had previously married, and deserted, a woman in Canada. She was Millicent Milroy, a schoolteacher of Guelph, who died aged 95 in 1985. Further checking reveals that Millicent's story is well known in Ontario, and she was the subject of a number of press reports in the 1970s.

Apparently, the couple met in October 1919 when Edward was Prince of Wales, and soon afterwards Edward wrote to Mackenzie King, the Canadian Prime Minister, saying that he was planning to marry a Canadian girl. Edward's equerry, Alan Lascelles (in a letter to his wife), also mentioned being introduced to a certain 'Miss Mulrey'. Millicent Milroy then moved from Guelph to Alberta, near to Edward's Canadian ranch, where he was regularly stationed between 1920 and 1927. In 1933 Millicent returned to the old Scots settlement at Guelph, and current local residents claim to have seen her marriage certificate. They attest that it was registered as a morganatic marriage (whereby children cannot inherit their father's status or property). Indeed, Millicent's GP, Dr Jan Hodsil, said she was sworn to secrecy in the matter by the Canadian Board of Ethics.

Millicent's next-door neighbour, Mary Calder, confirmed that the Royal Canadian Mounted Police ransacked the Milroy house and took everything after Millicent died. Her Will, however, is now held in the archives of Guelph Library, and her 1985 gravestone was inscribed by the local stonemasons, Campbell and Polloch. Standing in a cemetery at Cambridge, Ontario (about an hour's drive from Toronto), its inscription reads: 'Millicent A.M.M.M., P.St. – daughter of James and Helen Milroy, 1890-1985, wife of Edward VIII, Duke of Windsor 1894–1972'.

Whether the marriage reports are true or false, it is clear that the Buckingham Palace staff were not surprised when questioned about them a few years ago by the Canadian writer Veronica Ross. Even they could not be certain, for the general irresponsibility of the late Duke of Windsor was an embarrassment which left no room for surprises. They neither confirmed nor denied the story of Millicent and Edward, saying only that it was 'impossible to disprove'.

A Salvaged Dynasty

Edward's legacy to his unfortunate brother Albert (who became King George VI) was that of a tumbling monarchy – an institution which had fallen from its once solid German pedestal. It had become a monarchy of scandal and avoidance of duty; Edward's abdication was insulting to the community, and was naturally equated with failure and shame. This was a difficult inheritance for the unprepared George VI; he had never been trained for kingship, his health was not good, and he suffered with a speech impediment. There is little doubt that without Elizabeth Bowes-Lyon at his side the monarchy would have crumbled. Here, at last, was a lady to admire – but Elizabeth was no product of Hanover. She sprang from an old Jacobite family, and to accommodate her becoming Duchess of York, her father even resigned from the Royal Stuart Society. To a point, Elizabeth's marriage was mildly embarrassing to British Jacobites, but the good lady certainly proved her traditional worth by salvaging an establishment that would not otherwise have survived.

It is perhaps necessary, however, to clarify HM The Queen Mother's position with regard to her strategically advertised Scottish blood. Elizabeth is the daughter of the 14th Earl of Strathmore and Kinghorn, Baron Glamis (died 1944). She was born, according to the local church plaque, in Saint Paul's Walden, Hertfordshire, on 4 August 1900. Her father, Claude, was born in London, and her grandfather, Claude (13th Earl), was born in Redbourn, Hertfordshire. His father, Thomas (12th Earl), was born in Durham; his father, Thomas (11th Earl and brother of John, 10th Earl), in Saint Paul's Walden, and his father, John (9th Earl), in Rainton, County Durham. Only by tracing back to his father, Thomas (8th Earl), do we find a Scottish birth in 1704.

It is evident, therefore, that the heavily publicised Scottish blood of the Queen Mother is very much on the thin side, and her line had persisted well south of the Border for six generations, with marriages into Durham and Hertfordshire families. Yet for all that, the Government decided to play the 'Scots card' against the ever-increasing threat of Scottish nationalism. The intensive propaganda used by Westminster to convince the Scots that they had a Scottish queen was undoubtedly well conceived, and it worked to the extent that it is widely believed that Elizabeth Bowes-Lyon was born at Glamis Castle.

It is not even certain that Elizabeth was born in Hertfordshire for, contrary to the local church plaque, her birth certificate states that she was born in London. But the birth does not appear to have occurred at Lord Glamis' Grosvenor Gardens apartment, and the actual location of the event remains a mystery. Elizabeth's intriguing birth certificate was not even dated until seven weeks after Her Majesty's birth, because her father had been playing cricket in Scotland at the time!

In an attempt to draw a distinction between the Saint Paul's Walden legend, the London certificated record, and the Glamis Castle fantasy, the question of Elizabeth's mysterious birth was recently put to the officials of Clarence House. Their vague answer was, 'It doesn't really matter where she was born, or whether there were some inaccuracies'.[1] But it certainly mattered to the Scots in 1936–7, when a collapsing Germanic dynasty was given a whole new credibility on the basis of Queen Elizabeth's Scottish birthright.

The Battenberg Dilemma

When George and Elizabeth's eldest daughter, Princess Elizabeth, became romantically involved with Philip of Greece, a whole new round of intrigue and subterfuge began. This centred around an attempt to veil Philip's personal background – for, despite the contrived press reports of the time, Philip had not a drop of Greek blood in his veins. His place of birth was simply a matter of physical location, but in real terms his descent was Germanic-Danish. When Philip and Elizabeth were betrothed, Philip had no surname; indeed he was quite stateless, except for a tenuously afforded citizenship of Denmark. This arrangement had its roots in the House of Schleswig-Holstein-Sonderburg-Glucksbürg.

Philip's father, Andrew, was the son of the Danish Prince Wilhelm (second son of Christian IX). Wilhelm had moved to Greece in 1863 to fill a well-touted vacancy for a king; he managed to become George I of the Hellenes, but was assassinated in 1913. One of his brothers-in-law was Tsar Alexander III of Russia, and another was Queen Victoria's son Edward VII. Wilhelm's own eldest son (Philip's uncle) succeeded as Constantine I of Greece, until deposed in 1917 for refusing to join the Allies against Germany. Three years later he was returned to office, but abdicated again in 1922.

Shortly after Philip's birth in 1921, his father, Prince Andrew, was involved in a serious military blunder against the Turks, in which 40,000 Greek soldiers died and 1.5 million citizens were obliged to flee their homes. In the wake of this, Andrew (along with five of his ministers and a general) was arrested, charged with treason, and brought before a military tribunal. He was accused of abandoning his position when in contact with the enemy, and the tribunal found him guilty. His colleagues were subsequently executed by firing-squad on 22 November 1922, but Andrew was saved by way of a British rescue mission instigated by the Foreign Secretary, Lord Curzon. Andrew and his wife, Alice, along with Philip and his sisters, were carried away aboard HMS *Calypso*, and the family was registered as being 'perpetually banished' from Greece.

With Philip's marriage to Elizabeth Windsor pending in 1946, it was necessary that he should secure an acceptable nationality and adopt a suitable family name, and so in February 1947, for the price of £10 (along with hundreds of incoming war refugees), Philip obtained British naturalization. For his surname he chose that of his maternal uncle, Lord Louis Mountbatten. However, despite all attempts to smoke-screen the issue, it was clear that (just as the Saxe-Coburg-Gotha name had been changed to Windsor during the First World War) 'Mountbatten' was also an elected substitute for the family's original German name of 'Battenberg'. In fact, Philip's mother was Princess Alice of Battenberg.

As if that were not enough to consider in the wake of the Duke of Windsor affair, and with the war recently over, there was more to come. Alice's heritage was easy enough to disguise since she had a female ancestry (through the Marchioness of Milford Haven) from Queen Victoria; but Philip had four elder sisters who had continued the Hesse tradition, and when they were married in the 1930s Philip's maternal family was substantially inclined towards Nazism.

Sophie, the youngest sister, was married to Philip of Hesse's brother – the ardent Nazi, Christopher of Hesse. He was a close friend of Hermann Goering, and became Prussian Ministerial Director and Head of Goering's *Forschungsamt* intelligence service in Berlin. It was at Christopher's own castle that the Edward of Windsor documents were found. Cecile, the second youngest sister (who died with her husband in 1937), was married to George Donatus, heir to the Duchy of Hesse. His brother, Prince Louis, was appointed Cultural Attaché to the German Embassy in London under Von Ribbentrop, and Louis' express duty was to provide a personal link between the Third Reich and the British royals. Theodora, Philip's next sister, was married to Berthold, Margrave of Baden, a German officer in the French incursion. The eldest sister, Margarita, was the wife of Gottfried, Prince of Hohenlohe-Langenburg, a corps commander in the Austrian invasion.

Shortly after Philip and Princess Elizabeth became privately engaged in 1946, death sentences were imposed at Nuremberg on Goering and Von Ribbentrop. Philip's brother-in-law, Christopher of Hesse, escaped a Nuremberg sentence only because he had previously been killed in his plane over Italy.

King George VI was so nervous about his daughter's tinder-box relationship that the Buckingham Palace Private Secretary,

Sir Alan Lascelles, issued a formal denial of any engagement between Philip and Elizabeth. Meanwhile, the propaganda machine went into action, quite truthfully, with tales of Philip's days at Dartmouth College and his commendable service in the British Navy.

Although King George had his reservations about the liaison, Philip's uncle, Louis Mountbatten of Burma, was pushing hard for Philip's marriage to the heiress of Windsor. Through his nephew's male line, he wanted to change the British dynasty from Windsor to his own House of Battenberg/Mountbatten. In February 1947 Philip renounced his Greek inheritance and was no longer a prince, simply Lieutenant Mountbatten. But the prospect of being the 'last' Windsor was anathema to King George, who took all necessary steps to prevent the Mountbatten take-over by ensuring that Philip was not granted the style of 'Prince' in Britain; his status was, therefore, confined to being Duke of Edinburgh.

When Philip and Elizabeth were married on 20 November 1947, every effort was made to suppress the truth of Philip's German heritage – but one month later, on 19 December, Philip of Hesse (who had been seized by the Americans for war crimes) was brought before the Tribunal at Frankfurt. In Britain, his trial had minimal press coverage, and he was not linked in any way with the royal consort who was vaguely described as being 'formerly of Greece'.

On 7 February 1952 King George VI died while Philip and Elizabeth were abroad. Lord Louis wasted no time in announcing that the House of Mountbatten had succeeded to the throne of Britain. This view was upheld by the editor of *Debrett's Peerage,* with whom Mountbatten had been liaising over the preparation of his family lineage. As confirmed only recently in the *Daily Express* (4 September 1990), this editor, L G Pine, wrote in the press that Philip, 'by adopting his mother's anglicized family name when he was naturalised, had upon his marriage effectively replaced the Royal Family name of Windsor with his own new surname'.

Fortunately for the Windsors, King George's *letters patent* (under the Great Seal) had checked this dynastic change to some degree – though not entirely. Previously, Philip and Elizabeth's son Charles (born 1948) had been christened simply 'Prince

Charles of Edinburgh' – not Charles Windsor. Similarly, their daughter Princess Anne's birth registration (1950) contained no surname. It was not until 21 April 1952 that Prime Minister Sir Winston Churchill made a related announcement. He stated that the Royal House, in spite of its Mountbatten marital status, would continue in the female line as the 'House of Windsor'. Five years later, in 1957, Queen Elizabeth II conferred the distinction of 'Prince' upon her husband in recognition of their 10th wedding anniversary. Then in 1959 the Queen relented a little further by changing the general family name to 'Mountbatten-Windsor' – which is actually the equivalent of 'Battenberg–Saxe-Coburg-Gotha'.

The Stone of Destiny

In 1953, HM Queen Elizabeth II of Great Britain had been ceremonially crowned in England – but she almost wasn't. Prior to the event, Scottish nationalists removed the Coronation Stone from Westminster, in order to carry it back to Scotland where it belonged. Many Scots claimed that the Hanoverian descent of Windsor was still not accepted north of the Border. Geoffrey Fisher, the Archbishop of Canterbury, roared away on the radio, intimating that the Scots should give back the stone, and it was duly returned. But the stone removed from Westminster was not, as supposed, the sacred Stone of Destiny. It was the substitute which King Edward I had acquired in 1296, and which had sat, thereafter, beneath the coronation chair at Westminster Abbey. The true Stone of Destiny was hidden by the Abbot of Scone in the 13th century, and has remained secreted ever since.

Seemingly, many of the ancient Saxon Kings of England, in descent from Alfred the Great to Edmund Ironside (died 1016), were crowned upon a stone which was kept at the Church of Kingston-upon-Thames. However, none of the incoming Norman or Plantagenet kings had that privilege until Edward I stole the bogus stone from Scotland.

What the unsuspecting Edward had actually removed to England was a piece of sandstone cut from a monastery doorway. This is why the medieval Scots never asked for this particular stone to be returned. However, Edward I did manage to steal the original Scottish Regalia of King Alexander III, along with the venerated Black Rood (crucifix) of St Margaret, which was held to contain a fragment of the Holy Cross. It is of particular significance to note that when the Westminster stone was offered back to Bruce and the Scots at the 1328 *Treaty of Northampton*, the offer was declined. Indeed, the English never thought to enquire about the stone upon which Bruce had himself sworn his Oath of Fealty. A request was made, nevertheless, for the Holy Rood – but the English claimed that this had been lost.

Quite recently, the Westminster stone was returned to Scotland after 700 years, and (despite its being a sham artifact) the gesture was portrayed by Parliament as one of long-sought recognition for the Scots. But nothing could be further from the truth! The stone was not 'given' back to the Scots; neither are future coronations of British monarchs planned to be in Scotland. The Westminster Parliament and the English Crown officials have simply decided to house the stone in Scotland, to be removed back to London as and when necessary. As such, it constitutes no more than a museum piece that will serve as a visible daily reminder of Scotland's subjugation.

When the day of Elizabeth Mountbatten-Windsor's coronation arrived in 1953, she (like countless monarchs before) sat on the Coronation Throne with a piece of masonry rubble beneath her and a substitute Crown of Saint Edward on her head (Oliver Cromwell had melted down the original crown prior to the 1660 Stuart Restoration). Much against the wishes of the Anglican clergy, the Moderator of the Church of Scotland was involved in order to save the Queen's embarrassment against the Scottish patriots – but there was more embarrassment to follow when the new monarch was crowned as 'Queen Elizabeth II'. At this, the Scots let loose their considerable annoyance and disbelief: how could the Queen possibly be the 'second' Elizabeth of Great Britain? The Scots had never had a 'first' Elizabeth! Were the English suggesting that Elizabeth I Tudor of England had reigned over Scotland as well?

Regardless of the anomaly, Elizabeth II it was to be – but when the 'E II R' initials appeared in Scotland, anything bearing them was vandalized. Post-boxes were a favourite target, and they were regularly exploded during the small hours. Eventually Sir Thomas Innes of Learney, Lord Lyon King of Arms, diplomatically pronounced that the Scottish Post Office, its mail vans and pillar-boxes, would bear the Crown of Scotland only, and wherever displayed the 'E II R' initials were to be immediately removed. In the light of this experience, and in view of Charles Edward Stuart's Holyrood coronation in September 1745, it will be interesting to see what happens if the House of Windsor attempts to give the Scots a 'second' King Charles III.

In due time, Queen Elizabeth came to Edinburgh to honour the Scottish Regalia. The Scots had elected to mark the occasion with an impressive ceremony, but to their astonishment a contrary note was received from the Home Office, instructing them to keep the affair as simple as possible. Nevertheless, in true Scottish spirit, they went about their respectful plan, and when the day arrived, all concerned wore Scottish State dress; the High Kirk of Saint Giles was resplendent in medieval colours, and the Stewart Crown (on a deep red cushion) was guarded by the Duke of Hamilton and the Countess of Errol, High Constable of Scotland. The Church was packed with people who had come to see the Crown of the Scots presented to the English monarch. They envisaged a truly splendid occasion, but were thoroughly disappointed.

A fanfare announced the arrival of Her Majesty, and the pageant was set to begin. Within the ceremonially bedecked High Kirk, the finely dressed officers and congregation awaited the grand entrance of the sovereign monarch – but who was this at the doorway? In walked Queen Elizabeth, wearing an everyday blue raincoat, and carrying a handbag!

With the initial embarrassment over, there followed the moment when the Queen was supposed to touch the Crown of the Scots – and it was then that the royal handbag came into its own as it swung into the attack. Were it not for the quick action of the cushion-bearer, the Crown would likely have been sent crashing to the stone floor below. Since that time, and in accordance with custom, the Windsors have maintained their annual visits to Edinburgh – but despite this tradition, the walls of Holyrood House retain their timeless legacy of Stewart Scotland, and they have no Hanoverian empathy whatever.

20

Sovereign Rights and Entitlements

Château du Moulin

Julius, 5th Count of Albany

Returning now to my own 19th-century forebears, the Stewart story can be brought down to the present day.

In the wake of the adventurous Istanbul train journey, Charles Benedict Stuart's son, Prince Julius Anthony Henry, 5th Count of Albany, was often a guest of the Sultan of Constantinople. Julius was my great-grandfather, and by 1892 had reverted to the original *Stewart* spelling of our ancestral name. He dispensed with the French corruption, *Stuart*, which had long prevailed in the royal line. (In Italy, we had always been called *Stuardo.*)

At about the same time the family sold Stuarton House in Rome, and moved to our old estate in the Belgian Ardennes near Spa. In those days my family was still relatively wealthy, largely due to the impressive banking connections of Julius' mother, Louise Dalvray, who had inherited part of her father's fortune. We also maintained significant political influence through the Stuart Household Order of the Knights of Saint Germain. The Ardennes property had originally been given to Princess Louise Marie in 1692 by her godfather, King Louis XIV of France, and it was at this same Château du Moulin that I was raised – a truly delightful castle with about 20 rooms, set within 120 acres of rich farming land, traversed by a river.

HRH Prince Julius Anthony Henry Stewart, 5th Count of Albany, from a painting by Theo van Rysselberghe 1898

Anthony, 6th Count of Albany

Having become a Belgian National under the protection of the Royal House of Saxe-Coburg, my great-grandfather was married on 10 January 1898. His wife was Marie Joanna, daughter of Claude Philippe Vandenbosch de Monpertigen (originally from the Netherlands) and Marie, Comtesse de Lannoy. They had three children: my great-uncle, Prince Anthony James Stewart, 6th Count of Albany, born in 1898; my great-aunt Ursula Marie Anne, Baroness of Renfrew, born on 18 March 1901; and my grandfather, Julius Joseph James Stewart of Annandale, Prince of

Scotland, born in 1906. By that stage of our history all the family were settled into the Protestant faith.

It is important to mention that from December 1913 (with the First World War looming) each successive Stewart heir has signed a sworn declaration to the effect that 'the House of Stewart recognizes the House of Saxe-Coburg (subsequently Windsor) as having sole right to the English Crown of Saint Edward. In turn, the Stewart interest remains in due entitlement to the original Kingdom of Scots'.

The senior legitimate succession fell to my grandfather, Prince Julius Joseph James Stewart, Lord of Annandale and sovereign heir-presumptive. On 21 May 1932 he married Germaine Eliza Segers de la Tour d'Auvergne, *de jure* Princess of the Duchy of Bouillon, and Duchess of Albany in her own right. Germaine Eliza was the lineal descendant and heiress of Aglae de Rohan Walkinshaw-Stuart (Charlotte of Albany's daughter) and her husband Jehan de la Tour d'Auvergne, Comte de Bouillon.

By the marital union of Julius Joseph and Germaine Eliza, both the legitimate and legitimated lines from Charles III became permanently attached. Then on 11 November 1934 Princess Germaine presented her husband with their only child – a daughter christened Renée Julienne, and styled Lady Derneley. In time, she was destined to become my mother.

During the Second World War both my great-uncle and grandfather were prominent in the Belgian Resistance, and Hubert Pierlot, Prime Minister of Belgium in exile (first in North Africa and then in London), was a close friend of the family. In 1940 Pierlot sent word to Château du Moulin a few days before the invasion of Belgium by German troops. He advised my family to leave the castle in case of reprisals, but they were initially unable to heed his advice. In later years my mother told me of how the sky above our home was filled with German planes, and there were tanks almost at the front steps. She and the others were lucky to escape with their lives, and our house was seized to become an enemy headquarters for the area. For a time the Stewarts removed to Brussels with some bare essentials, but my great-grandfather, Julius Anthony, died in the following year, and his widow, Marie Joanna, was found dead a few months later in a bomb-shattered house.

My grandfather, Prince Julius Joseph, was a member of the

Underground Army which repatriated wounded British and American soldiers to Britain, while helpless Jews were evacuated to Portugal and Switzerland. Using the assumed name of Dee, he was eventually discovered by the Gestapo and taken to the cellars of the Palais de Justice for interrogation. Fortunately, he was not treated too badly and, after a short confinement he was released, having been shot through the hand.

By September 1944 the Germans had left Belgium, and Hubert Pierlot was reinstated as Prime Minister. At his behest, the surviving Stewarts were driven back to their castle in the Ardennes, where on 11 November a celebration ball was held. Life at Château du Moulin resumed its peaceful routine thereafter, but with fewer residents than before. The links with Brussels remained, however, and only quite recently in 1982 the city celebrated the 50th marriage anniversary of my grandparents. On that occasion, Prince Julius Joseph Stewart and Princess Germaine Eliza de Sedan were personally entertained by the capital authorities of Belgium.

Today, there are several family lines descended from Charles Edward Stuart's son Prince Edward James, 2nd Count of Albany. They include the Counts of Derneley (by descent from Prince Henry Frederick Alexander, younger brother of Prince Charles Benedict James), and the Demidoff Stewarts, Dukes of Coldingham (by descent from Prince Claude Henry, younger son of Prince Charles Benedict, brother of Prince Julius Anthony Henry 1874–1941). Among the descendants of Charlotte of Albany are the Polish families of Sobolewski and Sobiesierski, and the Barons Lafosse de Chatry – female-line heirs to the Royal House of Bourbon-France. Foremost, however, in the legitimate senior descent of the ancient Royal House of Stewart is the line as hitherto detailed – the descent which is now settled very firmly on myself as the 7th Count of Albany.

The Stewart Heritage

In 1955 my mother, Princess Renée Julienne, Lady Derneley, became engaged to her cousin Gustave Joseph Clement Fernand Lafosse de Blois de Chatry – a scion of the Royal House of Bourbon-France, and a descendant of Charlotte of Albany's

Délivré en exécution de l'article 16 de la Constitution.

Afgeleverd in uitvoering van artikel 16 der Grondwet.

Nous soussigné certifions que
Wij ondergeteekende verklaren dat

Son Altesse Royale le Prince Julius Joseph Jacques Stewart, Seigneur d' Annandale, né a Laeken, le 16 Mars 1906, fils de SAR le Prince Julius Antoine Henri Stewart, Comte d' Albanie, et de Jeanna Marie Vandenbosch de Monpertingen

Et

Germania Elisa Segers de la Tour, Princesse de Sedan, née à Bouillon, le 24 Avril 1908, fille de Henri Jean Baptiste Segers et de Marie Suzanna Dejaeghere de la Tour d' Auvergnes

ont contracté mariage, devant Nous, Officier de l'État civil de Bruxelles, deuxième district,
voor Ons, Ambtenaar van den Burgerlijken Stand, hebben huwelijk aangegaan te Brussel, tweede district,

le 21 Mei 1932
den

Bureau D — № 4290. — 1930.

The marriage certificate of Prince Michael's grandparents, Prince Julius Joseph James Stewart of Annandale and Princess Germaine Eliza de la Tour d'Auvergne in May 1932

daughter Marie Beatrice. In 1956 Renée was created Princess Royal of Strathearn, and on 5 May that year she and Gustave were married. I arrived on the scene on 21 April 1958 – but my parents separated in 1963, and I remained their only offspring.

It has occasionally been put to me in recent years that, although my mother held the Stewart royal heritage, it would perhaps be more logical that I had inherited my father's name. However, in order to perpetuate the succession, mine was indeed the Stewart inheritance as the senior heir. My situation is identical to that of Britain's present Charles Windsor, Prince of Wales, whose own dynastic descent is traced though his mother, Queen Elizabeth. The main difference between us lies in the method of nominal inheritance. Immediately after my birth in 1958, the Belgian State confirmed that I should bear my mother's name, whereas in Prince Charles's case, it was not until 1952 (four years after his birth) that the Westminster Parliament recognized his privilege.

All legal steps were taken by the Royal Houses of Stewart and Windsor to ensure perpetuity of the lines, and both offspring (Charles and myself) were regarded as lawful heirs to kingship. For Charles the entitlement was *de facto* (a matter of Fact – whether by Right or not) – but my own entitlement is expressly *de jure* (by automatic Right).

Michael, 7th Count of Albany

My great-uncle Anthony James, 6th Count of Albany, died in 1963. He had married Jeanette Van Haal in the 1940s, but they had no children, and so I duly inherited the family titles, 7th Count of Albany, Count Stuarton, Duke of Kendal and Kintyre, 26th Lord High Steward of Scotland. Indeed, I had already been termed *Septième Comte d'Albanie* on my birth certificate, as is standard European procedure for the eldest son in line.

Given that my father left us when I was very young, I was glad enough not to have been granted his name, particularly since he left us in a state of financial chaos. He had somehow managed to squander the family inheritance, and I can well recall that dreadful afternoon of 22 December 1968 when our château was invaded by his creditors; my father had been gone five years by then. At the age of ten, I would gladly have let them do their worst with him, but the family decided to uphold our reputation by honouring all the commitments on his behalf – and the debt was phenomenal. There were six of us then, including my grandmother and my great-uncle's widow. When uncle Anthony James died, we each inherited £200,000 [equivalent to about £1.75m each in today's purchasing terms] – and so the total went into the rescue pot, along with all our other assets. But even that was not enough, and we were obliged to sell Château du Moulin, having held the property for 276 years.

My parents were divorced in 1969, by which time my mother and I had moved from a 20-room castle to a cheaply rented two-room flat in Brussels. From the age of five I had been individually tutored at home, but suddenly I was sharing a class teacher with 25 other children. Mother had been working full-time for five years, and continued to do so – which brings us back to where this book began. Having experienced the best and the worst of times, I left my last school in Soignies with the same longing that had persisted since my early days at the Ardennes estate – and I intended, against whatever odds, to retrace my ancestors' footsteps to Scotland.

I well remember my fifth birthday, with its customary party, cake and candles, and how, while my grandfather was cutting the cake, my godmother asked me what I would like to do when grown-up. I did not think the question odd, nor answered with the customary 'fireman' or 'train-driver'. 'When I am 18, I shall leave, to live and die in Scotland', I said. My mother could hardly believe that her infant son was handing in his notice! But whatever prompted my decision on that day, I certainly kept the appointment.

Goodbye to Brussels

My ambition never changed. I read books about Scotland, I bought pictures of Scotland, and I listened regularly to BBC radio to become accustomed to the language. When I left the room, Mother would re-tune to a French-speaking station, and when I returned I would switch back to the British channel. There was such a rivalry of interests that it became a family joke, and eventually I bought my own radio, which was permanently tuned to BBC News, plays and, of course, *The Archers.* I would even sing songs in English at college, accompanied by my friend Christian on his guitar. Actually, they were hardly in English at all, with just the odd recognizable English word thrown in, but they sounded good to the others.

By the middle of 1975 I was working for an insurance broking company in Brussels, and it was my ambition to save as much of my earnings as possible, so as to fund my journey. But saving is not that easy in a city environment, where living standards are high, and their upkeep expensive. Nevertheless, from my early days I had earned the nickname 'Perseverance'; even as a small child I had saved birthday money, Christmas money, and whatever other cash came along, rarely spending without good reason. And so it was that, within a year, I decided the time had come to pack my bags for Scotland.

I gave Thilly and Ritweger notice in August 1976, but preferred not to make any announcement to my parents until the last. Under Belgian law employees are entitled to a free afternoon each week after serving notice, and at the first opportunity I changed my Belgian money for British currency, and wrote letters to some prominent people in Scotland, informing them of my intention. Goodness knows what they must have thought on receiving the letters for as I was soon to discover, the majority of people in Britain had absolutely no idea that we Stewarts still existed.

Back home I was quite unaware that my parents had discovered my plan. But early that same evening the entry bell rang, and my father demanded that I let him in. He had not crossed our threshold for years, but there he was – and within no time my mother appeared, exclaiming, 'He's off to Scotland, of all places!'. Stewarts do not often raise their voices, but that day the whole apartment building rang with word of my impending departure!

Somehow I must have foreseen the possibility of such an encounter, for earlier that day I had photocopied all my papers, leaving only the copies in my room. I was, therefore, neither surprised nor particularly bothered when my father was directed to search my belongings for any documents that I would need to take with me. He found only the copies, which he tore to shreds in his anger – whereupon he left the flat, and mother went about her business. At that, I retired to my room, and determined that I would leave in the morning.

Next day, instead of going to my office, I went to the Station du Nord, where I bought a one-way ticket to London. I returned to the apartment to collect my suitcase, and left an explanatory note on the dining-table: 'Gone to Scotland. Will be okay. Love, Michael'.

Before long I was on the train to Ostende, from where I took the ferry to Dover. By that time the excitement of the adventure had taken hold of me, and I knew that until I reached Scotland all else would pale into the ordinary – as indeed did the famous white cliffs and the city of London where I spent my first night, longing to board the train for Edinburgh.

As the train approached the Scottish Border I felt an enormous sense of relief – a relief that only a Scottish heart can feel. The back of my neck was tingling, and I looked about to see how my fellow travellers were behaving. The general level of conversation increased; the once sober people were smiling, and the quiet ones began to hum Scottish tunes. Even the tea suddenly tasted better as we rounded the rugged coastline, and at last we pulled into Edinburgh's Waverley Station.

Whereas London had left me somewhat nonplussed, majestic Edinburgh gave me a shock of joy. It was comparable with Imperial Vienna, and a true jewel in the crown of Europe – the seven hills, the towering Castle, the Royal Mile, the New Town, and the constant reminders of history at every turn. But shame on those councillors who allowed Princes Street to be so defaced with its modern shop façades.

The following day I went to Elgin, where I was lucky to find a vacant hotel room with the tourist season being in full swing. It was there that I was confronted with the 'egg and tea' dilemma, but I have other fond memories of this visit. When the lady led me upstairs to my room, we passed a magnificent dark wood carving of the Scottish Coat-of-Arms. Finding this within a private residence almost overwhelmed me, for it was indicative of the true patriotism of the Scots. But there was more, and on being shown into my room my attention was directed to a very uncommon portrait of Henry Stewart, Lord Darnley. It was like looking into a mirror, and I could hardly believe it. 'Yes, this is undoubtedly my room', I exclaimed – and the lady agreed.

So, there I was in August 1976, with my feet firmly settled on Scottish soil – and I was only 18. *The Scotsman* newspaper claimed, for some reason, that I was on a three-week visit, but I had staked everything I owned on the trip, and could not have afforded a return passage if I wanted. Scotland had been my lifelong ambition, and this was not about to change. In the early 1970s I had met with Eamon de Valera, who was twice Prime Minister of the Irish Free State, and I told him then, in Brussels, that I would one day live in Scotland. I remembered that conversation on my arrival, and I was never so pleased that my hitherto edifying years had taught me so much about self-sufficiency and social awareness.

Over 20 years later I have spent over half my life in Scotland. My only protracted trip away was caused by conscription for Belgian National Service, when I spent eight months abroad at my regiment's centre of transmission. I hasten to mention, however, that the passion and parental anger which accompanied my leaving Brussels in 1976 soon subdued, and normal family relationships were resumed before long.

Politics and a Passport

Once fully settled in Scotland, it took me no time at all to develop a keen interest in Scottish politics. I had learned a good deal of Scots history beforehand, but I now had the chance for personal involvement. Quite early on I met Wendy Wood, then leader of the 'Scottish Patriot', who became a most cherished friend and ally. One evening, while toasting bread on her fire, Wendy announced that 'Freedom' was the ultimate 'Right' of the Scottish Nation – and this message has lingered with me ever since. I enquired as to how people could further such a right when so many were concerned enough with straightforward survival. She gave me no magic recipe, but I learned from her that rights, if not granted, had to be won.

At that time in 1977, spirits were running high with regard to possible Scottish Devolution – too high as it transpired. Early that year there were hopes for a Westminster Bill which, while not granting anything close to independence, would at least make some concession towards self-administration. But the Bill came and went, to be conveniently buried by the protagonists of the Union.

Back in 1974, the Scottish National Party had secured over 30 per cent of the vote, winning 11 seats. They had also come second in 42 constituencies, with Labour ahead in 35 of these, and the Conservatives trailing. As a result of this, the Labour Government announced its intention to establish a Scottish Assembly. Traditionally, the Labour Party had long opposed the idea, although the Tories had expounded the virtues of the concept for some years. Seemingly, in 1976 both parties were in agreement, and everyone's hopes were raised, but the Labour back-benchers got cold feet in a guillotine motion, and the Tories changed their minds altogether; in fact they opposed the proposal simply to embarrass the Labour Government!

Since that time, the Scots have lived on hopes and broken promises. Recently, the Labour Party has been waving the flag once more for a separate Scottish Parliament – albeit somewhat feebly after the untimely death of John Smith, whose leadership promise is already being sidestepped. Now, the new Labour Government talks only of a devolved Parliament, responsible to Westminster, and with limited powers.

In terms of renewed independence, there is little doubt that Scotland is fit enough to stand on her own. We are the only European Union nation with an oil supply sufficient for ourselves and others. At present our waters stock more fish than those of many other nations put together. We are well placed for agricultural production, and have good markets for lamb, wool and, of course, our world-wide 'water of life'. Over and above these things, we have very worthwhile invisible assets such as tourism. Yet our shipbuilding and manufacturing industries are being constantly hammered into the ground by a distant Government which benefits more from it all than do the Scots people themselves. In 1976, Scotland was the 10th richest country in the world. Now, because of short-sighted Westminster politics, we are sliding down the scale in about 23rd position (with Britain about 18th overall). Within the tie of the Union, we retain control over less than 11 per cent of the revenue raised in Scotland, and the noose is tightening.

It was during the year following the Scottish Assembly fiasco that I was called to Belgium for National Service, but I returned to Scotland in due time for my 21st birthday in 1979. On my coming of age I was installed as Knight Grand Officer of the Supreme Military Order of the Temple of Jerusalem, and Knight Grand Commander of the Chivalric Military Order of the Temple of Jerusalem. The press and media were there in readiness when I attended the Soiree of the White Cockade at the Saltyre Society in Edinburgh. Honoured guests of the evening included Chevalier Commander T N Bazalgette (a Trustee of the Royal Stuart Society in London), Lady Compton Mackenzie (widow of the late Sir Compton Mackenzie), William Merrelees OBE (ex-Chief Constable of Edinburgh), Dame Wendy Wood of the Scottish Patriot, and Chevalier David Stevenson of the Order of Saint Lazarus.

From that moment, public awareness of my existence was heightened as further press and broadcasting ensued. On 11 July 1979 a significant milestone was reached when the Government finally acknowledged my presence after 300 years of family exile, and the *Glasgow Evening Times* duly reported that 'Westminster is unable to prevent Prince Michael James Stewart from using his titles'.

Subsequently, I was invested as a Knight Grand Cross and Collar of the Imperial Order of St George, for which Order I was Grand Prior in Scotland for a year. King Hassan I of Afghanistan also honoured me as a Knight Grand Commander of the Royal Durrani Order of the Crown of Amanullah, and I was then elected Patron Grand Officer of the International Society of Commission Officers for the Commonwealth (founded in Geneva in 1946). Originally this position had been reserved for HRH Prince Charles, but it was decided by the Society's executive to entrust me with the post instead. They stated that it would afford me 'the respect and support of many people throughout the Commonwealth'.

Meanwhile I still had to maintain a roof over my head – a small flat which my friends had christened 'Château Stewart'. The problem was that, by then, I was heavily involved with all manner of Scots-related activities, which left me very little time in which to earn my keep. I compromised very nicely by working in an Edinburgh tartan shop, and this enabled me to meet residents and tourists alike on a daily basis. In latter years, I have worked for the Leukaemia and Cancer Children's Fund, and am currently involved as Patron of the Albany House Trust, a charitable organization which promotes Scottish tradition, culture, and performing arts.

In May 1981 I reached a second milestone when corresponding with the Home Office on a political matter. Having signed myself simply as 'Chevalier Commander Michael Stewart', I was politely addressed in reply as 'Count of Albany' and 'Lord High Steward'. I decided, therefore, to test the ground with regard to the possibility of gaining future British national citizenship, but was not at all sure whether my princely status would be acknowledged in these Islands. However, there was no better way to find out than by applying for a British Visitor's Passport, for this would clearly oblige the Home Office to investigate my heritage, if they had not done so already. The investigations took some while, but in due course the Government Department wrote in confirmation of my birth-date and titular names, and before long my passport was issued in the name of 'HRH Prince Michael James Alexander Stewart of Albany'.

International Law

I then determined to examine my overall situation in Britain under International Law, and so I contacted the International Parliament for Safety and Peace. The official response was that since King George III had formally recognized the 'Count of Albany' title in Britain, then I was theoretically entitled to sit in the House of Lords. However, it was explained that to facilitate this privilege I would have to swear an Oath of Fealty to the House of Windsor.

Over a period of time, correspondence travelled back and forth between my office and Downing Street, and I was pleased enough to be addressed from No 10 as 'Lord High Steward' and 'Count of Albany'. Albeit I was not a *de facto* (operative) king, and even though a technical matter of family honour precluded me from accessing the House of Lords, I was accepted as a rightful Prince of the Royal House of Stewart.

In October 1985 my status and legitimate descent were further confirmed by the Orthodox Patriarch of Slavs. In the following month, the President of the International Parliament

(Mediterranean Security), endorsed by the United Nations, ratified my legal rights as Head of the Royal House of Stewart and Head of the Celtic Church of the Sacred Kindred of Saint Columba.

Under International Law, my titles were verified on 4 November 1985 as being Prince and Lord of Scotland, Duke of Kintyre, Prince of Ireland, France, Poland and Jerusalem, Duke of Normandy, Aquitaine and Touraine, legitimate titular claimant to the Throne of Scots, and legal Pretender to the Throne of Britain. Additionally, my individual sovereign entitlements were confirmed[1] and documented as:

1 The 'Jus Imperii' – the right to command.
2 The 'Jus Majestatis' – the right to be honoured, respected and protected.
3 The 'Jus Honorum' – the right to reward merit and virtue with honours and titles, without offence to the State.
4 The 'Jus Gladii in Pectore and in Potentia' – the overall *de jure* right of sovereignty, albeit suspended in practical terms of the present alternative regime.

Under the terms of the 'Jus Majestatis', I retain the express right to grant knighthoods in the Chivalric Orders created by my family in exile, namely:

a) The Noble Order of the Guard of Saint Germain – created in 1692 by King James VII.
b) The Stewart Order of Saint George – created in 1717 by King James VIII.
c) The Jacobite Order of the Crown of Hibernia – created in 1783 by King Charles III.

Under the terms of the 'Jus Honorum', I retain the additional right to create Jacobite titular distinctions in the tradition of my kingly ancestors.

In short, under International Law, although my monarchical position is suspended in practical terms by virtue of a prevailing alternative house, the *de jure* entitlements still exist by right of sovereign heritage. Hence, the 'Jus Gladii In Pectore and In Potentia' exists 'by right' but not in practice; only the pretention remains – from which derives the definition 'pretender'. Irrespective of this, I may always preserve the 'Jus Majestatis' and the 'Jus Honorum' to full effect because the sovereign remains *Fan Honorum,* with the right to be honoured, respected and protected according to International Law. As far as titular distinctions and knightly honours are concerned, the rules are simply that, in granting such merit awards, I may not offend the State or my royal cousins in England.

I fully realize that I cannot please everyone, and that despite all my legally confirmed heritage there will be some who will continue to blinker themselves to my existence. Yet the fact remains that after 300 years I am the first in a previously disregarded legitimate line of *de jure* Princes and High Stewards of Scots to achieve nominal reinstatement without too much interference from the British Government or the reigning House of Windsor. Neither have I met with opposition from the Lyon Court, with which I hold a satisfactory position of *status quo,* while officers of the Lord Lyon, the Scottish Council of Chiefs, and the Baronial Council have all been guests at my functions. I am similarly afforded free ongoing access to numerous international Ambassadors, Consuls General and other diplomats with whom I am well acquainted.

I appreciate that there will always be those staunch Unionists who will close their minds and never come to terms with my position. But, be that as it may, my legacy is already acknowledged by the authorities directly concerned. Whether or not Scotland ever achieves a renewed independence, my recognized standings as Prince of Scotland, Lord High Steward, and Count of Albany are sufficient to facilitate my personal involvement in matters which concern the civil rights, liberties and welfare of the Nation – and it is my inherited duty to be so involved.

If Scotland's independence is achieved in the future, then it will be for the people to ascertain whether or not a Constitutional Monarchy is also desirable. In such a circumstance, as defined by the *Declaration of Arbroath,* the individual 'choice' of a constitutional monarch should also rest with the sovereign Community of the Realm. In 1913 the Royal House of Stewart formally resigned its English interests to the succession from King George V (the succession of Hanover-Saxe-Coburg-Gotha: subsequently Windsor). However, our Scottish interests have since been fully retained by the sworn legal declarations of each successive Count of Albany.

My position at the Head of the Celtic Church was fully ratified in 1985 following the death of my grandfather, Julius Joseph James, in Brussels. He held the traditional reins as Lay Abbot and 56th Archpriest of the Holy Celtic Church of the Sacred Kindred of Saint Columba. I was presented with the opportunity to continue that tradition by my cousin, the titular King of Armenia, and the continuing honour was subsequently granted and confirmed by the Prince-Patriarch of the Orthodox Church of the Slavs. At this, I became 57th Archpriest and Temporal Head of Scotland's ancient Druidic-Christian Church of the Culdees.

Meanwhile, my separate rapport with the Roman Church had been somewhat strained since 1979. At that time, I had been formally advised against attending the Pope's reception party in Dublin after the murder of Lord Louis Mountbatten. Notwithstanding this, when my Celtic honour was received in 1985, Pope John Paul II was reminded that my veins carried Polish blood, and that I held a titular claim to the Polish Crown by right of my Sobieski inheritance. Being Polish himself, the Pope, therefore, acknowledged my status and invoked 'God's abundant blessings' – thereby restoring my relationship in that quarter.

Big Brother is Watching

Although I have not experienced too much interference from the national authorities through all my years in Britain, I must now tell of the one occasion when this was not the case. As previously detailed, I was issued with a British Visitor's Passport in 1986. The passport was not, however, automatically renewable. Furthermore, its provisions afforded travel only within Europe, or to the British Crown colony of Bermuda – not to America or the Commonwealth countries.

Some years later, I still had a British Visitor's Passport, having reapplied annually, and it was still issued in the name of 'HRH Prince Michael James Alexander Stewart of Albany'. But in January 1991 I was invited to be Chief for the day at the Costa Messa Highland Games near Los Angeles. I had nearly four months in which to obtain a full ten-year British Passport before the Games in May, and I had absolutely no reason to suppose there would be a problem. I was a recognized British Citizen (as detailed in my annual passport), with a National Insurance number, and had paid my taxes in Scotland for 15 years. According to the law, anyone who has been a British resident for ten years was entitled to a permanent British Passport – everyone except me that is!

In the first instance, the Home Office informed me that, outside of normal practice, I should take my original Belgian Passport to the Belgian Embassy in London, where it would be renewed. This seemed a little strange when I had applied for a British passport, but I went all the same, and was shown to the Consular Office where I handed over my long outdated document, together with my old ID card. These were promptly destroyed by an official, who informed me that neither would be renewed. Somewhat stunned, I left the Embassy realizing that something was afoot, and that I was not destined to receive a full passport from anyone. What was most infuriating was that the British Passport Office had already cashed my cheque for a document that I never received!

It had never occurred to me that I was regarded as any sort of threat to the British authorities, but clearly they did not want me going to America. I was baffled, however, as to why the Belgian Embassy should take the Home Office stance in the matter. But then I was reminded that Britain and Belgium share the same Royal Family – the German House of Saxe-Coburg. 'What did you expect?' my mother asked. 'You have spoken so often on behalf of Scotland; the English State officials are bound to want to prevent you going to America and the Commonwealth'. And so I had to cancel my United States engagement.

Initially, I did nothing more – but then at 8 o'clock one morning two CID officers appeared at my door. 'We've come to talk about your passport,' said one; to which I replied, 'What passport?'. However, I ushered them in, and awaited their news. Little was I to know that this meeting was to be a true eye-opener as to the lengths that our State commanders will go in an endeavour to intimidate an individual.

There was no conversation from the men, simply statements and accusations, the first of which was, 'We believe you tried to acquire a British Passport under false pretences.' I reminded them that I had carried an annually reissued British Visitor's

Passport for ten years, and that as a recognized British citizen I was fully entitled to a renewable passport. Having satisfactorily dealt with that matter, I was told, 'We believe you tried to acquire a British Passport to further your claim to the Scottish Crown'. Quite apparently, it was known that I had a legitimate claim, but I was not prepared to be drawn on this because it had absolutely nothing to do with my passport application. I merely answered that, as a free citizen, I had a right to travel the free world. Or was Great Britain no longer a part of the 'free' world? There was no response – only a question: 'Where do you keep your file?'.

The file to which the officer referred was the one in which I keep my personal papers: birth certificate, baptism certificate, lawyers' correspondence and the like. I decided that this was really none of their business, but in the absence of a reply, one of the men looked straight at my lower desk drawer, and said, 'It is here'. How on earth would he have known that? And then it dawned upon me: some days earlier I had returned home to find that my key would not unlock my own front door. The caretaker explained that the lock had been tampered with, and I had to buy a replacement. So that's how they knew – they had been before! Since then my personal file has been lodged, with full security, elsewhere.

Not wishing to pursue any course of antagonism, I gave the file to the officer. He simply flicked through the papers, rhetorically asking, 'You do like keeping letters, don't you?'. 'Why should I not keep letters?'. I responded. 'There is correspondence there from No 10 Downing Street. Would you not keep such letters?'. With that, he snapped the file shut, and informed me that we were all off to the police station to progress their enquiries.

Once arrived, the officers directed me to an interview room, where they produced two 60-minute cassette tapes. 'I do have a job to go to', I explained, 'And I really can't remain here with you for two hours'. Using the recording machine to advantage, I announced that the whole exercise was an absolute waste of taxpayers' money, and a waste of my time and theirs. And, surprisingly, that was the end of it. Quite suddenly, their whole impetus was lost. They explained that they were only doing their job, and politely offered to drive me back home, after which I never heard from them again.

The Plot Thickens

Something dramatic must have sparked this very strange episode, and upon investigation I discovered precisely what had happened. The whole thing had arisen because of my involvement with the Knights Templars in Scotland.

Although I was a hereditary Templar from birth, the Grand Prior for Scotland had decided that I should be formally invested in Scotland in 1979. By virtue of this, the Grand Prior, Francis Sherry, determined that traditional Jacobite ideals would be retained within the Order. Many of the Templars were members of the Scottish National Party, and at that time the SNP had 11 members at Westminster, with Scottish Independence high on the political agenda. My involvement (although wholly non-political) was, therefore, being closely watched from the South, and there were those who decided to implement a plan of action to discredit me, just as had been done to my ancestor Charles Edward Stuart.

A programme of 'infiltration' became the order of the day, and quite soon the Scottish Templars had been penetrated by those determined to undermine the organization. As a result, an anti-Michael faction became apparent, and a report was submitted by them to the Templar hierarchy claiming that the British Sovereign authorities were preparing to take action against me. This, of course, did not happen, and the report was duly dismissed – but the subversive element formed their own Neo-Teutonic clique, and subsequently issued a series of physical threats in an attempt to hound me from public life. As the years passed, heated disagreements became so common that a break-away Templar movement was formed, disassociating itself from my friends in the original Order so as to pursue their anti-Michael campaign. Not only that, but verbal and written assaults were also made against the Grand Prior and his honourable colleagues. (As I mentioned earlier, there are numerous unofficial Templar-styled organizations in existence, and these must not be confused with the legitimate chartered Order.)

One member of the treacherous faction was a printer, and another had access to the press, and so with these attributes to their benefit the high-point of their carefully contrived plan went into action. This brings us to 1991, the year of my police encounter.

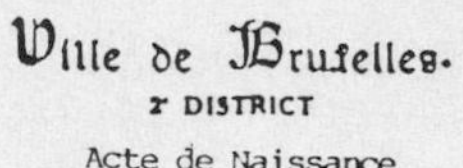

Ville de Bruxelles. — 2e DISTRICT — Acte de Naissance

Stad Brussel. — 2e DISTRICT — Geboorteakte

L'an mil neuf cent cinquante
Het jaar duizend negenhonderd
huit le vingt et un Avril, a neuf heure cinquante minutes,..

après constatation, Nous,
na vaststelling, stellen Wij,
Maurice Marchal, Echevin délégué,.........................

de la Ville de Bruxelles, dressons l'acte de naissance
van Stad Brussel, de geboorteakte op van
de Son Altesse Royale, le Prince

Michael Jacques Stewart, septième Comte d'Albanie, né le vingt et un Avril, à six heure dix minutes, Chaussée de la Hulpe, 169, fils de Gustave Joseph Fernand Clément Lafosse de Chatry, Baron de Chatry, Comte de Blois et de Saint Victor, né a Anvers le six Janvier Mil neuf cent trente cinq et de Son Altesse Royale, la Princesse Renée Julienne Stewart, Princesse Royale de Strathearn, née a Berchem Sainte Agathe le onze Novembre mil neuf cent trentè quatre, conjoints domiciliés à Bruxelles Avenue Jean Sobieski, 36. Sur la déclaration du père. En présence de Francois Pelsmaekers, sans profession, agé de Septante quatre ans, domicilié à Watermael Boitsfort et de Humbert Mutti, Directeur Technique, agé de Cinquante quatre ans, domicilié a Auderghem.

Après lecture, Nous avons signé avec le déclarant et les témoins.

VILLE DE BRUXELLES – STAD BRUSSEL

Pour extrait conforme :, – Voor gelijkluidend uittreksel :
Bruxelles II, le
Brussel II. 21/04/1958
Pour l'Officier de l'Etat civil.
Voor de Ambtenaar van de Burgerlijke Stand.
Le fonctionnaire délégué.
De gemachtigde Ambtenaar.

The City of Brussels birth certificate of HRH Prince Michael James Stewart, 7th Count of Albany (Son Altesse Royale, le Prince Michael Jacques Stewart, septième Comte d'Albanie), dated April 1958

Quite out of the blue, gentlemen from the *Sunday Mail* and *Sunday Express* arrived on my doorstep, explaining that they had been provided with copies of my birth certificate – a birth certificate which was numbered 549, and which named me as Michael Lafosse (Lafosse being my father's name). There had never been such a document, and the copy presented to the press was an outright forgery. I explained this to the reporters, and showed them Home Office correspondence which correctly cited me as HRH Prince Michael James Stewart of Albany – correspondence which also confirmed my date and place of birth. They announced that they knew my mother's name to be Dee (not Stewart), whereupon I explained that Dee was a name used by my grandfather in the Belgian Resistance in World War II. As for my mother, HRH Renée Julienne, Princess Royal of Strathearn, she had only recently attended a Scottish function in the company of the Consul General of the United States.

Despite my endeavours to convince the reporters of the truth, they had already planned their respective articles which duly appeared in the national press. These not only showed photographed extracts from the forged certificate, but also attacked me personally, and gave numerous quotes of things I had never said. As I was soon to discover, the background events which led up to this were the very reason for the police involvement when I made my passport application. However, my annual British Visitor's Passport was once again correctly reissued on 5 October 1991.

After that the reprisals became positively vicious. My front door was vandalized, unsavoury items were pushed through my letter-box, and the wheels of my car were unbolted, so that the vehicle collapsed when next being driven. Quite suddenly the police were on my side, and it was suggested that I take legal action to prosecute the known perpetrators, who were identified by my neighbours. I truly hope that the editors of the *Sunday Mail* and *Sunday Express* will learn a lesson from this, for by entertaining the malicious fabrications of deceitful fraudsters they engendered a series of events which could so easily have lead to some innocent person being injured or killed.

Contrary to the fake document reproduced in the Sunday papers in 1991, my birth certificate (issued in Brussels on 21 April 1958) does not bear any number, whilst naming me from the outset as *'Son Altesse Royale, le Prince Michael Jacques Stewart, Septième Comte d'Albanie'* (*see* opposite). As previously detailed, I was afforded my mother's name with the agreement of the King of the Belgians, even though a deal had been struck in 1892 exempting the Stewarts from being subjects of the Belgian

Crown. This very agreement was upheld in 1978 when, although serving my time in Belgian National Service, I was not required to salute the Belgian flag. A Habsburg cousin, with whom I was stationed, was afforded the same exemption.

During the Second World War, the *de jure* King of Yugoslavia was born in a London hotel. For the purpose of this event, the relevant floor of that hotel was designated by the British State as being, in effect, Yugoslavia. In view of this, Prince Alexander was deemed to have been born in Yugoslavia, not in Britain. By way of such political strategy, and through situations of exile, as in the Stewart case, many members of dispossessed royal houses have been subjected to being citizens of States other than of our choosing – if indeed we are allowed to be citizens of any State at all. For my part, I am no longer a Belgian citizen since I have resided, through choice, in Scotland for 20 years. However, although by general law I am a British citizen, I am afforded no status of naturalization.

In January 1996 I decided to apply for British Nationality. I completed and submitted the necessary form, but nothing happened. Eventually the Home Office informed me that my application had been lost. Another form was requested, but it did not arrive until January 1997. Once again, this was duly completed and submitted – only to meet with no response whatever. Now, a year and many phone calls later, the matter is still outstanding. Meanwhile, British Visitor's Passports have themselves become obsolete, and my permanent passport problem has not yet been resolved. This means, of course, that I now have no alternative but to pursue the matter at an international level.

Constitutional Privacy

Big Brother may have been watching me, but since 1991 I have been watching back. My apartment had been forcibly entered and searched, and my papers probably photographed, so I decided to investigate the extent of people's rights and liberties in this regard. What I discovered was that Big Brother was not only watching me – he is actually watching all of us.

Few people are aware that personal telephone calls (private or business) can be, and are, monitored from time to time by the

State authorities. There are key words that can trigger an automatic interest – words such as Queen, Royal Family, Prime Minister, Westminster, IRA, SNP, Scottish Independence, and so on. It is perfectly possible for the relevant State Department to build up personal profiles on anyone in Britain – and such profiles do indeed exist for the majority. All of this is managed through telephone records, credit card and bank card receipts, tax submissions, etc. From these can be determined social habits, political activities, consumer preferences, civic priorities, family interests, and the like.

Quite apart from video cameras in our towns and cities, they are also on the open road, recording our vehicle movements on a permanent basis. There are ever more low-flying helicopters to be seen, with their occupants recording the activity below, while selected policemen are evident with their cameras and video recorders at public gatherings and the most peaceful of demonstrations. Indeed, ex-police officers such as the former Chief of the Metropolitan Police, Sir John Smith, have expressed particular concern at the increasing invasion of citizens' privacy. We are watched in the street, we are watched in our cars, and we are watched inside a growing number of public and private buildings. Our Post Office mail can be intercepted, and it has recently been announced that there is also an operative right to intercept any Internet E-mail communication. Our phone calls are known, much of our individual spending is computerized, and all the extracted information is centralized in State-held files. Yet, none of the information in these individual profiles is safeguarded by the Data Protection Registrar.

We, the people, are journeying down a one-way street; we are not permitted to see our personal profiles, or to know their contents – and this area of State officialdom is regarded as being none of our business! We are told by the authorities that more technology means less bureaucracy, but this is quite untrue. There is actually more bureaucracy, and it currently takes twice the number of staff to operate and administer that technology than it did before the event. We are told that the avid camera activity is an aid against crime – but it presupposes that we are all criminals by recording each and every one of us, prying into our daily lives. If the authorities are really interested in security and crime prevention, then a return to proper policing methods and an adequately staffed Police Force might help in this regard!

In the final analysis, we are all pawns in a political chess game, with our individual game positions updated by cameras, electoral registers and the like. While we move around the board, our movements are filmed and recorded by those in charge of the game. As time goes by, we become ever more dehumanized, to the extent that we shall soon experience a total lack of privacy, even within the confines of our own homes. Quite apparently, what each of Britain's nations desperately requires is a 'Privacy Law' – a law embodied within a people's Written Constitution. The alternative is total subjugation to dictatorial State authority.

21

The Stewart Renaissance

Europe and the Council of Princes

In Strasburg, June 1992, the House of Habsburg Austria relinquished its presidency of the European Council of Princes (Conseil Européen des Princes) – an office it had retained for 46 years. Instead, I was unanimously elected to the presidential office in my capacity as Head of the Royal House of Stewart. The Council is a specialist consultative organization which advises on constitutional and civil rights matters, and at its helm I now represent a combined delegation of European royal houses. This is a great honour for the House of Stewart, and is uniquely significant for Scotland. The Council was originally founded in 1946 as the International Council of Government, with delegates from both functional and deprived sovereign families, and there are currently 33 participant members.

Being established immediately after the Second World War, the Council's objective was to resist the rise and spread of Communism in the West, and for that purpose substantial funds were provided from the USA. Later, the Council became deeply involved at an international parliamentary level, and was especially concerned with the maintenance of people's rights and freedoms in Europe. Since the British, unlike other nations, had no Written Constitution to uphold, the social and community ideals of the Council were to no one's advantage in Britain. This is still the case since there are no British constitutional clauses which can override unjust European Union dictates. As a result, Britain suffers continually from impositions that can be legally avoided in other countries. It is, therefore, not surprising that the House of Windsor declined its invitation to participate from the outset.

With the introduction of the Common Market and the EEC, the International Council became less active in respect of individual countries, and much of its new thinking was applied to Europe as a whole. Then, in view of the establishment of the European Parliament, the International Council of Government was restyled to become the European Council of Princes. The Council was re-registered in Brussels in 1992 by Prof Yasmin Hohenzollern, Prinzezin Von Lansleburg, Président UTE (Union Télévision Européen) – EEC (now EU) Communications. Princess Yasmin is of Imperial descent from Emperor Frederick I Barbarossa (1152–90) and the House of Hohenstaufen.

The Council is presently concerned that the European Parliament frequently oversteps its mandate, and this is demonstrated by the imposition of central dictates upon individual countries which should be treated separately within a European framework for the common good. Consequently, a primary aim of the Council of Princes is that elected EU ministers should be seen to uphold their personal obligations. These Euro-MPs (MEPs) are chosen by vote of the people, and they are supposed to represent the interests of their individual electorates within Europe. But this is not what happens: having gained their elected positions of influence, the MEPs are often seen to represent Europe within their constituencies of election – supporting centrally promoted measures and mandates that are not to the benefit of their electorates.

At present Scotland is both badly and under-represented by her MEPs, and this anomaly must be addressed. With regard to Britain as a whole, it is plain that, with 60 per cent of national exports going to Europe, we should be working towards a proper reward for the British workforce, rather than providing an endless gravy-train for the bureaucrats.

If the European Union is to succeed, then its progress must not be hindered by statutes and dictates which impinge upon the time-honoured sovereignty of individual nations – or which adversely affect the regional communities within those nations. It is perfectly possible to maintain a unity which affords the freedom to trade and expand within each other's countries, but this must be achieved with far less bureaucracy and political imposition than has been suffered to date by people who deserve far better treatment. Broad-based, prohibitive legislation which does not suit the individual psyche of nations must be curtailed; it serves no general benefit, and is wholly destructive to the welfare and morale of the member states' electorates.

Scottish Independence

Scotland's separate identity is preserved by way of my attachment to the royal Council, since I hold my presidency expressly as the Stewart Prince of Scots. However, Scotland is gradually losing her identity within the wrap of the British Union. Few people these days realize just how much of international importance has emanated from Scotland – inventions and foundations which should give us enormous prestige – but reference books and encyclopedias are, by Union design, generally quiet about these matters, and Scotland's worldwide significance is thereby suppressed. I have, therefore, in Appendix XI of this book, listed some of the more notable Scottish accomplishments.

Under the government of Westminster, Scotland's public services and backbone industries have been demolished, while Scottish culture and heritage are overshadowed and constantly disregarded by insensitive and non-representative Governments. Without a Written Constitution, there are no defined parameters of democracy, and the nation's civil rights and liberties are conveniently ignored, while the people's contentions and proposals are continually overruled.

Plainly, a majority of Scots recognize that this destructive process must be resisted if Scotland's traditions and character are to survive. Such resistance can only be fully effective through sound political argument, a rational progress towards full independence within Europe, and a reinstatement of Scotland's own separate Written Constitution. The Constitution could then uphold all the ideals which are so dear to the hearts of the community (*see* Constitutional Model in Appendix XII). It would afford security and protection for the liberty and welfare of the people, while at the same time promoting an equality of individual rights – not the all too familiar class-structured laws of property and wealth.

Under such circumstances, there could indeed be a restoration of Scotland's political, industrial, economic and social dignity. There would also exist the right of freedom to re-establish the nation's own Constitutional Monarchy. Ideally, this should be a non-political working monarchy, operating in close liaison with an executive advisory council. A truly representative Scottish Parliament would comprise a single Citizens' Estate (*see* Appendix XIII), and the electorate should have the social advantage of proportional representation with a single transferrable vote in multi-member constituencies. In respect of individual issues, voters would then be able to select a preferential order of candidates in each constituency, irrespective of party allegiance. By this route, all important matters would receive adequate representation at the people's behest.

With her own reinstated elected Parliament, an independent Scotland would, I trust, benefit from a Government which was wholly geared to Scottish interests. I would hope to see strategic investment to modernize the infrastructure, thereby creating new employment while encouraging outside investment in our own industries. I would anticipate a fairer tax system, along with restructured educational and health services, so that the nation can be properly served. We already have our own banks and legal system, and by salvaging our financial destiny there is no reason why Scotland could not emerge as the Switzerland of the North. The European Scots Colleges, once so renowned, could be reinstated in centres like Paris, Rome and Madrid, so that our students might study at a truly international level. In such an environment, not only would Scotland have an individual voice within the European Union, but she would also be separately represented at the United Nations.

From 1979 to 1996 no less than £27,000m of Westminster revenue was generated in Scotland. That's nearly £6m per head of Scotland's population – around £350,000 per year, each! With this amount of revenue removed, Scotland currently retains less than 11 per cent of her total generated income. Meanwhile, individual Scots have been constantly reminded to tighten their belts through an ongoing period of wage restraint, while the Westminster politicians and their Public Service colleagues have granted themselves substantial pay increases.

But what of those not fortunate enough to be in employment?

And what about the thousands now without homes – or those battling with negative equity because they bought their properties on a false governmental promise of security? Britain's homeless cannot obtain employment because they have no fixed address. They cannot vote because they have no fixed address. They cannot draw Social Security benefits because they have no fixed address. But what did the Conservative Government minister say when questioned in 1996 about the homeless in the streets of London? 'Well, they're mostly Scottish', he explained – as if Scots didn't really count in the general equation. As a result, prior to Christmas that year, a great many Scots were 'repatriated' across the Border to Scotland. Repatriated! Where did this word come from? What happened to the Union?

The fact is that the Union only exists when it suits the English authorities; otherwise it is completely ignored with Scots automatically classified as second-class citizens. The Labour Party leader recently stated, twice in the same radio interview, that Scotland's traditions are different to those of Britain! I presume he meant England. Is not Scotland a part of Britain? In fact, comments such as these prove, time and time again, that Scotland is not really taken seriously at Westminster. So it's time that *we* took ourselves seriously.

A Worldwide Kingdom of Scots

Since 1707 Scotland has had no recognition as a free country within the British Islands, and no separate identity on the global scene. Westminster's attempts to suppress the Scottish image within the Union have been constant and unyielding. Despite this, other nations in Europe and the Commonwealth still recognize the importance of maintaining autonomous links with Scotland as a realm in her own right. Not the least of reasons for this is the extensive bond of Scottish heritage which exists throughout the world; this is primarily the case in such countries as America, Canada and Australia, to which places there was large-scale Scots emigration after Culloden. In Europe also, generations of families have sprung from those who followed their kings into exile. At present, around 5 million people reside in Scotland, but this number is exceeded by the Scots in Los

Angeles, New York City, North Carolina and Virginia. Add to this the remainder of America plus the rest of the world, to a total of some 42 million, and it emerges that there is truly a 'Worldwide Kingdom of Scots'.

The 1689 *Bill of Rights* directs that British monarchs can only hold office with 'parliamentary consent' – but it is worth looking at how parliamentary influence affected the English Crown before that date. Following England's period under the Saxons and Danes, William the Conqueror took the crown by force-of-arms in 1066, and the Norman and Plantagenet dynasties ensued. By descent from Edward III's son, John of Gaunt, Henry VII's 1485 Tudor succession was approved by Parliament. When James VI Stuart of Scots succeeded as James I of England in 1603, he too was invited with the consent of Parliament. Then later in 1689, after James VII (II) was deposed, the *Bill of Rights* came into force, and Parliament's consent of future monarchs became law.

Thus it can be seen that, despite the 1689 Bill, parliamentary consent had long been a prerequisite for succession. In later times, Charles Edward Stuart's hereditary prerogative was vastly superior to that of the Hanoverian Georges, but as the *Bill of Rights* dictated, even the most impressive right of lineage was, and still is, overruled by the required 'consent' of Parliament. King Edward VIII Windsor, for example, was unable to secure such vital parliamentary support, and was ousted in favour of his brother, Prince Albert, who succeeded as King George VI.

Scotland's early history is, in fact, no different, for when Robert the Bruce held the throne, the Stewarts had no obvious claim to the Scottish Honours despite their long heritage as kings' deputies. The immediate Stewart ancestry was of Scots-Breton nobility, but although the Stewarts had become Lord High Stewards of Scotland, there was no automatic right to succession. Walter, 6th High Steward, married Bruce's daughter Marjorie, and it was their son (through the Bruce female line) who became Robert II, founder of the Royal House of Stewart in 1371. In practice, this was achieved simply because Walter's son had the 'consent' of the primary representatives of the people – denoting that the parliamentary precedent existed even in those days.

It can be deduced, therefore, that no matter how strong or technically correct is an individual claim, there are no automatic rights to a crown in Britain. This applies to the descendants of

Bruce's appointed predecessor John Balliol, to the heirs of the Saxon King Harold, and indeed to my own Stewart succession. Constitutionally, the same would apply to the lines of Sigismund in Poland and Gustavus in Sweden, along with numerous others. Even the House of Windsor reigns only with the express approval of Parliament. Under International Law, *de jure* sovereign entitlements may be conferred in respect of first-in-line successors to established royal houses, but although these entitlements are expressly relevant in many important areas of operation, their holders can only achieve monarchical status by Government invitation and parliamentary consent.

Within an independent Scotland, the traditional spirit of the Scots could truly be revived; so too could the popular ideals of Robert the Bruce. His Constitution (as upheld by all succeeding Stewart Kings) placed the rights and liberties of people first and foremost. To this end, any future King or Queen of Scots should be committed to swear an 'Oath of Fealty' to the Nation – a 'Vow of Service' to the people – not the other way about, as is the case in the English feudal tradition.

It was clearly laid down in the *Declaration of Arbroath* that sovereignty should rest wholly with the people of the Community of the Realm of Scotland, and that they (through their Government representatives) could 'choose' a king to uphold their emancipation. However, this Constitutional Right was removed, without regard for the people of Scotland, by a series of strategically programmed events which culminated in the 1707 *Treaty of Union.*

Scotland's position today is not unlike that of Norway in the 19th century, when Norway was detrimentally tied to Sweden and Denmark. After lengthy debate, the problem could only be solved by Norway's own declaration of independence and the installation of an autonomous Parliament. Then in 1905 (to finally gain freedom from the disruptive controls of the Swedish Crown) there followed the establishment of Norway's own Constitutional Monarchy.

In Scotland such measures rest, of course, with the will of the people, but if true independence is deemed necessary and desirable then these are the historically proven routes to that end. If the 'Flower of Scotland' is to bloom again, the people's will must be put forward as a matter of undisputed majority requirement. At present, this requirement is veiled by thoroughly disproportionate political representation, and such will be the case so long as the present political structure exists. Meanwhile, Scottish culture and traditions persist against enormous odds; Clan societies flourish internationally, while the poems of Robert Burns and the Jacobite songs are cherished in many lands. Indeed, the tartan and pipes are constant reminders of an ever-lingering heritage which is the envy of the world. (The oldest piece of checked cloth – or tartan – found in Scotland dates from about 325 AD.) In America, the Commonwealth, and in continental Europe, numerous electorates live within constitutional frameworks that are modelled on Scotland's own original; yet for all that, the very people whose individual national rights are continually denied are the Scots themselves.

In 1995 I was offered the opportunity to gain the Crown of Estonia, which I politely declined because my interests are confined solely to the welfare of Scotland. Following subsequent national press reports, I was asked in a BBC radio interview what it meant to me to be the Prince and heir-apparent to the Crown of Scots. My answer was straightforward: it means working with a total commitment to the interests of the Scottish Nation. Since coming to Scotland in 1976 I have endeavoured to champion Scotland's cause at home and abroad – but there have been no clashing broadswords or loud rebellion as in days of old.

It was by no chance that I was elected to chair the European Council of Princes; this was a positive stance by others of significant international influence to make known their continuing high regard for Scotland's own traditional Royal House of Stewart. At no time since my arrival in Scotland have I lingered in the wings awaiting Scottish Independence, nor for the convenience of a reinstated Scottish Parliament, but have determinedly persevered throughout in the Scottish national interest, with no small results to date. Henceforth, it remains both my will and my duty to continue in the honoured service of the Community of the Realm of Scotland.

By the People – For the People

More than 300 years from my family's moment of exile, the patriotic Scots still cling to the lingering memory of their own independent kingdom. Scotland rings with the music and poetry of the Stewarts and the Jacobite days, and families exude passion in all corners of the realm. They sing of the Stewarts – they love us, or hate us, they lose their tempers and debate us, and they even cry for us. One way or another, the Stewart heritage is filled with emotion, and the reason is plain to all: quite unlike England's imposed House of Hanover, the Royal House of Scotland was created 'by' the Scottish people 'for' the Scottish people – and in this regard, nothing has really changed. For as long as the Scots remember the Stewarts, so too will Stewart hearts be firmly centred in Scotland.

During the many years of my campaigning for Scotland's right to be properly represented on the world stage, many people have asked me which future system of government I support for Scotland – partial devolution or total independence? I am a strong advocate of Scottish Independence. This is not because of the possibility of my becoming King, since this could only occur if the Community of the Realm of Scotland elected me to succeed to the Honours of Scotland following a plebiscite. I support Independence simply because it would lift us from the mire into which successive Unionist Governments have strategically manoeuvred us through the past 40 years. Now is the time to consider a few home truths about Scotland's position within the constraint of the Union.

I will not dwell upon the Thatcher and Major policies of hard-line Conservatism imposed on the Scottish nation. Suffice to say, most of us are more than glad to see the back of Conservative rule and, all being well, we shall not suffer it again. But we still face a very uncertain future. The first of May 1997 was undoubtedly a milestone for the British Unionist Labour Party, or 'New Labour' as it is now called. On that day, Scotland returned a customary majority of Labour MPs, along with a number of Liberal Democrats and Scottish Nationalists. On the face of it, the Conservative and Unionist Party appears to have been sent packing; but it is not that simple, and a different picture emerges on studying the voting figures.

There were more than 4,100,000 people on the Scottish electoral register in May (which is quite high for a country with a population of less than 5.5 million), and the votes were cast as follows: over 1,200,000 electors voted for Labour; over 645,000 voted for the Scottish Nationalists; over 400,000 voted Conservative, and over 300,000 voted Liberal Democrat. These figures reveal that more than a million people did not bother to vote, but more importantly they reveal that the Conservatives (who acquired no seats) actually gathered more votes than the apparently successful Liberal Democrats. The Scottish National Party also achieved more votes than the Liberal Democrats, but are now under-represented, while the Liberal Democrats, with the lowest overall vote, are subsequently over-represented. It is clear, therefore, that a system of proportional representation is a much needed requirement for an equitable Scottish political system.

The promise of a referendum for a Scottish Parliament was a necessary catalyst to swing the Scottish vote in favour of the Labour Party, and it worked. But in England the strategy was of a different kind. Prime Minister Tony Blair simply told the most influential supporters of the Conservative Party (the businesses, banking institutions, and the corporates) that New Labour would take a route towards Conservative-style policies – and that worked as well. Few of us imagined that the Blair agenda would attract such overwhelming support, or that the Conservatives would be so soundly defeated. We all remember Tony and Cherie Blair walking along Downing Street; it was an emotional moment – a triumphal entrance, full of hope – and many supposed that the political honeymoon would last for a good while. However, some of us directly concerned with politics realized that Labour's approbation would be short-lived, as the new policies are based on the very same legislative measures that brought the nations of Great Britain to a disgraceful level of poverty and uncertainty.

Two particular groups were destined to feel the immediate effects of these so-called new policies – the unemployed and the students in higher education. These two groups have always been vulnerable, whatever the party in power, but never more so than under the Government today. The new system for students, or 'the package' as Scotland's Bryan Wilson kept calling New Labour's proposal on the TV programme *Trial by Night,* adds yet a further penalty to the untenable Conservative regime of 'education by privilege' rather than education by right. Imagine a graduate beginning his or her professional life with two substantial debts: the first a State-inflicted millstone in return for an education, and the second a financial burden necessary to provide house and home. The concept and the very mechanics of the New Labour 'package' are wholly preposterous, and constitute an insult to those keen young students who wish to better themselves at a university.

As for the unemployed, the matter is similarly inequitable. Presently, while drawing benefit, they are required to go on job schemes of 18 hours a week for a wage of £10 per week (an average of 55 pence an hour) – less than some workers earn in Third World countries. This is required for 12 consecutive weeks, during which period they are not recorded in the official unemployment register. Should they decline, they are threatened with having their standard entitlement cut by 40 per cent from £49.15 a week to £29.55 a week (*The Scotsman*, 3 May, 1997). Any second failure to comply with the regulations risks a termination of all rights to benefit, even though insurance contributions have been previously and regularly made to secure the right to such entitlement.

In actual fact, the New Labour honeymoon was brought to a very swift conclusion within weeks of their installation when Mohammed Sarwar, the Asian Labour MP for Govan, was suspended following allegations of bribes taken during the election campaign. This was soon followed by the suicide of Gordon McMaster, Labour MP for Paisley South, after allegations of a homosexual affair. Then there was the 'double standards' debate when New Labour, having received a cool £1 million from the Formula One chiefs, allowed the motor racing fraternity to continue tobacco advertising when they had banned other sports from the practice. We are told that Tony Blair knew nothing about this immense donation to the campaign fund, but it was clearly no secret to other members of his party. This does not bode well for a new Government whose officials saw fit to withhold information from their leader at the outset. Neither does it portray Mr Blair as a competent leader if he can be so easily duped by his own colleagues.

By August 1997 the Labour members in Scotland were campaigning in favour of a Scottish Parliament with tax varying powers, and both the Scottish National Party and the Liberal Democrats supported the concept, although for very different reasons. The SNP saw it as the first step towards full Scottish Independence, while the Liberal Democrats saw it as a first step towards a Federal State of Britain. Meanwhile, the unrepresented Conservatives waved the Union flag and prophesied resultant high taxes, while enrolling the Bank of Scotland's Bruce Patullo to back their claim in public. This enraged a number of the Bank's customers, who promptly took their accounts elsewhere, and the majority of Scottish businesses indicated their support for Labour's devolution plan. For a time, the political climate in Scotland was quite euphoric – but then, on 31 August, Diana, Princess of Wales, died tragically in Paris, and the British nations were stunned to the extent that all political matters paled against the overwhelming grief of mourning. Scotland's campaigning was set aside for a whole week in respect for the betrayed mother of the royal heirs – the people's princess who, against all odds, had captivated the hearts of nations worldwide.

Those who took the initial brunt of Diana's demise were Queen Elizabeth and her immediate family; some perceived them as uncaring when they paraded the young princes, William and Harry, to Crathie Church, Balmoral, on the morning after their mother's death; and yet Diana received no mention in the service. The Queen then refused to lower the Buckingham Palace flag to half-mast, and the public were shocked and angered by an unfeeling display of cold-hearted obstinacy.

Many people suggested that Diana's death was perhaps more mysterious than it had first appeared, and conspiracy theories were inevitably proposed and debated. However, the important point is that if people genuinely trusted and respected their governing establishment, such claims would never be conceived in the first place. That apart, the close liaison of Diana Frances (née Spencer) with Dodi Fayed was clearly a significant threat to the establishment *status quo.* The power lords would have been considerably troubled by the prospect of a future Diana Fayed, Princess of Wales – a princess who might well have borne more children. Perhaps these children would have been raised in the Muslim faith – offspring who, in the future, would be able to claim the King as their brother.

The subsequent national mourning of Diana's death was reminiscent of the feeling which followed President Kennedy's assassination in 1963. If anything, it was a more heightened experience, for the loss of Diana was somehow more unbelievable, and the public emotion at her funeral reminded many of the day when Argentina's Maria Eva de Peron, another champion of the oppressed, was laid to rest in 1952. The moving speech given by Diana's brother Charles, Earl Spencer, held back nothing in reminding the royal 'firm' that William and Harry were only half Mountbatten – Windsor, and that the Spencer family saw it as their duty to uphold and perpetuate the socially motivated upbringing begun by the princes' mother. The noble Earl was heartily applauded within and without Westminster Abbey, and Queen Elizabeth's own personal announcement of sadness was regarded as being 'too little too late'. Like the spirit of her ancestor, Mary, Queen of Scots, Diana's own unique legacy of caring will haunt the Royal Family for all time. She will be affectionately remembered just as she had wished – as the people's own 'Queen of Hearts', and her romantic island repose will, no doubt, add to the mystique. Indeed, the nation has, in Diana, a truly compassionate 'Lady of the Lake' – a devoted and humanitarian Grail Queen.

Prince William will indeed succeed to the Crown of St Edward, but not simply because he is his father's heir; he will succeed in the hearts and minds of the populace because he is his mother's son. Young Prince Harry, with his Spencer characteristics, will doubtless add to the popularity of a house which, in time to come, might well feel justified in dropping the Germanic Mountbatten-Windsor name for that of Spencer, thereby honouring the English people in memory of Diana Frances. It must be remembered that their father, Charles, Prince of Wales, holds his present heirship in his own mother's line, not in the line of his father. Just as the people of Scotland look forward to a brighter future in the 21st century, so too are the people of England and Wales due for a new light to shine, and the House of Hanover-Saxe-Coburg–Windsor's light is fading fast.

Five days after Diana's funeral, history was made in Scotland when our citizens voted overwhelmingly in favour of a devolved Scottish Parliament with tax varying powers. This was yet another rebuttal of the Conservatives' opposition agenda which, despite all polls and opinions, had still not come to terms with Scottish political aspirations.

With Scottish devolution in prospect, Labour's Scottish Secretary, Donald Dewar, has now elected to buy a Scottish and Newcastle Brewery property to house the new Parliament. But, why should the taxpayers be happy with this when money has already been spent in transforming the impressive Royal High School in Regent Terrace for the purpose? We are now told that this is too small for 144 members plus civil servants' offices, but it stands opposite St Andrews House which has perfectly adequate office accommodation. Mr Dewar is now being considered as a likely First Minister for Scotland, and this title is itself an indication of New Labour's lack of traditional awareness, for the leader of the Scottish Parliament should rightly be called Lord High Chancellor. In any event it is both arrogant and patronizing for the Government to presume that a devolved Scottish Parliament should be a Labour controlled institution with a 'Yes Prime Minister' attitude. This is not conducive to paving Scotland's route into the 21st century. Far better for the Scottish nation would be a leader with integrity enough to challenge the political greed of the London Government – a leader who would uphold his or her brief to champion the social, industrial, economic and sovereign rights of the Scots against the vested interests of Westminster politicians.

There is, however, one undeniable fact about the referendum result in that the Government will be using Scotland as a guinea-pig to prove to the political establishment of England that if future proportional representation can work in Scotland, it can also work in England. But the problem faced by Tony Blair is that his Labour Government might not be elected for a second term, and the pendulum might very quickly swing back towards the Conservative Party in England. Where would that leave Scotland? The answer is straightforward in that provision could be made for the possibility to be avoided. In order not to see Scottish politics being tampered with again by way of policies favouring the greater Kingdom of England, the way forward for Scotland (as identified in Norway in 1905) would be to become totally independent, either as a Republic or as a Kingdom with a Constitutional Monarchy.

Republicanism has its supporters on all sides in Scotland, not the least of whom is Roseanna Cunningham, Scottish Nationalist MP for Perth. However, it was apparent at the SNP Conference at

Rothesay, Bute, in September 1997, that the Party leader, Alex Salmond, had not been expecting Ms Cunningham to make such a strong stand on the matter. Alex Salmond is a great believer in the advantages of Constitutional Monarchy (such as those of Belgium, Luxembourg, Spain, the Netherlands, Denmark, Sweden and Norway), and he is fully aware of what such regimes offer the people, with their Constitutional Monarchs being the upholders and guardians of popular Written Constitutions. It is a proven fact that Constitutional kings and queens do act in the interest of the people they represent, and they are seen to stand against parliamentary policies which might infringe upon the civil rights and liberties of their nations. Republican protagonists tend to forget that the precepts of 'liberty, fraternity and equality' are not prerogatives of modern republicanism; they were practised first and foremost in Scotland following the 1320 *Declaration of Arbroath.* This Written Constitution was upheld through the generations until 1688, when James VII of Scots (II of England) was sent into exile by the Westminster establishment in order to introduce English feudalism into Scotland with the collaboration of the Duke of Argyll.

A President of Scotland would be politically partisan, whereas a Scottish Constitutional Monarch would not be, since the office (as in Europe) would be outside the party structure. The margin of security offered by a Written Constitution relies upon two factors. The first is that national sovereignty must rest with the people, and secondly, the constitutional parameters relating to both Crown and Parliament must be well defined. While Parliament must be able to legislate, the authority of such legislation must never infringe upon the general welfare of the people. When any such infringement of rights is perceived, the Crown representative, acting as champion of the people's Constitution, would necessarily act to bring the ministers back to the drawing board. My own concept of this procedure would be for the Monarch, or Guardian of the Realm, to operate in conjunction with a Privy Council (*see* Appendix XIII). The Council would act as a second parliamentary house, and would be vested with a Constitutional College which could advise upon the revision of Bills within the boundaries of the Constitution.

There are, in practice, certain aspects of pure republicanism which engender social and political extremes such as racism and fascism. Consider the situations in France, Germany and the USA, where violence against non-French, non-German, and non-Anglo-European Americans, respectively, is commonplace. Each of these countries is an outright republic, and each suffers from similar problems which ultimately relate to political legislation that cannot be checked by a people's constitutional champion. Idealistic as a Republic of Scotland might appear to some, these same dangers would soon become apparent, and would herald the first step towards a police state rather than a people's state.

Scottish culture would suffer as well within a republican environment. Scotland has, after all, an extremely old monarchic tradition – older even than England, France, Spain or any other country in eastern or western Europe. Are we to forsake all this in our quest for independence? Surely not, for the independent Scotland secured by Robert the Bruce was that of a constitutional kingdom, not a party-political republic. Indeed, insular republicanism is quite foreign to the traditional Scottish psyche, and our history has proved that in matters of security, protection, liberty, welfare and equality, our Constitutional Monarchs served the people better than has any subsequent presidency of a republican state. True democracy is an environment which allows people to participate in the political welfare of their country – not just in theory but in practice. True independence is a route towards greater self-determination for all who participate, and there is little individual esteem for the citizens of dictatorial republics.

There are, of course, those who proclaim that Scotland could never survive by herself, without the mythical subsidies from Westminster. In this regard, however, a look at some facts and figures will enable us to see things in their proper perspective. Scotland's population is just under 5.5 million and, as stated by Lord Alistair McAlpine (former Treasurer of the Conservative Party), Scotland has a Gross Domestic Product of £50 billion. Our business and financial sectors employ some 206,000 individuals, while managing about £135.8 billion. This places Scotland among the world's top 25 richest countries, and our capital, Edinburgh, is the 5th financial centre in Europe, 14th in the world. But, as previously mentioned, the national budget passed back from Westminster to fund the Scottish infrastructure (the so-called Scottish Bloc) equals less than 11 per cent of the Scottish revenue sent to the Chancellor of the Exchequer in London. In other words, Westminster retains over 89 per cent of Scotland's revenue to buttress the rest of the United Kingdom, and our own budget is scheduled to be further decreased by 1999.

At present, the fastest-growing industry in Scotland is tourism, and our banking system is now solidly anchored worldwide, owning foreign banks, and proving itself to be no bar to Scottish independence. Scotland's infrastructure is run by 12,000 civil servants, and we export more per head of population than the English. Taking into account that Europe takes 60 per cent of Britain's exported goods and services, and bearing in mind that Scotland is the United Kingdom's biggest exporter, it therefore makes economic sense to remain within the European Union, and to preserve our links with the 325 million valued buyers on the Continental mainland. It is relevant also to mention at this stage that International Law recognizes the fact that the oil recovered from the Scottish sea is, indeed, Scotland's oil, in the same way that offshore oil recovered in the Middle East belongs to the individual states concerned.

Scotland's educational system is in many ways different to that of England, and in the main it is better. Scotland's legal system is the envy of Europe, and France's Judge Lévy can be quoted as saying, 'It is hoped that it would become the legal system of Europe as soon as possible'. Scotland's Christian institutions, be they Presbyterian, Catholic or Episcopal, are also quite distinct from those of England. In essence, everything within the social, political, industrial and religious structure of Scotland proves that our country has so little in common with England that it is really not worth our while to remain within the stranglehold of the United Kingdom. Indeed, England recoups far more from Scotland than has ever been reciprocated.

We have now voted in favour of a devolved Parliament, and from now on we must consider all the relevant facts on their own merits, rather than continue to be the pawns of cross-Border political propaganda. The time has come for us to put the residents and workforce of Scotland first, and to set our sights firmly towards constitutional change for the betterment and well-being of future generations. I am convinced that there is an important place within Europe for an independent Kingdom of Scots with a traditional Stewart monarchy. As of old, the monarch's primary function would be to uphold the Written

Constitution on behalf of the Community of the Realm. In such an establishment, Scotland would be governed 'by' the Scots 'for' the Scots. There would be a freely elected parliamentary structure, and a democratically effective system of proportional representation. Under such circumstances, Scotland could enter the 21st century free from sectarian interests and proud of her achievements. This might seem idealistic to some, but it is a much needed ideal if we desire Scotland to survive the political turmoil of the next millennium.

Nemo Me Impune Lacessit (No one touches me with impunity) is the motto of the ancient Stewart Kingdom of the Scots. Let us live by this ancestral wisdom, or the little respect we have left will be swept from beneath our feet. The legend of our Arms, *In Defens* (as identified above the Royal Crest of Scotland), is what Scotland's lawful monarchy stood and often died for – in defence of the civil rights and equalities of a fraternal people. It was for flying this individual banner of liberty that my ancestor James VII was hounded and deposed by an alien Parliament whose English ministers had no concept whatever of the Scots' social tradition.

For the longest time, Scotland has been presented with no constructive and lawful alternative to her sufferance as the lesser relation of the British Union – but this book has been written expressly to highlight a remedy for this unfortunate lack of choice. I may not be able to unify the entire nation, but as the rightful Prince and High Steward of the Scots, and as the direct senior descendant of our Patriot King, Robert the Bruce, I can certainly help to encourage Scotland's traditional spirit of self-determination and independence. Indeed, it is my express duty and privilege to serve the nation in this regard.

NOTES AND REFERENCES

Chapter 2

1 Gilmour, William W, *Famous Scots*, William Maclellan, Glasgow, 1979, p 33
2 Graves, Robert, *The White Goddess*, Faber & Faber, London, 1961, p 51
3 The Vatican Archives, Rome

Chapter 3

1 Gardner, Laurence, *Bloodline of the Holy Grail*, Element Books, Shaftesbury, 1996, ch. 12, p 190 (hardback edition)
2 The Flemish-Burgundian Archives, Bibliothèque Royale, Brussels, Belgium

Chapter 4

1 The Diocesan Archives of Angers, France
2 *The Scots Magazine*, August, 1997

Chapter 5

1 Gardner, Laurence, *Bloodline of the Holy Grail*, ch. 16, p 260
2 Rose Croix, *Archives of the Frères Ainés de la Rose Croix*, Bibliothèque Nationale, Paris
3 The Vatican Archives, Rome
4 The 1320 *Declaration of Arbroath* at H M Register House, Edinburgh

Chapter 6

1 The *Beaucant* Records of the Chivalric & Military Order of the Temple of Jerusalem, Scotland
2 Douglas, Sir Robert of Glenbervie, *The Peerage of Scotland*, at The British Library, London
3 Donaldson, Gordon, and Morpeth, R S, *A Dictionary of Scottish History*, John Donald, Edinburgh, 1977, p 198
4 The Vatican Archives, Rome
5 Douglas, Sir Robert of Glenbervie, *The Peerage of Scotland*
6 The Spanish National Archives, Madrid
7 The Vatican Archives, Rome
8 Archives Nationales, Paris

9 *The Privy Seal Register of Scotland*
10 Donaldson, Gordon, and Morpeth, R S, *A Dictionary of Scottish History*, p 220

Chapter 7

1 *Archives d'Aubignie*, Berri, France
2 Archives Nationales, Paris
3 Donaldson, Gordon, and Morpeth, R S, *A Dictionary of Scottish History*, p 58
4 Archives Nationales, Paris
5 Archives Nationales, Paris
6 Douglas, Sir Robert of Glenbervie, *The Peerage of Scotland*
7 *The Privy Seal Register of Scotland*
8 The Vatican Archives, Rome
9 Archives Nationales, Paris
10 Archives Nationales, Paris
11 The Masonic Archives, at Freemasons' Hall, Edinburgh

Chapter 8

1 Adam, Frank, *The Clans, Septs and Regiments of the Scottish Highlands* (rev, Sir Thomas Innes of Learney), Johnston & Bacon, Edinburgh, 1970, p 127
2 Archives Nationales, Paris
3 Fenwick, Hubert, *The Auld Alliance*, Roundwood Press, Warwick, 1971, p 10
4 Archives Nationales, Paris
5 Zweig, Stefan, *Marie Stuart*, Brodart & Taupin, Paris, 1973, p 79
6 The Vatican Archives, Rome
7 Alderman, Clifford Lindsey, *Death to the King*, Bailey Bros & Swinfer, Falconstone, 1973, p 8

Chapter 9

1 *The Diaries of Samuel Pepys* at The British Library, London
2 Trevor, Meriol, *The Shadow of a Crown*, Constable, London, 1988, p 99
3 Mathieu, Cardinal F D, *Jacques II trahis par Innocens XI*, Vatican Archives, Rome, 1904

Chapter 10

1 Mathieu, Cardinal F D, *Jacques II trahis par Innocens XI*
2 Archives Nationales, Paris
3 Mathieu, Cardinal F D, *Jacques II trahis par Innocens XI*
4 Trevor, Meriol, *The Shadow of a Crown*, p 261

5 The *Beauceant* Records of the Chivalric & Military Order of the Temple of Jerusalem, Scotland
6 Archives Napoléon, Paris
7 Archives Nationales, Paris
8 Mathieu, Cardinal F D, *Jacques II trahis par Innocens XI*
9 Mathieu, Cardinal F D, *Jacques II trahis par Innocens XI*
10 Mathieu, Cardinal F D, *Jacques II trahis par Innocens XI*
11 Morton, H V, *In Search of Scotland*, Methuen, London, 1929, pp 231–2
12 Archives Nationales, Paris
13 Mackay, James A, *Robert Bruce, King of Scots*, Robert Hale, London, 1974, p 149
14 Vitelleschi, Marchesa, *A Court in Exile*, Hutchinsons, London, 1903, p 36

Chapter 11

1 Trevor, Meriol, *The Shadow of a Crown*, p 261
2 Cook, E Thornton, *Their Majesties of Scotland*, p 397
3 Donaldson, Gordon, and Morpeth, R S, *A Dictionary of Scottish History*, p 6
4 The House of Commons Archives, Westminster

Chapter 12

1 The House of Lords Archives, Westminster
2 Archives Nationales, Paris
3 Cronin, Vincent, *Louis XIV*, Reprint Society, London, 1965, p 191
4 Vitelleschi, Marchesa, *A Court in Exile*, p 73
5 Holy Roman Archives at Vienna, Austria
6 *Craccas* Newspaper, 16 May 1718, Rome

Chapter 13

1 Marshall, Rosalind K, *Bonnie Prince Charlie*, H M Stationery Office, Edinburgh, 1988, p 150
2 The House of Lords Archives, Westminster
3 Morton, H V, *In Search of Scotland*, p 133
4 Gardner, Barry, and Evans, David, *Thomas Anderson: King's Officer and Jacobite Gentleman*, Brendon Arts, Exmoor, 1992, pp 1–2
5 Scott, Paul Henderson, *Andrew Fletcher and the Treaty of Union*, John Donald, Edinburgh, 1992, App B p 231
6 Cook, E Thornton, *Their Majesties of Scotland*, p 398
7 Trevor, Meriol, *The Shadow of a Crown*, p 261
8 Gardner, Laurence, *Bloodline of the Holy Grail*, ch. 19, p 315

Chapter 14

1 Archives Nationales, Paris
2 Castries, Duc de, *The Kings and Queens of France*, Weidenfeld and Nicolson, London, 1979, pp 218–19
3 Marshall, Rosalind K, *Bonnie Prince Charlie*, pp 129–130
4 *Burke's Peerage, Baronetage and Knightage*
5 The House of Lords Archives, Westminster
6 The Masonic Archives at Freemasons' Hall, Edinburgh

Chapter 15

1 The Vatican Archives, Rome
2 Lavalette, Comte Antoine Marie Chaman de, *Memoires et souvenirs de Marguerite Marie Thérèse d'Audibert de Lussan, Comtesse de Massillan et d'Albanie*, Archives Nationales, Paris, 1831
3 Steuart, A Francis, *The Neopolitan Stuarts*, in *English Historical Review*, 1903
4 Lavalette, Comte Antoine Marie Chaman de, *Memoires et souvenirs de Marguerite Marie Thérèse d'Audibert de Lussan, Comtesse de Massillan et d'Albanie*
5 The Vatican Archives, Rome
6 The Vatican Archives, Rome
7 Archives Nationales, Paris
8 The *Stuart Papers* at Windsor
9 *Memoirs of Cardinale Ercole Consalvi*, Bibliothèque Nationale, Paris, 1864
10 The House of Lords Archives, Westminster
11 The Vatican Archives, Rome

Chapter 16

1 Archives Napoléon, Paris
2 Antoine, Robert, Chevalier de Beauterne, *La vie du Prince Edouard Jacques Stuart d'Albanie*, Bibliothèque Nationale, Paris, 1846
3 The Senate Archives, Washington, USA
4 Archives Nationales, Brussels, Belgium
5 The Vatican Archives, Rome
6 Archives Napoléon, Paris
7 Archives Napoléon, Paris
8 Archives Napoléon, Paris
9 Archives Napoléon, Paris
10 The Vatican Archives, Rome
11 The Masonic Archives at Freemasons' Hall, Edinburgh
12 Foissy, Msr (Avocat), *Les Comtes d'Albanie depuis 1766*, at the Archives Nationales, Notorial Registers Acts, Paris, 1830

Chapter 17

1 Archives Nationales, Paris
2 The Senate Archives, Washington, USA
3 The House of Lords Archives, Westminster
4 Sherry, Francis A, *The Rising of 1820*, William Maclellan, Glasgow, 1974 (general coverage)
5 The Danish National Archives, Copenhagen
6 The House of Lords Archives, Westminster

Chapter 18

1 Brotonne, Léonce de, *Les Stuarts et leurs alliances*, Paris, 1834
2 Duperre, *Letters of Admiral Duperre*, Archives Nationales, Paris
3 Choquier, *Letters of Baron Surlet de Choquier*, Archives Nationales, Brussels, Belgium
4 The Vatican Archives, Rome
5 The Vatican Archives, Rome
6 Massue, Melville Henry, 9th Marquis de Ruvigny et Raineval, *The Jacobite Peerage, Baronetage, Knightage and Grants of Honour*, London, 1904, and Charles Skilton, Edinburgh, 1974
7 Armoises, Madame Olivier des, *Un rapport sur la mort ètrange du 4ième Comte d'Albanie le Prince Charles Benoix Stuart à Monsieur le Ministre des Affaires Etrangère a Paris*, Archives Nationales, Paris, 1898

Chapter, 19

1 Zec, Donald, *The Queen Mother*, Sidgwick & Jackson, London, 1990, p 13

Chapter 20

1 The International Parliament for Safety and Peace, Palermo, Sicily – Inc. USA

APPENDICES

APPENDIX I

King James IV and the Great Michael

Crowned at Scone in June 1488, after the death of his father at the Battle of Sauchieburn, James became the sixth Stewart King of Scots, being the fourth of his name in the kingly line, and fifth of his name overall. The name 'James' was little recorded prior to 1300 in Scotland, and it was probably used by the Stewarts because of their connection with the tradition of St James the Great. In 1253, James the High Steward's father, Alexander of Dundonald, went as a pilgrim to Santiago de Compostella in Spain (Sant lago = Saint James), and most likely named his son James as a result. St James, reputed to have preached there shortly before his death, was much venerated by the Spanish, and in 1508 King James IV continued the connection by commissioning the merchant mariner Robert Barton to offer a silver ship, weighing 31.5oz, to the shrine of St James.

The 'silver ship' may well have represented James IV's intention to unite the princes of Christendom in opposition to the Ottoman Turks who had succeeded the Seljuk Turks in their occupation of Jerusalem. The Crusades were over by then, but James sent his ambassador to Pope Julius II, with his proposal to construct a great warship so that he could personally lead another Crusade. In recognition of James's sincerity, the Pope sent him a consecrated hat and sword early in 1507, along with the title 'Protector of the Christian Faith'. The diplomatic correspondence to this effect continued between the King of Scots and the Courts of Europe until as late as 24 May 1513, when James sought a peaceful unification with Henry VIII Tudor of England.

In preparation for his ambitious Crusade, James busied himself with the construction of a Royal Fleet, the first ship of which was the *Margaret*. She was a four-master of around 600 tons, carrying 25 guns and named after his wife Margaret Tudor, the sister of Henry VIII. Her keel had been laid in about 1502, and the specialist shipwrights, John Lorans and Jennen Diew, were appointed from France to oversee the project. The *Margaret*'s launch proved difficult because of the sand-bar at Leith, and so a new royal dockyard was established a mile or so westward at Newhaven. There, work was immediately commenced on the premier ship of Scotland, the *Great Michael*.

The shipwright who replaced Lorans and Diew was the Frenchman, Jacques Terrel, who undertook to work from the King's blueprint. Not only was the *Great Michael* to incorporate guns below decks, and all the latest developments in maritime armaments, but she was also to accommodate a small army capable of sustaining a long sea voyage. Scotland was unable, however, to meet the demands for the timber needed for such a major enterprise, and so Terrel had to scour the forests of Denmark and France to obtain the majority of wood for the hull and masts.

The building yard was styled by digging out a hollow to accommodate a cradle for the keel, and traces of this were identified on the *c*1690 *Plan of Leith and Approaches*. This was presented to the Rt Hon St James Fleming, Lord Provost of Edinburgh, and dedicated by Captain Greenvile Collins, Hydrographer to the King. Pulled from the dock with great ceremony on the morning of 24 October, the *Great Michael* was reported in the contemporary *History of Scotland* by Robert Lindsay of Pitscottie (1436–1565) to be:

> so strong, and of so great length and breadth, namely 240 feet and 36 feet within the sides. She was 10 feet thick in the wall, outted jests of oak in her wall, and boards on every side, so stark and so thick that no cannon could go through her.

However, this dreadnought of her age, who had stripped Scotland of oak, excepting the royal hunting forest of Falkland, and was designed to front a great Crusade, was soon to become a pawn in the struggle between England and France.

After her launch, but still requiring her masts stepped and her superstructure completed, the *Great Michael* was towed upstream to safety (out of reach of enemy ships) to her fitting-out basin at the Pow of Airth near Kincardine. There, a shallow dock had been prepared, and after adjustments of the ship's ballast, she was to sit on the mud while her cowbrigging and upper works were completed. The area was named Dublarlands, probably due to the watery conditions in which the artisans had to work. Then, when the *Great Michael* was finally ready for service, she was brought back to Newhaven, taking on more guns at Blackness, *en route*. At Newhaven, her hull was fired to remove any worm, and once re-tallowed she lay behind Inchkeith Island, to be stocked with provisions and generally made ready.

A carrack of 1,000 tons or more, the *Great Michael* required four masts upon which to hang sails to produce enough power to drive her bullish hull through the stormy northern seas. Her small sprit sails forward, and her mizzen and bonaventure mizzen masts aft, were lateen rigged (triangular and about 45° to the mast) to assist with steerage. The forward and main masts were fitted with top sails, but the main mast was also fitted with a topgallant sail, and all were square-rigged for power. These top masts were stepped at the fighting tops, so that any damage could be rectified without having to replace the whole mast. The fighting tops were to be manned by archers, who would also be well stocked with javelins and pestilence that could be released from windward to cause great annoyance to the enemy, thereby giving the *Great Michael* a significant advantage. Small swivel-guns were also housed in the fighting tops, so as to rain down shot upon any borders. From these top masts were flown the great standards of Scotland, and pennants of the Royal House of Stewart. The lion rampant, flown only by the monarch, was heavily embroidered and fringed, requiring 992m of cloth, and the flags overall cost the princely sum of £72 7s 6d [about £26,500 by today's value].

The main deck was about half the length of the ship, and below it was the lower deck – both well stocked with cannon founded in Edinburgh by Robert Bortwick. The fore and after castles consisted of up to six decks, all stocked with smaller armaments. In fact, James IV boasted that the *Great Michael* had 16 pits of cannon on either side – more cannon than ever the King of France took to a siege. It is likely that the side cannon, mounted on several decks, were large breach-loading, cast-iron guns, painted with red lead and oiled over to protect them from the ravages of salt water. It is also likely that the guns were secured against recoil, but not run through the hull since the gunports had to be lined with leather to prevent them from catching fire. The more powerful guns were great bronze basilisks, capable of 'firing a stone shot bigger than a great penny loaf one and a half miles'. These were mounted on trollies, two in the stern and one in the forecastle. They were run out through the gunports after being muzzle loaded, and though primarily used as sternchasers for defence, they could be well adapted for bombardment, as in the siege of Carrickfergus. The shock to the vessel when these great guns were fired was far better absorbed through the length of the hull than would have been the case if mounted on the ship's broadsides.

Despite James's ambition to lead his Crusade, he was overtaken by the political scene closer to home, and he was subjected to relentless pleas from Louis XII of France to assist him against the expansionist policies of England's Henry VIII. Dr Nicholas West, Henry's Ambassador to Scotland, was also seeking the support of the Scottish Fleet, and he constantly harried King James, although to no avail. At that stage, both the French and English kings had lost their premier ships, *La Cordelière* and the *Regent*, during a sea battle on 9–10 August 1512.

Responding in favour of King Louis, the Scottish Fleet of 16 large ships and 10 smaller ships sailed for France, with King James on board the *Great Michael*. He led the way as far as the Isle of May, where he transferred command of the Fleet to the Earl of Arran. The *Great Michael* was victualled to support a crew of some 300 sailors and gunners, while also billeted on board were 1,000 soldiers. Hundreds of barrels of fresh fish, cheese, beer, wine, biscuits, and fresh-baked local bread were necessary to keep the mariners fit and ready for battle, and King James supplied salted meat as his personal contribution. Fresh water was, of course, always a problem at sea, and in this regard extra supplies were taken on board while at anchor off the Isle of Bute. This was subsequent to having dealt a severe blow to the English garrison at Carrickfergus in Ireland, where the great warship experienced her first battle action.

Subsequently, the *Great Michael*, with her French pilot Philippe Rouxell, led the storm-tossed Fleet to the safety of Brest. The three premier ships of Scotland, the *Great Michael*, the *Margaret* and the *James*, then formed a strong and effective deterrent to the English Navy, and were to lead an attempt to seize Henry VIII on his return to England from France. Only the severest of weather saved him, and forced the Franco-Scots ships to return to harbour. But Henry was not happy to know that the *Great Michael* lay in wait somewhere, and so in 1514 he captured and interrogated the 18-year-old Frenchman, Boudouin Pucher, who reported that the ship was at the haven of Honfleur. Then in 1522, he captured master mariner Dougall Campbell, who had served on the *Great Michael* under her master Stephen Valois, and he reported her to then be at Brest.

And so, neither King James IV nor the *Great Michael* took part in any Holy Land Crusade, and the ship served her remaining life as the primary warship of the French Navy until about 1527. She was referred to as *La Michelle – La Grande Nef d'Ecosse*, and her last master was Vice Admiral l'Artigue of France.

APPENDIX II

The Declaration for Liberty of Conscience
Issued by James VII (II) Stuart – 4 April 1687

It having pleased Almighty God not only to bring us to the Imperial Crown of these Kingdoms through the greatest difficulties, but to preserve us by a more than ordinary Providence upon the Throne of our royal ancestors, there is nothing now that we so earnestly desire as to establish our government on such a foundation as may make our subjects happy, and unite them to us by inclination as well as duty – which we think can be done by no means so effectually as by granting to them the Free Exercise of their Religion for the time to come. And add that to the Perfect Enjoyment of their Property (which has never been in any case invaded by us since our coming to the Crown). Which, being two things men value most, shall ever be preserved in these Kingdoms, during our reign over them, as the truest methods of their peace and glory.

We cannot but heartily wish (as it will be easily believed) that all the people of our dominions were members of the Catholic Church. Yet, we humbly thank God it is (and hath of long time been) our constant sense of opinion (which upon diverse occasions we have declared) that conscience ought not to be constrained, nor people forced in matters of mere religion. It has ever been contrary to our inclination – as we think it is to the interest of governments which it destroys, by spoiling trade, depopulating countries and discouraging strangers. And finally, that it never obtained the end for which it was employed.

We, therefore – and out of our princely care and affection for all our loving subjects (that they may live at ease and quiet), and for the increase of trade and encouragement of strangers – have thought fit, by virtue of our royal prerogative, to issue forth this declaration of indulgence – making no doubt of the concurrence of our two Houses of Parliament, when we shall think it convenient for them to meet.

In the first place, we do declare that we will protect and maintain our archbishops, bishops and clergy, and all other of our subjects in the Church of England, in the Free Exercise of their Religion – as by law established – and in the quiet and full enjoyment of all their possessions, without any molestation or disturbance whatsoever.

We do likewise declare that it is our royal will and pleasure that, from henceforth, the execution of all, and all manners of, penal laws (in matters ecclesiastical) for not coming to the Church, or not receiving the sacrament, or for any other nonconformity to the religion established, or by reason of the exercise of religion in any manner whatsoever, be immediately suspended; and the further execution of the said penal laws is hereby suspended.

And to the end that, by the Liberty hereby granted, the Peace and Security of our Government in the practice thereof may not be endangered, we have thought fit, and do hereby straitly charge and command all our loving subjects, that we do freely give them leave to meet and serve God after their own way and manner – be it in private houses or places purposely hired or built for that use, so that they take especial care that nothing be preached or taught amongst them which may, in any ways, tend to alienate the hearts of our people from us or our Government. And that their meetings and assemblies be peaceable – openly and publicly held – and all persons freely admitted to them. And that they do signify and make known, to some one or more of the next Justices of the Peace, what place or places they set apart for those uses.

And, forasmuch as we are desirous to have the benefit of the services of our loving subjects (which by the law of nature is inseparably annexed to and inherent in our royal person), and that none of our subjects may for the future be under any discouragement or disability (who are well inclined and fit to serve us) by reasons of some oaths or tests that have been administered on such occasions, we do hereby further declare that it is our royal will and pleasure that the oaths commonly called the Oaths of Supremacy and Allegiance, and also the several Tests and Declarations mentioned in the Acts of Parliament made in the 25th and 30th years of the reign of our late royal brother, King Charles II (the *Test Acts* of 1673 and 1678), shall not at any time hereafter be required to be taken, declared or subscribed by any person whatsoever who is, or shall be, employed in any office or place of trust – either civil or military – under us or in our Government.

And we do further declare it to be our pleasure and intention, from time to time hereafter, to grant our royal dispensation, under our great seal, to all our loving subjects so to be employed, who shall not take the said Oaths, or subscribe or declare the said Tests or Declarations, in the above mentioned Acts and every of them.

James R

APPENDIX III

1706 Vote on the Union of Scottish and English Parliaments

Nobles – *For*

Earl of Seafield (Chancellor)
Marquis of Montrose
Duke of Argyll
Marquess of Tweedale
Marquess of Lothian
Earl of Mar (Secretary)
Earl of Loudon
Earl of Crawford
Earl of Sutherland
Earl of Rothes
Earl of Mortoun
Earl of Eglinton
Earl of Roxburgh
Earl of Haddington
Earl of Galloway
Earl of Wemyss
Earl of Dalhousie
Earl of Leven
Earl of Northesk
Earl of Balcarres
Earl of Forfar
Earl of Kilmarnock
Earl of Kintore
Earl of Dunmore
Earl of Marchmont
Earl of Hynford
Earl of Cromarty
Earl of Stair
Earl of Roseberry

Nobles – *Against*

Duke of Atholl
Duke of Hamilton
Marquess of Annandale
Earl of Errol
Earl Marischal
Earl of Buchan
Earl of Glencairn
Earl of Wigton
Earl of Strathmore
Earl of Selkirk
Earl of Kincardine
Viscount Stermont
Viscount Kilsyth
Lord Semple
Lord Oliphant
Lord Balmbrino
Lord Blantyre
Lord Barganey
Lord Belhaven
Lord Colvin
Lord Kinnaird

Nobles – *For*	**Nobles** – *Against*
Earl of Glasgow	
Earl of Hopetoun	
Earl of Delorain	
Earl of Hay	
Viscount Duplin	
Viscount Garnock	
Lord Forbes	
Lord Elphinstoune	
Lord Ross	
Lord Torphicen	
Lord Fraser	
Lord Banff	
Lord Elibank	
Lord Duffus	
Lord Rollo	

Barons – *For*	**Barons** – *Against*
Sir Robert Dicksone of Inverask	George Lockhart of Carnwath
William Nisbet of Dirletoun	Sir James Foulis of Collington
John Cockburn jnr of Orminston	Andrew Fletcher of Saltoun
Sir John Swinton of that Ilk	Sir Robert Sinclair of Longformacus
Sir Alexander Campbell of Cessnock	Sir Patrick Home of Renton
Sir William Ker of Green Head	Sir Gilbert Elliot of Minto
Archibald Douglas of Cavers	William Baillie of Lamington
William Bennet of Grubbet	John Sinclair jnr of Stevenson
John Murray of Bowhill	John Sharp of Hoddam
John Pringle of Haining	Alexander Fergusson of Isle
William Morrison of Preston Grange	Alexander Gordon of Pitlurg
George Baillie of Jervis Wood	John Forbes of Culloden
Sir John Johnstoun of Wester Hall	Thomas Hope of Rankieller
William Douglas of Dornock	James Carnegie of Phinhaven
William Stewart of Castle Stewart	James Ogilvie jnr of Boyne
John Stewart of Sorbie	Sir Henry Innes jnr of that Ilk
John Montgomery of Wree	John Brisbane of Bishopstone
Sir Robert Pollock of that Ilk	William Cochran of Kilmarnock
William Dalrymple of Glen Muir	Sir Humphrey Colhoun of Luss
John Hadden of Glen Agies	Sir John Houstoune of that Ilk
Mungo Grahame of Gorthy	John Grahame of Killaney
Sir Thomas Burnet of Leyes	James Grahame of Buchlyvie
William Seton jnr of Pitmeddon	Thomas Sharp of Houston
Alexander Grant jnr of that Ilk	Sir Patrick Murray of Auchtertyre

Barons – *For*

Sir Kenneth MacKenzie
Angus MacLeod of Cathol
John Campbell of Mammore
Sir James Campbell of Auchinbreck
James Campbell jnr of Arkinglass
Sir William Anstruther of that Ilk
James Halyburton of Pitcur
Alexander Abercrombie of Glasgow
William Maxwell of Cardross
James Dunbar jnr of Hemprigs
John Bruce of Kinross
Robert Stewart of Tillycoultry

Barons – *Against*

John Murray of Strowan
Sir David Ramsay of Balmain
James More of Stoniewood
David Bethune of Balfour
Patrick Lyon of Auchter House
David Graham yngr of Fintry
Alexander Mackgie of Dalgown
Alexander Douglas of Eagleshaw

Burgesses – *For*

Sir Patrick Johnstoun
John Serymhowe
Col Areskin
John Muir
James Scott
Patrick Bruce
Sir James Smollet
William Carmichael
Daniel Mackleod
John Ross
Sir David Dalrymple
Patrick Ogilvie
William Alvis
John Urquhart
James Spittle
Daniel Campbell
Robert Douglas
George Dalrymple
Sir John Areskin
Patrick Moncrieffe
George Munro
Sir Andrew Home
William Coltran
Sir Peter Halket
Sir Alexander Ogilvie
John Clerk
Sir Hugh Dalrymple

Burgesses – *Against*

Robert Inglis
Alexander Robertson
John Black
Walter Stewart
Alexander Watson
Hugh Montgomery
Alexander Edgar
James Oswald
Robert Johnstoune
Alexander Duff
Francis Mollison
Walter Scott
Robert Kellie
John Hutchinson
Walter Sutherland
Dougal Stewart
Archibald Shiels
George Brodie
John Lyon
George Spence
Sir David Cunningham
William Johnstoune
John Carruthers
George Home
Robert Frazer
John Bayne
James Bethun

Burgesses – *For*

George Allardyce
Roderick MacKenzie
Sir James Stewart
Sir Robert Forbes
Alexander Maitland
Charles Campbell

APPENDIX IV

Jacobite Clans of the 'Forty-five'

As mentioned in the main text, the Clans were to some extent divided in the 1745–6 campaign. It is, therefore, not possible to give a comprehensive list of Clans which wholeheartedly supported one side or the other, even though there were many cases of total support or significant majority. Of the Hanoverian faction, the most apparent was Clan Campbell, who carried with them many of the Grants, Rosses, Mackays and Sutherlands of the northern and central Highlands. From the west, the Macleods and Mackenzies were also allied to Hanover, along with the Macdonalds of Sleat – although in general the Macdonalds were keenly Jacobite.

Prominent in the Jacobite ranks were the Macdonalds of Glengarry, Keppoch and Clanrannald, and the Camerons, Macleans, and Stewarts of Appin. The Jacobite allegiance of these Clans was further heightened by their traditional hatred for Clan Campbell, and for those other Clans whose faithless chiefs had benefitted through subservience to the English feudal regime. There were also numerous smaller Jacobite families, such as the Macdonalds of Glencoe and the MacLachlans, who were attached to the larger Clan units, while some banded together to form allied regiments such as the Atholl Brigade. Others who joined forces were the MacGillivrays, Farquharsons and MacBeans who united under Lady Mackintosh.

Additionally, many clansmen came together to form regiments under common leaders such as Lord Lewis Gordon and

Lord Ogilvie, while some cavalry troops were provided by a Franco-Irish contingent. However, the horse regiments of Lords Elcho, Balmerino and others actually fought on foot at Culloden.

At risk of missing out some Clans whose members might justly feel their family names should be featured, a representative list of those Clans wholly, predominantly, or significantly Jacobite at the time of Culloden includes:

Cameron	Gunn	MacLachlan
Chattan	Hay	MacLaren
Chisholm	Johnston	Maclean
Drummond	McColl	MacNab
Duncan	Macdonald	MacPherson
Erskine	MacGillivray	MacRae
Farquharson	MacGregor	Murray
Fletcher	MacIntyre	Ogilvie
Forbes	Mackenzie	Oliphant
Fraser	MacInnon	Robertson
Gordon	MacKintosh	Stewart of Appin

The Jacobite Battle Order – 16 April 1746

Charles Edward Stuart (Charles III) – Commander-in-Chief
John William O'Sullivan – Adjutant and Quartermaster

LEFT WING	CENTRE	RIGHT WING
Duke of Perth	**Lord John Drummond**	**Lord George Murray**
Macdonalds	Chisholm	Stewart of Appin
of Glengarry	Edinburgh Volunteers	Cameron
of Keppoch	MacLachlan	Atholl
of Clanrannald	MacLean	
	Farquharson	
	Chattan	
	Mackintosh	
	Fraser	

Artillery Ordnance Master: John Finlayson

RESERVE

Franco-Irish Picquets	Fitz-James Horse
Scots Royals (France) or	Baggot's Hussars
Perth Regiment	Kilmarnock's Horse

Glenbucket's Regiment
Lewis Gordon's Regiment
Ogilvie's Regiment
Gordon of Avuchie's Regiment

Strathallan's Perthshire Horse
Pitsilgo's Banffshire Horse
Elcho's Life Guards
Balmerino's Horse

APPENDIX V

Royal Declaration and Regency Commission
Issued by James VIII Stuart – 23 December 1743

James VIII, by the grace of God, King of Scotland, England, France and Ireland, Defender of the Faith, etc. To all our loving Subjects of what degree or quality soever – Greeting.

Having always borne the most constant affection to our ancient Kingdom of Scotland, from whence we derive our royal origin, and where our progenitors have swayed the Sceptre with glory through a longer succession of kings than any monarchy on earth can at this day boast of, we cannot but behold, with the deepest concern the miseries they suffer under a foreign usurpation, and the intolerable burdens daily added to their yoke, which become yet more sensible to us when we consider the constant zeal and affection the generality of our Subjects of our ancient Kingdom have expressed for us on all occasions, and particularly when we had the satisfaction of being ourselves among them.

We see a Nation always famous for valour, and highly esteemed by the greatest of foreign potentates, reduced to the condition of a Province under the specious pretence of an Union with a more powerful neighbour. In consequence of this pretended Union, grievous and unprecedented taxes have been laid on and levied with severity in spite of all the representatives that could be made to the contrary; and these have not failed to produce the poverty and decay of trade which were easily foreseen to be the necessary consequences of such oppressive measures.

To prevent the just resentment which could not but arise from such usage, our faithful Highlanders, a people always trained up and inured to arms, have been deprived of them. Forts and citadels have been built and garrisoned where no foreign invasion could be apprehended, and a military government has been effectually introduced as into a conquered country. It is easy to foresee what must be the consequences of such violent and unprecedented proceedings if a timely remedy be not put to them. Neither is it less manifest that such a remedy can ever be obtained, but by our Restoration to the Throne of our ancestors into whose royal hearts such destructive maxims could never find admittance.

We think it needless to call to mind how solicitous we have ever been, and how often we have ventured our royal person to compass this great end which, with the divine providence seems now to have furnished us with the means of doing effectually, by enabling our good Subjects in England to shake off the yoke under which they have likewise felt their share of the common calamities. Our former experience leaves us no room to doubt of the cheerful and hearty concurrence of our Scots Subjects on this occasion towards the perfecting of the great and glorious work; but that none may be deterred by the memory of past miscarriages from returning to their duty and being restored to the happiness they formerly enjoyed. We, in this public manner, think fit to make known our gracious intentions towards all our people.

We do, therefore, by this our Royal Declaration, absolutely and effectually pardon and remit all treasons and other crimes hitherto committed against our royal Father or ourselves; from the benefit of which Pardon we except none but such as shall, after the publication hereof, wilfully and maliciously oppose us or those who shall appear, or endeavour to appear, in arms for our service.

We further declare that we will, with all convenient speed, call a free Parliament that, by the advice and assistance of such an assembly, we may be enabled to repair the breaches caused by so long an usurpation, to redress all grievances and to free our people from the unsupportable burden of the Malt Tax, and all other hardships and impositions which have been the consequences of the pretended Union, that so the Nation may be restored to that Honour, Liberty and Independency which it formerly enjoyed.

We likewise promise, upon our royal Word, to protect, secure and maintain all our Protestant Subjects in the free exercise of their religion, and in the full enjoyment of their Rights, Privileges and Immunities, and in the secure possession of all churches, universities, colleges and schools conformable to the laws of the land.

All this we shall be ready to confirm in our first Parliament in which we promise to pass any Act or Acts that shall be judged necessary to secure each private person in the full possession of his liberty and property to advance trade, to relieve the poor, and to establish the general welfare and tranquillity of the Nation. In all such matters we are fully resolved to act always by the advice of our Parliaments, and to value none of our Titles so much as that of Common Father of our People, which we shall ever show ourselves to be by our constant endeavours to promote the quiet and happiness of all our Subjects. And we shall be particularly solicitous to settle, encourage and maintain the fishery and linen manufactory of the Nation, which we are sensible may be of such advantage to it, and which we hope are works reserved for us to accomplish.

As for those who shall appear more signally zealous for the recovery of our just Rights and the prosperity of their Country, we shall take effectual care to reward them according to their respective degrees and merits; and we particularly promise, as aforesaid, our full free and general pardon to all officers, soldiers and sailors now engaged in the service of the usurper, whether of the sea or land, provided that, upon the publication hereof, and before they engage in fight or battle against our forces, they quit the said unwarrantable service and return to their duty, in which care we shall pay them all the arrears that shall be at that time due to them from the usurper. We shall grant to the officers the same commissions that they shall then bear, if not higher, and to all soldiers and sailors a gratification of a whole year's pay for their forwardness in promoting our service.

We shall further promise and declare that the vassals of such as shall, without regard to our present Declaration, obstinately persist in their rebellion, and thereby forfeit all pretensions to our royal Clemency, shall be delivered from all servitude they were formerly bound to, and shall have grants and charters of their lands to be immediately held of the Crown provided they, upon the publication of this, our Declaration, declare openly for us and join heartily in the Cause of their Country.

And, having thus declared our gracious intentions to our loving Subjects, we do hereby require and command them to be assisting to us in the recovery of our Rights and of their own Liberties. And that all our Subjects from the age of sixteen to sixty do, upon the setting up of our Royal Standard, immediately repair to it, or join themselves to such as shall first appear to us in their respective Shires; and also to seize the horses and arms of all suspected persons and all ammunition, forage, and whatever else may be necessary for the use of our forces.

We also strictly command all receivers, collectors or other persons who may be seized of any sum or sums of money levied in the name, or for use in the name, of the usurper, to retain such sum or sums of money in their hands till they can pay them to some person of distinction appearing publicly for us and demanding the same for our use and service, whose receipt or receipts shall be a sufficient discharge for all such collectors, receivers, or other persons, their heirs, etc.

Lastly, we do hereby require all Sheriffs of Shires, Stewards of Stewartries, and their respective deputies, Magistrates of Royal Boroughs, and Bailies of Regalities, and all others to whom it may belong, to publish this, our Declaration, at the Market Crosses of their respective towns and boroughs, and there to proclaim us, under the penalty of being proceeded against according to the Law for their neglect of so necessary and important a duty.

Whereas we have a near prospect of being restored to the Throne of our ancestors by the good inclinations of our Subjects towards us, and whereas, on account of the present situation of this Country, it will be impossible for us to be in person at the first setting up of our Royal Standard, and even for some time after. We, therefore, esteem it for our service, and the good of our kingdoms and dominions, to nominate and appoint, as we hereby nominate, constitute and appoint, our dearest son, Charles, Prince of Wales, to be sole Regent of our Kingdoms of England, Scotland and Ireland, and of all other our dominions during our absence.

It is our will and intention that our said dearest son should enjoy and exercise all that power and authority which, according to the ancient Constitution of our Kingdom, has been enjoyed and exercised by former Regents. Requiring all our faithful Subjects to give all due submission and obedience to our Regent aforesaid as immediately representing our royal person, and acting by our authority. And we do hereby revoke all commissions of Regency granted to any person or persons whatsoever. And lastly, we do hereby dispense with all formalities and other omissions that may be herein contained, declaring this, our Commission, to be as firm and valid, to all intents and purposes, as if it had passed our Great Seals, and as if it were according to the usual style and forms.

James R

APPENDIX VI

Eighteenth-century Jacobite Societies in England and Wales

Society	Location	Operative
Aberystwyth	Wales	1709–10
Bulkeley	Anglesey	1722–47
Beaufort Club	London	1723
Beaufort Hunt	Badminton, Glos	From 1740
Benn's Club	London	1700s
Brothers Club	London	1710–14
Bucks Society	Liverpool	1760–70
Burford's Club	London	1722
Caryll Club	London	1749
Cheshire Gentlemen	Cheshire	1715–49
Cheshire Hunt	Cheshire	From 1763
Confederate Hunt	Wynnstay, Wales	1754–8
The Corporation	Rochdale, Lancs	1760
Cowper's Cabal	London	1722
Crosby Bowling Club	Liverpool	1700
Cycle of the White Rose	Wynnstay, Wales	1710–1869
Dove Society	Wales	1700s
Freemasons (Tory lodges)	General	1700s
Gang Warily	Wales	1700s
Gloucestershire Society	Gloucestershire	1657–1840
Hard Whites	Preston, Lancs	1700s
Hell Fire Society	Norwich	1751
Hill Top Boys	Walsall, Staffs	1750
Honourable Brotherhood	London	1711
Honourable Incorporation	Chester	1700s / 1800s
Jemmy's Men	Norwich	1751
Kerry Hunt	Wales	1700s
Loyal Brotherhood	Badminton, Glos	1700s

Society	Location	Operative
Loyal Society	Bristol	1713–14
Mock Corpn of Ardwick	Manchester	1767
Mock Corpn of Sefton	Liverpool	1774–8
Mock Corpn of Walton	Preston, Lancs	1702–1830
Montgomery Club	Wales	1700s
Oak Society	London	1740–52
October Club	London	1710–14
Oyster & Parched Pea Club	Preston, Lancs	1771–1841
Sea Serjeants	South Wales	1726–63
John Shaw's Club	Manchester	From 1740
Shrewsbury Hunt	Shropshire	1769–99
Steadfast Society	Bristol	1737–45
John Stewart's Club	Manchester	1735–1892
Tarporley Hunt	Cheshire	From 1762

APPENDIX VII

Transcript of Interview
Charles III Stuart and George Washington's envoys
November 1782

From the private papers of the Manorwater family is taken the following extract from the conversation transcript supplied by the Hon Charles Hervey-Townshend, Britain's later Ambassador to The Hague. Charles Edward Stuart, along with Hervey-Townshend and Comtesse Marguerite de Massillan, met with the United States representatives at the Palazzo San Clemente, Florence.

Charles III – And now, having won, you have the greatest of human experiments before you. Your business is to show that the Saxon stock is adaptable to a republic.

Mr Fish – We are not pedants, and have no desire to dispute a form of Constitution. A people may be as free under a king as under a senate. Liberty is not the lackey of any type of government.

Comtesse Marguerite – Are these not strange words from a member of a race whom I thought had wedded to the republicanism of Helvidius Priscus!

Hon Hervey-Townshend – As a loyal subject of a monarchy, I must agree with our American friends. But your hands are tied, for I cannot picture the establishment of a House of Washington – and if not, where are you to turn for your sovereign?

Mr Galloway – We are experimenters, as you say Sir, and must go slowly. In the meantime, we have an authority which keeps peace and property safe. We are at leisure to cast our eyes round and meditate on the future.

Charles III – Then, gentlemen, you take an excellent way of meditation in visiting this museum of old sovereignties [Europe]. Here you have the relics of any government you please – a dozen republics, tyrannies, theocracies, merchant confederations, kingdoms, and more than one empire. You have your choice.

Comtesse Marguerite – I am tolerably familiar with the land and, if I can assist you, I am at your service.

Mr Galloway – Sir, we have letters, one especially which gives us the authority to offer the Crown of America to the rightful King of Great Britain. I have told you that we in America are not yet wholly republicans, although there are those among our people who favour a republic. But they are still a minority. We may have got rid of a king who misgoverned us, but we have no wish to get rid of kingship. We want a king of our own choosing, and would get with him all the ancient sanctions of monarchy. You, Sir, are the most illustrious royal stock of Europe, and are (if legitimacy goes for anything) the rightful King of Great Britain, France and Ireland. Even in the eyes of those republicans, you are the most powerful candidate for their favour.

Comtesse Marguerite – It seems to me that there is nothing more potent as an appeal to the American pride than to say, 'We have got rid of King George, and choose of our own free will the older line and King Charles'. It is a chance not to be ignored.

Charles III – Gentlemen, I am somewhat of your opinion in matters of government, but look at me – I am an old man, old before my time. I have suffered something from fortune. I have sojourned forty years in the wilderness of exile. I have my failings, and very few virtues left. Anyway, this is what they say about me! What about the succession?

Comtesse Marguerite – You have always believed that you must be a king at all costs, for the good of the people. Give them a king and, during the remaining years of your life, there will be time to settle the problem of succession. Besides, you have a daughter.

Mr Fish – Sir, we have the opportunity to start afresh, with a clean page to write upon. We believe that the way abides peacefully in a royal house, with cyphers who dignify without obstructing a popular Constitution. We come to you with the reasoned conclusion of the men who achieved liberty. General Washington shares our views, and has asked Mr Hamilton to send us on this mission.

Mr Sylvester (1) – You say you are an old man – but so much the better. We do not wish a young king who may be fractious. An old man tempered by misfortune is what our purpose demands.

Mr Sylvester (2) – You say you have failings – no virtues. Sir, a man cannot lead his life for even forty years and retain his virtues. As for the gossips regarding your character, I have heard them but I do not credit them. I have not forgotten Preston and Derby, and meeting you merely proves my views.

Mr Fish – As for the fact that you have no legitimate posterity, Sir – you may remarry, father a son or a daughter. But this happens to be the chiefest recommendation – I will speak plainly, Sir: we need a breathing space, and that would enable us to take the House of Stuart on trial. After all, we have no intention to saddle our people for good with a race that would prove burdensome. Should you fail us, we could look elsewhere for a better monarch.

Charles III – Gentlemen, at the eleventh hour of my life you are asking this old man to become your king. Ten or fifteen years ago I would have said yes, but now I fear I have to refuse it. I do not know whether I would be fit to rule over your people. I have travelled far; I was even begged to join your Party in '75, but even then I refused, with hope to regain Scotland and England while the usurper's troops were fighting on your side of the Ocean. It would not last long, I fear, to give you that needed breathing space. My wife has left me – making my kingship the laughable joke of Europe. It would not be fair on your fellow Americans. Nay, Sir, you and your friends tell Mr Hamilton and General Washington that I was flattered by the thought, but I am too old. I have failed most of my life, and have no wish to fail more. Thank you gentlemen, but this is my answer – my last word on the subject. Let us think no more upon it.

APPENDIX VIII

Stuart Secretaries of State in Exile 1689–1777

1689 (Jan–25 Aug)	John, 1st Earl of Melfort, KT – Principal Secretary
1689	Hon Henry Browne – Secretary for England
	Father Lewis Innes – Secretary for Scotland
	Sir Richard Nagle – Secretary for Ireland
1690	Sir James Montgomery – Secretary for Scotland
1693–4 (June)	John, 1st Duke of Melfort, KT
	Joint with Charles, 2nd Earl of Middleton
1694 (June)–6	Charles, 2nd Earl of Middleton
	Joint with John Caryll
1696–1702	Charles, 2nd Earl of Middleton
1702–3	John Caryll
1703–13 (24 Dec)	Charles, 2nd Earl of Middleton
1713 (24 Dec)–15 (July)	Sir Thomas Higgons
1715 (July)–16 (March)	Henry, 1st Earl of Bolingbroke
1716 (March)–24	John, 1st Duke of Mar, KG KT
1724–7 (3 April)	John, 1st Earl of Inverness, KT
1727	Sir John Graeme
1727–47	James, 1st Earl of Dunbar, KT
1747–59	Daniel, 1st Earl of Lismore, KG
1759–63	John, 1st Earl of Alford
1763–4	James Edgar
1764–8	Andrew Lumisden
1768–77	John, 3rd Lord Caryll, KT

APPENDIX IX

Natural Offspring of Charles Edward Stuart

The two key offspring of Charles Edward Stuart detailed in the main text are 1753: Charlotte, Duchess of Albany (legitimated) – daughter of Clementina Walkinshaw, and 1786: Edward James, Count Stuarton (legitimate) – son of Marguerite de Massillan. Apart from these, however, Charles Edward had a number of illegitimate children. These children are detailed below, along with information regarding certain of their descendants. They are also given in Appendix XIV–Charts A–E: 'Natural Offspring of Charles Edward Stuart'.

THE SCHOOL

Firstly, it is worth mentioning the Jacobite orphanage where some of these offspring were raised: the residential school of Berse Drelincourt, near Wrexham in Wales. This imposing Georgian residence was built in 1715 for Mary Drelincourt, widow of Pierre, Dean of Armagh. The house was subsequently passed to Pierre and Mary's daughter Anne who, from 1739, was married to Hugh, 3rd Viscount Primrose, ancestor of Lord Rosebery. Anne was an ardent Jacobite campaigner who regularly corresponded with Charles Edward under the name of 'Miss Fines'. Following her husband's early death in 1741, Lady Anne Primrose also retained their house in Essex Street, London, which was visited by Charles Edward in September 1750.

A close Jacobite ally of Lady Primrose was Dr William King, Principal of St Mary Hall, Oxford. They were part of a well-organized ring of English and Welsh Stuart supporters led by the

Duke of Westmorland, Lord Barrymore and the Duke of Beaufort. In the Welsh sector (which included the Shropshire and Cheshire border country) there were two prominent Jacobite societies to which many of the nobility and gentry belonged. In the south were the Sea Serjeants of Carmarthenshire and Pembrokeshire, whose headquarters was the Masonic lodge at the Red Lion in Market Street, Carmarthen. The north operated through the Cycle of the White Rose, headed by Sir Watkin Williams Wynn, Bart, Lord Lieutenant and MP for Denbighshire. The Cycle's headquarters was Sir Watkin's house at Wynnstay, Wrexham; then (following his death in 1749) at his widow's property, Llangedwyn Hall, near Oswestry. Sir Watkin's widow was Frances, daughter of George Shakerley of the Carmarthen Sea Serjeants and Anne Bagot of Blythefield. Various other houses in the region were also important to the Jacobite endeavour – houses such as Marbury Hall, Cheshire (the home of James Barry, Earl of Barrymore), Malpas Hall, Cheshire (belonging to the Stuart envoy, Richard Minshull), Blythefield Hall, Staffordshire (seat of the Bagot family), and Stoneleigh Abbey (baronial seat of the Leighs of Warwick).

In 1747, the year after the Battle of Culloden, Berse Drelincourt became an operative charity school, and it specialized in the secret residential education of children born to Jacobite nobility. Close by, Mary Drelincourt had founded and endowed Berse Church (known as Madame's Chapel) in 1742, and an underground tunnel ran between the two properties. Technically, the school was established as an orphanage for girls, but there were boys resident as well, and for reasons of strict security Anne Drelincourt (Lady Primrose) was the sole and absolute director, allowing no visitors whatever.

Lady Primrose had been involved with the Jacobite cause during the 1745 Rising, and she befriended Flora MacDonald, who aided Charles Edward's flight to Skye. Indeed, following Flora's imprisonment in England it was Lady Anne who secured her release and gave her financial aid.

Berse Drelincourt became a safe haven for the offspring of exiled high-ranking Jacobites, whose lives were at risk from Hanoverian assassins in Europe. In this regard, Lady Primrose made numerous trips abroad to bring back infants under her care. Her confederate in this regard was Eleanor Oglethorpe, the

Marquise de Mézières, of Westbrook House in Godalming, Surrey. Eleanor was the sister of the Crown agent James Oglethorpe, founder of Georgia, USA. She housed Charles Edward on various occasions in the 1750s when he made surreptitious visits to England.

Lady Anne Primrose died in 1775, but Berse Drelincourt continued as a charity school, although on a more open basis and for girls only, in line with an Indenture which Anne had drawn up some years earlier. The house remained an educational school until about 1950, when it was partially vacated and fell into disrepair. The present owners have, however, spent many years restoring the house and gardens, and are currently compiling a detailed history of this important establishment.

The Finsthwaite Princess

At the Grand Ball, Holyrood House, on Monday 23 September 1745, Charles Edward Stuart (symbolically crowned titular Charles III on the previous day) was introduced to Lady Clementina Walkinshaw, daughter of John, Laird of Barrowfield, and Catherine Paterson of Bannockburn. Charles and Clementina were immediately attracted, and following the Jacobite success at the Battle of Falkirk (17 January 1746) Charles lodged at the Patersons' Bannockburn House, where Clementina tended his wounds. Having lost the Battle of Culloden (16 April 1746), Charles returned to France, by which time Clementina was pregnant, with her baby expected in the October. She and Charles had sworn a contractual declaration of common-law wedlock in the February, with Clementina promising to follow the Prince 'wherever he might be pleased to summon her, and whatever might betide'. This was why the later French registers recorded her as Lady Stuart (*see* Chapter 18).

Their daughter was duly born, whereupon Lady Primrose and Dr William King were consulted about her safe upbringing. At that time, Berse Drelincourt was some months away from fulfilling its charity school purpose, and so the Stuart baby was lodged with Dr King's brother and sister-in-law in Lakeland. Dr King's brother lived at a large farmhouse at Finsthwaite, near Lake Windermere, and his brother's wife (née Taylor) was related to the Backhouses who had another house nearby. [Both properties, Finsthwaite House and July Flower Tree respectively, are still there.] It was agreed that these two families would take care of the girl, whose name was locally recorded as Clementina Johannes Sobieska Douglas (the last name being a common incognito of Charles Edward).

Lady Primrose arranged for both houses to be refitted (with funding provided by Charles Edward) and prior to the baby's arrival ornate staircases, oak panelling, intricate plasterwork, and secret passages were all installed 'for the reception of an illustrious person'. For posterity, young Clementina Douglas arrived with a bronze medal (dated 1719) gifted by her grandfather, John Walkinshaw of Barrowfield. The medal commemorated the marriage of James Francis Edward (James VIII) and Clementina Sobieska – the parents of Charles Edward Stuart.

Unfortunately, Clementina Douglas did not live beyond the age of 24, and she died unmarried in May 1771, having moved to nearby Waterside, Newby Bridge. On her death, she left her medal to a local friend, Jane Penny, and by 1913 it was owned by Rev Charles Townley, MA, Hon Canon of Carlisle. In that year he restored Clementina's grave in Finsthwaite churchyard where her large marble cross bears the epitaph, 'Behold thy King cometh'.

Charles Godefroid de Rohan

During the latter 1740s Charles Edward entered into an affair with Princess Marie Anne Louise de Talmont in Paris, but there was no offspring from this liaison. However, in 1748 his new mistress, Princess Marie Louise de Rohan-Guéméné, bore him a son. She was his first cousin and the wife of Jules Hercule de Rohan, Duc de Montbazon. During 1747, while Jules Hercule was away in the Low Countries, Charles had taken a summer residence at St Oeun, near Paris, and often dined with Marie Louise and her mother-in-law at the Hôtel de Guéméné in the Place Royale. As the weeks passed, so the relationship grew, with passionate letters passing between Marie Louise and Charles. Clandestine meetings were frequent, and Madame de

Guéméné enlisted the aid of Marie Louise's father, the Duc de Bouillon, in an attempt to end the affair. But it was too late – Marie Louise was already pregnant.

She was parentally compelled to write to Charles stating that she must never see him again, but she also wrote other contrary letters which she smuggled to him in secret: 'They keep a constant watch on me . . . Remember, I am bearing your child, and I am suffering because of you. If you stop loving me it will be more than I can endure. But if you still love me, we will somehow keep in touch'. An agonizing series of events followed, leading to Charles being subjected to verbal and physical attacks from Madame de Guéméné, to the extent that he was obliged to relinquish his attachment to Marie Louise before her husband returned.

On 28 July 1748 a son was born to Marie Louise and Charles Edward. He was quietly christened at the Church of St Paul as Charles Godefroid de Rohan – but the press reporters were silenced. Even the social chronicles which always recorded such events within noble families made no mention of the child. To those neighbours and relations who could not be ignored, the boy was portrayed as the lawful son of Marie Louise and her husband Jules Hercule de Montbazon, Prince de Rohan-Guéméné. However, Jules Hercule's mother, Madame de Guéméné, knew the truth, and was naturally concerned that her legitimate grandson, three-year-old Henri, might be compromised in terms of property, title and finance. She decided, therefore, that Henri's new half-brother should become the responsibility of his natural father, Charles Edward Stuart, and plans were made to put this into effect.

Charles Godefroid de Rohan was said to have died, aged only six months, at 9pm on 18 January 1749, and by the following afternoon his casket was buried in the Crypt of St Louis at the Convent des Feuillants, Paris. The hurried funeral was strictly private; the newspapers made no mention of the event, and the family observed no period of mourning thereafter. Even Charles Edward's own notes of the era bear not the slightest mention of any calamity.

Emperor Napoleon had the little coffin opened 60 years later in 1809, only to find it completely empty. He was not surprised at this because he had previously been informed by Jules Hercule's brothers, Louis and Ferdinand de Rohan, that Charles Godefroid had been secreted out of the country soon after his birth. He had, in fact, been conveyed by Lady Anne Primrose to the secure environment of Berse Drelincourt.

Having been placed under the financial support of his real father, Charles Godefroid's assumed family name was discarded, and he became known more correctly as Charles Stewart. In time, he had two offspring – and we shall return to the first of these children, a son, in the section entitled 'Sobieski-Stuarts'. The second child, however, was a daughter called Sophia Elizabeth, and in 1821 she married Lieut Gen John Chester-Bagot, grandson of Sir Walter Wagstaffe Bagot, 5th Baronet of Blythefield (the Bagots being one of the families mentioned above). Sophia was then aged about 25, having been born *c*1795, and she produced three daughters and two sons: Sophia, John, Mary, Barbara and Heneage. Heneage continued the Bagot family name, but his brother, Col John, assumed the name St Leger, after Col John St Leger, who had founded the classic English flat race in 1776.

Lucy

During the early 1750s, Charles Edward spent a good deal of time in England and Wales. These visits were largely related to the ultimately doomed Elibank Plot to assault St James's Palace in London, but they were more precisely concerned with the Carmarthen Riots which were designed to draw military attention westwards prior to November 1752 when the London assault was planned. Although the Elibank Plot came to nothing, the continuing riots caused chaos in South Wales and the West of England right through to 1755.

While in south Wales, Charles was under the protection of the influential Sea Serjeants who ran the Tory Jacobite lodges in Pembroke and Carmarthen, and early in 1750 he was resident in Trevigan (Llanrian parish, St Davids) with a Sea Serjeant landowner called Propert. Squire Propert had an unmarried 18-year-old daughter with whom Charles had an affair, and their daughter, Lucy, was born later that year. Henceforth, Miss

Propert was claimed to have secretly married, but no one ever saw her husband, and she remained at Trevigan until her death, aged 44, in 1775.

Meanwhile, young Lucy was well provided for in her early years by way of an arrangement with Charles Edward's colleague, Frederick, Prince of Wales, who died the year after Lucy's birth. (Frederick was a Stuart sympathizer, despite being the son and heir of King George II.) By the age of 16, however, Lucy had become the mistress of Frederick's son Edward Augustus, Duke of York, much to the dismay of Edward's most renowned mistress, the notorious Kitty Fisher.

Kitty was the leading courtesan of her day, and she used to charge Edward 100 guineas a night for her services – chasing him from the room on one occasion when he offered her only 50 guineas! Being so coveted in high society, Kitty Fisher could not understand Edward's preoccupation with Lucy, and she presumed in her arrogance that Lucy must be charging a good deal less, failing to recognize that there was rather more to the relationship than a paying agreement. So one night Kitty arranged for Lucy's purse to be secreted from the royal bedroom in order to check the amount of money within. There was none – hence, the nursery rhyme:

Lucy Locket lost her pocket; Kitty Fisher found it.
Not a penny was there in it – but a ribbon round it.

A year later, on 17 September 1767, Edward Augustus died at the Prince of Monaco's palace, but not before he had married the expectant Lucy, who was transported back to Wales. There, on 15 March 1768, at the Castle of Haverfordwest, she gave birth to their son William, but died in childbirth.

Edward's brother King George III then came to the rescue, and placed young William in the care of a palace retainer whose name the boy assumed, to become known as William Groves. He was sent to Eton, where King George regularly visited him in the early 1780s, and then went on to Oriel College, Oxford, taking his BA on 23 June 1791. Afterwards, he took Holy Orders, ordained by Beilby Porteous, Bishop of London, on 14 August 1791 in Fulham Palace Chapel. Subsequently, William became a Chaplain to Queen Victoria's father, Edward, Duke of Kent (son of George III), but he left the royal household when Edward died in January 1820, to take up the Rectory of Kingsnorth in the archdeaconry of Canterbury.

By 1851, when the Rev William Groves died aged 83 at Bexley, Kent, he had become Curate of St Margaret's, Westminster – and he left to the Church a sworn manuscript which gave the full details of his life and royal descent.

Chevalier Douglas

In June 1752 Clementina Walkinshaw was in Dunkirk (preparing to become a canoness of a noble chapter in Douai) when Charles Edward sent word that she should join him in Ghent. Clementina duly obeyed in accordance with her earlier vow, and early in October 1753 their daughter Charlotte was born in Liège. The Jacobite Secretary, James Edgar, was not at all happy about the relationship because Clementina's sister was a lady-in-waiting to the Princess of Wales, and he reckoned that Clementina might be a Hanoverian agent. In this regard, he received a letter from his nephew John, dated 14 January 1754, stating, 'Clementina has got in with the Prince; has borne two children to him, and got an extreme ascendant over him'.

We have already learned about the Finsthwaite daughter, but who was the 'second' child borne to Clementina? Could it be the same child mentioned in the *Dictionary of National Biography* – the son who was baptized by Bishop Gordon? It most certainly was, and this son had also been removed from Charles and Clementina in earlier times. Indeed, Charles Edward was so concerned at the loss of these children that (as confirmed in the University of London archive) he wrote the following note on 6 November 1753 with regard to Charlotte: 'A marque to be put on ye child iff I part with it. I am pushed to ye last point, and so won't be cajioled any more'.

Mary Ward

As detailed in the main text, Clementina and Charlotte left Charles Edward in 1760, subsequent to which Charles went to stay at Bouillon, where yet another child was conceived and born. This time, his mistress was not a relation or a chance acquaintance, but had been expressly brought to Charles by his agents Guérin and Jones. Charles Edward's instructions were that he required 'a woman aged 20–5, with good bourgeois sentiments, of good health, and educated, without great property, but with good teeth, an agreeable figure, and a knowledge of music'.

The mistress was duly found for Charles, and their daughter Mary was born in 1761 at the Château de Carlsbourg, Bouillon. She was carried almost immediately to Berse Drelincourt by Eleanor Oglethorpe, a Jacobite emissary, who worked with the famed Stuart agent Dr Samuel Johnson.

Dr Johnson had a lodger called Levet at his London house, and the lodger's brother was the Rev R Levet, who (in 1744) had been succeeded by Rev Michael Ward as Rector of Blythefield, Staffordshire. Rev Ward was a close friend of Sir Walter Wagstaffe Bagot of Blythefield, whom Dr William King had succeeded as MP for Oxford University.

Although Lady Primrose ran the Wrexham orphanage, the men who organized the outside affairs of the Jacobite children were the doctors King and Johnson. Hence, through their efforts, Charles Edward's daughter Mary was eventually placed in the care of Rev Michael Ward, whose family name she adopted.

In time, one of Sir Walter Wagstaffe Bagot's sons (also Walter) became the new Rector of Blythefield. He firstly married Anne Swinnerton, but after her untimely death Walter married Mary Ward, by whom he had eight children.

One of Rev Walter's elder brothers was Charles Bagot, who assumed the surname of Chester in 1755 upon the death of Sir Charles Bagot-Chester, Bart. In 1765 he married Catherine Legge (daughter of Hon Heneage, son of William, 1st Earl of Dartmouth), and it was their fourth son, Lieut Gen John Chester-Bagot, who married Sophia Elizabeth Stewart (daughter of Charles Godefroid de Rohan-Stuart – *as given above*).

Sobieski-Stuarts

It has been previously mentioned that Charles Edward Stuart's eldest son, Charles Godefroid (who died in 1820), had two children. The younger of these was the aforesaid Sophia Elizabeth, and her brother was called James. He was born in Tuscany in 1773, and in 1810 he assumed the style Comte d'Albanie – a style that was to progress to his heirs, who became prominent figures in Scotland.

At the time of James's birth, Charles Edward was married to Louise of Stolberg, and they were then in Siena, having moved from Rome earlier that year. Prior to their departure, Bishop Gordon had written that he suspected Louise to be pregnant, but there was no resultant child, and the doctors subsequently proclaimed her to be barren. Louise was, nevertheless, unwell at the time (as reported in the *Florentine Journal*), and this fuelled the unfounded suspicion of her confinement.

Charles Godefroid (then aged 25 and known as Charles Stewart) was married to a descendant heiress of George Hay of Muiresk (brother of the 10th Earl of Erroll) who had died at Avignon, France, in about 1628. However, when Charles Godefroid's younger half-sister, Charlotte of Albany, heard about the impending birth she became concerned about her own position. So in May 1773 she and her mother, Clementina, journeyed from Meux to see Charles Edward in Rome. The degree of urgency was extraordinary because Clementina had previously been banned from entering Rome – but still she came, to face the wrath of the Cardinal Secretary of State who ordered her out of the city.

In the previous month, Hanoverian Intelligence had reported that Charles Edward had met privately at the Rome Opera House with the captain of a British warship. The captain was a colleague of Charles Edward's second son Chevalier Douglas, and arrangements were made at the meeting to secrete the new Stuart child from Italy when it was born.

In the event, a Jacobite exile known as Dr Beaton was approached one evening by a gentleman outside the Florentine Convent of St Rosalie, near Pisa. He was asked to lend his professional help with an accouchement for the Stuart cause, and was duly led to a room where he delivered the baby. Then, later that same night, he saw the gentleman again, travelling in a carriage with a woman who bore a wrapped infant in her arms. Beaton confirmed that this was not the mother of the child, but a much older woman. Subsequently, it was related that a cloaked woman, carrying a tiny baby, had stepped from an unmarked coach near Porto Franconi. She was rowed out to a British warship which, without delay, sailed away to the west.

The ship's master was Admiral John Carter Allen (whom Charles had met at the Opera House), and the woman was Lady Anne Primrose. The eventual destination for young James Stewart was, once again, Berse Drelincourt where his father had been raised.

James was not long at the orphanage though, for within two years Lady Primrose died and the school came under new management. In 1775, the secretive Jacobite days of Berse Drelincourt were over, and James was adopted by the benevolent Admiral, to become known as Thomas Allen. He too joined the Navy, and at the age of 19 he married Catherine Matilda (a daughter of Rev Manning of Godalming, Surrey – a colleague of Eleanor Oglethorpe) by whom he had two sons, John and Charles, and a daughter, Catherine.

Eventually, John and Charles Allen both married, and Charles had children, but throughout their lives the brothers were extremely close. They each had a marked Stuart resemblance, and Charles was so like his late royal namesake that he modelled for Thomas Duncan's famous painting of Prince Charles Edward entering Edinburgh after the 1745 Battle of Prestonpans. Having fought with Napoleon against the British at Waterloo, the brothers settled in London where they studied to become fluent in Scots Gaelic, and moved in circles of high society.

In 1822 Charles Allen and his father James d'Albanie (alias Thomas Allen) were presented to King George IV in Edinburgh, whereupon Sir Walter Scott was dismayed to see Charles wearing the badge of the House of Erroll. By 1825 both Charles and John were in Edinburgh, where they were welcomed by the nobility, befriending the Marquess of Bute, the Earl of Moray, Lord Lovat, and numerous Clan chiefs. Indeed, their only adversaries were Hanoverian sympathizers such as Sir Walter Scott, who disputed not their Stuart descent but their right to wear the insignia of the Hays of Erroll. As we have seen, the brothers were descended (through Charles Godefroid's wife) from George Hay of Muiresk, and in this regard they claimed their line to be senior to the prevailing Hay High Constables of Scotland (*see* Note on page 380).

From the time of Culloden until 1788, the wearing of tartan and Highland dress had been forbidden in Scotland, but King George IV had revived the tartan fashion by wearing a kilt for his Edinburgh visit. Although there were some numbered patterns around at the time, most of the original Clan designs had been lost, and it was in partially solving this problem that the brothers gained their ultimate reputation, to be known thereafter as the 'Sobieski-Stuarts'. In 1828 they produced a copy of an ancient Scottish manuscript which contained a list of traditional Clan tartans, and these were resurrected for manufacture. The manuscript had been transcribed in 1721 from an original at the Scots College of Douai in France – a 16th-century compilation by Sir Richard Urquhart. Then in 1845 John and Charles Sobieski-Stuart produced a monumental volume called *The Costume of the Clans*, from which more than 50 of today's approved tartans have been reproduced.

In 1838 Lord Lovat had granted the brothers the island of Eilean Aigas on the River Beauly, and they were ultimately buried at the nearby Eskdale Chapel. Here, John and Charles lie beneath a Celtic cross which bears a joint epitaph detailing the fraternal Sobieski-Stuart Counts of Albany: John, born 14 June 1795; died 13 February 1872. Charles, born 4 June 1797; died 25 December 1880. The epitaph concludes: 'They were lovely and pleasant in their lives, and in their deaths they were not divided'.

NOTE: George of Muiresk was the brother of William Hay, 10th Earl of Erroll, who died in 1636 to be succeeded by his son Gilbert, 11th Earl. However, Gilbert died without issue in 1674, nominating his cousin John as his successor. But John Hay was not of the main Erroll descent; he was descended from the 2nd wife of the 16th-century 8th Earl in the line of Keillour. Nevertheless, despite protests from the family of the 10th Earl's brother George Hay, the cousin line of John inherited the earldom. It was, therefore, because of their descent from George Hay that the Sobieski-Stuart brothers insisted on wearing the badge of Erroll in Scotland.

As shown in the Appendix XIV Chart, 'Natural Offspring of Charles Edward Stuart: C', Charles Sobieski-Stuart's son, Charles Edward d'Albanie, married (16 May 1874) Lady Alice Mary Emily Hay, daughter of William, 18th Earl of Erroll.

COUNT ROEHENSTART

Although Charles Edward's daughter, Charlotte of Albany, never married, she did have a long-standing lover in Ferdinand de Rohan, Prince de Guéméné, Archbishop de Bordeaux, Archduc de Cambrai. Their two daughters, Marie Beatrice and Aglae Clementine, have already been mentioned, but Charlotte also had a son called Charles Edward Maximilien. He is perhaps better known, however, as Count Roehenstart – a corruption of Rohan Stuart.

Roehenstart always portrayed himself as Charlotte's lawful son, but he was of course illegitimate. Following the death of his grandmother, Clementina Walkinshaw, he was raised in the care of Baron Korff (a title which, from time to time, Roehenstart assumed himself).

It is well known that Roehenstart fabricated much of his family history in an attempt to legitimate his position in the eyes of the law – and in doing this he made sure that all those from whom he claimed descent were long dead. In the event, however, his plan failed, and he never achieved the social recognition afforded to his well-married (though equally illegitimate) sisters.

Roehenstart led a wandering existence for most of his life, travelling to many parts of the world, including Russia and America. He was married twice, firstly to an Italian, Marie Antoinette Sophie Barbuoni (as given in the *Stuart Papers at Windsor* and the *Almanach de Gotha*). His second wife, after Marie's death, was an Englishwoman, Louisa Constance Smith. There were no children by either marriage, and the *Roehenstart Papers* confirm that there were no illegitimate children either.

The unfortunate Count died after a coach accident in Scotland in 1854. The coach, travelling from Inverness to Edinburgh, lost a wheel and overturned at Inver, near Dunkeld. Among the men thrown from the top was Roehenstart, who was carried to the Atholl Hotel in Dunkeld. After a few days, he was much improved, and sent some money to the women of Inver who had helped him – but then quite suddenly on 28 October he collapsed and died. Although never proven, it has been suggested that his death in care was perhaps an assassination. Roehenstart was subsequently buried in the ruined nave of the Dunkeld

Cathedral of St Columba, where his gravestone was wrongly inscribed, giving his age as 73 rather than 70.

NOTE: There has been an immense amount of genealogical nonsense written about Count Roehenstart, not the least of which appears in the 1953 *Notes and Queries* which are often cited in this regard. The *Notes and Queries* entry was written by an American gentleman named Sydney Horace Lee Washington, who claimed to be a descendant of Count Roehenstart – but he was not. He was, however, descended from the Stuarts by way of his mother Helen (1874–1940), a descendant of Mary, the daughter of Charles Edward Stuart's son Charles John Thomas (Chevalier Douglas). Helen's husband (S H L Washington's father) was Charles Jules Auguste Françoise Marie Leboeuf Buonaparte – alias The Hon Horace Lee Washington.

APPENDIX X

Proclamation and Call to the People
(The 1820 Rising) From the Glasgow Archives

Friends and Countrymen, we have been reduced to take up arms for the redress of our common grievances. Our principles are few, and founded on the basis of our Constitution. Equality of Rights (not of property) is the object which we contend, and which we consider as the only security for our liberty and lives. 'Liberty or Death' is our motto, and we have sworn to return home in triumph, or return no more.

Soldiers – shall you plunge your bayonets into the bosoms of your fathers and brothers? Come then at once, to free your Country and your King from the power of those who have held them too long in thraldom.

We declare inviolable all public and private property in the present state of affairs and, during the continuation of so momentous a struggle, we earnestly request all of you to dissent from labour from and after this day, the 1st April, and wholly in the recovery of their rights; and consider it as the duty of every man not to recommence until he is in the possession of those rights which distinguish the free man from the slave – viz, that of giving the consent to the law by which he is governed. We, therefore, recommend the proprietors of Public Works, and all others, to stop the one and shut up the others until order is restored – as we will be accountable for no damage which may be sustained, and which, after this public information, they can have no claim to. And we hereby give notice to all those who shall be carrying arms against those who intend to regenerate their Country and restore its inhabitants to their native dignity.

We shall consider them as traitors to the Country, and enemies of the King – and treat them as such.

By Order of the Committee of Organization for the Formation of a Provisional Government – Glasgow, April 1st 1820.

APPENDIX XI

Scotland's International Accomplishments

Few people are fully aware of the significant contributions made by Scots to the international world – contributions which have helped to set the scene for modern life. This Appendix is by no means exhaustive but it will, I trust, give a good overview of some areas of invention and foundation where Scots have led their respective fields through the centuries. Readers will doubtless know of many examples which I have not included. However, all is embraced within the traditional saying:

Wha's like us?
Damn few, and they're a' deid!

The Englishman, in the home he calls his 'castle', slips into his favourite raincoat – patented by chemist Charles Mackintosh, from Glasgow, Scotland.

En route to his office, he strides along the English lane – surfaced by John Macadam of Ayr, Scotland.

He drives a British-made car, fitted with tyres invented by John Boyd Dunlop of Dreghorn, Scotland.

At the office, he receives his mail bearing adhesive stamps invented by James Chalmers of Dundee, Scotland.

During the day, he uses the telephone invented by Alexander Graham Bell, born in Edinburgh, Scotland.

At home in the evening, his daughter pedals her bicycle, invented by Kirkpatrick Macmillan, blacksmith of Dumfries, Scotland.

> He watches the news on TV, an invention of John Logie Baird of Helensburgh, Scotland, and hears an item about the United States Navy, founded by John Paul Jones of Kirkbean, Scotland.
>
> He has now been reminded too much of Scotland, and in desperation he picks up the Bible, only to find that the first man mentioned in the good book is a Scot, King James VI, born in Edinburgh Castle, Scotland, who authorized the translation.
>
> Nowhere can the Englishman turn to escape the ingenuity of the Scots. He could take to drink, but the Scots make the best in the world.
>
> He could take a rifle to end it all, but the breech-loading rifle was invented by Captain Patrick Ferguson of Pitfours, Scotland.
>
> If he escaped death, he might find himself on an operating table, injected with penicillin, discovered by Alexander Fleming of Darvel, Scotland, and given an anaesthetic discovered by Sir James Young Simpson of Bathgate, Scotland.
>
> Out of the anaesthetic, he would find no comfort in learning that he was as safe as the Bank of England, founded by William Paterson of Dumfries, Scotland.
>
> Perhaps his only remaining hope would be to get a transfusion of guid Scottish blood, which would entitle him to ask: 'Wha's like us?'.

Many Scots have the above legend somewhere at home, maybe hanging on a wall to remind visitors that the Scottish Nation has introduced more than a nominal creative share to the civilized world. But this well-known list is not the half of it. Just think of our other accomplishments:

In America

The *New York Herald* was founded by James Gordon Bennet (whence, the 'Gordon Bennet' expression), a native of Banffshire, Scotland.

The famous Pinkerton Detective Agency was founded by Allan Pinkerton (1819–84), born in Glasgow, Scotland.

The Rev John Witherspoon, a Scottish Presbyterian minister, born in Gifford, near Haddington, Scotland, was the only clergyman to sign the American Declaration of Independence, and was a founder of the institution that became Princeton University.

Robert Burns celebrated George Washington's birthday with an ode – and Washington himself had an ancestry back to William I the Lion of Scots.

Richard Oswald, born in Dumfriesshire, negotiated the Peace Treaty at the end of the War of Secession.

North Carolina's first Governor was the Scots-born William Drummond.

The American fir tree was identified in 1825 by David Douglas, born at Scone, in Scotland.

The first monument to Abraham Lincoln on Britain's side of the Atlantic is to be found in Edinburgh's Calton Cemetery.

An Ayrshire man, John Paul Jones (1747–97), founded the United States Navy.

In Canada

Brown and Gilmore, both from Scotland, founded Quebec's first newspaper.

Alexander Muir, born in 1830 at Lesmahagow, Scotland, composed both the words and music for *The Maple Leaf*.

Lord Strathcona (1820–1914), a Scot, pioneered the Canadian Pacific Railway.

The great Canadian River Fraser is called after Simon Fraser, a native of New York, born of Scottish parents.

The explorer Sir Alexander Mackenzie of Stornoway (1763–1820) gave his name to Canada's River Mackenzie.

It was the endowment of James McGill (1744–1813), born in Glasgow, which founded McGill University, Montreal – one of Canada's leading seats of learning.

Canada's first Prime Minister (Tory) was the Glasgow-born Sir John Macdonald (1815–91), and the second Prime Minister (Liberal) was Alexander Mackenzie (1822–92), born at Logierait, near Dunkeld, Scotland.

In Australia, New Zealand and Tasmania

Western Australia's capital is Perth – so-named after its Scottish counterpart.

New Zealand's financial capital is Dunedin – named after Edinburgh, the capital city of Scotland.

Brisbane, in Queensland, is named after the Scots-born general, Sir Thomas Macdougall Brisbane (1773–1860), of the Brisbanes of Bishopton, Scotland. He was a soldier and a talented astronomer, and strove to improve conditions for convicts by substituting useful labour for the treadmill, offering tickets of leave for good conduct. Brisbane also introduced many breeds of horse, wine, sugar cane and tobacco crops at his own expense, and became Governor of New South Wales.

The Macquarie Islands, 500 miles south-west of New Zealand, were named after Scots-born Lachlan Macquarie (1761–1824), who also became Governor of Australia's New South Wales in 1809. He retained this office for 12 years, during which time the city of Sydney was developed, and the town of Bathurst was founded in the Territory's interior. With intent to secure social equality for convicts with free settlers, Macquarie established civil courts and a bank.

The highest peak in Tasmania is called Ben Lomond, in remembrance of its Scottish namesake.

The foundations, which supported the development of the

Australian woollen industry, were laid by John Macarthur of Scottish ancestry.

The first Governor General of Australia was Lord Hopetoun (1860–1908), a Scotsman.

In France

Scots-born John Law established the first Bank of France, the 'Banque Generale', in 1716.

The famous 'Banner of Jeanne d'Arc' was painted by James Polwarth, a Scot.

The 'Garde Ecossaise' was a distinctly Scots Guard, retained as the private bodyguard of the Kings of France until the death of Louis XVIII.

Scots were granted French Nationality by Louis XII in 1515, and this legislation was effective until 1906 when the Westminster Parliament insisted that it should be rescinded.

John Stewart, Earl of Buchan (1380–1424), defeated the English at Baugé, and was appointed Constable of France.

The Stuart Dukes d'Aubignie were from a branch of the Royal House of Stewart; and the Douglas family held the title, Duke of Touraine, for three generations.

In India

In 1882 the geographer Sir William Hunter, a native of Dundee, Scotland, planned and implemented India's first national census.

Scotsman Alan Octavian Hume founded the Indian Congress Party which won India's independence in August 1947.

In Poland

Prince James Francis Edward Stuart married Maria Clementina Sobieska of Poland, the granddaughter of King Jan III. A few years earlier, Prince James (titular King James VIII of Scots) had been offered the Crown of Poland.

Poland's *Songs of Revolt* were written by the Scottish poet Thomas Campbell (1777–1844), who espoused the cause of Polish freedom.

In Russia

The Russian Navy was founded by Samuel Greig (1735–88), born in Scotland, and was largely manned with Scottish officers.

One of Peter the Great's Commanders-in-chief was Patrick Gordon of Aucheuchries in Buchan, the commander of Russia's successful campaign against the Turks.

The Tsars employed Scottish physicians for generations. Catherine the Great's physician was Scots-born Dr John Rogerson, while the Scotsman Dr James Wylie was Tsar Alexander I's personal physician, as well as being President of the St Petersburg and Moscow Medical Academies.

The Cameron Gallery can be found in the Royal Palace at St Petersburg, and it was established by Catherine the Great to commemorate the Scots in her service.

In the Nordic Kingdoms, Scandinavia and Finland

Scotland's Queen Margaret was the 'Maid of Norway'. Two Scottish Kings, James III and James VI, married Danish princesses.

In the 17th century, many Scots emigrated to Sweden in order to follow the banner of King Gustavus II Adolphus in the Thirty

Years War. When the war ended, thousands of Scots uprooted to become traders and merchants along the Baltic coast, and deep into Russia and Poland. Gothenburg was established as a trading base, and many of today's prominent families in Sweden can trade their ancestry from the Scots settlers.

One of these emigrant Scots was Robert Douglas, who became a Field Marshal in the Swedish Army. His grandson entered Russian service, and in 1717 was made Governor General of Finland by Peter the Great. By the 1800s, the head of the family, Count Ludvig Douglas, was a distinguished Foreign Minister, and his son was Commander-in-chief of the Swedish Army during the Second World War.

The Arts and Architecture

In 1763, an art school was founded in Glasgow by the brothers Robert and Andrew Foulis (1707–76 and 1712–75, respectively). This led to the founding of the Glasgow Academy of Fine Arts nine years before the Royal Academy came into being.

In the world of photography, David Octavius Hill (1802–70) was the first artist to use calotypes for portraiture on a large scale. The models would be lit by Hill, while his colleague Adamson developed and printed the negatives. Hill's camera-portraits are now treasured among the finest ever made.

Few outside Glasgow realize that the masterwork of Charles Rennie Mackintosh (1868–1928), the City Art College, is referred to as 'The Mother of Modern European Architecture'.

John Grierson, a Scot, was the founder of the British documentary film movement.

Following a visit to Staffa in 1829, Mendelssohn was inspired to write the world-famous *Fingal's Cave*.

The first grand piano was made by John Broadwood (1732–1812), a native of Edinburgh, who led the world in the manufacture of this instrument. Two of the greatest pianists of their era, Frederic Lamond (one of Liszt's last pupils) and Eugen d'Albert, were both from Glasgow.

Scotland can boast of the one song sung with enthusiasm throughout the world – a song suitable for every occasion: *Auld Lang Syne*. The *Skye Boat Song*, and numerous others, are also sung by Scots worldwide, and our pipe bands are a proud Scottish export.

The first war memorial in Britain, the Scottish National War Memorial at Edinburgh Castle, was designed by the Scotsman Sir Robert Stoddart Lorrimer (1864–1922). Coventry Cathedral was designed by Sir Basil Spence (1907–76), born in India of Scottish parents.

Banking and Finance

Banking today would amount to nothing were it not for Scotsmen. John Napier of Merchiston (1550–1617), born in Edinburgh Castle, invented both logarithms and the decimal point. The Bank of England was founded in 1694 by the Scotsman William Paterson (1658–1719), and the Bank of Scotland followed in 1695.

By 1746 Scotland had three chartered corporations engaged in banking with limited liability (England had, until 1996, only one). Scotland's banks pioneered in several directions, including: banking on the limited liability principle; the early adoption and extension of note issue to a point where gold and silver were practically redundant; the progressive elaboration of the branch agency concept; the introduction of cash credit (overdraft); the practice of payments of interest upon deposits; the early adoption of large-scale joint stock banking; exchange stabilization between Edinburgh and London; the banking practice of willingness to hold each other's notes in times of stress – a principle upheld by central banks in international fields.

The author of the social credit plan for reforms in the monetary system, advocating debt-free credit creation, was the Scotsman,

Major C H Douglas, probably the greatest economist of modern times.

Let us not forget that it was Adam Smith of Kirkcaldy (1723–90), author of *The Wealth of Nations*, who stated that 'Labour is the only universal, as well as the only accurate, measure of value – the only standard by which we can compare the relative values of commodities at all times and in all places'. In economic circles, Adam Smith is regarded as the 'Father of political economy'.

The first ever savings bank was instituted by the Rev Henry Duncan (1774–1846), born at Lochrutton, Kirkcudbrightshire, and established in 1810 at Ruthwell in Dumfries.

The father of the Investment Trust movement was Robert Fleming from Scotland.

The Prairie Cattle Company Limited, though Edinburgh based, was from Dundee, and was the first large-scale joint stock venture in Texas cattle ranching. Without Scottish financial involvement, there would have been no state of Texas.

By 1884, three-quarters of foreign aid and colonial investment companies were of Scottish origin.

Twenty-two years before the Rochdale co-operators owned their store in 1844, it was Alexander Campbell, from Kintyre, who was the first to advocate the Co-op dividend principle of distributing dividends on purchases at the Cambuslang Co-operative.

It was the Scottish philosopher David Hume (1711–76), considered to be one of the greatest philosophers, who wrote, 'To mortgage the public revenues, and to trust that posterity will pay off their incumbrances contracted by their ancestors, is madness'.

In 1970, Scotland managed to export beyond Britain goods and services to the worth of some £776m (about £148 per head of population) – a world record which, to date, Scotland has retained and surpassed, having given a surplus of £27 billion to the British Exchequer between 1979 and 1996.

Engineering, Maritime and Exploration

Scotland can also boast many great engineering achievements. Among the best-known works of Thomas Telford (1757–1834), a native of Eskdale, are the Caledonian Canal and the Menai Suspension Bridge, while his design for the high level Dean Bridge in Edinburgh was his last work before his retirement.

Born at Phantassie, East Lothian, was the Scottish civil engineer John Rennie (1761–1821), who engineered the Kennet, Avon, Rochdale and Lancaster canals. He designed and constructed the breakwater at Plymouth, built London's Waterloo Bridge, and also designed London Bridge, which was built after his death.

Born in Kelso, Sir William Fairbairn built the Conway and Menai tubular bridges in 1845. Another Kelso man, Sir James Brunlees, laid the first railway line across the Alps.

Spencer Wilkes, a resident of Islay, was the first President of the Rover Motor Company. Indeed, the Rover was first tested on the hills and beaches of Islay.

The Tay's second bridge and the Forth Railway Bridge were built by Sir William Arrol (1839–1913), born in Houston, Renfrewshire. The Railway Bridge, built between 1883 and 1890 on the cantilever principle, is 1½ miles long (*c*2.41k), of which one mile is spanned by the cantilevers. The main span is 1710ft (*c*521m), while the rail level stands 158ft (*c*48m) above high water. The Forth Road Bridge (built about three-quarters of a mile upstream between 1958 and 1964) is the largest suspension bridge in Europe, being over 1½ miles long (*c*2.4k) with approach viaducts, and the central span between the towers is 3,300ft long (*c*1,005m), standing 512ft (*c*155.5m) above mean river level, with headroom varying from 150 to 163ft (*c*45.6 to 49.6m).

The father of the famed 18th-century explorer, Captain James Cook, was a Scotsman who had settled in Yorkshire. Indeed Cook's Scottish origins may well have been the reason for his giving several of the islands which he discovered Scottish names, such as New Hebrides and New Caledonia.

The first white man to cross Australia, south to north in 1862, was John McDowell Stuart (1815–66) from Dysart, Fife. He achieved this on his third attempt.

Glasgow-born James Mollison made the first solo east–west crossing of the North Atlantic in 1931. The first solo circumnavigation of the world in a sailing vessel was made by Captain Chay Blyth of Hawick, who subsequently rowed across the Atlantic in 1966, together with John Ridgway.

The 19th-century missionary and explorer, Dr David Livingstone, was a Scot.

The first manned balloon ascent in Britain was made on 27 August 1784 by the Scotsman James Tyler.

King James IV created the Scottish Navy, and his descendant, Charles II, created the English Navy. By 1580 Scotland had sea laws compiled by Sir James Balfour, Lord President of the Court of Session (Scotland) – and Admiralty and maritime laws are based on this. Ten years later, William Welwood, Professor of Law at St Andrews University (who seemingly discovered the principle of the siphon in 1577), published *The Sea Laws of Scotland*.

The first two steam-boats in Europe were designed by Scotsmen: the *Charlotte Dundass* by William Symington (1763–1831), and the *Comet* (Europe's first sea-going steam-powered vessel, sailing between Glasgow and Oban) by Henry Bell (1767–1830), a native of Torpichen near Bathgate.

The largest private shipyard was established in Govan, and was owned by John Elder, a Glasgow marine engineer who was the first to experiment with, and adopt, compound steam engines. The *Marjorie*, built by William Denny on Clydeside, was the first steam-boat to cross the Channel, while the Clyde's first iron sea-going ship was built by the Glasgow shipbuilders Tod & MacGregor in 1837. Although an innovation, it was viewed with some scepticism by many at the time.

The first paddle-steamer to cross the Atlantic was the *Sirius*, built at Leith, near Edinburgh. A co-founder of the P&O Line

(Peninsula and Orient), the world's largest passenger line, was the Shetlander, Arthur Anderson, who subsequently became chairman of the company, and endowed the Educational Institute at Lerwick in 1862.

The first steamer on the River Thames was the *Margery*, built by William Denny & Brothers of Dumbarton – the same firm that built the first welded ship in Britain, the *Robert the Bruce*, in 1933. Apparently, the River Thames police force was founded by Scotsman Patrick Colquhoun.

Hugh Clapperton (1788–1827), who led the expeditions from Tripoli, across the Sahara to the River Niger and various parts of Nigeria, was born in Annan.

Dr Mungo Park (1771–1806), a qualified physician born at Foulshiels near Selkirk, went to Africa in 1795, and journeyed from Senegal to Niger, and from Gambia to Niger in 1805, drowning in the Niger at Boussa during an attack by natives.

James Bruce of Kinnaird (also known as 'of Abyssinia') was born in Stirlingshire. Having become Consul in Algiers in 1763, he ventured up the Nile in 1768 to reach Abyssinia, finding the sources of the Bahr-el-Azrek, or Blue Nile. His written account of his travels (published in five volumes in 1790) was considered so incredible by his peers that they accused him of writing fiction.

Inventions, Electronics and General

The vacuum flask (present-day Thermos) was invented by Sir James Dewar (1842–1923). Iron milk vessels came into use thanks to a Biar of the Shotts Iron Works. Charles Mackintosh of Glasgow (1766–1843) gave the world waterproof cloth; and the kaleidoscope was invented by Scotsman Sir Robert Brewster.

The hot-blast furnace, which revolutionized the iron industry, was invented by James B Neilson, while coal-gas lighting was invented by William Murdoch (1754–1839), born at Bellow Mill near Old Cumnock.

The Rev Patrick Bell of Carmylie, Forfarshire (1799–1869), invented the first reaping machine in about 1831, and his invention was followed in the USA by McCormick's reaper. It was Andrew Meikle (1719–1811), born at Houston Mill near Dunbar, who invented the threshing machine for removing husks from grain in 1788. In 1737 the winnowing machine was invented by Andrew Roper of Hawick.

The machine for making fishing nets was invented by James Paterson of Musselburgh, where the world's first factory to mechanically manufacture fishing-nets was founded.

It can be said that the Industrial Revolution was ushered in by 28-year-old James Watt (1736–1819), who was born in Greenock. He invented the first steam machine, while a Scotsman's grandson, George Stephenson, invented the steam locomotive.

James 'Paraffin' Young founded the world's first oil industry (the shale oil industry in Scotland's West Lothian) when he invented a successful way to manufacture paraffin. His patents were subsequently used to process oil when it was discovered in America.

The Scots were also the first to put academic sciences into the manufacture of chemicals for commercial sale, and the Scots funded Britain's first modern science-based industry in the shape of the chemical industry, one of the most versatile in the world.

Glasgow professor, William Thompson (1824–1907), later Lord Kelvin, made outstanding discoveries in thermodynamics, electricity and navigation. He laid the first Atlantic cable, and sent and received the first signals ever transmitted between Europe and America.

Scotsmen gave their names to two of the six basic international standards of measurement: the 'Watt' (unit of energy), and the 'Degree Kelvin' (unit of temperature). Both Alexander Graham Bell (1847–1922 : inventor of the telephone) and John Logie Baird (1886–1946 : inventor of the television) were born in Scotland – the former in Edinburgh, and the latter in Helensburgh.

Radio location, or as it is better known, Radar, was pioneered by Sir Robert Alexander Watson-Watt (1892–1973), and it was this which helped the Allied Forces to win the Second World War.

James Nasmyth (1808–90), born in Edinburgh, invented the steam hammer, probably the most important invention of its day. It was due to the Edinburgh citizen, James Clerk Maxwell (1831–79), and his researches into magnetism and electricity, that Heinrich Hertz' production of electricity waves and Guglielmo Marconi's wireless telegraphy came into being.

The linen printing industry was transformed into a machine trade by the invention of cylinder printing in 1783 by the Scotsman, Thomas Bell. The introduction of bronze coinage was due to Thomas Graham. 'Graham's Law' of colloid chemistry enunciating the law of gaseous diffusion, is named after him, while the discovery of both specific and latent heat, as well as the discovery of carbonic gas and the distinction between fixed and common air, was due to Joseph Black, a chemist of Scottish extraction born in Bordeaux, France.

One of the modern pioneers of the Town and Country Planning concept was Sir Patrick Geddes (1854–1933), born in Perth. The oldest post-medieval high tower flat can be found in Edinburgh.

Golf has been played in Scotland since the early 1400s. Although the Mecca of the game of golf is St Andrews, the world's oldest golf course is in Musselburgh. The first Golf International (Scotland versus England) was played at Leith Links under the patronage of King James VII.

The dates for John Boyd Dunlop (*see* page 385) are 1840–1921. Similarly, the dates for John MacAdam are 1756–1836.

Publishing and Literature

It was George Dalgarno, an Aberdonian, who invented the first artificial international language, published in 1651. The first circulating library (lending books for a small fee) was established in Edinburgh in 1725 by Allan Ramsay – and it was not until 1740 that a similar operation was begun in London.

The first rotary press was invented by Thomas Nelson from Edinburgh (1822–92), and it was exhibited by him at the International Exhibition of 1851. His idea was later adopted by John III Walter of the *London Times* – speaking of which, the *Glasgow Herald* is older than *The Times*, which was established in 1788.

The Glasgow Junior Chamber of Commerce is the largest in Europe, and the Glasgow Chamber of Commerce is the oldest in the Commonwealth.

It was Hugh Maxwell, a Scotsman, who invented the printer's roller, without which the printing industry would never have progressed. The renowned *Encyclopedia Britannica* was in origin a Scottish undertaking: Bell & MacFarquhar of Edinburgh published the first edition between 1768 and 1771, with William Smellie as Editor, and James Howe (the deaf-and-dumb son of a Stirling minister) was involved with the illustrations. Even the *New English Dictionary* was created by Sir James Augustus Henry Murray (1837–1915), born in Denholm. He also edited the sections A–D, H–K, O, P and T.

Sir Arthur Conan Doyle (1859–1930), the detective story novelist, was born in Edinburgh, where he studied medicine under Joseph Bell, who provided the prototype for the famous character Sherlock Holmes.

The author Thomas Carlyle (1795–1881) was born in the village of Ecclefechan in Dumfriesshire. The popular novels, *Treasure Island, Kidnapped, The Master of Ballantrae, Dr Jekyll and Mr Hyde*, and others were written by Robert Louis Stevenson of Edinburgh (1850–94). James Barrie (1860–1937), born at Kirriemuir, wrote the great children's play *Peter Pan*. Scotland's own bard, Robert Burns (1759–96), is a worldwide favourite, and declaimed every year is his *Address to a Haggis*. Sir Walter Scott (1771–1832) is said to have invented the concept of the historical novel.

Hugh MacDiarmid (died 1978) – who also wrote under the name of C M Grieve – is one of Scotland's most internationally acclaimed poets. Present-day Irvine Welsh (of *Trainspotting* fame) has become internationally known through the Hollywood film adaptations of his books.

The *Edinburgh Review*, founded in 1802, was the first critical and political review, and among its features were essays by England's Lord Macaulay (1800–59). The leading philosophical magazine, *Mind*, was founded by the Scottish philosopher Alexander Bain, while *The Economist* magazine was founded in 1843 by the Hawick economist and politician James Wilson.

The world's first-ever war correspondent was the Scotsman William Howard Russell, correspondent for *The Times* in the Crimean War.

Medicine

It is interesting to note that when King's College (now Aberdeen University) was founded in 1495, it included a Chair of Medicine – the first in Britain, more than 40 years before Cambridge, and nearly 50 years before Oxford followed suit.

Sir Charles Bell (1774–1842), born in Edinburgh, was the first investigator and author of *The Nervous System of the Human Body. Domestic Medicine,* the first English-language book of its kind, was written by William Duncan of Ancrum, Roxburghshire, and was published in 1769.

Born at Blantyre near East Kilbride, John Hunter (1728–93) is the acknowledged founder of modern surgery. Sir James Young Simpson (1811–70) introduced the use of chloroform in childbirth, gaining the displeasure of the Scottish clergy, who maintained that he was violating the divine will, and quoted to him from Genesis: 'I will greatly multiply thy sorrow and thy conception; in sorrow thou shalt bring forth children'. Undeterred, Simpson continued his work, and the first child born under chloroform was named Anaesthesia. Some 30,000 people attended Simpson's funeral – a great tribute to a great man.

It has previously been mentioned that Sir Alexander Fleming (1881–1955) discovered penicillin. However, he also discovered lysozyme, an anti-bacterial agent in tears and saliva.

The discovery of the malarial parasite by Sir Ronald Ross, of Scottish ancestry, laid the foundations for combating malaria. For his work in this field he won the Nobel Prize in 1902.

Although born in Essex, England, Lord Lister, a professor at Edinburgh and Glasgow Universities, worked at Glasgow Royal Infirmary, from where his findings on the cause and prevention of septic infection in wounds emanated. Insulin was isolated by Dunkeld-born Dr J R Macleod.

The ultimate brain surgery pioneer was Sir William McEwan, born in Rothesay, and by 1893 nineteen patients were recorded as having undergone operations for brain abscess treatment. Eighteen of these were cured and survived, whereas a 100 per cent mortality rate was otherwise generally recorded for the same condition.

Politics and Military

Up to 1 May 1707 and the Treaty of Union, Scotland had a Written Constitution – the *Declaration of Arbroath*. This dated back to 1320, and was the oldest written constitution in Europe. It proclaimed that the entire Community of the Realm of Scotland was born equal.

James Keir Hardie (1836–1915), born at Bellshill, was the founder of the Scottish Parliamentary Labour Party in 1888, and of the Independent Labour Party in 1893. In each case, the first words on the parties' agenda state: 'To promote the ideal of an independent Scotland'. At that time, neither party had any formal connection with the Trade Union movement. In 1900, all the socialist groups in Britain – the ILP, the Fabian Society, and the Social Democrat Federation – joined in representation with the Trade Unions, and set up the Labour Representation Committee, electing James Ramsay Macdonald (later Prime Minister) as its first Secretary.

The 1906 election saw 29 LRC candidates elected out of the 50 who stood, and the Labour Party was born.

Britain's first constitutionally recognized Prime Minister was Sir Henry Campbell-Bannermann, a Glasgow draper and subsequently Lord Provost of Glasgow. Scotland has, in fact, given Britain six Prime Ministers: Arthur James Balfour (held office 1902–5), Sir Henry Campbell-Bannerman (1905–8), Andrew Bonar Law (1922–3), James Ramsay Macdonald (1924; 1929–31; 1931–5), Sir Harold Macmillan (1957–63), and Sir Alec Douglas Hume (1963–4).

The oldest active military regiment in Britain, and probably the oldest in Europe, is the Royal Scots – the first regiment of foot. This evolved from regiments in French service, and was variously known as the Regiment d'Hebron, the Regiment de Douglas, the Douglas Ecossais, the Earl of Dumbarton's Regiment of Foot, the Royal Regiment of Foot, the Lothian Regiment, and (due to its antiquity) was often referred to as Pontius Pilate's bodyguard.

In the years 1797 to 1837, Skye alone gave to the British Army 21 Lieutenant-Generals, 48 Lieutenant-Colonels, 600 majors, captains and subalterns, and around 10,000 private soldiers. During the same period, Skye also provided for the Civil Service, a Governor General of India, four governors of colonies, a chief baron of England, and a Lord of Session. In fact, the Duke of Wellington might not have defeated Napoleon's army at Waterloo were it not for the Scots regiments.

Two eminent Scots held the highest posts during the Second World War. They were Air Chief Marshal Sir Hugh Dowding (Head of Fighter Command), born in Moffat, Dumfriesshire, and Marshal of the Royal Air Force, Arthur William Tedder, born at Glenguin in Stirling. He was the Deputy Supreme Commander of the Allied Expeditionary Forces under America's General Dwight Eisenhower.

* * *

I trust that these examples will serve to remind all Scots, at home and abroad, that Scotland is perfectly well-equipped to become an independent Nation once again.

APPENDIX XII

Model for a Scottish Written Constitution
Based on European examples with a working Constitutional Monarchy

The following Constitutional model is a document which I would recommend all Scots, particularly those at home, to study in depth. It offers far more to the Scottish Nation and people than has ever been afforded or proposed by any of the political parties operative in Scotland.

Please note that a House of Lords is not included within this Constitutional framework. It has been replaced by a system whereby the electorate is afforded the opportunity to fully participate in legislative matters relating to the political affairs of Scotland. There is, in fact, nothing quite like this conceptual Written Constitution existing anywhere in Europe. It is a unique document which would safeguard the civil rights and liberties of all Scots and others residing in Scotland from the less constructive legislation emanating from either Brussels or Strasburg.

The modern concept of government is one which facilitates an enhancement of people's lifestyles within and without the working environment. This can only be achieved if the various aspects of legislative power are properly defined so as to uphold this enhancement from one generation to the next. In so doing, we can ensure that the revenue from Scotland's direct and indirect resources is distributed far more equitably than has been the case to date.

Title 1: ON SCOTLAND – COMPONENTS AND TERRITORIES

Article 1

Scotland is a State made up of Constituencies, Regions and Districts.

Article 2

Scotland is made up of 72 Constituencies within 12 Regions and their inherent Districts.

Title 2: ON THE SCOTS AND THEIR RIGHTS

Article 3

The title of 'Scot' is held by birthright, and may otherwise be acquired, preserved and lost according to rules determined by Civil Law.

The Constitution, and the other laws relative to political rights, determine which are, apart from this title, the necessary conditions for the exercise of these rights.

Article 4

Naturalization is accorded by the Legislative Power.

Article 5

Scots citizens are equal before the Law. They alone are eligible for civil and military service, but for the exceptions which could be made by law for special cases.

Article 6

Enjoyment of the rights recognized for Scots should be ensured without discrimination. To this end, laws and decrees guarantee notably the rights and freedoms of ideological and philosophical minorities.

Article 7

Individual freedom is guaranteed.

No one can be prosecuted except in the cases provided for by Scots Law, and in the form prescribed by Scots Law.

Article 8

No punishment can be made or given except in pursuance of the Law.

Article 9

The domicile is inviolable. No unauthorized or unsolicited visit to the inhabitant's residence can take place except in the cases provided for by Scots Law, and in the form prescribed by Scots Law.

Article 10
No one can be deprived by the State of his or her property except in the case of expropriation for a public purpose, in the cases and manner established by Scots Law, and in return for a fair indemnity paid beforehand.

Article 11
Criminal punishment by confiscation of assets is not lawful. Requisition of assets is confined to Court Orders concerning indebtedness.

Article 12
Civil death (capital punishment) is abolished. It cannot be brought back into force.

Article 13
Freedom of worship, public practice of the latter, as well as freedom to demonstrate one's opinions on all matters, are guaranteed, except for offences contrary to Scots Law committed when using this freedom.

Article 14
No one can be obliged to contribute in any way whatsoever to the acts and ceremonies of a religion against his or her will.

Article 15
The State does not have the right to intervene either in the nomination or in the installation of ministers of any religion whatsoever, nor to forbid these ministers from corresponding with their superiors, from publishing their acts, except, in the latter case, taking into consideration normal responsibilities in matters of press and publication.

Article 16
Everyone has the right to the respect of his or her private and family life, except in the cases and conditions determined by Scots Law.

Article 17
Everyone has the right to lead a life in conformity with human dignity. To this end, the laws, decrees and rulings guarantee – taking into account corresponding obligations, economic, social and cultural rights – and determine the conditions for exercising them.

These rights include notably:

i The right to employment and to a free choice of professional activity in the framework of a general employment policy with a minimum wage structure;

ii A level of employment that is as stable and high as possible. The right to fair terms of employment and to fair remuneration. Also, the right to information, consultation and collective negotiation;
iii The right to belong to an independent, non-politically affiliated Trade Union, lawfully established to assist the personal and financial well-being of members;
iv The right to social security, to health care, and to social, medical and legal aid;
v The right to have decent accommodation. Homelessness is to be abolished as soon as such abolition can be effectively and financially implemented by Scots Law;
vi The right to enjoy the protection of a healthy environment;
vii The right to enjoy cultural and social fulfilment.

Article 18

State Education is free, and will be maintained at a high standard.

The Community of the Realm of Scotland sustains the concept of schooling based on a broad religious proclivity of parents.

If a Regional or District organizing authority wishes to delegate competency in one of several autonomous bodies, it can only do so by decree adopted by a two-thirds majority vote of councillors.

Everyone has the right to education with the respect of fundamental rights and freedoms. Access to State education is free until the end of obligatory school age.

Article 19

The Press is free, but must adhere to the provisions of a Privacy Clause respecting the rights of private and family life of every individual within the confines of the Realm of Scotland.

Article 20

Scots have the right to gather peaceably and without arms, in conformity with the laws that regulate the exercise of this right.

Open-air meetings are entirely subject to police regulations.

Article 21

Everyone has the right to address petitions, signed by one or more persons, to the public authorities.

Constituted bodies are alone able to address petitions in a collective name.

Article 22

The confidentiality of letters is inviolable unless believed to threaten the security of the State.

The Law determines which nominated representatives can violate the confidentiality of letters entrusted to the postal service.

Article 23
Civil Servants must be indemnified by insurance related to professional liability, excepting the Armed Forces.

Article 24
No prior authorization is necessary to take legal action against Civil Servants because of their public office, except with regard to what has been ruled concerning Government Ministers and members of local governments.

Article 25
Everyone has the right to consult any administrative document and to have a copy made, except in the cases and conditions stipulated by Scots Law.

Title 3: ON POWER
Article 26
i All power emanates from the Nation with whom Sovereignty rests;
ii National Sovereignty is upheld, represented and observed by the Constitutional Monarch, the King or Queen of Scots.

Article 27
The State authority only has power in matters that are formally attributed to it by the Constitution and the laws carried in pursuance of the Constitution itself.

Article 28
The Legislative Power is exerted collectively by the King or Queen of Scots, the Citizens' Estate and the Privy Council.

Article 29
The Executive Power, as stipulated by the Constitution, belongs to the King or Queen of Scots, Guardian of the Realm.

Article 30
Local Government structure is created by Scots Law. It cannot be changed until a majority of those voting in a National Referendum give such leave.

Article 31
Judiciary Power is free from Executive influence, and can only be influenced by legislation.

Rulings and court decisions are carried out in the name of the King or Queen of Scots, Guardian of the Realm.

Article 32
Interests which are exclusively of a District or Regional nature are as defined by legislation, and as according to the principles established by the Constitution.

Section I: ON THE CITIZENS' ESTATE

Article 33
The members of the Citizens' Estate are elected directly by citizens who have attained the age of 18, and do not fall within the categories of exclusion stipulated by Scots Law.

Each elector has the right to only one vote.

Article 34
The establishing of the constituencies or electoral colleges of the Privy Council is governed by Scots Law.

Elections regarding the Citizens' Estate are carried out by the system of Proportional Representation that the Law determines.

The ballot is voluntary and secret.

Article 35
The Citizens' Estate is made up of 144 members.

Proportional Representation has a single transferrable vote in multi-member constituencies to facilitate voters' own preferential selection of candidates.

The Law determines the electoral constituencies. It also determines the conditions required to be an elector, as well as those for carrying out of electoral operations.

Article 36
To be eligible, one must:

i be a Scottish citizen;
ii enjoy all civil and public rights;
iii have attained the age of 18;
iv be a legally eligible resident in Scotland.

No other conditions of eligibility can be required.

Article 37

The members of the Citizens' Estate are elected for five years.

The House is renewed every five years.

Article 38

Each member of the Citizens' Estate benefits from an annual salary to be determined from time to time.

Members of the Citizens' Estate are allowed no additional fee or salary-paying employment, so as to ensure there will be no vested interests contrary to their publicly elected roles.

Members have the right to free travel on all means of transport operated or contracted by the State.

Members also have the right to travel expenses when using other transport on State business.

Members who are suspended through allegation of misconduct will be suspended without pay until their name is cleared by Law, at which time full retrospective salary will be reinstated.

Section II: ON THE PRIVY COUNCIL

Article 39

The Privy Council is made up of 100 Privy Councillors.

The Privy Council is an advisory body, free from party politics, with the right to initiate legislation which must be referred to the Citizens' Estate, and can only become law when passed by the Citizens' Estate.

The Privy Council has the right to revise legislation, and to refer it back to the Citizens' Estate for acceptance.

Each Privy Councillor represents an interest according to his or her Electoral College.

Article 40

In order to be appointed as Privy Councillor by the Electoral Colleges one must:

i be a Scottish citizen;
ii enjoy civil and political rights;
iii have attained the age of 18;
iv be a legally eligible resident in Scotland.

Article 41

Privy Councillors do not receive a State salary.

They do have the right to be reimbursed for any related expenses, and to be compensated for any loss of income caused by Privy Council duties.

They also have the right to free travel on all means of transport operated or contracted by the State.

Title 4: ON LEGISLATIVE POWER

Article 42

Legislative Power is jointly exercised by the King or Queen of Scots, the Citizens' Estate and the Privy Council for:

i The granting of naturalization;
ii Laws relative to the civil and penal responsibilities of the Government Ministers;
iii State budgets and accounts;
iv The establishment of Armed Forces quotas.

Article 43

Each branch of the Legislative Power has the right of initiative.

Draft Bills submitted at the King or Queen's initiative are brought to the Citizens' Estate, then forwarded to the Privy Council.

Draft Bills relating to the approval of Treaties submitted on the King or Queen's initiative are introduced to the Privy Council, and afterwards transmitted to the Citizens' Estate.

Article 44

A draft Bill may be adopted only after having been voted on article by article.

The Citizens' Estate and Privy Council have the right to amend and to sub-divide those articles and amendments proposed.

Article 45

A parliamentary consultation Commission, composed on an equal basis of members of the Citizens' Estate and the Privy Council, settles competency conflicts which may arise between them and may, with mutual agreement, extend the study periods at all times.

Lacking majority representation by either of the two groups comprising the Commission, the latter must statute on a two-thirds majority basis.

A law determines the composition and functioning of the Commission, in addition to a method of calculating the time periods.

Article 46

The authoritative interpretation of Scottish laws remains the sole competency of the Scots Judiciary and the Scots judicial system.

Title 5: ON THE CONSTITUTIONAL MONARCHY AND THE GOVERNMENT

Section I: ON THE KING OR QUEEN OF SCOTS – GUARDIAN OF THE REALM

Article 47

The Monarch's constitutional powers are hereditary through the direct, natural and legitimate male descent from King James VI Stewart. Failing that, by female descent.

A qualifying descendant who marries without the King or Queen's consent or, in the absence thereof, without the consent of those exercising the Monarch's powers in cases provided for by the Constitution, shall be deprived of rights to the Crown.

His or her lost rights may nonetheless be re-established by the King or Queen of Scots. Or in the absence thereof, by those exercising the Monarch's powers in cases provided for by the Constitution, in the event of agreement on the part of the Citizens' Estate and the Privy Council.

Article 48

The King or Queen of Scots may not act as Head of another State.

Article 49

The Monarch's sovereign person is inviolable.

Article 50

The Civil List for the duration of each reign is established by the Citizens' Estate.

The Monarch is accountable to the Exchequer.

Article 51

Upon the King or Queen's death, the Citizens' Estate and the Privy Council meet without convocation ten days following the decease at latest. Should either have been previously dissolved, and should the convocation in the Dissolution Act have been made for a time later than the tenth day following the decease, then the Citizens' Estate and Privy council are to return to their functions until the establishment of those destined to replace them.

From the moment of the Monarch's death, and until the taking of Oath by his or her successor to the Throne, or by the Regent, the Monarch's constitutional powers are to be exercised, in the name of the Sovereign People, by the Committee of the Articles, and under its responsibility.

Article 52
The King or Queen of Scots attains his or her majority on attainment of his or her 18th year of age.

The Monarch may accede to the throne only after having taken the following Oath of Fealty before the united Citizens' Estate and Privy Council:

'I, ..., ...th of my name, King/Queen of Scots, Guardian of the Realm of Scotland, do swear to uphold and observe the Constitution, laws, civil rights and liberties of the Scottish Nation and People; to preserve our national independence, and to protect Scotland's territorial integrity.'

Article 53
Should upon the Monarch's death, his or her successor be under age, the Citizens' Estate and Privy Council will meet as a single assembly, for the purpose of Regency and guardianship.

Article 54
Should the King or Queen of Scots be unable to reign, the Committee of the Articles, having observed this inability, will immediately summon the Citizens' Estate and the Privy Council, to provide Regency and guardianship in unity.

Article 55
Regency may be conferred on only one person, preferably of the Royal House if of age.

The Regent may take office only after having sworn the Oath as specified.

Article 56
Should the Throne become vacant, the Citizens' Estate and Privy Council, debating as one assembly, temporarily ensure regency until their reconvening. This meeting must take place within two months. The new House and Council, debating as one assembly, will provide permanent cover for the vacancy.

Section II: ON THE GOVERNMENT

Article 57
The King or Queen of Scots appoints and dismisses his or her Government and Cabinet in consultation with the Lord High Chancellor, High Commissioners and Commissioners of the Committee of the Articles.

The Government offers its resignation to the Monarch if the Citizens' Estate, by an absolute majority of its members, adopts a motion of disapproval, proposing to the King or Queen the nomination of a successor to the Lord High Chancellor, or proposes the nomination of a successor within three days of the rejection of a motion of confidence. The Monarch names the proposed successor as Lord High Chancellor, who takes office the moment the new Government is sworn in.

Article 58
Scots resident in Scotland may alone be Government Ministers. The term 'Scot' relates to Constitution Article 3.

Article 59
No immediate member of the Royal Family may be a Government Minister.

Article 60
The Inner and Outer Committees, being the Government Ministers, including the Cabinet, consist of 16 members at most.

Article 61
Government Ministers have access to the Citizens' Estate and the Privy Council, and must be heard whenever they so request.

The Citizens' Estate may demand the presence of Government Ministers. The Privy Council may request their presence for discussion of a motion or draft Bill, or for the exercise of its right to investigate.

For other matters, the Privy Council may request Government Ministers' presence.

Article 62
High Commissioners and Commissioners are responsible before the Citizens' Estate. None may be prosecuted or pursued on account of opinions expressed in the line of duty.

Article 63
The Citizens' Estate has the right to accuse Government Ministers and to confront them before the Judicial Supreme Court of Appeal; the latter alone having authority to judge them, Chambers assembled, except for that which is statuted by Law, regarding the exercising of a civil suit by a victimized party, and regarding crimes and misdeeds which Government Ministers may have committed outside their line of duty.

Cases of responsibility are determined by Scots Law, as are the sentences and the manner of proceeding against them, either on the basis of accusations introduced in the Citizens' Estate or on the basis of a civil suit emanating from a victimized party.

Title 6: ON TEMPORARY DISPOSITION

Until being covered by the law hitherto described, the Citizens' Estate holds discretionary powers to accuse a Government Minister, and the Supreme Court of Appeal to judge him or her in those cases established by penal laws and by the application of those sentences foreseen.

Article 64

The King or Queen of Scots, on consultation, appoints and dismisses Secretaries of State.

The latter are members of the Government. They are not part of the Council of Ministers. They are deputies to the Ministers.

The Monarch determines their attributions and the limits within which they may engage in countersigning.

Constitutional provisions which apply to Government Ministers apply equally to Secretaries of State.

Section III: ON RESPONSIBILITIES

Article 65

Neither King nor Queen of Scots has powers other than those formally attributed to him or her by the Constitution, and by the specific laws established by virtue of the Constitution.

Article 66

No actions of the Monarch may take effect without the countersignature of a Government Minister who, in so doing, takes the responsibility upon himself.

Article 67

The King or Queen of Scots bestows ranks within the Armed Forces.

He or she appoints individuals to general administrative functions and to Foreign Affairs, but for those exceptions established by Scots Law.

He or she appoints individuals to other functions only by virtue of specific provisions of a law.

Article 68

The King or Queen of Scots establishes regulations and decrees required for the execution of laws, without ever having the power to either suspend the laws themselves, or to dispense from their execution.

He or she has, however, the right of advice at weekly meetings with the Lord High Chancellor.

Article 69
The Monarch sanctions and promulgates laws as presented by the Citizens' Estate.

He or she has the right to annul or reduce sentences pronounced by Judges, in accordance with the advice of a Parole Board, except for that which is statuted relative to Government Ministers and members of Regional and District Governments.

Article 70
The King or Queen of Scots may mint money in keeping with the Scots Law.

Article 71
The King or Queen of Scots may confer titles of nobility, while remaining unable to attach privileges to the latter.

Article 72
The King or Queen of Scots may give military orders within the limits prescribed by Scots Law.

Article 73
The present power of the Lord Lyon, King of Arms, remains inviolable, as do the powers of the Baronial Council of Scotland and the Scottish Council of Chiefs.

Title 7: ON REGIONAL AND DISTRICT COUNCILS

Article 74
The Councils are composed of elected representatives.

Each Regional and District Council is composed of members elected directly as members of the concerned District Council, or as members of a Regional Council.

Article 75
Council members are elected for a period of five years.

Council elections take place every five years.

Article 76
Elections, as well as the compositions and functioning of Councils, are fixed by Scots Law.

Article 77
The Councils establish by law:

i Cultural issues;

ii Education, with the exception of the:
 a determination of the beginning and end of mandatory school age;
 b minimum standards for the grading of diplomas.

Title 8: ON JUDICIARY POWER

Article 78
Courts hold exclusive competency with respect to conflicts involving Civil Rights issues.

Article 79
The Scottish Judiciary Power is inviolable.

Title 9: ON REGIONAL AND DISTRICT INSTITUTIONS

Article 80
Regional and District institutions are governed by Scots Law.
 The Law applies the following principles:

i The direct election of Regional and District Council members;
ii The attribution to Regional and District Councils all that which is in the Regional or District interest, without prejudice to the approval of their actions in cases and following that manner determined by Scots Law;
iii The decentralization of attributions in favour of Regional and District institutions;
iv The publicizing of Regional and District Council meetings within the limits established by Scots Law;
v The publicizing of accounts and budgets;
vi The intervention of overseeing authorities or of the legislative power, to prevent violations of the Law or harm to public interests.

Article 81
The drafting of Civil Acts, and maintenance of registers being exclusively to the attributions of District authorities.

Title 10: ON INTERNATIONAL RELATIONS

Article 82
The King or Queen of Scots, in consultation, manages international relations, without prejudice to the ability of Districts and Regions to engage in international co-operation, including the signature of

Treaties, for those matters within their responsibilities as established by the Constitution and in virtue thereof.

The Monarch commands the Armed Forces, and determines the state of War and the cessation of hostilities. He or she notifies the Citizens' Estate and the Privy Council as soon as State interests and security permit, and adds those messages deemed appropriate.

Article 83
The King or Queen of Scots concludes Treaties, which may take effect only following the approval of the Citizens' Estate and the Privy Council.

Article 84
The Citizens' Estate and Privy Council are informed from the beginning of negotiations concerning any revision of the Treaties establishing the European Union, in addition to Treaties and Acts which may have modified or completed the latter. They are aware of the planned Treaty prior to signature.

Title 11: ON FINANCE

Article 85
Taxes to the benefit of the State may be imposed only by virtue of Scots Law.

The Law determines those exceptions of proven necessity.

The Law can suppress the taxes either wholly or partially.

Article 86
A Tax may be established by a Region only following Council decision.

The Law determines those exceptions of proven necessity.

The Law can suppress the taxes either wholly or partially.

Article 87
Taxes to the benefit of the Nation State are agreed on an annual basis by the Government.

Rules which determine them remain valid for one year if they are not renewed.

Article 88
No privileges with regard to taxes can be established except by Scots Law.

Article 89
Each year the Citizens' Estate rules on the approval of State accounts, and votes on the National Budget.

The Citizens' Estate and the Privy Council establish their respective allocations on an annual basis.

All State receipts and expenditure must be included in the National Budget, and included in the accounts.

Article 90

Under no circumstances may a pension for State services be attributed other than by sole virtue of a law.

Article 91

i Members of the State Audit Office are nominated by the Citizens' Estate for a duration established by Scots Law. The Office is established by Scots Law;

ii This Office is responsible for the examination and for the liquidation of general administration accounts working for the Public Treasury. It must see that no budgetary item is surpassed, and that no transfers take place;

iii The Office also oversees operations relative to the establishment and to the perception of State income, including tax collection. It establishes the accounts of the various State administrations, and is responsible in this regard for the collection of all required information and accounting items;

iv General accounts of the State are submitted to the Citizens' Estate with State Audit Office observations;

v The Scottish Banking System is inviolable unless changed through legislation.

Title 12: ON THE ARMED FORCES AND POLICE FORCE

Article 92

Armed Forces recruitment methods are determined by Scots Military Law. The Law also establishes matters of promotion, and the rights and obligations of military personnel.

Article 93

Military quotas are voted annually. The law establishing them remains valid for one year if not renewed meanwhile, but it is annually established in any event.

Article 94

The organization and procedures of the Police are the subject of a law.

Article 95

Under no circumstances may foreign troops be admitted within the service of the State, or occupy or cross through the territory other than on the sole basis of Scots Law.

Article 96
Military personnel may be deprived of rank, honours and pensions only in the manner described by Scots Law.

Title 13: GENERAL DISPOSITIONS

Article 97
i The Constitution may not be wholly or partially suspended;
ii All legislations emanating from the Parliament of the European Union deemed to impeach or violate the Constitution of the Community of the Realm of Scotland may be rejected and amended by the Citizens' Estate so as to protect the sovereign rights of the Scottish Nation and people.

Article 98
Constitutional texts are established in English and Scots Gaelic.

Article 99
All foreigners on Scottish soil benefit from that protection provided to persons and property, save for those exceptions provided for by Scots Law.

Article 100
The Scottish Nation adopts the Saltyre Cross as its national flag.

The Coat of Arms depicts the motto: *Nemo Me Impune Lacessit* (No one touches me with impunity).

Article 101
The City of Edinburgh is the capital of Scotland, and the headquarters of the Government.

Title 14: ON THE REVISION OF THE CONSTITUTION

Article 102
The Legislative Power has the right to declare a warranted constitutional revision of those matters which it determines.

Following such a declaration, the Citizens' Estate and the Privy Council are dissolved by full right. They are reconvened anew.

The Citizens' Estate and Privy Council statute of common accord with the King or Queen of Scots on those points submitted for revision.

In such case, the Citizens' Estate and Privy Council may debate only provided that two-thirds of the membership of each are present. No change may be adopted unless voted on by a two-thirds majority.

Article 103

No constitutional revision may be undertaken or pursued during times of war, or when the Citizens' Estate and/or Privy Council are presented from meeting freely on State territory.

Article 104

During a Regency, no changes may be brought to the Constitution regarding the Constitution or the constitutional powers of the Scottish Monarch.

Article 105

Under no circumstances may a written or verbal order from the King or Queen of Scots diminish the responsibilities of a Government Minister.

APPENDIX XIII

Constitutional Structure

For an Independent Democratic Scottish Government

Permanent Officers

Lord Chamberlain

Auditor General

The Monarch or Guardian of the Realm

Constitutional with Privy Council

The Scottish Academy

Advisory and Honorary Council

Membership awarded for services to Scotland
Specialists for advice, research commissions, etc
Standing Committees with Legal and Constitutional expertise

Lord High Chancellor

Committee of the Articles

GOVERNMENT

The Inner Committee

Lord High Commissioners

(A)	(B)	(C)	(D)
TREASURY	**HOME AFFAIRS**	**FOREIGN AFFAIRS**	**DEFENCE**

Responsible to the Lord High Chancellor

Armed Forces	European Affairs
(D)	(C)
Scottish Affairs	Trade
(A)	(C)

The Outer Committee

High Commissioners

Highlands and Islands	Agriculture Forestry & Fisheries	Post & Telecom-munications	Art Schools & Education	Health & Social Services	Employment & Industrial Development	Research & Technology	Transport
(B)	(B)	(B)	(B)	(B)	(B)	(B)	(B)

PARLIAMENT

Chairman of the Assembly

Estate Convener

The Citizens' Estate

Public Commissioners

The Community of the Realm

Rights of Franchise to all Adult Residents

Proportional Representation with Single Transferable Vote in multi-member constituencies to facilitate voters' own preferential selection of party candidates

NATIONAL ASSEMBLY

APPENDIX XIV

Additional Genealogical Charts

The amount of material contained in this particular Appendix might be regarded by some as excessive. However, no book has so far published for public consumption the full genealogical details of the Royal House of Stewart. It is considered important, therefore, to make this Appendix as complete as possible, so as to support and enhance the lineage charts within the main text.

While few of Europe's royal houses allowed their daughters to marry into the aristocracy, landed gentry, or the mercantile world, the Royal House of Scotland was an exception to the rule, thereby identifying itself as a monarchy *of* the people *for* the people.

Many people of Scottish descent will find themselves to be in a lineage from Robert II, Robert III, James I, James II, or the various natural children of James IV and James V. As such, they will be connected to the Stuart Kings of Britain, and can therefore be considered indirectly collateral to myself and the thousands of legitimate descendants from James VI. Furthermore, it will be recognized that their ancestry is rather more complex than is generally supposed, for the blood of the majority of Scots has become quite cosmopolitan through the ages.

The Native Kings of Britain

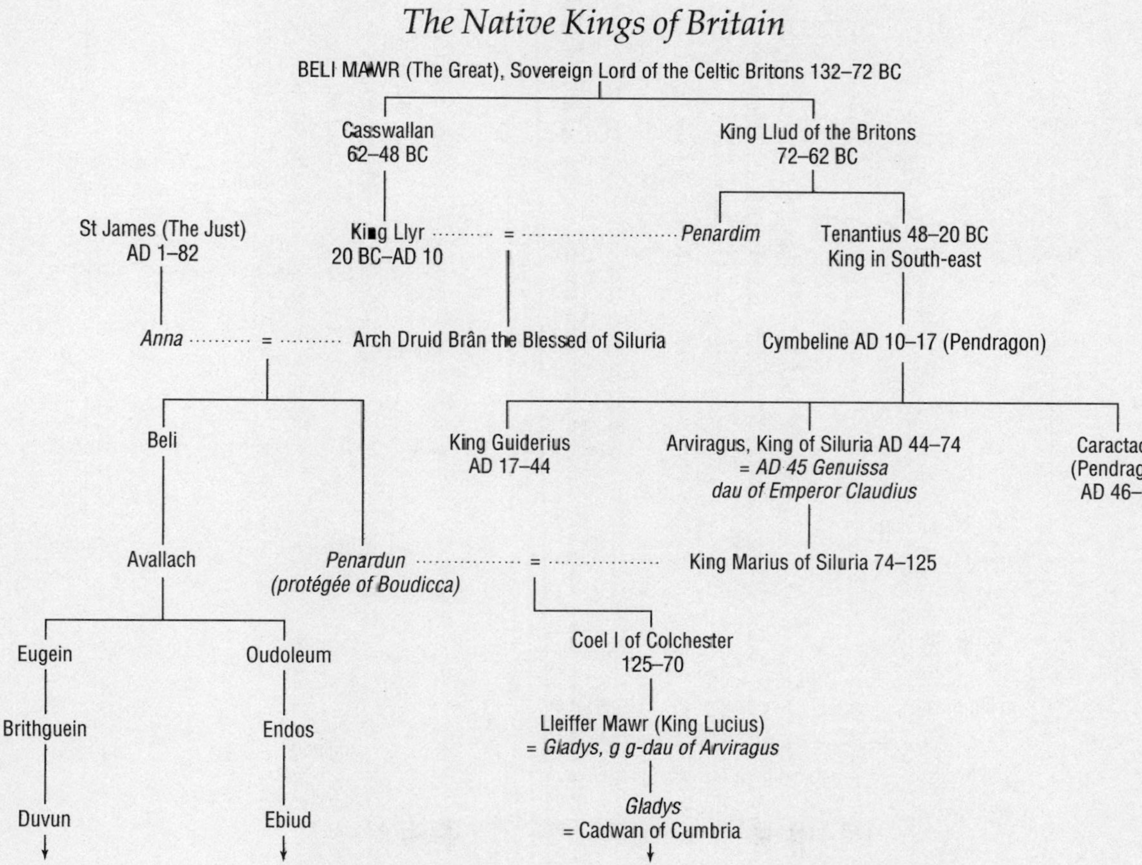

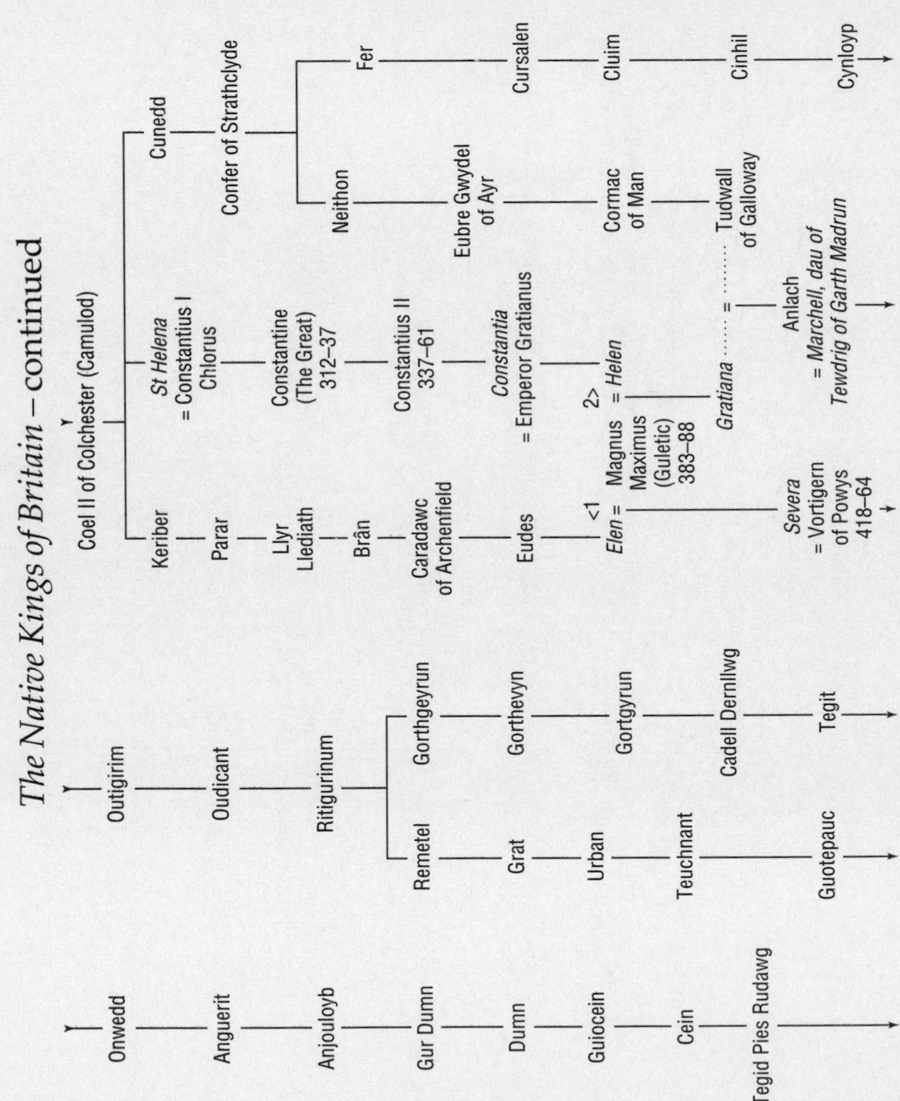
The Native Kings of Britain – continued
Onwedd
Anguerit
Anjouloyb
Gur Dumn
Dumn
Guiocein
Cein
Tegid Pies Rudawg
Outigirim
Oudicant
Ritigurinum
Remetel
Grat
Urban
Teuchnant
Guotepauc
Gorthgeyrun
Gorthevyn
Gortgyrun
Cadell Dernllwg
Tegit
Coel II of Colchester (Camulod)
Keriber
Parar
Llyr Llediath
Brân
Caradawc of Archenfield
Eudes
Elen = Magnus Maximus (Guletic) 383–88
<1
2>
= Helen
Severa = Vortigern of Powys 418–64
St Helena = Constantius I Chlorus
Constantine (The Great) 312–37
Constantius II 337–61
Constantia = Emperor Gratianus
Gratiana .... = ... Tudwall of Galloway
Anlach = Marchell, dau of Tewdrig of Garth Madrun
Cunedd
Confer of Strathclyde
Neithon
Eubre Gwydel of Ayr
Cormac of Man
Fer
Cursalen
Cluim
Cinhil
Cynloyp

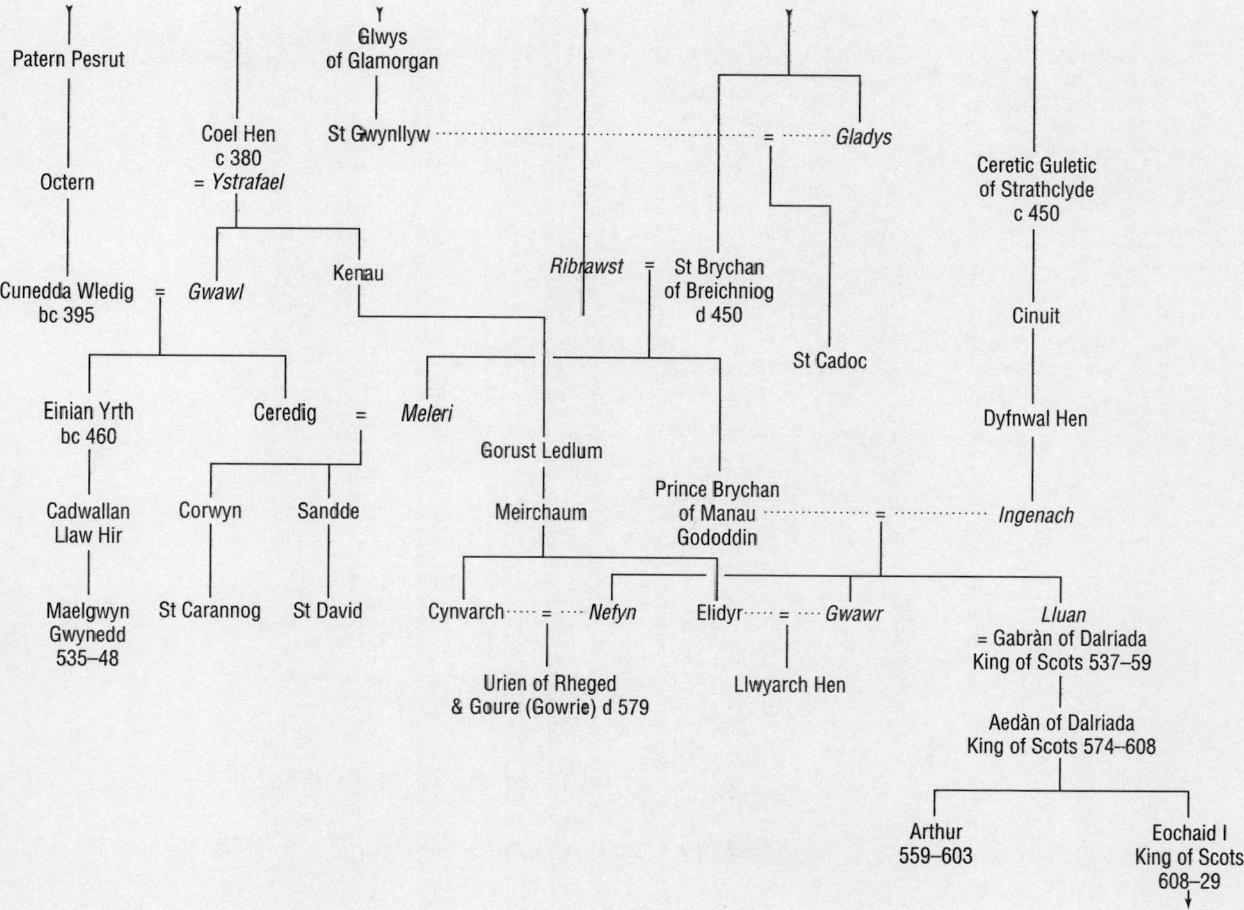
Patern Pesrut
Octern
Cunedda Wledig
bc 395
= *Gwawl*
Coel Hen
c 380
= *Ystrafael*
Kenau
Glwys
of Glamorgan
St Gwynllyw
= *Gladys*
Ribrawst
= St Brychan
of Breichniog
d 450
St Cadoc
Ceretic Guletic
of Strathclyde
c 450
Cinuit
Dyfnwal Hen
Ingenach
Prince Brychan
of Manau
Gododdin
Einian Yrth
bc 460
Ceredig
= *Meleri*
Gorust Ledlum
Meirchaum
Cadwallan
Llaw Hir
Corwyn
Sandde
Maelgwyn
Gwynedd
535–48
St Carannog
St David
Cynvarch
= *Nefyn*
Elidyr
= *Gwawr*
Lluan
= Gabràn of Dalriada
King of Scots 537–59
Urien of Rheged
& Goure (Gowrie) d 579
Llwyarch Hen
Aedàn of Dalriada
King of Scots 574–608
Arthur
559–603
Eochaid I
King of Scots
608–29

Descent to Margaret Atheling, wife of Malcolm III of Scots

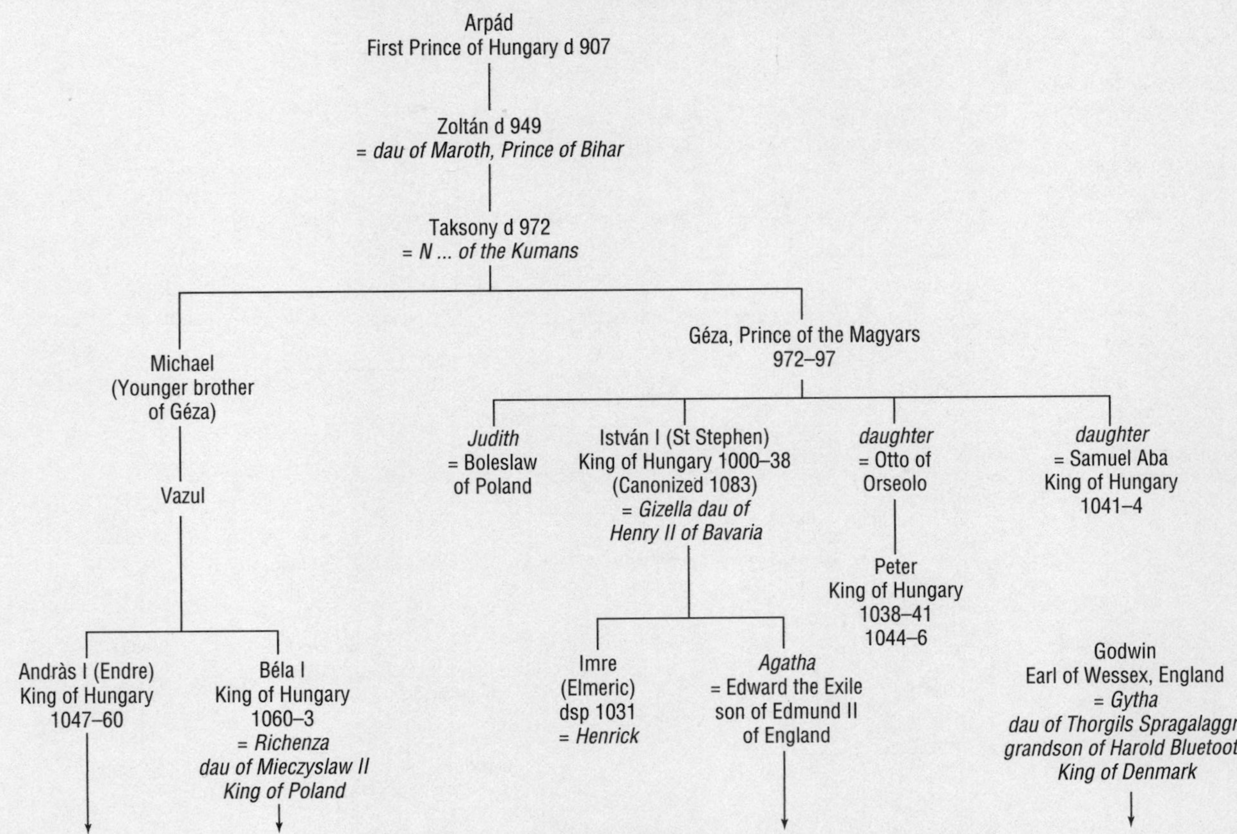

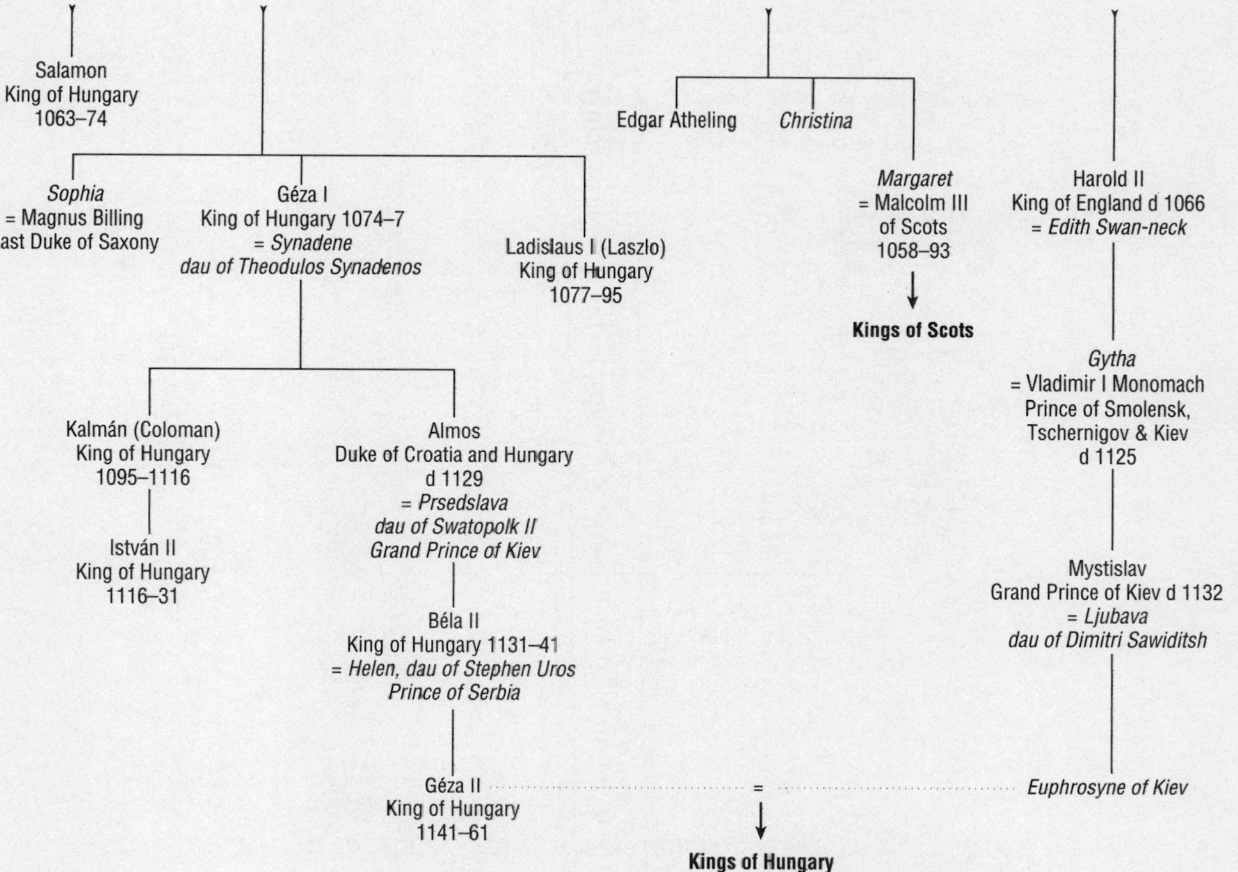
Salamon
King of Hungary
1063–74
Sophia
= Magnus Billing
Last Duke of Saxony
Géza I
King of Hungary 1074–7
= Synadene
dau of Theodulos Synadenos
Ladislaus I (Laszlo)
King of Hungary
1077–95
Edgar Atheling
Christina
Margaret
= Malcolm III
of Scots
1058–93
Kings of Scots
Harold II
King of England d 1066
= Edith Swan-neck
Gytha
= Vladimir I Monomach
Prince of Smolensk,
Tschernigov & Kiev
d 1125
Kalmán (Coloman)
King of Hungary
1095–1116
István II
King of Hungary
1116–31
Almos
Duke of Croatia and Hungary
d 1129
= Prsedslava
dau of Swatopolk II
Grand Prince of Kiev
Béla II
King of Hungary 1131–41
= Helen, dau of Stephen Uros
Prince of Serbia
Mystislav
Grand Prince of Kiev d 1132
= Ljubava
dau of Dimitri Sawiditsh
Géza II
King of Hungary
1141–61
=
Euphrosyne of Kiev
Kings of Hungary

Descent to Maud (Matilda) de Lens, wife of David I of Scots

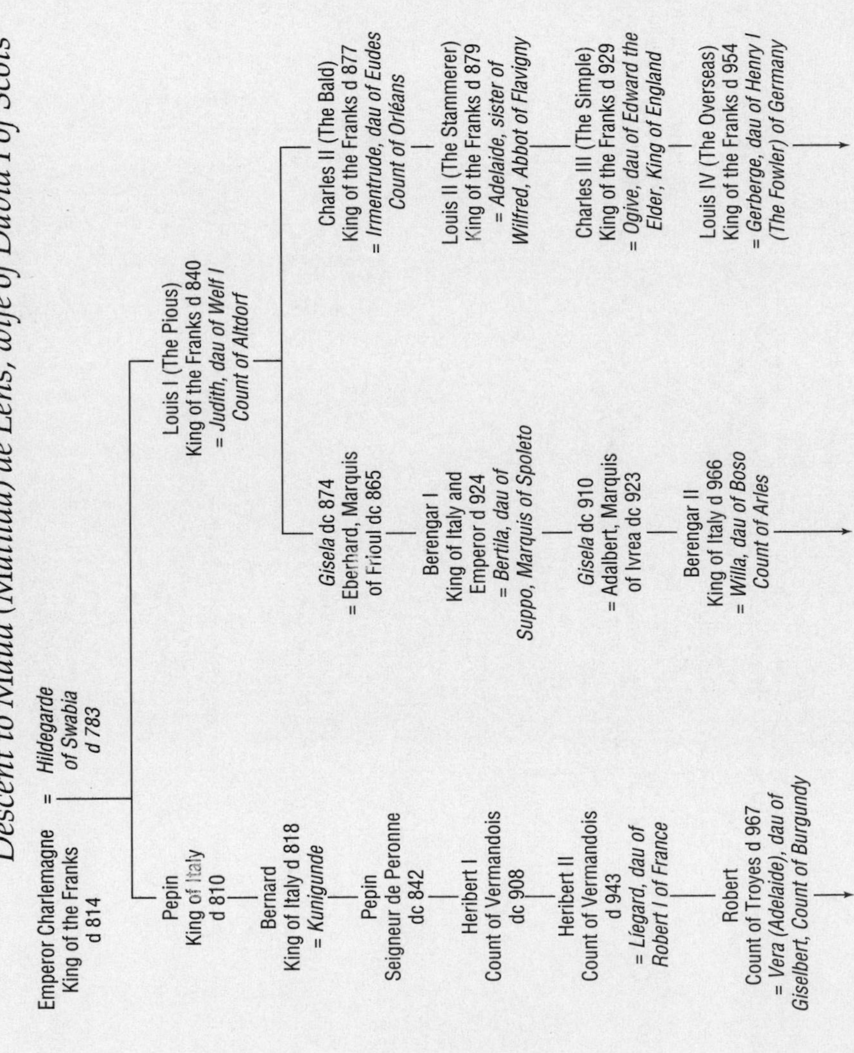

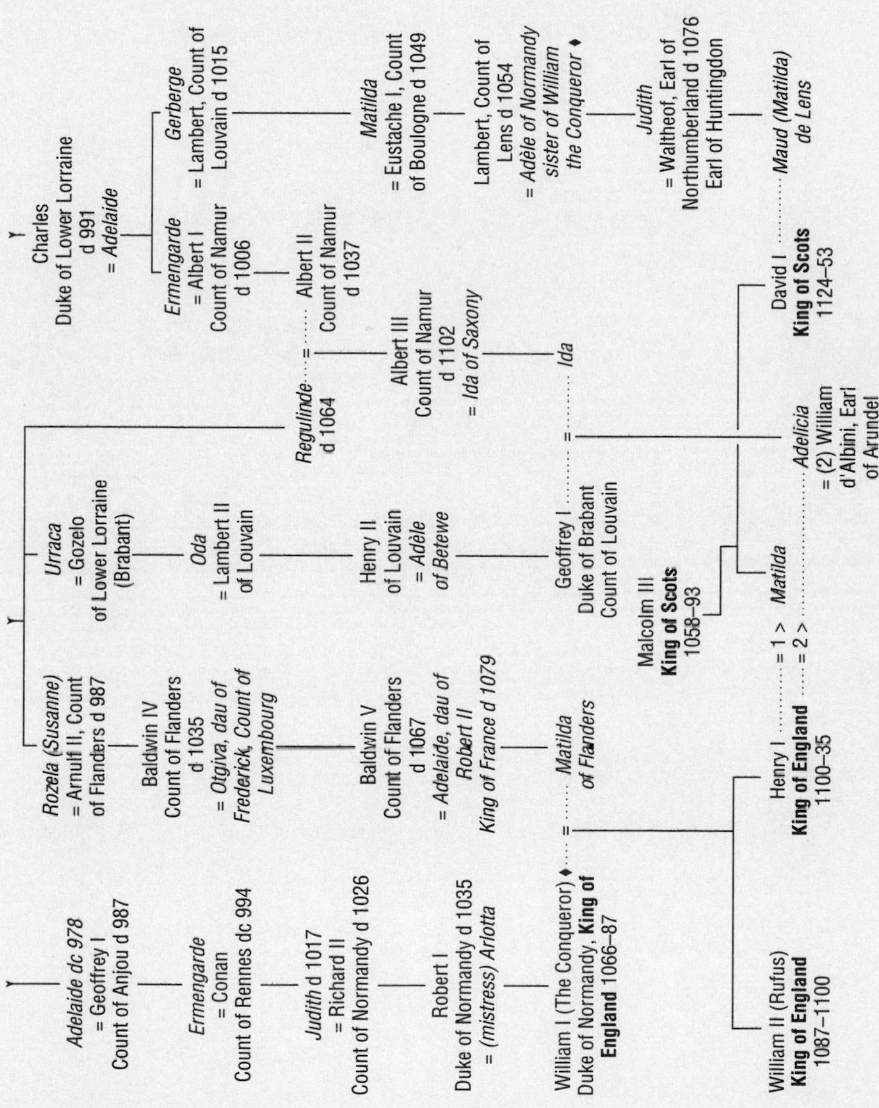

Adelaide dc 978
= Geoffrey I
Count of Anjou d 987
Ermengarde
= Conan
Count of Rennes dc 994
Judith d 1017
= Richard II
Count of Normandy d 1026
Robert I
Duke of Normandy d 1035
= (mistress) Arlotta
William I (The Conqueror) ♦
Duke of Normandy, King of England 1066–87
Rozela (Susanne)
= Arnulf II, Count of Flanders d 987
Baldwin IV
Count of Flanders
d 1035
= Otgiva, dau of Frederick, Count of Luxembourg
Baldwin V
Count of Flanders
d 1067
= Adelaide, dau of Robert II
King of France d 1079
Matilda
of Flanders
Urraca
= Gozelo
of Lower Lorraine
(Brabant)
Oda
= Lambert II
of Louvain
Henry II
of Louvain
= Adèle
of Betewe
Geoffrey I
Duke of Brabant
Count of Louvain
Regulinde
d 1064
Charles
Duke of Lower Lorraine
d 991
= Adelaide
Ermengarde
= Albert I
Count of Namur
d 1006
Albert II
Count of Namur
d 1037
Albert III
Count of Namur
d 1102
= Ida of Saxony
Ida
Gerberge
= Lambert, Count of Louvain d 1015
Matilda
= Eustache I, Count of Boulogne d 1049
Lambert, Count of Lens d 1054
= Adèle of Normandy sister of William the Conqueror ♦
Judith
= Waltheof, Earl of Northumberland d 1076
Earl of Huntingdon
William II (Rufus)
King of England
1087–1100
Henry I
King of England
1100–35
= 1 >
= 2 >
Malcolm III
King of Scots
1058–93
Matilda
Adelicia
= (2) William d'Albini, Earl of Arundel
David I
King of Scots
1124–53
Maud (Matilda)
de Lens

Descent to Ermengarde de Beaumont, wife of William I (the Lion) of Scots

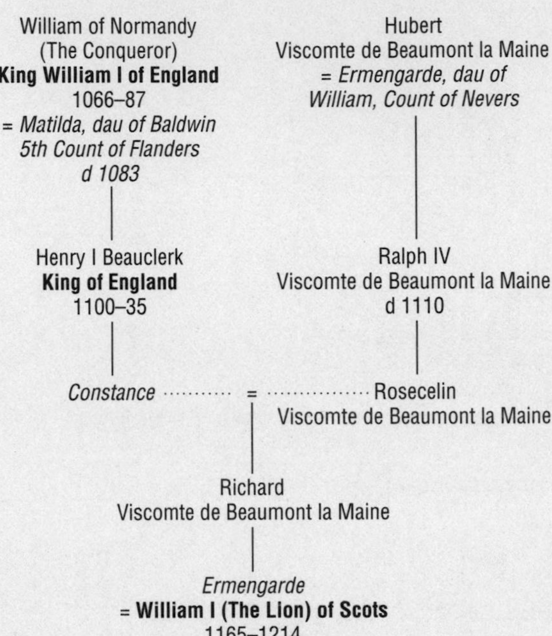

Descent to Marjorie Bruce, mother of Robert II Stewart of Scots

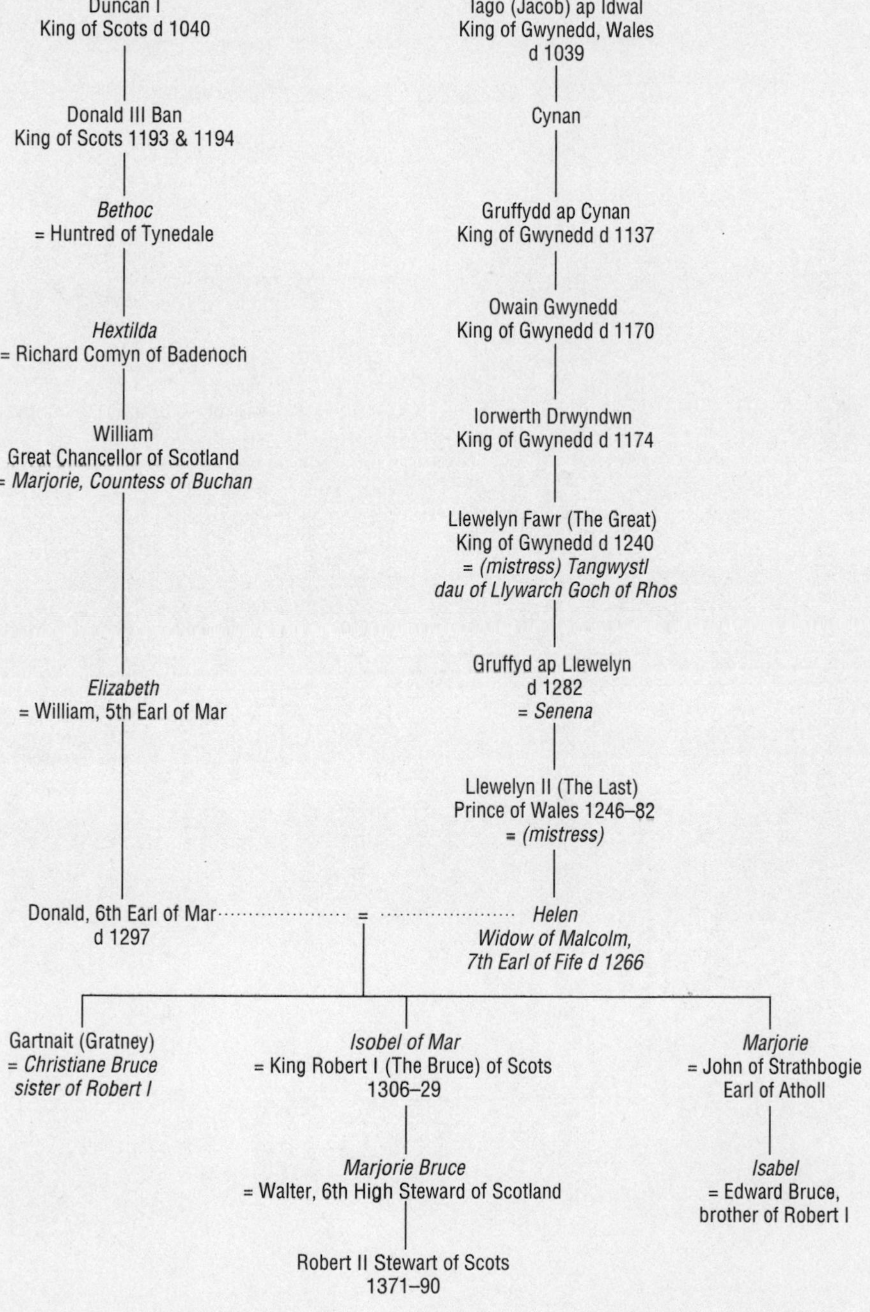

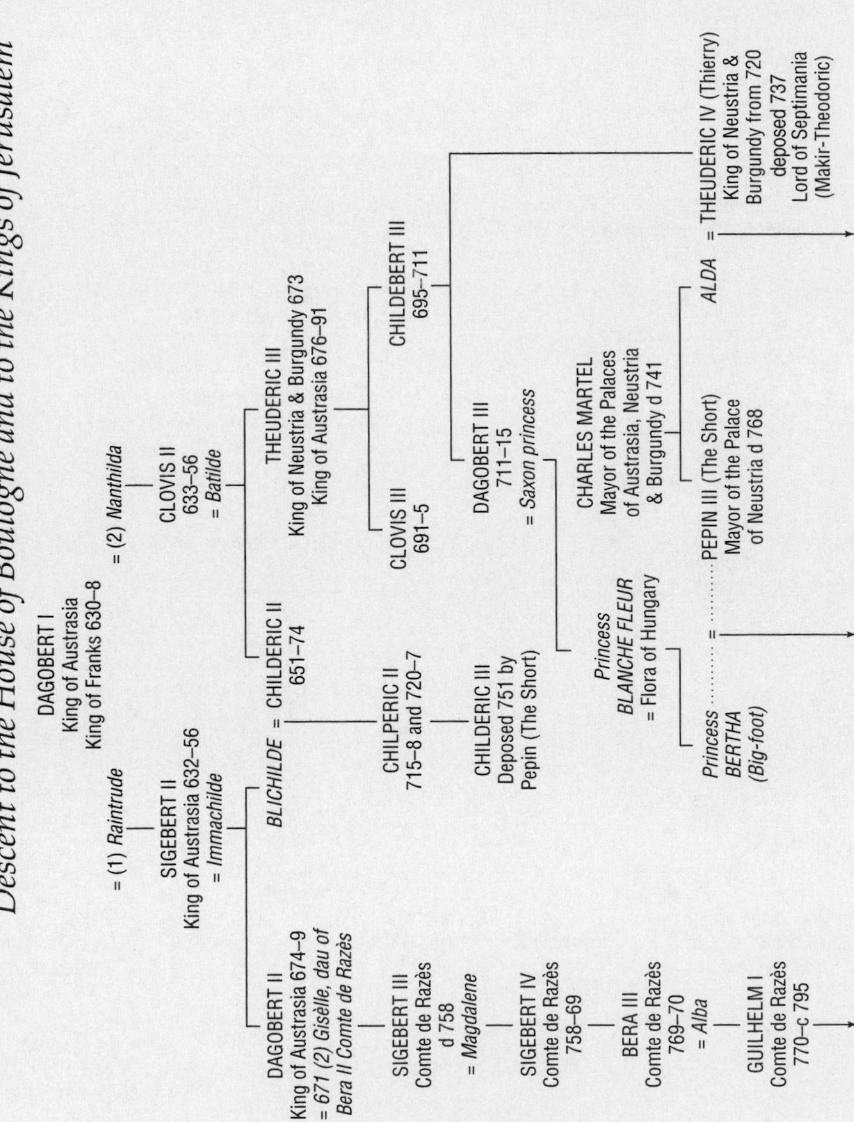
Descent to the House of Boulogne and to the Kings of Jerusalem
DAGOBERT I
King of Austrasia
King of Franks 630–8
= (1) Raintrude
= (2) Nanthilda
SIGEBERT II
King of Austrasia 632–56
= Immachilde
CLOVIS II
633–56
= Batilde
DAGOBERT II
King of Austrasia 674–9
= 671 (2) Gisèlle, dau of
Bera II Comte de Razès
BLICHILDE = CHILDERIC II
651–74
THEUDERIC III
King of Neustria & Burgundy 673
King of Austrasia 676–91
SIGEBERT III
Comte de Razès
d 758
= Magdalene
CHILPERIC II
715–8 and 720–7
CLOVIS III
691–5
CHILDEBERT III
695–711
SIGEBERT IV
Comte de Razès
758–69
CHILDERIC III
Deposed 751 by
Pepin (The Short)
DAGOBERT III
711–15
= Saxon princess
BERA III
Comte de Razès
769–70
= Alba
Princess
BLANCHE FLEUR
= Flora of Hungary
CHARLES MARTEL
Mayor of the Palaces
of Austrasia, Neustria
& Burgundy d 741
GUILHELM I
Comte de Razès
770–c 795
Princess
BERTHA
(Big-foot)
=
PEPIN III (The Short)
Mayor of the Palace
of Neustria d 768
ALDA = THEUDERIC IV (Thierry)
King of Neustria &
Burgundy from 720
deposed 737
Lord of Septimania
(Makir-Theodoric)

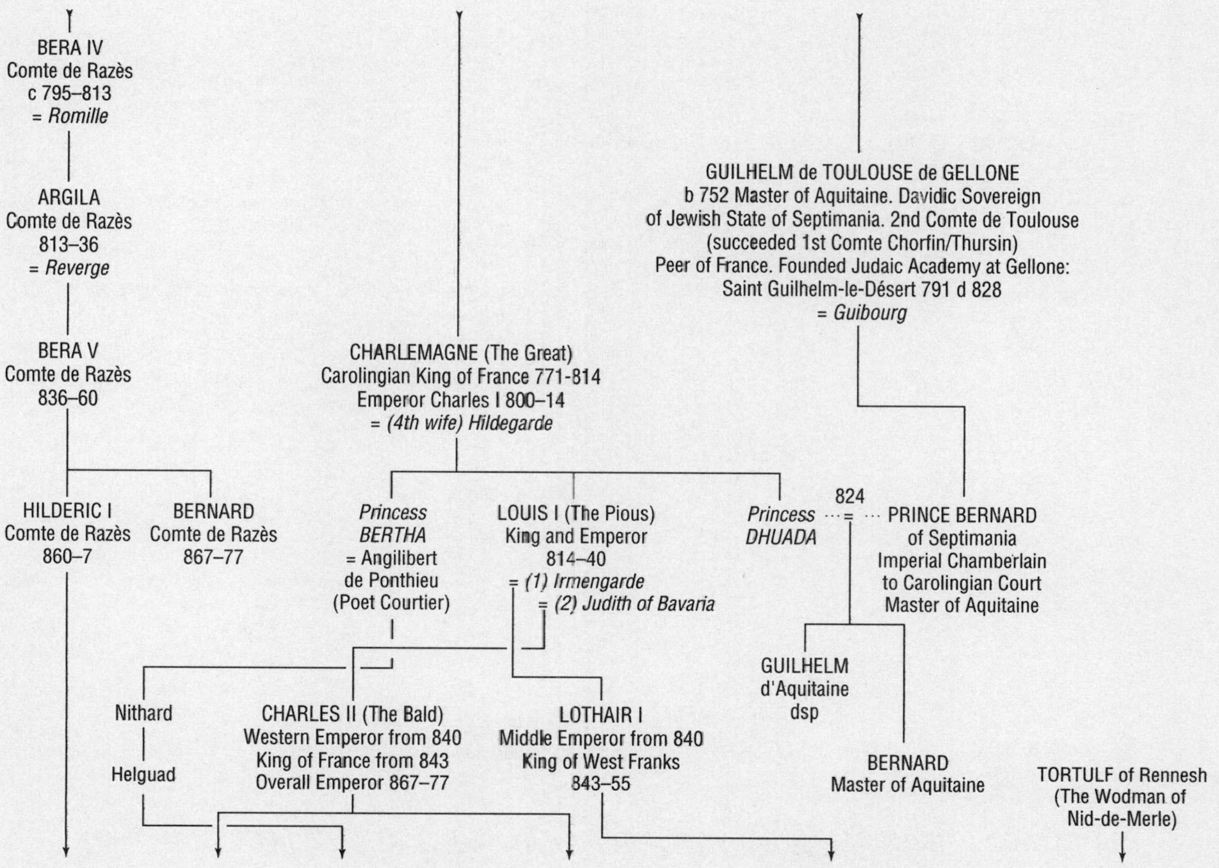
BERA IV
Comte de Razès
c 795–813
= *Romille*
ARGILA
Comte de Razès
813–36
= *Reverge*
BERA V
Comte de Razès
836–60
HILDERIC I
Comte de Razès
860–7
BERNARD
Comte de Razès
867–77
CHARLEMAGNE (The Great)
Carolingian King of France 771-814
Emperor Charles I 800–14
= *(4th wife) Hildegarde*
Princess
BERTHA
= Angilibert
de Ponthieu
(Poet Courtier)
LOUIS I (The Pious)
King and Emperor
814–40
= *(1) Irmengarde*
= *(2) Judith of Bavaria*
Princess
DHUADA
824
= PRINCE BERNARD
of Septimania
Imperial Chamberlain
to Carolingian Court
Master of Aquitaine
GUILHELM de TOULOUSE de GELLONE
b 752 Master of Aquitaine. Davidic Sovereign
of Jewish State of Septimania. 2nd Comte de Toulouse
(succeeded 1st Comte Chorfin/Thursin)
Peer of France. Founded Judaic Academy at Gellone:
Saint Guilhelm-le-Désert 791 d 828
= *Guibourg*
Nithard
Helguad
CHARLES II (The Bald)
Western Emperor from 840
King of France from 843
Overall Emperor 867–77
LOTHAIR I
Middle Emperor from 840
King of West Franks
843–55
GUILHELM
d'Aquitaine
dsp
BERNARD
Master of Aquitaine
TORTULF of Rennesh
(The Wodman of
Nid-de-Merle)

Descent to the House of Boulogne and to the Kings of Jerusalem – continued

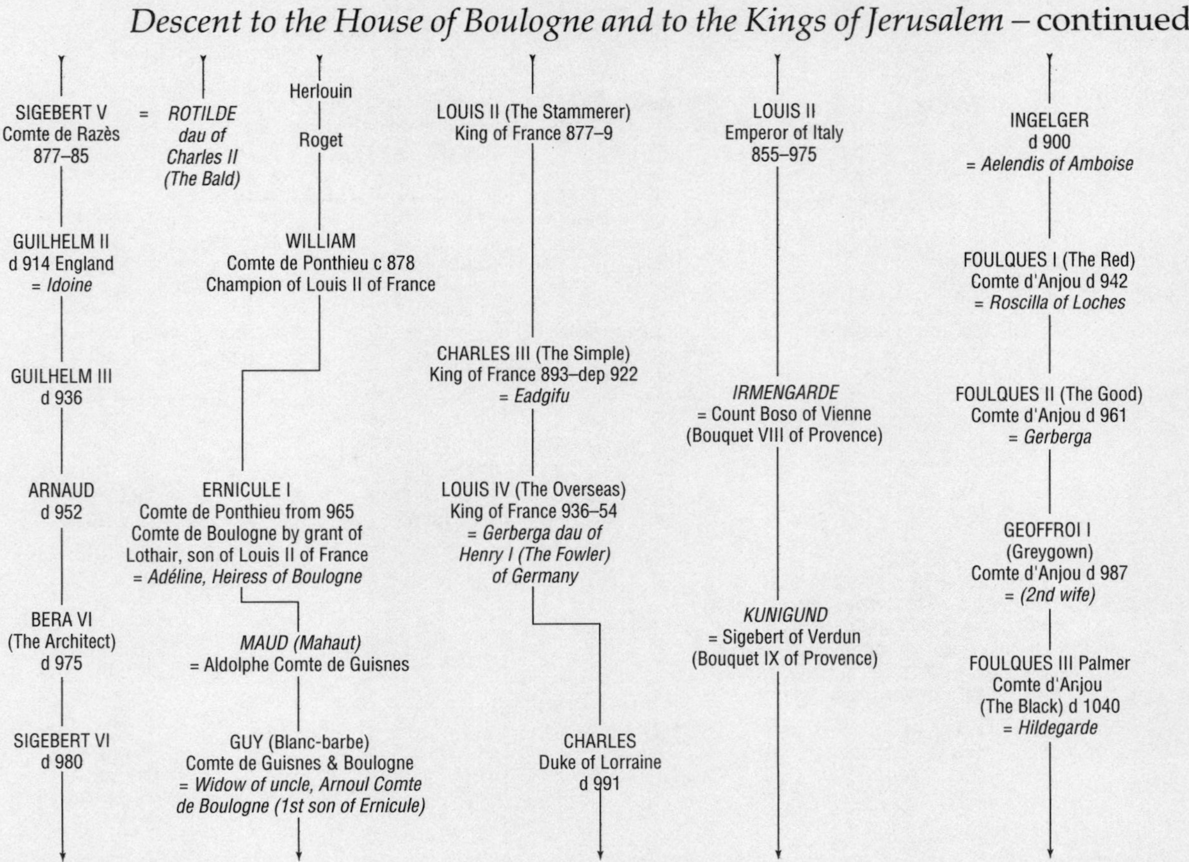

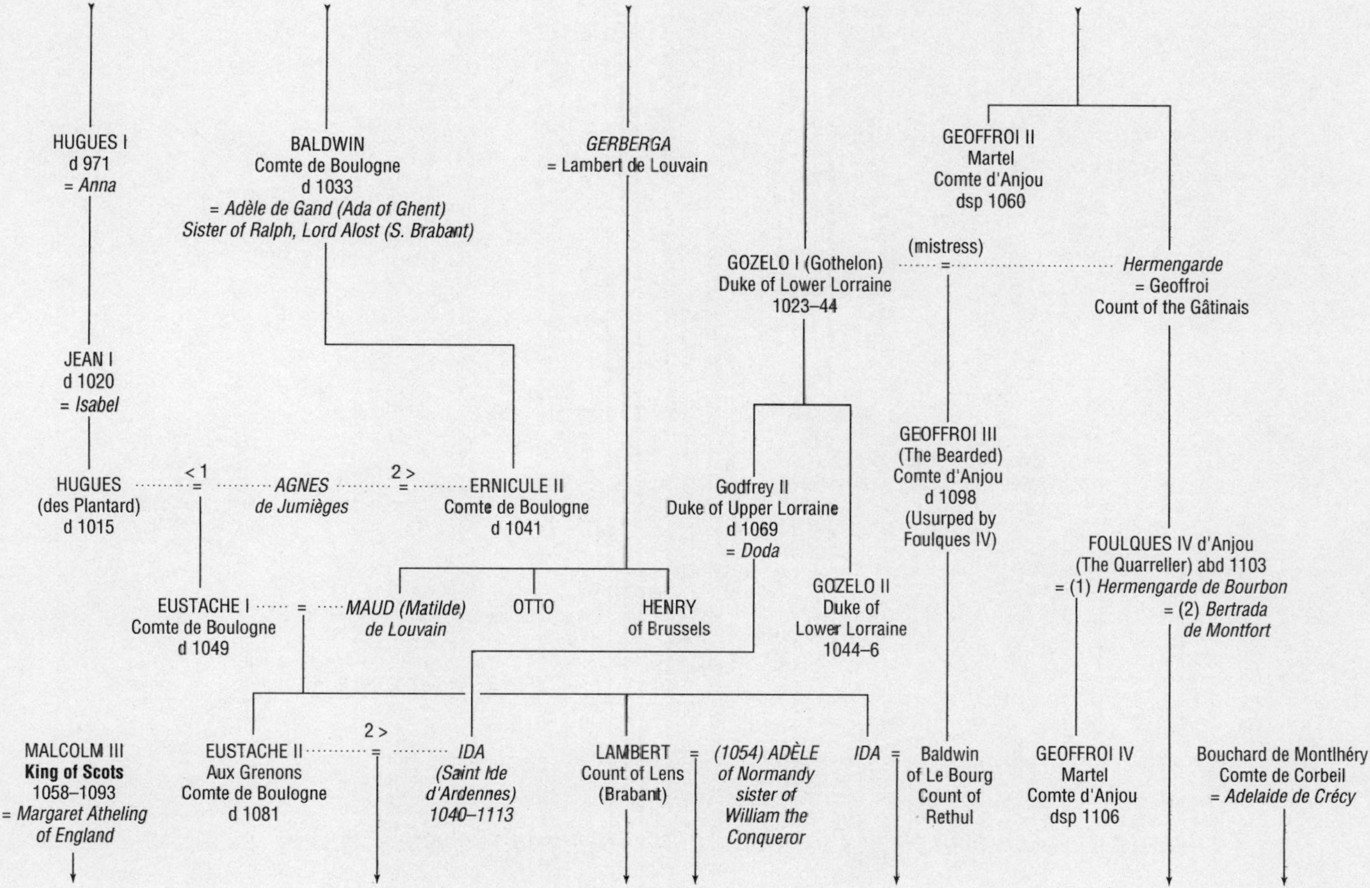
HUGUES I
d 971
= *Anna*
BALDWIN
Comte de Boulogne
d 1033
= *Adèle de Gand (Ada of Ghent)*
Sister of Ralph, Lord Alost (S. Brabant)
GERBERGA
= Lambert de Louvain
GEOFFROI II
Martel
Comte d'Anjou
dsp 1060
GOZELO I (Gothelon)
Duke of Lower Lorraine
1023–44
(mistress) = *Hermengarde*
= Geoffroi
Count of the Gâtinais
JEAN I
d 1020
= *Isabel*
HUGUES
(des Plantard)
d 1015
<1 = *AGNES*
de Jumièges
2> = ERNICULE II
Comte de Boulogne
d 1041
Godfrey II
Duke of Upper Lorraine
d 1069
= *Doda*
GEOFFROI III
(The Bearded)
Comte d'Anjou
d 1098
(Usurped by
Foulques IV)
FOULQUES IV d'Anjou
(The Quarreller) abd 1103
= (1) *Hermengarde de Bourbon*
= (2) *Bertrada*
de Montfort
EUSTACHE I
Comte de Boulogne
d 1049
= *MAUD (Matilde)*
de Louvain
OTTO
HENRY
of Brussels
GOZELO II
Duke of
Lower Lorraine
1044–6
MALCOLM III
King of Scots
1058–1093
= *Margaret Atheling*
of England
EUSTACHE II
Aux Grenons
Comte de Boulogne
d 1081
2> = *IDA*
(Saint Ide
d'Ardennes)
1040–1113
LAMBERT
Count of Lens
(Brabant)
= *(1054) ADÈLE*
of Normandy
sister of
William the
Conqueror
IDA = Baldwin
of Le Bourg
Count of
Rethul
GEOFFROI IV
Martel
Comte d'Anjou
dsp 1106
Bouchard de Montlhéry
Comte de Corbeil
= *Adelaide de Crécy*

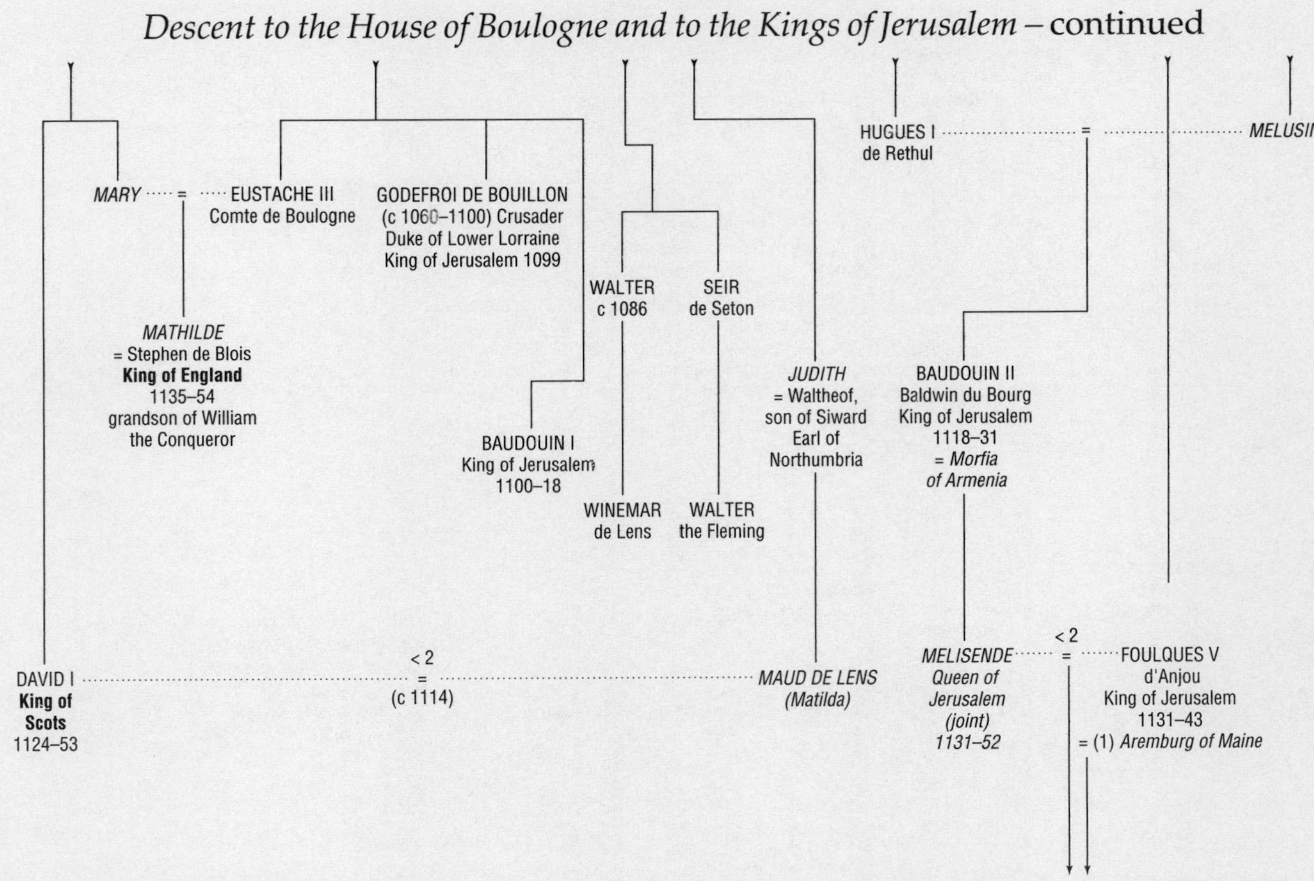
Descent to the House of Boulogne and to the Kings of Jerusalem – continued
MARY = EUSTACHE III
Comte de Boulogne
GODEFROI DE BOUILLON
(c 1060–1100) Crusader
Duke of Lower Lorraine
King of Jerusalem 1099
HUGUES I
de Rethul
= MELUSINE
WALTER
c 1086
SEIR
de Seton
MATHILDE
= Stephen de Blois
King of England
1135–54
grandson of William
the Conqueror
JUDITH
= Waltheof,
son of Siward
Earl of
Northumbria
BAUDOUIN II
Baldwin du Bourg
King of Jerusalem
1118–31
= Morfia
of Armenia
BAUDOUIN I
King of Jerusalem
1100–18
WINEMAR
de Lens
WALTER
the Fleming
DAVID I
King of
Scots
1124–53
< 2
=
(c 1114)
MAUD DE LENS
(Matilda)
MELISENDE
Queen of
Jerusalem
(joint)
1131–52
< 2
=
FOULQUES V
d'Anjou
King of Jerusalem
1131–43
= (1) Aremburg of Maine

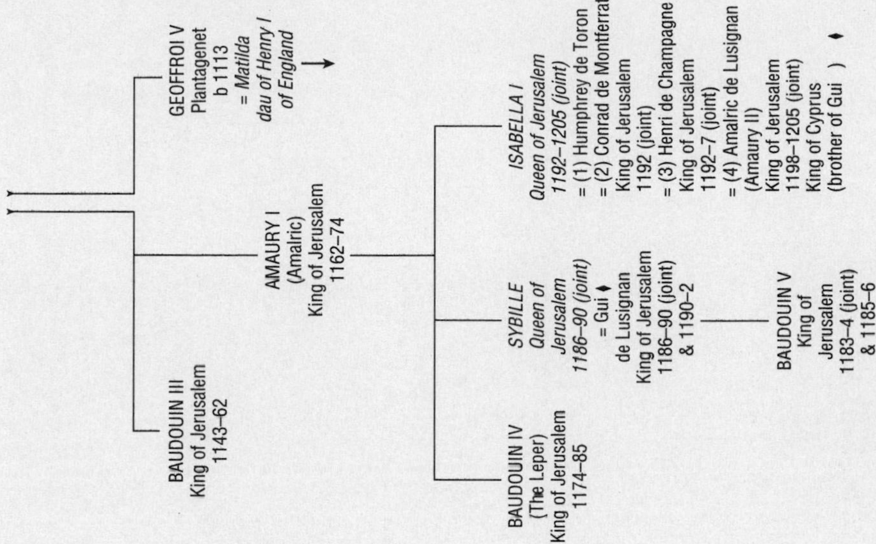
GEOFFROI V
Plantagenet
b 1113
= *Matilda*
dau of Henry I
of England
BAUDOUIN III
King of Jerusalem
1143–62
AMAURY I
(Amalric)
King of Jerusalem
1162–74
BAUDOUIN IV
(The Leper)
King of Jerusalem
1174–85
SYBILLE
Queen of
Jerusalem
1186–90 (joint)
= Gui
de Lusignan
King of Jerusalem
1186–90 (joint)
& 1190–2
BAUDOUIN V
King of
Jerusalem
1183–4 (joint)
& 1185–6
ISABELLA I
Queen of Jerusalem
1192–1205 (joint)
= (1) Humphrey de Toron
= (2) Conrad de Montferrat
King of Jerusalem
1192 (joint)
= (3) Henri de Champagne
King of Jerusalem
1192–7 (joint)
= (4) Amalric de Lusignan
(Amaury II)
King of Jerusalem
1198–1205 (joint)
King of Cyprus
(brother of Gui)

Contemporary Monarchs 1066–1688

SCOTLAND		ENGLAND		FRANCE	
SCOTS				**CAPETIANS**	
LULACH of Moray Step-son of Macbeth	1057–8			ROBERT II Son of Hugh Capet = *Constance of Provence*	996–1031
		NORMANS			
MALCOLM III Canmore Son of Duncan I = 1 *Ingibjorg Atheling* = 2 *Margaret the Saxon*	1058–93	WILLIAM I (The Conqueror) Duke of Normandy = *Matilda of Flanders*	1066–87	HENRI I Son of Robert II = *Anne of Kiev*	1031–60
DONALD III BAN Brother of Malcolm III	1093–4 (dep)	WILLIAM II (Rufus) Son of William I (Unmarried)	1087–1100	PHILIP I Son of Henri I = (1) *Bertha of Holland*	1060–1108
DUNCAN II Son of Malcolm III and Ingibjorg	1094				
DONALD III BAN (Restored)	1094–7				
EDGAR Son of Malcolm III and *Margaret Atheling*	1097–1107				
ALEXANDER I Brother of Edgar = *Sybilla, natural dau of Henry I of England*	1107–24	HENRY I (Beauclerk) Brother of William II = *Maud, daughter of Malcolm III of Scots*	1100–35	LOUIS VI (The Fat) Son of Philip I = (2) *Adelaide of Savoy*	1108–37

DAVID I (The Saint) Brother of Alexander = *Matilda of Huntington*	1124–53	STEPHEN Count of Blois Grandson of William I = *Matilda of Boulogne*	1135–54	LOUIS VII (The Young) Son of Louis VI = (2) *Alix of Champagne*	1137–80
		PLANTAGENETS			
MALCOLM IV (Maiden) Grandson of David I (Unmarried)	1153–65	HENRY II (Curtmantel) Grandson of Henry I = *Eleanor of Aquitaine* *Ex 1st wife of Louis VII* *of France*	1154–89		
WILLIAM I (The Lion) Brother of Malcolm IV = *Ermengarde de Beaumont*	1165–1214	RICHARD I (Lionheart) Son of Henry II = *Berengaria of Navarre*	1189–99	PHILIP II (Augustus) Son of Louis VII = *Isabella of Hainault*	1180–1223
		JOHN (Lackland) Brother of Richard I = *Isabel of Angoulème*	1199–1216		
ALEXANDER II Son of William I = *Mary of Picardy*	1214–49	HENRY III Son of John = *Eleanor of Provence*	1216–72	LOUIS VIII (Lionheart) Son of Philip II = *Blanche of Castile*	1223–6
				LOUIS IX (Saint Louis) Son of Louis VIII = *Margaret of Provence*	1226–70
ALEXANDER III Son of Alexander II = *Margaret, dau of* *Henry III of England*	1249–86			PHILIP III (The Bald) Son of Louis IX = *Mary of Brabant*	1270–85
MARGARET *(The Maid of Norway)* *Granddaughter of* *Alexander III, daughter* *of Eric II of Norway* *(Unmarried)*	1286–90	EDWARD I (Longshanks) Son of Henry III = *Eleanor of Castile*	1272–1307	PHILIP IV (The Fair) Son of Philip III = *Joan of Navarre*	1285–1314

Contemporary Monarchs 1066–1688 – continued

JOHN BALLIOL Gt grandson of Earl of Huntingdon (bro of William the Lion) = *Isobel de Warenne* *dau of John, Earl of Surrey*	1292–6			LOUIS X (The Headstrong) Son of Philip IV	1314–16
WILLIAM WALLACE Guardian of the Realm	1296–1306			PHILIP V (The Tall) Son of Philip IV	1316–22
ROBERT I (The Bruce) Gt g-grandson of Earl of Huntingdon (bro of William the Lion) = (1) *Isabel of Mar* = (2) *Elizabeth of Ulster*	1306–29	EDWARD II (Caernarvon) Son of Edward I = *Isabella of France* *daughter of Philip IV*	1307–27	CHARLES IV Son of Philip IV	1322–27
				VALOIS	
DAVID II Son of Robert I and *Elizabeth*	1329–32	EDWARD III (Windsor) Son of Edward II = *Philippa of Hainault*	1327–77	PHILIP VI Nephew of Philip IV Son of Count Charles de Valois = (1) *Joan of Burgundy*	1328–50
EDWARD BALLIOL Son of John Balliol	1332–41			JOHN II (The Good) Son of Philip VI	1350–64
DAVID II (Restored)	1341–71				
ROBERT II Son of Walter, 3rd High Steward, and Marjorie Bruce = *Elizabeth dau of Sir Adam* *Mure of Rowallan*	1371–90	RICHARD II (Bordeaux) Son of the Black Prince, and Grandson of Edward III dsp	1377–99	CHARLES V (The Wise) Son of John the Good = *Joan of Bourbon*	1364–80

ROBERT III [John, Earl of Carrick] Son of Robert II = *Annabella, dau of John Drummond of Stobhall*	1390–1406	HENRY IV (Bolingbroke) [House of Lancaster] Son of John O'Gaunt (Duke of Lancaster), and Grandson of Edward III = *Mary de Bohun*	1399–1413	CHARLES VI (The Mad) Son of Charles V = *Isabeau of Bavaria* *(Their daughter, Katherine, married Henry V of England)*	1380–1422
JAMES I Son of Robert III = *Joan Beaufort of Somerset, g-dau of John O'Gaunt*	1406–37	HENRY V (Monmouth) [House of Lancaster] Son of Henry IV = *Katherine de Valois, daughter of Charles VI of France*	1413–22		
JAMES II Son of James I = *Maria, daughter of Arnold van Egmond, Hertog van Gelre, Graaf van Zutphen*	1437–60	HENRY VI (Windsor) [House of Lancaster] Son of Henry V = *Margaret, daughter of Rayner, Duke of Anjou, Titular King of Jerusalem* (Deposed by Edward Duke of York)	1422–61	CHARLES VII (The Well Served) Son of Charles VI = *Mary of Anjou*	1422–61
JAMES III Son of James II = *Margaret, daughter of Christian I of Denmark*	1460–88	EDWARD IV [House of York] Son of Sir Richard Plantagenet, in descent from John O'Gaunt's brother, Lionel, Duke of Clarence = *Elizabeth, daughter of Richard Widville, Earl Rivers*	1461–83	LOUIS XI Son of Charles VII = *Charlotte of Savoy*	1461–83
		EDWARD V [House of York] Son of Edward IV Murdered before coronation, along with brother, Richard dsp	1483	CHARLES VIII Son of Louis XI = *Anne of Brittany*	1483–98

Contemporary Monarchs 1066–1688 – continued

JAMES IV Son of James III = *Margaret Tudor, daughter of Henry VII of England*	1488–1513	RICHARD III [House of York] Killed at Bosworth Field Son of Sir Richard Plantagenet, and brother of Edward IV = *Anne, daughter of Richard Neville, Earl of Warwick*	1483–85	LOUIS XII [Duke of Orleans] Grand-nephew of Chales VI = 1 *Joan of Valois* = 2 *Anne of Brittany, widow of Charles VIII*	1498–1515
		TUDORS			
JAMES V Son of James IV = (2) *Marie de Guise-Lorraine, daughter of Claude, Duc de Guise*	1513–42	HENRY VII Son of Edmund Tudor Earl of Richmond *[in descent from Katherine de Valois, widow of Henry V, and her 2nd husband Owen Tudor]* and Margaret Beaufort, gt g-dau of John O'Gaunt = *Elizabeth of York, daughter of Edward IV*	1485–1509	FRANCOIS I Cousin of Louis XII = (1) *Claude de France dau of Louis XII* = (2) *Eleanor of Austria*	1515–47
MARY, QUEEN OF SCOTS *Daughter of James V and Marie de Guise-Lorraine* = (1) Francis, the Dauphin, Francis II of France Son of King Henri II = (2) Henry Stewart, Lord Darnley, Duke of Albany Son of Matthew, Earl of Lennox = (3) James Hepburn Earl of Bothwell, Duke of Orkney	*1542–87*	HENRY VIII Son of Henry VII = (1) *Catherine, daughter of Ferdinand V of Aragon and Castille* = (2) *Anne, daughter of Sir Thomas Boleyn, Earl of Ormonde* = (3) *Jane, daughter of Sir John Seymour, and sister of Edward, Duke of Somerset* = (4) *Anne of Cleves* = (5) *Catherine Howard* = (6) *Catherine Parr*	1509–47	HENRI II Son of Francois I = *Catherine de Medici*	1547–59

		EDWARD VI Son of Henry VIII and *Jane Seymour* (Unmarried)	1547–53	FRANCOIS II Son of Henri II (As Dauphin and King, Francis was the first husband of *Mary Stuart, Queen of Scots*) dsp	1559–60
		JANE GREY *Daughter of Henry Grey,* *Duke of Suffolk, and* *g-dau of Henry VII* *[Inherited the Crown by Will of Edward VI]* *(Executed)*	1553		
		MARY I *Daughter of Henry VIII* *and Catherine of Aragon* = Philip II of Spain *dsp*	1553–8	CHARLES IX Son of Henri II ∴ Brother of Francis II dsp	1560–74
JAMES VI Son of *Mary Queen of Scots* and Lord Darnley **JAMES I of England from 1603**	1567–1625	*ELIZABETH I* *Daughter of Henry VIII* *and Anne Boleyn* *(Unmarried)*	1558–1603	HENRI III Son of Henri II ∴ Brother of Francis II dsp	1574–89
		STUARTS KINGS OF BRITAIN		**BOURBONS**	
JAMES VI of Scots became James I of England on Union of Crowns in 1603 [*see* ENGLAND column] →		**[Union of Scots and English Crowns]**		HENRI IV Son of Antoine de Bourbon and Jeanne, Queen of Navarre = *(2) Marie de Medici* (Their daughter, Henriette, married Charles I of Britain)	1589–1610
		JAMES I (VI of Scots) Son of Mary Queen of Scots and Henry Stewart, Lord Darnley = *Anne, daughter of Frederick II of Denmark and Norway*	1603–25		

Contemporary Monarchs 1066–1688 – continued

		CHARLES I Son of James I (VI) = *Henriette Marie, daughter of Henri IV of France* (Executed)	1625–49	LOUIS XIII Son of Henri IV [Policies under Cardinal de Richelieu 1624–42] = *Anne of Austria*	1610–43
		[Commonwealth Declared – 1649]		LOUIS XIV (The Sun King) Son of Louis XIII [Policies under Cardinal Mazarin until 1661] = *Maria Theresa, Infanta of Philip IV of Spain*	1643–1715
		Oliver Cromwell Lord Protector	1653–8		
		Richard Cromwell Lord Protector	1658–9		
		[Stuart Restoration – 1660]			
CHARLES II ♦ Crowned at Scone as King of Scots before later becoming also King of England	1651–85	CHARLES II ♦ Son of Charles I = *Katherine of Braganza, Infanta of John IV of Portugal* *dsp (legit)*	1660–85		
Since James VII did not abdicate, the *de jure* Scottish succession progressed, to the present day, through his son, James Francis Edward Stuart – *See Charts*: DESCENT TO CHARLES EDWARD STUART and COUNTS OF ALBANY		JAMES II (VII of Scots) Brother of Charles II = (1) *Anne, daughter of Edward Hyde, Earl of Clarendon* = (2) *Mary D'Este, daughter of Alphonso IV of Modena* (Deposed by Whig Revolution)	1685–8		

Descent to Joan Beaufort wife of James I of Scots and to Margaret Tudor wife of James IV of Scots

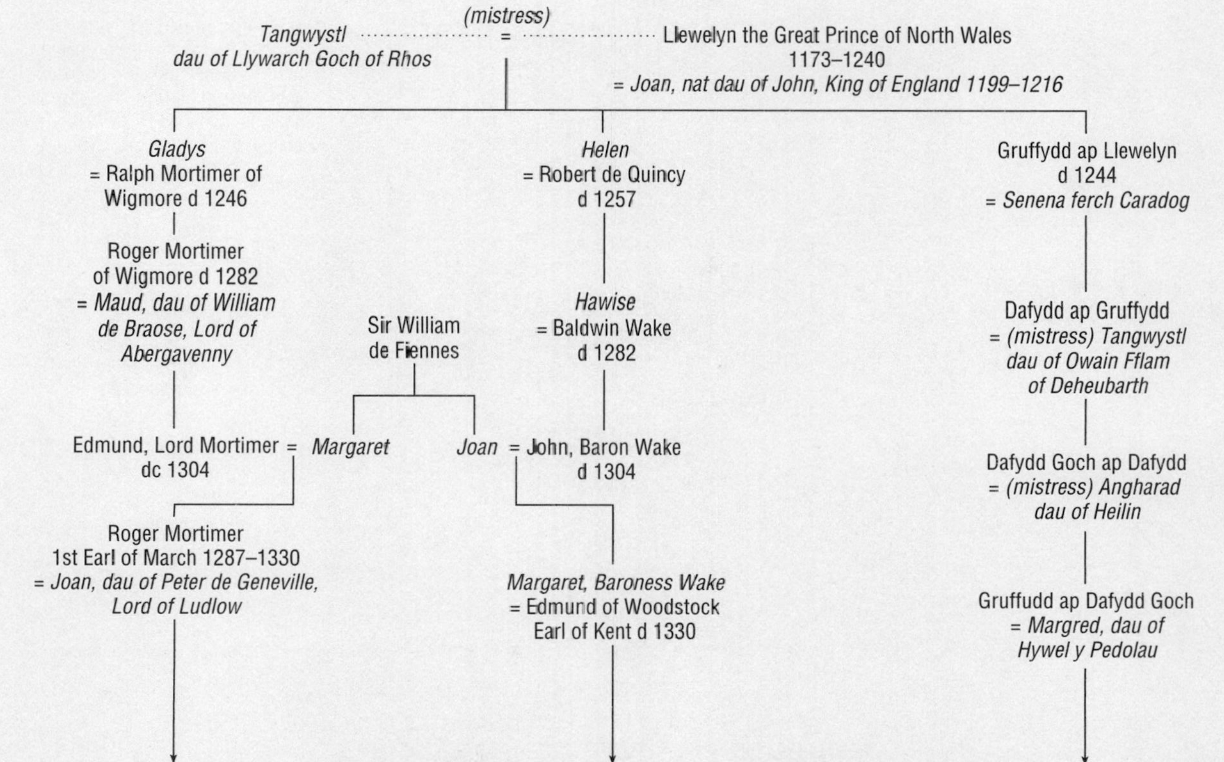

Descent to Joan Beaufort – continued

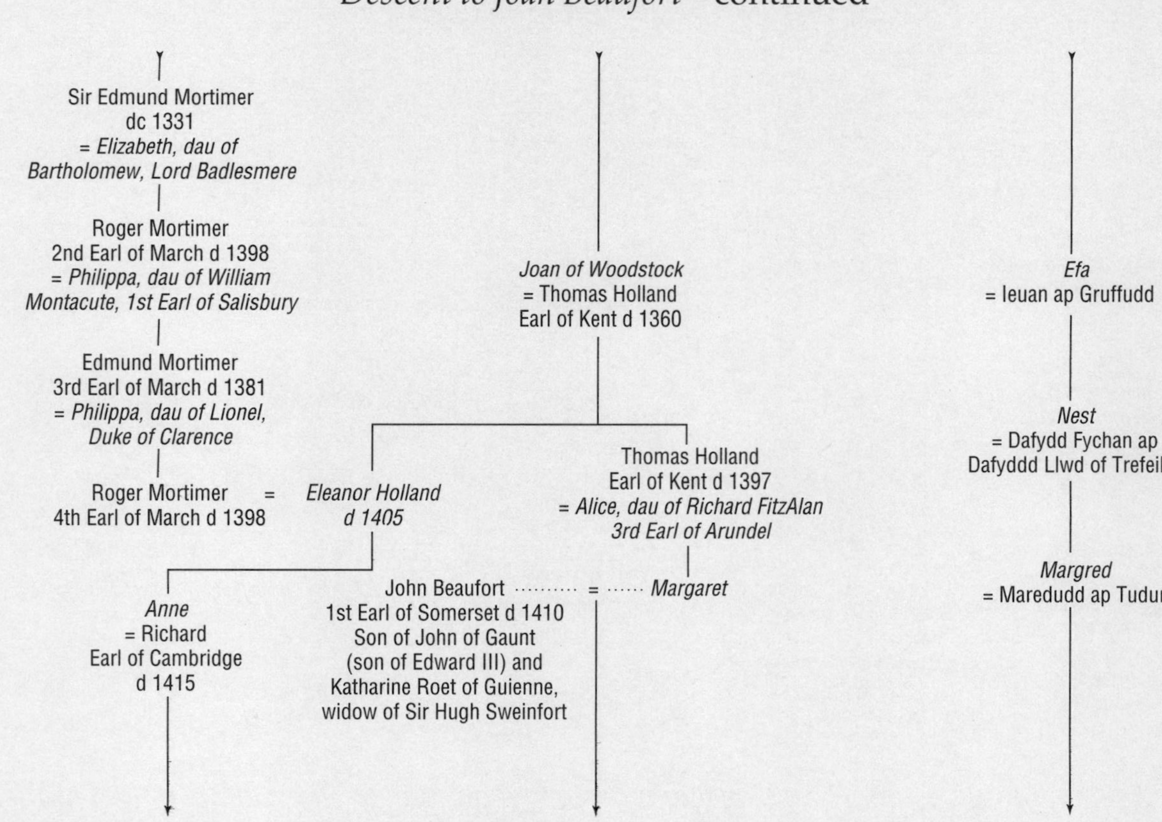

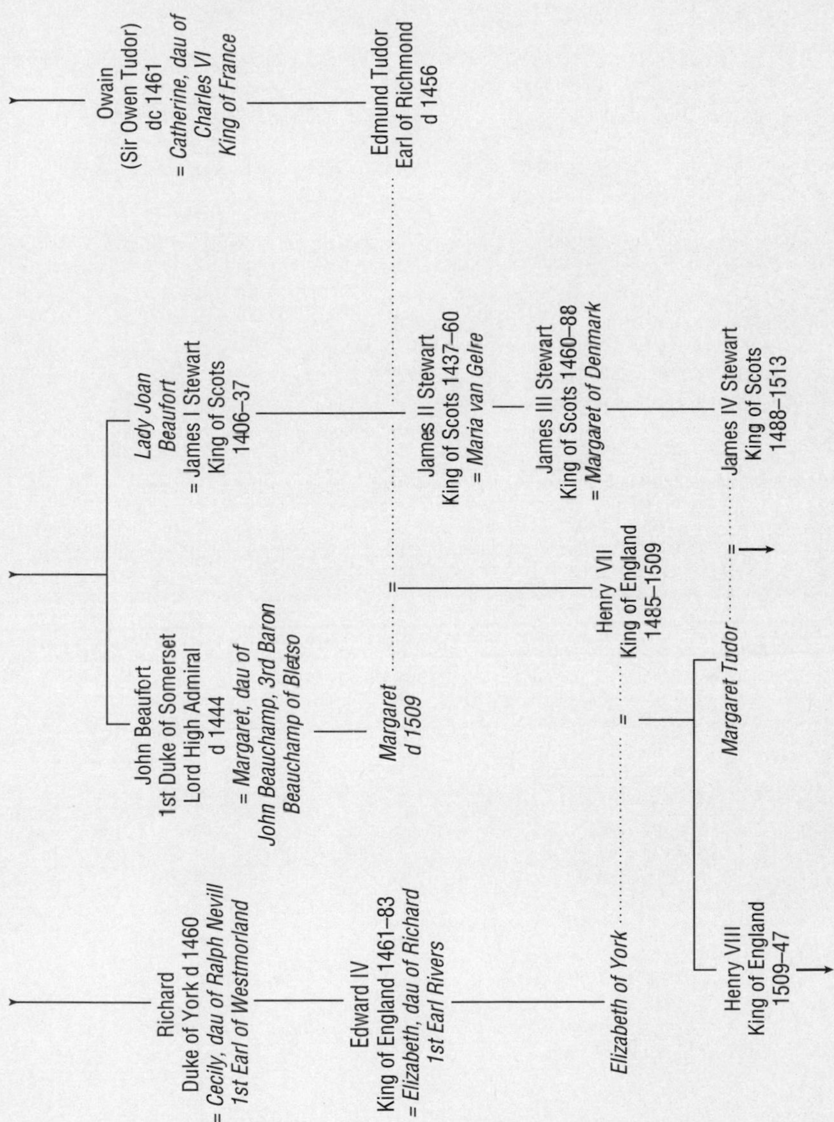

Richard
Duke of York d 1460
= Cecily, dau of Ralph Nevill
1st Earl of Westmorland
John Beaufort
1st Duke of Somerset
Lord High Admiral
d 1444
= Margaret, dau of
John Beauchamp, 3rd Baron
Beauchamp of Bletso
Lady Joan
Beaufort
= James I Stewart
King of Scots
1406–37
Owain
(Sir Owen Tudor)
dc 1461
= Catherine, dau of
Charles VI
King of France
Edward IV
King of England 1461–83
= Elizabeth, dau of Richard
1st Earl Rivers
Margaret
d 1509
James II Stewart
King of Scots 1437–60
= Maria van Gelre
Edmund Tudor
Earl of Richmond
d 1456
Elizabeth of York
Henry VII
King of England
1485–1509
James III Stewart
King of Scots 1460–88
= Margaret of Denmark
Henry VIII
King of England
1509–47
Margaret Tudor
James IV Stewart
King of Scots
1488–1513

Descent to Maria van Gelre, wife of James II Stewart of Scots and to Mary, Queen of Scots

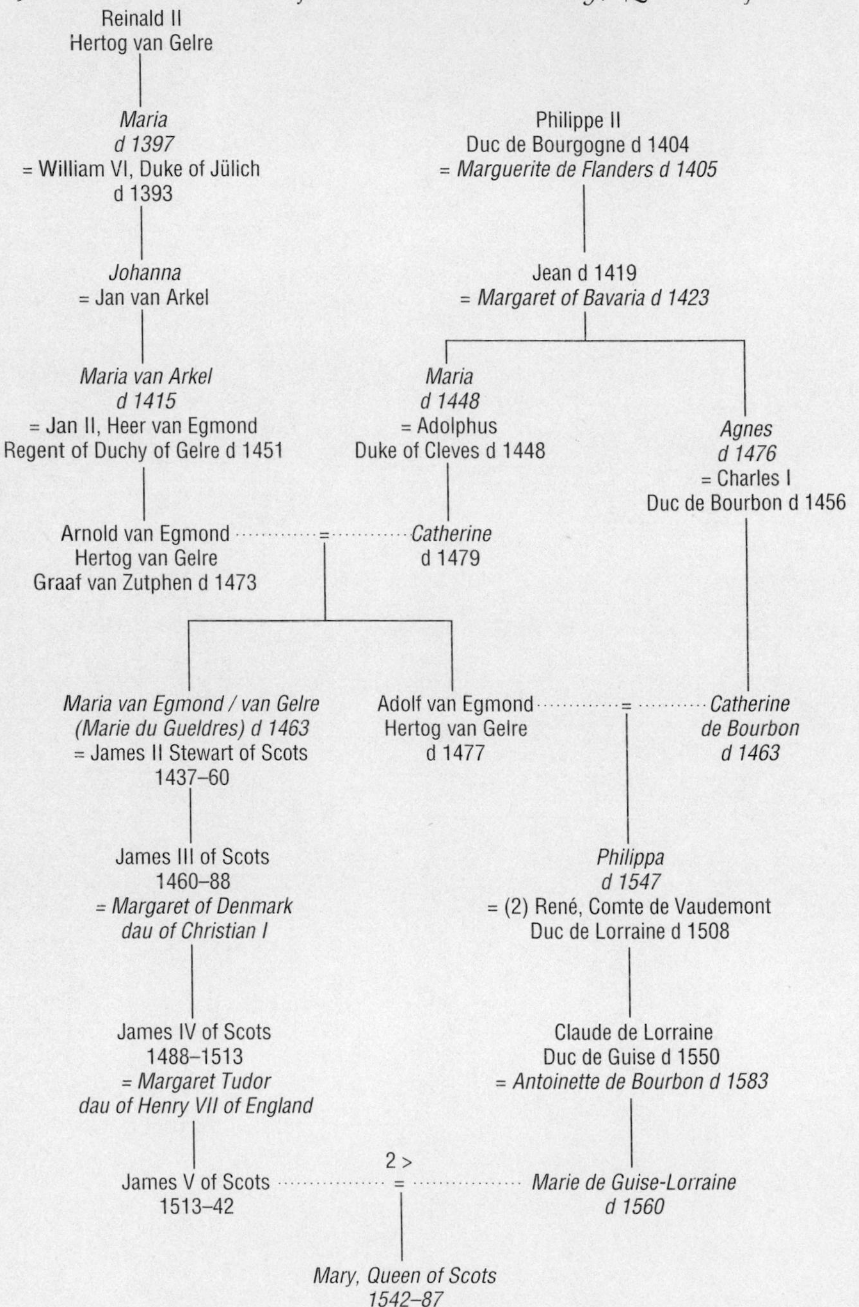

Descent to Marie de Guise-Lorraine, wife of James V of Scots

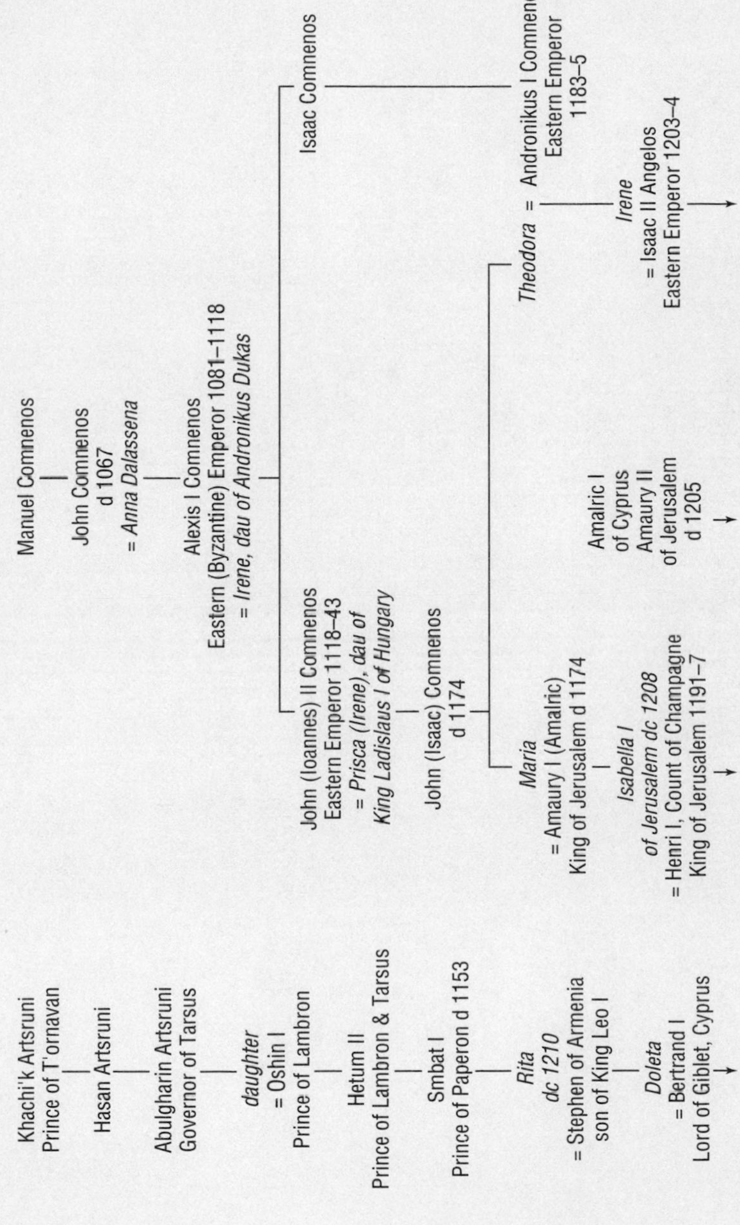

Descent to Marie de Guise-Lorraine Wife of James V of Scots – continued

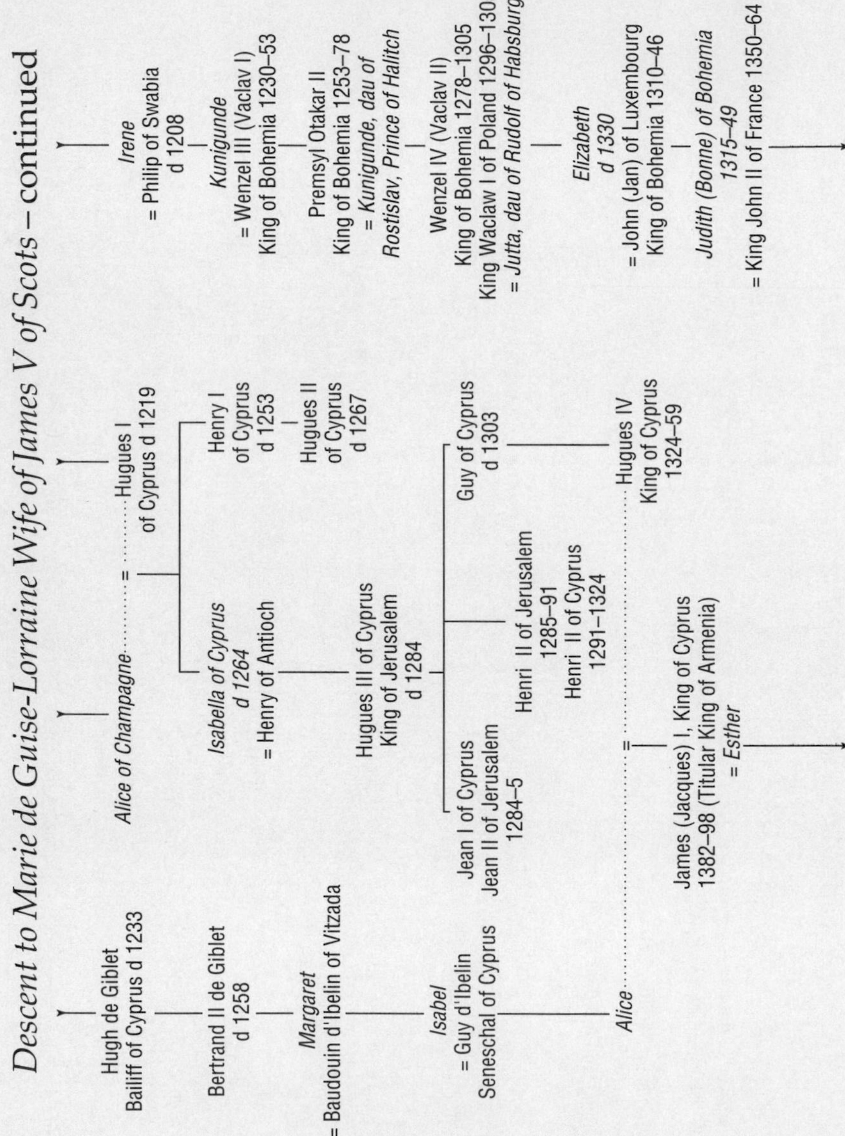

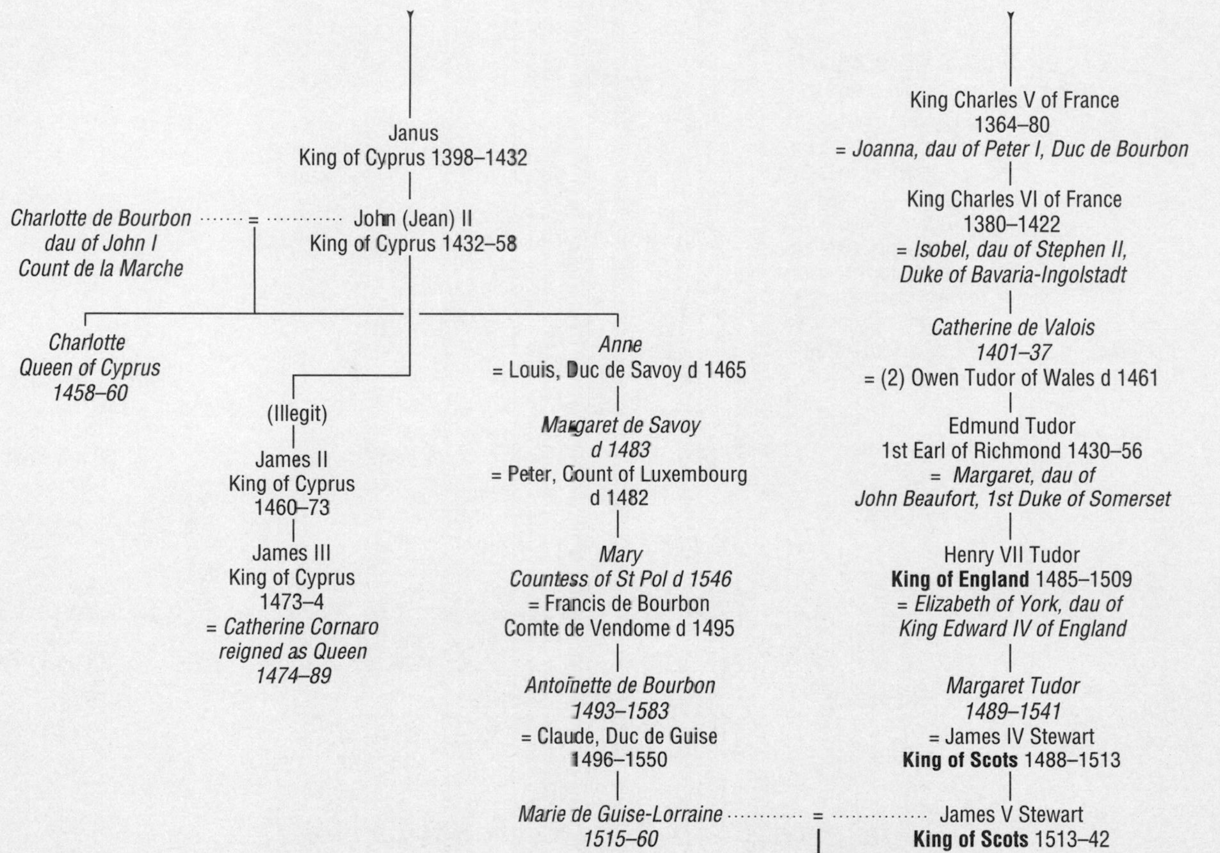
Janus
King of Cyprus 1398–1432
Charlotte de Bourbon
dau of John I
Count de la Marche
=
John (Jean) II
King of Cyprus 1432–58
Charlotte
Queen of Cyprus
1458–60
(Illegit)
James II
King of Cyprus
1460–73
James III
King of Cyprus
1473–4
= Catherine Cornaro
reigned as Queen
1474–89
Anne
= Louis, Duc de Savoy d 1465
Margaret de Savoy
d 1483
= Peter, Count of Luxembourg
d 1482
Mary
Countess of St Pol d 1546
= Francis de Bourbon
Comte de Vendome d 1495
Antoinette de Bourbon
1493–1583
= Claude, Duc de Guise
1496–1550
Marie de Guise-Lorraine
1515–60
=
King Charles V of France
1364–80
= Joanna, dau of Peter I, Duc de Bourbon
King Charles VI of France
1380–1422
= Isobel, dau of Stephen II,
Duke of Bavaria-Ingolstadt
Catherine de Valois
1401–37
= (2) Owen Tudor of Wales d 1461
Edmund Tudor
1st Earl of Richmond 1430–56
= Margaret, dau of
John Beaufort, 1st Duke of Somerset
Henry VII Tudor
King of England 1485–1509
= Elizabeth of York, dau of
King Edward IV of England
Margaret Tudor
1489–1541
= James IV Stewart
King of Scots 1488–1513
James V Stewart
King of Scots 1513–42

Monarchs from the 1688 Whig Revolution

GREAT BRITAIN		FRANCE
[*de jure*] **STUART**	[*de facto*] **ORANGE/STUART**	**BOURBON**
JAMES VII (II) d 1701 [no abdication] = *Mary Beatrix D'Este of Modena*	**WILLIAM III** 1689–1702 Duke of Orange (Dutch) Son of William of Nassau and *Mary Stuart, dau of Charles I* And = *MARY II (Stuart)* 1689–94 *Dau of James VII (II) and 1st wife, Anne Hyde dsp*	
JAMES VIII (III) 1701–66 Son of James VII Stuart = *Princess Maria Clementina Sobieska of Poland*	***ANNE*** *(Stuart)* 1702–14 *Dau of James VII (II) and Anne Hyde of Clarendon dsp*	
	HANOVER	
	GEORGE I 1714–27 [House of Guelph] Duke of Brunswick-Luneburg Son of Elector of Hanover (German) = *Sophia Dorothy, dau of George William, Duke of Zelle*	**LOUIS XV** 1715–74 G g-son of Louis XIV Son of Louis, Duke of Burgundy (d 1712), son of Louis the Dauphin (d 1711) [Policies under Cardinal Fleury to 1743] = *Marie Leczinska of Poland* *Mistresses:* (1) *Jeanne, Mme de Pomadour* (2) *Marie, Mme du Barry* FRENCH COLONIES (CANADA/INDIA) LOST DURING SEVEN YEARS WAR 1756–63

CHARLES III 1766–88
Count of Albany
Son of James VIII Stuart
= *Comtesse Marguerite de Lussan de Massillan*

HENRY I (IX) 1788–1807
Henry Benedict
Cardinal, Duke of York
Bro of Charles III Stuart
dsp

JAMES IX (IV) 1807–45
Edward James
2nd Count of Albany
Son of Charles III Stuart
= *Maria Emmanuel Pasquini of Italy*

GEORGE II 1727–60
Duke & Elector of Hanover
Son of George I
= *Whilhelmina Caroline, dau of John Frederick, Margrave of Brandenburgh-Anspach*

GEORGE III 1760–1820
King of Hanover
(Grandson of George II)
Son of Frederick, Prince of Wales
= *Sophia Charlotte, dau of Charles, Duke of Mecklenburg-Strelitz*

GEORGE IV 1820–30
King of Hanover
Son of George III
= (2) *Caroline Amelia, dau of Charles William Ferdinand, Duke of Brunswick-Wölfenbuttel*
Predeceased by daughter
No male heir

LOUIS XVI 1774–93
Grandson of Louis XV
Son of Louis the Dauphin (d 1765)
= *Marie Antoinette, daughter of Emperor Francis I and Maria Theresa*
Both Louis and *Marie Antoinette* guillotined (1793) in Revolution

FRENCH REVOLUTION 1789–99 ABOLISHED ABSOLUTE MONARCHY IN FRANCE. SUPREME COURT *PARLEMENT OF PARIS* ABOLISHED IN 1792 WHEN **FIRST REPUBLIC** PROCLAIMED

LOUIS XVII 1793–5
Nominal King of France
Son of Louis XVI
Died in prison

LOUIS XVIII 1795–1824
Count of Provence
Nominal King of France
Uncle of Louis XVII
Brother of Louis XVI
Lived in exile until 1814

Monarchs from the 1688 Whig Revolution – continued

HENRY II (X) 1845–69
Henry Edward Benedict
3rd Count of Albany
Son of James IX Stuart
= *Agnes Beatrix de Pescara of Italy*

CHARLES IV 1869–87
Charles Benedict James
4th Count of Albany
Son of Henry II Stuart
= *Louis Jeanne Francoise Dalvray of France*

FROM DECEMBER 1913, LEGAL DECLARATIONS SWORN AND SIGNED BY STUARTS/STEWARTS RELINQUISHING RIGHTS TO ENGLISH CROWN OF SAINT EDWARD, BUT RETAINING RIGHTS TO THE HEREDITARY KINGDOM OF SCOTS

WILLIAM IV 1830–7
King of Hanover
Brother of George IV
= *Amelia Adelaide, dau of George Frederick, Duke of Saxe Meiningen*
Predeceased by daughters
No male heir

VICTORIA 1837–1901
(Alexandrina Victoria)
Regina et Imperiatrix
Niece of William IV
Dau of his brother, Edward, Duke of Kent, and Princess Victoria Mary, dau of Francis Frederick, Duke of Saxe-Saalfeld-Coburg
= Francis Albert, Prince of Saxe-Coburg-Gotha. Son of Ernest I of Saxe-Coburg and Gotha

COUP D'ÉTAT BY **NAPOLEON BUONAPARTE** BROUGHT REVOLUTION TO AN END IN NOV 1799. HE WAS CONSUL FROM 1802, AND EMPEROR NAPOLEAN I OF THE FRENCH 1804–15 d 1821

CHARLES X 1824–30
Count of Artois
Brother of Louis XVI and Louis XVIII
English exile in Revolution
Returned to France 1824
Abdicated 1830

ORLEANS

Louis Philippe 1830–48
Elected (Citizen King) of the French.
Son of Duke of Orleans.
Abdicated, d (England) 1850

HENRY III of Scots 1887–1941
(XI of England 1887–1913)
Julius Anthony Henry
5th Count of Albany
Son of Charles IV Stuart
= *Maria Joanna Vandenbosch of Flanders*

SAXE-COBURG-GOTHA

EDWARD VII 1901–10
[Albert Edward]
Son of Queen Victoria
= *Princess Alexandra, dau of Christian IX of Denmark*

WINDSOR

FAMILY NAME CHANGED TO WINDSOR IN FIRST WORLD WAR (1917) TO VEIL GERMAN HERITAGE. WINDSOR WAS THE SURNAME OF KING EDWARD III (d 1377)

GEORGE V 1910–36
Son of Edward VII
= *Princess Mary of Teck*

EDWARD VIII 1936
Duke of Windsor
1st son of George V
= *Mrs Wallis Simpson*
Abdicated

BOURBON *de jure* succession:

Henri V of France 1830–83
Comte de Chambord
Grandson and Testamentary
Nominee of Charles X
Son of Charles, Duc de Berri
by 2nd wife. dsp

1848 REVOLUTION PROCLAIMED **SECOND REPUBLIC** WITH 44 SUCCESSIVE GOVERNMENTS BETWEEN 1918 AND 1940

de jure

LOUIS XIX 1883–1918
Louis Xavier Ferdinand
Duc d'Aquitaine
Half-nephew of Henri V
G-son of Charles, Duc de Berri
by 1st wife, *Amy Brown*
(no male Issue)

JACQUES I 1918–75
James, Duke of Segovia
2nd son of Alfonso XIII of Spain
Bourbon Linear Nominee of Louis XIX
= *Emmanuela, dau of Roger de Dampierre, Marquis of San Lorenzo*

Monarchs from the 1688 Whig Revolution – continued

JAMES X of Scots 1941–63
Anthony James
6th Count of Albany
Son of Henry III Stewart
dsp

ALEXANDER IV of Scots 1963–
Michael James Alexander
7th Count of Albany
Grand-nephew of James X Stewart
Grandson of Julius Joseph James Stewart of Annandale.
Son of *Renée Julienne Stewart, Princess Royal of Strathearn*, and Baron Gustave Lafosse de Blois de Chatry

GEORGE VI 1936-52
[Prince Albert]
2nd son of George V
= *Elizabeth Bowes-Lyon, dau of Claude, Earl of Strathmore*

ELIZABETH II 1952–
Daughter of George VI
= (1947) Philip (Duke of Edinburgh), son of Prince Andrew, son of King George I of Greece. Great-grandson of Christian IX of Denmark. Descended in female line via mother, *Princess Alice of Battenberg*, from the German House of Hesse, and from *Queen Victoria*

When Saxe-Coburg-Gotha became Windsor in WWI, the BATTENBERG name was also changed to Mountbatten. Philip assumed the name of MOUNTBATTEN on gaining British citizenship in 1947

FRANCE FELL TO GERMANY IN SECOND WORLD WAR. LIBERATED IN 1944. DE GAULLE ESTABLISHED PROVISIONAL GOVERNMENT. **FOURTH REPUBLIC** PROCLAIMED IN 1946

DE GAULLE RECALLED AS PRESIDENT OF THE **FIFTH REPUBLIC** 1958. RESIGNED 1969

ALFONSE I 1975–89
Alfonso, Duc d'Anjou & Cadiz
Son of Jacques I
= *Carmen, dau of Christopher Martinez-Bordiu de Villaverde*

LOUIS XX 1989–
Louis Alfonso
Duc d'Anjou and Cadiz
2nd son of Alfonse I

Walkinshaw Descent

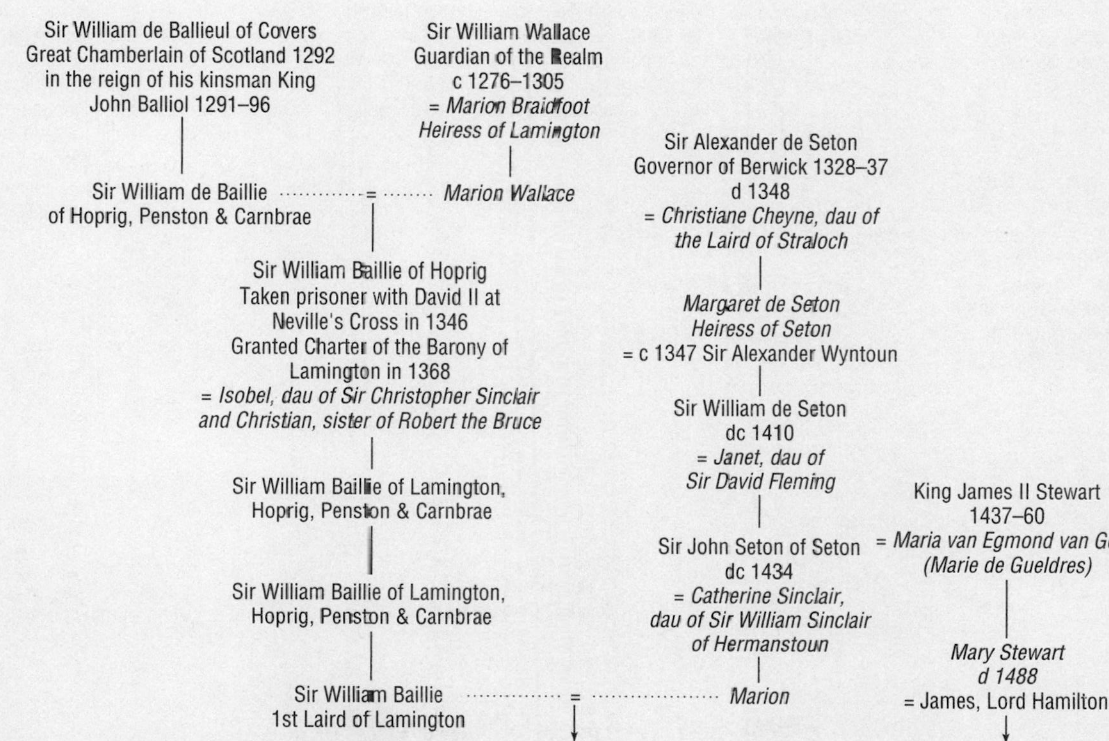

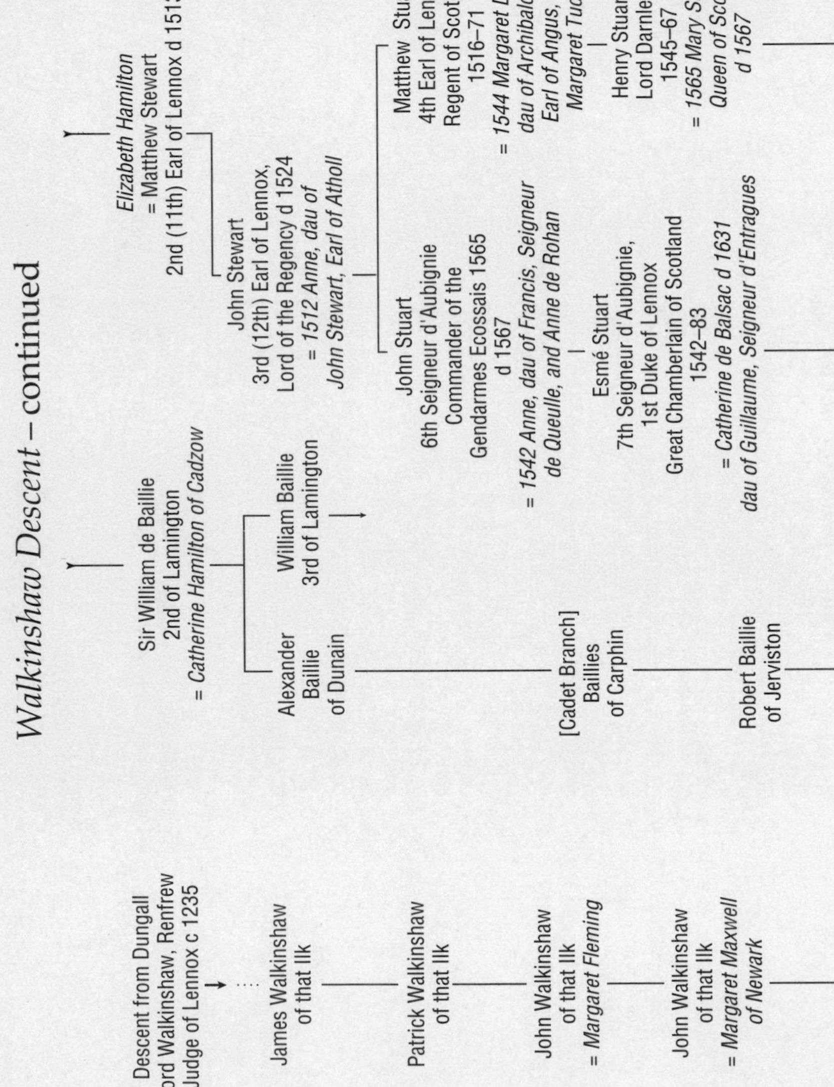
Walkinshaw Descent – continued
Descent from Dungall
Lord Walkinshaw, Renfrew
Judge of Lennox c 1235
James Walkinshaw
of that Ilk
Patrick Walkinshaw
of that Ilk
John Walkinshaw
of that Ilk
= *Margaret Fleming*
John Walkinshaw
of that Ilk
= *Margaret Maxwell*
of Newark
Sir William de Baillie
2nd of Lamington
= *Catherine Hamilton of Cadzow*
Alexander
Baillie
of Dunain
William Baillie
3rd of Lamington
[Cadet Branch]
Baillies
of Carphin
Robert Baillie
of Jerviston
Elizabeth Hamilton
= Matthew Stewart
2nd (11th) Earl of Lennox d 1513
John Stewart
3rd (12th) Earl of Lennox,
Lord of the Regency d 1524
= *1512 Anne, dau of*
John Stewart, Earl of Atholl
John Stuart
6th Seigneur d'Aubignie
Commander of the
Gendarmes Ecossais 1565
d 1567
= *1542 Anne, dau of Francis, Seigneur*
de Queulle, and Anne de Rohan
Esmé Stuart
7th Seigneur d'Aubignie,
1st Duke of Lennox
Great Chamberlain of Scotland
1542–83
= *Catherine de Balsac d 1631*
dau of Guillaume, Seigneur d'Entragues
Matthew Stuart
4th Earl of Lennox
Regent of Scotland
1516–71
= *1544 Margaret Douglas*
dau of Archibald, 6th
Earl of Angus, and
Margaret Tudor
Henry Stuart
Lord Darnley
1545–67
= *1565 Mary Stuart*
Queen of Scots
d 1567

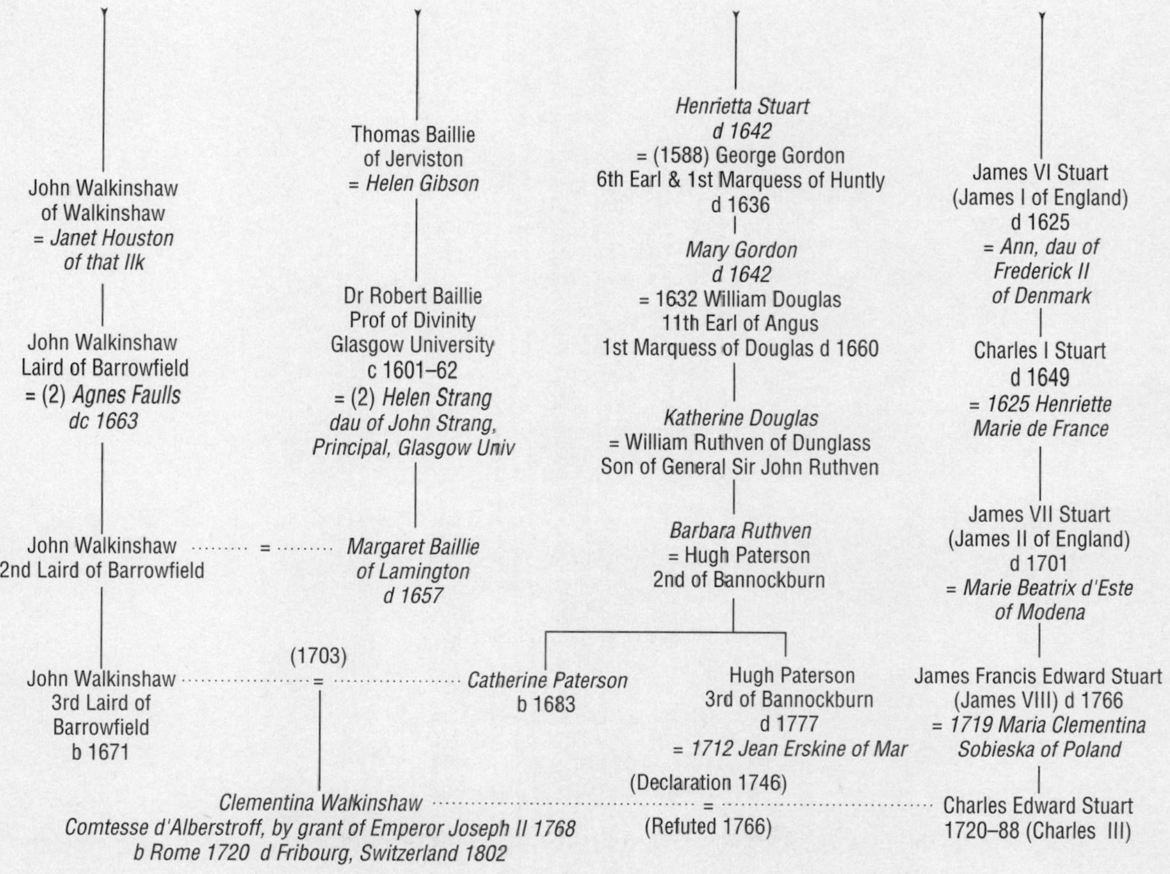
John Walkinshaw
of Walkinshaw
= Janet Houston
of that Ilk
John Walkinshaw
Laird of Barrowfield
= (2) Agnes Faulls
dc 1663
John Walkinshaw
2nd Laird of Barrowfield
=
John Walkinshaw
3rd Laird of
Barrowfield
b 1671
(1703)
=
Clementina Walkinshaw
Comtesse d'Alberstroff, by grant of Emperor Joseph II 1768
b Rome 1720 d Fribourg, Switzerland 1802
Thomas Baillie
of Jerviston
= Helen Gibson
Dr Robert Baillie
Prof of Divinity
Glasgow University
c 1601–62
= (2) Helen Strang
dau of John Strang,
Principal, Glasgow Univ
Margaret Baillie
of Lamington
d 1657
Henrietta Stuart
d 1642
= (1588) George Gordon
6th Earl & 1st Marquess of Huntly
d 1636
Mary Gordon
d 1642
= 1632 William Douglas
11th Earl of Angus
1st Marquess of Douglas d 1660
Katherine Douglas
= William Ruthven of Dunglass
Son of General Sir John Ruthven
Barbara Ruthven
= Hugh Paterson
2nd of Bannockburn
Catherine Paterson
b 1683
Hugh Paterson
3rd of Bannockburn
d 1777
= 1712 Jean Erskine of Mar
(Declaration 1746)
=
(Refuted 1766)
James VI Stuart
(James I of England)
d 1625
= Ann, dau of
Frederick II
of Denmark
Charles I Stuart
d 1649
= 1625 Henriette
Marie de France
James VII Stuart
(James II of England)
d 1701
= Marie Beatrix d'Este
of Modena
James Francis Edward Stuart
(James VIII) d 1766
= 1719 Maria Clementina
Sobieska of Poland
Charles Edward Stuart
1720–88 (Charles III)

Bruce Descent to Stolberg-Guedern, Scots Maternal Route to Louise de Stolberg

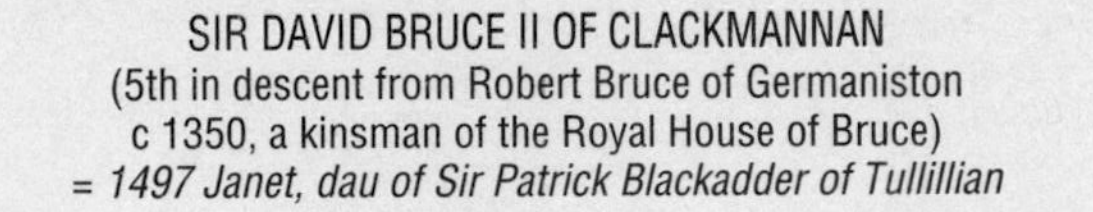

SIR DAVID BRUCE II OF CLACKMANNAN
(5th in descent from Robert Bruce of Germaniston
c 1350, a kinsman of the Royal House of Bruce)
= *1497 Janet, dau of Sir Patrick Blackadder of Tullillian*

|

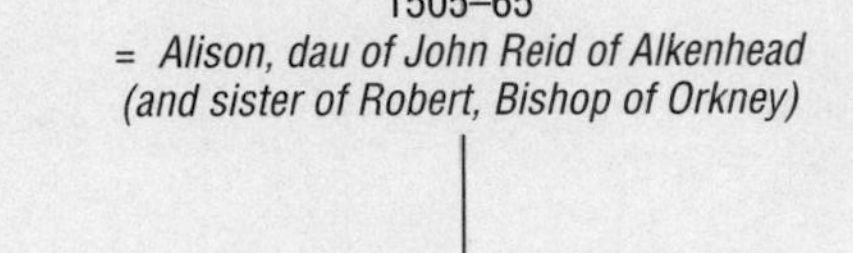

EDWARD BRUCE OF BLAIRHALL
1505–65
= *Alison, dau of John Reid of Alkenhead*
(and sister of Robert, Bishop of Orkney)

|

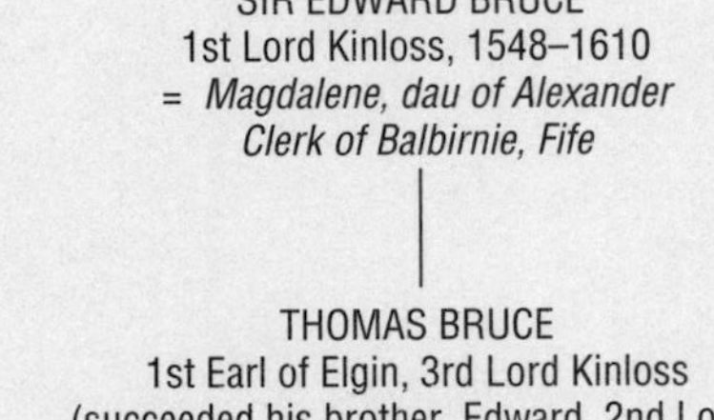

SIR EDWARD BRUCE
1st Lord Kinloss, 1548–1610
= *Magdalene, dau of Alexander*
Clerk of Balbirnie, Fife

|

THOMAS BRUCE
1st Earl of Elgin, 3rd Lord Kinloss
(succeeded his brother, Edward, 2nd Lord)
1599–1663
= *1622 Anne, dau of Sir Robert*
Chichester of Raleigh, Devon

↓

ROBERT BRUCE
2nd Earl of Elgin, 1st Earl of Ailesbury
d 1685
= *1646 Lady Diana Grey, dau of Henry*
1st Earl of Stamford

THOMAS BRUCE
3rd Earl of Elgin, 2nd Earl of Ailesbury
d 1741 Brussels
= *2nd 1700 Charlotte d'Argenteau, Countess*
d'Esseneux, Baroness de Melsbroek, Flanders d 1710

MARIA THERESA CHARLOTTE BRUCE
= Maximillian Emanuel, Prince de Hornes

ELIZABETH DE HORNES
= Gustavus, Prince de Stolberg-Guedern

PRINCESS LOUISA MAXIMILLIENE DE STOLBERG-GUEDERN
Countess of Albany, Baroness Renfrew dsp 1824
= 1772 Charles Edward Stuart (Charles III), div 1784

D'audibert de Lussan Route 1 to Marguerite de Massillan

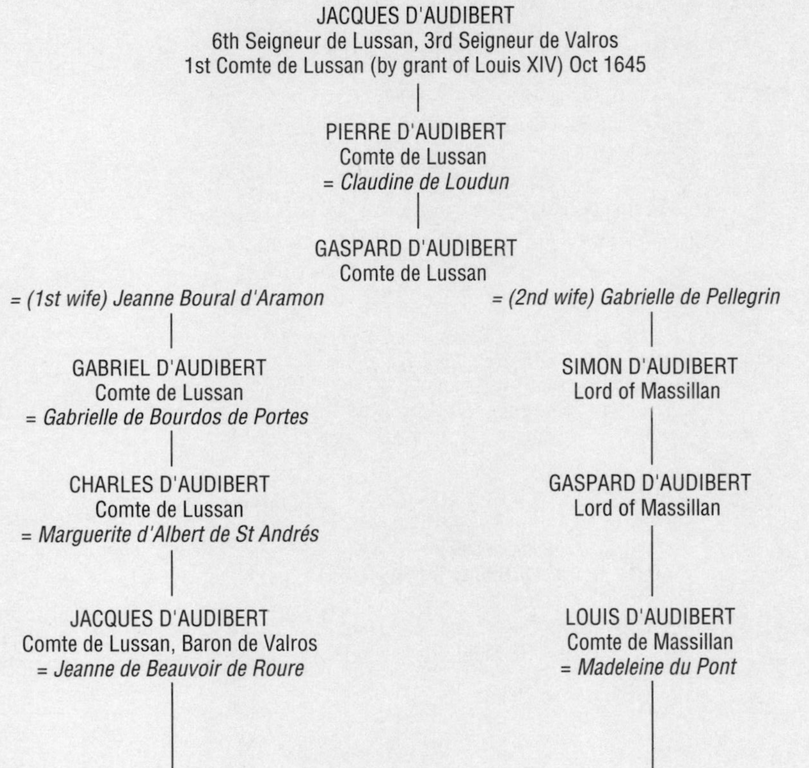

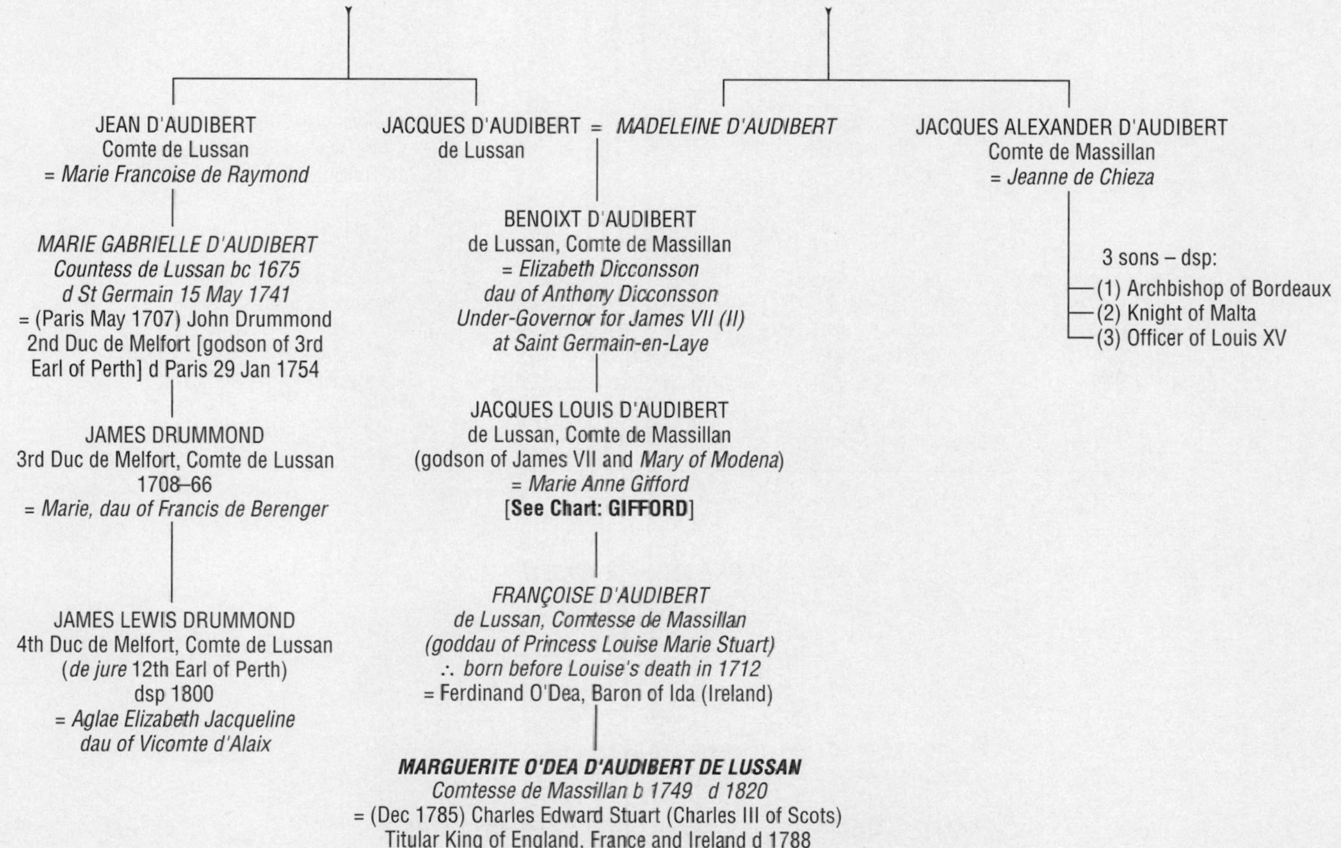
JEAN D'AUDIBERT
Comte de Lussan
= Marie Francoise de Raymond
MARIE GABRIELLE D'AUDIBERT
Countess de Lussan bc 1675
d St Germain 15 May 1741
= (Paris May 1707) John Drummond
2nd Duc de Melfort [godson of 3rd
Earl of Perth] d Paris 29 Jan 1754
JAMES DRUMMOND
3rd Duc de Melfort, Comte de Lussan
1708–66
= Marie, dau of Francis de Berenger
JAMES LEWIS DRUMMOND
4th Duc de Melfort, Comte de Lussan
(de jure 12th Earl of Perth)
dsp 1800
= Aglae Elizabeth Jacqueline
dau of Vicomte d'Alaix
JACQUES D'AUDIBERT = MADELEINE D'AUDIBERT
de Lussan
BENOIXT D'AUDIBERT
de Lussan, Comte de Massillan
= Elizabeth Dicconsson
dau of Anthony Dicconsson
Under-Governor for James VII (II)
at Saint Germain-en-Laye
JACQUES LOUIS D'AUDIBERT
de Lussan, Comte de Massillan
(godson of James VII and Mary of Modena)
= Marie Anne Gifford
[See Chart: GIFFORD]
FRANÇOISE D'AUDIBERT
de Lussan, Comtesse de Massillan
(goddau of Princess Louise Marie Stuart)
∴ born before Louise's death in 1712
= Ferdinand O'Dea, Baron of Ida (Ireland)
MARGUERITE O'DEA D'AUDIBERT DE LUSSAN
Comtesse de Massillan b 1749 d 1820
= (Dec 1785) Charles Edward Stuart (Charles III of Scots)
Titular King of England, France and Ireland d 1788
JACQUES ALEXANDER D'AUDIBERT
Comte de Massillan
= Jeanne de Chieza
3 sons – dsp:
(1) Archbishop of Bordeaux
(2) Knight of Malta
(3) Officer of Louis XV

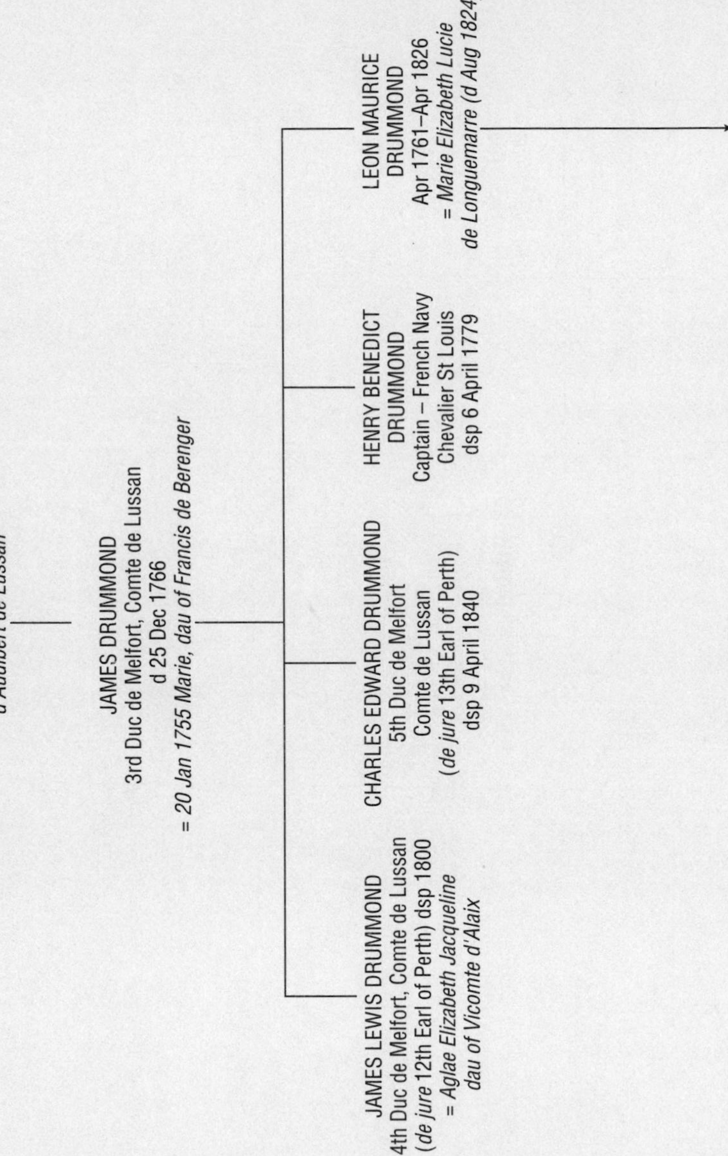
Supplement to d'Audibert de Lussan Chart
From *Marie Gabrielle d'Audibert de Lussan*
JAMES DRUMMOND
3rd Duc de Melfort, Comte de Lussan
d 25 Dec 1766
= *20 Jan 1755 Marie, dau of Francis de Berenger*
JAMES LEWIS DRUMMOND
4th Duc de Melfort, Comte de Lussan
(*de jure* 12th Earl of Perth) dsp 1800
= *Aglae Elizabeth Jacqueline dau of Vicomte d'Alaix*
CHARLES EDWARD DRUMMOND
5th Duc de Melfort
Comte de Lussan
(*de jure* 13th Earl of Perth)
dsp 9 April 1840
HENRY BENEDICT DRUMMOND
Captain – French Navy
Chevalier St Louis
dsp 6 April 1779
LEON MAURICE DRUMMOND
Apr 1761–Apr 1826
= *Marie Elizabeth Lucie de Longuemarre (d Aug 1824)*

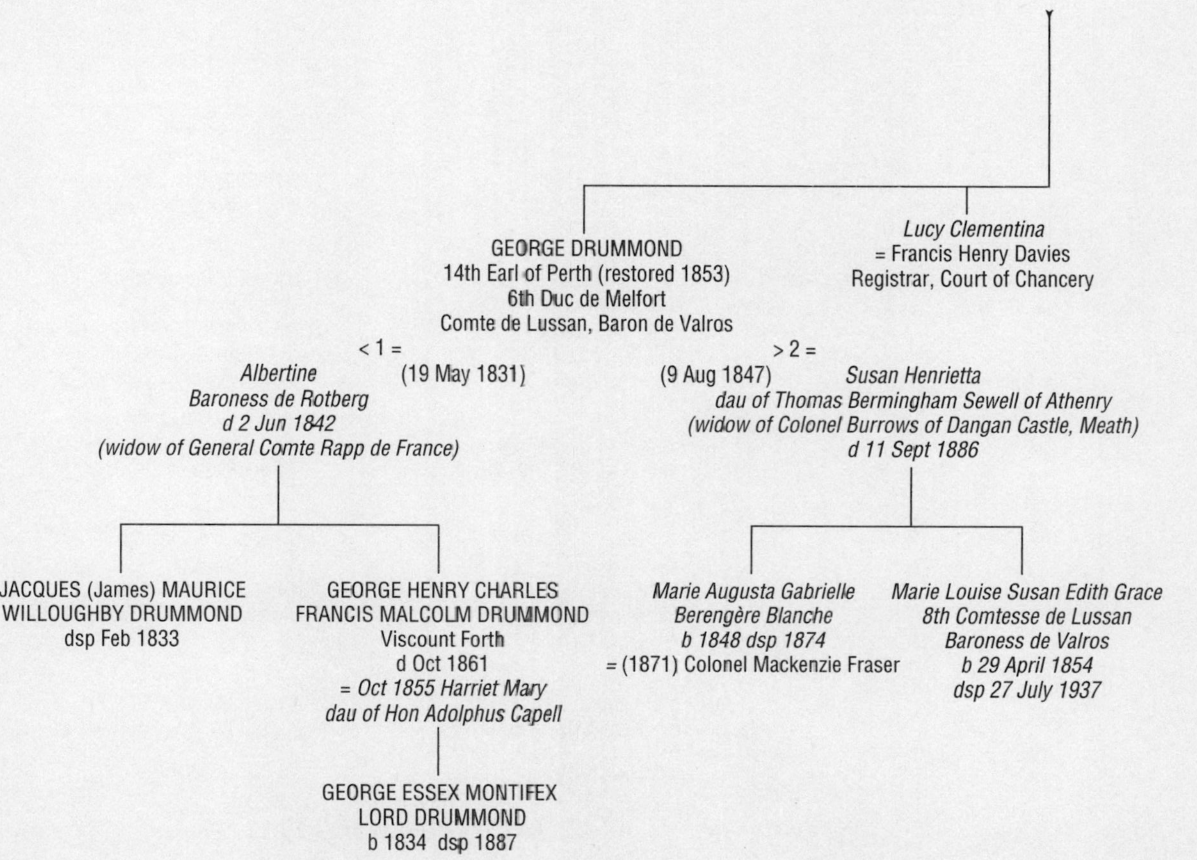
GEORGE DRUMMOND
14th Earl of Perth (restored 1853)
6th Duc de Melfort
Comte de Lussan, Baron de Valros
Lucy Clementina
= Francis Henry Davies
Registrar, Court of Chancery
< 1 =
(19 May 1831)
Albertine
Baroness de Rotberg
d 2 Jun 1842
(widow of General Comte Rapp de France)
> 2 =
(9 Aug 1847)
Susan Henrietta
dau of Thomas Bermingham Sewell of Athenry
(widow of Colonel Burrows of Dangan Castle, Meath)
d 11 Sept 1886
JACQUES (James) MAURICE
WILLOUGHBY DRUMMOND
dsp Feb 1833
GEORGE HENRY CHARLES
FRANCIS MALCOLM DRUMMOND
Viscount Forth
d Oct 1861
= *Oct 1855 Harriet Mary*
dau of Hon Adolphus Capell
GEORGE ESSEX MONTIFEX
LORD DRUMMOND
b 1834 dsp 1887
Marie Augusta Gabrielle
Berengère Blanche
b 1848 dsp 1874
= (1871) Colonel Mackenzie Fraser
Marie Louise Susan Edith Grace
8th Comtesse de Lussan
Baroness de Valros
b 29 April 1854
dsp 27 July 1937

Gifford, route 2 to Marguerite de Massillan

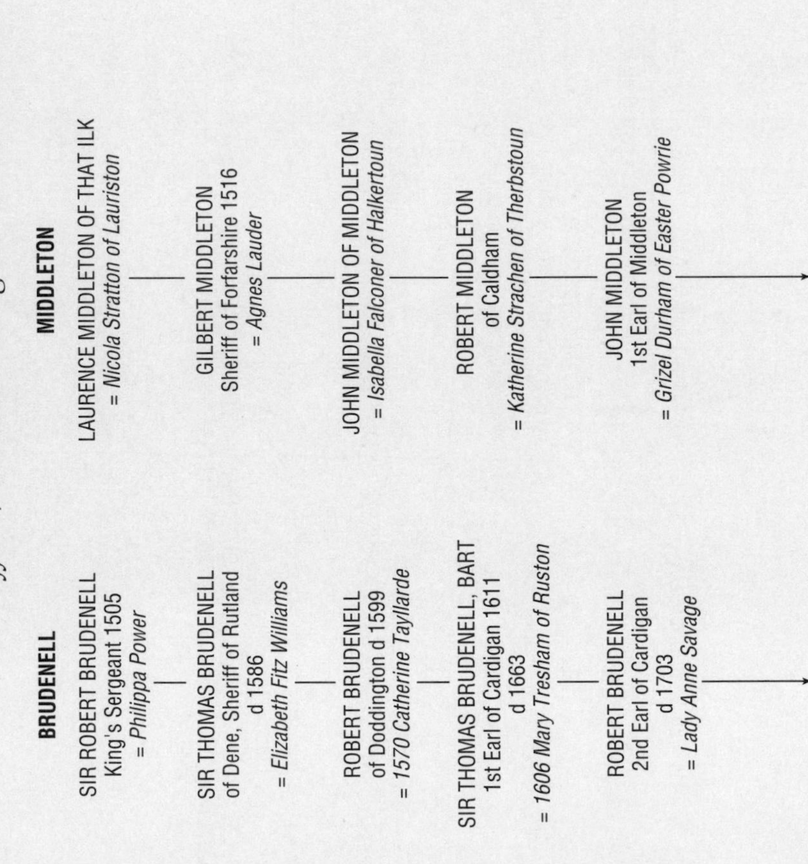

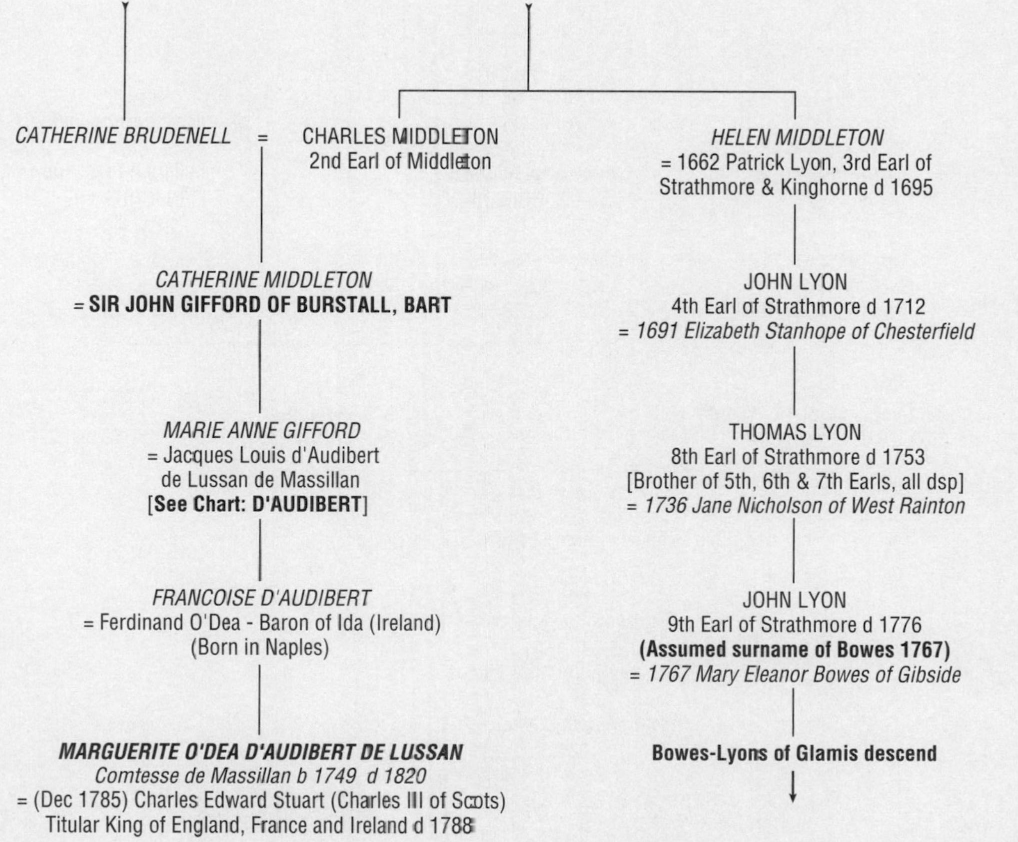
CATHERINE BRUDENELL = CHARLES MIDDLETON
2nd Earl of Middleton
HELEN MIDDLETON
= 1662 Patrick Lyon, 3rd Earl of
Strathmore & Kinghorne d 1695
CATHERINE MIDDLETON
= SIR JOHN GIFFORD OF BURSTALL, BART
JOHN LYON
4th Earl of Strathmore d 1712
= 1691 Elizabeth Stanhope of Chesterfield
MARIE ANNE GIFFORD
= Jacques Louis d'Audibert
de Lussan de Massillan
[See Chart: D'AUDIBERT]
THOMAS LYON
8th Earl of Strathmore d 1753
[Brother of 5th, 6th & 7th Earls, all dsp]
= 1736 Jane Nicholson of West Rainton
FRANCOISE D'AUDIBERT
= Ferdinand O'Dea - Baron of Ida (Ireland)
(Born in Naples)
JOHN LYON
9th Earl of Strathmore d 1776
(Assumed surname of Bowes 1767)
= 1767 Mary Eleanor Bowes of Gibside
MARGUERITE O'DEA D'AUDIBERT DE LUSSAN
Comtesse de Massillan b 1749 d 1820
= (Dec 1785) Charles Edward Stuart (Charles III of Scots)
Titular King of England, France and Ireland d 1788
Bowes-Lyons of Glamis descend

De Forano, Counts of Albany Chart: Supplement 1

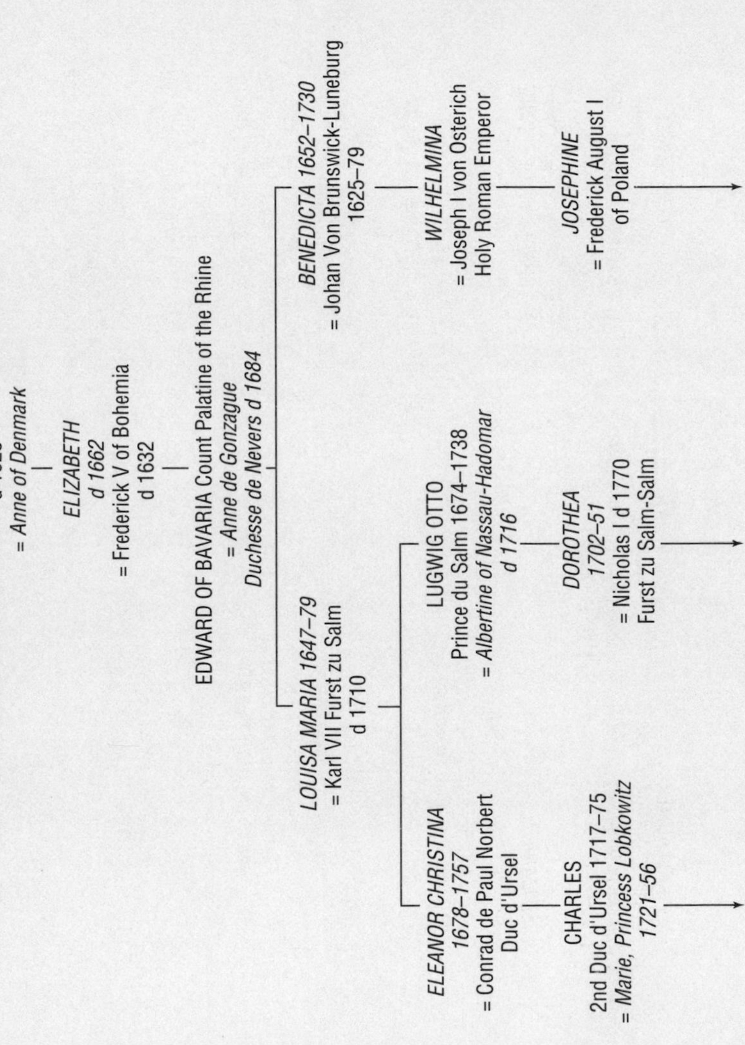

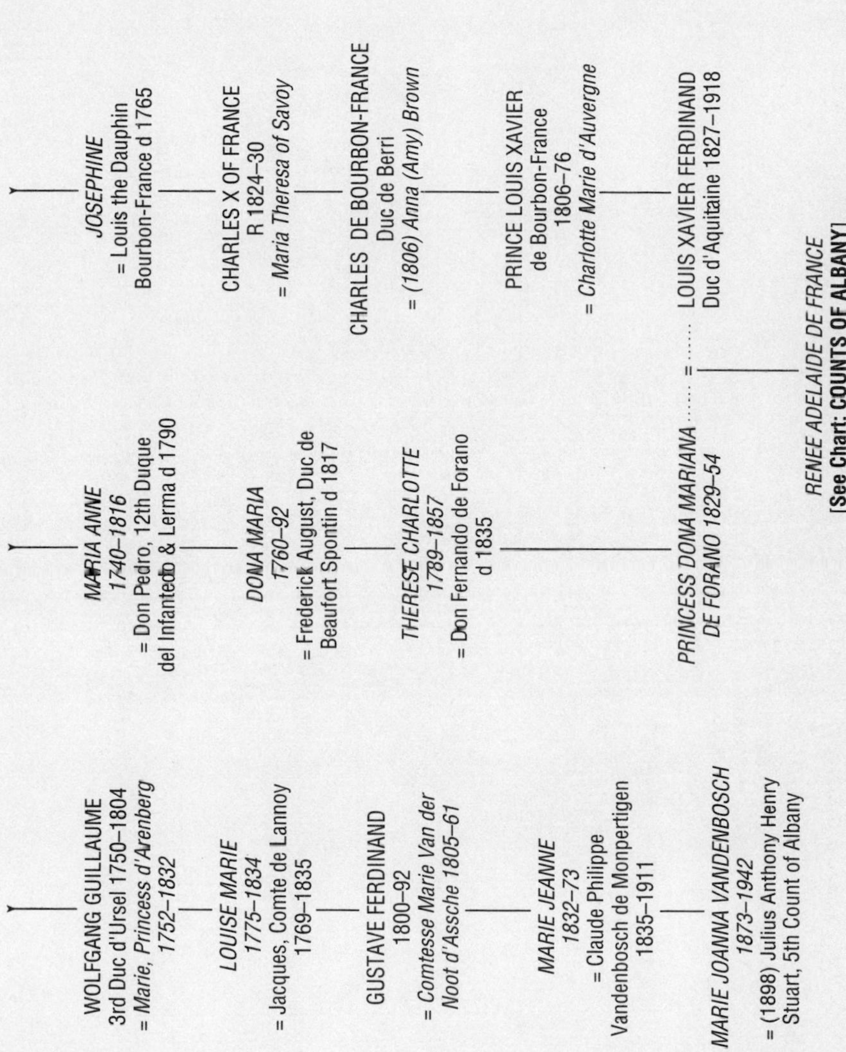
WOLFGANG GUILLAUME
3rd Duc d'Ursel 1750–1804
= Marie, Princess d'Arenberg
1752–1832
LOUISE MARIE
1775–1834
= Jacques, Comte de Lannoy
1769–1835
GUSTAVE FERDINAND
1800–92
= Comtesse Marie Van der
Noot d'Assche 1805–61
MARIE JEANNE
1832–73
= Claude Philippe
Vandenbosch de Monpertigen
1835–1911
MARIE JOANNA VANDENBOSCH
1873–1942
= (1898) Julius Anthony Henry
Stuart, 5th Count of Albany
MARIA ANNE
1740–1816
= Don Pedro, 12th Duque
del Infantado & Lerma d 1790
DONA MARIA
1760–92
= Frederick August, Duc de
Beaufort Spontin d 1817
THERESE CHARLOTTE
1789–1857
= Don Fernando de Forano
d 1835
PRINCESS DONA MARIANA
DE FORANO 1829–54
=
JOSEPHINE
= Louis the Dauphin
Bourbon-France d 1765
CHARLES X OF FRANCE
R 1824–30
= Maria Theresa of Savoy
CHARLES DE BOURBON-FRANCE
Duc de Berri
= (1806) Anna (Amy) Brown
PRINCE LOUIS XAVIER
de Bourbon-France
1806–76
= Charlotte Marie d'Auvergne
LOUIS XAVIER FERDINAND
Duc d'Aquitaine 1827–1918
RENEE ADELAIDE DE FRANCE
[See Chart: COUNTS OF ALBANY]

Albany Cadet Branches, Counts of Albany Chart: Supplement 2

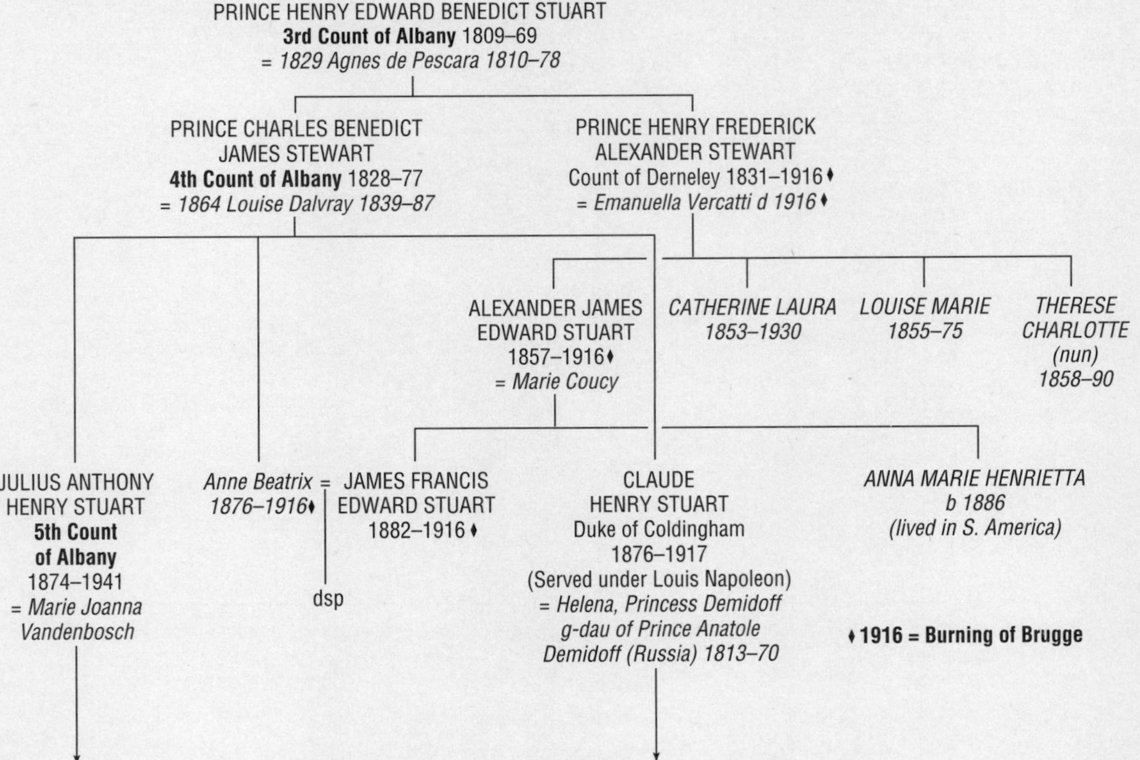

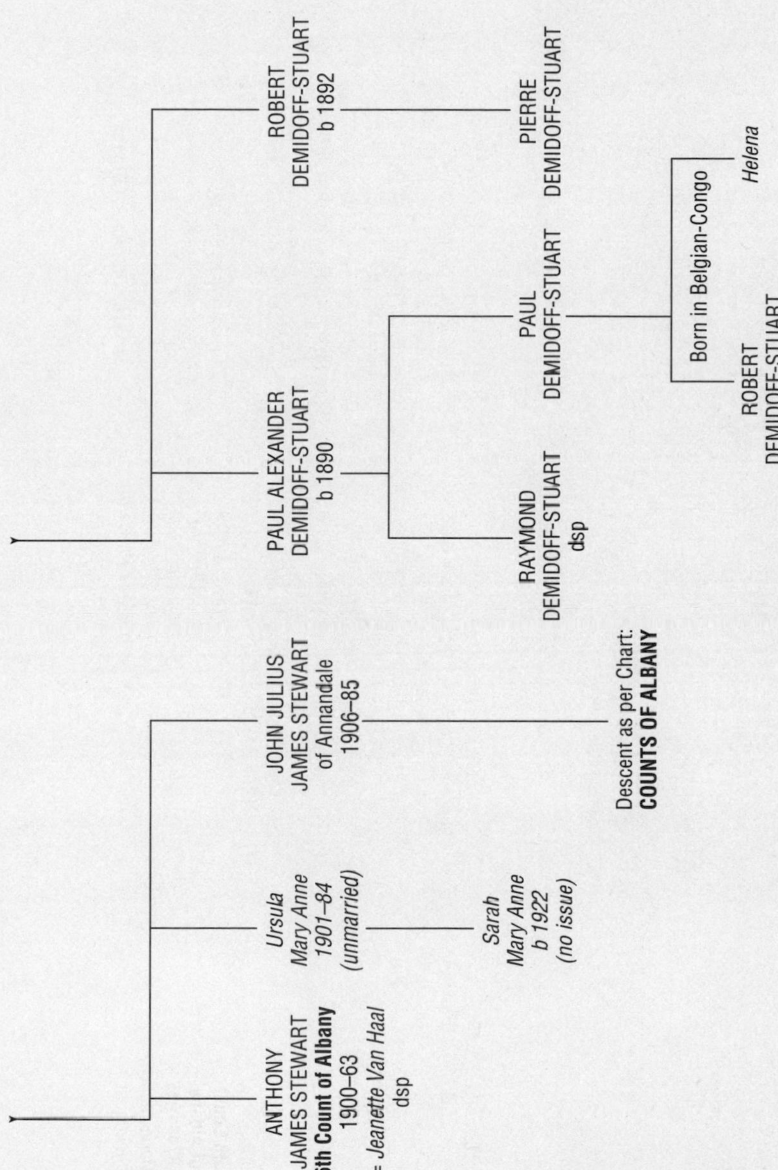
ANTHONY
JAMES STEWART
6th Count of Albany
1900–63
= Jeanette Van Haal
dsp
Ursula
Mary Anne
1901–84
(unmarried)
Sarah
Mary Anne
b 1922
(no issue)
JOHN JULIUS
JAMES STEWART
of Annandale
1906–85
Descent as per Chart:
COUNTS OF ALBANY
PAUL ALEXANDER
DEMIDOFF-STUART
b 1890
RAYMOND
DEMIDOFF-STUART
dsp
PAUL
DEMIDOFF-STUART
Born in Belgian-Congo
ROBERT
DEMIDOFF-STUART
Helena
ROBERT
DEMIDOFF-STUART
b 1892
PIERRE
DEMIDOFF-STUART

Natural Offspring of Charles Edward Stuart

Chart A

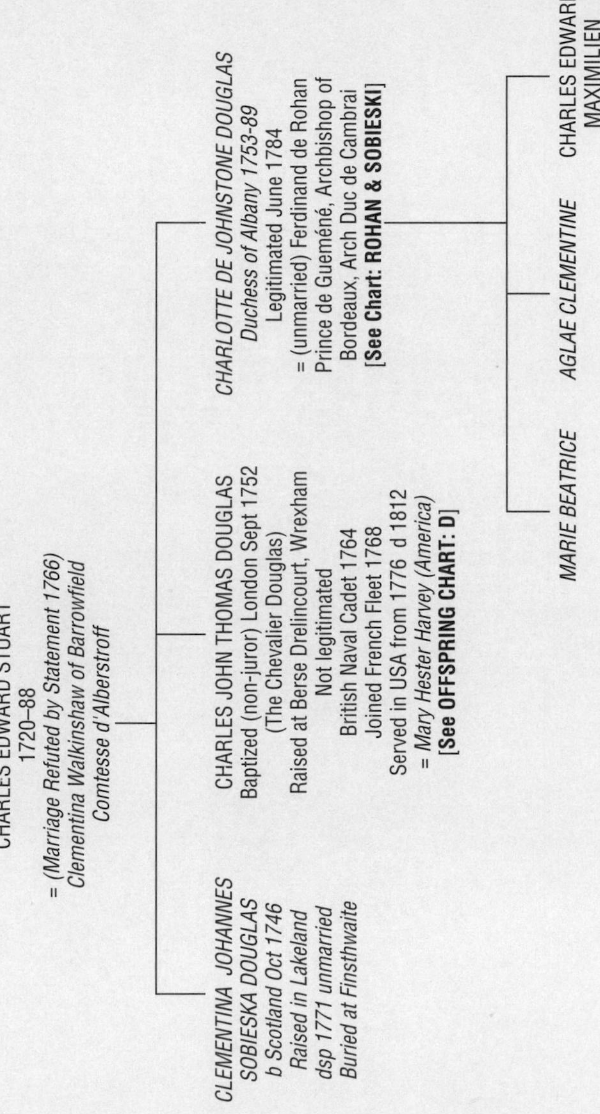

Chart B

CHARLES EDWARD STUART
1720–88
= *(mistress 1750)*
Dau of Squire Propert of Trevigan, Pembrokeshire
1730–75

|

Lucy
(Raised at Berse Drelincourt, Wrexham)
Mistress of Edward Augustus, Duke of York
son of King George III
= Secretly married in Monaco to Duke Edward prior to his death in 1767

|

Rev William (Groves)
b Haverfordwest, March 15 1768
Placed in care of George III's retainer, Groves
Educated at Eton and Oriel College, Oxford in 1780s
Took Holy Orders. Ordained, London 1791
Curate of St Margaret's Westminster
1791–1820, Chaplain to Queen Victoria's father, Edward, Duke of Kent
d 1851

Chart C

CHARLES EDWARD STUART
1720–88
= *(Mistress) Marie Louise de Rohan Guéméné, née de la Tour d'Auvergne, Duchesse de Montbazon d 1781, daughter of Duc de Bouillon and Princess Maria Charlotte Sobieska, maternal aunt of Charles Edward Stuart*
[**See Chart: ROHAN & SOBIESKI**]

CHARLES GODEFROID DE ROHAN
b 28 July 1784
Removed to safety by Louis & Ferdinand de Rohan following Aix la Chapelle Treaty and Charles Edward's removal from Paris in Dec 1748. Publicly recorded as having died in infancy with mock burial Jan 1749. Subsequently raised at Berse Drelincourt, Wrexham, as CHARLES STEWART d 1820

= *m in France to descendant heiress of George Hay of Erroll, Baron of Muiresk, who died at Avignon c 1628*

(= *mother unknown*)

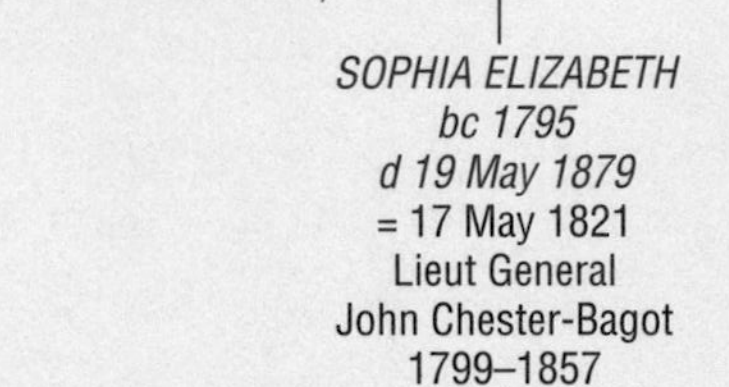

SOPHIA ELIZABETH
bc 1795
d 19 May 1879
= 17 May 1821
Lieut General
John Chester-Bagot
1799–1857

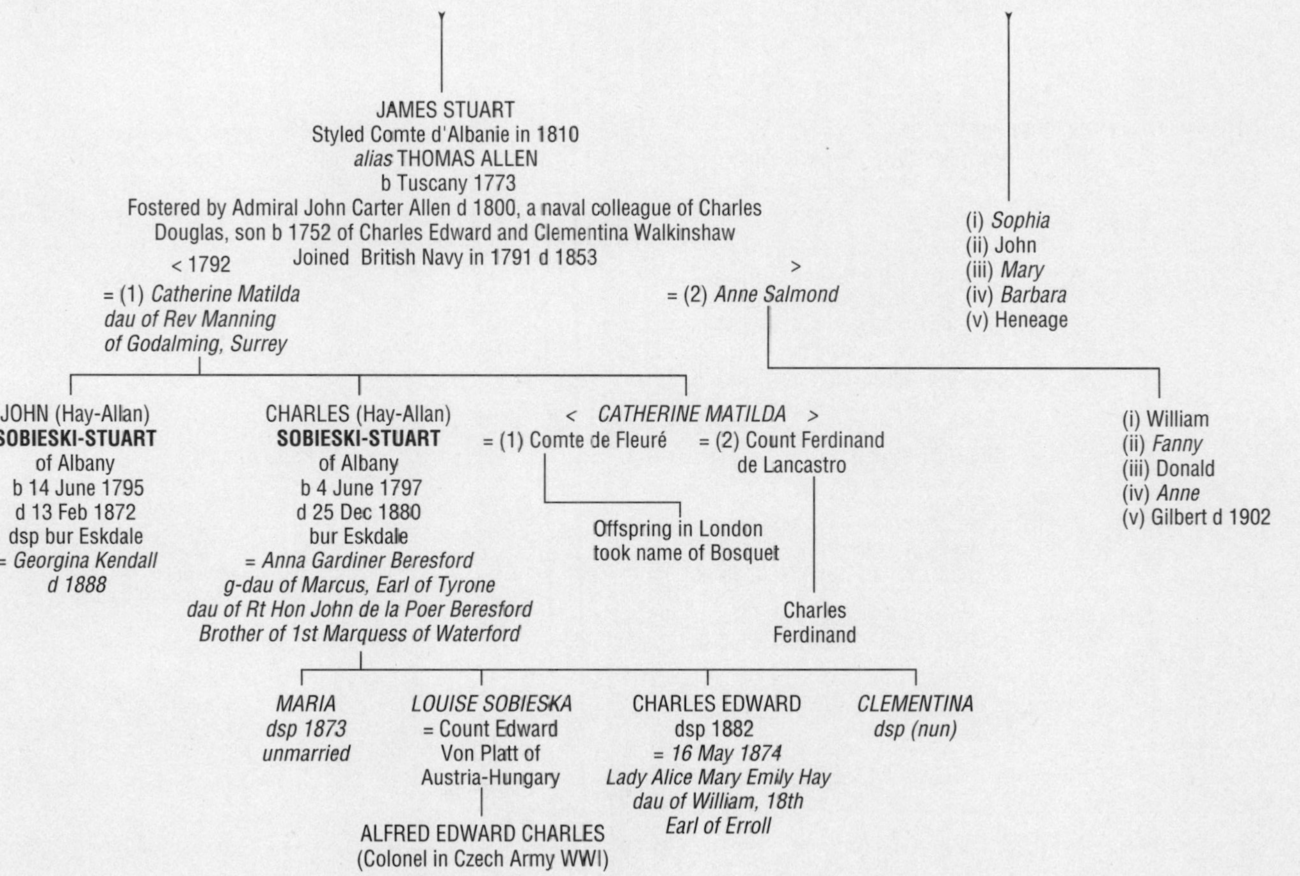
JAMES STUART
Styled Comte d'Albanie in 1810
alias THOMAS ALLEN
b Tuscany 1773
Fostered by Admiral John Carter Allen d 1800, a naval colleague of Charles
Douglas, son b 1752 of Charles Edward and Clementina Walkinshaw
Joined British Navy in 1791 d 1853
< 1792
>
= (1) *Catherine Matilda*
dau of Rev Manning
of Godalming, Surrey
= (2) *Anne Salmond*
(i) *Sophia*
(ii) John
(iii) *Mary*
(iv) *Barbara*
(v) Heneage
JOHN (Hay-Allan)
SOBIESKI-STUART
of Albany
b 14 June 1795
d 13 Feb 1872
dsp bur Eskdale
= *Georgina Kendall*
d 1888
CHARLES (Hay-Allan)
SOBIESKI-STUART
of Albany
b 4 June 1797
d 25 Dec 1880
bur Eskdale
= *Anna Gardiner Beresford*
g-dau of Marcus, Earl of Tyrone
dau of Rt Hon John de la Poer Beresford
Brother of 1st Marquess of Waterford
< *CATHERINE MATILDA* >
= (1) Comte de Fleuré
= (2) Count Ferdinand
de Lancastro
Offspring in London
took name of Bosquet
Charles
Ferdinand
(i) William
(ii) *Fanny*
(iii) Donald
(iv) *Anne*
(v) Gilbert d 1902
MARIA
dsp 1873
unmarried
LOUISE SOBIESKA
= Count Edward
Von Platt of
Austria-Hungary
ALFRED EDWARD CHARLES
(Colonel in Czech Army WWI)
CHARLES EDWARD
dsp 1882
= *16 May 1874*
Lady Alice Mary Emily Hay
dau of William, 18th
Earl of Erroll
CLEMENTINA
dsp (nun)

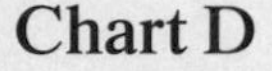

Chart D

KING CHARLES I STUART 1625–1649

KING CHARLES II 1660–85
= *(Mistress) Marguerite Duchesse de Rohan*

James (Giacomo) de Rohano-Stuardo
Principe de Boveria (Legitimated 1667)
= *Theresa Corona of Naples*

Giacomo Enrico
de Rohano-Stuardo
= *Lucia Minelli della Riccia (Rome)*

Giuseppe
= *MARIE DE NEUHOFF*
Titular Queen of Corsica
Dau of King Theodore of Corsica

CHARLES (CARLO) MARIE
(assumed) BUONAPARTE d 1785
= *Maria Letizia Ramolino d 1836*

KING JAMES VII 1685–88

JAMES FRANCIS EDWARD STUART (JAMES VIII) d 1766

CHARLES EDWARD STUART 1720–88
= *Clementina Walkinshaw of Barrowfield*
Comtesse d'Alberstroff

CHARLES JOHN THOMAS DOUGLAS
Baptized (non-juror) London Sept 1752
(The Chevalier Douglas)
Raised at Berse Drelincourt, Wrexham
Not Legitimated
British Naval Cadet 1764
Joined French Fleet 1768
Served in USA from 1776 d 1812
= *Mary Hester Harvey (America)*

Mary
= (1) John Randolph 1773–1833 div
= (2) 1805 Colonel James McKibben (Franklin Co)

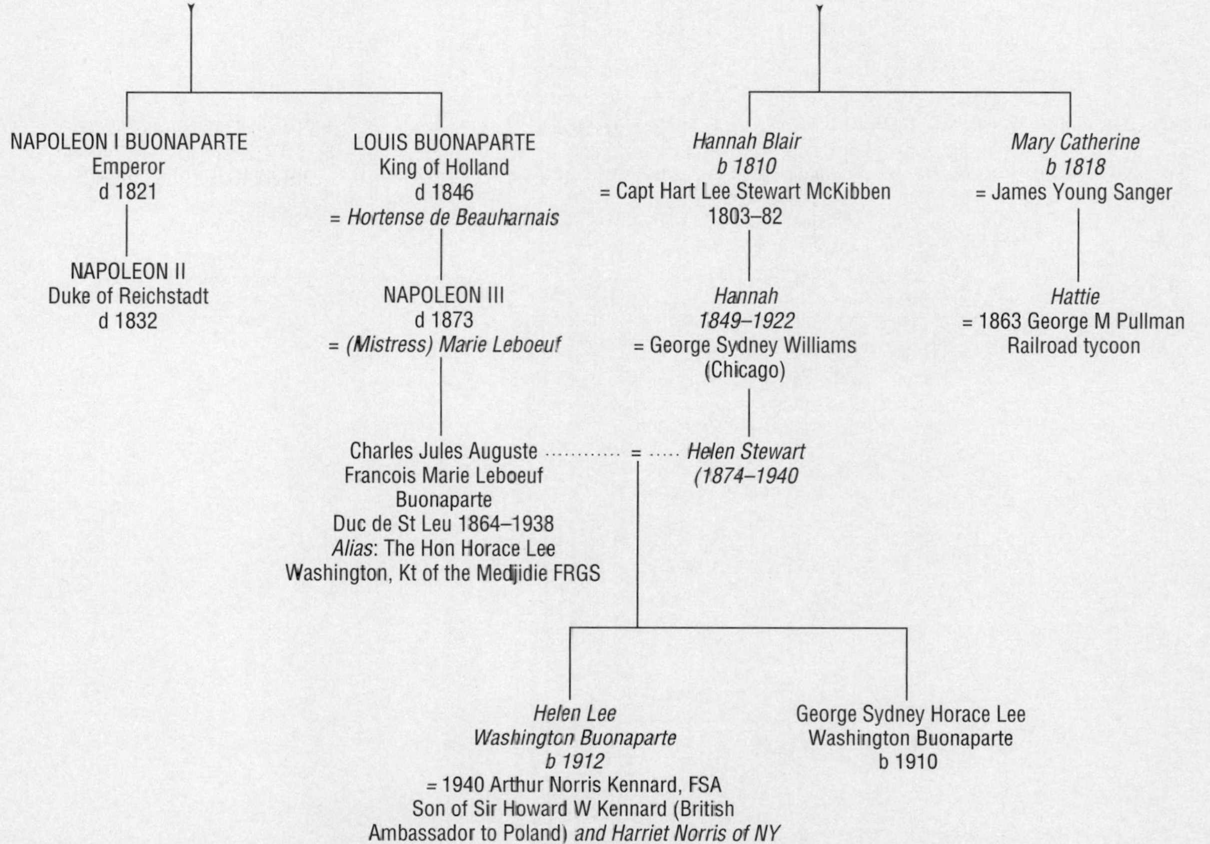
NAPOLEON I BUONAPARTE
Emperor
d 1821
LOUIS BUONAPARTE
King of Holland
d 1846
= *Hortense de Beauharnais*
Hannah Blair
b 1810
= Capt Hart Lee Stewart McKibben
1803–82
Mary Catherine
b 1818
= James Young Sanger
NAPOLEON II
Duke of Reichstadt
d 1832
NAPOLEON III
d 1873
= *(Mistress) Marie Leboeuf*
Hannah
1849–1922
= George Sydney Williams
(Chicago)
Hattie
= 1863 George M Pullman
Railroad tycoon
Charles Jules Auguste .... = ... *Helen Stewart*
Francois Marie Leboeuf
Buonaparte
Duc de St Leu 1864–1938
Alias: The Hon Horace Lee
Washington, Kt of the Medjidie FRGS
(1874–1940)
Helen Lee
Washington Buonaparte
b 1912
= 1940 Arthur Norris Kennard, FSA
Son of Sir Howard W Kennard (British
Ambassador to Poland) *and Harriet Norris of NY*
George Sydney Horace Lee
Washington Buonaparte
b 1910

Chart E

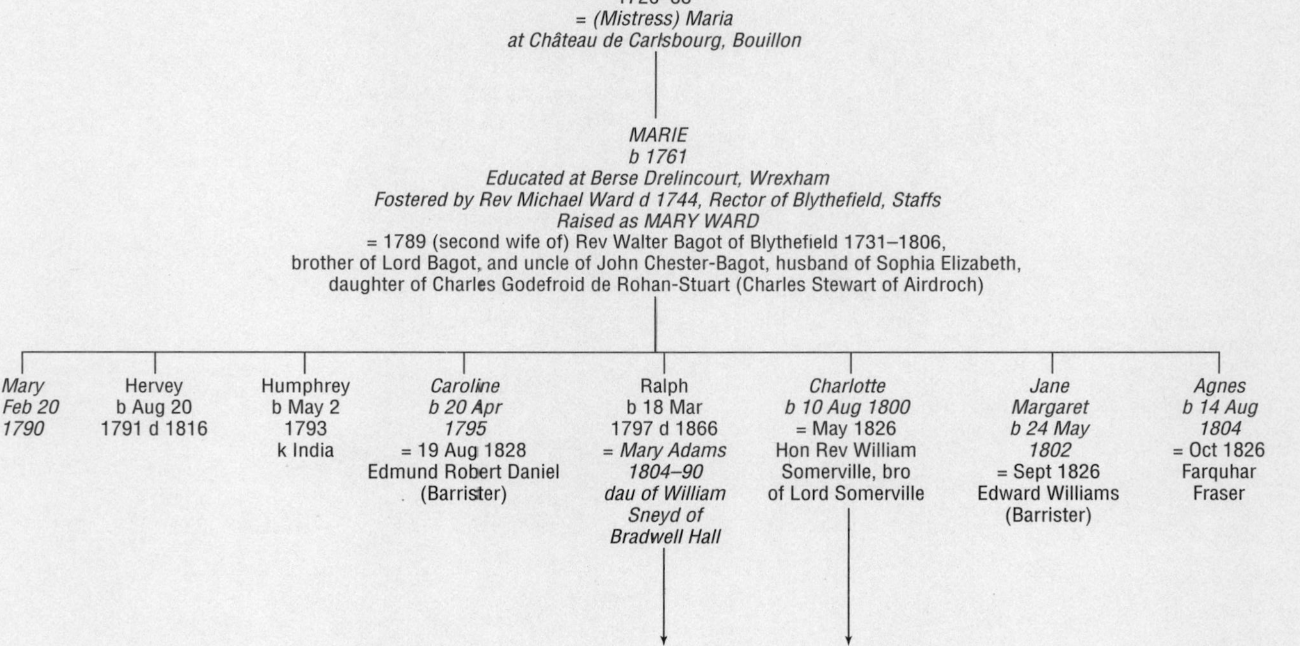
CHARLES EDWARD STUART
1720–88
= (Mistress) Maria
at Château de Carlsbourg, Bouillon
MARIE
b 1761
Educated at Berse Drelincourt, Wrexham
Fostered by Rev Michael Ward d 1744, Rector of Blythefield, Staffs
Raised as MARY WARD
= 1789 (second wife of) Rev Walter Bagot of Blythefield 1731–1806,
brother of Lord Bagot, and uncle of John Chester-Bagot, husband of Sophia Elizabeth,
daughter of Charles Godefroid de Rohan-Stuart (Charles Stewart of Airdroch)
Mary b Feb 20 1790
Hervey b Aug 20 1791 d 1816
Humphrey b May 2 1793 k India
Caroline b 20 Apr 1795 = 19 Aug 1828 Edmund Robert Daniel (Barrister)
Ralph b 18 Mar 1797 d 1866 = Mary Adams 1804–90 dau of William Sneyd of Bradwell Hall
Charlotte b 10 Aug 1800 = May 1826 Hon Rev William Somerville, bro of Lord Somerville
Jane Margaret b 24 May 1802 = Sept 1826 Edward Williams (Barrister)
Agnes b 14 Aug 1804 = Oct 1826 Farquhar Fraser

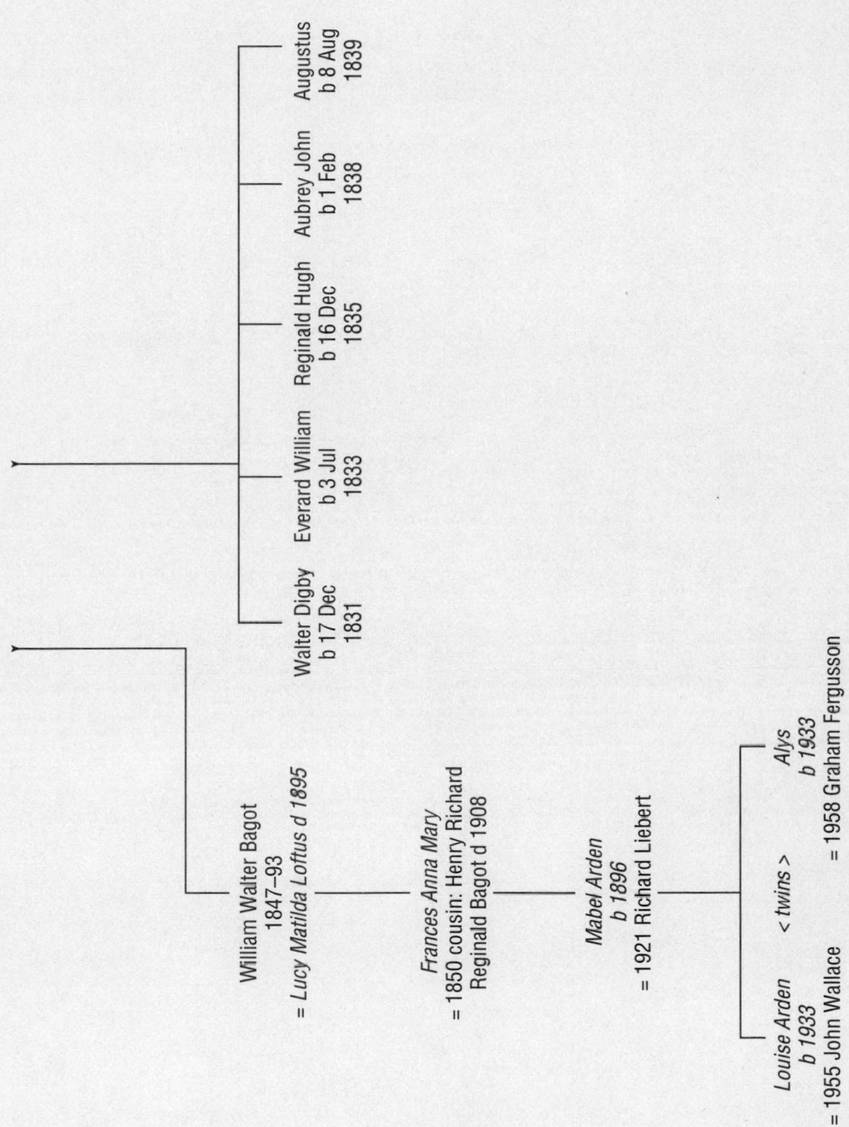
Walter Digby
b 17 Dec
1831
Everard William
b 3 Jul
1833
Reginald Hugh
b 16 Dec
1835
Aubrey John
b 1 Feb
1838
Augustus
b 8 Aug
1839
William Walter Bagot
1847–93
= *Lucy Matilda Loftus d 1895*
Frances Anna Mary
= 1850 cousin: Henry Richard
Reginald Bagot d 1908
Mabel Arden
b 1896
= 1921 Richard Liebert
Louise Arden
b 1933
= 1955 John Wallace
< twins >
Alys
b 1933
= 1958 Graham Fergusson

The Diverted Stuart Succession

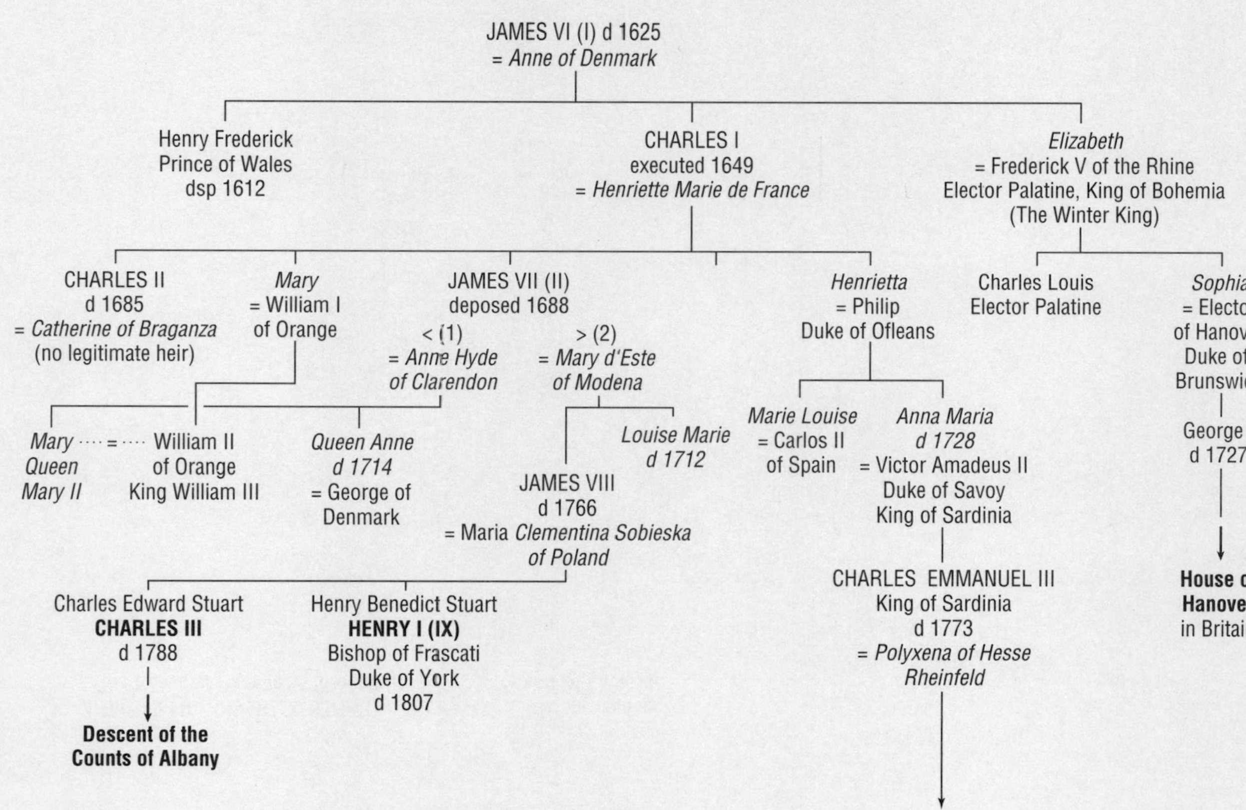

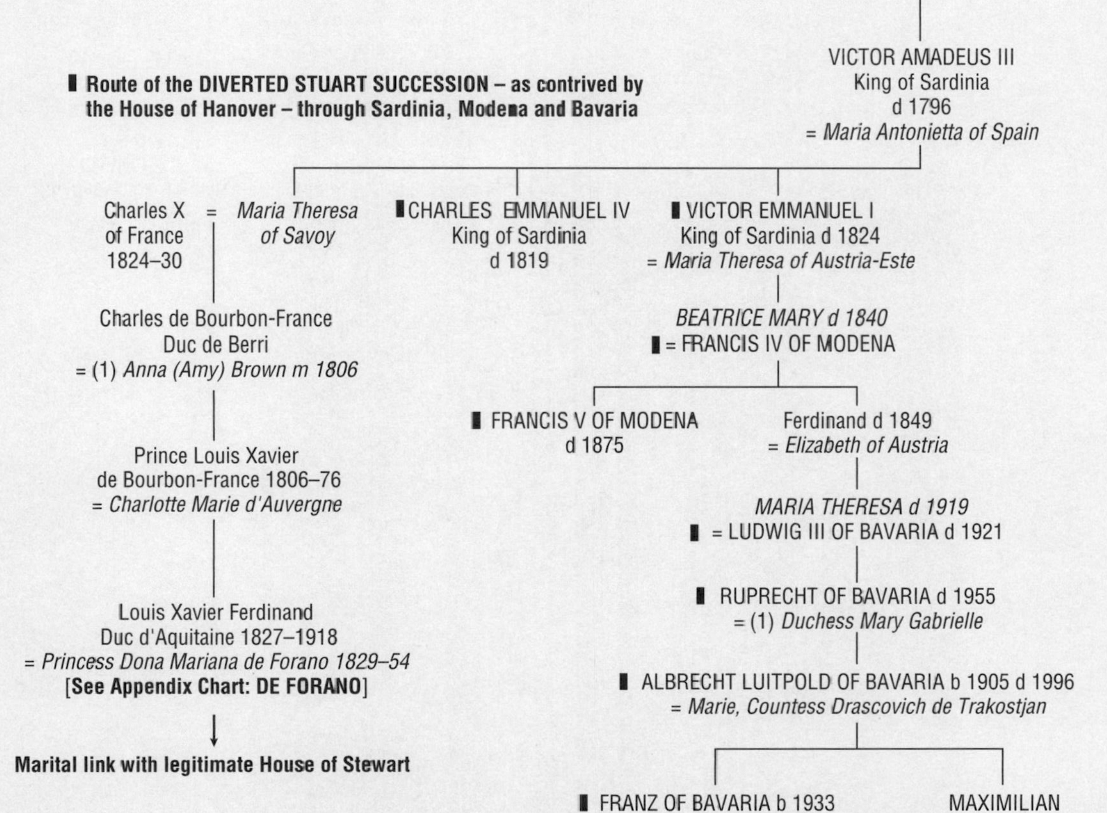
■ Route of the DIVERTED STUART SUCCESSION – as contrived by the House of Hanover – through Sardinia, Modena and Bavaria
VICTOR AMADEUS III
King of Sardinia
d 1796
= Maria Antonietta of Spain
Charles X of France 1824–30 = Maria Theresa of Savoy
■ CHARLES EMMANUEL IV
King of Sardinia
d 1819
■ VICTOR EMMANUEL I
King of Sardinia d 1824
= Maria Theresa of Austria-Este
Charles de Bourbon-France
Duc de Berri
= (1) Anna (Amy) Brown m 1806
BEATRICE MARY d 1840
■ = FRANCIS IV OF MODENA
■ FRANCIS V OF MODENA
d 1875
Ferdinand d 1849
= Elizabeth of Austria
Prince Louis Xavier
de Bourbon-France 1806–76
= Charlotte Marie d'Auvergne
MARIA THERESA d 1919
■ = LUDWIG III OF BAVARIA d 1921
■ RUPRECHT OF BAVARIA d 1955
= (1) Duchess Mary Gabrielle
Louis Xavier Ferdinand
Duc d'Aquitaine 1827–1918
= Princess Dona Mariana de Forano 1829–54
[See Appendix Chart: DE FORANO]
■ ALBRECHT LUITPOLD OF BAVARIA b 1905 d 1996
= Marie, Countess Drascovich de Trakostjan
Marital link with legitimate House of Stewart
■ FRANZ OF BAVARIA b 1933
MAXIMILIAN

APPENDIX XV

The Forgotten Monarchy of Scotland
(Key to colour plate 7)

1 King Robert I – The Bruce
2 Castle Stalker on Loch Laich
3 Sir William Wallace
4 Stirling Castle
5 Charles Edward Stuart (*Bonnie Prince Charlie*)
6 Flora MacDonald
7 Viscount Graham of Claverhouse (*Bonnie Dundee*)
8 Prince Michael Stewart of Albany
9 Edinburgh Castle
10 Mary, Queen of Scots
11 James VII (II) Stuart
12 James IV Stewart

Sir Peter Robson, Ut St Gm, Royal Albany, 1 Main St, Sparta, Ontario NOL 2H0, Canada

BIBLIOGRAPHY

Adam, Frank, *The Clans, Septs and Regiments of the Scottish Highlands*, (rev, Sir Thomas Innes of Learney), Johnston & Bacon, Edinburgh, 1970

Alderman, Clifford Lindsey, *Death to the King*, Bailey Bros & Swinfer, Falconstone, 1973

Anderson, Alan Orr, *Early Sources of Scottish History* (rev), Paul Watkins, London, 1990

Angers, *Diocesan Archives of Angers*, France

Antoine, Robert, Chevalier de Beauterne, *La vie du Prince Edouard Jacques Stuart d'Albanie*, Bibliothèque Nationale, Paris, 1846

Antonelli, *Letters of Cardinale Antonelli* (1806–76), Vatican Archives, Rome

Arbroath, *The Declaration of Arbroath 1320*, H M Register House, Edinburgh

Armoises, Madame Olivier des, *Un rapport sur la mort étrange du 4ième Comte d'Albanie le Prince Charles Benoix Stuart à Monsieur le Ministre des Affaires Etrangère à Paris*, Archives Nationales, Paris, 1898

Arnot, Hugo, *The History of Edinburgh From the Earliest Time to the Present Day* , Robinson & Co, London, 1785

Aubignie, *Archives d'Aubignie*, Berri, France

Bain, J, *A Calendar of Documents Relating to Scotland*, H M Stationery Office, Edinburgh 1881–88

Beccaria-Bonesana, *Letters of Marchese Cesare Beccaria-Bonesana (1735–94)*, Archivo Storico, Rome

Belmonte, Cardinal Pignatelli de, *Préambules et articles d'abdication des droits à la couronne de St Edouard d'Angleterre de SAR le Prince Julius Antoine Henri Stewart, 5ième Comte d'Albanie, signé a Bruxelles le 12 Novembre 1913*, Vatican Archives, 1919

Benedictine *Records of the Diocese of Arras*, Arras, France

Benedictines, The Order of, Rome

Bielorussia, *Records of the Orthodox Church of Bielorussia*, Archives Palermo, Sicily

Bordeaux, *Records of the Archbishopric of Bordeaux*, France

Bourmont, *Letters of General de Bourmont (1830)*, Services Historiques de l'armée de Terre, Château de Vincennes, France
Brady, Dr William Mazière, *Anglo-Roman Papers*, 1890
British Embassy, *19th-century Dispatches of the British Embassy in Paris*, Archives of HM Foreign Office, London
Brotonne, Léonce de, *Les Stuarts et leurs alliances*, Paris, 1834
Buonaparte, *Dispatches of General Giuseppe Buonaparte to Consul Napoleon Buonaparte in Paris, 1792*, Archives Napoléon, Paris
Burke's Peerage, Baronetage and Knightage
Castries, Duc de, *The Kings and Queens of France*, Weidenfeld and Nicolson, London, 1979
Cesarini, *Diaries of Cardinale Angelo Cesarini*, Diario di Roma, Vatican Archives
Cesari Rocca, Count Colonna de, *L'armorial des Stuarts et des Comtes Albanie en exil*, Archives Nationales, Paris, 1893
Chateaubriand, *Letters of René François, Vicomte de Chateaubriand (1803), Consul of France in Rome*, Archives Napoléon, Paris
Choquier, *Letters of Baron Surlet de Choquier*, Archives Nationales, Brussels, Belgium
Coleridge, E H, *The Life of Thomas Coutts*, John Lane, London, 1920
Collier, W D, *The Scottish Regalia*, H M Stationery Office, 1970
Consalvi, *Memoirs of Cardinale Ercole Consalvi*, Bibliothèque Nationale, Paris, 1864
Cook, E Thornton, *Their Majesties of Scotland*, John Murray, London, 1928
Coutts, *Letters of Thomas Coutts, Banker*, Coutts Bank Archives, London
Cronin, Vincent, *Louis XIV*, Reprint Society, London, 1965
Denmark, *The Danish National Archives*, Copenhagen
Dickinson, William Croft, *Scotland From the Earliest Times*, Thomas Nelson, Edinburgh, 1961
Dominicans, The Order of, Rome
Donaldson, Gordon, and Morpeth, R S, *A Dictionary of Scottish History*, John Donald, Edinburgh, 1977
Douglas, Sir Robert of Glenbervie, *The Peerage of Scotland MS*, 1764
The Baronetage of Scotland MS, The British Library, London, 1798
Dottin, Abbé George, *La Religion des Celtes*, Bibliothèque Nationale, Paris, 1904
Dradffen, George S, MBE, *Pour le Foy*, 1949, at Freemasons' Hall, Edinburgh
Duperre, *Letters of Admiral Duperre*, Archives Nationales, Paris
English Historical Review, 1903, The British Library, London
Etudes Heraldiques, Société des, Records of, *Généalogiques et Sigillographiques de Belgique*, National Library of Scotland, Edinburgh, 1949
Fenwick, Hubert, *The Auld Alliance*, Roundwood Press, Warwick, 1971
Fesch, *Letters of Cardinale Giuseppe Fesch to Emperor Napoleon I*, Archives Napoléon, Paris

Figgis, John Neville, *The Divine Right of Kings*, Harper Torchbooks, London, 1965
Flanders, *Flemish-Burgundian Archives*, Bibliothèque Royale, Brussels, Belgium
Foissy, Msr (Avocat), *Les Comtes d'Albanie depuis 1766*, Archives Nationales, Notorial Registers Acts, Paris, 1830
France, *Grande Famille de France*, National Library of Scotland, Edinburgh
France, *Records of the Grand Armorial de France (1830, 1938, 1952)*, National Library of Scotland, Edinburgh
Franciscans, The Order of, Rome
Freemasonry, *The Masonic Archives*, Freemasons' Hall, Edinburgh
Gardner, Barry, and Evans, David, *Thomas Anderson: King's Officer and Jacobite Gentleman*, Brendon Arts, Exmoor, 1992
Gardner, Laurence, *Bloodline of the Holy Grail*, Element Books, Shaftesbury, 1996
Gentleman's Magazine, The, September 1807, The British Library, London
Gilmour, William W, *Famous Scots*, William Maclellan, Glasgow, 1979
Gould, Robert Frere, *The History of Freemasonry*, Caxton, London, 1933
The Atholl Lodges, at Freemasons' Hall, Edinburgh
Graves, Robert, *The White Goddess*, Faber & Faber, London, 1961
Haswell, Jock, *James II, Soldier and Sailor*, Hamilton, London, 1972
Hervey-Townshend, *Letters of the Hon Charles Hervey-Townshend (1782)*, The Manorwater Archives, private collection
Hewison, James King, *The Isle of Bute in the Olden Time*, William Blackwood, Edinburgh 1895
Holy Roman Archives, Vienna, Austria
Hugo, *The Letters of Victor Hugo (1831)*, Archives Nationales, Paris
Italy, *Records of the Istituto Genealogico Italiano*, Florence, Italy
Jackson, A F C, *Rose Croix*, Lewis Masonic, Shepperton, 1980
Jackson, Keith B, *Beyond the Craft*, Lewis Masonic, Shepperton, 1980
Jesus Christ, The Order of, Rome
Jones, Bernard E, *Freemasons' Book of the Royal Arch*, George Harrap, London, 1957
Keating, Geoffrey, *The History of Ireland* (1604), (trans David Comyn and Rev P S Dineen), Irish Texts Society, London, 1902
Lamoriçière, *Reports of General Christophe de Lamoriçière (1806–65)*, Services Historiques de l'armée de Terre, Château de Vincennes, France
Lavalette, Comte Antoine Marie Chaman de, *Mémoires et souvenirs de Marguerite Marie Thérèse d'Audibert de Lussan, Comtesse de Massillan et d'Albanie*, Archives Nationales, Paris, 1831
Lehmahowski, *Memoires of Colonel Lehmahowski of the Polish Army*, Knightown Library, Indiana, USA
Lesseps, *Letters of Ferdinand de Lesseps (1805–94)*, Archives Nationales, Paris
Little, Bryan, *The Monmouth Episode*, Werner Laurie, London, 1956

Lumbruso, Baron Alberto, *Miscellanea Stuardo d'Albanie*, Archivo Storico di Sardinia, 1899

Lyonet, Mgr. Jean Paul François, *Napoleonian Records of Cardinale Giuseppe Fesch*, Vatican Archives, Paris, 1841

Macdonald, *Souvenirs du Maréchal Etienne Jacques Joseph Alexandre Macdonald, Duc de Tarente*, Bibliothèque Nationale, Paris, 1892

Mackay, James A, *Robert Bruce, King of Scots*, Robert Hale, London, 1974

Mackenzie, Sir George, *The Antiquity of the Royal Line of Scotland*, H M Printers, Edinburgh 1685

MacMannus, Cathal, *Annals of Ulster (15th century)*, (ed W M Hennessey and R MacCarthy), Fermanagh, Dublin, 1887–1901

Mannes Papers, The, Royal House of Stewart (Notorial Acts, 1965)

Marshall, Rosalind K, *Bonnie Prince Charlie*, H M Stationery Office, Edinburgh, 1988

Massue, Melville Henry, 9th Marquis de Ruvigny et Raineval, *The Jacobite Peerage, Baronetage, Knightage and Grants of Honour*, London, 1904, and Charles Skilton, Edinburgh, 1974

The Royal Blood of Britain, TC & EC Jack, London, 1903

Mathieu, Cardinal F D, *Jacques II trahis par Innocens XI*, Vatican Archives, Rome, 1904

McLaren, Moray, *The Capital of Scotland*, Douglas & Foulis, Edinburgh, 1950

Meneval, *Napoleonian Records of Baron Claude François de Meneval*, Archives Napoleon, Paris, 1831

M'Firbis, Dudley, *The Duan Albanach (11th century)*, Irish MS Society, 1650

Michael, H R H Prince, of Greece, *Crown Jewels of Britain and Europe*, Peerage Books, London, 1990

Montholon, *Napoleonian Records of Comte Charles François Tristan de Montholon*, Archives Napoléon, Paris, 1847

Morton, H V, *In Search of Scotland*, Methuen, London, 1929

Moscova, *Records of the Princes de la Moscova in America*, US Senate Archives, Washington

Munro, R W, *Gazetteer of Scotland*, Johnston & Bacon, Edinburgh, 1973

Murray, John, 7th Duke of Atholl, *Chronicles of the Atholl and Tullibardine Families*, Ballantyne, London, 1908

Napoleon, *Letters of Emperor Napoleon I to Henry I (IX) 1803–1807*, Archives of the Archbishopric of Frascati, Italy

Nineteenth Century Review, The, 1897, at The British Library, London

Norvins, Jacques Margret de Montbreton de, *Souvenirs Romain des Comtes Princiers d'Albanie en Belgique*, Bibliothèque Nationale, Paris, 1897

O'Farril, *Letters of Monsieur O'Farril to Emperor Napoleon I (1808)*, Archives Napoléon, Paris

Oman, Carola, *Mary of Modena*, Hodder & Stoughton, London, 1962

Orléans, *Letters of Henry d'Orléans, Duc d'Aumale, to Louis Philippe I of France*, private collection, Orléans Royal Family, Paris

Orthodox Church of the Slavs, The, *Records of*, Palermo, Italy

Paeologue, Maurice, *Memorie inedito di Principe Enrico Stuardo*, Florence, Istituto Genealogico Italiano, Florence

Paul, James Balfour, Lord Lyon, King of Arms, *Ordinary of Scottish Arms*, 1903, National Library of Scotland, Edinburgh

The Scots Peerage 1904–1914, National Library of Scotland, Edinburgh

Pepys, *Diaries of Samuel Pepys*, at British Library, London

Pergami, *Letters of Bartolomeo Pergami to Caroline, Princess of Wales (wife of George IV)*, Windsor Castle

Pierlot, *Letters of Hubert Pierlot, late Prime Minister of the Kingdom of the Belgians*, Archives Nationales, Brussels, Belgium

Polignac, *Letters of Jules de Polignac, First Minister of France*, Archives Nationales, Paris, 1830

Poniatowski, *Dispatches to King Charles X of France from Prince Poniatowski*, Archives Nationales, Paris

Pryde, G S, *The Treaty of Union Between Scotland and England 1707*, Thomas Nelson, London, 1950

Rohan-Guéméné Ferdinand de (Grand Almoner of Empress Josephine de Beauharnais), *Ecclesiastical History of the Archbishop of Bordeaux*, Bordeaux, France 1809

Rose Croix, *Archives of des Ainês de la Rose Croix*, Bibliothèque Nationale, Paris

Round, J Horace, *Calendar of Documents Preserved in France 918–1206*, Eyre & Spottiswoode, London 1899

Rouvroy, *Letters of Claude Henri de Rouvroy, Comte de Saint Simon (1760–1825)*, Archives Nationales, Paris

Rovere, *Letters of Mamiani della, Count Terenzio (1802–85)*, Archivo Storico, Rome

Saint Germain, *The Jacobite Records of Saint Germain en Laye*, Stewart family Trustees and the Noble Order of the Guard of St Germain

Saint Lorenzo, *Records of the Church of St Lorenzo*, Lucina, Rome

Saint Paul's, *Records of Old Saint Paul's – Edinburgh*, Archives of the Scottish Episcopal Church, St Mary's Cathedral, Edinburgh

Schwarzenberg, *Dispatches to King Charles X of France from Prince Schwarzenberg*, Archives du Ministère des Affaires Etrangères, Paris

Scotland, *The Great Seal Register of Scotland*, H M Register House, Edinburgh

Scotland, *The Privy Seal Register of Scotland*, H M Register House, Edinburgh

Scott, Paul Henderson, *Andrew Fletcher and the Treaty of Union*, John Donald, Edinburgh, 1992

Seton, Walter, *Relations of Henry, Cardinal York, with the British Government*, The Royal Historical Society, London, 1919

Sforza, Giovani, *Della origine della famiglia principesco Stuardo d'Albanie*, Archivo Baron Lumbroso, Italy, 1895

Sherry, Francis A, *The Rising of 1820*, William Maclellan, Glasgow, 1974

Skene, William Forbes (ed),*Tracts of Dalriada; Chronicles of the Picts and Scots; Chronicles of the Picts; Chronicles of the Scots*, H M General Register House, Edinburgh, 1867
Celtic Scotland, David Douglas, Edinburgh, 1886–90
Spanish National Archives, Madrid
Stephani, Frederic de, *Un rapport sur les origines des Princes Stuart d'Albanie à Rome à Monsieur le Ministre de l'Instruction et des Cultes de l'Empire Français*, Turin 1859, Archives du Ministère des affaires Etrangères, Paris
Stevenson, Joseph (trans), *The Chronicle of Melrose (12th century)*, in *Church Historians of England*, 1856
Steuart, A Francis, *The Neopolitan Stuarts*, in *English Historical Review*, 1903
Stuart, *The Stuart Papers* at Windsor
Stuart, *Letters of Lord Stuart, British Ambassador to Paris (1830)*, Archives of H M Foreign Office, London
Sussex, *Letters of Prince Augustus Frederick, Duke of Sussex*, Windsor Castle
Teil, Baron Joseph du, *Rapports militaire du Prince Edouard Stuart d'Albanie sur les batailles de l'Empereur Napoléon I*, Archives Napoléon, Paris, 1890
Templars, *The Beauceant Records of the Chivalric & Military Order of the Temple of Jerusalem*, Scotland
Temple, *Statutes of the Religious and Military Order of the Temple*, The Grand Conclave, Edinburgh, 1844
Torlonia, *Letters of Roman Banker*, Torlonia, Archives Napoléon, Paris
Torre, Federico, *Memorie storiche della Casa Reale Stuardo*, Milan, Archivo Storico, Rome
Trevor, Meriol, *The Shadow of a Crown*, Constable, London, 1988
Vitelleschi, Marchesa, *A Court in Exile*, Hutchinsons, London, 1903
Voltaire, *Précis du siècle de Louis XV*, Bibliothèque Nationale, Paris, 1769
Ward, J S M, *Freemasonry and the Ancient Gods*, Simpkin, Marshall, Hamilton & Kent, London, 1921
Watson, *Private Papers of Sir Robert Watson*, Principal of Scots College, Archives Napoléon, Paris, 1806
Watson, W J, *The History of the Celtic Place Names of Scotland*, William Blackwood, Edinburgh, 1926
Westminster, *Archives of the House of Lords*, Westminster, London
Archives of the House of Commons, Westminster, London
Zec, Donald, *The Queen Mother*, Sidgwick & Jackson, London, 1990
Zweig, Stefan, *Marie Stuart*, Brodart & Taupin, Paris, 1973

INDEX